THE KING AND THE BEAST™

A Student New Testament

Contemporary English Version

Thomas Nelson Publishers
Nashville

Contents

Many thanks to Ken Abraham, primary author of the following special student materials. Ken is a former pastor and drummer with the Christian group Abraham, and is the author of several books for young people.

CONTENTS

(Characters in stories are fictitious. Any resemblance to real persons, living or dead, is coincidental.)

THE KING AND THE BEAST

The beast is on the prowl. He lurks and he hides behind harmless-looking things. He's looking for a chance to attack God's children.

The beast ought to know better. King Jesus has already defeated him. King Jesus has beaten the beast! Not just "one of these days." Jesus is Lord and King today!

Jesus Is King

That's what this book is all about. In Matthew and Revelation and all the great stuff in between, one message keeps coming through. Jesus is King. He rules!

Sure, the beast is still trying to bully people into believing that he controls the world. But he's fighting a losing battle. In fact, he has already lost. Jesus won the war when he died on the cross, paying the price for our sins. Then, he proved he is God by rising from the dead three days later.

Who Is the Beast?

Actually, you might say there's more than one "beast." The biggest one is Satan. In this book you'll see him for the punk he really is. The devil is a liar, a cheat, a robber, and a murderer. But he is no match for Jesus. The devil is a defeated foe. King Jesus is Master of the universe.

Two other beasts you will discover are in the book of Revelation. You've probably heard about these beasts. Horror stories are told about them. Movies make them appear larger than life. These two beasts are called "the Antichrist and the False Prophet."

These beasts are bad news. For a while it will look as if they are going to conquer the King's people. But wait till you see what King Jesus does to these devilish dudes. (Here's a hint: check out Revelation 19.19–21!) King Jesus is Master of heaven and earth.

But the most frightening beast you will face in this book is "the beast" within yourself. As you read The King and The Beast, you will see yourself in the mirror of God's word. You might find some things that make you uncomfortable. That's okay. The King will show you what to do about those things. If you allow him, King Jesus will be the Master of *your life.*

1

In *The King and The Beast,* you will see how deadly sin is. You will also learn how you can be forgiven of sin and freed from it. You will discover how the devil tries to deceive and destroy you and your friends. But most of all, you will see how a King loved you enough to leave his heavenly "castle," to come and fight the beast for you. Because King Jesus has beaten the beast, you can be free.

Come on along! You're going to appreciate *The King and The Beast.* It's an exciting, *true* adventure story. As you read, allow the King to defeat the beast in *your* life—today, tomorrow, and forever!

Unusual Stories in *The King and The Beast*

▶ A guy who was so hungry he almost ate pig food (Luke 15.16)

▶ A fellow who fell asleep during church, then fell out a window (Acts 20.7–12)

▶ A lake of fire (Revelation 20.14, 15)

▶ A book-burning party (Acts 19.17–20)

▶ Huge hailstones that weigh a hundred pounds (Revelation 16.21)

▶ A strange diet (Matthew 3.4)

▶ The blasting and the blessing (Acts 5.1–16)

▶ An angel who argued with the devil (Jude 9)

DOWN WITH THE DEVIL!

Are you afraid of the devil? A lot of your friends are, you know. They're scared stiff that Satan (another name for the devil) and his demons are going to beat up on them. Even some Christians think more about the devil than they do about Jesus.

Don't give the devil so much credit. Sure, he's real, and yes, he's a nasty enemy, but don't forget that the devil and his demons are defeated! Jesus won the war when he died on the cross and arose from the grave that first Easter weekend a long time ago.

Now, if you are trusting in Jesus, "God's Spirit is in you and is more powerful than the one that is in the world" (1 John 4.4). That means you don't have to fear the devil. You have about as much chance of being possessed by a demon today as you do of being attacked by King Kong in the mall parking lot!

Isn't That Being Cocky?

No, it's understanding and *believing* that Jesus is stronger than the devil and his demons. No demonic power on earth or in hell can stand at the name of Jesus.

Satan is known by many names in the Bible. Some of them are:

- Your enemy, the devil (1 Peter 5.8)
- The old snake, who fools everyone on earth (Revelation 12.9)
- The god who rules this world (2 Corinthians 4.4)
- The evil one (Matthew 13.38)
- A murderer and liar (John 8.44)
- A roaring lion (1 Peter 5.8)

Some of your friends may think that Satan is a big joke, or that it's cool to worship the devil. But you can see from some of his names that the devil plays for keeps. Don't mess with him.

On the other hand, Satan tries to scare us into thinking that he is as powerful as Jesus. He attempts to strike fear into our hearts through rock music that deals with the occult, through album covers that show witches and other demonic symbols, and, of course, through gross monster movies, featuring some madman who gets his power from the pits of hell.

3

Get the Straight Stuff

But if you read the Bible, you'll get the real picture. And not a bit of it will cause you to have nightmares. Why? Because in every battle with the devil or his demons, it is obvious that Jesus is the Master of the universe. Jesus always beats the devil!

For example, one day Jesus had barely gotten out of the boat after crossing Lake Galilee when a man with evil spirits came running up to him (see Mark 5). This guy was a mess—so much that the town had written him off as a hopeless case. They had tried to tame him by tying him up with chains and clamping him down with leg irons. But when the demons surged through the man's body, he broke the chains and smashed the leg irons as if they were made of string. Finally, everyone said, "There's nothing more we can do with him," so they threw him out of town, to live in the graveyard.

That's where Jesus found him. The man with evil spirits was a maniac; he was running around day and night, yelling, and cutting himself with sharp stones.

Jesus Is the One in Charge

Jesus could have passed by the poor fellow. But he didn't. He wasn't put off by the man's bad actions. Nor was he afraid. Jesus simply took command and cast the spirits out of the man. Instantly, the man was well. Jesus let the demons enter into a herd of hogs that was feeding on the hillside. The pigs promptly ran down the steep bank and were drowned in the lake.

Do you see who was in charge? Not the demons. They had to go where Jesus told them. He is the Master. He is Lord.

It is not the Christian who needs to fear the devil and his agents. It's the other way around: the demons tremble and bow at the presence of Jesus!

THE BIBLE: NO ORDINARY BOOK!

You've probably wondered, **"What's so special about the Bible?"** After all, other religions have their "holy books." What makes the Bible any different from them?

The Bible is an amazing book. Every year, it is a best-seller. It so far outsells every other book that the people who make up the best-seller lists don't even include it anymore.

Modern books can't compare with the Bible. For one thing, the Bible was written by some forty different men, over a time span of nearly two thousand years, under the direction of one editor, the Holy Spirit. Some of the fellows who wrote the Bible were highly educated. Others had never been off the farm. A few were fishermen. At least one was a doctor. One was a tax collector. Several were government officials. Only a few were what we would call teachers. Most of these authors never met each other.

Who Did That?

Yet the Bible has unity. It's almost as though someone was putting it all together. Someone was! That someone was the Holy Spirit.

The writers wrote the words, but the ideas came from God. That's why the Bible is called God's word.

Think about it. If you were able to pick out forty of your friends and ask them to write on such subjects as religion, morals, science, the creation of the world, the meaning of life, and the end of the world, you would think that their ideas would all be different. But the Bible isn't that way. Its writers and subjects flow together perfectly.

The Joke's On Them

Oh, sure, some skeptics have tried to make fun of the Bible. Some have said that it isn't true. Others say it is all a matter of your opinion. Few of these skeptics, however, have ever read the Bible for themselves. They simply repeat somebody else's opinion. Most of these critics do not know Jesus personally. No wonder they are skeptical. You can always enjoy a book more when the author is your friend.

Still, the Bible has stood up to blow after blow from a lot of people who should know better. Some of the stories of this in history are funny. For example, about 250 years ago, a famous skeptic named Voltaire held a Bible in his hand and said, "In one hundred years, this book will be forgotten, eliminated!"

Guess what? Almost one hundred years later, Voltaire's house was bought and made into offices for the Geneva *Bible* Society! The group began shipping Bibles out of Voltaire's former home. Before long, they had grown into an international Bible distribution network.

The great preacher, Paul, wrote to his young friend Timothy about how good it is to know God's word. Paul said:

Keep on being faithful to what you were taught and to what you believed. After all, you know who taught you these things. Since childhood, you have known the Holy Scriptures that are able to make you wise enough to have faith in Christ Jesus and be saved. Everything in the Scriptures is God's Word. All of it is useful for teaching and helping people and for correcting them and showing them how to live. The Scriptures train God's servants to do all kinds of good deeds. (2 Timothy 3.14–17)

You can believe the Bible. Jesus did. He quoted from it often. He mentioned twenty-four different books of the Old Testament.

History and science continue to confirm the Bible's accuracy, too. Hundreds of prophecies have already come to pass, and others will be fulfilled, possibly in your lifetime.

Most of all, the Bible is amazing because God still uses his word to change people's lives today.

WHAT GREAT PEOPLE HAVE SAID
ABOUT THE BIBLE

66 The New Testament is the best Book the world has ever known or will know. 99 —Charles Dickens

66 I have known ninety-five great men of the world in my time, and of these, eighty-seven were followers of the Bible. 99 —William E. Gladstone

66 I am profitably engaged in reading the Bible. Take all of this Book upon reason that you can, and the balance by faith, and you will live and die a better man. 99 —Abraham Lincoln

66 If we abide by the principles taught in the Bible, our country will go on prospering. 99 —Daniel Webster

66 The first and almost the only Book deserving of universal attention is the Bible. I speak as a man of the world . . . and I say to you, 'Search the Scriptures.' 99 —John Quincy Adams

66 It is impossible to rightly govern the world without God and the Bible. 99 —George Washington

66 A thorough knowledge of the Bible is worth more than a college education. 99 —Theodore Roosevelt

66 All that I am I owe to Jesus Christ, revealed to me in His divine Book. 99 —David Livingstone

66 Hold fast to the Bible as the sheet-anchor of your liberties; write its precepts in your hearts, and practice them in your lives. To the influence of this book we are indebted for all the progress made in true civilization, and to this we must look as our guide in the future. 99 —Ulysses S. Grant

66 The Bible is a book in comparison with which all others in my eyes are of minor importance; and which in all my perplexities and distress has never failed to give me light and strength. 99 —Robert E. Lee

❝ This great book . . . is the best gift God has given to man. . . . But for it we could not know right from wrong. ❞ —Abraham Lincoln

❝ After more than sixty years of almost daily reading of the Bible, I never fail to find it always new and marvelously in tune with the changing needs of every day. ❞ —Cecil B. DeMille

❝ Sin will keep you from this Book. This Book will keep you from sin. ❞ —Dwight L. Moody

❝ Nobody ever outgrows Scripture; the Book widens and deepens with our years. ❞ —Charles Haddon Spurgeon

HOW TO GET THE MOST OUT OF YOUR BIBLE

The New Testament is not written in some secret code. It is written in everyday words for ordinary people. It wasn't written to *conceal* (hide) God's plan. It was written to *reveal* (to make open) God's plan. It is clear enough for any of us to understand and to live by.

Who Wrote the New Testament?

Weren't the people who wrote the Bible just fallible human beings? Of course they were. But God showed them what to write.

The New Testament, like the Old Testament, is God's word. God *inspired* men to write the Bible! The word *inspired* means "God-breathed." In other words, God gave people the thoughts, and they wrote his words on paper. That's why we call the Bible *God's* word, and not simply *Matthew's* word, or *John's* word, or another apostle's word.

God inspired men to write his message. The writers came from many walks of life. John and Peter were fishermen. Luke was a doctor. Matthew had been a tax collector. Paul was a mean man who used to cause Christians trouble, until one day, he met the risen, glorious King Jesus! Paul's life was never the same. He became a great missionary. (Check out his story in Acts 9.1–30.)

James and Jude were Jesus' brothers. Mark also knew the good news firsthand. He was a young man when he met Jesus. Later, possibly with Peter's help, he remembered the story well. His version of the good news is a fast-paced, action-packed adventure. Mark was also a co-worker with Paul.

Amazingly, God used this varied group of Jesus' followers to write exactly what he wanted in the New Testament, exactly the way he wanted it said.

Why Should I Read the Bible?

Why? Because God wants to talk to you. Two ways God normally will speak to you are through prayer (talking with God) and through the written words of his Bible. As you read through his word, he will speak to your heart, your mind, and your conscience.

What Will God Say to Me?

As you read the New Testament, you will discover:

- Who Jesus is
- What Jesus said and did
- How much he loves you
- What God is like
- What makes God happy or sad
- How to get to know God better, and much more!

You will see how you can be forgiven of your sins and how you can forgive others. The New Testament tells you how to live happily. It gives you courage even in the face of death. It tells you how to get ready for heaven.

The Bible also answers important questions such as:

- "Where did I come from?"
- "Why am I here on earth, anyhow?"
- "Where am I going?"
- "How can I find and know the truth?"

Most important of all, the New Testament tells you how you can know Jesus and be saved forever. Jesus wants you in his family. He wants you to know him better. By reading the New Testament, you will become his friend. You will learn what it is going to be like to live with Jesus in heaven . . . forever!

REASONS WE CAN TRUST THE BIBLE

1. *Jesus said that we could* (Matthew 5.18; John 10.35).

2. *Fulfilled prophecies.* The Bible has hundreds of prophecies that have been fulfilled word for word. Some of these prophecies were predicted hundreds of years in advance. For example, the prophet Micah said that the Christ would be born in Bethlehem (Micah 5.2), and Jesus was (Matthew 2.5, 6).

3. *Archeology and history* prove the accuracy of the New Testament. Critics have tried to disprove the Bible, but they can't. For example, enough evidence exists for the resurrection of Jesus Christ to prove it in any fair trial.

4. *No "loose canons."* The early Christians who gathered the books together that are included in the original Bible (called the canon of Scripture), were very careful. Many books were written about Jesus during the first few centuries after his resurrection. Some of them are interesting to read, but they are not *Scripture.* The groups that approved the New Testament books checked and prayed about them and tested them against each other. They wanted to make sure that only those books that were inspired by God got into the Bible.

❝ Somebody told me that the Bible is full of errors. How do I know I can trust the Bible? ❞

No Errors in the Bible

Skeptics often talk about the errors in the Bible. Usually, if you ask them to give you an example of one of those errors, they can't name one. They just "heard" somebody else say the Bible isn't true.

The Bible does have some things that *look* like errors. After closer study, many of these things can be explained. For example, in John's gospel, Jesus chased the merchants out of the temple in the early part of the story (John 2.13–16). In Matthew's account, Jesus did this near the end of his ministry (Matthew 21.12–14). One of the writers must be wrong. Right?

Not necessarily. Possibly, Jesus cleared the temple twice. Another explanation could be that John was writing about the *truth* of what Jesus did, and may not have been concerned about *when* Jesus did it.

Apparent differences in the Bible are not really contradictions, just more than one way of looking at an event or idea.

Other skeptics say, "With all the copying of the New Testament manuscripts, how do we know that the writers didn't change or miss anything?" It's true that in Bible times, they didn't have printing presses as we do today. Every copy of the Bible had to be copied by hand. And yes, every once in a while, a copyist made an error. Most of these errors were very minor. Usually, they had to do with the spelling of one word.

But of the thousands of manuscripts and parts of manuscripts that modern archeologists have discovered, none of them contain major doctrinal differences. In other words, the New Testament that you have is the same information between Matthew and Revelation that the Christians had in the first century. You can trust your Bible. It's true.

How Should I Read My Bible?

Read some of the New Testament every day. Some people like to read several chapters. Others prefer to read one or two pages. Some read only a few sentences or paragraphs. It's not how *much* you read that matters. It's how much of God's word you understand and put into practice in your life.

Most new students of the Bible find that it is better to begin by reading a few minutes each day. Set a reachable goal of reading through the New Testament in one year. You will probably read it through several times.

No, God won't zap you if you miss reading for a day. But, you will feel spiritually weak. Have you ever gone without eating for a day? You can survive. But if you stop eating for long, you begin to get sick. The same thing happens spiritually if you neglect reading your Bible.

Not only that. The New Testament is Jesus' love letter to you. Aren't you excited when you get some mail from a good friend? Read a little of your love letter every day.

If you have never read the New Testament before, start with John's Gospel. Then read the Acts of the Apostles. Then go back to Matthew's Gospel and read it before moving on to some of Paul's letters and the rest of your New Testament.

Pray before you begin, and ask God to speak to you through his word. Ask him to show you what he wants you to know. Ask him to give you ways to make Scripture work in your everyday life.

Read your New Testament slowly. Sure, you want to get the whole story, but take your time. After each paragraph, ask yourself, "What does this mean and what does it have to do with me?"

A Notebook Helps

Keep a notebook handy while you read the New Testament. If you have questions, jot them down. You can ask your pastor later, or maybe you will find the answer yourself as you read more.

Seek to answer three main questions as you read:

✓ *"What does this part of the Scripture actually say?"*

✓ *"What does the passage mean?"*

✓ *"How can I put this truth to work in my life?"*

Let's look at each of these questions more closely.

"What Does the Scripture Say?"

When you study the Scripture, ask the questions that every good news reporter asks: Who? What? When? Where? and Why?

✓ *Who* is speaking? Who is being addressed?

✓ *What* is being said or done?

✓ *When* is the action taking place?

✓ *Where* is the action taking place?

✓ *Why* is this important to the writer? Why is he convinced that this is true?

"What Does the Passage Mean?"

Again, ask yourself the same sort of questions you would if you were studying any other important book:

✓ What did the passage mean to its original readers?

✓ What is the main point of the passage?

✓ Why is this even in the Bible? Why did God have the writer include this?

✓ How does this point connect with what has been said before it?

✓ Also, what do other biblical portions say about this (if anything)?

✓ If this was written for a specific need, what general principle can be learned?

"How Can I Put This Truth to Work in My Life?"

Reading the Bible merely to gain knowledge is noble, but it won't change your life. If you are to be a better person, more like Jesus and closer to him, you will want to *apply* what you have read.

With all due respect, as you read the New Testament, keep asking yourself, "So what? What difference does this make to me? Or to my family, friends, school, town, or world?"

To apply what you read, you must put it into practice in your daily life. Otherwise, the exciting truths you discover in your New Testament will soon grow dull. And why should God uncover any new gems for you if you haven't used what he has already given to you?

To apply the truth you have learned, ask yourself some more tough questions. You may want to record the answers to these in your notebook:

✓ What does this passage *teach* me about Jesus? About God? About the Holy Spirit? About myself?

✓ Does the passage show me any *sin* that I need to confess or turn away from? Is there a need for *restitution* (making a wrong right, if possible—for example, paying back money that you have stolen, or apologizing to somebody whom you have hurt)?

✓ Is the Spirit speaking to me about my *attitude*? How should I change it?

✓ Is there a *command* for me to obey? How? What action does God want me to take?

✓ Is there a *promise* in the passage that I can believe and live by? Does the promise have a condition attached? If so, how do I go about meeting it?

✓ Is there an *example* for me to follow, or an example of something to be avoided?

✓ Is there something here I should *pray* about? What can I praise the Lord for as a result of this truth?

You don't have to ask yourself these questions for every verse. Just keep them in mind. Better yet, write them in your notebook and try to answer as many of the questions as possible when you read your New Testament. It especially helps to write out your response to a passage: what do you plan to do, when, and how?

Memorize As Much Scripture As You Can

You may be thinking, "Oh, I could never memorize anything." Yes, you can! It's easy and it's fun.

We memorize songs, recipes, sports statistics, all kinds of numbers, computer keys, dramatic parts, football plays, and speeches. How much more valuable is the word of God in our hearts and minds?

Write some key verses on cards and carry them with you wherever you go. When you have a chance—such as in the lunch line, waiting for a traffic light, or riding a bus—pull out a card and review your verses. You will be amazed at how quickly you learn!

Memorizing Scripture is a vital part of doing battle with the beast. Whenever the devil tries to tempt you, just quote an appropriate Bible verse to him. He won't stay long. On the other hand, many times when you're under attack, you don't have time to pull out your Bible and say, "Well, I know there is a promise in here somewhere that applies to this situation!" Better to prepare ahead of time by memorizing key verses.

Would God Really Send Me to Hell for Being Bad?

God doesn't send people to hell for being bad. If he did, heaven would be one lonely place. People go to hell because they reject Jesus Christ as Savior and Lord. If a person rejects Jesus, the natural result is sin. Usually, the reason they reject him is *because* of sin, too. The Bible says, "Sin pays off with death. But God's gift is eternal life given by Jesus Christ our Lord" (Romans 6.23).

God never intended for you to go to hell. Hell was created as a place of punishment for the devil and his angels (Matthew 25.41). If you go to hell, it will be your own fault, not God's. Because he loves you, he has made a way of escape. "He wants everyone to turn from sin and no one to be lost" (2 Peter 3.9).

Does Hell Really Exist?

Count on it. You may not hear much about hell these days, unless someone is telling someone else to go there. But hell is for real.

One fellow blamed hell for keeping him away from church. "I don't like to go to church and hear all that preachin' about hellfire and brimstone," he said. It could be that he hadn't been to church in a while, because many preachers today rarely speak about hell. Many congregations don't want to hear about it. But the Bible mentions hell quite a bit. In fact, Scripture has three times as much to say about God's justice, judgment, wrath, and punishment of sin as it says about the love and mercy of God. But, then, who's counting?

WHAT IS HELL LIKE?

Jesus told a story in Luke 16.19–31 about "Lazarus and the Rich Man." In it, you can find several facts about what it is like in hell. (Scholars wonder whether Jesus was saying that the events in the story really happened. But the point is that Jesus included these details:)

- The rich man was *awake*. He wasn't in some state of sleep.
- He was able to *see*. He looked up and saw Lazarus and Abraham far off from him, apparently in heaven (16.23).
- He could *speak*. He begged Abraham to have pity upon him, but it was too late (16.24).
- He was *thirsty* (16.24).
- He was *suffering terribly* in the fire (16.23, 24).
- He *could not escape*. Abraham told him, "There is a deep ditch between us, and no one from either side can cross over" (16.26).
- The rich man had *memories*. He could remember his family and even asked Abraham to warn them about the awfulness of hell (16.28). This may be one of the worst aspects of hell. The person who rejects Jesus will be able to remember the chances he or she had to trust Christ, but decided not to.

16

Four Words, One Idea

The Bible has four different words for hell. The word used most often for "hell" in the Old Testament is *sheol.* Sheol is a dark, gloomy underworld. It is the place of the dead. Nothing is said about fire and brimstone, but sheol is not exactly the kind of place where you would enjoy living forever.

In the New Testament, the word *hades* means much the same as sheol. Another word, *tartarus,* is used once by the Apostle Peter. It describes the place where disobedient angels were sent when they sinned (2 Peter 2.4).

The most common word for hell in the New Testament is *Gehenna.* Ten of the eleven times it is used, it comes from the mouth of Jesus himself. *Gehenna* means "a final place of punishment for the ungodly."

These four words might not all refer to precisely the same location. But the idea is definitely that *heaven* is the place to be.

The Garbage Dump of Human History

Originally, *Gehenna* referred to a place, the valley of Hinnom, located just outside of Jerusalem. Years before Jesus was born, it was where human sacrifices were offered to the heathen god Molech. By the time of Christ, it had become the garbage dump of Jerusalem. The open garbage pile attracted all sorts of bugs, maggots, worms, rats, and other vermin. To help reduce the health hazard, the garbage was set on fire all the time. Fire, smoke, and awful smells were always part of Gehenna.

When Jesus wanted to describe the horrors of hell in human terms, he used the word *Gehenna.* He called it a place of everlasting punishment; a place of outer, absolute darkness. It is the garbage dump of human history.

Hell Is No Party

One foolish fellow said, "I don't want to go to heaven. I want to go to hell. That's where all the party animals will be. That's where the booze will be flowing and the drugs and the wild and crazy women will be."

Oh, really?

Seven times in the Gospels, Jesus referred to hell as a place where people are weeping and gnashing their teeth. He called it a furnace of fire. Maybe he had the garbage dump in mind when he said, "The worms there never die, and the fire never stops burning" (Mark 9.48). It doesn't sound much like a party.

I Thought God Was Love!

He is. But he isn't a mellow, "I wouldn't hurt a fly" type of God. Some people say, "Well, I believe in Jesus, but I don't believe in hell!"

Too bad for them. What they fail to realize is that most of what we know about hell comes from the mouth of Jesus himself.

It was Jesus Christ who said, "If you say that someone is worthless, you will be in danger of the fires of hell" (Matthew 5.22). It was Jesus Christ who rebuked his friends for fearing what mere men could do to them: "Don't be afraid of people. They can kill you, but they cannot harm your soul. Instead, you should fear God who can destroy both your body and your soul in hell" (Matthew 10.28).

Christ warned that hell is a place to be avoided at all costs (see Matthew 5.21–30). First, you should avoid the horrors of hell yourself. You can do that by trusting Jesus as your Savior, and showing you have done so by living the way he tells you in the Bible.

Second, you should also try to help your friends and family to find Jesus. He wants to save *them* from the fires of hell, too. Jesus gave his life for you. To be a Christian means that you care about the things Christ cares about. One of the things you can be sure he is concerned about is seeing your friends and family saved. You should be, too.

Bad News; Good News

The **bad news** is that being good will never get you into heaven. In fact, the Bible teaches that doing good deeds won't give you any "brownie points" with God at all. You can't earn your way into God's family.

The **good news** is that God has already done all that is needed in order to save you from sin and pay your way into heaven. The Apostle Paul explained it this way to his helper, Titus:

> God our Savior showed us
> how good and kind he is.
> He saved us because
> of his mercy,
> and not because
> of any good things
> that we have done.
>
> God washed us by the power
> of the Holy Spirit.
> He gave us new birth
> and a fresh beginning.
> God sent Jesus Christ
> our Savior
> to give us his Spirit.
>
> He did this so that
> the kindness of Jesus
> would make us acceptable
> to God
> and give us the hope
> of eternal life. (Titus 3.4–7)

If you could work your way out of sin's grasp, or earn your ticket into heaven, then God would be in debt to you. He would owe you something for what you have done. But the Bible makes it clear that God doesn't owe anything to anyone. Compared to how good he is, all of our good thoughts, words, and deeds "are like filthy rags" (quoting Isaiah 64.6 in the Old Testament).

Are You Good Enough to Get into Heaven?

A lot of people say, "Hey, I'm not such a bad person. I live a pretty good life. Surely, God will let me into his heaven."

Unfortunately, that person has missed an important point. It's not how *bad* you are; it's how *good* are you? Are you good enough for God to allow you to enter into heaven, a place where there is no sin, no dirty thoughts, no selfishness, no evil actions, and nothing displeasing to God? It's not how many sins you have committed; the question is: "Have you *ever* sinned?" If you've ever sinned (and all of us have), you need a Savior.

Usually, we compare ourselves with other people. It's easy to point at someone else and say, "Well, at least I'm not as bad as he is!" or "I know I live a lot better than she does." But God compares us to Jesus. How do you measure up next to *him*?

Sink or Swim

Think of it this way: Three guys are trying to swim from California to Hawaii. The first to make it will win a fantastic prize. One man is a thief, a gambler, and a drug addict. The second fellow is a successful businessman. The third is a preacher who was formerly a star on his college swim team, years ago.

All three men dive into the water at the same time. The first man, the crook, swims hard and fast . . . for about twenty yards. Then, he runs out of energy and starts gasping for breath and gulping gallons of salty sea water. Friendly fishermen fish the fellow out of the foam.

The second man, the white-collar type, swims about 150 yards before he, too, has to be rescued from the sea.

The third man, the good swimmer, moves smoothly through the water for more than two miles. Then, coughing and sputtering, he, too, has to be hauled aboard a boat.

Even though one contestant was better than another, all of them fell short. Not only were they not good enough to win the prize, but all three of them had to be rescued. They all needed to be saved, or else they would have drowned.

That's what the Bible means when it says, "All of us have sinned and fallen short of God's glory" (Romans 3.23). Just being a little better than someone else doesn't help if you're drowning. And the Bible says we *are* about to die! We are all "going down for the last time" when Jesus comes along and offers his hand. By reaching out to him, you can be saved.

Jesus is strong enough to save you from the downward pull of sin. He is good enough to get you into heaven. He won't force you, but if you take ahold of his hand and trust him with your life, he will save you here and now. He will also take you safely with him to heaven.

Now that's good news!

---

8 MIRACLES THAT SHOW JESUS IS MORE POWERFUL THAN NATURE

- Jesus turned water into wine (John 2.1–10).

- He calmed a bad storm (Matthew 8.22–27; Mark 4.35–41; Luke 8.22–25).

- He fed more than 5,000 people with only five loaves of bread and two small fish (Matthew 14.13–21; Mark 6.31–44; Luke 9.12–17; John 6.5–15).

- He walked on the water in the middle of a lake (Matthew 14.22–33; Mark 6.45–52; John 6.16–21).

- He fed more than 4,000 people (Matthew 15.29–39; Mark 8.1–9).

- He told Peter where to catch a fish with a coin in its mouth (Matthew 17.24–27).

- He caused the disciples to haul in a huge catch of fish (Luke 5.1–11)

- And then there was another big catch of fish (John 21.1–11).

Is There Really a Heaven?

Most people believe in heaven. Many people who don't believe in hell believe in heaven. It is the ultimate goal of life.

But where is heaven? What does it look like? How can we get there? Why don't the astronauts bump into it in outer space? Good questions.

Preachers used to warn people about being so heavenly-minded that they were no earthly good. You probably haven't heard that lately. Nowadays, most Christians are so wrapped up in and attached to *this* world, few ever think or talk much about heaven. Until the earth shakes. Then people tend to look up.

The Bible says quite a bit about heaven. The subject is mentioned fifty-two times in the book of Revelation alone! Hundreds of other references to heaven are sprinkled through the Scripture.

Granted, when the Bible speaks of heaven, the writers are not always referring to eternal bliss. Many times the term is used simply to describe the skies above us.

Jesus sometimes used the phrase "kingdom of heaven." By this, he meant his spiritual kingdom, not necessarily an eternal resting place (see Matthew 5.3; 10.7; 16.19).

But the Bible also pictures a *place* called heaven. This is the "home" of God.

What Is Heaven Like?

What do we know about heaven? Why should we want to go there?

Most importantly, we know that *heaven is the home of Jesus.* Yes, his Spirit lives within the hearts of all true believers. But in heaven, you will see Jesus, alive and in person! When Jesus returns to earth, every person who ever lived will see him—even those who crucified him. Quoting the prophets Daniel and Zechariah, the Apostle John wrote:

> Look! He is coming with the clouds. Everyone will see him, even the ones who stuck a sword through him. (Revelation 1.7)

Whew! What a thought! You are going to see the King! A common fellow was invited to dinner by England's royal family. At the dinner, the man could barely eat, because his stomach was fluttering so badly. Can you imagine being in the presence of the King of kings?

No Excuses This Time!

You will be there—count on it. And you won't be late. You may be a pro at putting things off until some other time, but this is one meeting you will not miss. You may avoid Jesus Christ all of your life on earth. You may attempt to shut him out of your life. You may ignore him. You may reject him. But the one person you can count on meeting someday, whether you want to or not, is Jesus Christ.

On that day, if you know Jesus (which is evidenced by living for him), he will welcome you into your heavenly home. If you don't know him, you will hear him say words that will haunt you forever in hell: "Get out of my sight, you evil people!" (Matthew 7.23).

Your Future Home

Not only is heaven Jesus' home, it is your future home, too. The night before he was killed, Jesus told his disciples, "Don't be worried! Have faith in God and have faith in me. There are many rooms in my Father's house. I wouldn't tell you this, unless it was true. I am going there to prepare a place for each of you. After I have done this, I will come back and take you with me. Then we will be together" (John 14.1–3).

Can your mind imagine the place that the all-powerful King Jesus is preparing for you? It will be beyond our wildest dreams!

Check It Out!

In Revelation, John describes heaven (sometimes referred to as the "New Jerusalem" or the "holy city") as a huge cube. It is about fifteen hundred miles in each direction, including fifteen hundred miles high! (Revelation 21.16). The main building material in the city is pure gold (21.18). The New Jerusalem has walls of jasper (21.18). It has twelve gates, three entrances on each side (21.21).

An unusual river is there, too. It is crystal clear, and its waters give life. "On each side of the river are trees that grow a different kind of fruit each month of the year. The fruit gives life, and the leaves are used as medicine to heal the nations" (22.1, 2).

Interpreters differ about how much of John's vision of heaven should be taken literally. Some of it could be symbolic. But there is no question that John describes a gorgeous place.

What Will We Do in Heaven?

Nobody knows for sure what we will do in heaven. Billy Graham has often said that he thinks part of our time in heaven will be spent working. Work *is* a joyous activity when it's done in the right spirit. Other teachers say that we may also be ruling over some parts of God's universe. Maybe so, but the Bible doesn't say these things specifically.

What the Bible does say is that in heaven we will have complete freedom to fellowship with our God. John writes prophetically:

> . . . God's home is now with his people. He will live with them, and they will be his own. Yes, God will make his home among his people. (Revelation 21.3)

True Praise and Worship

One of the most fun and exciting activities of heaven will be entering into a new level of praise and worship of the Lord. We will join the four living creatures of Revelation 4.8 who never stop singing, "Holy, holy, holy is the Lord, the all powerful God, who was and is and is coming!"

We will sing along with heaven's twenty-four elders who "kneeled down before the one sitting on the throne. And as they worshiped the one who lives forever, they placed their crowns in front of the throne and said, 'Our Lord and God, you are worthy to receive glory, honor, and power. You created all things, and by your decision they are and were created'" (Revelation 4.10, 11; see also 5.11–13).

Praise is going to be the "language" of heaven. Worship will no longer be "worked up." It will flow naturally to God from the hearts of his people.

What *Won't* Be in Heaven?

It is interesting to note what will *not* be in heaven:

- There will be no more *hassles with Satan* (Revelation 20.10)
- No *sea* (21.1; some Bible scholars believe this means we will no longer be separated from our loved ones)
- No *tears* are in heaven, either; nor is there any *death, suffering, crying, or pain* (21.4)
- Neither will there be any *temple* (21.22)
- No *sun*, no *moon* (21.23)

- No *night,* no *closing* of the city gates (21.25)
- Nothing *unworthy* (21.27)
- No one who is *dirty-minded* (21.27)
- No one who tells *lies* (21.27)
- No *curse* of sin; it will be broken (22.3)

Heaven Is a Holy Place

Everything about heaven is holy. The Lord of heaven is holy. The angels and the other creatures who are worshiping the Lord Jesus are holy. The redeemed saints of God are holy. Everything and everyone in heaven is holy!

If that is the case (and it is), obviously not everybody is going to go to heaven. That's why Jesus warned:

Go in through the narrow gate. The gate to destruction is wide, and the road that leads there is easy to follow. A lot of people go through that gate. But the gate to life is very narrow. The road that leads there is so hard to follow that only a few people find it. (Matthew 7.13, 14)

How Can You Get to Heaven?

There is only one way to heaven. That is through Jesus Christ. He must get you in or you won't get in at all. You don't go to heaven because you have more good points than bad marks against your name. No, the people who are going to heaven really deserved to go to hell. But they called out to Jesus and he saved them.

You must be born again to get into heaven. Not just a member of a church, but a member by faith of what the Bible calls "the body of Christ." If you have never been born again, or if you are not sure that you have, this is a good time to make sure.

How to Be Born Again

Jesus never gave us a formula for being born again. Sometimes, he works in different ways. Generally though, to become a born-again Christian, four acts of your will are involved:

1. You must ADMIT that you are a sinner and that you want to be saved.

2. You must REPENT of your sins. This means that you are willing to turn away from your sins. The word *repent* means to turn around completely.

3. You must BELIEVE that Jesus died on the cross *for you* and that he arose from the dead.

4. You must RECEIVE Jesus into your life. The best way to do this is simply to ask him to come in. Tell Jesus you want to trust him from now on. Thank him for saving you right now.

Is Jesus Really the *Only* Way to Get to Heaven?

Is Jesus the *only* way to get to heaven? Yes. "But those people who worship other deities are very sincere!"

Lots of people are sincere. Many have great faith in their gods. But faith in a false god is foolish. Your faith is only as good as the god in which it is placed. That's where Jesus shines.

Jesus Christ claimed to be God. He allowed himself to be worshiped as God, something no other Jewish person would dream of doing. When Thomas said to Jesus, "You are my Lord and my God" (John 20.28), Jesus did not say, "No, Thomas, don't call me that." Jesus accepted Thomas' worship. So Jesus believed in his own deity.

Jesus often said that he was the Son of God (for an example, see John 3.16–18). He said things about himself that, if they were not true, would have meant he was dishonest or even crazy. Some people want to think of Jesus as merely a great moral teacher. Jesus did not stop there. He said he was God.

He never claimed to be *one* of the ways you could find God and get to heaven. He said, "I am *the* way." He stated it clearly:

> "I am the way, the truth, and the life!" Jesus answered. "Without me, no one can go to the Father." (John 14.6)

Are these simply the rantings of a madman? No way! Jesus not only claimed to be God, he proved it by the miracles he did. Most of all, he proved it by dying on the cross and rising from the dead. That's what makes Jesus so different from other religious leaders.

WHAT ABOUT THE CRUSADES, SLAVERY, AND THE INQUISITION?

Could Christians be so cruel toward other people? Sadly, yes. In history, so-called "Christians" have sometimes treated members of other religious groups terribly. Those who did such things either didn't know the true Jesus, or were dreadfully deceived. Jesus has never commanded his followers to kill Moslems, keep slaves, persecute Jews, or hurt anyone else.

Awful things such as the Crusades, slavery, and the Inquisition are the result of sinful people using Christianity for their own purposes. That is still going on today. You hear it every so often. People claiming to be Christians hurt others in the name of religion. But that is not true Christianity. Don't blame Jesus, his teachings, or true Christians for such sinful actions. The people doing these things do not really know Christ, or else they are choosing to live in sin.

"What makes Jesus any different than Buddha or Mohammed or Confucius?"

Mohammed believed himself a prophet. Buddha called himself a seeker. (Too bad he never found the truth.) Confucius never claimed to be anything more than a wise teacher. All of these religious leaders are dead and buried. Only Jesus is alive.

Nowadays, it gets confusing to hear many people using the same terms as Christians, but not believing that Jesus is God. Moslems, for example, accept Jesus as a prophet and a great teacher, but they deny that Jesus is God. Yet you see and hear them talking about praying to God.

Many people say that the Islamic god and the Christian God are the same. That is impossible. God is God, period. And Jesus proved that he is God. If you don't believe that Jesus is who he says he is, you don't really believe God. You may believe your ideas *about* God, but your ideas will never save you. Only Jesus can do that.

---

3 PEOPLE RAISED FROM THE DEAD BY JESUS

- Jairus's daughter (see Mark 5.22–43)
- A widow's son in the town of Nain (see Luke 7.11–15)
- Jesus' friend Lazarus (see John 11.1–44)

SIN: A CRIME OF THE HEART

Sin is serious stuff. Many Christians think lightly of sin. They say, "Aw, it's not so bad." Or "What's the difference? Nobody's perfect." Or "Everybody is doing it!"

Watch out! The Bible doesn't say that at all. It says that God hates sin. He allowed his only son, Jesus, to die for your sins. Obviously, God takes sin seriously.

What Is Sin?

Scholars have all sorts of definitions for sin. Some of them are helpful; others are confusing. Here is a simple one: *"Sin is willful disobedience to God."* When you know what is right and you willfully decide to do wrong, that is sin. James puts it this way: "If you don't do what you know is right, you have sinned" (James 4.17).

The word that Jesus used most often when he talked about sin means "to miss the mark." It is as though you were aiming at a target, but you missed. Your shot fell short. That's what the Scripture means when it says, "All of us have sinned and fallen short of God's glory" (Romans 3.23). We tried to hit God's mark, but we missed.

Okay. So we've all sinned. What can you do about it? How can you get free from sin and its effects? The Bible says, "If we say that we have not sinned, we are fooling ourselves, and the truth is not in our hearts. But if we tell God about our sins, he can always be trusted to forgive us and take our sins away" (1 John 1.8, 9). Wow! God will forgive us for sinning. Isn't that great news?

Why Is Sin So Serious?

Sin is serious because it is always an offense toward God. Whether you sin against yourself or someone else, it still offends God. He hates sin. He knows that it can kill you, and he loves you enough to tell you the truth. When you sin, it's like spitting in Jesus' face. It is *his* law— and his heart—that you are breaking.

What Does It Mean to Repent of My Sins?

To repent of your sins means more than merely feeling sorry that you did something wrong. We tend to think that to admit our failure is

29

all that is necessary. We assume that we can pray a few sorrowful words or shed a few tears and everything will be fine. Oh, no it won't! To say you are sorry for your sins is a good place to start but a bad place to stop. You should also ask God to forgive you.

"I'm sorry" is simply a statement of fact. To repent means to "turn around," to "turn away" from your sin. Lots of people are sorry for their sin, but they won't turn away from it. In the New Testament, even Judas, the disciple who betrayed Jesus, was sorry for what he had done. But he didn't ask Jesus for forgiveness. Nor did he turn away from his sin. Instead, he went out and hanged himself (Matthew 27.5).

On the other hand, think of the story Jesus told about the "prodigal son." The son said, "I will . . . go to my father and say to him, 'Father, I have sinned against God in heaven and against you'" (Luke 15.18). He was forgiven.

If you want to be forgiven of your sin, *turn* to God. Tell him all about it. Ask him to forgive you. He will! Stop playing spiritual games. Quit blaming everyone else for your sin. Take responsibility for your own actions and attitudes. Make up your mind that you are turning away from sin. Then do it. The Holy Spirit will help you (see p. 110).

What If I Sin Again?

Unfortunately, you probably will sin again. You're not in heaven yet. Sometimes, you may fail. When you do, here are three things to remember:

1. Keep "short accounts" with God. In other words, when the Holy Spirit shows you that you have thought, said, or done something displeasing to God, be quick to confess that sin. Tell God about it. Admit what you have done and tell God that you are sorry—truly sorry.

2. Ask God to forgive you. Don't worry. He won't get disgusted with you. Not if you are serious about repenting. Then, turn away from that sin. Ask God to give you the power to turn around.

3. Own up to what you have done. Make right what is wrong (if possible).

The Apostle John gives you another hint: "My children, I am writing this so that you will not sin. But if you do sin, Jesus Christ always does the right thing, and he will speak to the Father for us" (1 John 2.1). That's good news!

WHAT'S THE DIFFERENCE BETWEEN A SIN AND A MISTAKE?

It all depends on your motive. Most of us don't mean to make mistakes. We just do. On the other hand, sin is willful. It is voluntary. You don't have to do it. You sin because you *want* to do it. It is a decision of your will.

An old story illustrates this truth. A little boy helped his dad to pick some onions from their garden. After they pulled the onions, the father and son washed, sorted, and laid them out to dry on the back porch.

"Good job, son," the father said, as he gently patted his boy on the back. "Thanks for helping me."

Later that month, the boy was out in the garden by himself. He looked, and to his surprise, found more onions growing in the place where he and his dad had already picked the onions previously!

"Oh, boy! Dad's gonna love this," he thought, as he pulled the onions from the ground. He took the onions into the house and washed them under the faucet. As he did, the boy noticed that these onions weren't nearly as large as the ones he and his dad had picked a few weeks earlier. Still, he couldn't wait to see his father's face when he saw the onions.

Surprise, Surprise!

When the father arrived home from work, the boy met him at the door. "Dad! Look what I found in the garden today. More onions!" His father allowed the boy to pull him through the kitchen and onto the back porch. There, the man's smile turned to a scowl.

"What's wrong, Dad? Look at the onions I found. Didn't I do good? Look, I cleaned them just like we did the other ones."

"Son, these onions aren't ready to be picked yet," the father answered. "While you were at school, I planted some more onions in that part of the garden. Now, they're ruined. It's too late in the year to plant any more. I appreciate your work. I know you meant well. But what you did was wrong."

What Was It?

Now, here's the question: Did the boy sin? Or did he merely make a mistake? People who see God only as a heavenly Judge might say, "Yes, the boy sinned. He did wrong. He must be punished."

Those who see God not only as Judge but also as heavenly Father would say, "No, the boy's heart was clean. He didn't mean to do wrong. His motives were pure. Yes, he made a mistake, but he did not deliberately disobey his father. In fact, he had hoped to please him." So in this case we have a mistake, not a sin.

Still, a parent corrects a child who has done something wrong, even with pure motives, to try to keep the mistake from happening again. Likewise, God disciplines and teaches his children.

But God can't allow willful sin to go unpunished. So he allowed his Son, Jesus, to take the punishment for your sins. By faith in him, you can receive forgiveness of sin and eternal life in fellowship with your Father in heaven.

WHO DO YOU THINK YOU ARE?

How you see yourself is one of the key factors in your life. Some people refer to this as their self-image, or self-esteem.

What Is Self-Esteem?

Self-esteem is that deep-down feeling you have about your personal worth. It's how you regard yourself. It's your opinion of your own value. It's that feeling that says, "I like myself" or "I dislike myself."

Your self-image is much like a self-portrait of yourself. It is who and what you picture yourself to be. It's what you think of *you*.

Why Does It Matter?

The reason your self-concept is so important is: you will probably talk, act, and react like the person you *think* you are. Oh, sure, even with a poor self-concept you may break out of the pattern and belt one out of the park—or ace the big test—or get a date with your dreamboat.

On the other hand, even guys and girls with good self-images blow it from time to time. Usually, though, your mind will complete the picture you tell it to paint of yourself.

If you see yourself as ugly, fat, stupid, or slow, you will probably act that way. If your self-worth is low, you may think of yourself as a born loser, a washout, a filthy, unforgiven sinner. You may think that you are unworthy of God's love or anybody else's.

You may slip into the habit of putting yourself down. Here are a few of the phrases that a person with poor self-esteem often uses:

66 I can never do anything right. 99

66 Why me? 99

66 I'll never amount to anything. 99

66 I guess God loves me, but I sure can't stand myself. 99

66 Oh, I'm such a klutz! 99

❝ I'm good for nothing. **❞**

❝ Everything I touch, I mess up. **❞**

❝ What a rotten person I am. **❞**

❝ God could never use somebody like me. **❞**

Sound familiar?

On the other hand, if you know that you *matter* to God, that he created you in his image and he really *cares* about what happens to you, then you can feel good about yourself. Your self-image begins to rise when you remember that God loves you. Not only does he love you, he *likes* you, too! He thinks you are pretty special. You are a one-of-a-kind miracle, made by the Master.

Because of that, you can honestly say, "Thanks, Lord, for creating me. I know you have a purpose for making me the way you did. I'm glad to be me. I'd rather be me than any other person on earth. Thanks Lord, for what you are going to do in and through my life."

COMMON ERRORS CONCERNING SELF-CONCEPT

1. Thinking too highly of ourselves

This leads to sinful pride. *Pride* points to self. It is an attitude of superiority, "I'm better than you are." It is an inflated opinion of one's self.

Pride causes us to feel that *we* should be like God. *We* want to choose which of his commands we will obey. *We* want to call the shots—to do our own thing—rather than what God wants us to do.

This sort of self-pride is sinful. It caused Adam and Eve to rebel against God.

2. Thinking too lowly of ourselves

We tend to wallow in low self-esteem. We know that we are "fallen sinners," so we think we are worthless. Like Adam and Eve, we feel naked and ashamed, and we fear being exposed.

Understand: When you have sinned, you ought to feel badly about what you did. If you have hurt someone else, or yourself, or God, no wonder you don't feel good about yourself. You don't need to "accept yourself." You need to repent and make things right.

But once you're forgiven, it's over and in the past. Don't keep giving yourself a hard time about it. Sometimes a person you hurt won't want to "forgive and forget." You can only ask. Even if the person would rather stay mad, you want to know you've done all you could. God knows too.

3. Eating humble pie

True humility is one of the best qualities a person can have. But some people confuse godly humility with putting themselves down.

You know this sort of person. They go around dragging themselves through the dirt. "Be a doormat for Jesus" is their motto. But their fake humility is an insult to Christ. Honest humility notes our strengths and our weaknesses, good times and bad times, and gives God the glory in both (see Romans 8.28).

4. Poor, poor, pitiful me!

Other people confuse true humility with feeling sorry for themselves. "I can't do anything right. I think I'll eat some worms!" They think they are being humble, when in fact, their self-pity is only pride turned upside down.

Others have difficulty accepting a compliment. They say "Aw, shucks. It was nothin'." Or, "I'll bet I couldn't do that again in a million years!"

When someone says something nice about you, all you need to say is, "Thank you." That's *it.*

Of course, as a Christian, you know that it is "Christ in you" who does the work (Colossians 1.27). If anything of value is going to get done, he must do it. Still, he does his work *through* you. Simply accept it when somebody gives you a word of encouragement for a job well done. (Just don't get cocky about it; he used a donkey one time too, remember?)

5. Whiners and blowhards

Whiners spend most of their time advertising their mistakes. "Did I mess up?" "Was that all right? I think I blew that last part."

In a weird way, whiners are trying to get somebody else to support their own self-esteem. They really crave compliments and flattery, but their self-images are so low they are afraid to ask for an honest opinion. They hang negative comments out on the line, hoping that someone will come along and take them down. Usually, no one does.

Blowhards are the opposite. They keep telling you how great they are. Blowhards are always right, at least in their own minds. They're showoffs, and often they're loud, crude, and rude.

Strangely, both whiners and blowhards suffer from low self-esteem. They are constantly trying to draw the attention to *themselves.* What they are really saying is: "Help! I need attention. Please look at me!"

People with good self-images have healthy respect for God and healthy regard for themselves.

They don't need to crawl and they don't need to boast. They can do without expensive toys or trinkets. They know who they are in Christ, so they can afford to be modest. Their self-esteem doesn't depend upon whether or not they "win" in the eyes of the world. Their view of themselves is based upon the source of all truly lasting success, Jesus Christ.

TIPS TO IMPROVE YOUR SELF-CONCEPT

Improving your self-image may take some time and some work, but with God's help, you can do it. Here are some suggestions that will help, too.

1. Remember, God loves you and accepts you, no strings attached.

Sure, sometimes he gets angry about some of the things you do, but he will never stop loving you. He wants you in his family. YOU MATTER TO GOD!

2. Get a grip on God's forgiveness.

It's tough to feel good about yourself when you know you are dirty on the inside. Forgiveness is needed.

First, seek and receive God's forgiveness. Admit what you have done, and ask him to forgive you. Tell him that you are willing to turn away from that evil. Ask him for his power to help you avoid that same sin in the future. (You have to mean this. Don't play games.)

Second, seek forgiveness from those you may have hurt. You might be surprised at how fast most people are to forgive. (*Most* people.)

Third, you must forgive yourself. This is harder to do than you might think. But remind yourself that God has forgiven you. If Jesus loves and forgives you *(and he does),* then you can love and forgive yourself.

Fourth, you must extend forgiveness to those who have hurt *you.* Even if they never find out about it, forgive them from your heart. You'll feel as though a thousand pounds were lifted from your shoulders. Remember, Jesus said, "If you forgive others for the wrongs they do to you, your Father in heaven will forgive you. But if you don't forgive others, your Father will not forgive your sins" (Matthew 6.14, 15). Try it! You'll discover that your sense of self-worth will soon begin to rise.

3. Find a friend in whom you can confide.

You don't need many friends to help improve your self-image. But if you can find even one with whom you can share your inner feelings, it may be a large step forward for your self-esteem. This friend should be somebody you trust. They should also be someone who will tell you the truth about yourself.

Don't think you are a weirdo for seeking help. Just the opposite is true. We all need encouragement. Someone who can and will give you a positive boost in this area may be an answer to prayer.

4. Read.

Read the stories of some of the people who have truly had an impact upon their world, people such as Abraham Lincoln, D. L. Moody, Thomas Edison, Billy Graham, and others. Read about people who have done what you would like to do. Read about how human and fallible they were. Learn from them. If they are still living, listen to them speak, in person or on tape.

5. Smile.

Not only does it improve your self-image, it will make you more interesting to others.

6. Dress up your appearance.

Your outward appearance does make a statement, to others, and to yourself. You don't have to dress in fancy clothes or in some strange style. Just wear what makes you feel good about yourself.

7. Don't believe the devil.

The Bible says that Satan tries to accuse God's people night and day (Revelation 12.10). "You're never going to get it together," he whispers. "You've messed up too many times. You've been too bad."

Remember, THE DEVIL IS A LIAR! Tell him to get lost.

The apostle Paul tells us:

Let the Spirit change your way of thinking and make you into a new person. (Ephesians 4.23, 24)

Cheer up and feel good about *you.* God is on your side.

I'M ALL
STRESSED OUT

Stress. A lot of us feel it. Parents, teachers, businessmen, even pastors. Teenagers are especially sensitive to stress. Stress at home, at work, at school with your friends, pressure from your peers, difficult decisions about dating, drugs, sex, or alcohol, grappling with your grades . . . whew! The stress can really get to you.

What Causes Stress?

Most stress in your life can be traced to one of three sources:

✓ Other people

✓ Events or circumstances

✓ Inner confusion or frustration

Other people can put pressure on you in many different ways. Parents can pressure you to do better at school, to get a part-time job, or to be home on time. Brothers and sisters (especially younger and sisters) can be a source of stress, too.

Sometimes other people simply bother you. Stress strikes when your friends have ignored you, criticized you, or attempted to get you to do something you'd rather avoid.

Events and circumstances, especially those over which you have no control, pour on the pressure. For example, you pass your driver's test, but don't have a car of your own to drive. Your parents need theirs, and not many friends will allow you to borrow an automobile. So, you're stuck. All dressed up and no way to go.

STRESS FINDER

Stress can sneak up on you. Many times you don't even notice it until it's too late. But being aware of a few signs of stress can help you avoid being caught by surprise.

Read over the list below and think back over the past few days or weeks. Then check off those signs you have noticed in your life recently. More than three checkmarks, and you may be headed for burnout. Review the suggestions, and if necessary, seek help:

❑ Extreme tension between you and your parents

❑ Temper tantrums

❑ Headaches

❑ Avoiding being with other people

❑ Frequent stomach knots or pains

❑ Problems with your peers

❑ Nightmares

❑ Too much sleep

❑ Too little sleep

❑ Declining interest in enjoyable activities

❑ Attempting to escape your problems through music, movies, and TV, or drugs, sex, alcohol, or the occult.

Or, you studied like mad for that big test, and you really did pretty well, but "Billy the Brain" blew the curve by blitzing the test and scoring a perfect paper. Another "C" for you.

Or, you've been hoping and praying for a date to homecoming, but nobody wants to go with you. What's the result? Frustation, anger, and, you guessed it, more pressure.

Sometimes the stress comes from **turmoil inside** that you can't explain. It's just there. Fear of failure, or rejection, or not being popular, or that you aren't smart enough or good-looking, or that you won't be able to succeed in the career you want to pursue. All of these things bring about stress.

How Can You Handle Stress?

1. Notice the warning signs. Your heart always seems to be racing. Your stomach feels as though it is tied in knots. These are often the first warnings of too much stress.

2. Recognize that everyone gets stressed out once in a while. Even strong Christians have to deal with the pressures of life. The pressures don't go away with age. They simply take a different form.

3. Try various methods of coping. When the pressure is on, some people will close their eyes and relax for a few minutes. Others suggest that you blink hard. This breaks the train of thought that has been racing through your mind. Sometimes it helps to take a deep breath and let it out very slowly. Do this several times and you will begin to feel your body relaxing.

Take a walk. Take a break. Change your routine or usual pattern of doing things. Often, physical exercise is a great stress reducer. Go swimming or jogging. Play some basketball.

Check your diet. Are you eating healthy, or are you stuffing your body with junk food? It does make a difference.

4. Realize that there are some things you can't control. For example, you can't control whether or not your parents will get a divorce, but you can control whether or not you will get to school or work on time. Concentrate on those things you *can* change, not the ones you can't.

5. Seek support. Everyone needs to talk with someone who cares. Don't be bashful about seeking help from someone who has been where you are right now. Possibly your parents, pastor, or youth leader can relate to what you are going through. Be willing to go to them and ask for their advice. They may never know you are hurting unless you talk to them. Your friends may be able to help, too, but keep in mind, their views are probably close to your own. Otherwise, you wouldn't be friends.

6. Talk to God. This is your first line of defense against stress. When you pray, talk honestly with the Lord. Tell him what you are feeling, and ask for his help. He understands, and he can help.

Sometimes the best part of praying takes place when you simply keep quiet and listen for God to speak to your heart and mind. He tells us in his word, "Be still, and know that I am God" (Psalm 46.10). In other words, relax and listen. Allow him to help.

Why Am I So Depressed?

Depression is difficult to define. Yet it is one of the most common complaints among Christians. Depression is an emotional condition, but it affects our spiritual condition as well. Generally, it is described as feelings of distress, failure, hopelessness, gloom, despair, dejection, sadness, boredom, and an inability to cope. Basically, it's a very "yukky" feeling.

What Causes Depression?

- Sometimes people who are prone toward depression have a poor self-image. They feel badly about themselves, so it is hard to feel good about much else.
- Sometimes depression is caused by feelings of guilt or shame, self-criticism, or embarrassment. If these feelings are the result of sin, the sin should be confessed to the Lord. Often, depression will go away when a person knows that he or she is forgiven.
- Sometimes self-pity causes depression. Maybe you are feeling sorry for yourself because you made a wrong decision. Or you flunked a test. Or you didn't get to do something you wanted to do. Watch out. This kind of depression leads to sin.
- Sometimes, though, none of the above reasons are the cause of the depression. You simply feel "down" and you don't really have a good reason. You are not alone. Some of the great Christians in past generations battled the beast of depression all their lives. John Wesley, Hudson Taylor, Charles Spurgeon, and Amy Carmichael are just a few of many "world-changing" Christians who fought periodic bouts with depression.

Is Depression a Sin?

It's not a sin to get depressed. But it might be a sin to *stay* depressed—especially if the depression is caused by self-centeredness.

Keep in mind, people don't simply "snap out of" depression. It may take time. Be patient with yourself. Perhaps a physical, chemical imbalance in your body is the cause. If you seem always depressed, an exam by a doctor may be the place to start. Check your diet carefully. Are you eating right? Getting enough sleep? Exercising?

Other Possibilities

Are you a perfectionist? You say nothing ever seems quite good enough for you? If so, you will probably be depressed much of your life.

Do you have some wrong concepts about God? Maybe you have been taught that you can never please him; that you must always work harder and harder; that you are doomed to be a failure in your spiritual life. If so, no wonder you get depressed! God is not like that. He loves you, period. You don't have to earn his love. Nothing you ever do will keep God from loving you.

Whatever the reason for your depression, don't ignore it. If you find yourself often feeling down for long periods of time, seek counsel. Your pastor will be able to help, but the first step will be up to you.

Also, spend some time talking honestly to God in prayer. Tell him your *real* feelings, not just things you think you are supposed to say. Read regularly from your Bible, not as a duty, but approach the Bible as a life energizer. It is.

God wants to deliver you from depression. If you will let him, he will.

❝ You can make more friends in two months by becoming interested in other people than you can in two years by trying to get other people interested in you. ❞ —Dale Carnegie

Why Am I So Lonely?

Loneliness is one of the worst feelings in life. It's that awful, isolated feeling you get, sometimes even in a crowd. You feel unwanted, rejected, unnecessary. No matter how hard you try, you sense that you just don't belong. You feel like the third passenger in a Corvette.

Lonely people usually have a hard time talking to other people. They lack confidence in themselves. "Who would want to talk with me?" the lonely person wonders.

This makes for a cruel merry-go-round in their relationships. They are lonely because they *can't* talk to others, and they *won't* talk to others because they feel so badly about themselves. So they *don't* talk. They just keep going around and around on a lonely merry-go-round.

Help! I Want to Get Off!

How can you get off that ride?

1. Begin by reading some of the Bible every day. When you read God's word, you sense his presence. When you know that *he* is with you, even when it *looks* like you are alone, you are no longer lonely. Your Best Friend is right there with you.

2. Get involved within your local church or youth group. Think about what you can give to the group, rather than what you can get. Just being around other Christians is a help. Laugh. Have fun. Try new things. Tell somebody else about the joy you have found in Jesus.

3. If possible, mend any "broken fences" with your own family. Maybe the reason you feel so alone is because you broke off your relationship with your family. Do whatever you can to patch things up.

4. Keep in close touch with a youth leader, pastor, or a friend you trust. Ask this person to honestly tell you when you are sliding into self-pity or other negative attitudes that would cause people not to want to be around you.

5. Take the Lord at his word:
The Lord has promised that he will not leave us or desert us. That should make you feel like saying, "The Lord helps me! Why should I be afraid of what people can do to me?" (Hebrews 13.5, 6).

6. Make sure you are in a right relationship with the Lord. If you are "out of sync" with God, it will affect all of your other friendships. It becomes easy to retreat into your own feelings. You don't want to talk. You feel dirty on the inside. But if you have God's peace in your heart, that will shine through your face. Other people will want to be around you.

7. Sometimes you must work at getting along with people. One of the best ways to do this is by asking questions. Everybody has a story to tell, but most people don't have anyone who will listen. Draw the other person out. Get him or her talking, then be sure to listen and show interest.

8. Work at expressing your own feelings and thoughts. Many people are afraid to say what they think for fear of saying something silly. Try starting a sentence with "I feel" or "I think" and then simply express what you feel. You may be right or wrong. Still, if it is an honest statement, nobody will be able to dispute it. It is what *you* feel.

9. Look people in the eye when you talk to them. Besides building your confidence, it will say to the person with whom you are talking, "I'm interested in what you are saying. I want to hear more." Have you ever talked to a person who, while talking with you, is looking over your shoulder or around the room? How did it make you feel? Unimportant? Frustrated? Angry?

10. When you feel shy and timid, and you sense yourself wanting to retreat into a lonely corner, stop. Pray right there. Ask God for an extra dose of confidence. He will give you the help you need.

How Can I Find Friends Who Like Me for Who I Am?

One thing is for sure: you won't make true friends by letting down your values or by going along with the crowd. Sure, you'll get some attention for a while that way. But not for long, And the attention you get won't make you feel great about yourself. Nowadays, people respect someone who dares to "go against the flow."

Where Can I Meet Friends?

New friends might be just about anywhere! You usually make your closest friends where you spend most of your time. Here are some tips:

1. School, work, sports teams or events, and church activities are some possibilities. *Go where the kind of friends you want hang out:* Christian concerts, working with the church youth group, missions trips, or just goofing off together.

   God *could* send friends to your door without you having to do anything. Most likely, though, he won't. He expects you to do your part. If you insist upon wasting your time watching television, you might as well go out and buy an inflatable friend, prop it up in the corner, and pretend "he" or "she" is your best friend. But if you want to meet real people who aren't plastic, go where they are.

2. *Be a bit bold.* Don't be bashful about saying hello to new people at school or church. But if the person turns down your attention, back off. Don't be a pest.

3. *Let your friendships grow and multiply.* Don't take advantage of your friends, but allow them to introduce you to *their* friends. Do the same for them.

4. The old saying is true: *"To have a friend you must be a friend."* Take an interest in your friends. Let them know that they are important to you. Send a card or a note of encouragement once in a while. Most everybody loves to get mail, especially when it's telling them that they matter to someone else. Tell your friends why you admire or appreciate them. Don't flatter, just be yourself. Be a friend.

5. Most important, make sure Jesus is *Lord of your friendships.* Keep first things first. Look at Matthew 6.25–34 and check out your priorities as you read.

How Can I Be a Good Friend?

Everyone says that to have friends, you must *be* a friend. But what does that really mean? How can you be the kind of person other people want to be near? Here are some places to start:

1. Be a servant.

Try to serve others, rather than looking to have your needs met. Give, rather than seeking to get. Help someone else, instead of always expecting someone to help you. Most people tend to think about themselves. When they are looking for friends, they look for people who might be able to help them. If you are a helping kind of person, you'll have plenty of friends.

"But what about *my* needs?"

God is the only one who can meet your deepest needs. By giving his Son, Jesus, to die for your sins, God proved that he loves you (Romans 5.6–8). Other people can *help* you feel loved or wanted, and it's okay to enjoy them doing so. But when you *need* other people's love or acceptance more than God's, it's an insult to him.

Not only that, other people will let you down. Even your best buddy will disappoint you. But Jesus never will. He will be there every time you need him.

Instead of trying to get others to do what you want, try to serve them. How? By putting others first, rather than yourself. You will be able to do that because you know that Jesus loves and accepts you without any strings. As you serve others, you'll be surprised how many people want to be your friend.

2. Be real.

It's okay to let other people know that you hurt, that you don't have all the answers, that you're not always feeling on top of the world about everything. Some people think that being a Christian means that you never have a problem. If that were true, Jesus would have made a poor Christian!

People got mad at Jesus. Some people even cursed at him. Some of his best friends let him down. They betrayed him when he needed them most. But Jesus didn't get his self-worth from other people. He got it from his heavenly Father.

Jesus could risk being let down by his friends. Why? Because his trust was in God. He knew that if he was rejected or disappointed by other people, he was still loved and accepted by the one that mattered most, his heavenly Father.

3. Be available.

Friends need to be there for each other. If you are never around when your friends need help or encouragement—guess what? They probably won't be there for you, either.

4. Be loyal.

Nobody likes a person who is two-faced. Some people play games with their friendships. They are your friend as long as you're with them. But when you turn your back, watch out! You don't need that sort of friend, and you certainly don't want to *be* that kind of friend.

5. Be honest.

If your friends can't or won't be honest with you, find a better quality of friends. Likewise, if you find yourself stretching the truth to impress your friends, you are not being honest. Honesty isn't the best policy when it comes to friendship. It's the *only* policy.

6. Be yourself.

Think about it. If everyone in town loved you because you convinced them that you were so talented, so rich, so athletic, or something else, and you really weren't—who would those people be loving? Not you. They'd be loving the fake you.

That's why even if you could pull it off (which most people can't), it is always silly to pretend you are someone or something you are not. You want to be loved for who you really are.

Not only that, *you* are a one-of-a-kind original. The world has never seen another you. You are unique. God made you that way on purpose. He gave you unique gifts, talents, and personality traits to be used for his glory. You have a lot to give to any friendship. You've got *you!*

GOD IS NOT OPPOSED TO SEX

God created sex. He thinks it is a great idea. God is not opposed to sex.

God is against the *misuse* of sex. He hates sexual immorality.

God always speaks favorably about sex when it is within marriage. But the Bible condemns *all* sexual activity outside the bonds of marriage. God's word says, "Have respect for marriage. Always be faithful to your partner, because God will punish anyone who is immoral or unfaithful in marriage" (Hebrews 13.4).

This Is Serious!

God labels all sexual conduct outside of marriage as sin. Yes, he is serious. The Apostle Paul said, "Don't you know that evil people won't have a share in the blessings of God's kingdom? Don't fool yourselves! No one who is immoral or worships idols or is unfaithful in marriage or is a pervert or behaves like a homosexual will share in God's kingdom" (1 Corinthians 6.9, 10).

Whew! Do you get the message that God doesn't want you messing around with sexual immorality?

All through the Bible, God specifically says the same thing about sex before marriage or sex outside of marriage. He says it is wrong. Check this out:

> Don't be immoral in matters of sex. That is a sin against your own body in a way that no other sin is. Surely you know that your body is a temple where the Holy Spirit lives. The Spirit is in you and is a gift from God. You are no longer your own. God paid a great price for you. So use your body to honor God. (1 Corinthians 6.18–20)

God Is Not a Killjoy

Why should God care about your sex life? Why does he give you such strict instructions concerning your sexuality? Doesn't he want you to enjoy one of life's greatest pleasures? Is he trying to cramp your style? Does he want to hurt you? To make you miserable? Is he trying to keep you frustrated all the time?

No way! God wants the *best* for you. He wants you to enjoy your sexuality to the fullest—at the right time and with the right person—

your marriage partner! God wants you to enjoy every gift he has given you. To enable this, he has given you some guiding rules and regulations in his word. These principles will keep you from hurting yourself or harming anyone else.

When you live your life according to God's will, you're happy. When you choose to disobey, you're miserable.

7 Reasons to Avoid Premarital Sex

1. God said so. You can read what he said. Look up these Scriptures:
   1 Thessalonians 4.3–8
   Ephesians 5.3–5
   Colossians 3.5, 6
   1 Corinthians 6.9–20

2. If you limit your physical expressions in a dating relationship, it will allow you time for something really important—TALKING! Many couples have explored each other's bodies, but have never gotten to know each other. It's almost a rule: The more physical your relationship *before* marriage, the less real communication.

3. People tend to lie in the heat of the moment. He or she may say something such as, "I love you! I need you! I can't stand it any longer. I've got to have you!" The next day at school or work that same person doesn't want to have anything to do with you.

   When somebody says to you, "If you loved me, you'd let me," look that person right in the eye and say, "If you loved me, you wouldn't ask."

4. Premarital sex can harm your future marriage. A good sexual relationship takes more than two sweating bodies locked in an embrace. It takes time, patience, and unconditional love. When these things are missing, as they almost always are in premarital sex, it can create a barrier blocking your future happiness. In premarital sex, poor patterns are established

that can cause a bitter taste toward sex. Sometimes married couples have mental "flash-backs" about premarital sexual experiences. Frequently, couples experience trouble in their marriages because they are comparing their mates with other sexual partners.

5. Premarital sex often results in premarital pregnancies. Over one million teenage girls get pregnant every year, despite modern methods of contraception (means of preventing a pregnancy). Many teens having sex don't use any protection, or they do not use contraceptives correctly. Besides, no form of contraception is absolutely foolproof.

Your best protection against premarital pregnancy is abstinence. That means not having sex before you're married.

There are no easy answers for a premarital pregnancy. Somebody always gets hurt. Society says it's okay to abort the baby if a girl gets pregnant outside of marriage. But most Christians agree that abortion is murdering an unborn baby. And God says murder is a serious sin.

Adoption, while it may be the best option, is still difficult. The young mother must carry her child for nine months, give birth, and then give the baby away.

6. Venereal disease is another major reason to avoid premarital sex. Nowadays, AIDS (Acquired Immune Deficiency Syndrome) gets most of the publicity. That's because if you get AIDS, you're dead. No cure exists, as of this writing.

But don't forget about "herpes." Nobody has found a cure for it yet, either. With herpes, you get sores in the private area of your body. These sores go away for a while. Then, like a monster in a bad horror movie, they keep coming back to haunt you again.

Many other venereal diseases are dangerous too, but AIDS and herpes can ruin your life.

Most people, but not all, who get these diseases catch them by having sexual contact with someone who has the disease. On the other hand, if you don't have sex outside of marriage, you will have little worry about ever catching a venereal disease.

7. Guilt is still a result of premarital sex. It always will be.

Jennifer is seventeen and sexually active. "My friends say it's okay to have sex. My teachers say it's okay as long as I use contraceptives. My mom even took me to the doctor to get a prescription for birth control pills. Everybody says it's okay—so why do I feel so guilty?"

Jennifer feels guilty because the Holy Spirit convicts us whenever we do something that is wrong. God says sex outside of marriage is wrong. If you disobey, one of the results will be guilt.

Premarital sex always leaves marks. Sometimes these marks mar a person for life. Avoid this mess. Keep yourself pure *before* marriage and faithful *in* marriage.

If you've already made some mistakes regarding premarital sex, remember that God loves you and wants to forgive you and cleanse you. This is just the sort of thing Jesus died for. You can come back to God whenever you want to. He won't push you away.

The Sad Story of Tim and Judy

Is sex okay if you're planning to marry your partner? That's what Tim and Judy thought. Tim was a student at a Bible college where he was studying for the ministry. Judy was a talented musician with a beautiful voice. They planned to be married right after their graduation.

During their senior year, Tim and Judy often ministered at many off-campus churches. Too bad they didn't practice what they preached. On the way back, they frequently indulged in sexual intimacies. At first, they limited themselves to heavy petting, prolonged kissing and caressing of each other. Before long, they went on to have sex. They told themselves (and each other) that it was okay, because soon they would be married.

"What difference does a piece of paper and a wedding make?" they said. "As far as we're concerned, we're married already. We just haven't had the ceremony yet."

Can you guess what happened to them? They broke up. The engagement ring was returned to the jeweler. Life was supposed to go on as usual.

The only problem was: neither of them could go on as normal. Even after they confessed their sins and asked forgiveness from God and each other, they knew something was different.

"Every time I'd see Tim on campus," Judy confessed, "I'd feel cheap." Judy finally couldn't take it any more. She dropped out of college with less than a semester to go before graduation. She stopped singing in churches and took a job that made no use of her musical talent.

Tim suffered too. "Even after I knew we were forgiven, the pain was still there. We thought sex was okay because we were going to get married. We were wrong! After we broke up, it was awful. Every time I saw Judy, my insides felt like they were going to come undone.

"We were both virgins before Judy and I started dating. We hadn't had sex with anyone. I think if we had waited, we might still be together today."

HOW TO UNPLUG THE SEXUAL PRESSURE COOKER

Here are some simple steps to help keep you pure sexually, or to help regain and maintain your sexual purity if you have failed in this area.

1. Avoid bad company.

Paul does not pull any punches when he warns us, "Don't fool yourselves. Bad friends will destroy you" (1 Corinthians 15.33). Take a look at the people with whom you spend most of your free time. What are their attitudes toward love, sex, marriage and dating?

The people you are "hanging out" with are going to have an impact on you. They can influence you positively or negatively. You want to be around other Christians so they can help lift you up, rather than pull you down. Also, if you are part of a Christian group, you can get positive peer pressure working for you, instead of always having to fight against negative peer pressure.

2. Avoid the "second look."

Sure, you are going to see things that you know are sexually exciting. Nowadays, sex is used to sell all sorts of things. Magazines, billboards, TV commercials, and lots of other sources blast away at your values. But you don't have to go looking for those things.

Likewise, when you see an attractive woman (or man), it is not wrong to think, "Wow, she (or he) sure is sharp!" But when you begin undressing that person in your mind, then your admiration has turned to lust. James, Jesus' brother, reminds us, "Don't blame God when you are tempted! God cannot be tempted by evil, and he doesn't use evil to tempt others. We are tempted by our own desires that drag us off and trap us. Our desires make us sin, and when sin is finished with us, it leaves us dead" (James 1.13–15).

3. Be careful of your conversation.

One of the better results of the "sexual revolution" is that we now talk more openly about sex. Still, be careful that you don't cheapen God's beautiful gift of sexuality. Never talk dirty about sex. A Christian should avoid conversations in which sexual subjects are being discussed in an obscene or profane way. This includes dirty jokes or comments that could be taken to have a double meaning (one being impure).

It's not wrong to talk about sex. Just be sure that your words are honoring to God who created the whole idea.

4. Be careful how you dress.

Your personal appearance makes a statement. You can represent the Lord well by dressing attractively and modestly. Or, you can transmit sexual signals that attract members of the opposite sex to your body. Remember, what looks good in God's sight may be quite different than what looks good in the sight of the world.

Before you go out the door, take a good look in a mirror. Ask yourself, "What message am I transmitting by my appearance?" If the message is not one that would please God, you would be better off to change your "look." God wants you to look good, so create a "look" that will honor him.

5. Guard your leisure time.

Most of us have more free time than guys and girls had in past generations. You may not believe that at times, but it's true. How you use your time can either make or break you. Remember King David? He had a sexual affair with Bathsheba when most of his best buddies were on the battlefield. He let down his guard and he lost his own battle against lust.

The same thing could happen to you, if you are not wise. Keep busy for God. When you are not busy, be careful about how you use your time off.

6. Think positively and purely.

Choose carefully what movies, videos, and television programs you see. You know what excites you sexually. It is silly to watch sexy movies and expect that you are going to be able to resist sexual temptation. In the battle between heaven and hell, the main arena is your mind!

Be careful what you read. Stay away from novels or magazines that cater to sexual fantasies.

"But I really enjoy the literature in *Playboy* and *Penthouse*," one guy said. Yeah, right. Who do you think you are kidding?

Many romance novels seek to attract an audience of young women by glamorizing premarital sex, extramarital affairs, and even homosexual affairs. Be careful, ladies! You don't need that sort of dirt in your mind.

The same is true of the music you hear. What you listen to will have a large influence on your attitudes about sex. Be wise. Anything that causes you to fantasize sexually, or to think in thought patterns that are in opposition to God's will, should be avoided.

Paul said, "Keep your minds on whatever is true, pure, right, holy, friendly, and proper. Don't ever stop thinking about what is truly worthwhile and worthy of praise" (Philippians 4.8).

7. Pet your dog, not your date!

We hardly talk about petting nowadays. Today, it's more like *advanced mauling!* Petting could be defined as "any intimate sex play short of sexual union." This includes any physical activity that is meant to excite sexual passion in another person.

The Scripture asks, "Can a man take fire to his bosom, and his clothes not be burned? Can one walk on hot coals, and his feet not be seared?" (Proverbs 6.27, 28). Obviously, the answer is no. Make that your answer on dates with regard to petting.

8. Avoid compromising positions.

Both guys and girls need to work at this. Young woman, if he puts his hands on your body where you know they should not be, gently but firmly move his hands. You don't need to bite him, slam his hand in the car door, or stick his finger in an electric socket. Just move his hands. He'll get the hint. If he doesn't, get rid of him!

The same goes for you guys. If a young woman makes sexual advances toward you, be man enough to put a stop to it.

Don't play compromising games. For example, don't lie

down on the floor together or on the couch to watch TV. Couples play these kinds of games all too frequently. Then they wonder how they ever got in trouble!

9. Pray before every date.

Maybe you've been praying *for* a date. That's a different sort of prayer!

This is for when you *are* going out with someone of the opposite sex. Before you leave the house, stop and pray. Your prayer doesn't have to be a long, drawn out affair. You don't have to sing the Doxology or pray for all the missionaries.

Just commit the date to the Lord and ask his blessing. Say something like, "Jesus, we thank you for this time to be together, and we want you to go with us on this date. Please bless our conversation and everything that we do. Thanks, Lord, for the good time we are going to have. Amen!"

That's it. You may want to pray together again when you return from your date. Keep it short and simple. Don't try to pray your way into or out of a good-night kiss. Just pray and thank the Lord for the good time he gave you.

10. Make Jesus Lord of your social life.

No, Jesus won't call somebody up on the phone and ask that person out for you. But he will guide your decision-making process about whom you should date, or whether you should be dating at all. Remember, Jesus loves you and wants the *best* for you.

Is It Wrong to Date
Non-Christians?

Good, godly men and women have different views regarding this matter. Some see no harm at all in dating unbelievers. "After all," they say, "how are we ever going to win our friends to Christ if we always hang around only with other Christians?" Others say no Christian should ever date anyone who is not a Christian also.

Those who lean toward the second position base their opinion on Paul's warning in 2 Corinthians 6.14, 15:

> Stay away from people who are not followers of the Lord! Can someone who is good get along with someone who is evil? Are light and darkness the same? Is Christ a friend of Satan? Can people who follow the Lord have anything in common with those who don't?

Paul is saying that certain things in life just don't mix. Namely: a believer and an unbeliever. In Paul's time, large oxen were used to help plow the fields. Usually, two oxen were "yoked" together, which greatly increased the amount of work that the farmer could get done.

Sometimes, though, an ox and a bull were yoked together. This never worked well. The ox was strong and used to the yoke, but the bull often tried to pull in a different direction from the one in which the master wanted them to go. The two animals would make a lot of noise and put forth a huge amount of energy, but little useful work was done for the master.

This is the picture Paul paints of the Christian who is in an intimate relationship with an unbeliever.

Obviously, God is opposed to the marriage of a Christian and a non-Christian. But what about just dating an unbeliever?

The answer depends upon the people involved, what dating means to you, and your own mental, emotional, physical, and spiritual maturity levels. What are you looking for in the dating relationship? What are your future goals, desires, and ideas about marriage?

Check out your motives, too. If you are a born-again Christian, why do you want to date a non-Christian? Are you trying to "keep one foot in the world"?

A Few Things for Sure

Some people should definitely *not* date a nonbeliever. If you are a Christian who is seriously searching for a marriage partner, you'd better keep your dating within the family of God. You know God's command to "stay away from people who are not followers of the Lord." To marry a non-Christian would be sinful.

Someone else who should avoid dating non-Christians is the person who falls in love easily. You know the type. If you are a person whose emotions can be easily played upon, it would be unwise to date a non-Christian. You would be playing with fire.

If your "Mr. (or Miss) Wonderful" is not a Christian, you may find yourself suddenly forced to choose between your love for Christ and your love for that person. It's a hard and painful choice.

Positively Speaking

Positively, dating between two Christians can be far more fun anyhow! Much can be shared between two believers, even on a casual date. It just makes sense. The chances of enjoying your dates and pleasing God at the same time are much greater when two Christians are working together toward the same goal.

Certainly you can have non-Christians as friends. And yes, you should be telling them about Jesus. But your closest relationships should be among fellow believers.

COMMON EXCUSES: WHY CHRISTIANS GO OUT WITH UNBELIEVERS

- "Because there aren't any Christian guys around my town!"

- "Christian girls are boring. They never want to have any fun."

- "A lot of Christian guys are sort of twinky and twerpy."

- "I never used to date non-Christians. But lately, it seems that most of the Christians won't go out with me. So, I've started dating nonbelievers. I decided it would be better to date non-Christians than not to date at all."

- "Christian guys are just as bad as nonbelievers. I went out with a guy from church last week and I spent most of the evening trying to keep his hands off me. I thought Christian guys were better behaved, but I might as well have been with an unbeliever."

- "Christian guys just don't ask me out."

RISKS YOU RUN WHEN YOU DATE A NON-CHRISTIAN

There are many risks to dating nonbelievers. Here are a few of the more common ones:

1. **What are you going to do if you fall in love?**
The Scripture is clear: "Can people who follow the Lord have anything in common with those who don't?" (2 Corinthians 6.15). Yet the fact is: Christians do fall in love with nonbelievers. Many sincere Christians have played "Russian roulette" with their emotions—and have lost. They dated a non-Christian, they fell in love, and then they willfully chose to disobey God. They went ahead with a marriage that God clearly opposed. You can't disobey God and still expect his blessing!

2. **"Missionary dating" rarely works.**
Some naive Christians expect to have a positive impact upon the nonbelievers they date. Every once in a while, non-Christians do find Christ as a result of dating a Christian. When it does work that way, everybody makes a big deal about it. That's because it rarely happens!

Most "evangelistic dates" end in failure for both parties. Often, the non-Christian doesn't understand, and the Christian feels frustrated because his or her witnessing efforts fell upon "deaf" ears.

3. **You probably won't convert your partner.**
Sometimes a Christian goes ahead and marries an unbeliever thinking, "I'll convert him (or her) later." Maybe miracles can still happen. But there's no guarantee. The devil has deceived many into believing that it will somehow be easier to persuade an unbeliever to become a Christian *after* the wedding. That's usually not how it turns out.

Thousands of Christians who have lived with, or are living with a non-Christian mate could tell you the truth. It's even tougher to convert your partner when you're married.

4. **Dating an unbeliever can become addictive.**
You think that you could break off the relationship with an unbeliever rather easily. But what happens is that suddenly you

60

are faced with a choice. On the one hand there's a person you can see, feel, hear, and touch. On the other hand there's Jesus, whom you have never physically seen, or felt, or heard with your ears, or touched with your hands. You may discover, to your horror, that you are "hooked" on an unbeliever.

5. You may fall out of fellowship.

It's no secret that most non-Christians are not comfortable in church. They are "out of their element." Therefore, if you are dating an unbeliever, you may be tempted to spend less time in church yourself. You begin hanging out with the unbelieving crowd, and before long, you begin to slide spiritually.

6. You may lose out with Jesus.

Dating non-Christians will almost always create a drag on your spiritual life. Soon, it becomes easier to miss church and to spend less time fellowshiping with other believers. Your Bible sits unopened. The time you used to spend in prayer is taken up by other things. Before long, you've allowed Jesus to be crowded right out of the center of your heart.

7. You're living in different worlds.

As a Christian, you are a child of God. Without Jesus, your unbelieving date is a child of the devil (see John 8.44). If you should get married, guess who becomes your spiritual father-in-law?

Would you really want to be bound to someone who cannot or will not understand your faith in Jesus? Your values are likely to be different. Your attitudes toward love, sex, and commitment in marriage may be worlds apart.

Let's be honest. It's tough enough for two Christians to maintain a pure and holy relationship. Why trouble yourself by dating a non-Christian? The price tag is too high!

THE ABORTION BATTLE

More and more pregnant young women are choosing to abort their babies. Why? First, because it's *legal.* On January 22, 1973, the United States Supreme Court said it was okay to kill an unborn baby. Since then, an average of one and a half million babies have been destroyed *every year.* That's over four thousand babies a day.

The United States has allowed more people to be killed through abortions than have died in all of our wars put together. Only a tiny percentage of those abortions were performed to protect the health of the mother. Most were done to free young couples from the responsibilities of premarital pregnancies and parenthood.

That's the second reason why abortions are on the rise. Today, many young adults think of abortion as a "last ditch" method of birth control. Their attitude is: "If I get pregnant, I can always get an abortion."

Often, this appears to be the easiest way out rather than facing parents, friends, and the knowing looks of others in school or in town. Saving face, no matter what the cost, is the crucial issue.

A Fetus Is a Pre-Born Baby

Have you ever noticed that most people who are in favor of abortion never talk about the *baby?* They talk about the *fetus,* which is Latin for "unborn child." Why? Because "terminating a fetus" sounds like getting rid of some sort of toxic waste product. Destroying a *baby* sounds much different, doesn't it?

Actually, from the moment of conception, the instant your life began, your tiny one-celled "fetus" had all the ingredients for *you.* In that one cell were the characteristics that make up your height, the color of your hair and eyes, and your many other traits. All of *you* was already there. Only time and food were necessary for you to grow into the "larger" person you are today.

When somebody talks about aborting a fetus, don't let them kid you. They are talking about killing a human child. Furthermore, an aborted baby suffers a brutally painful death. In one type of abortion, the baby is burnt to death by a salt-water solution injected into the mother. In another method of abortion, the baby is pulled from its mother's womb, often literally, tearing the baby's little body apart.

Doctors are trying to devise new, less painful methods of abortion. Some of these will involve pregnant women taking pills or receiving injections. Still, the fact remains, when a woman aborts a baby, a life is being destroyed.

What Does the Bible Say about Abortion?

First, the Bible makes it plain that murder is a sin. As part of the Ten Commandments, God says, "You shall not murder" (Exodus 20.13). Abortion merely to avoid an unwanted pregnancy is murder, whether the government says so or not.

Beyond that, God places immense value upon human life. An unborn baby has the potential to become a fully developed person. God is the one who is forming the child in the mother's womb, not the doctors or the government. King David described it this way:

> For You formed my inward parts; You covered me in my mother's womb. I will praise You, for I am fearfully and wonderfully made; marvelous are Your works, and that my soul knows very well. My frame was not hidden from You, when I was made in secret, and skillfully wrought in the lowest parts of the earth. (Psalm 139.13–15)

Not only does David say that God is involved in this process, but David tells us that God had a plan for our lives even before we were born:

> Your eyes saw my substance, being yet unformed. And in Your book they all were written, the days fashioned for me, when as yet there were none of them. (Psalm 139.16)

God told his prophet Jeremiah something similar. He said, "Before I formed you in the womb I knew you; before you were born I sanctified you; I ordained you a prophet to the nations" (Jeremiah 1.5).

The Bible always talks about an unborn child as a baby, not as a fetus, or a problem, or "an accident." (For a beautiful example of this, turn to Luke 1.39–45.)

AFTER AN ABORTION

Maybe you or a person close to you has already had an abortion. Perhaps you didn't know any better. Or, maybe you knew it was wrong. Your conscience screamed at you like a siren, but you were afraid to do anything else. Whatever the case, here are a few things a person who has had an abortion should know:

- God has not given up on you. He still loves you, even though you have sinned.

- Abortion, although horrible, is *not* the unpardonable sin. You can be forgiven. If you (or your friend) are willing to confess your sins to the Lord, he has promised to forgive you (see 1 John 1.9).

- If you (or your friend) have never trusted Jesus as your Savior, this would be an excellent time to start. Admit to God that you are a sinner. Tell him that you are willing to turn away from your sin. Believe that Jesus died on the cross for you, to pay the price for your sins. Ask him to come into your life.

- Now that you (or your friend) are forgiven, "go and do not sin anymore." Read the story about the woman who was caught in bed with a man who was not her husband (John 8.3–11). Notice how tenderly, yet how firmly Jesus dealt with her. He forgave her when everyone else wanted to kill her. He'll do the same for you.

Is Homosexuality a Sin?

Here are a few comments often heard: "Homosexual relationships are just as normal as heterosexual relationships." "God doesn't judge a person according to his or her sexual preferences." "If God didn't want people to be gay, he wouldn't have made them that way."

"You Christians are a bunch of homophobiacs. Just because you are sexually repressed, don't bother those who are free to express their true feelings." "Homosexuality is an alternate lifestyle. It's merely a different sexual orientation."

These are common statements being made about homosexuality today. Are the people who say such things right? What does the Bible say about homosexuality?

What Is Homosexuality?

A homosexual is a person who is sexually attracted to those of his or her own sex. Male homosexuals are often referred to as "gay," although the term is often used to include males and females. Female homosexuals are sometimes referred to as "lesbians." Homosexuality is a complex problem, and one that is misunderstood by many both in and out of the church. It is a lifestyle practiced by millions. But that does not make it normal. Nor does it mean that homosexuality should be accepted as slightly unusual behavior, any more than drunkenness, murder, robbery, or rape should be viewed as only slightly abnormal.

What Does the Bible Say?

Is homosexuality a sin? The Bible says it is.

Homosexual acts are strongly condemned in both the Old and New Testaments. Nowhere in the Bible is homosexuality regarded as any-

---

IF YOU ARE TEMPTED TOWARD HOMOSEXUALITY

If you are a homosexual or feel yourself tempted toward homosexual acts, it is important to understand that God loves you. He hates the sin of homosexual actions, but he loves you.

Some people try to excuse their immoral behavior by saying, "Well, I can't help it. I was born that way."

Yes, you can help it. If you still feel homosexual temptations pulling at you, even though you are a Christian, you must resist those desires just as a heterosexual person must resist the temptations to immorality. Resisting is difficult but not impossible, if it's done by the power of the Holy Spirit.

Real deliverance will result as you stay in continuous, close contact with Jesus. He will give you the power to resist temptation and to live a holy life.

Radical change often requires time. Your progress may be a process. If you fail, ask Jesus for forgiveness, and allow him to restore you once again.

thing other than sinful activity. Although homosexual acts are not singled out as being worse than other sins, those who do such things are always included in God's judgment and condemnation.

The Old Testament towns of Sodom and Gomorrah were destroyed because of their awful sinfulness. Part of this was revealed by some of the townspeople's intent to have homosexual relations with God's angels! (See Genesis 19.1–25; also Judges 19.13—20.48.)

In the Old Testament, God left no doubt about his feelings toward homosexual conduct. He warned, "You shall not lie with a male as with a woman. It is an abomination" (Leviticus 18.22). A few chapters later God says, "If a man lies with a male as he lies with a woman, both of them have committed an abomination. They shall surely be put to death. Their blood shall be upon them" (Leviticus 20.13). You don't get the impression that God views homosexuality as an "alternate lifestyle," do you?

The ungodly nations around God's people promoted homosexual activities. They even endorsed homosexual prostitution (see 1 Kings 14.24; 22.46).

Get With the Times?

Some people say, "Well, that's the Old Testament. We New Testament believers are not under those laws any more."

Granted, but the Apostle Paul didn't think it made much difference in this case. In his letter to the Christians at Rome, he described both male and female homosexual behavior as evil and shameful. Check it out for yourself in Romans 1.26–32.

While you are at it, flip the pages over to 1 Corinthians 6.9. There, Paul includes perverts and homosexuals along with those who will *not* share in God's kingdom. (This is assuming that they refuse to turn from their sins and be saved.)

Why Would God Condemn Homosexual Acts?

God is probably against homosexual conduct for the same reason he is against premarital sex and extramarital sex: God is firmly in favor of marriage and the family. Sex is meant to be the ultimate expression between a man and a woman, committed to each other for life, in marriage. All sex outside of marriage, homosexual or heterosexual, is sin.

Is There Hope
For a Homosexual?

Yes there is! In fact, the same passage in which Paul lists all sorts of immoral acts, including homosexuality, says, "Some of you used to be like that. But now the name of our Lord Jesus Christ and the power of God's Spirit have washed you and made you holy and acceptable to God" (1 Corinthians 6.11). Did you catch that? *Washed. Holy. Acceptable to God.*

What he is saying is that no person is beyond hope. No perversion is beyond cure. No homosexual sin or heterosexual sin will keep a person from God if he or she honestly repents and finds forgiveness.

A Word to the Church Concerning Homosexuals

God does not want anyone to be bound by homosexuality. He wants to help those who are. Yet many Christians who will tolerate a drunk, a murderer, or a thief have little love or concern for those who are struggling with the sin of homosexuality. This is not right. Remember, we are all saved by God's good grace toward us, not our own goodness.

The good news about Jesus is the homosexual's only hope. But if the church's attitude turns the homosexual away, he or she may die in sin, and God will hold us accountable for the help we didn't care enough to give.

As Christians, we cannot condone the sin of homosexuality. Nevertheless, as with any sinful situation, we are to hate the sin but love the sinner. In other words, when and where people are hurting, our job, as Christians, is to be helping.

HOW TO AVOID
THE AIDS PLAGUE

Lots of people are talking about AIDS these days. Nearly every day, you hear another news report about it, see a story about AIDS in a magazine, or hear some expert warning people about it on a talk show. What is the truth about AIDS? Here are some frequent questions and some factual answers.

What Is AIDS?

AIDS is a short term for a disease with a long name: Acquired Immune Deficiency Syndrome. When a person gets AIDS, his or her body's immune system is broken down by the disease. As a result, the body cannot protect itself against infections and certain kinds of cancer.

It is caused by a virus with another long name: human immunodeficiency virus, often referred to as HIV. Simply, HIV is the virus that causes AIDS.

How Do People Usually Get AIDS?

AIDS is spread mainly in two ways: (1) through semen-to-blood contact; (2) through blood-to-blood contact. Most people get AIDS as a result of sexual activity with an infected person, or through dirty needles and syringes used by intravenous drug abusers. (Intravenous drug users inject drugs directly into their veins.)

It is also *possible* to get AIDS by deep, "French kissing," if infected blood should mix in saliva, due to bleeding gums or cuts in the mouth.

Similarly, it is *possible* to get AIDS from an infected doctor or dentist. It is also possible for a pregnant mother with AIDS to pass on the infection to her baby. These cases, however, are rare compared to the total number of people who get AIDS. Most get AIDS through sexual contact.

How People *Don't* Get AIDS

You *don't* get AIDS by hugging a person with AIDS. Nor do you get it by shaking hands, being sneezed on, using the same toilet or water fountain, or even eating from the same dishes that an AIDS-infected person has used.

Isn't AIDS a Homosexual Disease?

Yes and no.

Yes, when it was first discovered in America, many of the victims of AIDS were male homosexuals (that is, men who had sexual relations with other men).

No, AIDS is not just a homosexual disease. Heterosexuals (people who are sexually attracted to members of the opposite sex) get AIDS, too. AIDS is not confined to one group or location. It has turned up in all 50 states in the U.S. and in 132 countries.

In the U.S., AIDS is more common among homosexuals. But even that statistic is rapidly changing as the disease spreads. In some other countries, AIDS has already infected as many women as men, and more heterosexuals than homosexuals.

Can Anybody Get AIDS?

Anyone who is sexually active is a target for AIDS. The AIDS symptoms may not show up in a person's body for five to eight years (or longer) *after* they are infected. That means, if you have sex with *anybody,* you are open to the disease if your partner has had sex with anyone else but you within the past eight years! In other words, you may not know whether *you* have been infected for eight years after having sexual relations with someone. Any person who is infected with the HIV virus, whether or not they have symptoms of AIDS, can still infect another person.

Can't Condoms Keep Me from Getting AIDS?

Not really. No condom is 100 percent safe. Condoms can come off during sex. They can also break. They must also be used correctly in order to be effective.

Simply put: there is no such thing as "safe sex" outside of a faithful marriage commitment.

Can AIDS Be Cured?

No. Not yet, anyhow. Research is going forward, but right now, everybody who gets AIDS dies within a few years. They are the walking dead. More than half of those who have contracted AIDS have already died. Fifty percent of AIDS victims die within a year after the disease fully develops. Ninety-five percent die within two years.

How Can I Avoid Getting AIDS?

Easy. Don't do drugs, and keep yourself sexually pure before marriage and completely faithful to your partner within marriage. If you will do that, your chances of getting AIDS are almost (but not quite) zero. Yes, it is possible that you could contract the disease through some freak accident in which your blood was infected by someone with AIDS. But the chances are very small.

In other words, if you live the way God tells you in his word, you have little to fear from AIDS. No wonder the Apostle Paul wrote, "Dear friends, God is good. So I beg you to offer your bodies to him as a living sacrifice, pure and pleasing. That's the most sensible way to serve God. Don't be like the people of this world, but let God change the way you think. Then you will know how to do everything that is good and pleasing to him" (Romans 12.1, 2).

Is AIDS God's curse upon us for the immorality of our world? Could be, but nobody knows for sure. All sin is offensive to God, so one might wonder why he would devise a special punishment for sexual sins.

One thing is certain: AIDS is a logical result of sin. When you choose to live in disobedience to God, you die. You are dying while you're still alive. The Bible says, "You cannot fool God, so don't make a fool of yourself! You will harvest what you plant. If you follow your selfish desires, you will harvest destruction, but if you follow the Spirit, you will harvest eternal life" (Galatians 6.7, 8).

What's a Christian to Do?

In Jesus' day, leprosy was an awful skin disease. It was so bad that nobody wanted to be near a person who had it. That person was known as a leper.

Most people ran away from the lepers in Jesus' day. Healthy people feared that they would "catch" leprosy if they got close to a leper. By law, when a leper walked down the street, he or she had to warn people to stay away. They rang handbells and cried out, "Unclean! Unclean!"

But Jesus loved lepers, too. He reached out to them in love and healed them. (For an example look at Mark 1.40–42.)

In our day, AIDS victims are thought of as "unclean." Few people want to be near someone who has AIDS. Many are afraid that if they touch an AIDS victim, they, too, will catch the disease. This is not true. But what's a Christian to do?

Talk Is Cheap

The AIDS problem may be your best chance to put your Christian *talk* into *actions*. Many AIDS victims think Christians hate them. You can *show* them that you care, by reaching out to them with the love of Jesus.

How can you do this? Maybe somebody you know has AIDS. You could visit that person at home or in the hospital. Talk to that person. Spending time with a dying AIDS victim is a ministry that almost anyone can perform. You don't have to have all the answers. Just being there shows you care.

Remember, all AIDS patients are dying—fast. Many are dying without Jesus. Maybe you can tell the person you visit about the Lord who loved lepers. He still loves them today.

Ties That Bind

Jennifer was sad and depressed. That wasn't unusual. Lately, Jennifer always felt rotten.

Her problem dated back to before she was a teenager. In her pre-teens, her body began to change. Her friends' bodies were changing, too, but not as quickly as Jennifer's. She wasn't quite thirteen yet, but she was already becoming a woman.

About that time, her dad began to pick on her. One night he entered her bedroom while she was sleeping and awakened her. He started touching Jennifer on parts of her body and in ways that she didn't think right.

The next morning, he acted as if everything were normal, especially when Jennifer's mom was around. But more and more, her dad began treating her differently.

Often, he would curse and swear at her. He called her bad names in front of her friends. He made fun of her rapidly growing body. He yelled a lot, too. He constantly warned her that she "better never come home pregnant."

At first, Jennifer did not try to resist her father's sexual advances. She felt guilty about it, but after all, he was her dad. Maybe this was his way of expressing how much he cared for her.

As she grew older, she learned that the things her dad was doing were not normal. Most dads didn't treat their daughters that way. Still, she didn't know how to stop him. She was afraid to tell her mom. She knew that nobody in school would believe her.

After a while, Jennifer began believing that it

HOW CAN I FORGIVE SOMEONE WHO HURT ME?

Is there someone you have been holding "on the hook" for a long time? Maybe somebody hurt you deeply and deserves to be punished.

Remember, the Apostle Paul says:

Don't mistreat someone who has mistreated you. But try to earn the respect of others, and do your best to live at peace with everyone. Dear friends, don't try to get even. Let God take revenge. In the Scriptures the Lord says, "I am the one to take revenge and pay them back." (Romans 12.17–19)

Your job is to forgive. Forgiveness is a choice. Right now, say to yourself and to God, "I choose to forgive that person for the hurt he (or she) did to me."

Ask God to forgive *you* if you have been holding onto a hurt or hatred. Ask his forgiveness for feeling so bitter toward that person who hurt you. Then ask him to fill your heart with *his* love for that person.

Does it sound impossible? It's not. Jesus will help you!

must be her fault that her dad was doing such things. She began to see herself as a bad person.

At school, Jennifer's social life was awful, especially her friendships with guys. She was a pretty girl, so she was asked out a lot. Mostly, she turned the guys down. She knew her dad would not approve. Those dates she did accept turned into nightmares. She felt every guy she dated only wanted to abuse her sexually. Many of them did.

In college, Jennifer found a relationship with Jesus Christ. Only then was she able to be free from the family ties that bound her in the past. She found the forgiveness that she needed, as well as the love and acceptance.

One day, Jennifer was reading her Bible and she found a story Jesus told in Matthew 18. As Jennifer read the story, she realized that she needed to forgive her dad. It was hard to do, but Jesus gave her the strength to forgive her father for all the times he had hurt her.

Take a minute to read what Jennifer read, in Matthew 18.21–35.

Jesus told this story about a man who wouldn't forgive. It ends with the angry king turning the unforgiving man over to be tortured in jail. The point is: It is foolish to think God will forgive you if you won't forgive the person who offended you.

When Jennifer found forgiveness of her own sins, Jesus gave her the inner power to forgive others . . . even her dad. As a result, the chains of the past were broken, and Jennifer was free.

If there are painful memories in your past, don't find fault. Don't look for someone to blame. Find forgiveness and get free!

WHAT IS ABUSE?

The term *abuse* covers a wide group of subjects these days. Some of the most common forms of abuse are: verbal, physical, and sexual abuse.

Verbal Abuse

This is where one person is always saying terrible things to or about another. The abuser may curse or swear, yell or scream. The verbal abuser does not just get mad once in a while. He or she often gets furious, sometimes violently angry.

Verbal abusers like to call people terrible names. By putting down someone else, they think they are building themselves up. They also blame other people for their troubles. Most verbal abusers refuse to take responsibility for their own actions.

Physical Abuse

This includes undue hitting, punching, kicking, pulling hair, slapping, or any cruel or undeserved punishment. Physical abuse is not normal spanking. Most parents have to spank their kids once in a while. God commands parents to correct and discipline their children. He also tells kids to obey their parents (see Ephesians 6.1–3). But the abuser spanks too hard and too often, many times for no real reason except to vent his or her anger.

Other kinds of physical abuse may include being locked in a room, purposely not given enough food, or being badly beaten with a belt, board, or some other object.

Sexual Abuse

Sexual abuse does not always have to include sexual intercourse. Sexual abuse can include someone touching or exposing the private parts of another person's body. Sometimes sexual abuse can be committed by somebody in the victim's own family (a father or mother, a brother or sister, a step-parent, or a relative). Girls are not the only ones being abused. Many boys have also been abused.

All three of the above abuses are *sin*.

I Know Someone Being Abused

What should you do if you know a victim of abuse?

DON'T IGNORE IT!
This is very important. Don't pretend that it isn't happening. Don't try to find an excuse or reason for the abuse. It is not right, any way you look at it.

GET HELP.
Go and tell a "neutral" person, someone you trust, what you think is going on. This person could be a pastor, youth leader, guidance counselor, or teacher.

The abused person has little hope of getting free unless the offender is stopped. That's why you must tell somebody. Once the problem is reported to the proper authorities, the abused person and the abuser can get help. (By the way, *never* tell a lie about abuse. Accusing someone falsely is called slander. It is a serious crime and a violation of one of the Ten Commandments.)

What Spiritual Advice Should I Give an Abused Person?

1. *Tell* the victim of abuse that even though he or she may feel dirty, a victim is not a bad person. Someone may have been forced or tricked into doing bad things, but that doesn't make that person evil. He or she may feel confused, but that's not the same as being crazy.

   What happened was wrong, but the victim was not responsible. An abused person doesn't need to feel guilty, worthless, helpless, or afraid. It was right to tell about the problem.

2. *Remind* the abused person of God's love. "God loves you" are powerful words. Tell the victim of abuse that he or she is special. Jesus cares about that person and so do you.

3. *Pray* with and for the abused person. Commit the problem to the Lord. Encourage the victim to forgive the abuser. It will do no good to hold onto hatred or bitterness. Forgiveness, though, does not mean that you should do nothing about the abuse. Continue the steps listed above.

4. *Encourage* the abused person to talk with a pastor. If he or she doesn't know a pastor, recommend yours and arrange an introduction.

Caution: Fragile

Abused girls and guys are fragile. They break easily because they have already been severely damaged. You can help in this situation only with lots of care and prayer.

Victims of abuse usually have a low self-image. They think that they are bad. They feel they don't matter. Often, they are depressed and frequently think of suicide. Unable to concentrate in school, they do poorly. Many run away from home. Some get involved with drugs or alcohol. Sometimes, abused people slip into other forms of sexual immorality because they feel that they are already "used."

Without the Lord Jesus Christ and his forgiveness, it is very hard for the abused to recover. Give them all the help and love that you can.

And if the abused person is *you,* take these words to heart:

- Don't ignore it!
- Get help.
- Remember that you are not a bad person.
- Jesus loves you and he will help you.
- Pray and commit the problem to him.
- Forgive the person who abused you.
- Talk to your pastor about the abuse soon!

What's Wrong With a Few Drinks?

Jesus turned some water into wine in the Bible. (To read about this event turn to John 2.1–10.) Doesn't that make it okay to drink?

Not exactly. First, the common "wine" in Jesus' time was probably similar to a mixture we call grape juice today. An ounce of grape juice was mixed with about two ounces of water. Some wines had as much as ten ounces of water for every two ounces of grape syrup.

Today's wines generally have a much higher alcoholic content. So do beer, wine coolers, and hard liquors. Modern alcoholic beverages receive a rating known as "proof." Many whiskeys, for example, are eighty to ninety "proof." The proof number is usually twice the percentage of alcohol in the drink. In other words, a drink with a "ninety proof" rating would be made up of forty-five percent pure alcohol! Some of the stronger wines in the Bible were only seven to ten percent alcohol.

Still, with even that low amount of alcohol, some wines of Bible times were strong enough to be used as medicines. Wine was also used as an antiseptic, to kill germs, by pouring it on a cut or wound. As an example of this, see the story of "the Good Samaritan" (Luke 10.25–37).

Paul also told Timothy to "take a little wine to help your stomach trouble" (1 Timothy 5.23). Today, that would be like your grandfather telling you to take a little bit of cough syrup for that cold you've been fighting.

Wine was also used as a painkiller in Jesus' day. It was especially strong when it was mixed with "gall," a bitter substance squeezed from a plant. This drink was offered to Jesus while he was on the cross, but he turned it down (Matthew 27.34).

DRINK THIS IN

The Old Testament, too, warns about the dangers of strong drink. Movies and TV make drinking look glamorous, but that's not the picture the Bible paints! Drink this in:

Who has woe?
Who has sorrow?
Who has contentions?
Who has complaints?
Who has wounds
  without cause?
Who has redness of
  eyes?
Those who linger long
  at the wine,
Those who go in search
  of mixed wine.
Do not look on the wine
  when it is red,
When it sparkles in the
  cup,
When it swirls around
  smoothly;
At the last it bites like a
  serpent,
And stings like a viper.
Your eyes will see
  strange things,
And your heart will
  utter perverse
  things.
Yes, you will be like
  one who lies down
  in the midst of the
  sea,
Or like one who lies at
  the top of the mast,
  saying:
"They have struck me,
  but I was not hurt;
They have beaten me,
  but I did not feel it.
When shall I awake,
  that I may seek
  another drink?"
(Proverbs 23.29–35)

77

Is Drinking a Sin?

The Bible doesn't say that drinking a glass of wine, or beer, or a mixed drink is a sin. It does say that it is wrong for a Christian to get drunk. Being drunk is listed right along with other major sins in the New Testament (see Romans 13.13; 1 Corinthians 6.9, 10; Galatians 5.19–21; and 1 Peter 4.3). Paul also taught that Christian leaders should never be drunk (1 Timothy 3.3; Titus 1.7).

Who Needs It Anyway?

A good question to ask yourself is: "Why do I want to drink anyway?" Most people don't like beer or whiskey the first few times they try it. They have to force themselves to enjoy the taste. But they still drink it. Why?

The truth is, many who feel they need to drink alcoholic beverages are immature. Often, they are insecure and have a poor self-image. They think that by drinking, they can escape themselves for a while and be less fearful, shy, or backward. When they drink, they sometimes say and do things that they wouldn't otherwise.

"What's wrong with that?" you may ask.

What's wrong is that *God wants you to find your freedom through Christ.* You don't need a drink to do that. Jesus wants you to feel better and to enjoy life naturally, as a result of *knowing him.*

Four Things to Think About

1. Remember, your body is a temple of the Holy Spirit. Alcohol destroys blood vessels and brain cells. Long-term drinking can also damage your liver. Is God pleased by that?

2. Drinking kills. Every year, nearly ten thousand young Americans under the age of twenty-five die in drinking-related traffic accidents. Besides that, alcohol is a leading cause of divorce, rape, child and wife abuse, and violent crime in America.

3. With this in mind, what message are you giving to your friends when you take a drink? Some people say, "Well, drinking doesn't bother me. I don't get drunk." Maybe so. Unfortunately, a lot of your friends can't stop with only one drink. Possibly, because of your bad example, they may end up getting in trouble, or worse.

4. The Apostle Paul gave us a good example to follow. He decided not eat or drink anything that would cause a weaker Christian to sin. He called this "the Law of Love." You can find his advice on this subject in Romans 14 and 15, and 1 Corinthians 8 through 10.

Beyond that, Paul said, "Don't destroy yourself by getting drunk, but let the Spirit fill your life" (Ephesians 5.18).

DEADLY RUSH

What do these people have in common: rock stars Elvis Presley, Janis Joplin, Jimi Hendrix, Keith Moon, and Sid Vicious; All-American basketball star Len Bias; pro football player Don Rogers; and actor John Belushi? You guessed it. They are all dead because of drugs.

Why Do People Take Drugs, Anyway?

Everyone knows drugs are dangerous. So why do people risk their lives for a momentary high?

Many guys and girls start taking drugs because of curiosity. "I just wanted to see what it was like."

More often, drugs are a key to acceptance among your peers. Wanting to belong to the group is normal and natural. For many youths, however, the approval of their peers is even more important to them than that of their parents. They'd do almost anything to be considered cool.

Be careful. Don't let your desire to be accepted by your friends drag you into a deadly drug trap.

Most teens get turned on to drugs by their own friends.

Unfortunately, drugs are readily available at most schools and teen hangouts. You don't have to go to the sleazy part of town to find them. They are all around you. The easy access to drugs makes them all the more tempting. Drug users come from all walks of life: rich kids, poor kids, bright kids, slower kids. All sorts of people get hooked. Hardly anyone *plans* on getting hooked; but millions of teenagers do.

The Big Escape

Some kids take drugs because they are trying to escape something. Maybe they're trying to run away from troubles at home or at school. Sometimes they are running from their own anger or loneliness.

In the movies or on TV, people who take drugs are often pictured as tough, hard, and mean. Some are. But most people who are involved in drug abuse are insecure and scared within. They may put up a pretty good front. They may look or act tough. Or maybe they try to act super-cool and sharp.

Inside, though, they are hurting. They are haunted by fear, guilt, frustration and other negative emotions.

Have you ever felt that way?

During the early teenage years, especially, you may feel awkward or ugly. Your body is changing. You're not a child anymore, but you're not an adult yet, either. You feel like you don't fit in anywhere. Your self-image goes down the tubes and drugs look like a way to temporarily escape the hassles.

Keep in mind, the devil wants to destroy you through drugs or anything else. He is a thief and liar. He's out to rob you and to kill you.

But Jesus came that you might have life in its fullest (John 10.10)—real life, not a fake, momentary, drug-induced "rush." Jesus wants to give you lasting peace. He said, "You will know the truth, and the truth will set you free" (John 8.32).

WHAT IS THE OCCULT?

The term "occult" is a catch-all term used to cover a variety of anti-Christian, demonic activities. The word means *secret,* or *concealed.* Some occult activities seem harmless at first, but they open the door to deeper involvement. Since these practices are demonic, or encouraged by the devil, as a Christian you will want to avoid them. Here are a few occult activities to stay away from:

1. **Reading of horoscopes**
This is part of a practice known as *astrology.* Astrology is much different than *astronomy,* which is a scientific study of the stars. Astrology is *not* a science. It is the belief that your future can be told by studying the position of the sun, moon, and planets with relation to the stars.

Horoscopes offer advice based on a chart with the signs of the zodiac, an imaginary path that the planets supposedly travel. Much of this advice is general and could apply to almost anyone. For example: "Today you will have an important decision to make. Make it wisely." You probably have important decisions to make every day!

On the other hand, any time you look for future direction apart from God, demonic influences are a possibility.

The Bible warns against astrology and horoscopes:

> If there is found among you . . . a man or a woman who has been wicked in the sight of the Lord your God . . . who has gone and served other gods and worshiped them, either the sun or moon or any of the host of heaven . . . then you shall bring out to your gates that man or woman who has committed that wicked thing, and shall stone to death that man or woman with stones. (Deuteronomy 17.2–5)

Ouch! Today, we don't punish people by stoning them, but you get the picture that God is not pleased with astrology or those who practice it.

The Lord said something similar through his prophet Isaiah. His words have a sarcastic tone to them:

> Let now the astrologers, the stargazers, and the monthly

prognosticators stand up and save you from what shall come upon you. Behold, they shall be as stubble, the fire shall burn them; they shall not deliver themselves from the power of the flame. . . . No one shall save you. (Isaiah 47.13–15)

2. Fortune telling

Fortune tellers claim to be able to tell you about your future by reading your palms, looking into a glass ball, reading tea leaves or cards.

3. Clairvoyance, mental telepathy, E.S.P. and psychic powers

This is the belief that certain people have "extra-sensory" abilities. They may be able to read somebody's mind, or "sense" when something is going to happen. Watch out for anything or anyone that promises to increase, develop, or tap your "psychic powers."

4. Witchcraft and spiritism

Witchcraft is an old, false, anti-Christian system of rituals and chants. Witches claim they can contact and use powers from the unseen world. Spiritists are similar in that they make contact with the dead through a "medium." Those who practice witchcraft are included in Paul's list of people who will not be a part of God's forever family (Galatians 5.20).

5. Satanism

Worshiping the devil or asking him for help is very dangerous. Satan is the enemy of God. The devil plays for keeps.

6. Games involving the supernatural

Games such as Ouija boards and "Dungeons and Dragons" can also be doorways to trouble. The Bible never says that these things are silly little games. Nor does it say that they do not work. Satan can use them to hurt you. The Bible says to stay away from them. God wants you to get your direction from him.

Are Demons For Real?

Yes, unfortunately, demons are real. In the Bible, demons often tried to battle against Jesus. Wherever Jesus found demon activity, he drove them out. He delivered the demon-plagued person from his or her suffering. No demon could ever stand up to King Jesus.

What Is a Demon?

A demon is a fallen angel. When the angel Lucifer (now known as Satan) rebelled against God, a group of angels followed him. Nobody rebels against God and gets away with it...not even an angel. God threw the whole gang of these disobedient angels out of heaven. When Lucifer messed up, he took with him one third of the Lord's angels (see Revelation 12.4). Those fallen angels are now demons.

The devil is not some weird-looking dude holding a pitchfork and dressed in a red suit with a long tail. He probably doesn't have horns sticking out of his head.

Lucifer was one of the most beautiful and talented angels in heaven before he disobeyed God. A few other angels are spoken of individually in the Bible, but mostly, nobody knows for certain what angels look like. To give you a hint of their awesome power, one angel destroyed 185,000 Assyrian soldiers in one night (see 2 Kings 19.35 in the Old Testament). Demons, then, like Satan, may have kept much of their beauty and power that they had as angels.

What Do Demons Do?

Just as angels do the bidding of God, demons do much of the devil's dirty work. Demons do awful deeds of hatred, bitterness, and evil. In the New Testament, they were always hostile to human beings. At times, they were able to cause disease (Matthew 4.24; 12.22; 15.22; Luke 4.35) and mental illnesses (Mark 5.2–20; Luke 8.27–39). Demons often took on human abilities. They were able to talk, hear, think, feel, and act (see Matthew 8.31; 17.18; Mark 1.34; 5.12; Luke 8.32; 10.17).

Dealing with a Demon

Doing battle with a demon is nothing to play with. Here are some important tips to keep in mind.

1. Demons are powerful, but Jesus is more powerful!

Evil spirits are no match for King Jesus. If you are trusting in Jesus Christ, his Spirit is alive in you. The Bible says, "God's Spirit is in you and is more powerful than the one that is in the world" (1 John 4.4). That means that even though demons may be big and strong, Jesus in you is *bigger and stronger!* The meekest Christian who truly trusts in Jesus Christ casts fear into the "heart" of a demon. To be safe, though, you must put on the whole armor of God (see Ephesians 6.10–18).

2. Be careful.

Be sure that you are dealing with a demon before you try casting it out. Maybe some physical, emotional, or other spiritual problem is the real culprit. Some people try to blame demons for things for which they themselves are responsible.

3. Get help, if at all possible.

Dealing with a demon should never be done lightly. This is serious stuff. Demons hit back hard. In most cases where a person is set free, it has been because a group of Christians were praying *together* for that person, in the name of Jesus.

4. Be sure your own life is right with God.

Tend to this before trying to help someone else be delivered from a demon's influence. Demons fight dirty. If there is any area of unconfessed sin in your life, or any area of your life not under the control of the Holy Spirit, the demon will attack in that weak area. For an example of this see Acts 19.13–16.

5. Don't go demon-hunting.

This is war, and you need to be on the lookout for demons, but *don't* go making up demons where they don't exist. Just be ready to do battle if or when the enemy attacks.

6. Keep your eyes on Jesus.

Rather than worry about demons, keep focused on Jesus Christ. Make sure you are filled with his Spirit on a daily basis. Be joyful, not preoccupied with negatives. Yes, you can command demons to get out of your life or someone else's, but remember the real power is in the name and authority of Jesus (Acts 16.18).

Can a Christian Be Demon Possessed?

Many pastors and Bible teachers disagree over whether a believer in Jesus can be *possessed* by a demon. Perhaps we need to define terms.

Demon possession is when a person is under the *control* of a demon. Sometimes, a person who is demon-possessed seems to be two (or more) people. At one moment, he or she may be a calm, normal person. Then suddenly, without warning, he or she becomes enraged and may say or do evil things, often cursing Jesus. The demon-possessed person may speak in a strange voice and may be unusually strong.

Demons desire to do one thing: bring dishonor to the name of God. They will do anything to accomplish their purpose.

Demon oppression can be a common experience for many Christians. Here, the demon is attacking God's person or property. It may be that some forms of discouragement, depression, or unusual temptation are caused by such demonic activity.

Practically, the Bible does not make a distinction between demonic possession or oppression. All demonic influences must flee at the command of Jesus.

It makes sense that any area of your life that is not under the complete control of the Holy Spirit would be a target for an attack by an evil spirit. That's just one more good reason to stay filled up with the Spirit of Jesus.

You can do that by daily allowing Christ to have *full control* of your life. When the King is in his "temple" (you!), you have nothing to fear from demons.

WHAT IS A CULT?

Not all cult members shave their heads and sell books or flowers in public places. A cult is any group which denies that Jesus Christ came in bodily form, lived, died to save sinners, and rose again. Most cults deny that Jesus is God (see Colossians 1.15, 16).

Cults mix in half-truths that sound Christian, but are actually departures form the historical Christian faith. Cults deceive many people, especially those who do not study the Bible for themselves.

Cults thrive on ignorance and uncertainty. Christians who do not know what they believe—or why they believe—are prime targets for cults. Also, Christians who are discouraged or dissatisfied with their own churches often are attracted to cults. They are lured by the love and the life they see displayed by cult members.

"Gimme Something to Believe In"

Strangely, cults do not attract the "down-and-out" as much as the "up-and-out." Many cult members are upper-middle class, white, young men and women, ages eighteen to twenty-four. They often have grown up with "absent" parents and have a strong need for approval.

Many cultists are very sincere. They desire to see a better world and are frustrated at society's inability or unwillingness to change. Many cult members have had troubles in their families. Some lean toward a cult because of a recent failure in a relationship or job. Some have tried church and gotten "turned off." All cult members are looking for something spiritual to believe in.

Some Examples of Cults

By the definition above, the following groups are usually considered cults:

- *Transcendental Meditation (TM),* a kind of Hindu meditation that claims to provide inner peace and relief from stress, while claiming not to be a religion
- *Yoga,* a "cousin" to TM, also a form of Hinduism; the word "yoga" means "union," referring to the mythical state of "oneness of all things"
- *Baha'i,* a group that emphasizes mankind's supposed spiritual unity

- *The Unification Church,* sometimes called the "Moonies," referring to their founder, Sun Myung Moon; a group that often uses other community-oriented names to attract local interest
- *Hare Krishnas* (The International Society for Krishna Consciousness); often seen, with shaved heads and saffron robes, dancing and chanting on public streets
- *The "Children of God" or "Family of Love,"* known for promoting sexual promiscuity
- *The Divine Light Mission*
- *Erhard Seminars Training (EST)*
- *Rastafarians,* who believe that the late Ethiopian emperor Haile Selassie is their messiah
- . . . and of course there are many more than just these.

Cults Add to the Bible

A mind-boggling variety of cults operates in the U.S. and around the world. All teach their followers to worship false gods, or one god in a false form. Some look to their leader as their savior. Many teach a salvation by works: "If you chant these words, you might find God."

Cults add to what the Bible says. Beware. The Apostle Paul rebuked the Christians in Galatia for accepting such falsehood. He wrote:

> I am shocked that you have so quickly turned from God. . . . You have believed another message, when there is really only one true message. . . . I pray that God will punish anyone who preaches anything different from our message to you! (Galatians 1.6–8)

The main thing to remember about cult members is that they have been deceived. It will do little good to argue with them. The best thing you can do is show them the Scriptures that tell who Jesus is and that he died for our sins (John 3.16; Acts 4.12; and others). Keep pointing the person to the Bible as the absolute authority, *not* your church, or a pastor, or a television preacher.

Remember:

> Only Jesus has the power to save! His name is the only one in all the world that can save anyone. (Acts 4.12)

What's the New Age Rage?

Many Christians are confused about the "New Age" movement. Some are even afraid. They run around in a fuss, as if to say, "The New Agers are coming! The New Agers are coming!"

How silly. The New Age movement is not a gang of anti-Christian raiders out to destroy Christians. It is not even a well-organized group. It is simply another of Satan's twisted attempts to deceive those who are seeking spiritual truth.

What does a "New Age" person believe? It's hard to say. "New Agers" don't have a list of rules or commandments. They don't have an official sacred book. Basically, the New Ager says, "Hey guys. I'm not sure, but I think something else is out there!"

Then What's the Big Deal?

Still, the New Age movement is dangerous. While it has no distinct doctrine, the New Age denies Jesus Christ is God. Most forms of New Age teaching say, sooner or later, that *we* are gods. Beyond that, the movement believes that *everything* is god.

Let's say you go to an ice-cream shop for a sundae. The New Ager would say that the shop is god. *You* are god. The chocolate sundae you are eating is god. So it's sort of god sitting on god eating god for dessert. Is that far out, or what? The New Age movement would be funny if it weren't such a sad delusion.

But it's never funny when people believe a lie—especially when they lose their souls as a result.

What's New about New Age?

The New Age isn't really so new. It's a weird mixture of teachings based on Hinduism, Buddhism, other eastern religions, and the occult. In a way, it's old-fashioned, out-of-date *pantheism,* which says that everything is God.

From ancient times, men and women have worshiped rocks, trees, animals, clouds, volcanoes, other people, and all sorts of other objects. It is all idol worship: worshiping the created order, rather than the Creator. But think about it—if Satan would have named the New Age movement: "The Same Old Stupid Lies That We've Been Falling For These Past 2000 Years" nobody would want anything to do with it!

Satan wanted to be equal with God, rebelled against him, and got thrown out of heaven as a result. The devil duped Adam and Eve into making the same mistake of wanting to be more than what God created them to be. Ever since, people have tried to be their own gods. But we are not God. We are created beings. Only God is God.

Satan lures people into believing that by meditating, and making use of their own "inner potential," they can have god-like powers. Thousands have been deceived into thinking that they can "save" themselves. Others believe that a so-called "Christ" will come, bringing peace and prosperity to the world. But they are not talking about Jesus.

The danger of the New Age is that some of it *sounds* similar to biblical teaching. In many lies there is a kernel of truth. If a person doesn't know the truth of God's word, he or she can easily be misled. In the days ahead, don't be surprised if more and more books, movies, and music have "spiritual" themes. But the "spirit" will not be the Holy Spirit. It will be a spirit from hell.

What Are Some New Age Practices?

New Agers practice a variety of unusual rites, such as yoga, meditation, out-of-body experiences, and many more activities, so it is difficult to give a general list. Here are a few of the more familiar practices:

✓ *Channeling.* Channelers are people who claim to have or to be "spirit guides." They say that the spirit of someone who died can pass (channel) information through them back to you. The Bible says stay away from this stuff. The message is clear:

> There shall not be found among you anyone who makes his son or his daughter pass through the fire, or one who practices witchcraft, or a soothsayer, or one who interprets omens, or a sorcerer, or one who conjures spells, or a medium, or a spiritist, or one who calls up the dead. (Deuteronomy 18.10, 11)

Channelers often speak about "opening up to a higher self." Watch out! The only higher self you want to open up to is Jesus!

✓ *Crystals.* Many believers in the New Age have a collection of crystals. They place them in their homes, carry them in their purses, and put some in the car. These people are not merely collectors of fancy rocks. They believe that the crystals have power. They say that some crystals have power to heal diseases. Others, they believe, will bring you health, love, peace, or money. Strange, isn't it?

People who used to laugh at fads like "mood rings" are now buying colored stones to bring them happiness that only God can give.

✓ *"Holistic health" practices.* Again, many of these ideas sound good at first. But if you look carefully, you will find occult practices. Beware of health practices such as biofeedback, hypnosis, and psychic healing, that seem to draw on supernatural forces apart from God.

The Worst Danger of All

The New Age's worst danger is that it keeps people who are seeking spiritual truth from finding the real thing—a relationship with Jesus Christ. They get sidetracked into a New Age pit. Many are stuck in spiritual quicksand that is sucking them down to hell.

Nobody has ever found God through the New Age. They may have found a false god made in man's image, or some other image. Others may have found the Lord *in spite of* New Age teaching. But the New Age can never save anyone. It has no power to do so.

No one will ever have his or her sins forgiven through the New Age movement. Nobody will go to heaven as a result of the New Age. No one has been or ever will be *reincarnated,* to come back to earth as a different life form. The Bible says, "We die only once, and then we are judged" (Hebrews 9.27).

The New Age is not going to just go away. A lot of people are sold on it. Modern Christians need to know what a follower of Jesus believes and why. With so many people seeking spiritual truth, God may be able to use you to point New Agers to Jesus Christ, the one who said, "I am the Truth."

Can't I Be a Christian Without Reading the Bible?

To be a Christian means to be a follower of Jesus Christ. You trust in him. You want to do what he says, go where he leads you, and live the way he wants you to live.

How are you supposed to *know* all of this?

The best way to discover the truth about Jesus is to read the eye-witness accounts of those who knew him best. You will find those accounts in the New Testament. Four true stories are written by Matthew, Mark, Luke, and John. These books are known as the Gospels or "Good News."

In these exciting books, you will read about Jesus' supernatural birth at Bethlehem, his many miracles, and his awful death on the cross at Calvary. Then you will be amazed as Jesus does something that no other person has ever done under his or her own power. He arose from the dead!

Why Do I Need a Book to Tell Me about Jesus?

Jesus Christ shows us what God is like. In his time, all sorts of people saw him, heard him, and touched him. Twelve men actually lived with him for three years. But *we* were not there.

Without the New Testament, we would have to rely on "word of mouth" to learn about Jesus. As it passed down from Jesus' friends, one generation to the next, the story would have gotten confused. To prevent that from happening, God had Matthew, Mark, and Luke write the good news within thirty years of Jesus' death. John wrote his book before sixty years had passed.

This is important to know. Sometimes people ask, "Well, how can we be sure Jesus' friends wrote the true story?"

Easy. If they had written lies about Jesus, plenty of people were still alive who could have objected. But none did.

Testimony Is Evidence

Think of it this way. You may never have seen or heard President John F. Kennedy during his lifetime. All you know about him is what you have been told, what you have read, or what you have seen or heard in recorded clips. What, then, if someone wrote a book saying President Kennedy is alive and well?

How do you think people would react? They would certainly say the writer is either crazy or lying. Why? Because there are many people still alive who were witnesses when President Kennedy was assassinated.

Likewise, can you imagine the scene in Bible days when the gospel writers said, "Jesus is alive"—if he weren't? People would have laughed. They would have objected and said, "You men are insane. We saw Jesus on a cross. He's dead and buried in his tomb."

But they didn't. They couldn't! The body was gone. Jesus was and is *alive*.

If the enemies of Jesus could have proved that Jesus was dead and buried in a grave outside of Jerusalem, they would have ended Christianity before it got started. Instead, within a few years, people were taking the story of Jesus everywhere!

The New Testament is the true record of the great news about the risen Son of God. No Christian can do without it.

How Can I Know
the Will of God?

First of all, let's define terms. What do we mean by "God's will?" The Lord's *will* is what he *wants.*

The Bible says that God has a plan for the whole world. He is aware of everything that is happening on earth. He is in charge of world history and current events. Nothing happens without him causing it or allowing it.

That's nice to know. Usually, however, when we talk about seeking God's will, we are searching for specific answers to such questions as:

"What does God want *me* to do?"

"Where does he want me to work?"

"Should I go to college? If so, where?"

"Whom does he want me to marry?"

"Does God even desire for me to be married, or should I stay single?"

Some Christians don't believe that God deals with us that specifically. They say that he has a general plan for your life, and that as long as you make your decisions based upon the Bible, he will approve and bless you. Other Christians believe that God is *very* specific about your important decisions, but not as concerned about the minor details of your life. A bit of both views are right.

How Will God Guide Me?

God could speak to you any way he chooses. He could call you up on the telephone, or talk to you through a lamp shade . . . if he wanted to do so. In the Old Testament we see that God spoke to Moses through a burning bush (Exodus 3.1—4.16), and he once used a donkey to speak to a fellow named Balaam (Numbers 22.28–35). We can't limit how God can speak to us.

Still, when you are seeking God's guidance in making any decision, you should ask three important questions:

1. **What Does the Bible Say about This?**
Current events or inner feelings may give you a hint about what God wants you to do. Nevertheless, your first source in finding God's will is God's *word* (check out 2 Timothy 3.16, 17).

God will never give you guidance that goes against what he has already given you in the Bible. That's one reason why it is vital that you become familiar with Scripture. It tells you God's will for your life. Isn't that great? You don't have to wonder how God wants you to live. He tells you straight-out in the Bible.

Whenever you wonder whether or not you should do something that you know goes against God's word, the answer is easy. *No!*

For example, should you steal food from the cafeteria, or rip off the place where you work? Of course not. How do you know? Because God's word says so: "If you are a thief, quit stealing. Be honest and work hard, so you will have something to give to needy people" (Ephesians 4.28). That's straight stuff, isn't it? He says it even more bluntly in the Old Testament: "You shall not steal" (Exodus 20.15). That's number eight on God's Top Ten List.

Not only does Scripture tell you what *not* to do, the Bible tells you what God *wants* you to do. Look at how clear his word is: "Stop being bitter and angry and mad at others. Don't yell at one another or curse each other or ever be rude. Instead, be kind and merciful, and forgive others, just as God forgave you because of Christ" (Ephesians 4.31, 32).

2. What Do Wise Counselors Say?

The second question you should ask when you are trying to determine what God wants you to do is: "What do wise counselors say?"

All through his word, God tells you to seek the advice of wise spiritual leaders. He cautions: "The way of a fool is right in his own eyes, but he who heeds counsel is wise" (Proverbs 12.15).

Your spiritual counselors may include your parents (if they are Christians), your pastor, a church youth leader, your Sunday School teacher, or a professional Christian counselor. Talk to one or more of these leaders when you are trying to make a decision on a matter.

Ask your counselors if they can point out any Scriptures that deal with your decision. Also, ask them if they have had any personal experiences that might be helpful.

Listen carefully when your spiritual leaders instruct you. If someone in authority corrects you, don't go running from one counselor to another. Ask God if this is his advice to you. He will often speak to you through your spiritual leaders.

Be careful here. Even good people can give you bad advice. You are seeking *godly* counsel. If someone gives you advice that doesn't line up with God's word, let it go in one ear and out the other. Forget it.

3. What Does Common Sense Say?
God gives each of us an incredible brain. He expects us to use it.

Don't depend upon your own ideas, but don't ignore them either. God may be trying to tell you something. Similarly, you should consider events and circumstances, but always in light of God's word.

God wants you to use your common sense. Just remember, many times God's direction goes beyond what common sense says. That's why you need to pray for wisdom. The Bible says, "If any of you need wisdom, you should ask God, and it will be given to you" (James 1.5).

Other Ways God Might Guide You

Besides the Bible, wise leaders, and common sense, God may use other methods to guide you. Again, keep in mind, God's guidance always goes along with what God's word says. In addition to his word, he may direct you through:

✓ *Inner Feelings*
Sometimes you can't explain it, you just know inside that something is the right or wrong thing to do. You may hear somebody else say, "I just felt *led,*" or "I have a peace about it." These inner impressions often come from God.

Be careful, though. Satan also tries to use inner feelings to confuse you. If you are not sure whether your "leadings" are from God, go back to your three main sources of guidance: the Bible, godly counselors, and your own common sense. Ask God to show you, to confirm, whether or not your inner feelings are from him.

Besides the devil, inner feelings can come from other questionable sources. They may be the result of spiritual immaturity, your own emotions, stress, lack of sleep, or eating too much pizza!

That's why inner feelings should always be confirmed before acted upon.

✓ Supernatural Direction

Can God use dreams, visions, voices, miraculous events, "fleeces" (asking God to confirm a certain course of action by giving specific signs), or other unusual methods? He sure can! Does he? Probably not as often as many people think he does. Always check these supernatural signs against the Bible. Ask yourself, "Has God ever before directed anybody this way?" "Is this sign being repeated to me?" "Is it confirmed by mature spiritual leaders?"

Never trust supernatural signs if they go contrary to God's word. Also, beware of the person who tells you, "God told me to tell you. . . ." If you are listening for God's voice, he can show *you* his choice.

✓ Opened and Closed Doors

Circumstances may be part of God's guidance, but be wise. Never base a decision on circumstances alone. Your best bet is to push gently on those open doors. If they open further, step carefully through them. If they slam in your face, back off. Don't try to break the door down.

Again, you must use common sense. For example, you want to get married and you love the color yellow. One day, you see the "love of your life" and he or she is wearing a *yellow* sweater. "It must be the will of God!" you assume. That's not God. That's dumb.

✓ Your Personal Desires

Christians often make two contrasting mistakes about their personal dreams, goals, and desires. The first mistake is to assume that because *we* want to do something, it must be God's will. The second mistake is to assume that because we *want* to do something, it is *not* God's will. Both assumptions can easily be wrong.

Many times, God gives us exactly what we want, *if* it will glorify him, and not conflict with other things he has for us. God wants our lives to be filled with joy. He doesn't want us to be miserable.

God gives each of us gifts and talents. It makes sense that we will enjoy using those things for his glory. He wants you to enjoy where you work, the person you marry, the place where you live, and even the food you eat.

Just because you like something, don't rule it out as part of God's will for you. It might be!

What Does the *Old* Testament Have to Do with Jesus?

If we want to read the story of Jesus, we turn to the New Testament. But if we want to truly understand why Jesus did the things he did, we also need to know about the Old Testament. It is part of God's word to us, too.

A *testament,* or covenant, is a promise. It is an agreement between two parties that tells what each will do in the relationship. The Old Testament is the story of God's dealings with his people under the old promise. Under the old promise, God's people offered sacrifices of meat and grain as a sign of their repentance (turning from sin). Then God sent his son, Jesus, to begin a new covenant, the *new* agreement, the New Testament. Jesus gave his life as the ultimate sacrifice. Now God's people no longer have to offer the blood of goats and lambs to show they are sorry for their sins. Jesus gave his blood to pay the price for everyone's sin.

Jesus knew all about God's first agreement with his people. Everything he did in the New Testament was based upon God's old covenant. For example, as you read Matthew's story of the Good News, notice how quick he is to remind his readers that Jesus came to fulfill the Old Testament promises of God.

The Old Testament in Small Sections

The Old Testament has thirty-nine books. That's a lot of books and may seem too big to handle. To help you understand it, let's divide the Old Testament into several smaller sections:

1. The **Law of Moses** (sometimes simply referred to as "The Law"). This section tells how the relationship between God and people began. In it, you'll find the stories of Adam and Eve, Noah, Abraham, Joseph, Moses, and many more. The Law includes the first five books of the Bible:

   - Genesis
   - Exodus
   - Leviticus
   - Numbers
   - Deuteronomy

2. The **Historical Books.** All of the Old Testament books can be placed in a historical setting. The Historical Books, however, pick up the story of God's people after they came out of slavery in Egypt, and crossed into the land God had promised them. The books tell about Joshua, Gideon, Samson, David, Solomon, and dozens of other heroes (and villains) who lived during the early times of the nation of Israel. The Historical Books include:

- Joshua
- Judges
- Ruth
- 1 & 2 Samuel
- 1 & 2 Kings
- 1 & 2 Chronicles
- Ezra
- Nehemiah
- Esther

3. The **Writings.** This section includes books of wisdom, songs, and poetry:

- Job
- Psalms
- Proverbs
- Ecclesiastes
- Song of Solomon

4. The **Prophets.** Prophets not only predicted the future; they also brought God's word to their own times and situations. You might say most of the books of prophecy are more *forth*-telling than *fore*-telling. The prophets describe how God feels when his people disobey. They also promise what he will do when his people repent (when they turn back to him and turn away from their sin).

On the other hand, the Old Testament prophets told of a day when the Messiah (Christ) would come. They described in detail what the Christ would do. When Jesus came, he fulfilled hundreds of these prophecies. Many of the prophet's predictions have already come true. Others remain yet to happen. And they will! The prophetical books include:

- Isaiah
- Jeremiah

- Lamentations
- Ezekiel
- Daniel
- Hosea
- Joel
- Amos
- Obadiah
- Jonah
- Micah
- Nahum
- Habakkuk
- Zephaniah
- Haggai
- Zechariah
- Malachi

What Did Jesus Say about the Old Testament?

Some people thought that Jesus would do away with the Old Testament. He didn't. He said the opposite:

> Don't suppose that I came to do away with the Law and the Prophets. I did not come to do away with them, but to give them their full meaning. Heaven and earth may disappear. But I promise you that not even a period or comma will ever disappear from the Law. Everything written in it must happen. (Matthew 5.17, 18)

The Old Testament was the Bible of Jesus' day. He accepted it as Scripture. Jesus often referred to the Old Testament. He quoted it regularly to settle religious arguments with his enemies. Some of his final words, as he died on the cross, were verses from the Old Testament. (Jesus quoted Psalms 22.1 and 31.5. You can read this in Mark 15.34 and Luke 23.46.)

Jesus also taught his disciples from the Old Testament. Many of the stories he told had their roots in the Old Testament. Even when Jesus was telling his disciples about his second coming, he used word pictures drawn from the Old Testament (see Matthew 24.29–31).

Jesus believed the Old Testament. His life, ministry, death, and resurrection were all based on it. The New Testament is built firmly on the foundation of the Old Testament.

3 Faith-Builders When You Have Doubts

Almost all believers have questions and doubts about their faith at one point or another. Jesus never became angry with his friends because of their doubts. When their doubts turned to *unbelief,* however, he sternly corrected them.

When you have questions or doubts, here are three reminders that will help boost your faith:

1. Look at the physical world around you.

This earth could not have "just happened" by some cosmic accident. Imagine that thousands of auto parts were floating around out in space, and one day they all fell to earth in the form of a brand new sports car. Pretty silly, huh?

Now multiply that by the billions of objects on earth that have complex designs, and you begin to realize how silly it would be to believe that the world "just happened." No, it didn't "just happen." God created the heavens and the earth.

2. The resurrection of Jesus Christ.

When you have doubts, just remember, *Jesus arose from the dead.* Nobody has ever been able to explain that one away (although many have tried). Over five hundred people *saw* Jesus alive within a short time after he had been crucified, pronounced dead, and buried.

3. Jesus has changed your life.

A changed life is still the best proof of Christianity. When you are tempted to doubt, remember what Jesus has already done for you. Some people may not understand. Others may not believe you. But nobody can argue with you when you can honestly say, "Jesus changed my life!"

4 Reasons You Can Be Sure Jesus Is Risen from the Dead

The resurrection of Jesus Christ is the central issue of Christianity. Unlike other religions such as Islam or Buddhism, Christianity rises or falls with the resurrection. Even the Apostle Paul said, "And if Christ was not raised to life, our message is worthless, and so is your faith. . . . But Christ has been raised to life" (1 Corinthians 15.14, 20).

The Resurrection Really Happened

The resurrection of Jesus Christ is a historical fact. Here are four reasons why you can be sure of it:

1. **The tomb was empty**

The testimonies of Matthew, Mark, Luke, John, Peter and Mary all agree: on the Sunday after Jesus was crucified, his tomb was empty. Jesus was gone.

What happened?

Some say the women and the disciples went to the wrong tomb. But if that were true, why couldn't the Jewish authorities take them to the "right" tomb and produce the embalmed body of Jesus?

Some say that Jesus didn't really die on the cross, that he just "appeared" to die. That's an insult to the Roman soldiers, who knew how to kill a man, and knew a dead man when they saw one. Not only that, it doesn't explain how Jesus rolled the stone away. Nor does it explain how a severely beaten, battered, and bloody Jesus could have the energy or the ability to convince everyone that he had risen miraculously from the grave.

Others say that the appearances of Jesus must have been hallucinations. The disciples and others who "saw" Jesus after he had been crucified, they say, were just "seeing things." But that doesn't make sense either. Besides the impossibility of mass hallucinations, it still doesn't explain where the real body of Jesus was or is.

Some say that somebody stole Jesus' body. But who would have wanted it? His friends? They were afraid to even come near the cross when Jesus was dying. It is unlikely that they would have been brave enough to tangle with the Roman guards posted at the grave (Matthew 27.62–66).

The enemies of Jesus would have had no reason to steal his dead body either. Even if they had, when the disciples began preaching that Jesus was alive, his enemies could have ended Christianity with one deadening thud. All they had to do was produce the body. But they couldn't. He was alive!

2. The change in the lives of Paul and James

Some skeptics say that Jesus appeared only to his loyal followers after the resurrection. But that is not true. He appeared to two very strict Jews, Paul and James.

Paul, known as Saul before he met the risen Jesus, hated everything about Jesus. He hated those who said that Jesus was alive, and he had legal permission from the Jewish leaders to persecute any Jews who were followers of Jesus. But then Jesus himself appeared to Saul as he was on his way to Damascus (Acts 9).

Saul was converted. He later became known as "Paul," and spent the rest of his life telling people about the Lord Jesus.

James was Jesus' brother, but he had not believed in Jesus. Yet James became a leader in the early Christian church. What happened? The Apostle Paul explains:

> Christ died for our sins, as the Scriptures say. He was buried, and three days later he was raised to life, as the Scriptures say. Christ appeared to Peter, then to the twelve. After this, he appeared to more than five hundred other followers. Most of them are still alive, but some have died. He also appeared to James, and then to all of the apostles. Finally, he appeared to me, even though I am like someone who was born at the wrong time. (1 Corinthians 15.3–8)

3. The eyewitness accounts

Within a few days of his execution, all sorts of people were claiming to have seen Jesus, alive from the dead! Think of the list:

- Mary Magdalene
- Peter
- John

- the other disciples
- Thomas (the skeptic)
- the two travelers on the road to Emmaus (Luke 24.29)
- five hundred others
- Saul of Tarsus (some time later than the others)

All of these people said the same thing: "Jesus is alive!"

4. The effect on the people who saw Jesus

Have you ever wondered what happened to the disciples? Tradition tells us that all of them, except for John, died violent deaths rather than deny that Jesus is alive. John lived the longest after Jesus' death. He died of natural causes. The others gave their testimonies with their lives.

Skeptics object, "Yes, but men and women often give their lives for a cause they believe in. That's no proof that Jesus arose."

True, many people will die for something they *believe* to be true, but people will not lay down their lives for something they *know* to be false. Yet, one by one, each of the disciples gave up their lives. If Jesus had not risen, wouldn't at least one of them have said, "Wait a minute! Why should I die for a lie about a dead man?"

But they didn't. They were convinced that Jesus is alive. You can have that same confidence.

No one can *prove* that Jesus is alive any better than Jesus himself. Scripture says: "So you will be saved, if you say that God raised Jesus Christ from death, and if you believe this with all your heart. God will accept you and save you, if you truly believe this and tell it to others" (Romans 10.9, 10).

---

66 Christianity begins where religion ends . . . with the resurrection. 99 —Anonymous

"When Are You Coming Back, Jesus?"

The world has not seen the last of Jesus Christ! He came once in human history and the Bible says he will come again.

Over two hundred prophecies predicted Jesus' *first* coming. For instance, the Bible predicted that he would:

✓ be born into the family of Judah

✓ be born to a virgin

✓ be born in Bethlehem

✓ go down to Egypt

✓ heal the sick

✓ be rejected by his own people

✓ be betrayed by a friend

✓ be sold for thirty pieces of silver

✓ be crucified with sinners

✓ be pierced in his side

✓ be raised from the dead

✓ ascend into heaven

Every single prophecy concerning the *first* coming of Jesus was fulfilled! So far so good.

Now: the Bible also has over three hundred prophecies about the *second* coming of Jesus Christ. So, what do you think the chances are that those prophecies will be fulfilled? That's right: one hundred percent of God's promises will come to pass, quite possibly in your lifetime.

"Do You Expect Me to Believe That?"

Yes! The biblical prophets of God have never made an error yet. Skeptics sometimes say, "Aw, I don't believe Jesus is coming back to earth!"

Hope they're not too disappointed. He's coming anyhow. And the skeptics' belief or unbelief won't change that fact. Of course, it may change where they spend eternity . . . but it won't affect Christ's coming one way or the other.

When Is Jesus Coming?

Jesus' disciples were wondering that same thing. One day, they asked Jesus directly: "When will this happen? What will be the sign of your coming and of the end of the world?" (Matthew 24.3).

Jesus didn't tell his disciples that he would return on a specific date. Any time you read or hear of people saying they know the date when Jesus is coming, beware. Jesus didn't set a date. He said that no one knows the day or the hour (Matthew 24.36). He did give us certain signs to look for, though.

No one sign by itself is the signal that Jesus is coming. But placed together, they paint a pretty clear picture of what the world will be like just before Jesus returns. The idea is: When you see these things happening, get ready!

What Are Some of the Signs?

1. False messiahs and false prophets (Matthew 24.5, 11, 24).
Jesus said that many would come claiming to be him, saying that they are the Christ, the Messiah. These false prophets will fool a lot of people. "They will even try to fool God's chosen ones" (Matthew 24.24).

We are seeing this today. Left and right, east and west, cult figures claim to be Christ. Sun Myung Moon, Jim Jones, and Charles Manson have tried to be so-called messiahs. New cults are springing up all around the world. Although false teachers have flourished since the day of Jesus, most cults have grown up only within the past two hundred years.

Jesus said it would be this way just before he returns.

2. Wars and threats of wars (Matthew 24.6, 7).
Some people say, "We've always had wars. Wars are part of our world's history." And they're right. But two factors should be noted:

A. War is no longer a local affair. It is global. Even if our country isn't involved, television grimly reminds us of the wars going on around the earth. Now, people in all parts of the world can watch war on live TV.

B. We now have the potential to literally destroy the world. The stuff that once made up science fiction stories has become reality. At the end of World War II, General

Douglas MacArthur warned, "We have had our last chance. If we do not now devise some greater and more equitable system, Armageddon will be at our door." The soldier's words were prophetic. Today, the world is "armed to the teeth," ready for the final conflict.

In August, 1945, the United States dropped the first atomic bomb to be used in war, on the Japanese city of Hiroshima. In the city of 500,000 people, 70,000 were killed instantly. Another 70,000 were injured and many of that number died in the hours that followed.

An area of 4.7 square miles (over 3,000 acres) in the downtown part of the city was completely leveled. Shock waves blasted from the center of the explosion at speeds of over 600 miles per hour. The waves crumbled walls that were more than a mile from town. Heat waves *millions* of degrees in intensity melted flesh, stone, and anything else in their path.

The really scary part is that the bomb dropped on Hiroshima was a small one compared to what we have today. It was equal to about 20,000 tons of dynamite, not exactly a firecracker, but only *one-fiftieth* of a megaton. Now, however, the world's superpowers are armed with *one-hundred megaton* nuclear warheads. It's a wonder anyone sleeps at night!

3. Famines (Matthew 24.7).

Jesus said that before his coming, the world would once again know severe famine. "People will starve to death," he said. Today, despite lots of hunger relief projects and many fine Christian-oriented relief agencies, millions of people still starve to death. Before another day passes, 10,000 human beings will die of starvation. Ten thousand more will die tomorrow, and the next day, and the next.

The population of the earth is getting larger. Five billion people are on earth right now. At the same time, the world's food supply is getting smaller, often because of human selfishness, but also because of such things as acid rain, pollution, global warming, and changing weather patterns, causing many areas to experience severe lack of water. You don't need to be brilliant to figure out this equation:

More People + Less Food = Famine.

Jesus said it would be that way. That doesn't mean we

should do nothing and let people die. Christians should be leading the way to help feed and clothe a needy world. But still, we should recognize the signs of the times.

Other Signs of the Times

4. Earthquakes in various places (Matthew 24.7).

5. Many will give up (Matthew 24.10).
Not only will they give up, but Jesus said that they would betray and hate each other.

6. Evil will spread and love will grow cold (Matthew 24.12).

7. The good news will be preached in all the world (Matthew 24.14).
Jesus didn't say that everyone would *believe* the good news. He didn't even say that every *person* would hear. Many make that mistake. They think that every person in the world must receive the good news before Jesus returns. That is not what Jesus said. Read the verse carefully for yourself:

> When the good news about the kingdom has been preached all over the world and told to all nations, the end will come. (Matthew 24:14)

While much mission work remains to be done in foreign countries and in our own, we are the first generation to truly have the potential of seeing Jesus' words fulfilled any day now.

8. Jerusalem is back under Jewish control (Luke 21.24).
"So what?" you might ask. Simply this: Jesus foretold that "Jerusalem will be overrun by foreign nations until their time comes to an end." He was telling his disciples that this was another sign to look for in regard to his return.
You might not realize it, but until recently, the Jews were not in control of Jerusalem. The country of Israel did not even exist! It had been overrun, just as Jesus predicted. Then, on May 14, 1948, David Ben-Gurion read Israel's Declaration of Independence, re-establishing the Jewish nation. But much of Jerusalem was still controlled by non-Jews.

Then in June, 1967, in the historic "Six-Day War," Israel reclaimed the entire city of Jerusalem. They regained control of the area where God's temple once stood. (This is where the Moslem shrine known as the Dome of the Rock now stands. So there are some ways in which Jerusalem is still in Gentile *hands* even though it is under Israeli *government*.)

"When are you coming back, Jesus?" He'll come back when Jerusalem is fully back under Jewish control. Our generation could be seeing the beginning of the end of this age.

What Should We Do?

Jesus concluded his discussion of his return with a great word of hope. He said, "When all of this starts happening, stand up straight and be brave. You will soon be set free" (Luke 21.28).

He also gave a stern warning: "Watch out and keep praying that you can escape all that is going to happen and that the Son of Man will be pleased with you" (Luke 21.36).

Who Is the Holy Spirit?

The Holy Spirit is not a godly "ghostbuster." Nor is he a Christian version of "Casper the Friendly Ghost." He is the third person of the Holy Trinity, which includes the Father, the Son (Jesus), and the Holy Spirit.

The Holy Spirit is not an "it." He is not "the Force." Jesus always referred to the Spirit as "he" or "him." In other words, the Holy Spirit is as personal as Jesus himself. Here are some of the things the Holy Spirit does:

- He can speak (Acts 13.2)
- He guides us (John 16.13)
- He understands and can communicate (1 Corinthians 2.9–12)
- He can be lied to (Acts 5.3)
- He can be resisted (Acts 7.51)
- He can be grieved (made sad) (Ephesians 4.30)
- He can be insulted (Hebrews 10.29)
- He can be spoken against (blasphemed) (Matthew 12.31)

What Else Does the Holy Spirit Do?

He shows the world the truth about sin and God's justice and judgment (John 16.8). He will show you what is true (John 16.13). Most important, the Holy Spirit always directs the glory to Jesus (John 16.14); the Spirit does not draw the attention to himself.

- He teaches you what Jesus wants you to know (John 14.26; 16.7–15)
- He helps you to know Jesus better (1 Corinthians 2.1–13)
- He helps you to think as Christ does (1 Corinthians 2.16)

HOW CAN GOD BE THREE IN ONE?

The word "Trinity" is not in the Bible. It is only our attempt to describe the three aspects of God. The idea of God being three persons in one is difficult for us to understand.

Some people have tried to explain it by comparing the Trinity to an egg. The egg has three parts, the yolk, the white, and the shell, yet it is all the same egg. But that's really not an adequate explanation.

Others have compared the Trinity to three forms of water. Water can be a liquid, a vapor (steam), or a solid (ice), but it is all water. It is just in a different form. Similarly, God exists in three forms: our heavenly Father; Jesus, the Son; and the Holy Spirit. But the water-steam-and-ice comparison is as weak as the one about the egg.

Our best efforts always fall short of explaining the Trinity. It is a mystery that God himself will have to explain to us someday, when we see him face to face.

In the meantime, we believe that God is three persons in One because Jesus did, and he should know! Some of his last words to his disciples before he was lifted up into heaven were: "Go to the people of all nations and make them my disciples. Baptize them in the name of the Father, the Son, and the Holy Spirit . . ." (Matthew 28.19).

110

- He helps you to avoid sin and do what is right (1 Corinthians 6.11)

The Spirit Our Helper

God has given his Holy Spirit to us to help us live holy lives. When Jesus walked the earth in person, he could only be at one place, at one time. Now he can be with all of us, by his Spirit. The Spirit helps us to do what Jesus wants us to do.

To do this, the Holy Spirit produces *spiritual fruit* in our lives. Paul tells us what this "fruit" is like: "God's Spirit makes us loving, happy, peaceful, patient, kind, good, faithful, gentle, and self-controlled" (Galatians 5.22).

The Holy Spirit also gives each believer a *spiritual gift* or gifts (see 1 Corinthians 12.4–11; other gifts are listed in Ephesians 4 and Romans 12). These gifts are to be used to build up the entire body of Christ. The Spirit doesn't give out God's gifts so you can be a "Spiritual Lone Ranger." No, he wants you to use your gifts to help others to grow more like Jesus.

Christ In You

To sum up, the Holy Spirit is the Spirit of God, alive in you. God wants to fill your life with the Spirit's presence (Ephesians 5.18). If you will allow him, he will create in you the character of Jesus. It will still be you, but in a real way, Jesus will be at the center of your life. He will be in charge. The Holy Spirit gives us the inner power to be like Jesus and to represent him in our world.

What Is the Unforgivable Sin?

Jesus performed many miracles by the power of the Holy Spirit. His enemies, however, said that these wonderful things were actually done by the power of Satan working through Jesus! This was a serious mistake. It shows how hard their hearts had become to the Holy Spirit. They gave the devil credit for deeds that only the Lord could do. This prompted a strong statement from Jesus. Look at it again:

> I tell you that any sinful thing you do or say can be forgiven. Even if you speak against the Son of Man, you can be forgiven. But if you speak against the Holy Spirit, you can never be forgiven, either in this life or in the life to come. (Matthew 12.31–32)

Whew! We may not understand everything that Jesus meant, but we know enough! First, anyone who willfully and consistently rejects the work of the Holy Spirit can never find forgiveness. Second, anyone who hardens himself or herself to the point where they prefer to glorify Satan by giving him credit for the Holy Spirit's work is in serious danger of committing the unpardonable sin.

Three suggestions: (1) Never give the devil credit for anything that the Holy Spirit may have done. (2) Be extremely careful about saying something is "of the devil," just because you don't understand it. (3) Keep your heart sensitive to the Holy Spirit. Don't allow yourself to grow hard, or calloused to his voice. When he speaks to you, listen and obey. If he convicts you of some sin, don't ignore it. Confess it. Repent—that means turn away from it—now! Don't allow layers of sin to build up to the point where you can no longer hear the voice of God's Spirit. That could be deadly, now and forever.

On the other hand, if you still sense God speaking to your heart, give thanks. He wants to forgive you. He wants you in his family. He hasn't given up on you! And he won't.

Why Do I Need to Go to Church? Can't I Worship God at Home?

Sure, you could worship God at home. In fact, most of the early New Testament churches met in someone's home. A church can be anywhere two or more believers gather together in Jesus' name to worship him and to obey his commands.

Today, most Christians attend worship services held in a church building. But the church is not the building. The church is the body of believers gathered in Jesus' name.

Going to church can be a great encouragement to you. You should attend a church where the people are worshiping the Lord Jesus, and aren't hung up on worshiping one another or themselves.

What's It All About?

Sometimes, though, people get confused. They don't understand what the church is about. They are easily bored by it all. They are missing the point. The church isn't someplace you *go*. It is something you *are*. It is not the steeple. It's the people.

It would be interesting to take a survey outside such a church next week, as the people are leaving.

"Were you in church?" you ask.

"Yes, of course," they reply with a self-righteous sniff.

"Why?" you ask.

"Well, we always do it. It's the Sabbath, after all."

"But what were you doing in there?" you continue to probe.

"Oh, I don't know. But we've been doing it for years!"

That's not the church. In the New Testament, the church is called a body (see 1 Corinthians 12.12–31). It has life. It has movement. It is an organism, not just an organization. That's the kind of church you don't want to miss.

Maybe that's why the writer to the Hebrews says:

> Some people have gotten out of the habit of meeting for worship, but we must not do that. We should keep on encouraging each other, especially since you know that the day of the Lord's coming is getting closer. (Hebrews 10.25)

113

Sure, you could attend "Bedside Baptist" this week. Or maybe you'll make it to "Mattress Methodist." You could even get out of bed and watch four hours of prime-time preaching.

But no amount of sleep and no amount of television religion can compare to the fellowship you can enjoy simply by gathering together with a bunch of believers to worship the Lord.

Somebody put it this way: "The difference between watching a church service on TV and going to church is like the difference between calling your guy or girl on the phone and actually going out on a date."

7 PROBLEMS OF 7 CHURCHES

In Revelation 2.1 to 3.22, seven letters are dictated by the risen Lord Jesus. He told these things to John in a vision, and commanded him to write them down.

In each of the letters, Jesus warned his followers about a problem. See how much the problems sound like our churches today:

1. They didn't have as much love (for the Lord) as they used to (Revelation 2.4).

2. They were afraid to suffer for Jesus (2.10).

3. They were following false teachings (2.14, 15).

4. They had problems with immorality (2.20, 21).

5. They were almost dead spiritually (3.1–3).

6. They were tempted to give up (3.11).

7. They were lukewarm spiritually (3.15, 16).

Still, Jesus gave them (and us!) a promise. He said:

I correct and punish everyone I love. So make up your minds to turn away from your sins. Listen! I am standing and knocking at your door. If you hear my voice and open the door, I will come in and we will eat together. Everyone who wins the victory will sit with me on my throne, just as I won the victory and sat with my Father on his throne. (Revelation 3.19–21)

ISN'T THE CHURCH FILLED WITH HYPOCRITES?

There certainly are a lot of hypocrites in the church. But don't worry, there's always room for one more!

Ha ha, very funny. But let's talk about hypocrisy. Hypocrites are people who say they believe one thing, but their lives show something else. Haven't you ever done that? We all have.

The word "hypocrite" comes from the ancient Greek. It means "an actor playing a part." When Greek actors acted, they wore masks to show what their character looked like. Often, one actor played two or three parts. During the play, he would wear several different masks.

The word "hypocrite" came to mean "someone whose real self and motives are masked." Maybe that is what Jesus had in mind when he talked about religious hypocrites.

No Hiding Place

Hypocrisy is nothing new. In Jesus' day, as in ours, religious people tried to impress each other by showing how "spiritual" they were. If they were fasting (going without food for a brief time to help focus on God), they would walk around with sad, "hungry" looks on their faces. When they prayed, they would pray long, loud prayers—especially if anyone else was watching or listening. Some of them even wore Bible verses in tiny boxes, strapped to their foreheads or arms.

Hypocrites still attend church today. You probably know some of them. They like to be admired for their religious deeds, or how much they know about the Bible. They make rules that they think other Christians should follow. They are critical of others, proud, and self-righteous. Hypocrites pretend that they're perfect. Sometimes they act as though no problem is big enough to bother them. They are just afraid to take down their masks and stop pretending.

But Jesus wasn't fooled. He knew what the hypocrites were like on the *inside.* Jesus knew their hearts. He knew what their attitudes were like. He knew that they didn't want to please God so much as they wanted the approval of people.

It's possible to do the right thing with a wrong motive for the wrong reason, or with wrong attitudes in our hearts. Jesus knows when we do that. He examines our motives. He not only knows *what* we do. He knows *why* we do it.

115

What About You?

It's easy to talk about somebody else being a hypocrite. How about you? How do your friends see you? Do your words and your actions line up? Or do you say that you believe one thing, but live quite differently? Watch out! Jesus didn't play games with hypocrites who looked and sounded pure on the outside, but had filthy attitudes within. He wants his followers to *get real*.

In Matthew 6.1–18, Jesus gives us some ideas about how we can keep from being hypocrites. Check them out.

HOW CAN I BECOME A CHRISTIAN?

A jailer at Philippi asked Paul the most important question in life: "What must I do to be saved?" (Acts 16.30). Paul answered him, "Have faith in the Lord Jesus and you will be saved! This is also true for everyone who lives in your home" (16.31). The jailer believed Paul's message about Jesus and the good news. The jailer became a Christian and so did his family members. You can, too!

To be a Christian means to be a follower of Jesus Christ. A Christian believes that Jesus is God's Son. Since Jesus was God in a human form, he was able to be the sacrifice for your sins. Jesus became the bridge between his heavenly Father and you.

Jesus was crucified and was buried. Then, he was raised from the dead. This proved that Jesus was *and is* God's Son. Today, Jesus is alive with God the Father in heaven. One day, perhaps very soon, he will return to earth to take his followers to live forever with him in heaven. Then there will follow a series of earth-shaking events, including the final judgment and the setting up of God's eternal kingdom.

That's Radical!

When you become a follower of Jesus, it is a radical commitment. You are saying, "Jesus, I believe in you. I trust you with my life. I want to live for you. I believe that you died on the cross to take my place, so I could be forgiven. Because of that, I am willing to turn away from my sinful way of living to follow you."

Jesus said that this is such a radical step, it is like being "born from above" or "born again" (John 3.3). Being born again means much more than getting a fresh start in life. It is not merely "turning over a new leaf." It is more like ending one way of life and starting another. You end your old sinful ways and begin living the way Jesus wants.

One night a religious man named Nicodemus came to talk with Jesus. Nicodemus admitted that Jesus was a great teacher who had come from God. But Jesus cut right to the heart. He answered Nicodemus's question before the man asked it:

> Jesus replied, "I tell you for certain that you must be born from above before you can see God's kingdom!" (John 3.3)

Nicodemus didn't understand. He thought Jesus was talking about a *physical* rebirth. Jesus was talking about a *spiritual* rebirth. Just as you have been born into your parents' family, you must also be born into God's family.

But Aren't We All Part of God's Family?

Not everybody is part of God's family. We have all been made in the image of God. That means we are made something like him. But just being similar to God doesn't make you part of his family. The way you get to be part of God's family, or born from above, is by trusting in Jesus. That's the *only* way.

The Apostle John explains what Jesus did:

> He came into his own world, but his own nation did not welcome him. Yet some people accepted him and put their faith in him. So he gave them the right to be the children of God. They weren't God's children by nature or because of any human desires. God himself was the one who made them his children. (John 1.11–13)

---

66 I hear all sorts of terms talking about being a Christian: born again, born from above, saved, in Christ, and others. What do they all mean? Aren't all Christians born again? **99**

What Does It Mean to Be a Christian?

People use several terms to describe a life following Christ. Some simply use the term *Christian:* to be a follower of Christ. Some say they have been *saved.* By this they mean that they have been saved *from* sin, the devil and hell, and saved *to* Jesus and heaven. Others say they are *in Christ,* meaning that they are living with Jesus in their lives. All of these are biblical terms.

Other people say, "Well, I'm not sure whether I am a born-again Christian or not. I go to church. I'm a good person. Isn't that enough?"

Not really. You normally *know* whether you have made a commitment to someone or not. For example, are you married? You know. It is the same with Jesus. If you have committed yourself to him, you *know* it. It's not "I think so" or "I hope so"; it's an "I know so" relationship.

Going to church is a good thing to do, but it doesn't necessarily mean that you are a Christian. The late songwriter Keith Green used to say, "Sitting in church doesn't make you a Christian any more than sitting in McDonald's makes you a hamburger!" You must receive Jesus into your life. Trust him. Commit yourself to him. If you do this, you will be born again, saved, a Christian.

John's Gospel sums up what this means:

> God loved the people of this world so much that he gave his only Son, so that everyone who has faith in him will have eternal life and never die. God did not send his Son into this world to condemn its people. He sent him to save them! No one who has faith in God's Son will be condemned. But everyone who does not have faith in him has already been condemned for not having faith in God's only Son. (John 3.16–18)

How Can I Be Saved?

Having faith in Jesus is the only way you can be saved. But having faith is not just saying, "Yeah, sure, I believe." It is believing that Jesus died on the cross to pay the penalty for your sins. You should have had to die because of your sins, but Jesus took your place (Romans 6.23). Do you believe that?

Having faith in Jesus means that you also believe in your heart that God raised him from the dead (Romans 10.9, 10). Do you believe that? If not, read the accounts in the Gospels again until you understand and believe that Jesus died and rose again.

Having faith in Jesus also means that you invite Jesus to come into your life. It's similar to when a man and a woman "invite each other into their lives" on their wedding day. They are saying to each other: "You are the one I want. You are the one I will live for. I don't want any other lovers. You are the only one for me. Everything I have and everything I am, I give to you. I commit myself to you. I trust you with my life. I ask you to receive me into your life. I receive you into mine."

When you invite Jesus into your life, it is a similar promise, only his promise to you lasts forever! He will never take it back. He will even help you to keep the promises you have made to him. When you trust Jesus, you will never be disappointed (Romans 10.11).

Let's Do It!

If you want to become a Christian, you can right now.

▶ *Ask Jesus to forgive your sins.*
Pray something such as: "Jesus, I'm sorry for my sins. Please forgive me. Please give me the power to turn away from sin. I don't want to live badly anymore. I am willing to let you help me turn away from sinful things."

▶ *Tell Jesus that you trust him.*
Pray: "Lord, I give my life to you. I may not understand everything about what that means, but I know I want you in my life. I commit myself to you. I believe the Bible when it says that you have committed yourself to me."

▶ *Tell him that you believe he is alive from the dead.*
Pray: "Jesus, I believe you are alive. I believe that you died for me and you rose from the dead. I believe you have proven that you are God. By trusting in you, I can have eternal life, too. Give me that eternal life, starting today. Help me to love you and to live for you. You are the one I want. Please receive me. I receive you. I believe I am a Christian. I am saved. I am born again."

Where Are All the Flashing Lights?

When you become a Christian, you may or may not experience intense feelings. Your *feelings* are not the most important part of being a Christian. It's your *commitment* that counts. If you honestly give yourself to Jesus, he accepts you. A bride and groom may not *feel* any different right after the wedding, but they are. They have made a commitment. They have pledged themselves to each other. Whether they feel like it or not, they are married.

The same is true for you. You have committed yourself to Jesus. Jesus has committed himself to you. It's more than mushy-gushy feelings. It is an act of your will. You have decided to follow Jesus. Congratulations! You have made the right choice.

SUGGESTIONS TO HELP YOU GET STARTED IN YOUR CHRISTIAN LIFE

1. *Read your Bible* every day, if at all possible. Begin with John's Gospel and read regularly. It won't take long to read the whole New Testament. Then get a copy of the complete Bible with

the Old Testament. As you read, ask the Lord to speak to your heart, your mind, and your conscience. He will. Ask him to teach you from his word. He will!

2. *Pray every day.* Prayer is talking with God. You don't need to use big words, or "religious-sounding" phrases. Just talk to God as you would talk to a good friend. Be respectful. After all, he is *God!* But be yourself, too. If you don't understand something, ask him about it.

Tell him where you hurt. Tell him about the things that make you happy. He is interested in every part of your life. He wants to hear from you.

As you read your Bible, God will speak to you. As you pray, you can talk with him. It is two-way communication.

3. *Tell someone what you have done.* As soon as possible, tell someone else about the commitment you have made to Jesus. Private promises are too easy to break. Make your promise public property. Tell someone who knows you very well. This will do two things:

First, if the person you tell is not a Christian, you will be a "witness" to him or her. The one you tell may want to meet Jesus too!

Second, whether or not the person is a Christian, by stating your commitment to another person, you put yourself on record. That person is going to watch you, to see if your commitment is real.

You don't have to know everything about the Bible or understand all that your promises hold. Just tell the truth. Say something such as: "I'm not sure of all the details yet, but one thing I'm certain of: I have committed my life to Jesus Christ. From now on, I'm going to live for him. I'm going to live the way he wants me to live."

4. *Go to church.* Start this weekend, if not before! Find a church where the Bible is taught and preached. Your new Christian life is going to be exciting and the church will be a big part of it. The church is your "spiritual family." God will give you many "brothers" and "sisters" to enjoy as part of his family. You will want to be with them as often as possible.

When you are first born from above, you are similar to a new baby. The baby needs to be fed, to be cared for, to grow. In a spiritual sense, as a "newborn Christian," you need to grow.

The best place for this is with your spiritual "family," where you can build friendships and have fun. So find a church where you can continue to learn how to follow Jesus more closely.

5. *Help others to find Jesus.* You can do this by telling them about Jesus. Tell them the good news. Again, you don't need to wait until you know more. Just tell them what you know. When you find something good, you want to tell somebody else. And you have found the best. You have found Jesus!

Another way to help others find Jesus is by inviting them to go to church with you. After the service, you can talk about what you heard. You can also invite your friends to fun activities such as Christian concerts or small group Bible studies.

6. *Allow Jesus to work through your life.* Maybe there is something you can do for the Lord as an expression of your love for him. Can you sing or play an instrument? Can you teach? Would you be willing to help with the children at church, or visit the shut-ins (people who are sick, old, or for some other reason can't get to church)? Remember, the things you do for Jesus don't save you. But now that you are saved, surely there is something you can do for him. After all he has done for you, you will want to show him your thanks somehow.

The real excitement in your Christian life, however, is not just doing things for Jesus. It comes when you allow Jesus to do things in and through *your* life! He may use you to speak words of encouragement to someone. He may use you to help someone else receive food or shelter. He may use you to tell someone the Good News. That's what the Christian life is all about—Jesus Christ alive in you!

You don't have to be especially talented in order for Jesus to use you. It's not your *ability* that he is looking for. It's your *availability.* Tell him, "Jesus, I'm available to you. Here's my life. You are welcome to work through me any way you wish. I just want to bring honor and glory to your great name!"

New Birth Certificate

Giving your life to Jesus is something you will want to remember the rest of your life. To help you celebrate your decision, fill out the information on this page. In a way, it is your "spiritual birth certificate."

_____

Your Name

_____

Place

_____

Date

Today, I have committed my life to Jesus Christ. This is what Jesus means to me:

_____

_____

_____

_____

Signature

THE BIBLE FOR
TODAY'S
FAMILY

CONTEMPORARY ENGLISH VERSION

New Testament
with Application Notes

Thomas Nelson Publishers
Nashville

TRANSLATING THE CONTEMPORARY ENGLISH VERSION

Translation it is that opens the window, to let in the light; that breaks the shell, that we may eat the kernel; that puts aside the curtain, that we may look into the most holy place; that removes the cover of the well, that we may come by the water ("The Translators to the Reader." King James Version, 1611).

The Bible was written to be read! This means that a faithful translation of the Bible must be both *reliable* and *readable*. It must be a text that can be trusted and one that is suitable for both public and private reading, and also for memorizing.

The *Contemporary English New Testament* was translated with these goals in mind. Every attempt has been made to produce a text that is faithful to the *meaning* of the original and that can be read with ease and understanding by readers of all ages. The translators of the *King James Version* had similar aims. According to the introduction that was published in the earliest editions of the *KJV*, the translators realized that a Hebrew or Greek word could not always be translated in the same way. They also knew that in order to make the *meaning* clear for their readers, they must often use a *form* that was very different from that of the original languages, but still true to the sacred text. That same translation principle has been followed in the *CEV*.

Like all reliable translations, the *Contemporary English New Testament* is made directly from the original Greek and is not an adaptation of any existing translation or translations. But not everyone who knows the biblical languages can do for today's readers what the *KJV* translators hoped to do for their own generation. Almost any scholar can produce a literal rendering of the original languages. But this is only the *first* step in the translation process. Two important questions must still be asked: "What do the words mean?" and "What is the most accurate and natural way to express this meaning in contemporary English?"

Not only was the Bible written to be read. It was written to be *understood*. But many readers fail to understand the meaning of a passage, because the translation itself keeps them from doing so. For example, "a kind of firstfruits of all he created" (James 1.18) may faithfully represent the *form* of the Greek text, but the *meaning* is certainly not clear, except for the reader who has special training in biblical backgrounds.

Traditional translations use words such as *justification, righteousness, redemption, reconciliation, propitiation, atonement, salvation, sanctification,* and *repentance.* All of these words are absent from the *Contemporary English Version.* One reason for this absence is that they are not used in everyday English. But there is an even more important reason: these are nouns, but they describe *actions* that God or people do. For example, the word *salvation* means "God saves people." *Repentance* is more difficult, because it refers to more than one event: Someone sinned and then turned from sin. In the *CEV,* each of these words may be translated in several different ways, depending on the special meaning they may have in a particular verse.

Many people are surprised to learn that one of the hardest words to translate is *grace!* The word is simple enough to pronounce, but it must always be explained. This is because in the New Testament *grace* means something far different from what it does in ordinary speech. The main problem is that the phrase "the grace of God" describes an event, and it means: "God is kind to us in a way that we do not deserve."

Acts 20.32 will show the difference between the way *grace* appears in traditional translations and how it is restructured by the *Contemporary English Version.* By following the form of the Greek text and using traditional language, the verse may be translated: "Now I commit you to God and to the word of his grace, which can build you up and give you an inheritance among all those who are sanctified."

"The word of his grace" is difficult for several reasons: (1) "word" means "message"; (2) "of" merely shows that there is some relation between "word" and "grace," but it does not tell what the actual relation is; and (3) "grace" is an event, not an object.

There are also other problems in the verse: (1) "build you up" is not contemporary English usage; (2) "inheritance" is used in the special biblical sense of "what belongs to God's people"; (3) "those who are sanctified" is a New Testament way of referring to God's people; and (4) in the Greek text the pronoun "which" refers to "word," rather than to "grace."

In the *Contemporary English Version* every word, phrase, and clause of the original was carefully studied by the translators. Then, with equal care, they tried to find the best way to translate the verse so it could be easily read and understood. As a result, the form is very different, but the meaning is both *accurate* and *clear:* "Now I place you in God's care. Remember the message about his great kindness! This message can help you and give you what belongs to you as God's people."

The translators of the *Contemporary English Version* believe, as did the translators of the *King James Version:* ". . . this is the word of God, which we translate . . . we affirm and avow . . . (it) contains the word of God, no it *is* the word of God." At every stage in the translation process, the guidance of the Holy Spirit has been sought, and all who use this translation are encouraged to seek the same guidance. After all, "the prophets did not think these things up on their own, but they were guided by the Spirit of God" (2 Peter 1.12).

The *Contemporary English Version* New Testament has been translated directly from the Greek text published by the United Bible Societies (third edition, corrected, 1983). Drafts of the *Contemporary English Version* New Testament in its early stages were sent for review and comment to a number of biblical scholars, theologians, and educators representing a wide variety of denominations. In addition, drafts were sent for review and comment to all English-speaking Bible Societies and more than forty UBS translation consultants around the world. Final approval of the text was given by the American Bible Society's Board of Managers upon recommendation of its Translations Subcommittee.

Difficult words are explained in the list of *Words to Know*. Items *of special interest* are told about the New Testament and about each book in it. A *quick look* at the contents is also provided for each of these books.

Three kinds of notes are included: (1) notes that explain important differences in the Greek manuscripts, (2) notes that give another translation of the Greek text, and (3) notes that provide helpful information about Bible history and customs.

ABOUT THE NEW TESTAMENT

In the first century A.D., Christians and Jews used the same Scriptures, which Christians later called the Old Testament. Both of these communities of faith usually used these Scriptures in a Greek translation (called the Septuagint) instead of in the original languages of Hebrew and Aramaic. This collection of sacred writings in Greek was the Bible of the early Christians. They found proof in these writings that Jesus is the Messiah and the Son of God, and they also found there how God wanted them to live.

Later in the first century, Christians started writing the books that would become the New Testament. These were the books about the life and teaching of Jesus (called Gospels), the letters of Paul and others, and the books of the Acts of the Apostles and Revelation. All of these were written in Greek, which was a language that people all over the Roman empire could understand. By the second century, these books were widely used by Christians for preaching, teaching, worshiping, and telling about their faith.

The writings of the New Testament are arranged in an order that gives the greatest value to the four books (Gospels) about Jesus, since they tell about his life and teaching, his miracles, his saving death on a cross, and his rising to life. These four Gospels (Matthew, Mark, Luke, and John) take up almost half of the New Testament, which is another reason why they are placed first.

The Acts of the Apostles follows the four Gospels. It actually continues the Gospel of Luke and shows the connection between the ministry of Jesus and the mission of the early church. Acts also shows how the followers of Jesus answered the question of whether Gentiles could also become Christians.

The letters of Paul follow next, and they are arranged roughly in order of their length (from Romans to Philemon). Most of these letters were written to churches Paul had started, and in them he deals with problems that had come up. Paul's letters are then followed by a group of writings known as the "general letters," because they are mostly addressed to a general audience and were to be circulated to other followers. These letters are also arranged roughly in order of their length (from Hebrews to 3 John and Jude).

Revelation is the last book in the New Testament, and it was written to give hope and encouragement to Christians who were suffering because of their faith. It is also a prophecy and contains visions of how God will punish evil people and reward his faithful followers.

The New Testament is the world's most widely read book! More than 70 million copies are printed throughout the world each year, and the complete New Testament has been translated into more than seven hundred languages.

How can a book that is almost two thousand years old be in such demand and influence so many lives today? Why are people so interested in a young Jewish carpenter named Jesus, who lived his short life without going more than seventy miles from the small village where he was born? The New Testament is in demand because it tells the good news about Jesus Christ! And this good news is God's powerful way of saving *everyone* who has faith in Jesus. In the New Testament we learn that God is kind and that he loved the people of this world so much that he sent Jesus Christ into the world to save us all.

For these reasons, and many more, people keep coming to the New Testament for the light and power it gives for daily living. Jesus promised his followers that God's Spirit would always guide them to understand the message of the Scriptures. And so, in the New Testament we are not reading dead words from the past. Here we meet Jesus Christ, the living Word of God.

Table of Contents

MATTHEW TELLS THE GOOD NEWS

ABOUT THIS BOOK

The Sermon on the Mount (5.1—7.28), the Lord's Prayer (6.9–13), and the Golden Rule (7.12: "Treat others as you want them to treat you") are all in this book. It is perhaps the best known and the most quoted of all the books that have ever been written about Jesus. That is one reason why Matthew was placed first among the four books about Jesus called Gospels.

One of the most important ideas found here is that God expects his people to obey him, and this is what is meant by the Greek word that appears in many translations as *righteousness*. It is used seven times by Matthew, but only once by Luke, and not at all by Mark. So it is an important clue to much of what Matthew wants his readers to understand about the teaching of Jesus.

Jesus first uses this word at his own baptism, when he tells John the Baptist, "We must do all that God wants us to do" (3.15). Then, during his Sermon on the Mount, he speaks five more times of what God's people must do to obey him (5.6,10,20; 6.1,33). And finally, he reminds the chief priests and leaders of the people, "John the Baptist showed you how to do right" (21.32).

Matthew wanted to provide for the people of his time a record of Jesus' message and ministry. It is clear that the Old Testament Scriptures were very important to these people. And Matthew never fails to show when these texts point to the coming of Jesus as the Messiah sent from God. Matthew wrote this book to make sure Christians knew that their faith in Jesus as the Messiah was well anchored in the Old Testament Scriptures, and to help them grow in faith.

Matthew ends his story with the words of Jesus to his followers, which tell what they are to do after he leaves them:

I have been given all authority in heaven and on earth! Go to the people of all nations and make them my disciples. Baptize them in the name of the Father, the Son, and the Holy Spirit, and teach them to do everything I have told you. I will be with you always, even until the end of the world. (28.19–20)

A QUICK LOOK AT THIS BOOK

The Ancestors of Jesus
(Luke 3.23–38)

1 Jesus Christ came from the family of King David and also from the family of Abraham. And this is a list of his ancestors. 2-6aFrom Abraham to King David, his ancestors were:

Abraham, Isaac, Jacob, Judah and his brothers (Judah's sons were Perez and

Jesus had a family

(1) Jesus is the real Son of God from heaven. But he is also a real man who had an earthly family. Matthew lists many people who had been in Jesus' ancient family for 2,000 years. Jesus

Zerah, and their mother was Tamar), Hezron;

Ram, Amminadab, Nahshon, Salmon, Boaz (his mother was Rahab), Obed (his mother was Ruth), Jesse, and King David.

6b-11From David to the time of the exile in Babylonia, the ancestors of Jesus were:

David, Solomon (his mother had been Uriah's wife), Rehoboam, Abijah, Asa, Jehoshaphat, Jehoram;

Uzziah, Jotham, Ahaz, Hezekiah, Manasseh, Amon, Josiah, and Jehoiachin and his brothers.

12-16From the exile to the birth of Jesus, his ancestors were:

Jehoiachin, Shealtiel, Zerubbabel, Abiud, Eliakim, Azor, Zadok, Achim;

Eliud, Eleazer, Matthan, Jacob, and Joseph, the husband of Mary, the mother of Jesus, who is called the Messiah.

17There were fourteen generations from Abraham to David. There were also fourteen from David to the exile in Babylonia and fourteen more to the birth of the Messiah.

The Birth of Jesus
(Luke 2.1–7)

18This is how Jesus Christ was born. A young woman named Mary was engaged to Joseph from King David's family. But before they were married, she learned that she was going to have a baby by God's Holy Spirit. 19Joseph was a good man*a* and did not want to embarrass Mary in front of everyone. So he decided to quietly call off the wedding.

20While Joseph was thinking about this, an angel from the Lord came to him in a dream. The angel said, "Joseph, the baby that Mary will have is from the Holy Spirit. Go ahead and marry her. 21Then after her baby is born, name him Jesus,*b* because he will save his people from their sins."

22So God's promise came true, just as the

agood man: Or "kind man," or "man who always did the right thing." *bname him Jesus*: In Hebrew the name "Jesus" means "the Lord saves."

needed the help of his parents and other family members to grow up in the world in a way that pleased God. Matthew's long list also helps us to see that the birth of Jesus had been in the mind of God for a very long time.

Joseph and Mary believed God

(18) Mary and Joseph were a young couple who trusted God. Even though they didn't understand all that God was going to do, they knew they must believe that their Son from heaven would do a great work. In our own lives we don't always understand what God is doing. But it is more important to trust God than to think we have to understand everything.

What did they name Mary's Son?

(21) They named him Jesus, meaning "The Lord Saves." It was a well-known name— the name Joshua is just a different spelling of it. The second part of Jesus' name is Christ (or Messiah), meaning "Anointed One." This meant that God himself filled the life of Jesus in a very special way that made him able to do all the works God sent him to do. But Matthew also reminds us that Jesus was called Immanuel—"God with us."

prophet had said, 23"A virgin will have a baby boy, and he will be called Immanuel," which means "God is with us."

24After Joseph woke up, he and Mary were soon married, just as the Lord's angel had told him to do. 25But they did not live together before her baby was born. Then Joseph named him Jesus.

The Wise Men

2 When Jesus was born in the village of Bethlehem in Judea, Herod was king. During this time some wise menc from the east came to Jerusalem 2and said, "Where is the child born to be king of the Jews? We saw his star in the eastd and have come to worship him."

3When King Herod heard about this, he was worried, and so was everyone else in Jerusalem. 4Herod brought together all the chief priests and the teachers of the Law of Moses and asked them, "Where will the Messiah be born?"

5They told him, "He will be born in Bethlehem, just as the prophet wrote,

6'Bethlehem in the land
    of Judea,
you are very important
    among the towns of Judea.
From your town
    will come a leader,
who will be like a shepherd
    for my people Israel.'"

7Herod secretly called in the wise men and asked them when they had first seen the star. 8He told them, "Go to Bethlehem and search carefully for the child. As soon as you find him, let me know. I want to go and worship him too."

9The wise men listened to what the king said and then left. And the star they had seen in the east went on ahead of them until it stopped over the place where the child was. 10They were thrilled and excited to see the star.

cwise men: People famous for studying the stars.
dhis star in the east: Or "his star rise."

Where was Jesus born?
(1) Jesus was born in the town of Bethlehem in Judea. Bethlehem had a great history. There King David was born a thousand years earlier to a family begun by a couple named Boaz and Ruth. Boaz was a wealthy Hebrew farmer, but Ruth was from a hated Gentile race who came to true faith in the God of the Bible. Jesus descended from that great family.

Wise men worshiped Jesus
(9) Even thinkers in faraway Persia—called Iran today—had been expecting a great King to be born in Palestine. Jewish ancestors of Jesus had told the Persians about the coming Savior. So when Persian scholars, called magi (pronounced MAJ-eye), saw a special star in their sky they believed that the King's birth was near. They traveled hundreds of miles across the desert to worship Jesus.

11When the men went into the house and saw the child with Mary, his mother, they kneeled down and worshiped him. They took out their gifts of gold, frankincense, and myrrh[e] and gave them to him. 12Later they were warned in a dream not to return to Herod, and they went back home by another road.

The Escape to Egypt

13After the wise men had gone, an angel from the Lord appeared to Joseph in a dream. The angel said, "Get up! Hurry and take the child and his mother to Egypt! Stay there until I tell you to return, because Herod is looking for the child and wants to kill him."

14That night Joseph got up and took his wife and the child to Egypt, 15where they stayed until Herod died. So the Lord's promise came true, just as the prophet had said, "I called my son out of Egypt."

The Killing of the Children

16When Herod found out that the wise men from the east had tricked him, he was very angry. He gave orders for his men to kill all the boys who lived in or near Bethlehem and were two years old and younger.

17So the Lord's promise came true, just as the prophet Jeremiah had said,

18"In Ramah a voice was heard
    crying and weeping loudly.
Rachel was mourning
    for her children,
and she refused
to be comforted,
    because they were dead."

The Return from Egypt

19After King Herod died, an angel from the Lord appeared in a dream to Joseph

God protected his Son
(13) Wicked people envy and fear the good. King Herod was such an evil person. He was not the lawful king or even a Jew. He had been given the Jewish throne by the Roman conquerors for political reasons, so he was afraid when he heard that the true King was being born. Then Herod tried to kill Jesus by murdering a lot of boy babies in Bethlehem. But God had a plan for Jesus' life, so his parents took him away to Egypt. God is a hiding place for all who love him.

---

[e]*frankincense, and myrrh*: Frankincense was a valuable powder that was burned to make a sweet smell. Myrrh was a valuable sweet-smelling powder often used in perfume.

while he was still in Egypt. 20The angel said, "Get up and take the child and his mother back to Israel. The people who wanted to kill him are now dead."

21Joseph got up and left with them for Israel. 22But when he heard that Herod's son Archelaus was now ruler of Judea, he was afraid to go there. Then in a dream he was told to go to Galilee, 23and they went to live there in the town of Nazareth. So the Lord's promise came true, just as the prophet had said, "He will be called a Nazarene."*f*

The Preaching of John the Baptist
(Mark 1.1–8; Luke 3.1–18; John 1.19–28)

3 Years later John the Baptist started preaching in the desert of Judea. 2He

f He will be called a Nazarene: The prophet who said this is not known.

Bloom where you're planted
(20) Jesus' family didn't return to Bethlehem when they came back from Egypt. They went to live far away in the northern farming and fishing district of Galilee. Growing up in the town of Nazareth like other boys, Jesus became a helper in the carpenter shop of Joseph, his earthly father. God usually gives us families so we can learn together. But if you're all alone in the world God cares about you in a very special way.

Let your life count for Jesus
(1) John baptized people in the Jordan River when they told of their sorrow for their sins. By baptizing people

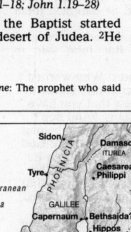

Palestine

said, "Turn back to God! The kingdom of heaven[g] will soon be here."[h]

3John was the one the prophet Isaiah was talking about, when he said,

"In the desert someone
is shouting,
'Get the road ready
for the Lord!
Make a straight path
for him.' "

4John wore clothes made of camel's hair. He had a leather strap around his waist and ate grasshoppers and wild honey.

5From Jerusalem and all Judea and from the Jordan River Valley crowds of people went to John. 6They told how sorry they were for their sins, and he baptized them in the river.

7Many Pharisees and Sadducees also came to be baptized. But John said to them:

You bunch of snakes! Who warned you to run from the coming judgment? 8Do something to show that you have really given up your sins. 9And don't start telling yourselves that you belong to Abraham's family. I tell you that God can turn these stones into children for Abraham. 10An ax is ready to cut the trees down at their roots. Any tree that does not produce fruit will be chopped down and thrown into a fire.

11I baptize you with water so that you will give up your sins.[i] But someone more powerful is going to come, and I am not good enough even to carry his sandals.[j] He will baptize you with the Holy Spirit and with fire. 12His threshing fork is in his hand, and he is ready to separate the wheat from the

John showed that God must wash away their sins. John was not afraid to stand alone and tell the world that Jesus is the Son of God who takes away people's sins. Be prepared always to show by the way you act that Jesus loves those around you and will take away their sins if they ask him.

Where is the Jordan River?

(5) This river runs 70 miles to the Dead Sea from Lake Galilee. It was across this river that the ancient Jews miraculously passed into their promised land many hundreds of years before Jesus was born.

---

[g]*kingdom of heaven*: In the Gospel of Matthew "kingdom of heaven" is used with the same meaning as "God's kingdom" in Mark and Luke. [h]*will soon be here*: Or "is already here." [i]*so that you will give up your sins*: Or "because you have given up your sins." [j]*carry his sandals*: This was one of the duties of a slave.

husks.*k* He will store the wheat in a barn and burn the husks in a fire that never goes out.

The Baptism of Jesus
(Mark 1.9–11; Luke 3.21, 22)

13Jesus left Galilee and went to the Jordan River to be baptized by John. 14But John kept objecting and said, "I ought to be baptized by you. Why have you come to me?" 15Jesus answered, "For now this is how it should be, because we must do all that God wants us to do." Then John agreed. 16So Jesus was baptized. And as soon as he came out of the water, the sky opened, and he saw the Spirit of God coming down on him like a dove. 17Then a voice from heaven said, "This is my own dear Son, and I am pleased with him."

Jesus and the Devil
(Mark 1.12, 13; Luke 4.1–13)

4 The Holy Spirit led Jesus into the desert, so that the devil could test him. 2After Jesus went without eating*l* for forty days and nights, he was very hungry. 3Then the devil came to him and said, "If you are God's Son, tell these stones to turn into bread." 4Jesus answered, "The Scriptures say:
'No one can live only on food.
People need every word
    that God has spoken.' "
5Next, the devil took Jesus to the holy city and had him stand on the highest part of the temple. 6The devil said, "If you are God's Son, jump off. The Scriptures say:
'God will give his angels
    orders about you.

The King was a Servant
(13) John was surprised when Jesus himself came to the Jordan River to be baptized. But Jesus told John to baptize him anyway. That was how Jesus showed everybody he didn't come to lord it over people. Jesus the king made himself a servant of servants. People often try to be "number one." But Jesus warns us that the first will be last in his new kingdom.

Are you tested?
(1) Jesus was tested so that he could help us when we're "put to the test" by things that tempt us to sin. He fought the devil's temptations and won. Jesus knows and cares when someone asks us to do something wrong—or when we just feel like doing wrong. We can't fight our battles with sin all alone, but we lean on our great Savior—and he always helps us when we ask him to.

---

*k*His threshing fork is in his hand, and he is ready to separate the wheat from the husks: After Jewish farmers had trampled out the grain, they used a large fork to pitch the grain and the husks into the air. Wind would blow away the light husks, and the grain would fall back to the ground, where it could be gathered up. *l*went without eating: The Jewish people sometimes went without eating (also called "fasting") to show their love for God and to become better followers.

They will catch you
    in their arms,
and you will not hurt
    your feet on the stones.' "

7Jesus answered, "The Scriptures also say, 'Don't try to test the Lord your God!' "

8Finally, the devil took Jesus up on a very high mountain and showed him all the kingdoms on earth and their power. 9The devil said to him, "I will give all this to you, if you will bow down and worship me."

10Jesus answered, "Go away Satan! The Scriptures say:

'Worship the Lord your God
    and serve only him.' "

11Then the devil left Jesus, and angels came to help him.

Jesus Begins His Work
(Mark 1.14, 15; Luke 4.14, 15)

12When Jesus heard that John had been put in prison, he went to Galilee. 13But instead of staying in Nazareth, Jesus moved to Capernaum. This town was beside Lake Galilee in the territory of Zebulun and Naphtali.m 14So God's promise came true, just as the prophet Isaiah had said,

15"Listen, lands of Zebulun
    and Naphtali,
lands along the road
    to the sea and west
    of the Jordan!
Listen Galilee,
    land of the Gentiles!
16Although your people
    live in darkness,
they will see
    a bright light.
Although they live
    in the shadow of death,
a light will shine
    on them."

Stay out of unnecessary trouble
(12) Jesus had gone to the country of Judea, where he had been baptized by John the Baptist. But John was in prison because he preached the word of God. It was a bad time to be in Judea, and Jesus had much work to do before his death. So Jesus went back up to Galilee where he had grown up. Christians don't look for trouble. The time may well come to stand up and be counted for Jesus. Until then, we should ask God to give us the wisdom to avoid useless arguments.

---

mZebulun and Naphtali: In Old Testament times these tribes were in northern Palestine, and in New Testament times many Gentiles lived where these tribes had once been.

[17]Then Jesus started preaching, "Turn back to God! The kingdom of heaven will soon be here."[n]

Jesus Chooses Four Fishermen
(Mark 1.16–20; Luke 5.1–11)

[18]While Jesus was walking along the shore of Lake Galilee, he saw two brothers. One was Simon, also known as Peter, and the other was Andrew. They were fishermen, and they were casting their net into the lake. [19]Jesus said to them, "Come with me! I will teach you how to bring in people instead of fish." [20]Right then the two brothers dropped their nets and went with him.

[21]Jesus walked on until he saw James and John, the sons of Zebedee. They were in a boat with their father, mending their nets. Jesus asked them to come with him too. [22]Right away they left the boat and their father and went with Jesus.

Jesus Teaches, Preaches, and Heals
(Luke 6.17–19)

[23]Jesus went all over Galilee, teaching in the Jewish meeting places and preaching the good news about God's kingdom. He also healed every kind of disease and sickness. [24]News about him spread all over Syria, and people with every kind of sickness or disease were brought to him. Some of them had a lot of demons in them, others were thought to be crazy,[o] and still others could not walk. But Jesus healed them all.

[25]Large crowds followed Jesus from Galilee and the region around the ten cities known as Decapolis.[p] They also came from Jerusalem, Judea, and from across the Jordan River.

We must turn back to God
(17) God sees us as sheep who have strayed away from their shepherd. Sheep aren't very smart, so they sometimes wander off and get caught in bushes, or fall into holes, or get bitten by wolves. Jesus is our great Shepherd, and he wants to bring us back to where he can feed us and care for us. That means staying close to the other sheep, too. We all need to be part of a Christian church where God's word is taught and where we can learn to be strong members of the family of God.

The brothers dropped their nets
(20) Simon and Andrew dropped their nets to follow Jesus. James and John left their boat "right away." When Jesus called them, these men didn't try to hold on to their old way of life. Following Jesus was the one thing on their minds.

---

[n]*The kingdom of heaven will soon be here*: See the two notes at 3.2.   [o]*thought to be crazy*: In ancient times people with epilepsy were thought to be crazy.   [p]*the ten cities known as Decapolis*: A group of ten cities east of Samaria and Galilee, where the people followed the Greek way of life.

The Sermon on the Mount

5 When Jesus saw the crowds, he went up on the side of a mountain and sat down.q

Blessings
(Luke 6.20–23)

Jesus' disciples gathered around him,
2and he taught them:
3God blesses those people
    who depend only on him.
They belong to the kingdom
    of heaven!r
4God blesses those people
    who grieve.
They will find comfort!
5God blesses those people
    who are humble.
The earth will belong
    to them!
6God blesses those people
    who want to obey hims
    more than to eat or drink.
They will be given
    what they want!
7God blesses those people
    who are merciful.
They will be treated
    with mercy!
8God blesses those people
    whose hearts are pure.
They will see him!
9God blesses those people
    who make peace.
They will be called
    his children!
10God blesses those people
    who are treated badly
    for doing right.
They belong to the kingdom
    of heaven.t

Be a disciple

(1) Sometimes we think "disciples" were only the people that Jesus invited to be his special followers when he lived on earth. But Jesus is always looking for disciples. A disciple is a pupil in the school of Jesus. We are Jesus' disciples when we promise to follow and obey him for the rest of our lives. As we read about the disciples of Jesus' time we see that they had a lot to learn, and sometimes the lessons they learned were very hard ones. We too have much to learn, and we must spend time with Jesus in prayer and study if we are to be useful to him.

Who are the happy people?

(8) Some people think being happy is like having fun at an amusement park. Having *fun* is great, but real *happiness* is what we experience when God blesses us. Happiness is found by thinking and acting as this sermon describes. Many of the qualities listed are also found in God himself—who is perfectly happy. Yes, true happiness is to be like God and so be blessed (made happy) by God.

qsat down: Teachers in the ancient world, including Jewish teachers, usually sat down when they taught. rThey belong to the kingdom of heaven: Or "The kingdom of heaven belongs to them." swho want to obey him: Or "who want to do right" or "who want everyone to be treated right." tThey belong to the kingdom of heaven: See the note at 5.3.

11God will bless you when people insult you, mistreat you, and tell all kinds of evil lies about you because of me. 12Be happy and excited! You will have a great reward in heaven. People did these same things to the prophets who lived long ago.

Salt and Light
(Mark 9.50; Luke 14.34, 35)

13You are like salt for everyone on earth. But if salt no longer tastes like salt, how can it make food salty? All it is good for is to be thrown out and walked on. 14You are like light for the whole world. A city built on top of a hill cannot be hidden, 15and no one would light a lamp and put it under a clay pot. A lamp is placed on a lamp stand, where it can give light to everyone in the house. 16Make your light shine, so that others will see the good that you do and will praise your Father in heaven.

The Law of Moses

17Don't suppose that I came to do away with the Law and the Prophets.u I did not come to do away with them, but to give them their full meaning. 18Heaven and earth may disappear. But I promise you that not even a period or comma will ever disappear from the Law. Everything written in it must happen. 19If you reject even the least important command in the Law and teach others to do the same, you will be the least important person in the kingdom of heaven. But if you obey and teach others its commands, you will have an important place in the kingdom. 20You must obey God's commands better than the Pharisees and the teachers of the Law

Look and act like a Christian
(13) You are a Christian, you say. But does anyone else know it? Jesus doesn't employ secret agents. Christians "wear their hearts on their sleeves"—where everybody can see they really do love Jesus Christ. How? By what they say and what they do. Christians use their tongues to bless people, and their actions help people in trouble. If the world can't recognize a Christian on sight, maybe our Christianity isn't very real.

What good are laws?
(17) The *Lex Romana* (Law of the Romans) taught the world that a well-governed nation has fair laws. When respect for law breaks down, the nation itself fails. Some people believe they ought to be completely free to do whatever seems right—*to them.* We call the practice of that theory "anarchy." When anarchy rules, life and property are no longer sacred.

---

uthe Law and the Prophets: The Jewish Scriptures, that is, the Old Testament.

obey them. If you don't, I promise you
that you will never get into the kingdom
of heaven.

Anger

21You know that our ancestors were
told, "Do not murder" and "A murderer
must be brought to trial." 22But I promise you that if you are angry with someone,ᵛ you will have to stand trial. If you
call someone a fool, you will be taken
to court. And if you say that someone
is worthless, you will be in danger of
the fires of hell.

23So if you are about to place your
gift on the altar and remember that
someone is angry with you, 24leave your
gift there in front of the altar. Make
peace with that person, then come back
and offer your gift to God.

25Before you are dragged into court,
make friends with the person who has
accused you of doing wrong. If you
don't, you will be handed over to the
judge and then to the officer who will
put you in jail. 26I promise you that you
will not get out until you have paid the
last cent you owe.

Marriage

27You know the commandment
which says, "Be faithful in marriage."
28But I tell you that if you look at another
woman and want her, you are already
unfaithful in your thoughts. 29If your
right eye causes you to sin, poke it out
and throw it away. It is better to lose
one part of your body, than for your
whole body to end up in hell. 30If your
right hand causes you to sin, chop it
off and throw it away! It is better to
lose one part of your body, than for your
whole body to be thrown into hell.

ᵛ*someone*: In verses 22-24 the Greek text has "brother,"
which may refer to people in general or to other followers.

***Anger is the beginning of
murder***
(21) "Oh, I could just kill
you" are not idle words. Anger and murder go together.
If we really hate someone
enough, we even want to kill
that person. But there's another side to the double
edge of anger. Our angry
thoughts eat *us* up. People
have become very sick as
the effect of anger and hatred are allowed to build up
in the mind. Could this be
a warning that God himself
will judge hateful attitudes?

Marriage is sacred
(27) God created mar-
riage. So, like everything
else God created, marriage
is holy. All our promises are
serious, but there is no
promise on earth more serious than the promises we
make when we marry. When
we break our promises to
be faithful to our wives or
husbands, we are breaking
a vow we made before God.
God cares about the people
we hurt, and he will judge
us for hurting those closest
loved ones who trusted us.

Divorce
(Matthew 19.9; Mark 10.11, 12; Luke 16.18)

31You have been taught that a man who divorces his wife must write out divorce papers for her.w 32But I tell you not to divorce your wife unless she has committed some terrible sexual sin.x If you divorce her, you will cause her to be unfaithful, just as any man who marries her is guilty of taking another man's wife.

Promises

33You know that our ancestors were told, "Don't use the Lord's name to make a promise unless you are going to keep it." 34But I tell you not to swear by anything when you make a promise! Heaven is God's throne, so don't swear by heaven. 35The earth is God's footstool, so don't swear by the earth. Jerusalem is the city of the great king, so don't swear by it. 36Don't swear by your own head. You cannot make one hair white or black. 37When you make a promise, say only "Yes" or "No." Anything else comes from the devil.

Our promise should be enough
(33) God really rules the world, so we can never be sure we will be allowed to do all we wish. That's why we say, "Till death do us part" when we marry. So we should be careful not to take vows to God we may not be able to keep. But our own "yes" or "no" should be the trustworthy answer of one honest person to another. Otherwise we ought to keep quiet.

Revenge
(Luke 6.29, 30)

38You know that you have been taught, "An eye for an eye and a tooth for a tooth." 39But I tell you not to try to get even with a person who has done something to you. When someone slaps your right cheek,y turn and let that person slap your other cheek. 40If someone

Not fighting back
(38) Jesus teaches us not to pay back one hurt with another one. We ought to take it when we are harmed, and know that God will see that justice is done in the end. This has always been a very hard teaching for people to live by.

wwrite out divorce papers for her: Jewish men could divorce their wives, but the women could not divorce their husbands. The purpose of writing these papers was to make it harder for a man to divorce his wife. Before this law was made, all a man had to do was to send his wife away and say that she was no longer his wife. xsome terrible sexual sin: This probably refers to the laws about the wrong kinds of marriages that are forbidden in Leviticus or to some serious sexual sin. yright cheek: A slap on the right cheek was a bad insult.

sues you for your shirt, give up your coat as well. [41]If a soldier forces you to carry his pack one mile, carry it two miles.[z] [42]When people ask you for something, give it to them. When they want to borrow money, loan it to them.

Love
(Luke 6.27, 28, 32–36)

[43]You have heard people say, "Love your neighbors and hate your enemies." [44]But I tell you to love your enemies and pray for anyone who mistreats you. [45]Then you will be acting like your Father in heaven. He makes the sun rise on both good and bad people. And he sends rain for the ones who do right and for the ones who do wrong. [46]If you love only those people who love you, will God reward you for that? Even tax collectors[a] love their friends. [47]If you greet only your friends, what's so great about that? Don't even unbelievers do that? [48]But you must always act like your Father in heaven.

Giving

6 When you do good deeds, don't try to show off. If you do, you won't get a reward from your Father in heaven.

[2]When you give to the poor, don't blow a loud horn. That's what showoffs do in the meeting places and on the street corners, because they are always looking for praise. I promise you that they already have their reward.

[3]When you give to the poor, don't let anyone know about it.[b] [4]Then your gift will be given in secret. Your Father

Love others as God loved you

(43) God gave us life itself, and, as if that weren't enough, he even gave his own Son to die for us before we loved him. So then, can we not afford the small trouble of doing kind things for people around us? By loving even our enemies we show the world what God is like. Isn't that how he loved us?

Why do we give?

(1) Giving just to be seen by others doesn't impress God, and in the long run it doesn't impress people either. If we give just so the world can see what good people we are, those observing us soon realize that we're "all show" and no reality. Let's give for the right reason: that we want to help others because God first helped us.

---

[z]*two miles*: A Roman soldier had the right to force a person to carry his pack as far as one mile. [a]*tax collectors*: These were usually Jewish people who paid the Romans for the right to collect taxes. They were hated by other Jews who thought of them as traitors to their country and to their religion. [b]*don't let anyone know about it*: The Greek text has, "Don't let your left hand know what your right hand is doing."

knows what is done in secret, and he will reward you.

Prayer
(Luke 11.2–4)

5When you pray, don't be like those showoffs who love to stand up and pray in the meeting places and on the street corners. They do this just to look good. I promise you that they already have their reward.

6When you pray, go into a room alone and close the door. Pray to your Father in private. He knows what is done in private, and he will reward you.

7When you pray, don't talk on and on as people do who don't know God. They think God likes to hear long prayers. 8Don't be like them. Your Father knows what you need before you ask.

9You should pray like this:

Our Father in heaven,
    help us to honor your name.
10Come and set up your kingdom,
    so that everyone on earth
        will obey you,
    as you are obeyed
        in heaven.
11Give us our food for today.c
12Forgive our sins,
    as we forgive others.d
13Keep us from being tempted
    and protect us from evil.e

14If you forgive others for the wrongs they do to you, your Father in heaven will forgive you. 15But if you don't forgive others, your Father will not forgive your sins.

Worshiping God by Going without Eating

16When you go without eating,f don't try to look gloomy as those showoffs

How should we pray?
(5) God doesn't want beautiful speeches. He looks for sincere hearts. And this is the first thing to remember about prayer. God already knows our hearts, and our well-formed sentences aren't what count. Jesus shows that truthfulness in prayer is the important thing, not appearances. But he also reminds us that we have to care about the things God cares about. Otherwise our prayers will be selfish.

cour food for today: Or "the food that we need" or "our food for the coming day." dsins . . . others: Or "what we owe . . . what others owe." eevil: Or "the evil one," that is, the devil. Some manuscripts add, "The kingdom, the power, and the glory are yours forever. Amen." fwithout eating: See the note at 4.2.

do when they go without eating. I promise you that they already have their reward. 17Instead, comb your hair and wash your face. 18Then others won't know that you are going without eating. But your Father sees what is done in private, and he will reward you.

Treasures in Heaven
(Luke 12.33, 34)

19Don't store up treasures on earth! Moths and rust can destroy them, and thieves can break in and steal them. 20Instead, store up your treasures in heaven, where moths and rust cannot destroy them, and thieves cannot break in and steal them. 21Your heart will always be where your treasure is.

Light
(Luke 11.34–36)

22Your eyes are like a window for your body. When they are good, you have all the light you need. 23But when your eyes are bad, everything is dark. If the light inside you is dark, you surely are in the dark.

Money
(Luke 16.13)

24You cannot be the slave of two masters! You will like one more than the other or be more loyal to one than the other. You cannot serve both God and money.

Worry
(Luke 12.22–31)

25I tell you not to worry about your life. Don't worry about having something to eat, drink, or wear. Isn't life more than food or clothing? 26Look at the birds in the sky! They don't plant or harvest. They don't even store grain in barns. Yet your Father in heaven

This world is passing away
(19) Yes, scientists tell us that the earth will one day just die. There is a natural law that says everything in this world is going to wear out. So let us pay attention to the things that cannot die. God cannot die, and he has given us souls—an inner life—that can never die. He has prepared an eternal home for those who love him and who love the things he loves. It just makes sense to value the things that will last forever.

Money is a hard master
(24) People who have money for their master are never happy. No matter how long and how hard they struggle, they never get to the point where they feel they have enough. But those who have God for their master are able to be truly satisfied.

takes care of them. Aren't you worth more than birds?

27Can worry make you live longer?^g **28**Why worry about clothes? Look how the wild flowers grow. They don't work hard to make their clothes. **29**But I tell you that Solomon with all his wealth^h was not as well clothed as one of them. **30**God gives such beauty to everything that grows in the fields, even though it is here today and thrown into a fire tomorrow. He will surely do even more for you! Why do you have such little faith?

31Don't worry and ask yourselves, "Will we have anything to eat? Will we have anything to drink? Will we have any clothes to wear?" **32**Only people who don't know God are always worrying about such things. Your Father in heaven knows that you need all of these. **33**But more than anything else, put God's work first and do what he wants. Then all the other things will be yours as well.

34Don't worry about tomorrow. It will take care of itself. You have enough to worry about today.

Judging Others
(Luke 6.37, 38, 41, 42)

7 Don't condemn others, and God will not condemn you. **2**God will be as hard on you as you are on others! He will treat you exactly as you treat them.

3You can see the speck in your friend's eye, but you don't notice the log in your own eye. **4**How can you say, "My friend, let me take the speck out of your eye," when you don't see the log in your own eye? **5**You're nothing but showoffs! First, take the log out of your own eye. Then you can see how

Worry is a destroyer
(27) Worry doesn't help us improve our lives. A doctor will tell you that worry ruins your health and shortens your life. God is in charge of everything you see around you and everything you can't see. So isn't it reasonable to trust God in all things? Let's do our duty, and God will take care of the rest. This is the secret of a happy life.

Mind your own business
(3) This is often stern but good advice. Nobody likes people who meddle in the concerns of others. God did not appoint us to do his work of judging the worth of people. It is enough that we ourselves measure up to his standards of behavior. Anyway, we usually don't know enough about other people's business to judge them. But God knows and judges the hearts of all.

^g*live longer:* Or "grow taller." ^h*Solomon with all his wealth:* The Jewish people thought that Solomon was the richest person who had ever lived.

to take the speck out of your friend's eye.

6Don't give to dogs what belongs to God. They will only turn and attack you. Don't throw pearls down in front of pigs. They will trample all over them.

Ask, Search, Knock
(Luke 11.9–13)

7Ask, and you will receive. Search, and you will find. Knock, and the door will be opened for you. 8Everyone who asks will receive. Everyone who searches will find. And the door will be opened for everyone who knocks. 9Would any of you give your hungry child a stone, if the child asked for some bread? 10Would you give your child a snake if the child asked for a fish? 11As bad as you are, you still know how to give good gifts to your children. But your heavenly Father is even more ready to give good things to people who ask.

12Treat others as you want them to treat you. This is what the Law and the Prophets*i* are all about.

The Narrow Gate
(Luke 13.24)

13Go in through the narrow gate. The gate to destruction is wide, and the road that leads there is easy to follow. A lot of people go through that gate. 14But the gate to life is very narrow. The road that leads there is so hard to follow that only a few people find it.

A Tree and Its Fruit
(Luke 6.43–45)

15Watch out for false prophets! They dress up like sheep, but inside they are wolves who have come to attack you.

ithe Law and the Prophets: See the note at 5.17.

Look to the Lord for your answer

(7) Jesus means for us to *keep on* asking, searching, knocking—and the answer will come at last. God cares about our needs. Like a wise father, he doesn't spoil his children by giving them all they want when they want it. He supplies their needs and answers their wishes in the right ways and at the right times. In the meantime, let's keep talking to God about the things that concern us. God isn't deaf, and he will prove his love to us.

God's way is the best way

(13) Jesus said the godly way is truly the hard way to follow. That's because we easily prize the wrong things. Some people imagine such things as drugs, alcohol, and immoral living will bring them happiness. But do we need to be told that these things always lead to misery in the end? We make God's way hard for ourselves. God's way really is the road to the gate of everlasting joy and peace. If we miss that way, it is perhaps just because we follow the crowd instead of Jesus.

Actions speak louder than words

(15) There have always been a lot of talkers who claim to have new answers to life's questions that are better than God's answers. Many people went around preaching "new thought" in

16You can tell what they are by what they do. No one picks grapes or figs from thorn bushes. 17A good tree produces good fruit, and a bad tree produces bad fruit. 18A good tree cannot produce bad fruit, and a bad tree cannot produce good fruit. 19Every tree that produces bad fruit will be chopped down and burned. 20You can tell who the false prophets are by their deeds.

early times. They even wormed their way into the Christian church. But their empty words were like vapor that soon vanished. Many similar false prophets are around today. Let's just be patient. In good time we will see that all such claims to superior wisdom will come to an end. We know God's truth by its godly results.

A Warning
(Luke 13.26, 27)

21Not everyone who calls me their Lord will get into the kingdom of heaven. Only the ones who obey my Father in heaven will get in. 22On the day of judgment many will call me their Lord. They will say, "We preached in your name, and in your name we forced out demons and worked many miracles." 23But I will tell them, "I will have nothing to do with you! Get out of my sight, you evil people!"

Two Builders
(Luke 6.47–49)

24Anyone who hears and obeys these teachings of mine is like a wise person who built a house on solid rock. 25Rain poured down, rivers flooded, and winds beat against that house. But it did not fall, because it was built on solid rock.

26Anyone who hears my teachings and does not obey them is like a foolish person who built a house on sand. 27The rain poured down, the rivers flooded, and the winds blew and beat against that house. Finally, it fell with a crash.

28When Jesus finished speaking, the crowds were surprised at his teaching. 29He taught them like someone with authority, and not like their teachers of the Law of Moses.

Saying it doesn't make it true
(24) Those who make outward religious claims sometimes display a religion that is only skin-deep. Such people may deceive those around them with their words—and may even make a good try at deceiving themselves, but God cannot be deceived. What counts in the end is simple, daily obedience. Real faith produces people who do good and lovely things. What they build stands forever, because they build on the foundation of Jesus' words.

Jesus Heals a Man
(Mark 1.40–45; Luke 5.12–16)

8 As Jesus came down the mountain, he was followed by large crowds. 2Suddenly a man with leprosy[j] came and kneeled in front of Jesus. He said, "Lord, you have the power to make me well, if only you wanted to."

3Jesus put his hand on the man and said, "I do want to! Now you are well." At once the man's leprosy disappeared. 4Jesus told him, "Don't tell anyone about this, but go and show the priest that you are well. Then take a gift to the temple just as Moses commanded, and everyone will know that you have been healed."[k]

Jesus has the power
(2) The man with leprosy came to Jesus with the right idea: his getting healed depended only on Jesus' power and Jesus' wishes— not on what the man did to arrange for his healing. His eyes were on Jesus.

Jesus Heals an Army Officer's Servant
(Luke 7.1–10; John 4.43–54)

5When Jesus was going into the town of Capernaum, an army officer came up to him and said, 6"Lord, my servant is at home in such terrible pain that he can't even move."

7"I will go and heal him," Jesus replied.

8But the officer said, "Lord, I'm not good enough for you to come into my house. Just give the order, and my servant will get well. 9I have officers who give orders to me, and I have soldiers who take orders from me. I can say to one of them, 'Go!' and he goes. I can say to another, 'Come!' and he comes. I can say to my servant, 'Do this!' and he will do it."

10When Jesus heard this, he was so surprised that he turned and said to the crowd following him, "I tell you that in all of Israel I've never found anyone with this much faith! 11Many people will come from every-

Who is good enough for Jesus?
(8) The army officer was right. He was *not* good enough for Jesus. But we also should get the message—Jesus didn't come to us because we are good, but because we are sinners who need him. Nobody in church is good enough to be there. But we come to Jesus and become part of his family because he invites us to share his love and receive his forgiveness.

---

[j]*leprosy:* In biblical times the word "leprosy" was used for many different kinds of skin diseases.   [k]*everyone will know that you have been healed:* People with leprosy had to be examined by a priest and told that they were well (that is "clean") before they could once again live a normal life in the Jewish community. The gift that Moses commanded was the sacrifice of some lambs together with flour mixed with olive oil.

where to enjoy the feast in the kingdom of heaven with Abraham, Isaac, and Jacob. 12But the ones who should have been in the kingdom will be thrown out into the dark. They will cry and grit their teeth in pain."

13Then Jesus said to the officer, "You may go home now. Your faith has made it happen."

Right then his servant was healed.

Jesus Heals Many People
(Mark 1.29–34; Luke 4.38–41)

14Jesus went to the home of Peter, where he found that Peter's mother-in-law was sick in bed with fever. 15He took her by the hand, and the fever left her. Then she got up and served Jesus a meal.

16That evening many people with demons in them were brought to Jesus. And with only a word he forced out the evil spirits and healed everyone who was sick. 17So God's promise came true, just as the prophet Isaiah had said,

"He healed our diseases
and made us well."

Some Who Wanted to Go with Jesus
(Luke 9.57–62)

18When Jesus saw the crowd,*l* he went across Lake Galilee. 19A teacher of the Law of Moses came up to him and said, "Teacher, I'll go anywhere with you!"

20Jesus replied, "Foxes have dens, and birds have nests. But the Son of Man does not have a place to call his own."

21Another disciple said to Jesus, "Lord, let me wait till I bury my father."

22Jesus answered, "Come with me, and let the dead bury their dead."*m*

Serving Jesus
(15) Peter's mother-in-law was grateful to Jesus for healing her, and she got up and served him. Do we serve the Lord who has done so many kind things for us?

Have you traded in your old life?
(20) Jesus made himself poor so he could give us the riches of a new life to be spent forever with him. But in order to receive that *new* life, we have to leave the *old* life behind. That frightens some people until they see what Jesus is giving them to replace it. He will supply all our needs and assure us of a heavenly home as well.

---

l saw the crowd: Some manuscripts have "large crowd." Others have "large crowds." *m let the dead bury their dead*: For the Jewish people a proper burial of their dead was a very important duty. But Jesus teaches that following him is even more important.

A Storm
(Mark 4.35–41; Luke 8.22–25)

23After Jesus left in a boat with his disciples, 24a terrible storm suddenly struck the lake, and waves started splashing into their boat.

Jesus was sound asleep, 25so the disciples went over to him and woke him up. They said, "Lord, save us! We're going to drown!"

26But Jesus replied, "Why are you so afraid? You surely don't have much faith." Then he got up and ordered the wind and the waves to calm down. And everything was calm.

27The men in the boat were amazed and said, "Who is this? Even the wind and the waves obey him."

Don't be afraid of storms
(23) The world we grow up in is a frightening place sometimes, with its storms of poverty, crime, sickness, and death. The disciples feared the wind and the waves. They had to learn that Jesus is Lord of all, including storms. He is Lord over whatever frightens us. Our fears go away when we learn that Jesus is really in charge of all that happens.

Two Men with Demons in Them
(Mark 5.1–20; Luke 8.26–39)

28After Jesus had crossed the lake, he came to shore near the town of Gadara[n] and started down the road. Two men with demons in them came to him from the tombs.[o] They were so fierce that no one could travel that way. 29Suddenly they shouted, "Jesus, Son of God, what do you want with us? Have you already come to punish us?"

30Not far from there a large herd of pigs was feeding. 31So the demons begged Jesus, "If you force us out, please send us into those pigs!" 32Jesus told them to go, and they went out of the men and into the pigs. All at once the pigs rushed down the steep bank into the lake and drowned.

33The people taking care of the pigs ran to the town and told everything, especially what had happened to the two men. 34Everyone in town came out to meet Jesus. When they saw him, they begged him to leave their part of the country.

Sin makes people afraid of Jesus
(29) What strange behavior. These two men actually thought Jesus had come to punish them. The evil spirits who lived in the men had confused their thinking. But Jesus had come to save the men from the spirits that tormented them. Even the townspeople were confused. They weren't glad that the demon-possessed men were saved; rather, they were upset because the pigs had drowned. Their thinking was upside-down.

---

[n]*Gadara*: Some manuscripts have "Gergasa." Others have "Gerasa." [o]*tombs*: It was thought that demons and evil spirits lived in tombs and in caves that were used for burying the dead.

Jesus Heals a Crippled Man

(Mark 2.1–12; Luke 5.17–26)

9 Jesus got into a boat and crossed back
over to the town where he lived.[p]
2Some people soon brought to him a crippled man lying on a mat. When Jesus saw
how much faith they had, he said to the
crippled man, "My friend, don't worry!
Your sins are forgiven."
3Some teachers of the Law of Moses said
to themselves, "Jesus must think he is God!"
4But Jesus knew what was in their minds,
and he said, "Why are you thinking such
evil things? 5Is it easier for me to tell this
crippled man that his sins are forgiven or
to tell him to get up and walk? 6But I will
show you that the Son of Man has the right
to forgive sins here on earth." So Jesus said
to the man, "Get up! Pick up your mat and
go on home." 7The man got up and went
home. 8When the crowds saw this, they
were afraid[q] and praised God for giving
such authority to people.

Jesus Chooses Matthew

(Mark 2.13–17; Luke 5.27–32)

9As Jesus was leaving, he saw a tax collector[r] named Matthew sitting at the place
for paying taxes. Jesus said to him, "Come
with me." Matthew got up and went with
him.
10Later, Jesus and his disciples were having dinner at Matthew's house.[s] Many tax
collectors and other sinners were also there.
11Some Pharisees asked Jesus' disciples,
"Why does your teacher eat with tax collectors and other sinners?"
12Jesus heard them and answered,
"Healthy people don't need a doctor, but
sick people do. 13Go and learn what the
Scriptures mean when they say, 'Instead of
offering sacrifices to me, I want you to be
merciful to others.' I didn't come to invite

[p] *where he lived*: Capernaum. See 4.13. [q] *afraid*: Some manuscripts have "amazed." [r] *tax collector*: See the note at 5.46. [s] *Matthew's house*: Or "Jesus' house."

What was Jesus' real work?

(2) Jesus always put first things first. It's our way to put first things *last*. Our real problem is not our aches and pains. Our real problem is our sins. Some people may laugh at this, but they never ask themselves what caused human suffering in the days of Adam and Eve. Jesus knew sin was the cause. So he forgave the crippled man's sins, and then went on to illustrate his point by healing the man. Jesus is the Savior of both our souls and bodies. But even the bystanders missed his meaning.

Our bodies are important

(5) Our bodies are what we live in. This includes all the experiences we take for granted, like smelling a rose, tasting a good steak, hearing beautiful music, or viewing a lovely mountain scene. God gave us our bodies, so they're worth taking care of.

Jesus kept strange company

(11) Jesus never changed his lifestyle to suit his surroundings. He was always the same. Yet, if we can imagine it, Jesus was *the friend of sinners.* This was a fact that disgusted the religious leaders. They had completely misunderstood God's plan in sending his Son into the world—to seek and to save lost people. Not only that, but Jesus even

good people to be my followers. I came to invite sinners."

People Ask about Going without Eating
(Mark 2.18–22; Luke 5.33–39)

14One day some followers of John the Baptist came and asked Jesus, "Why do we and the Pharisees often go without eating,^{t} while your disciples never do?"

15Jesus answered:

The friends of a bridegroom don't go without eating while he is still with them. But the time will come when he will be taken from them. Then they will go without eating.

16No one uses a new piece of cloth to patch old clothes. The patch would shrink and tear a bigger hole.

17No one pours new wine into old wineskins. The wine would swell and burst the old skins.^{u} Then the wine would be lost, and the skins would be ruined. New wine must be put into new wineskins. Both the skins and the wine will then be safe.

A Dead Girl and a Sick Woman
(Mark 5.21–43; Luke 8.40–56)

18While Jesus was still speaking, a Jewish official came and kneeled in front of him. The man said, "My daughter has just now died! Please come and place your hand on her. Then she will live again."

19Jesus and his disciples got up and went with the man.

20A woman who had been bleeding for twelve years came up behind Jesus and barely touched his clothes. 21She had said to herself, "If I can just touch his clothes, I will get well."

22Jesus turned. He saw the woman and said, "Don't worry! You are now well be-

made apostles of such hated people as Matthew the tax collector. This sinner became the writer of the book about Jesus you are reading now.

New and old
(16) New and old cloth don't go together, and neither do new wine and old wineskins. Why did Jesus say this? He was showing his followers that now that he was here, something new was happening, and the old religious customs of the Jews would not be needed.

How much can we trust Jesus?
(21) A man had a dead daughter. A woman had a bleeding sickness. Both of them acted simply as if Jesus could and would immediately help them. Were they right to have such faith? Jesus says our blessings are the results of our faith in him. Have we really tested his ability to the utmost? Are there any limits to what he can do for our good if we trust him?

---

^{t}without eating: See the note at 4.2. ^{u}swell and burst the old skins: While the juice from grapes was becoming wine, it would swell and stretch the skins in which it had been stored. If the skins were old and stiff, they would burst.

cause of your faith." At that moment she was healed.

23When Jesus went into the home of the Jewish official and saw the musicians and the crowd of mourners,v 24he said, "Get out of here! The little girl is not dead. She is just asleep." Everyone started laughing at Jesus. 25But after the crowd had been sent out of the house, Jesus went to the girl's bedside. He took her by the hand and helped her up.

26News about this spread all over that part of the country.

Jesus Heals Two Blind Men

27As Jesus was walking along, two blind men began following him and shouting, "Son of David,w have pity on us!"

28After Jesus had gone indoors, the two blind men came up to him. He asked them, "Do you believe I can make you well?"

"Yes, Lord," they answered.

29Jesus touched their eyes and said, "Because of your faith, you will be healed." 30They were able to see, and Jesus strictly warned them not to tell anyone about him. 31But they left and talked about him to everyone in that part of the country.

Jesus Heals a Man Who Could Not Talk

32As Jesus and his disciples were on their way, some people brought to him a man who could not talk because a demon was in him. 33After Jesus had forced the demon out, the man started talking. The crowds were so amazed that they began saying, "Nothing like this has ever happened in Israel!"

34But the Pharisees said, "The leader of the demons gives him the power to force out demons."

v the crowd of mourners: The Jewish people often hired mourners for funerals. w Son of David: The Jewish people expected the Messiah to be from the family of King David, and for this reason the Messiah was often called the "Son of David."

Faith is important
(27) Here's another example. The blind men had faith in Jesus, and he said they could be healed because of their faith. The two men came to him confidently, with their hearts full of trust. It meant a lot to Jesus.

Beware of a hard heart
(34) Jesus had just freed a man from the power of a demon. Demons are evil spirits that can actually live inside people. Nearly everybody was glad for what Jesus had done. But the Pharisees resented Jesus because the crowds were following him instead of them. They should have been glad along with the crowds. But they loved their social position more than they loved God.

Jesus Has Pity on People

35Jesus went to every town and village. He taught in their meeting places and preached the good news about God's kingdom. Jesus also healed every kind of disease and sickness. 36When he saw the crowds, he felt sorry for them. They were confused and helpless, like sheep without a shepherd. 37He said to his disciples, "A large crop is in the fields, but there are only a few workers. 38Ask the Lord in charge of the harvest to send out workers to bring it in."

Jesus Chooses His Twelve Apostles
(Mark 3.13–19; Luke 6.12–16)

10 Jesus called together his twelve disciples. He gave them the power to force out evil spirits and to heal every kind of disease and sickness. 2The first of the twelve apostles was Simon, better known as Peter. His brother Andrew was an apostle, and so were James and John, the two sons of Zebedee. 3Philip, Bartholomew, Thomas, Matthew the tax collector,x James the son of Alphaeus, and Thaddaeus were also apostles. 4The others were Simon, known as the Eager One,y and Judas Iscariot,z who later betrayed Jesus.

Instructions for the Twelve Apostles
(Mark 6.7–13; Luke 9.1–6)

5Jesus sent out the twelve apostles with these instructions:

Stay away from the Gentiles and don't go to any Samaritan town. 6Go only to the people of Israel, because they are like a flock of lost sheep. 7As you go, announce that the kingdom of

xtax collector: See the note at 5.46.   yknown as the Eager One: The Greek text has "Cananaean," which probably comes from a Hebrew word meaning "zealous" (see Luke 6.15). "Zealot" was the name later given to the members of a Jewish group which resisted and fought against the Romans.   zIscariot: This may mean "a man from Kerioth" (a place in Judea). But more probably it means "a man who was a liar" or "a man who was a betrayer."

How much does Jesus care?
(36) Jesus saw the people as though they were sheep without a shepherd. Jesus, as he traveled through the towns of Galilee, was not just another kind man. He was the Lord from heaven. In heaven he and his Father had looked out on a needy, dying world. Then the Lord—the Son of God—said he would come and show his love for us. As the hymn says, Jesus came "out of the ivory palaces into a world of woe." He didn't blind us with his glory, but showed us a kind of love we had never seen before.

Jesus needed only a few
(5) A well-known advertisement announces, "The Marines are looking for a few good men." Many times an army's success depends more on its discipline than its numbers. A riotous mob is not an army. Jesus knew he could accomplish his goal with a handful of earnest people. So he chose twelve and instructed them. Yes, one of them would be a traitor, but that didn't hinder Jesus' plan. The apostle who cried out, "Christ gives me strength to face anything" (Philippians 4.13), speaks for all of us. As Jesus strengthens us, we conquer evil with the power of the good news.

heaven will soon be here.*a* 8Heal the
sick, raise the dead to life, heal people
who have leprosy,*b* and force out demons. You received without paying,
now give without being paid. 9Don't
take along any gold, silver, or copper
coins. 10And don't carry*c* a traveling bag
or an extra shirt or sandals or a walking
stick.

Workers deserve their food. 11So
when you go to a town or a village, find
someone worthy enough to have you
as their guest and stay with them until
you leave. 12When you go to a home,
give it your blessing of peace. 13If the
home is deserving, let your blessing remain with them. But if the home is not
deserving, take back your blessing of
peace. 14If someone won't welcome you
or listen to your message, leave their
home or town. And shake the dust from
your feet at them.*d* 15I promise you that
the day of judgment will be easier for
the towns of Sodom and Gomorrah*e*
than for that town.

Warning about Trouble
(Mark 13.9–13; Luke 21.12–17)

16I am sending you like lambs into
a pack of wolves. So be as wise as
snakes and as innocent as doves.
17Watch out for people who will take
you to court and have you beaten in
their meeting places. 18Because of me,
you will be dragged before rulers and
kings to tell them and the Gentiles about
your faith. 19But when someone arrests
you, don't worry about what you will
say or how you will say it. At that time
you will be given the words to say.
20But you will not really be the one

*An apostle makes hard
choices*

(16) The world is not always
a comfortable place for
those whom Jesus sends
here. Often being an apostle (or "sent one") means
prison, torture, hatred by
one's own family, and ha-
tred by the whole world.
Such a servant of Christ must
decide beforehand that he
or she is willing to pay such
a price for the privilege of
being sent. We are not better than our Master from
heaven who suffered all
these things for us.

awill soon be here: Or "is already here." *bleprosy*: See
the note at 8.2. *cDon't take along . . . don't carry*:
Or "Don't accept . . . don't accept." *dshake the dust
from your feet at them*: This was a way of showing
rejection. See Acts 13.51. *eSodom and Gomorrah*: During the time of Abraham the Lord destroyed these cities
because the people there were so evil.

speaking. The Spirit from your Father will tell you what to say.

21Brothers and sisters will betray one another and have each other put to death. Parents will betray their own children, and children will turn against their parents and have them killed. 22Everyone will hate you because of me. But if you remain faithful until the end, you will be saved. 23When people mistreat you in one town, hurry to another one. I promise you that before you have gone to all the towns of Israel, the Son of Man will come.

24Disciples are not better than their teacher, and slaves are not better than their master. 25It is enough for disciples to be like their teacher and for slaves to be like their master. If people call the head of the family Satan, what will they say about the rest of the family?

The One to Fear
(Luke 12.2–7)

26Don't be afraid of anyone! Everything that is hidden will be found out, and every secret will be known. 27Whatever I say to you in the dark, you must tell in the light. And you must announce from the housetops whatever I have whispered to you. 28Don't be afraid of people. They can kill you, but they cannot harm your soul. Instead, you should fear God who can destroy both your body and your soul in hell. 29Aren't two sparrows sold for only a penny? But your Father knows when any one of them falls to the ground. 30Even the hairs on your head are counted. 31So don't be afraid! You are worth much more than many sparrows.

Telling Others about Christ
(Luke 12.8, 9)

32If you tell others that you belong to me, I will tell my Father in heaven that you are my followers. 33But if you

Fear God, not other people
(26) Remember, everyone on earth is doomed to die. If we die in the service of Christ, that is a better death than living to a sick old age. People can destroy only our bodies; God is the Judge of our souls. But he cares very much for us. No servant of his ever died alone—Jesus himself stands near to give us a joyful death that is not an end but a beginning.

reject me, I will tell my Father in heaven that you don't belong to me.

Not Peace, but Trouble
(Luke 12.51–53; 14.26, 27)

34Don't think that I came to bring peace to the earth! I came to bring trouble, not peace. 35I came to turn sons against their fathers, daughters against their mothers, and daughters-in-law against their mothers-in-law. 36Your worst enemies will be in your own family.

37If you love your father or mother or even your sons and daughters more than me, you are not fit to be my disciples. 38And unless you are willing to take up your cross and come with me, you are not fit to be my disciples. 39If you try to save your life, you will lose it. But if you give it up for me, you will surely find it.

Rewards
(Mark 9.41)

40Anyone who welcomes you welcomes me. And anyone who welcomes me also welcomes the one who sent me. 41Anyone who welcomes a prophet, just because that person is a prophet, will be given the same reward as a prophet. Anyone who welcomes a good person, just because that person is good, will be given the same reward as a good person. 42And anyone who gives one of my most humble followers a cup of cool water, just because that person is my follower, will surely be rewarded.

John the Baptist
(Luke 7.18–35)

11 After Jesus had finished instructing his twelve disciples, he left and began teaching and preaching in the towns.*f*

Your troubles are Christ's troubles
(34) Sometimes we are tempted to think something is wrong with us, because telling about Jesus very often results in conflict. We call Jesus the "Prince of peace," but often his message brings trouble. Jesus didn't bring peace to everyone in his time. His generation hated him and put him to death. In spite of this, the miracle of God's kingdom was born in many hearts. We also can expect these different kinds of results in our own times.

Be kind to God's people
(40) When we meet a follower of the Lord Jesus, we ought to treat that person as well as we would treat Jesus himself. What acts of kindness have we done to a Christian lately for Jesus' sake?

f the towns: The Greek text has "their towns," which may refer to the towns of Galilee or to the towns where Jesus' disciples had lived.

²John was in prison when he heard what Christ was doing. So John sent some of his followers ³to ask Jesus, "Are you the one we should be looking for? Or must we wait for someone else?"

⁴Jesus answered, "Go and tell John what you have heard and seen. ⁵The blind are now able to see, and the lame can walk. People with leprosy^g are being healed, and the deaf can hear. The dead are raised to life, and the poor are hearing the good news. ⁶God will bless everyone who does not reject me because of what I do."

⁷As John's followers were going away, Jesus spoke to the crowds about John:

What sort of person did you go out into the desert to see? Was he like tall grass blown about by the wind? ⁸What kind of man did you go out to see? Was he someone dressed in fine clothes? People who dress like that live in the king's palace. ⁹What did you really go out to see? Was he a prophet? He certainly was. I tell you that he was more than a prophet. ¹⁰In the Scriptures God says about him, "I am sending my messenger ahead of you to get things ready for you." ¹¹I tell you that no one ever born on this earth is greater than John the Baptist. But whoever is least in the kingdom of heaven is greater than John.

¹²From the time of John the Baptist until now, violent people have been trying to take over the kingdom of heaven by force. ¹³All the Books of the Prophets and the Law of Moses^h told what was going to happen up to the time of John. ¹⁴And if you believe them, John is Elijah, the prophet you are waiting for. ¹⁵If you have ears, pay attention!

¹⁶You people are like children sitting in the market and ¹⁷shouting to each other,

"We played the flute,
    but you would not dance!

John announced Jesus' coming

(7) John the Baptist's ministry signaled the end of the Old Testament period. That is why Jesus said, "But whoever is least in the kingdom of heaven is greater than John" (verse 11). Jesus was announcing the kingdom of heaven. He himself is the King, and wherever he and his message come, his kingdom is in view. John was typical of an earlier time, a time that prepared the way for the King. John prepared the way, though even he did not fully understand the meaning of Jesus' coming (verse 3).

---

^gleprosy: See the note at 8.2.   ^hthe Books of the Prophets and the Law of Moses: The Jewish Scriptures, that is, the Old Testament.

We sang a funeral song,
    but you would not mourn!"
18John the Baptist did not go around eating and drinking, and you said, "That man has a demon in him!" 19But the Son of Man goes around eating and drinking, and you say, "That man eats and drinks too much! He is even a friend of tax collectors*i* and sinners." Yet Wisdom is shown to be right by what it does.

The Unbelieving Towns
(Luke 10.13–15)

20In the towns where Jesus had worked most of his miracles, the people refused to turn to God. So Jesus was upset with them and said:
    21You people of Chorazin are in for trouble! You people of Bethsaida are in for trouble too! If the miracles that took place in your towns had happened in Tyre and Sidon, the people there would have turned to God long ago. They would have dressed in sackcloth and put ashes on their heads.*j* 22I tell you that on the day of judgment the people of Tyre and Sidon will get off easier than you will.
    23People of Capernaum, do you think you will be honored in heaven? You will go down to hell! If the miracles that took place in your town had happened in Sodom, that town would still be standing. 24So I tell you that on the day of judgment the people of Sodom will get off easier than you.

Come to Me and Rest
(Luke 10.21, 22)

25At that moment Jesus said:
    My Father, Lord of heaven and earth, I am grateful that you hid all this from

Look out for pride
(20) The Jewish towns Jesus spoke to "had heard it all before." They were tired of hearing "divine messages." So they ignored Jesus' words and works. They thought they didn't need him because they had the religion of their ancestors. Tyre and Sidon, in the country of Phoenicia, had never heard the prophets or known God's Law. But, strange to say, the wicked cities of Tyre and Sidon were more open to Jesus.

Judgment is coming
(22) Most people don't like to hear about judgment. "Stories about Jesus and his love are all right," many seem to say, "but don't speak to us of judgment." Nevertheless the gracious, gentle Christ speaks more vividly about divine judgment than anyone in the Bible. So the world should take God's warnings seriously.

God loves ordinary people
(25) Abraham Lincoln is said to have commented, "God must have loved the common people, he made so many of them." The truth is, we are all quite ordinary if only we admit it. What makes us special is that God created us *all* in his likeness. Too often, what sets us apart is our pride. But Jesus blesses all who are willing to be ordinary for his sake.

---

itax collectors: See the note at 5.46. *jsackcloth . . . ashes on their heads*: This was one way that people showed how sorry they were for their sins.

wise and educated people and showed it to ordinary people. 26Yes, Father, that is what pleased you.

27My Father has given me everything, and he is the only one who knows the Son. The only one who truly knows the Father is the Son. But the Son wants to tell others about the Father, so that they can know him too.

28If you are tired from carrying heavy burdens, come to me and I will give you rest. 29Take the yokek I give you. Put it on your shoulders and learn from me. I am gentle and humble, and you will find rest. 30This yoke is easy to bear, and this burden is light.

A Question about the Sabbath
(Mark 2.23–28; Luke 6.1–5)

12 One Sabbath Jesus and his disciples were walking through some wheat fields.l His disciples were hungry and began picking and eating grains of wheat. 2Some Pharisees said to Jesus, "Why are your disciples picking grain on the Sabbath? They are not supposed to do that!"

3Jesus answered:

You surely must have read what David did when he and his followers were hungry. 4He went into the house of God, and then they ate the sacred loaves of bread that only priests are supposed to eat. 5Haven't you read in the Law of Moses that the priests are allowed to work in the temple on the Sabbath? But no one says that they are guilty of breaking the law of the Sabbath. 6I tell you that there is something here greater than the temple. 7Don't you know what the Scriptures mean when they say, "Instead of offering sacrifices to me, I want you to be merciful to others?" If you knew what this means, you would not

kyoke: Yokes were put on the necks of animals, so that they could pull a plow or wagon. A yoke was a symbol of obedience and hard work. *lwalking through some wheat fields*: It was the custom to let hungry travelers pick grains of wheat.

Jesus invites us to rest
(28) After a while, everybody gets tired of life, at least sometimes. This should remind us that God never intended us to travel this road by ourselves. Jesus wants to walk beside us and share our burdens. He took our greatest burden onto himself—our sins. Compared to that, the "burdens" he gives us are easy to carry.

The Pharisees were faultfinders
(2) The Pharisees were hard to please. All they could think about was their precious customs. They were proud because their ancestors had done great things for God. But the Pharisees themselves only seemed to spend their time finding fault with others. We must pray to be rescued from the kind of "religion" whose greatest strength is its ability to find fault.

The Sabbath is for doing good
(7) For most of us our "day of rest" is Sunday. We have lots of free time when we don't have to work. How do we use it—just for our own relaxation? If so, we're missing a chance to help others.

condemn these innocent disciples of mine. 8So the Son of Man is Lord over the Sabbath.

A Man with a Crippled Hand
(Mark 3.1–6; Luke 6.6–11)

9Jesus left and went into one of the Jewish meeting places, 10where there was a man whose hand was crippled. Some Pharisees wanted to accuse Jesus of doing something wrong, and they asked him, "Is it right to heal someone on the Sabbath?"

11Jesus answered, "If you had a sheep that fell into a ditch on the Sabbath, wouldn't you lift it out? 12People are worth much more than sheep, and so it is right to do good on the Sabbath." 13Then Jesus told the man, "Hold out your hand." The man did, and it became as healthy as the other one.

14The Pharisees left and started making plans to kill Jesus.

God's Chosen Servant

15When Jesus found out what was happening, he left there and large crowds followed him. He healed all of their sick, 16but warned them not to tell anyone about him. 17So God's promise came true, just as Isaiah the prophet had said,

18"Here is my chosen servant!
   I love him,
      and he pleases me.
   I will give him my Spirit,
      and he will judge
         the nations.
19He will not argue or shout
   or be heard speaking
      in the streets.
20He will not break off
      a bent twig
   or put out
      a faintly burning flame
   until he makes justice
      win the victory.
21All nations will place
      their hope in him."

The prophets described Jesus

(17) Jesus was not just an ordinary person who grew up to be great. His divine life and work were planned by God long beforehand in eternity past. This is why the prophet Isaiah was able to describe Jesus so clearly. God was in charge of history and of Isaiah, and God planned every word and deed of the life of Jesus.

Jesus and the Ruler of the Demons
(Mark 3.20–30; Luke 11.14–23; 12.10)

22Some people brought to Jesus a man who was blind and could not talk because he had a demon in him. Jesus cured the man, and then he was able to talk and see. 23The crowds were so amazed that they asked, "Could Jesus be the Son of David?"m

24When the Pharisees heard this, they said, "He forces out demons by the power of Beelzebul, the ruler of the demons!"

25Jesus knew what they were thinking, and he said to them:

Any kingdom where people fight each other will end up ruined. And a town or family that fights will soon destroy itself. 26So if Satan fights against himself, how can his kingdom last? 27If I use the power of Beelzebul to force out demons, whose power do your own followers use to force them out? Your followers are the ones who will judge you. 28But when I force out demons by the power of God's Spirit, it proves that God's kingdom has already come to you. 29How can anyone break into a strong man's house and steal his things, unless he first ties up the strong man? Then he can take everything.

30If you are not on my side, you are against me. If you don't gather in the harvest with me, you scatter it. 31-32I tell you that any sinful thing you do or say can be forgiven. Even if you speak against the Son of Man, you can be forgiven. But if you speak against the Holy Spirit, you can never be forgiven, either in this life or in the life to come.

A Tree and Its Fruit
(Luke 6.43–45)

33A good tree produces only good fruit, and a bad tree produces bad fruit. You can tell what a tree is like by the fruit it produces. 34You are a bunch of

mCould Jesus be the Son of David: Or "Does Jesus think he is the Son of David?" See the note at 9.27.

Whose side are we on?
(24) The Pharisees said Jesus was a servant of Satan. But Jesus showed them he couldn't be serving Satan and destroying Satan's works at the same time. The truth was that the Pharisees hated Jesus, but he showed them they were really denying the work of God's own Spirit. They were enemies of God and therefore enemies of Christ.

What you say can destroy you
(33) Jesus compared right speech to good fruit, and he compared evil speech to bad fruit. We don't take what we say seriously enough. It is just not true that "sticks and stones will break my bones, but names will never hurt me." Words do hurt and destroy the lives of others as well as ourselves.

evil snakes, so how can you say anything good? Your words show what is in your hearts. 35Good people bring good things out of their hearts, but evil people bring evil things out of their hearts. 36I promise you that on the day of judgment, everyone will have to account for every careless word they have spoken. 37On that day they will be told that they are either innocent or guilty because of the things they have said.

A Sign from Heaven
(Mark 8.11, 12; Luke 11.29–32)

38Some Pharisees and teachers of the Law of Moses said, "Teacher, we want you to show us a sign from heaven."
39But Jesus replied:
You want a sign because you are evil and won't believe! But the only sign you will get is the sign of the prophet Jonah. 40He was in the stomach of a big fish for three days and nights, just as the Son of Man will be deep in the earth for three days and nights. 41On the day of judgment the people of Nineveh[n] will stand there with you and condemn you. They turned to God when Jonah preached, and yet here is something far greater than Jonah. 42The Queen of the South[o] will also stand there with you and condemn you. She traveled a long way to hear Solomon's wisdom, and yet here is something much greater than Solomon.

Return of an Evil Spirit
(Luke 11.24–26)

43When an evil spirit leaves a person, it travels through the desert, looking for a place to rest. But when the demon

Signs from the Scriptures
(39) The Jewish Scriptures are full of wonderful stories, but they are more than stories—they are signs that point to Jesus. Jonah, Solomon, and many other great people from Israel's history show us things about what God planned to do when he sent his Son Jesus to save us.

Emptiness is not good
(43) It's one thing to "clean up" our lives by giving up sin. But we need to replace the bad things with good things. Learning from God's word, doing good to others, being more like Jesus—these are the things that should fill up a clean life.

[n]*Nineveh*: During the time of Jonah this city was the capital of the Assyrian Empire, which was Israel's worst enemy. But Jonah was sent there to preach, so that the people would turn to the Lord and be saved. [o]*Queen of the South*: Sheba, probably a country in southern Arabia.

doesn't find a place, 44it says, "I will go back to the home I left." When it gets there and finds the place empty, clean, and fixed up, 45it goes off and finds seven other evil spirits even worse than itself. They all come and make their home there, and the person ends up in worse shape than before. That's how it will be with you evil people of today.

Jesus' Mother and Brothers
(Mark 3.31–35; Luke 8.19–21)

46While Jesus was still speaking to the crowds, his mother and brothers came and stood outside because they wanted to talk with him. 47Someone told Jesus, "Your mother and brothers are standing outside and want to talk with you."p

48Jesus answered, "Who is my mother and who are my brothers?" 49Then he pointed to his disciples and said, "These are my mother and my brothers! 50Anyone who obeys my Father in heaven is my brother or sister or mother."

A Story about a Farmer
(Mark 4.1–9; Luke 8.4–8)

13 That same day Jesus left the house and went out beside Lake Galilee, where he sat down to teach.q 2Such large crowds gathered around him that he had to sit in a boat, while the people stood on the shore. 3Then he taught them many things by using stories. He said:

A farmer went out to scatter seed in a field. 4While the farmer was scattering the seed, some of it fell along the road and was eaten by birds. 5Other seeds fell on thin, rocky ground and quickly started growing because the soil was

pwith you: Some manuscripts do not have verse 47.
qsat down to teach: Teachers in the ancient world, including Jewish teachers, usually sat down when they taught.

Who are your real relatives?
(46) Family ties are usually close, and we may imagine there are no relationships closer than the ones within our families. But Jesus makes it clear that the family of God—of God's people— is on a higher level than any earthly ties. Our connection with our earthly family, if we have a family at all, may be only for a time. But our link to God's family is forever.

Spread the good news
(3) The saying is that "bad news travels fast." What is the best way to make sure the good news about Jesus is heard? Our kind deeds will be a great help. Jesus says we just have to keep on showing and telling everyone what a wonderful Savior we have. This story shows that some people will believe us and others will not. People are different in the way they hear what we say. But God guarantees that the good news we tell about Jesus will multiply itself in the lives of many.

not very deep. 6But when the sun came up, the plants were scorched and dried up, because they did not have enough roots. 7Some other seeds fell where thorn bushes grew up and choked the plants. 8But a few seeds did fall on good ground where the plants produced a hundred or sixty or thirty times as much as was scattered. 9If you have ears, pay attention!

Why Jesus Used Stories
(Mark 4.10–12; Luke 8.9, 10)

Next

10Jesus' disciples came to him and asked, "Why do you use nothing but stories when you speak to the people?"

11Jesus answered:

I have explained the secrets about the kingdom of heaven to you, but not to others. 12Everyone who has something will be given more. But people who don't have anything will lose even what little they have. 13I use stories when I speak to them because when they look, they cannot see, and when they listen, they cannot hear or understand. 14So God's promise came true, just as the prophet Isaiah had said,

> "These people will listen
> and listen,
>   but never understand.
> They will look and look,
>   but never see.
> 15All of them have
>   stubborn minds!
> Their ears are stopped up,
>   and their eyes are covered.
> They cannot see or hear
>   or understand.
> If they could,
> they would turn to me,
>   and I would heal them."

16But God has blessed you, because your eyes can see and your ears can hear! 17Many prophets and good people were eager to see what you see and to hear what you hear. But I tell you that they did not see or hear.

Stories were Jesus' way of teaching
(11) By telling stories, Jesus offered truth to people in a form that would be understood by those whose hearts God had prepared to receive it. Those whose hearts were not ready for the truth would just be puzzled.

Jesus Explains the Story about the Farmer
(Mark 4.13–20; Luke 8.11–15)

18Now listen to the meaning of the story about the farmer:

19The seeds that fell along the road are the people who hear the message about the kingdom, but don't understand it. Then the evil one comes and snatches the message from their hearts. 20The seeds that fell on rocky ground are the people who gladly hear the message and accept it right away. 21But they don't have deep roots, and they don't last very long. As soon as life gets hard or the message gets them in trouble, they give up.

22The seeds that fell among the thorn bushes are also people who hear the message. But they start worrying about the needs of this life and are fooled by the desire to get rich. So the message gets choked out, and they never produce anything. 23The seeds that fell on good ground are the people who hear and understand the message. They produce as much as a hundred or sixty or thirty times what was planted.

Weeds among the Wheat

24Jesus then told them this story:

The kingdom of heaven is like what happened when a farmer scattered good seed in a field. 25But while everyone was sleeping, an enemy came and scattered weed seeds in the field and then left.

26When the plants came up and began to ripen, the farmer's servants could see the weeds. 27The servants came and asked, "Sir, didn't you scatter good seed in your field? Where did these weeds come from?"

28"An enemy did this," he replied.

His servants then asked, "Do you want us to go out and pull up the weeds?"

29"No!" he answered. "You might also pull up the wheat. 30Leave the

weeds alone until harvest time. Then
I'll tell my workers to gather the weeds
and tie them up and burn them. But I'll
have them store the wheat in my barn."

Stories about a Mustard Seed and Yeast
(Mark 4.30–32; Luke 13.18–21)

31Jesus told them another story:

The kingdom of heaven is like what
happens when a farmer plants a mustard seed in a field. 32Although it is the
smallest of all seeds, it grows larger
than any garden plant and becomes a
tree. Birds even come and nest on its
branches.

33Jesus also said:

The kingdom of heaven is like what
happens when a woman mixes a little
yeast into three big batches of flour. Finally, all the dough rises.

The Reason for Teaching with Stories
(Mark 4.33, 34)

34Jesus used stories when he spoke to
the people. In fact, he did not tell them anything without using stories. 35So God's
promise came true, just as the prophetr had
said,

"I will use stories
    to speak my message
and to explain things
    that have been hidden
since the creation
    of the world."

Jesus Explains the Story about the Weeds

36After Jesus left the crowd and went inside,s his disciples came to him and said,
"Explain to us the story about the weeds
in the wheat field."

37Jesus answered:

The one who scattered the good seed
is the Son of Man. 38The field is the

---

rthe prophet: Some manuscripts have "the prophet
Isaiah." swent inside: Or "went home."

What can a seed do?
(31) The tiny mustard seed
grows and spreads its
branches. Likewise, the
Christian faith has grown
from its little beginnings to
fill the whole world with the
good news about Jesus.

What about the weeds?
(37) A good farmer tries to
keep his fields free from
weeds. God is like a farmer
in planting the seed that one
day results in many faithful
believers. But in spite of all
the good planting that God
does, evil grows along with
the good. But we shouldn't
worry too much. We just
keep on spreading the great
news about Jesus. God, the
greatest of all farmers, will
weed out the evil at last.

world, and the good seeds are the people who belong to the kingdom. The weed seeds are those who belong to the evil one, 39and the one who scattered them is the devil. The harvest is the end of time, and angels are the ones who bring in the harvest.

40Weeds are gathered and burned. That's how it will be at the end of time. 41The Son of Man will send out his angels, and they will gather from his kingdom everyone who does wrong or causes others to sin. 42Then he will throw them into a flaming furnace, where people will cry and grit their teeth in pain. 43But everyone who has done right will shine like the sun in their Father's kingdom. If you have ears, pay attention!

A Hidden Treasure

44The kingdom of heaven is like what happens when someone finds treasure hidden in a field and buries it again. A person like that is happy and goes and sells everything in order to buy the field.

A Valuable Pearl

45The kingdom of heaven is like what happens when a shop owner is looking for fine pearls. 46After finding a very valuable one, the owner goes and sells everything in order to buy that pearl.

A Fish Net

47The kingdom of heaven is like what happens when a net is thrown into a lake and catches all kinds of fish. 48When the net is full, it is dragged to the shore, and the fishermen sit down to separate the fish. They keep the good ones, but throw the bad ones away. 49That's how it will be at the end of time. Angels will come and separate the evil people from the ones who have done right. 50Then those evil people will be

How much is Jesus worth? (45) It is likely that the pearl in Jesus' story refers to himself. He is the King in the kingdom of God. The idea is that being in the kingdom is worth the very best of our lives. So let us be willing to exchange all that we value in life for Jesus' friendship. Whatever we treasure most comes second after him.

Good and bad together (49) Just as a fish net draws in all kinds of things—good fish, bad fish, seaweed, driftwood—so the Lord will make sure that his "good fish," believers, are finally separated from the evil that surrounds them now in the world. That should be a comfort to us.

thrown into a flaming furnace, where they will cry and grit their teeth in pain.

New and Old Treasures

51Jesus asked his disciples if they understood all these things. They said, "Yes, we do."

52So he told them, "Every student of the Scriptures who becomes a disciple in the kingdom of heaven is like someone who brings out new and old treasures from the storeroom."

The People of Nazareth Turn against Jesus
(Mark 6.1–6; Luke 4.16–30)

53When Jesus had finished telling these stories, he left 54and went to his hometown. He taught in their meeting place, and the people were so amazed that they asked, "Where does he get all this wisdom and the power to work these miracles? 55Isn't he the son of the carpenter? Isn't Mary his mother, and aren't James, Joseph, Simon, and Judas his brothers? 56Don't his sisters still live here in our town? How can he do all this?" 57So the people were very unhappy because of what he was doing.

But Jesus said, "Prophets are honored by everyone, except the people of their hometown and their own family." 58And because the people did not have any faith, Jesus did not work many miracles there.

The Death of John the Baptist
(Mark 6.14–29; Luke 9.7–9)

14 About this time Herod the ruler[t] heard the news about Jesus 2and told his officials, "This is John the Baptist! He has come back from death, and that's why he has the power to work these miracles."

3-4Herod had earlier arrested John and had him chained and put in prison. He did this because John had told him, "It isn't

[t]Herod the ruler: Herod Antipas, the son of Herod the Great (2.1).

Being popular is not the goal of life
(57) If we're popular we may be pleasing too many people. Jesus knew that most people would not appreciate him. Even though many heard him gladly, in the end he had only a handful of friends. But he reached his goal: he opened a way back to God for us. Doing the will of God, not pleasing people, is what life is about.

Evil often wins—for now
(3) Most of the great novels and stories of fiction are about the triumph of goodness. These stories show that people long for what they really don't see very much of—justice. John the Baptist was the victim of an awful injustice: he died at the mere wish of a young girl. Is there any justice? Yes. In the end God is the rewarder of those who love him. He will set all things right.

right for you to take Herodias, the wife of your brother Philip." 5Herod wanted to kill John. But the people thought John was a prophet, and Herod was afraid of what they might do.

6When Herod's birthday came, the daughter of Herodias danced for the guests. She pleased Herod 7so much that he swore to give her whatever she wanted. 8But the girl's mother told her to say, "Here on a platter I want the head of John the Baptist!"

9The king was sorry for what he had said. But he did not want to break the promise he had made in front of his guests. So he ordered a guard 10to go to the prison and cut off John's head. 11It was taken on a platter to the girl, and she gave it to her mother. 12John's followers took his body and buried it. Then they told Jesus what had happened.

The Herods

1. Herod "the Great," ruler of Judea from 37 to 4 B.C.; killed the boy babies of Bethlehem after Jesus was born (see Matthew 2)

2. Archelaus, son of no. 1, ruler of Judea from 4 B.C. to A.D. 6 (see Matthew 2.22)

3. Herod Antipas, son of no. 1, ruler of Galilee and Perea from 4 B.C. to A.D. 39; had John the Baptist beheaded; Jesus sent to him by Pilate (see Matthew 14; Luke 23)

4. Herod Philip, son of no. 1; lost his wife to his brother, no. 3 (see Matthew 14.3)

5. Philip, son of no. 1, ruler of Iturea and Trachonitis from 4 B.C. to A.D. 34 (see Luke 3.1)

6. Herod Agrippa I, grandson of no. 1, inherited no. 5's kingdom and ruled it from A.D. 37 to 44, and ruled Galilee from A.D. 39 to 44; killed James; put Peter in prison; killed by an angel (see Acts 12)

7. Herod Agrippa II, son of no. 6, ruled from A.D. 53 to 70; heard Paul's defense and rejected the good news (see Acts 25; 26)

Jesus Feeds Five Thousand
(Mark 6.30–44; Luke 9.10–17; John 6.1–14)

13After Jesus heard about John, he crossed Lake Galilee*u* to go to some place where he could be alone. But the crowds found out and followed him on foot from the towns. 14When Jesus got out of the boat, he saw the large crowd. He felt sorry for them and healed everyone who was sick.

15That evening the disciples came to Jesus and said, "This place is like a desert, and it is already late. Let the crowds leave, so they can go to the villages and buy some food."

16Jesus replied, "They don't have to leave. Why don't you give them something to eat?"

17But they said, "We have only five small loaves of bread*v* and two fish." 18Jesus asked his disciples to bring the food to him, 19and he told the crowd to sit down on the grass. Jesus took the five loaves and the two fish. He looked up toward heaven and blessed the food. Then he broke the bread and handed it to his disciples, and they gave it to the people.

20After everyone had eaten all they wanted, Jesus' disciples picked up twelve large baskets of leftovers.

21There were about five thousand men who ate, not counting the women and children.

Jesus Walks on the Water
(Mark 6.45–52; John 6.15–21)

22Right away Jesus made his disciples get into a boat and start back across the lake.*w* But he stayed until he had sent the crowds away. 23Then he went up on a mountain where he could be alone and pray. Later that evening, he was still there.

24By this time the boat was a long way from the shore. It was going against the

Does God care about our needs?
(19) Have you talked to God about the needs of your life? Jesus knew the needs of the crowd who followed him. The disciples spoke to Jesus about the need for food, so he used the small amount they had to feed many. Like a wise investor, God uses the little we have and multiplies it. So we prosper under God's care.

Jesus is Lord of nature
(24) God, not "Mother Nature," is in charge of the weather. On this occasion the wind blew and the waves rose high, but Jesus was Lord of the storm. Why do we fear the powers of nature? God made them all,

---

u crossed Lake Galilee: To the east side.   *v small loaves of bread*: These would have been flat and round or in the shape of a bun.   *w back across the lake*: To the west side.

wind and was being tossed around by the waves. 25A little while before morning, Jesus came walking on the water toward his disciples. 26When they saw him, they thought he was a ghost. They were terrified and started screaming.

27At once Jesus said to them, "Don't worry! I am Jesus. Don't be afraid."

28Peter replied, "Lord, if it is really you, tell me to come to you on the water."

29"Come on!" Jesus said. Peter then got out of the boat and started walking on the water toward him.

30But when Peter saw how strong the wind was, he was afraid and started sinking. "Lord, save me!" he shouted.

31Right away Jesus reached out his hand. He helped Peter up and said, "You surely don't have much faith. Why do you doubt?"

32When Jesus and Peter got into the boat, the wind died down. 33The men in the boat worshiped Jesus and said, "You really are the Son of God!"

Jesus Heals Sick People in Gennesaret
(Mark 6.53–56)

34Jesus and his disciples crossed the lake and came to shore near the town of Gennesaret. 35The people found out that he was there, and they sent word to everyone who lived in that part of the country. So they brought all the sick people to Jesus. 36They begged him just to let them touch his clothes, and everyone who did was healed.

The Teaching of the Ancestors
(Mark 7.1–13)

15 About this time some Pharisees and teachers of the Law of Moses came from Jerusalem. They asked Jesus, 2"Why don't your disciples obey what our ancestors taught us to do? They don't even wash their handsˣ before they eat."

and he'll help us to stand. The disappointments and sorrows of life are like storms. With Jesus beside us we can walk above those too.

Can Jesus heal our diseases?
(35) Many are living today who have been healed by Jesus' touch. But *we* have to touch *him* too. When the people touched Jesus' clothes, they didn't believe his clothes would heal them. They were showing their complete trust in him. Touching Jesus means believing he lives and that he always gives us what is best.

ˣwash their hands: The Jewish people had strict laws about washing their hands before eating, especially if they had been out in public.

³Jesus answered:

Why do you disobey God and follow your own teaching? ⁴Didn't God command you to respect your father and mother? Didn't he tell you to put to death all who curse their parents? ⁵But you let people get by without helping their parents when they should. You let them say that what they have has been offered to God.ʸ ⁶Is this any way to show respect to your parents? You ignore God's commands in order to follow your own teaching. ⁷And you are nothing but showoffs! Isaiah the prophet was right when he wrote that God had said,

⁸"All of you praise me
  with your words,
 but you never really
  think about me.
⁹It is useless for you
  to worship me,
 when you teach rules
  made up by humans."

We must follow God, not our customs
(5) Some believe that the custom described in this passage let people say that their belongings were devoted to God, and then keep them—but they could not give them to someone else. Jesus told sons and daughters who did this that they were only avoiding their duty to honor their parents, which was among the most important of God's laws about our duty to people. Such sons and daughters were hiding their sin under false religion.

What Really Makes People Unclean
(Mark 7.14–23)

¹⁰Jesus called the crowd together and said, "Pay attention and try to understand what I mean. ¹¹The food that you put into your mouth doesn't make you unclean and unfit to worship God. The bad words that come out of your mouth are what make you unclean." ¹²Then his disciples came over to him and asked, "Do you know that you insulted the Pharisees by what you said?"

¹³Jesus answered, "Every plant that my Father in heaven did not plant will be pulled up by the roots. ¹⁴Stay away from those Pharisees! They are like blind people leading other blind people, and all of them will fall into a ditch."

¹⁵Peter replied, "What did you mean when you talked about the things that make people unclean?"

ʸ*has been offered to God:* According to Jewish custom, when people said something was offered to God, it belonged to him and could not be used for anyone else, not even for their own parents.

16Jesus then said:

Don't any of you know what I am talking about by now? 17Don't you know that the food you put into your mouth goes into your stomach and then out of your body? 18But the words that come out of your mouth come from your heart. And they are what make you unfit to worship God. 19Out of your heart come evil thoughts, murder, unfaithfulness in marriage, vulgar deeds, stealing, telling lies, and insulting others. 20These are what make you unclean. Eating without washing your hands will not make you unfit to worship God.

What do you store up in your heart?
(16) We are more often concerned about what we put in our stomachs than how we fill our minds or hearts. It is too often what comes out of the mind or heart that hurts us and hurts those around us. Evil thoughts in the heart lead to sinful words and actions, and we become as bad for others as our thoughts are for us.

A Woman's Faith
(Mark 7.24–30)

21Jesus left and went to the territory near the cities of Tyre and Sidon. 22Suddenly a Canaanite womanz from there came out shouting, "Lord and Son of David,a have pity on me! My daughter is full of demons." 23Jesus did not say a word. But the woman kept following along and shouting, so his disciples came up and asked him to send her away.

24Jesus said, "I was sent only to the people of Israel! They are like a flock of lost sheep."

25The woman came closer. Then she kneeled down and begged, "Lord, please help me!"

26Jesus replied, "It isn't right to take food away from children and feed it to dogs."b

27"Lord, that's true," the woman said, "but even dogs get the crumbs that fall from their owner's table."

28Jesus answered, "Dear woman, you really do have a lot of faith, and you will be given what you want." At that moment her daughter was healed.

God hears the cry of faith
(23) Some people might say Jesus was not very kind to the Canaanite woman because he didn't grant her request right away. Jesus was teaching her and us that earnestness and sincerity matter to God. It is also important for us to find out for ourselves that we really mean what we pray for. When Jesus saw the woman's single-minded trust, he responded at once.

zCanaanite woman: This woman was not Jewish.
aSon of David: See the note at 9.27. bfeed it to dogs: The Jewish people sometimes referred to Gentiles as dogs.

Jesus Heals Many People

29From there Jesus went along Lake Galilee. Then he climbed a hill and sat down. 30Large crowds came and brought many people who were crippled or blind or lame or unable to talk. They placed them, and many others, in front of Jesus, and he healed them all. 31Everyone was amazed at what they saw and heard. People who had never spoken could now speak. The lame were healed. The crippled could walk, and the blind were able to see. Everyone was praising the God of Israel.

Jesus Feeds Four Thousand
(Mark 8.1–10)

32Jesus called his disciples together and told them, "I feel sorry for these people. They have been with me for three days, and they don't have anything to eat. I don't want to send them away hungry. They might faint on their way home."

33His disciples said, "This place is like a desert. Where can we find enough food to feed such a crowd?"

34Jesus asked them how much food they had. They replied, "Seven small loaves of bread*c* and a few little fish."

35After Jesus had told the people to sit down, 36he took the seven loaves of bread and the fish and gave thanks. He then broke them and handed them to his disciples, who passed them around to the crowds.

37Everyone ate all they wanted, and the leftovers filled seven large baskets.

38There were four thousand men who ate, not counting the women and children.

39After Jesus had sent the crowds away, he got into a boat and sailed across the lake. He came to shore near the town of Magadan.*d*

God wants us to be healed (30) In this world, we all get sick at times—and some day we'll die. Is this God's best for us? Not at all. Jesus made this point throughout his ministry. In God's kingdom there will be no more suffering because of disobedience. Those things will all be in the past, and we will have the glorious health that God planned for us.

Another feeding miracle (36) This is not the same as the feeding of the five thousand people told of in chapter 14. See chapter 16, where Jesus speaks of the two feedings separately.

c small loaves of bread: See the note at 14.17. *dMagadan*: The place is unknown, but it must have been on the east side of Lake Galilee.

A Demand for a Sign from Heaven
(Mark 8.11–13; Luke 12.54–56)

16 The Pharisees and Sadducees came to Jesus and tried to test him by asking for a sign from heaven. 2He told them:

If the sky is red in the evening, you say the weather will be good. 3But if the sky is red and gloomy in the morning, you say it is going to rain. You can tell what the weather will be like by looking at the sky. But you don't understand what is happening now.*e* 4You want a sign because you are evil and won't believe! But the only sign you will be given is what happened to Jonah.*f* Then Jesus left.

The Yeast of the Pharisees and Sadducees
(Mark 8.14–21)

5The disciples had forgotten to bring any bread when they crossed the lake.*g* 6Jesus then warned them, "Watch out! Guard against the yeast of the Pharisees and Sadducees."

7The disciples talked this over and said to each other, "He must be saying this because we didn't bring along any bread."

8Jesus knew what they were thinking and said:

You surely don't have much faith! Why are you talking about not having any bread? 9Don't you understand? Have you forgotten about the five thousand people and all those baskets of leftovers from just five loaves of bread? 10And what about the four thousand people and all those baskets of leftovers from only seven loaves of bread? 11Don't you know by now that I am not talking to you about bread? Watch out for the yeast of the Pharisees and Sadducees!

Miracles don't create faith
(2) Jesus once said that even if someone rose from the dead, many people still would not believe him. So, sure enough, when Jesus arose from the dead, they didn't believe. That's what Jesus was talking about when he mentioned what happened to Jonah: Jesus' resurrection would be like Jonah's rescue from the belly of the great fish. Faith is trust in God *himself*, not for what we want him to do for us.

False teaching spreads easily
(6) Like yeast that makes bread rise, false teaching gradually seems to take over whole societies. We hear all the time about unbiblical religious movements that become popular. Know why you believe in Jesus. Someone has said, "If you don't stand for something you'll fall for anything."

---

eIf the sky is red . . . what is happening now: The words of Jesus in verses 2 and 3 are not in some manuscripts. *fwhat happened to Jonah:* Jonah was in the stomach of a big fish for three days and nights. See 12.40. *gcrossed the lake:* To the east side.

12Finally, the disciples understood that Jesus was not talking about the yeast used to make bread, but about the teaching of the Pharisees and Sadducees.

Who Is Jesus?
(Mark 8.27–30; Luke 9.18–21)

13When Jesus and his disciples were near the town of Caesarea Philippi, he asked them, "What do people say about the Son of Man?"

14The disciples answered, "Some people say you are John the Baptist or maybe Elijahh or Jeremiah or some other prophet."

15Then Jesus asked them, "But who do you say I am?"

16Simon Peter spoke up, "You are the Messiah, the Son of the living God."

17Jesus told him:

Simon, son of Jonah, you are blessed! You didn't discover this on your own. It was shown to you by my Father in heaven. 18So I will call you Peter, which means "a rock." On this rock I will build my church, and death itself will not have any power over it. 19I will give you the keys to the kingdom of heaven, and God in heaven will allow whatever you allow on earth. But he will not allow anything that you don't allow.

20Jesus told his disciples not to tell anyone that he was the Messiah.

Jesus Speaks about His Suffering and Death
(Mark 8.31—9.1; Luke 9.22–27)

21From then on, Jesus began telling his disciples what would happen to him. He said, "I must go to Jerusalem. There the nation's leaders, the chief priests, and the teachers of the Law of Moses will make me suffer terribly. I will be killed, but three days later I will rise to life."

22Peter took Jesus aside and told him to

Jesus is the Son of God
(16) But isn't every believer a child of God? Yes, but not in the way Jesus is. He had lived in eternity with his Father and the Holy Spirit. Together the three are one God. Jesus the Messiah (or Christ) was born as a child in this world, and so became the God-Man. He is God in human form—this is how he became our Savior.

Jesus came to die
(21) Our idea of winning is living. Jesus' idea of winning was dying. That was Jesus' reason for coming into the world. It was his way of exposing Satan's lie that we are the hopeless prisoners of sin and death. Death would not be the end of the life of Jesus on earth. After three days he would rise to live again in even greater glory and power than before his death.

---

hElijah: Many of the Jewish people expected the prophet Elijah to come and prepare the way for the Messiah.

stop talking like that. He said, "Lord, surely God won't let this happen to you!"

23Jesus turned to Peter and said, "Satan, get away from me! You're in my way because you think like everyone else and not like God."

24Then Jesus said to his disciples:

If any of you want to be my followers, you must forget about yourself. You must take up your cross and follow me. 25If you want to save your life,[i] you will destroy it. But if you give up your life for me, you will find it. 26What will you gain, if you own the whole world but destroy yourself? What would you give to get back your soul?

27The Son of Man will soon come in the glory of his Father and with his angels to reward all people for what they have done. 28I promise you that some of those standing here will not die before they see the Son of Man coming with his kingdom.

The True Glory of Jesus
(Mark 9.2–13; Luke 9.28–36)

17 Six days later Jesus took Peter and the brothers James and John with him. They went up on a very high mountain where they could be alone. 2There in front of the disciples Jesus was completely changed. His face was shining like the sun, and his clothes became white as light.

3All at once Moses and Elijah were there talking with Jesus. 4So Peter said to him, "Lord, it is good for us to be here! Let us make three shelters, one for you, one for Moses, and one for Elijah."

5While Peter was still speaking, the shadow of a bright cloud passed over them. From the cloud a voice said, "This is my own dear Son, and I am pleased with him. Listen to what he says!" 6When the disciples heard the voice, they were so afraid that they fell flat on the ground. 7But Jesus came

See Jesus as he is

(2) The Son of God hid his glory by coming into this world as a man. He took upon himself the form of a servant. But on the mountain he showed himself to his disciples as he really is. Jesus is no longer the meek and lowly servant today. He is the King of Glory. We should realize he is no longer the suffering one, but the risen Christ who lives to share his life with us forever.

---

[i]*life*: In verses 25 and 26 the same Greek word is translated "life," "yourself," and "soul."

over and touched them. He said, "Get up and don't be afraid!" [8]When they opened their eyes, they saw only Jesus.

[9]On their way down from the mountain, Jesus warned his disciples not to tell anyone what they had seen until after the Son of Man had been raised from death.

[10]The disciples asked Jesus, "Don't the teachers of the Law of Moses say that Elijah must come before the Messiah does?"

[11]Jesus told them, "Elijah certainly will come and get everything ready. [12]In fact, he has already come. But the people did not recognize him and treated him just as they wanted to. They will soon make the Son of Man suffer in the same way." [13]Then the disciples understood that Jesus was talking to them about John the Baptist.

Jesus Heals a Boy
(Mark 9.14–29; Luke 9.37–43a)

[14]Jesus and his disciples returned to the crowd. A man kneeled in front of him [15]and said, "Lord, have pity on my son! He has a bad case of epilepsy and often falls into a fire or into water. [16]I brought him to your disciples, but none of them could heal him."

[17]Jesus said, "You people are too stubborn to have any faith! How much longer must I be with you? Why do I have to put up with you? Bring the boy here." [18]Then Jesus spoke sternly to the demon. It went out of the boy, and right then he was healed.

[19]Later the disciples went to Jesus in private and asked him, "Why couldn't we force out the demon?"

[20-21]Jesus replied:

It is because you don't have enough faith! But I can promise you this. If you had faith no larger than a mustard seed, you could tell this mountain to move from here to there. And it would. Everything would be possible for you.[j]

Our faith must be greater
(17) We forgive ourselves too easily for our weak faith. We feel the rightness of Jesus' remark here. We say great words about our mighty God, but we often live as though he were weak. Let's put away our unbelief and show by our lives that our God lives.

[j]*for you:* Some manuscripts add, "But the only way to force out that kind of demon is by praying and going without eating."

Jesus Again Speaks about His Death
(Mark 9.30–32; Luke 9.43b–45)

22While Jesus and his disciples were going from place to place in Galilee, he told them, "The Son of Man will be handed over to people 23who will kill him. But three days later he will rise to life." All of this made the disciples very sad.

Paying the Temple Tax

24When Jesus and the others arrived in Capernaum, the collectors for the temple tax came to Peter and asked, "Does your teacher pay the temple tax?"

25"Yes, he does," Peter answered.

After they had returned home, Jesus went up to Peter and asked him, "Simon, what do you think? Do the kings of this earth collect taxes and fees from their own people or from foreigners?"*k*

26Peter answered, "From foreigners."

Jesus replied, "Then their own people*l* don't have to pay. 27But we don't want to cause trouble. So go cast a line into the lake and pull out the first fish you hook. Open its mouth, and you will find a coin. Use it to pay your taxes and mine."

Who Is the Greatest?
(Mark 9.33–37; Luke 9.46–48)

18 About this time, the disciples came to Jesus and asked him who would be the greatest in the kingdom of heaven. 2Jesus called a child over and had the child stand near him. 3Then he said:

I promise you this. If you don't change and become like this child, you will never get into the kingdom of heaven. 4But if you are as humble as this child, you are the greatest in the kingdom of heaven. 5And when you

Obey the law
(24) Jesus agreed that the temple tax was not a good law. But he told Peter to pay it anyway. It was a small price to pay to avoid a foolish quarrel. If we are always demanding our rights, we just seem to be quarrelsome. Let's be willing sometimes to accept wrong for Jesus' sake. God supplies our needs somehow, as he supplied Jesus' and Peter's needs here in this passage.

You're important to God
(1) Self-importance is a pitiful sin. By pushing ourselves forward we really show how frightened we are. We're afraid of being forgotten, that people will ignore us, that we'll be lost in the crowd. So we try to be ahead of others. Christians can afford not to be "big shots"—we have a kingdom that will last forever. Our God won't forget us.

---

kfrom their own people or from foreigners: Or "from their children or from others." *lFrom foreigners . . . their own people*: Or "From other people . . . their children."

welcome one of these children because of me, you welcome me.

Temptations to Sin
(Mark 9.42–48; Luke 17.1, 2)

6It will be terrible for people who cause even one of my little followers to sin. Those people would be better off thrown into the deepest part of the ocean with a heavy stone tied around the neck! 7The world is in for trouble because of the way it causes people to sin. There will always be something to cause people to sin, but anyone who does this will be in for trouble.

8If your hand or foot causes you to sin, chop it off and throw it away! You would be better off to go into life crippled or lame than to have two hands and be thrown into the fire that never goes out. 9If your eye causes you to sin, poke it out and get rid of it. You would be better off to go into life with only one eye than to have two eyes and be thrown into the fires of hell.

The Lost Sheep
(Luke 15.3–7)

10-11Don't be cruel to any of these little ones! I promise you that their angels are always with my Father in heaven.m 12Let me ask you this. What would you do if you had a hundred sheep and one of them wandered off? Wouldn't you leave the ninety-nine on the hillside and go look for the one that had wandered away? 13I am sure that finding it would make you happier than having the ninety-nine that never wandered off. 14That's how it is with your Father in heaven. He doesn't want any of these little ones to be lost.

Don't be a stumbling stone
(6) We don't always see the things in our path that will trip us up. Temptation is like that. We aren't expecting it, but if we aren't careful we trip and fall into sin. It's also very important not to be a stumbling stone of temptation for others. By thoughtless things we do, we may cause others to sin.

God won't lose us
(12) We saw earlier how important we are to God. Jesus showed this very well in the story about the lost sheep. The shepherd valued that one sheep more than all the others. So he went and found it, wherever it was lost. That's the way God cares about each one of us—he never gives up till he finds the one who has wandered.

min heaven: Some manuscripts add, "The Son of Man came to save people who are lost."

When Someone Sins
(Luke 17.3)

15If one of my followers[n] sins against you, go and point out what was wrong. But do it in private, just between the two of you. If that person listens, you have won back a follower. 16But if that one refuses to listen, take along one or two others. The Scriptures teach that every complaint must be proven true by two or more witnesses. 17If the follower refuses to listen to them, report the matter to the church. Anyone who refuses to listen to the church must be treated like an unbeliever or a tax collector.[o]

Sin must be confessed

(15) "If I ignore it, maybe it will go away." Too often we think that way about something unpleasant—or even about something sinful. Sin breaks our relationship with God and others. We should confess our sins, not just to please others, but to please God. The kingdom of God cannot be the kingdom of God if sin is permitted. So let us help one another to do away with all things that offend God.

Allowing and Not Allowing

18I promise you that God in heaven will allow whatever you allow on earth, but he will not allow anything you don't allow. 19I promise that when any two of you on earth agree about something you are praying for, my Father in heaven will do it for you. 20Whenever two or three of you come together in my name,[p] I am there with you.

An Official Who Refused to Forgive

21Peter came up to the Lord and asked, "How many times should I forgive someone[q] who does something wrong to me? Is seven times enough?"

22Jesus answered:

Not just seven times, but seventy-seven times![r] 23This story will show you what the kingdom of heaven is like:

One day a king decided to call in his officials and ask them to give an account

---

[n]followers: The Greek text has "brother," which is used here and elsewhere in this chapter to refer to a follower of Christ. [o]tax collector: See the note at 5.46. [p]in my name: Or "as my followers." [q]someone: Or "a follower." See the note at 18.15. [r]seventy-seven times: Or "seventy times seven." The large number means that one follower should never stop forgiving another.

of what they owed him. 24As he was doing this, one official was brought in who owed him fifty million silver coins. 25But he didn't have any money to pay what he owed. The king ordered him to be sold, along with his wife and children and all he owned, in order to pay the debt.

26The official got down on his knees and began begging, "Have pity on me, and I will pay you every cent I owe!" 27The king felt sorry for him and let him go free. He even told the official that he did not have to pay back the money.

28As the official was leaving, he happened to meet another official, who owed him a hundred silver coins. So he grabbed the man by the throat. He started choking him and said, "Pay me what you owe!"

29The man got down on his knees and began begging, "Have pity on me, and I will pay you back." 30But the first official refused to have pity. Instead, he went and had the other official put in jail until he could pay what he owed.

31When some other officials found out what had happened, they felt sorry for the man who had been put in jail. Then they told the king what had happened. 32The king called the first official back in and said, "You're an evil man! When you begged for mercy, I said you did not have to pay back a cent. 33Don't you think you should show pity to someone else, as I did to you?" 34The king was so angry that he ordered the official to be tortured until he could pay back everything he owed. 35That is how my Father in heaven will treat you, if you don't forgive each of my followers with all your heart.

Be quick to forgive
(27) Christians are forgiven people. There can be no greater joy than to know God has forgiven our sins because of Jesus' death on the cross. Surely, then, forgiven people can afford to be great forgivers. Holding grudges isn't worthy of us who are children of a forgiving God. But if we can't forgive others, how can we expect to be forgiven?

Teaching about Divorce
(Mark 10.1–12)

19 When Jesus finished teaching, he left Galilee and went to the part of Judea

that is east of the Jordan River. [2]Large crowds followed him, and he healed their sick people.

[3]Some Pharisees wanted to test Jesus. They came up to him and asked, "Is it right for a man to divorce his wife for just any reason?"

[4]Jesus answered, "Don't you know that in the beginning the Creator made a man and a woman? [5]That's why a man leaves his father and mother and gets married. He becomes like one person with his wife. [6]Then they are no longer two people, but one. And no one should separate a couple that God has joined together."

[7]The Pharisees asked Jesus, "Why did Moses say that a man could write out divorce papers and send his wife away?"

[8]Jesus replied, "You are so heartless! That's why Moses allowed you to divorce your wife. But from the beginning God did not intend it to be that way. [9]I say that if your wife has not committed some terrible sexual sin,[s] you must not divorce her to marry someone else. If you do, you are unfaithful."

[10]The disciples said, "If that's how it is between a man and a woman, it's better not to get married."

[11]Jesus told them, "Only those people who have been given the gift of staying single can accept this teaching. [12]Some people are unable to marry because of birth defects or because of what someone has done to their bodies. Others stay single for the sake of the kingdom of heaven. Anyone who can accept this teaching should do so."

Jesus Blesses Little Children
(Mark 10.13–16; Luke 18.15–17)

[13]Some people brought their children to Jesus, so that he could place his hands on them and pray for them. His disciples told the people to stop bothering him. [14]But Jesus said, "Let the children come to me, and don't try to stop them! People who are

[s]*some terrible sexual sin:* See the note at 5.32.

Be faithful in marriage
(4) Family unity is very important for the purity of Christ's church. We prove our inability to love when we break our marriage promises. How can we say we love others if we don't even have Christian love for our spouses? Let's realize the importance of this and be sure to love our marriage partners until death.

Jesus cares about young people
(13) We make a big mistake if we think Jesus is only for adults. He asked children to come to him, and he prayed for them. Young people, just like older people, need to learn about Jesus. Parents should teach the Bible to their children at home, and take them to church. This is an important way by which God brings us to himself—by our parents' teaching and example.

like these children belong to God's kingdom."[t] 15After Jesus had placed his hands on the children, he left.

A Rich Young Man
(Mark 10.17–31; Luke 18.18–30)

16A man came to Jesus and asked, "Teacher, what good thing must I do to have eternal life?"

17Jesus said to him, "Why do you ask me about what is good? Only God is good. If you want to have eternal life, you must obey his commandments."

18"Which ones?" the man asked.

Jesus answered, "Do not murder. Be faithful in marriage. Do not steal. Do not tell lies about others. 19Respect your father and mother. And love others as much as you love yourself." 20The young man said, "I have obeyed all of these. What else must I do?"

21Jesus replied, "If you want to be perfect, go sell everything you own! Give the money to the poor, and you will have riches in heaven. Then come and be my follower." 22When the young man heard this, he was sad, because he was very rich.

23Jesus said to his disciples, "It's terribly hard for rich people to get into the kingdom of heaven! 24In fact, it's easier for a camel to go through the eye of a needle than for a rich person to get into God's kingdom."

25When the disciples heard this, they were greatly surprised and asked, "How can anyone ever be saved?"

26Jesus looked straight at them and said, "There are some things that people cannot do, but God can do anything."

27Peter replied, "Remember, we have left everything to be your followers! What will we get?"

28Jesus answered:

Yes, all of you have become my followers. And so in the future world, when the Son of Man sits on his glorious

What is goodness?

(22) The young man thought he had obeyed all the rules. But he was breaking God's very first commandment. He loved something more than God. The young man was a slave to his wealth. Each one of us must settle the question: what do I love most of all? Is anything more important than doing what God wants me to do?

[t]*People who are like these children belong to God's kingdom*: Or "God's kingdom belongs to people who are like these children."

throne, I promise that you will sit on
twelve thrones to judge the twelve tribes
of Israel. 29All who have given up home
or brothers and sisters or father and
mother or children or land for me will
be given a hundred times as much. They
will also have eternal life. 30But many
who are now first will be last, and many
who are last will be first.

Workers in a Vineyard

20 As Jesus was telling what the kingdom of heaven would be like, he said:
Early one morning a man went out
to hire some workers for his vineyard.
2After he had agreed to pay them the
usual amount for a day's work, he sent
them off to his vineyard.

3About nine that morning, the man
saw some other people standing in the
market with nothing to do. 4He said he
would pay them what was fair, if they
would work in his vineyard. 5So they
went.

At noon and again about three in the
afternoon he returned to the market.
And each time he made the same agreement with others who were loafing
around with nothing to do.

6Finally, about five in the afternoon
the man went back and found some others standing there. He asked them,
"Why have you been standing here all
day long doing nothing?"

7"Because no one has hired us," they
answered. Then he told them to go work
in his vineyard.

8That evening the owner of the vineyard told the man in charge of the workers to call them in and give them their
money. He also told the man to begin
with the ones who were hired last.
9When the workers arrived, the ones
who had been hired at five in the afternoon were given a full day's pay.

10The workers who had been hired
first thought they would be given more
than the others. But when they were

It pays to follow Jesus
(28) Cash will not be your
reward for following Jesus.
It will be something much
better than that. The friendship of Jesus is the greatest
reward anyone can know.
You can have his friendship
simply by giving yourself to
him. That isn't asking very
much when you consider
that you receive Christ himself in return. Besides, you
belong to God anyway.
What would you amount to
without him?

given the same, 11they began complaining to the owner of the vineyard. 12They said, "The ones who were hired last worked for only one hour. But you paid them the same that you did us. And we worked in the hot sun all day long!"

13The owner answered one of them, "Friend, I didn't cheat you. I paid you exactly what we agreed on. 14Take your money now and go! What business is it of yours if I want to pay them the same that I paid you? 15Don't I have the right to do what I want with my own money? Why should you be jealous, if I want to be generous?"

16Jesus then said, "So it is. Everyone who is now first will be last, and everyone who is last will be first."

God keeps his promises
(13) The five groups of workers in Jesus' story were paid what they were promised. Jesus teaches us here that we owe God our service, and he owes us only what he promised. He never had to ask us to share in his work at all. But our opportunity to serve him is itself a gift from him. So our reward is also his gift at the end of our life on earth.

Jesus Again Tells about His Death
(Mark 10.32–34; Luke 18.31–34)

17As Jesus was on his way to Jerusalem, he took his twelve disciples aside and told them in private:

18We are now on our way to Jerusalem, where the Son of Man will be handed over to the chief priests and the teachers of the Law of Moses. They will sentence him to death, 19and then they will hand him over to foreignersu who will make fun of him. They will beat him and nail him to a cross. But on the third day he will rise from death.

Jesus reminds us of his main purpose
(18) Yet another time Jesus spoke plainly of his coming death. God would allow wicked men to nail our Lord to a cross. But their evil work would be undone when he arose from the grave. Jesus wants us to know that without his death and resurrection his work would mean nothing. His great purpose was to die in our place for our sins, and so give us everlasting life with him.

A Mother's Request
(Mark 10.35–45)

20The mother of James and Johnv came to Jesus with her two sons. She kneeled down and started begging him to do something for her. 21Jesus asked her what she wanted, and she said, "When you come into your kingdom, please let one of my sons

---

uforeigners: The Romans, who ruled Judea at this time.
vmother of James and John: The Greek text has "mother of the sons of Zebedee." See 26.37.

sit at your right side and the other at your left."ʷ

²²Jesus answered, "Not one of you knows what you are asking. Are you able to drink from the cupˣ that I must soon drink from?"

James and John said, "Yes, we are!"

²³Jesus replied, "You certainly will drink from my cup! But it is not for me to say who will sit at my right side and at my left. That is for my Father to say."

²⁴When the ten other disciples heard this, they were angry with the two brothers. ²⁵But Jesus called the disciples together and said:

> You know that foreign rulers like to order their people around. And their great leaders have full power over everyone they rule. ²⁶But don't act like them. If you want to be great, you must be the servant of all the others. ²⁷And if you want to be first, you must be the slave of the rest. ²⁸The Son of Man did not come to be a slave master, but a slave who will give his life to rescueʸ many people.

Jesus Heals Two Blind Men
(Mark 10.46–52; Luke 18.35–43)

²⁹Jesus was followed by a large crowd as he and his disciples were leaving Jericho. ³⁰Two blind men were sitting beside the road. And when they heard that Jesus was coming their way, they shouted, "Lord and Son of David,ᶻ have pity on us!"

³¹The crowd told them to be quiet, but they shouted even louder, "Lord and Son of David, have pity on us!"

³²When Jesus heard them, he stopped and asked, "What do you want me to do for you?"

Who will be first?
(21) The mother's request seems selfish and petty. But this only shows how poorly Jesus' followers understood him at that time. They still thought their Messiah had come to give them earthly power. But Jesus' answer may have disappointed them. Greatness will be measured by unselfish service, not by being in control.

ʷ*right side . . . left*: The most powerful people in a kingdom sat at the right and left side of the king. ˣ*drink from the cup*: In the Scriptures a cup is sometimes used as a symbol of suffering. To "drink from the cup" is to suffer. ʸ*rescue*: The Greek word often, though not always, means the payment of a price to free a slave or a prisoner. ᶻ*Son of David*: See the note at 9.27.

33They answered, "Lord, we want to
see!"

34Jesus felt sorry for them and touched
their eyes. Right away they could see, and
they became his followers.

Jesus Enters Jerusalem
(Mark 11.1–11; Luke 19.28–38; John 12.12–19)

21 When Jesus and his disciples came
near to Jerusalem, he went to Bethphage on the Mount of Olives and sent two
of them on ahead. 2He told them, "Go into
the next village, where you will at once find
a donkey and her colt. Untie the two donkeys and bring them to me. 3If anyone asks
why you are doing that, just say, 'The Lorda
needs them.' Right away he will let you have
the donkeys."

4So God's promise came true, just as the
prophet had said,

5"Announce to the people
  of Jerusalem:
'Your king is coming to you!
He is humble
  and rides on a donkey.
He comes on the colt
  of a donkey.' "

6The disciples left and did what Jesus
had told them to do. 7They brought the donkey and its colt and laid some clothes on
their backs. Then Jesus got on.

8Many people spread clothes in the road,
while others put down branchesb which
they had cut from trees. 9Some people
walked ahead of Jesus and others followed
behind. They were all shouting,

"Hoorayc for the Son of David!d
God bless the one who comes
  in the name of the Lord.
Hooray for God
  in heaven above!"

10When Jesus came to Jerusalem, every-

The blind see
(34) Several times we find
Jesus giving people back
their sight. We might ask,
"Why didn't he give back
every blind person's sight?"
Some day he will, if only they
will trust him now as their
Lord and Savior. He was
showing at that time that, as
Lord, he has power to do
this if we believe. When we
have faith in Jesus we see
him and his greatness with
open eyes.

The King rode a donkey
(5) We would expect a king
to ride into town on a white
horse, with trumpets blaring
and lots of official ceremony. But the King of kings
himself was content to ride
a donkey. Jesus didn't need
and didn't want earthly
glory in order to be King.
He was King long before the
world was even created. But
Jesus showed that he was
willing to look unimportant
in order to conquer people's
hearts.

aThe Lord: Or "the master of the donkeys." bspread
clothes . . . put down branches: This was one way that
the Jewish people welcomed a famous person. cHoo-
ray: This translates a word that can mean "please save
us." But it is most often used as a shout of praise to
God. dSon of David: See the note at 9.27.

one in the city was excited and asked, "Who can this be?"

11The crowd answered, "This is Jesus, the prophet from Nazareth in Galilee."

Jesus in the Temple
(Mark 11.15–19; Luke 19.45–48; John 2.13–22)

12Jesus went into the temple and chased out everyone who was selling or buying. He turned over the tables of the money changers and the benches of the ones who were selling doves. 13He told them, "The Scriptures say, 'My house should be called a place of worship.' But you have turned it into a place where robbers hide."

14Blind and lame people came to Jesus in the temple, and he healed them. 15But the chief priests and the teachers of the Law of Moses were angry when they saw his miracles and heard the children shouting praises to the Son of David.d 16The men said to Jesus, "Don't you hear what those children are saying?"

"Yes, I do!" Jesus answered. "Don't you know that the Scriptures say, 'Children and infants will sing praises'?" 17Then Jesus left the city and went out to the village of Bethany, where he spent the night.

Jesus Puts a Curse on a Fig Tree
(Mark 11.12–14, 20–24)

18When Jesus got up the next morning, he was hungry. He started out for the city, 19and along the way he saw a fig tree. But when he came to it, he found only leaves and no figs. So he told the tree, "You will never again grow any fruit!" Right then the fig tree dried up.

20The disciples were shocked when they saw how quickly the tree had dried up. 21But Jesus said to them, "If you have faith and don't doubt, I promise that you can do what I did to this tree. And you will be able to do even more. You can tell this mountain to get up and jump into the sea, and it will.

Jesus appreciates true value

(12) The merchants in the temple thought their money was the greatest value. But Jesus set them straight about that. They were in God's house, and they must behave as they should or else get out. Then Jesus healed the blind and the lame in the temple. Churches today are also places for healing broken hearts with the good news about Jesus.

God has no limit

(19) Jesus used a fig tree to show his followers that he is Lord of all creation. If what we are asking God for is according to his will, there is no limit to what he can do for us when we have faith in him.

dSon of David: See the note at 9.27.

22If you have faith when you pray, you will be given whatever you ask for."

A Question about Jesus' Authority
(Mark 11.27–33; Luke 20.1–8)

23Jesus had gone into the temple and was teaching when the chief priests and the leaders of the people came up to him. They asked, "What right do you have to do these things? Who gave you this authority?" 24Jesus answered, "I have just one question to ask you. If you answer it, I will tell you where I got the right to do these things. 25Who gave John the right to baptize? Was it God in heaven or merely some human being?"

They thought it over and said to each other, "We can't say that God gave John this right. Jesus will ask us why we didn't believe John. 26On the other hand, these people think that John was a prophet, and we are afraid of what they might do to us. That's why we can't say that it was merely some human who gave John the right to baptize." 27So they told Jesus, "We don't know."

Jesus said, "Then I won't tell you who gave me the right to do what I do."

A Story about Two Sons

28Jesus said:
I will tell you a story about a man who had two sons. Then you can tell me what you think. The father went to the older son and said, "Go work in the vineyard today!" 29His son told him that he would not do it, but later he changed his mind and went. 30The man then told his younger son to go work in the vineyard. The boy said he would, but he didn't go. 31Which one of the sons obeyed his father?"

"The older one," the chief priests and leaders answered.

Then Jesus told them:
You can be sure that tax collectors[e]

A question for an answer
(23) The religious leaders thought they had trapped Jesus with their question. But he replied with a question they were afraid to answer. Whatever they answered would get them into trouble. So they gave what they hoped was a safe reply— "We don't know." So Jesus told them he wouldn't answer them either. Jesus turned the religious leaders' cleverness back on them.

[e]*tax collectors:* See the note at 5.46.

and bad women will get into the kingdom of God before you ever will! 32When John the Baptist showed you how to do right, you would not believe him. But these evil people did believe. And even when you saw what they did, you still would not change your minds and believe.

Renters of a Vineyard
(Mark 12.1–12; Luke 20.9–19)

33Jesus told the chief priests and leaders to listen to this story:

A land owner once planted a vineyard. He built a wall around it and dug a pit to crush the grapes in. He also built a lookout tower. Then he rented out his vineyard and left the country.

34When it was harvest time, the owner sent some servants to get his share of the grapes. 35But the renters grabbed those servants. They beat up one, killed one, and stoned one of them to death. 36He then sent more servants than he did the first time. But the renters treated them in the same way.

37Finally, the owner sent his own son to the renters, because he thought they would respect him. 38But when they saw the man's son, they said, "Someday he will own the vineyard. Let's kill him! Then we can have it all for ourselves." 39So they grabbed him, threw him out of the vineyard, and killed him.

40Jesus asked, "When the owner of that vineyard comes, what do you suppose he will do to those renters?"

41The chief priests and leaders answered, "He will kill them in some horrible way. Then he will rent out his vineyard to people who will give him his share of grapes at harvest time."

42Jesus replied, "Surely you know that the Scriptures say,

'The stone that the builders
    tossed aside
is now the most important
    stone of all.

Saying is not doing
(31) Some people are experts in talking about religion—they are even very correct in everything they say. But they don't practice what they say. We must be careful that we're not put to shame by those who can't *speak* well, but they *do* the will of God. We ought to learn and *know* God's word, but we must be even more careful to *obey* what God says.

This is something
the Lord has done,
and it is amazing to us.'
43I tell you that God's kingdom will be taken from you and given to people who will do what he demands. 44Anyone who stumbles over this stone will be crushed, and anyone it falls on will be smashed to pieces."f

45When the chief priests and the Pharisees heard these stories, they knew that Jesus was talking about them. 46They looked for a way to kill him. But they were afraid to arrest Jesus, because the people thought he was a prophet.

The Great Banquet
(Luke 14.15–24)

22 Once again Jesus used stories to teach the people:
2The kingdom of heaven is like what happened when a king gave a wedding banquet for his son. 3The king sent some servants to tell the invited guests to come to the banquet, but the guests refused. 4He sent other servants to say to the guests, "The banquet is ready! My cattle and prize calves have all been prepared. Everything is ready. Come to the banquet!"

5But the guests did not pay any attention. Some of them left for their farms, and some went to their places of business. 6Others grabbed the servants, beat them up, and killed them.

7This made the king so furious that he sent an army to kill those murderers and burn down their city. 8Then he said to the servants, "It is time for the wedding banquet, and the invited guests don't deserve to come. 9Go out to the street corners and tell everyone you meet to come to the banquet." 10They went out on the streets and brought in everyone they could find, good and bad alike. And the banquet room was filled with guests.

God blesses the ones who honor him
(43) This story is about the history of what happened during the time of the Bible. The owner of the world is God. He made the world and left it to be kept by his chosen people, Israel. But they mistreated God's messengers, the prophets. Then when the Jewish leaders killed their Messiah, God's son, God gave his blessing to his church, made up of Jews and Gentiles, mostly Gentiles. God will bless those who accept his son Jesus.

Are your sins covered?
(2) Jesus told the story of the banquet to show that not everybody is a citizen of God's eternal kingdom. Some people prove by their actions that their claims to be God's people are false. Others who may look good are only self-righteous. Their sins aren't covered—the way some of the guests weren't covered by the special wedding clothes that people were given to wear at wedding celebrations in those days. Those clothes were like the gift of Christ's own goodness that changes our hearts.

fpieces: Verse 44 is not in some manuscripts.

11When the king went in to meet the guests, he found that one of them was not wearing the right kind of clothes for the wedding. 12The king asked, "Friend, why didn't you wear proper clothes for the wedding?" But the guest had no excuse. 13So the king gave orders for that person to be tied hand and foot and to be thrown outside into the dark. That's where people will cry and grit their teeth in pain. 14Many are invited, but only a few are chosen.

Paying Taxes
(Mark 12.13–17; Luke 20.20–26)

15The Pharisees got together and planned how they could trick Jesus into saying something wrong. 16They sent some of their followers and some of Herod's followersg to say to him, "Teacher, we know that you are honest. You teach the truth about what God wants people to do. And you treat everyone with the same respect, no matter who they are. 17Tell us what you think! Should we pay taxes to the Emperor or not?"

18Jesus knew their evil thoughts and said, "Why are you trying to test me? You show-offs! 19Let me see one of the coins used for paying taxes." They brought him a silver coin, 20and he asked, "Whose picture and name are on it?"

21"The Emperor's," they answered.

Then Jesus told them, "Give the Emperor what belongs to him and give God what belongs to God." 22His answer surprised them so much that they walked away.

Life in the Future World
(Mark 12.18–27; Luke 20.27–40)

23The Sadducees did not believe that people would rise to life after death. So that

Let's do our civic duty
(17) The Pharisees thought Jesus might be a political troublemaker who taught people to resist the Roman government. Some Jews, called Zealots, hoped to overthrow the Romans. Was Jesus one of them? No—he surprised the Pharisees by telling them they should pay their taxes but keep their souls for God.

gHerod's followers: People who were political followers of the family of Herod the Great (2.1) and his son Herod Antipas (14.1), and who wanted Herod to be king in Jerusalem.

same day some of the Sadducees came to Jesus and said:

24Teacher, Moses wrote that if a married man dies and has no children, his brother should marry the widow. Their first son would then be thought of as the son of the dead brother.

25Once there were seven brothers who lived here. The first one married, but died without having any children. So his wife was left to his brother. 26The same thing happened to the second and third brothers and finally to all seven of them. 27At last the woman died. 28When God raises people from death, whose wife will this woman be? She had been married to all seven brothers.

29Jesus answered:

You are completely wrong! You don't know what the Scriptures teach. And you don't know anything about the

Life in heaven is different
(28) The Sadducees were trying to trick Jesus with their words. How could he ever answer such a question? But Jesus turned the tables on them by telling them they had the wrong idea about the life to come. There will be no marrying in heaven. They didn't believe in a resurrection. But in the Old Testament God said that he *is* worshiped by Abraham—years after Abraham had died. God cannot be worshiped by dead people. Abraham, Isaac, and Jacob are alive in heaven.

The Emperors of Rome

(The Roman empire was the "world superpower" when Jesus was born. People in areas all around the Mediterranean Sea had to pay taxes to Rome. The only army or navy in the area was Rome's. Here is a list of the Roman emperors during New Testament times, with the years they reigned:)

Augustus	31 B.C. to A.D. 14 (see Luke 2.1)
Tiberius	A.D. 14 to 37 (see Luke 3.1; Matthew 22.17; John 19.12)
Caligula	37 to 41
Claudius	41 to 54 (see Acts 11.28; 17.7)
Nero	54 to 68 (see Acts 25.11; 27.24; 28.19)
Galba	68 to 69
Otho	69
Vitellius	69
Vespasian	69 to 79
Titus	79 to 81 (invaded Jerusalem A.D. 70; see Matthew 24.2)
Domitian	81 to 96 (had John sent to Patmos; see Revelation 1.9)

power of God. [30]When God raises people to life, they won't marry. They will be like the angels in heaven. [31]And as for people being raised to life, God was speaking to you when he said, [32]"I am the God worshiped by Abraham, Isaac, and Jacob." [h] He is not the God of the dead, but of the living.

[33]The crowds were surprised to hear what Jesus was teaching.

The Most Important Commandment
(Mark 12.28–34; Luke 10.25–28)

[34]After Jesus had made the Sadducees look foolish, the Pharisees heard about it and got together. [35]One of them was an expert in the Jewish Law. So he tried to test Jesus by asking, [36]"Teacher, what is the most important commandment in the Law?"

[37]Jesus answered:

Love the Lord your God with all your heart, soul, and mind. [38]This is the first and most important commandment. [39]The second most important commandment is like this one. And it is, "Love others as much as you love yourself." [40]All the Law of Moses and the Books of the Prophets[i] are based on these two commandments.

About David's Son
(Mark 12.35–37; Luke 20.41–44)

[41]While the Pharisees were still there, Jesus asked them, [42]"What do you think about the Messiah? Whose family will he come from?"

They answered, "He will be a son of King David."[j]

[43]Jesus replied, "How then could the Spirit have David call the Messiah his Lord? David said,

---

The Law summed up
(37) Here are the Ten Commandments in brief. The most important of all the commandments is the first one. Love God. But people are made in God's likeness. So the second commandment is like the first. We can't say truly that we love God if we don't love people for the sake of God who made them.

Who is the Messiah?
(41) It was Jesus' turn to test the Pharisees. He asked them what seems like an easy question. Everybody knew the Messiah would come from the family of King David who lived a thousand years before. But Jesus confused the Pharisees by reminding them that David did not call the Messiah his descendant. David called the Messiah "my Lord." So how could David's descendant also be David's Lord? That really gave the Pharisees something to scratch their heads about.

---

[h] *I am the God worshiped by Abraham, Isaac, and Jacob*: Jesus argues that if God is worshiped by these three, they must still be alive, because he is the God of the living. [i] *the Law of Moses and the Books of the Prophets*: The Jewish Scriptures, that is, the Old Testament. [j] *son of King David*: See the note at 9.27.

⁴⁴'The Lord said to my Lord:
Sit at my right side^k
until I make your enemies
into a footstool for you.'
⁴⁵If David called the Messiah his Lord, how can the Messiah be a son of King David?"
⁴⁶No one was able to give Jesus an answer, and from that day on no one dared ask him any more questions.

Jesus Condemns the Pharisees and the Teachers of the Law of Moses
(Mark 12.38–40; Luke 11.37–52; 20.45–47)

23 Jesus said to the crowds and to his disciples:
²The Pharisees and the teachers of the Law are experts in the Law of Moses. ³So obey everything they teach you, but don't do as they do. After all, they say one thing and do something else.

⁴They pile heavy burdens on people's shoulders and won't lift a finger to help them. ⁵Everything they do is just to show off in front of others. They even make a big show of wearing Scripture verses on their foreheads and arms, and they wear big tassels^l for everyone to see. ⁶They love the best seats at banquets and the front seats in the meeting places. ⁷And when they are in the market, they like to have people greet them as their teachers.

⁸But none of you should be called a teacher. You have only one teacher, and all of you are like brothers and sisters. ⁹Don't call anyone on earth your father. All of you have the same Father in heaven. ¹⁰None of you should be called the leader. The Messiah is your only leader. ¹¹Whoever is the greatest should

A good teacher is a good doer
(3) Teachers or preachers might think they have done what God expects when others obey what they say. It may seem safe, but it's really very dangerous for teachers to teach others to obey what they themselves do not. It's easy for some leaders to think they're special just because they're leaders. They imagine they don't have to obey God themselves, just get others to.

---

^k*right side*: The place of power and honor. ^l*wearing Scripture verses on their foreheads and arms . . . tassels*: As a sign of their love for the Lord and his teachings, the Jewish people had started wearing Scripture verses in small leather boxes. But the Pharisees tried to show off by making the boxes bigger than necessary. The Jewish people were also taught to wear tassels on the four corners of their robes to show their love for God.

be the servant of the others. 12If you put yourself above others, you will be put down. But if you humble yourself, you will be honored.

13-14You Pharisees and teachers of the Law of Moses are in for trouble! You're nothing but showoffs. You lock people out of the kingdom of heaven. You won't go in yourselves, and you keep others from going in.m

15You Pharisees and teachers of the Law of Moses are in for trouble! You're nothing but showoffs. You travel over land and sea to win one follower. And when you have done so, you make that person twice as fit for hell as you are.

16You are in for trouble! You are supposed to lead others, but you are blind. You teach that it doesn't matter if a person swears by the temple. But you say that it does matter if someone swears by the gold in the temple. 17You blind fools! Which is greater, the gold or the temple that makes the gold sacred?

18You also teach that it doesn't matter if a person swears by the altar. But you say that it does matter if someone swears by the gift on the altar. 19Are you blind? Which is more important, the gift or the altar that makes the gift sacred? 20Anyone who swears by the altar also swears by everything on it. 21And anyone who swears by the temple also swears by God, who lives there. 22To swear by heaven is the same as swearing by God's throne and by the one who sits on that throne.

23You Pharisees and teachers are showoffs, and you're in for trouble! You give God a tenth of the spices from your garden, such as mint, dill, and cumin. Yet you neglect the more important matters of the Law, such as justice,

Let's not be showoffs

(13) Jesus called the leaders of his day by the right name—"showoffs." And they were worse than showoffs because they really had nothing to show off. Inside themselves they were morally rotten. What they were showing off wasn't real. The message is, beware of pretending to be something you're not. We may deceive ourselves, but we can't fool God.

Real godliness is costly

(23) A cheap religion is one that doesn't cost us very much. The leaders of Jesus' time made sure they could look very religious while at the same time living only for themselves. They paid their little tithes, but they were unjust, merciless, and unfaithful in their real duty.

---

mfrom going in: Some manuscripts add, "You Pharisees and teachers are in for trouble! And you're nothing but showoffs! You cheat widows out of their homes and then pray long prayers just to show off. So you will be punished most of all."

mercy, and faithfulness. These are the important things you should have done, though you should not have left the others undone either. [24]You blind leaders! You strain out a small fly but swallow a camel.

[25]You Pharisees and teachers are showoffs, and you're in for trouble! You wash the outside of your cups and dishes, while inside there is nothing but greed and selfishness. [26]You blind Pharisee! First clean the inside of a cup, and then the outside will also be clean.

[27]You Pharisees and teachers are in for trouble! You're nothing but showoffs. You're like tombs that have been whitewashed.[n] On the outside they are beautiful, but inside they are full of bones and filth. [28]That's what you are like. Outside you look good, but inside you are evil and only pretend to be good.

[29]You Pharisees and teachers are nothing but showoffs, and you're in for trouble! You build monuments for the prophets and decorate the tombs of good people. [30]And you claim that you would not have taken part with your ancestors in killing the prophets. [31]But you prove that you really are the relatives of the ones who killed the prophets. [32]So keep on doing everything they did. [33]You are nothing but snakes and the children of snakes! How can you escape going to hell?

[34]I will send prophets and wise people and experts in the Law of Moses to you. But you will kill them or nail them to a cross or beat them in your meeting places or chase them from town to town. [35]That's why you will be held guilty for the murder of every good person, beginning with the good man Abel. This also includes Barachiah's son

Let's have tender hearts
(29) The leaders would praise great people of the past, but Jesus reminded them that they would kill the people God sent in their own time. This applies to us today, too. It's not good enough to be proud of the great stories about Christians of the past. That's easy. But our hard hearts are shown if we don't love God's people who are living today.

[n]*whitewashed*: Tombs were whitewashed to keep anyone from accidentally touching them. A person who touched a dead body or a tomb was considered unclean and could not worship with the rest of the Jewish people.

Zechariah,° the man you murdered between the temple and the altar. 36I can promise that you people living today will be punished for all these things!

Jesus Loves Jerusalem
(Luke 13.34, 35)

37Jerusalem, Jerusalem! Your people have killed the prophets and have stoned the messengers who were sent to you. I have often wanted to gather your people, as a hen gathers her chicks under her wings. But you wouldn't let me. 38And now your temple will be deserted. 39You will not see me again until you say,

"Blessed is the one who comes
    in the name of the Lord."

The Temple Will Be Destroyed
(Mark 13.1, 2; Luke 21.5, 6)

24 After Jesus left the temple, his disciples came over and said, "Look at all these buildings!"

2Jesus replied, "Do you see these buildings? They will certainly all be torn down! Not one stone will be left in place."

Warning about Trouble
(Mark 13.3–13; Luke 21.7–19)

3Later, as Jesus was sitting on the Mount of Olives, his disciples came to him in private and asked, "When will this happen? What will be the sign of your coming and of the end of the world?"

4Jesus answered:

Don't let anyone fool you. 5Many will come and claim to be me. They will say that they are the Messiah, and they will fool many people.

6You will soon hear about wars and threats of wars, but don't be afraid.

Jerusalem's sin
(37) The city of Jerusalem had a special place in the heart of Jesus. But his heart was broken—the city would not have him. There would be great pain for them: they would soon be taken over by a cruel invading army. Can we learn from this and welcome Jesus better than Jerusalem did?

Our possessions are only for a time
(1) Old Scrooge in Charles Dickens' story *A Christmas Carol* woke up to realize he couldn't take his wealth to the grave. The Jews of Jesus' day greatly prized their temple. In fact the temple had almost come to take the place of God in their minds. For them, the worst thing Jesus could say was that the temple would be destroyed. But years later, that was exactly what God let happen. We need to have greater "life insurance" than buildings or cash.

°*Zechariah*: Genesis is the first book in the Jewish Scriptures, and it tells that Abel was the first person to be murdered. Second Chronicles is the last book in the Jewish Scriptures, and the last murder that it tells about is that of Zechariah.

These things will have to happen first, but that is not the end. [7]Nations and kingdoms will go to war against each other. People will starve to death, and in some places there will be earthquakes. [8]But this is just the beginning of troubles.

[9]You will be arrested, punished, and even killed. Because of me, you will be hated by people of all nations. [10]Many will give up and will betray and hate each other. [11]Many false prophets will come and fool a lot of people. [12]Evil will spread and cause many people to stop loving others. [13]But if you keep on being faithful right to the end, you will be saved. [14]When the good news about the kingdom has been preached all over the world and told to all nations, the end will come.

Trouble is coming

(9) Ever since Jesus went back to heaven the world has had continual trouble. Christians have not escaped. In fact Christians have suffered harshly for believing in Jesus, and untold numbers have died and are dying horribly. What can we say to this? Evil will have its day, but our safety is in God's presence where none of these things can trouble us.

The Horrible Thing

(Mark 13.14–23; Luke 21.20–24)

[15]Someday you will see that "Horrible Thing" in the holy place, just as the prophet Daniel said. Everyone who reads this must try to understand! [16]If you are living in Judea at that time, run to the mountains. [17]If you are on the roof[p] of your house, don't go inside to get anything. [18]If you are out in the field, don't go back for your coat. [19]It will be a terrible time for women who are expecting babies or nursing young children. [20]And pray that you won't have to escape in winter or on a Sabbath.[q] [21]This will be the worst time of suffering since the beginning of the world, and nothing this terrible will ever happen

[p]*roof*: In Palestine the houses usually had a flat roof. Stairs on the outside led up to the roof, which was made of beams and boards covered with packed earth.
[q]*in winter or on a Sabbath*: In Palestine the winters are cold and rainy and make travel difficult. The Jewish people were not allowed to travel much more than half a mile on the Sabbath. For these reasons it was hard for them to escape from their enemies in the winter or on a Sabbath.

again. 22If God doesn't make the time shorter, no one will be left alive. But because of God's chosen ones, he will make the time shorter.

23Someone may say, "Here is the Messiah!" or "There he is!" But don't believe it. 24False messiahs and false prophets will come and work great miracles and signs. They will even try to fool God's chosen ones. 25But I have warned you ahead of time. 26If you are told that the Messiah is out in the desert, don't go there! And if you are told that he is in some secret place, don't believe it! 27The coming of the Son of Man will be like lightning that can be seen from east to west. 28Where there is a corpse, there will always be buzzards.r

When the Son of Man Appears
(Mark 13.24–27; Luke 21.25–28)

29Right after those days of suffering,
"The sun will become dark,
and the moon
　　will no longer shine.
The stars will fall,
and the powers in the skys
　　will be shaken."
30Then a sign will appear in the sky. And there will be the Son of Man.t All nations on earth will weep when they see the Son of Man coming on the clouds of heaven with power and great glory. 31At the sound of a loud trumpet he will send his angels to bring his chosen ones together from all over the earth.

Jesus will return

(23) Every now and then we hear of some new cult or some new messiah. Jesus warns us not to be disturbed by these things that must come. We don't have to run after every religious fad. We know whom we have believed, and we have proved he can be trusted with our lives. We wait for his return when we shall be with him forever.

---

rWhere there is a corpse, there will always be buzzards: This saying may mean that when anything important happens, people soon know about it. Or the saying may mean that whenever something bad happens, curious people gather around and stare. But the word translated "buzzard" also means "eagle" and may refer to the Roman army, which had an eagle as its symbol. sthe powers in the sky: In ancient times people thought that the stars were spiritual powers. tAnd there will be the Son of Man: Or "And it will be the Son of Man."

A Lesson from a Fig Tree
(Mark 13.28–31; Luke 21.29–33)

32Learn a lesson from a fig tree. When its branches sprout and start putting out leaves, you know that summer is near. 33So when you see all these things happening, you will know that the time has almost come.ᵘ 34I can promise you that some of the people living today will still be alive when all this happens. 35The sky and the earth won't last forever, but my words will.

No One Knows the Day or Time
(Mark 13.32–37; Luke 17.26–30, 34–36)

36No one knows the day or hour. The angels in heaven don't know, and the Son himself doesn't know.ᵛ Only the Father knows. 37When the Son of Man appears, things will be just as they were when Noah lived. 38People were eating, drinking, and getting married right up to the day that the flood came and Noah went into the big boat. 39They didn't know anything was happening until the flood came and swept them all away. That is how it will be when the Son of Man appears.

40Two men will be in the same field, but only one will be taken. The other will be left. 41Two women will be together grinding grain, but only one will be taken. The other will be left. 42So be on your guard! You don't know when your Lord will come. 43Homeowners never know when a thief is coming, and they are always on guard to keep one from breaking in. 44Always be ready! You don't know when the Son of Man will come.

When will Jesus return?
(36) No one knows exactly when Jesus will come back according to the calendar and clock. But as the world becomes more violent, and disturbances increase, we are shown that the time is nearer. The main thing is to be ready and not be caught by surprise. We don't know when Jesus will return. Today's task is for us to be faithful in what God has given us to do.

ᵘ*the time has almost come*: Or "he (that is, the Son of Man) will soon be here." ᵛ*and the Son himself doesn't know*: These words are not in some manuscripts.

Faithful and Unfaithful Servants
(Luke 12.35–48)

⁴⁵Who are faithful and wise servants? Who are the ones the master will put in charge of giving the other servants their food supplies at the proper time? ⁴⁶Servants are fortunate if their master comes and finds them doing their job. ⁴⁷You may be sure that a servant who is always faithful will be put in charge of everything the master owns. ⁴⁸But suppose one of the servants thinks that the master will not return until late. ⁴⁹Suppose that evil servant starts beating all the other servants and eats and drinks with people who are drunk. ⁵⁰If that happens, the master will surely come on a day and at a time when the servant least expects him. ⁵¹That servant will then be punished and thrown out with the ones who only pretended to serve their master. There they will cry and grit their teeth in pain.

Don't forget about the Master

(45) It has been a long time since Jesus spoke these words, almost two thousand years. It would be easy for us to be like the unfaithful servant, to live as though Jesus will never come back. But he has promised he will. It could be today. Let's be ready.

A Story about Ten Girls

25 The kingdom of heaven is like what happened one night when ten girls took their oil lamps and went to a wedding to meet the groom.ʷ ²Five of the girls were foolish and five were wise. ³The foolish ones took their lamps, but no extra oil. ⁴The ones who were wise took along extra oil for their lamps.

⁵The groom was late arriving, and the girls became drowsy and fell asleep. ⁶Then in the middle of the night someone shouted, "Here's the groom! Come to meet him!"

⁷When the girls got up and started getting their lamps ready, ⁸the foolish ones said to the others, "Let us have

Be prepared at Jesus' coming

(1) Jesus' story is based on the marriage custom of his time. The girls were wedding attendants. All were waiting for the groom to arrive, but they fell asleep. Five wise girls had extra oil, but five foolish did not. Jesus teaches that we must be sure our commitment to him, the bridegroom, is great enough that we continue to be faithful until his coming.

ʷ*to meet the groom*: Some manuscripts add "and the bride." It was the custom for the groom to go to the home of the bride's parents to get his bride. Young girls and other guests would then go with them to the home of the groom's parents, where the wedding feast would take place.

some of your oil! Our lamps are going out."

⁹The girls who were wise answered, "There's not enough oil for all of us! Go and buy some for yourselves."

¹⁰While the foolish girls were on their way to get some oil, the groom arrived. The girls who were ready went into the wedding, and the doors were closed. ¹¹Later the other girls returned and shouted, "Sir, sir! Open the door for us!"

¹²But the groom replied, "I don't even know you!"

¹³So, my disciples, always be ready! You don't know the day or the time when all this will happen.

A Story about Three Servants
(Luke 19.11–27)

¹⁴The kingdom is also like what happened when a man went away and put his three servants in charge of all he owned. ¹⁵The man knew what each servant could do. So he handed five thousand coins to the first servant, two thousand to the second, and one thousand to the third. Then he left the country.

¹⁶As soon as the man had gone, the servant with the five thousand coins used them to earn five thousand more. ¹⁷The servant who had two thousand coins did the same with his money and earned two thousand more. ¹⁸But the servant with one thousand coins dug a hole and hid his master's money in the ground.

¹⁹Some time later the master of those servants returned. He called them in and asked what they had done with his money. ²⁰The servant who had been given five thousand coins brought them in with the five thousand that he had earned. He said, "Sir, you gave me five thousand coins, and I have earned five thousand more."

²¹"Wonderful!" his master replied. "You are a good and faithful servant.

Use your gifts effectively
(19) People who are wise in business try to invest their money where it earns more money. We think about that when we're about to put our savings in a bank, as we find out which one pays the most interest. Jesus expects us to be wise in the use of his gifts. The question for us is: How much has God been served by the way we spent our lives?

I left you in charge of only a little, but now I will put you in charge of much more. Come and share in my happiness!"

²²Next, the servant who had been given two thousand coins came in and said, "Sir, you gave me two thousand coins, and I have earned two thousand more."

²³"Wonderful!" his master replied. "You are a good and faithful servant. I left you in charge of only a little, but now I will put you in charge of much more. Come and share in my happiness!"

²⁴The servant who had been given one thousand coins then came in and said, "Sir, I know that you are hard to get along with. You harvest what you don't plant and gather crops where you have not scattered seed. ²⁵I was frightened and went out and hid your money in the ground. Here is every single coin!"

²⁶The master of the servant told him, "You are lazy and good-for-nothing! You know that I harvest what I don't plant and gather crops where I have not scattered seed. ²⁷You could have at least put my money in the bank, so that I could have earned interest on it."

²⁸Then the master said, "Now your money will be taken away and given to the servant with ten thousand coins! ²⁹Everyone who has something will be given more, and they will have more than enough. But everything will be taken from those who don't have anything. ³⁰You are a worthless servant, and you will be thrown out into the dark where people will cry and grit their teeth in pain."

The Final Judgment

³¹When the Son of Man comes in his glory with all of his angels, he will sit on his royal throne. ³²The people of all nations will be brought before him, and

Jesus will judge the world
(31) Lots of people may laugh and make a joke about Christ's coming. That's very tragic. Judgment is as certain as the sunrise. The nations of the world often ignore Jesus today. Have they thought about how they will answer the Lord when he sits on his judgment throne?

he will separate them, as shepherds separate their sheep from their goats.

33He will place the sheep on his right and the goats on his left. 34Then the king will say to those on his right, "My father has blessed you! Come and receive the kingdom that was prepared for you before the world was created. 35When I was hungry, you gave me something to eat, and when I was thirsty, you gave me something to drink. When I was a stranger, you welcomed me, 36and when I was naked, you gave me clothes to wear. When I was sick, you took care of me, and when I was in jail, you visited me."

37Then the ones who pleased the Lord will ask, "When did we give you something to eat or drink? 38When did we welcome you as a stranger or give you clothes to wear 39or visit you while you were sick or in jail?"

40The king will answer, "Whenever you did it for any of my people, no matter how unimportant they seemed, you did it for me."

41Then the king will say to those on his left, "Get away from me! You are under God's curse. Go into the everlasting fire prepared for the devil and his angels! 42I was hungry, but you did not give me anything to eat, and I was thirsty, but you did not give me anything to drink. 43I was a stranger, but you did not welcome me, and I was naked, but you did not give me any clothes to wear. I was sick and in jail, but you did not take care of me."

44Then the people will ask, "Lord, when did we fail to help you when you were hungry or thirsty or a stranger or naked or sick or in jail?"

45The king will say to them, "Whenever you failed to help any of my people, no matter how unimportant they seemed, you failed to do it for me."

46Then Jesus said, "Those people will be punished forever. But the ones who pleased God will have eternal life."

How will Jesus judge?
(40) What will Jesus care about when he sits as judge of the nations? He will want to know how someone treated his people. No matter how unimportant a person may seem in the eyes of the world, if that person is a child of God by faith in Jesus, then what someone does to that person is at the same time done to Jesus. It will be awful for those who are cruel to the ones who belong to him.

The Plot to Kill Jesus
(Mark 14.1, 2; Luke 22.1, 2; John 11.45–53)

26 When Jesus had finished teaching, he told his disciples, 2"You know that two days from now will be Passover. That is when the Son of Man will be handed over to his enemies and nailed to a cross."

3At that time the chief priests and the nation's leaders were meeting at the home of Caiaphas the high priest. 4They planned how they could sneak around and have Jesus arrested and put to death. 5But they said, "We must not do it during Passover, because the people will riot."

At Bethany
(Mark 14.3–9; John 12.1–8)

6Jesus was in the town of Bethany, eating at the home of Simon, who once had leprosy.x 7A woman came in with a bottle of expensive perfume and poured it on Jesus' head. 8But when his disciples saw this, they became angry. They said, "Why such a waste? 9We could have sold this perfume for a lot of money and given it to the poor."

10Jesus knew what they were thinking, and he said:

Why are you bothering this woman? She has done a beautiful thing for me. 11You will always have the poor with you, but you will not always have me. 12She has poured perfume on my body to prepare it for burial.y 13You may be sure that wherever the good news is told all over the world, people will remember what she has done. And they will tell others.

Judas and the Chief Priests
(Mark 14.10, 11; Luke 22.3–6)

14Judas Iscariotz was one of the twelve disciples. He went to the chief priests

Jesus faced the cross
(2) Once again Jesus reminded his followers that he would have to die the death of being nailed to a cross. But they didn't understand. It didn't seem possible that their Messiah would be put to death. Even Muslims today admit that someone was nailed to the cross, but "Jesus the prophet," they say, "could not have been put to death like that. God wouldn't have permitted it." Do we understand that without the death of God's Son we would have no hope of being saved from our sins? He took our punishment himself.

Give your best to Jesus
(10) The woman at Bethany was a puzzle to Jesus' disciples. They didn't understand what this woman did. Jesus was going to die, so she wanted to express her love and gratitude to him in a special act of sacrifice. The perfume was costly, but nothing was too good for Jesus. Can we not gladly pour out our lives for him?

---

xleprosy: See the note at 8.2. ypoured perfume on my body to prepare it for burial: The Jewish people taught that giving someone a proper burial was even more important than helping the poor. zIscariot: See the note at 10.4.

15and asked, "How much will you give me if I help you arrest Jesus?" They paid Judas thirty silver coins, 16and from then on he started looking for a good chance to betray Jesus.

Jesus Eats the Passover Meal with His Disciples
(Mark 14.12–21; Luke 22.7–13; John 13.21–30)

17On the first day of the Feast of Thin Bread, Jesus' disciples came to him and asked, "Where do you want us to prepare the Passover meal?"

18Jesus told them to go to a certain man in the city and tell him, "Our teacher says, 'My time has come! I want to eat the Passover meal with my disciples in your home.'"

19They did as Jesus told them and prepared the meal.

20-21When Jesus was eating with his twelve disciples that evening, he said, "One of you will surely hand me over to my enemies."

22The disciples were very sad, and each one said to Jesus, "Surely, Lord, you don't mean me!"

23He answered, "One of you men who has eaten with me from this dish will betray me. 24The Son of Man will die, as the Scriptures say. But it's going to be terrible for the one who betrays me! That man would be better off if he had never been born."

25Judas said, "Teacher, surely you don't mean me!"

"That's what you say!" Jesus replied. But later, Judas did betray him.

The Lord's Supper
(Mark 14.22–26; Luke 22.14–23; 1 Corinthians 11.23–25)

26During the meal Jesus took some bread in his hands. He blessed the bread and broke it. Then he gave it to his disciples and said, "Take this and eat it. This is my body."

27Jesus picked up a cup of wine and gave thanks to God. He then gave it to his disciples and said, "Take this and drink it.

A disciple gone bad
(16) It's hard to imagine how one of the twelve disciples could have done such a terrible thing. Judas, who had lived with Jesus day after day, betrayed him to die. But let's not be too quick to judge. The evil that was in Judas is in the heart of every person. Even sincere Christians who truly love Jesus betray him daily by a variety of ungodly thoughts, words, and actions.

The last meal together
(26) Taking a meal together is often a celebration of close friendship. The bond between Jesus and his disciples was even closer than they knew, for they still didn't understand what was going to happen to Jesus. In fact one of them, Judas, would even sell him out. At this time Jesus did something they would understand later. He invited them to eat and drink what stood for his very body and blood.

28This is my blood, and with it God makes his agreement with you. It will be poured out, so that many people will have their sins forgiven. 29From now on I am not going to drink any wine, until I drink new wine with you in my Father's kingdom." 30Then they sang a hymn and went out to the Mount of Olives.

Peter's Promise
(Mark 14.27–31; Luke 22.31–34; John 13.36–38)

31Jesus said to his disciples, "During this very night, all of you will reject me, as the Scriptures say,

'I will strike down
    the shepherd,
and the sheep
    will be scattered.'

32But after I am raised to life, I will go to Galilee ahead of you."

33Peter spoke up, "Even if all the others reject you, I never will!"

34Jesus replied, "I promise you that before a rooster crows tonight, you will say three times that you don't know me." 35But Peter said, "Even if I have to die with you, I will never say I don't know you."

All the others said the same thing.

Jesus Prays
(Mark 14.32–42; Luke 22.39–46)

36Jesus went with his disciples to a place called Gethsemane. When they got there, he told them, "Sit here while I go over there and pray."

37Jesus took along Peter and the two brothers, James and John.*a* He was very sad and troubled, 38and he said to them, "I am so sad that I feel as if I am dying. Stay here and keep awake with me."

39Jesus walked on a little way. Then he kneeled with his face to the ground and prayed, "My Father, if it is possible, don't make me suffer by having me drink from

a the two brothers, James and John: The Greek text has "the two sons of Zebedee." See 27.56.

Boasting is dangerous.
(33) Jesus made it clear that he would be arrested and the disciples would all leave him. Peter quickly announced his undying loyalty to his Master. He meant well, but he didn't know what he was promising. Later, he would learn how weak he was. Jesus knew how everybody would act, and Peter had to learn a lesson. We ought not to boast, but we should ask God to help us in the hard places.

Jesus didn't want to die
(39) What? But dying is what Jesus came to earth for. Yes, but it was the most grim assignment ever given to anyone. It was not only bodily pain that he faced,

this cup.*b* But do what you want, and not what I want."

40He came back and found his disciples sleeping. So he said to Peter, "Can't any of you stay awake with me for just one hour? **41**Stay awake and pray that you will not be tested. You want to do what is right, but you are weak."

42Again Jesus went to pray and said, "My Father, if there is no other way, and I must suffer, I will still do what you want."

43Jesus came back and found them sleeping again. They simply could not keep their eyes open. **44**He left them and prayed the same prayer once more.

45Finally, Jesus returned to his disciples and said, "Are you still sleeping and resting?*c* The time has come for the Son of Man to be handed over to sinners. **46**Get up! Let's go. The one who will betray me is already here."

Jesus Is Arrested
(Mark 14.43–50; Luke 22.47–53; John 18.3–12)

47Jesus was still speaking, when Judas the betrayer came up. He was one of the twelve disciples, and a large mob armed with swords and clubs was with him. They had been sent by the chief priests and the nation's leaders. **48**Judas had told them ahead of time, "Arrest the man I greet with a kiss."*d*

49Judas walked right up to Jesus and said, "Hello, teacher." Then Judas kissed him.

50Jesus replied, "My friend, why are you here?"*e*

The men grabbed Jesus and arrested him. **51**One of Jesus' followers pulled out a sword. He struck the servant of the high priest and cut off his ear.

52But Jesus told him, "Put your sword

but he would actually bear the punishment for the sins of the whole world. Jesus was a man, too, and as a man he hated the thought of such an awful death.

This had to happen
(52) Jesus didn't want his followers to resist his arrest. He could have stopped it by calling the armies of heaven to defend him. But he didn't. Jesus had to let his blood be shed on a cross, so that we sinners could have a way back to God.

---

bmaking me drink from this cup: In the Scriptures "to drink from a cup" sometimes means to suffer. See the note at 20.22.   *cAre you still sleeping and resting?*: Or "You may as well keep on sleeping and resting." *dthe man I greet with a kiss*: It was the custom for people to greet each other with a kiss on the cheek. *ewhy are you here?*: Or "do what you came for."

away. Anyone who lives by fighting will die by fighting. 53Don't you know that I could ask my Father, and right away he would send me more than twelve armies of angels? 54But then, how could the words of the Scriptures come true, which say that this must happen?"

55Jesus said to the mob, "Why do you come with swords and clubs to arrest me like a criminal? Day after day I sat and taught in the temple, and you didn't arrest me. 56But all this happened, so that what the prophets wrote would come true."

All of Jesus' disciples left him and ran away.

Jesus Is Questioned by the Jewish Council
*(Mark 14.53–65; Luke 22.54, 55, 63–71;
John 18.13, 14, 19–24)*

57After Jesus had been arrested, he was led off to the house of Caiaphas the high priest. The nation's leaders and the teachers of the Law of Moses were meeting there. 58But Peter followed along at a distance and came to the courtyard of the high priest's palace. He went in and sat down with the guards to see what was going to happen.

59The chief priests and the whole council wanted to put Jesus to death. So they tried to find some people who would tell lies about him in court.*f* 60But they could not find any, even though many did come and tell lies. At last two men came forward 61and said, "This man claimed that he would tear down God's temple and build it again in three days."

62The high priest stood up and asked Jesus, "Why don't you say something in your own defense? Don't you hear the charges they are making against you?" 63But Jesus did not answer. So the high priest said, "With the living God looking

What shall we do with Jesus?

(60) Here is one who went about doing good, arrested at a signal from his own former friend. They finally got two witnesses to speak against Jesus. The witnesses were needed to satisfy the law in this false trial. Of course the court had already decided what they would do. So Jesus confessed to his divine sonship. Then the leaders had their excuse to accuse him of insulting God. Think about this: What would the world do with Jesus if he were here like this today? Who would stand with him?

f some people who would tell lies about him in court: The Law of Moses taught that two witnesses were necessary before a person could be put to death. See verse 60.

on, you must tell the truth. Tell us, are you the Messiah, the Son of God?"[g]

64"That is what you say!" Jesus answered. "But I tell all of you,

'Soon you will see
the Son of Man
sitting at the right side[h]
of God All-Powerful
and coming on the clouds
of heaven.' "

65The high priest then tore his robe and said, "This man claims to be God! We don't need any more witnesses! You have heard what he said. **66**What do you think?"

They answered, "He is guilty and deserves to die!" **67**Then they spit in his face and hit him with their fists. Others slapped him **68**and said, "You think you are the Messiah! So tell us who hit you!"

Peter Says He Does Not Know Jesus
(Mark 14.66–72; Luke 22.56–62;
John 18.15–18, 25–27)

69While Peter was sitting out in the courtyard, a servant girl came up to him and said, "You were with Jesus from Galilee."

70But in front of everyone Peter said, "That's not so! I don't know what you are talking about!"

71When Peter had gone out to the gate, another servant girl saw him and said to some people there, "This man was with Jesus from Nazareth."

72Again Peter denied it, and this time he swore, "I don't even know that man!"

73A little while later some people standing there walked over to Peter and said, "We know that you are one of them. We can tell it because you talk like someone from Galilee."

74Peter began to curse and swear, "I don't know that man!"

Right then a rooster crowed, **75**and Peter remembered that Jesus had said, "Before a rooster crows, you will say three times

It's easy to "not know" Jesus

(70) Peter had boasted about his loyalty to Jesus. But later, with enemies all around, Peter found it easier to keep quiet and even say he didn't know Jesus. Are you a disciple of Jesus? Who knows that you are? Or do you hide your faith so as not to offend people?

---

[g]*Son of God*: One of the titles used for the kings of Israel. [h]*right side*: See the note at 22.44.

that you don't know me." Then Peter went out and cried hard.

Jesus Is Taken to Pilate
(Mark 15.1; Luke 23.1, 2; John 18.28–32)

27 Early the next morning all the chief priests and the nation's leaders met and decided that Jesus should be put to death. 2They tied him up and led him away to Pilate the governor.

The Death of Judas
(Acts 1.18, 19)

3When Judas learned that Jesus had been sentenced to death, he was sorry for what he had done. He returned the thirty silver coins to the chief priests and leaders 4and said, "I have sinned by betraying a man who has never done anything wrong."

"So what? That's your problem," they replied. 5Judas threw the money into the temple and then went out and hanged himself.

6The chief priests picked up the money and said, "This money was paid to have a man killed. We can't put it in the temple treasury." 7Then they had a meeting and decided to buy a field that belonged to someone who made clay pots. They wanted to use it as a graveyard for foreigners. 8That is why people still call that place "Field of Blood." 9So the words of the prophet Jeremiah came true,

"They took
> the thirty silver coins,
the price of a person
> among the people of Israel.
10They paid it
> for a potter's field,[l]
as the Lord
> had commanded me."

A tragic man's end
(5) Judas will always be a puzzle. Why did he sell Jesus out? Some people think he sincerely believed Jesus was bad for his country. Others say he wanted to make Jesus be more forceful in self-defense. But remember Judas was a thief, too. Great evil was at work deep in the life of this man. Judas would not even ask to be forgiven, choosing to kill himself instead.

---

[l]*a potter's field*: Perhaps a field owned by someone who made clay pots. But it may have been a field where potters came to get clay or to make pots or to throw away their broken pieces of pottery.

Pilate Questions Jesus
(Mark 15.2–5; Luke 23.3–5; John 18.33–38)

11Jesus was brought before Pilate the governor, who asked him, "Are you the King of the Jews?"

"Those are your words!" Jesus answered. 12And when the chief priests and leaders brought their charges against him, he did not say a thing.

13Pilate asked him, "Don't you hear what crimes they say you have done?" 14But Jesus did not say anything, and the governor was greatly amazed.

The Death Sentence
(Mark 15.6–15; Luke 23.13–26; John 18.39—19.16)

15During Passover the governor always freed a prisoner chosen by the people. 16At that time a well-known terrorist named Jesus Barabbas *j* was in jail. 17So when the crowd came together, Pilate asked them, "Which prisoner do you want me to set free? Do you want Jesus Barabbas or Jesus who is called the Messiah?" 18Pilate knew that the leaders had brought Jesus to him because they were jealous.

19While Pilate was judging the case, his wife sent him a message. It said, "Don't have anything to do with that innocent man. I have had nightmares because of him."

20But the chief priests and the leaders convinced the crowds to ask for Barabbas to be set free and for Jesus to be killed. 21Pilate asked the crowd again, "Which of these two men do you want me to set free?"

"Barabbas!" they replied.

22Pilate asked them, "What am I to do with Jesus, who is called the Messiah?"

They all yelled, "Nail him to a cross!"

23Pilate answered, "But what crime has he done?"

"Nail him to a cross!" they yelled even louder.

24Pilate saw that there was nothing he

A crowd loves a criminal
(15) The crowd had a choice. They could set either Jesus or Barabbas free. What could we expect of this mob? Of course they chose Barabbas. Crowds often love a crook. They're angry if the law robs them of their daring hero. Jesus was only a misunderstood stranger. "So hang him on a cross," they yelled, "and let the criminal Barabbas go."

---

jJesus Barabbas: Here and in verse 17 many manuscripts have "Barabbas."

could do and that the people were starting to riot. So he took some water and washed his hands[k] in front of them and said, "I won't have anything to do with killing this man. You are the ones doing it!"

25Everyone answered, "We and our descendants will take the blame for his death!"

26Pilate set Barabbas free. Then he ordered his soldiers to beat Jesus with a whip and nail him to a cross.

Soldiers Make Fun of Jesus
(Mark 15.16–21; John 19.2, 3)

27The governor's soldiers led Jesus into the fortress[l] and brought together the rest of the troops. 28They stripped off Jesus' clothes and put a scarlet robe[m] on him. 29They made a crown out of thorn branches and placed it on his head, and they put a stick in his right hand. The soldiers kneeled down and pretended to worship him. They made fun of him and shouted, "Hey, you king of the Jews!" 30Then they spit on him. They took the stick from him and beat him on the head with it.

Jesus Is Nailed to a Cross
(Mark 15.22–32; Luke 23.27–43; John 19.17–27)

31When the soldiers had finished making fun of Jesus, they took off the robe. They put his own clothes back on him and led him off to be nailed to a cross. 32On the way they met a man from Cyrene named Simon, and they forced him to carry Jesus' cross.

33They came to a place named Golgotha, which means "Place of the Skull."[n] 34There they gave Jesus some wine mixed with a

Jesus became a joke
(27) Who was this fool, they wondered—this man that Pilate called a king? They said he was a fanatic, good for an hour's fun. So the soldiers tormented him. Have you never heard the mob say it? "Oh, he's just one of those religious nuts." Many a lonely disciple has been pelted with garbage and foul language over the years. But Jesus stood in that place first.

[k]*washed his hands*: To show that he was innocent.
[l]*fortress*: The place where the Roman governor stayed. It was probably at Herod's palace west of Jerusalem, though it may have been Fortress Antonio north of the temple, where the Roman troops were stationed.
[m]*scarlet robe*: This was probably a Roman soldier's robe. [n]*Place of the Skull*: The place was probably given this name because it was near a large rock in the shape of a human skull.

drug to ease the pain. But when Jesus tasted what it was, he refused to drink it.

35The soldiers nailed Jesus to a cross and gambled to see who would get his clothes. 36Then they sat down to guard him. 37Above his head they put a sign that told why he was nailed there. It read, "This is Jesus, the King of the Jews." 38The soldiers also nailed two criminals on crosses, one to the right of Jesus and the other to his left.

39People who passed by said terrible things about Jesus. They shook their heads and 40shouted, "So you're the one who claimed you could tear down the temple and build it again in three days! If you are God's Son, save yourself and come down from the cross!"

41The chief priests, the leaders, and the teachers of the Law of Moses also made fun of Jesus. They said, 42"He saved others, but he can't save himself. If he is the king of Israel, he should come down from the cross! Then we will believe him. 43He trusted God, so let God save him, if he wants to. He even said he was God's Son." 44The two criminals also said cruel things to Jesus.

The Death of Jesus
(Mark 15.33–41; Luke 23.44–49; John 19.28–30)

45At noon the sky turned dark and stayed that way until three o'clock. 46Then about that time Jesus shouted, "Eli, Eli, lema sabachthani?"*o* which means, "My God, my God, why have you deserted me?"

47Some of the people standing there heard Jesus and said, "He's calling for Elijah."*p* 48One of them at once ran and grabbed a sponge. He soaked it in wine, then put it on a stick and held it up to Jesus.

49Others said, "Wait! Let's see if Elijah will come*q* and save him." 50Once again Jesus shouted, and then he died.

The King was nailed to a cross
(39) What a strange place for a king—on a cross. Even the people's leaders couldn't miss their chance to laugh at the idea. "Jesus saved others, so let's see him get himself down from that cross," they were saying. Then they laughed. The world is still laughing. What about ourselves? Are we different from that crowd? Has the King's death changed our lives?

---

oEli . . . sabachthani: These words are in Aramaic, a language spoken in Palestine during the time of Jesus. *pElijah*: In Aramaic the name "Elijah" sounds like "Eli," which means "my God." *qElijah will come*: Many of the Jewish people expected the prophet Elijah to come and prepare the way for the Messiah.

51At once the curtain in the temple[r] was torn in two from top to bottom. The earth shook, and rocks split apart. 52Graves opened, and many of God's people were raised to life. 53Then after Jesus had risen to life, they came out of their graves and went into the holy city, where many people saw them.

54The officer and the soldiers guarding Jesus felt the earthquake and saw everything else that happened. They were frightened and said, "This man really was God's Son!"

55Many women were looking on from a distance. They had come with Jesus from Galilee to be of help to him. 56Mary Magdalene, Mary the mother of James and Joseph, and the mother of James and John[s] were some of these women.

Jesus Is Buried
(Mark 15.42–47; Luke 23.50–56; John 19.38–42)

57That evening a rich disciple named Joseph from the town of Arimathea 58went and asked for Jesus' body. Pilate gave orders for it to be given to Joseph, 59who took the body and wrapped it in a clean linen cloth. 60Then Joseph put the body in his own tomb that had been cut into solid rock[t] and had never been used. He rolled a big stone against the entrance to the tomb and went away.

61All this time Mary Magdalene and the other Mary were sitting across from the tomb.

62On the next day, which was a Sabbath, the chief priests and the Pharisees went together to Pilate. 63They said, "Sir, we re-

The world shook as God's son died

(51) The death of Jesus was, along with his rising again to life, the central event of all history. As Jesus hung on the cross and the time of his death neared, the sky darkened and the earth shook. The world had been created through the Son of God (see John 1.3), and it was as if his creation was mourning his death.

Afraid of a dead man

(62) The chief priests and Pharisees weren't believers in Jesus, were they? They didn't expect him to rise again, did they? They weren't concerned about what the grieving disciples might do, were they? But see how fearful the Jewish leaders were, asking Pilate for guards and having the tomb officially sealed. Fear often comes from a guilty conscience.

---

[r]*curtain in the temple*: There were two curtains in the temple. One was at the entrance, and the other separated the holy place from the most holy place that the Jewish people thought of as God's home on earth. The second curtain is probably the one that is meant. [s]*of James and John*: The Greek text has "of Zebedee's sons." See 26.37. [t]*tomb . . . solid rock*: Some of the Jewish people buried their dead in rooms carved into solid rock. A heavy stone was rolled against the entrance.

member what that liar said while he was still alive. He claimed that in three days he would come back from death. 64So please order the tomb to be carefully guarded for three days. If you don't, his disciples may come and steal his body. They will tell the people that he has been raised to life, and this last lie will be worse than the first one."*u*

65Pilate said to them, "All right, take some of your soldiers and guard the tomb as well as you know how." 66So they sealed it tight and placed soldiers there to guard it.

Jesus Is Alive
(Mark 16.1–8; Luke 24.1–12; John 20.1–10)

28 The Sabbath was over, and it was almost daybreak on Sunday when Mary Magdalene and the other Mary went to see the tomb. 2Suddenly a strong earthquake struck, and the Lord's angel came down from heaven. He rolled away the stone and sat on it. 3The angel looked as bright as lightning, and his clothes were white as snow. 4The guards shook from fear and fell down, as though they were dead.

5The angel said to the women, "Don't be afraid! I know you are looking for Jesus, who was nailed to a cross. 6He is not here! God has raised him to life, just as Jesus said he would. Come, see the place where his body was lying. 7Now hurry! Tell his disciples that he has been raised to life and is on his way to Galilee. Go there, and you will see him. That is what I came to tell you."

8The women were frightened and yet very happy, as they hurried from the tomb and ran to tell his disciples. 9Suddenly Jesus met them and greeted them. They went near to him, held on to his feet, and worshiped him. 10Jesus said to them, "Don't be afraid! Tell my followers to go to Galilee. They will see me there."

The tomb was empty
(6) Nobody has ever been able to "explain away" how the tomb of Jesus became empty. He lay dead there, wrapped in special grave cloths—then he was gone. The soldiers told everyone the disciples stole the body of Jesus while they were sleeping. But the soldiers couldn't have known what happened when they were asleep. The Jewish authorities could not find the body of Jesus, but his disciples saw him alive.

u the first one: Probably the belief that Jesus is the Messiah.

Report of the Guard

11While the women were on their way, some soldiers who had been guarding the tomb went into the city. They told the chief priests everything that had happened. 12So the chief priests met with the leaders and decided to bribe the soldiers with a lot of money. 13They said to the soldiers, "Tell everyone that Jesus' disciples came during the night and stole his body while you were asleep. 14If the governorᵛ hears about this, we will talk to him. You won't have anything to worry about." 15The soldiers took the money and did what they were told. The Jewish people still tell each other this story.

What Jesus' Followers Must Do
(Mark 16.14–18; Luke 24.36–49; John 20.19–23; Acts 1.6–8)

16Jesus' eleven disciples went to a mountain in Galilee, where Jesus had told them to meet him. 17They saw him and worshiped him, but some of them doubted.

18Jesus came to them and said:

I have been given all authority in heaven and on earth! 19Go to the people of all nations and make them my disciples. Baptize them in the name of the Father, the Son, and the Holy Spirit, 20and teach them to do everything I have told you. I will be with you always, even until the end of the world.

ᵛ*governor:* Pontius Pilate.

A "tall tale"
(13) Imagine the Jewish leaders, expecting people to believe that the disciples actually smuggled the body of Jesus out of a guarded, sealed tomb with a heavy stone door. But that was their story—and a lot of people believed it because they wanted to. They needed a story and that was it.

Be soul winners
(19) Wherever we can, we must tell the great news that Jesus is alive. The Holy Spirit himself will convince people that this good news is true, and many will become Christians. Our lives also must show that Jesus is alive and living in us. That's a fact no one can deny when they really see it.

MARK TELLS THE GOOD NEWS

ABOUT THIS BOOK

This is the shortest of the four New Testament books that tell about the life and teachings of Jesus, but it is also the most action-packed. From the very beginning of his ministry, Jesus worked mighty wonders. After choosing four followers (1.16–20), he immediately performed many miracles of healing. Among those healed were a man with an evil spirit in him (1.21–28), Simon's mother-in-law (1.30,31), crowds of sick people (1.32–34), and a man with leprosy (1.40–45). Over and over Mark tells how Jesus healed people, but always in such a way as to show that he did these miracles by the power of God.

The religious leaders refused to accept Jesus. This led to conflicts (2.2–3.6) that finally made them start looking for a way to kill him (11.18). But the demons saw the power of Jesus, and they knew that he was the Son of God, although Jesus would not let them tell anyone.

This book is full of miracles that amazed the crowds and Jesus' followers. But, according to Mark, the most powerful miracle of Jesus is his suffering and death. The first person to understand this miracle was the Roman soldier who saw Jesus die on the cross and said, "This man surely was the Son of God!" (15.39).

This Gospel is widely thought to be the first one written. The many explanations of Aramaic words and Jewish customs in Mark suggest that Mark wrote to Gentile or non-Jewish Christians. He wants to tell about Jesus and to encourage readers to believe in the power of Jesus to rescue them from sickness, demons, and death. He also wants to remind them that the new life of faith is not an easy life, and that they must follow Jesus by serving others and being ready to suffer as he did.

The first followers of Jesus to discover the empty tomb were three women, and the angel told them:

Don't be alarmed! You are looking for Jesus from Nazareth, who was nailed to a cross. God has raised him to life, and he is not here. (16.6)

A QUICK LOOK AT THIS BOOK

1. The Message of John the Baptist (1.1–8)
2. The Baptism and Temptation of Jesus (1.9–13)
3. Jesus in Galilee (1.14—9.50)
4. Jesus Goes from Galilee to Jerusalem (10.1–52)
5. Jesus' Last Week: His Trial and Death (11.1—15.47)
6. Jesus Is Alive (16.1–8)
7. Jesus Appears to His Followers (16.9–20)

The Preaching of John the Baptist
(Matthew 3.1–12; Luke 3.1–18; John 1.19–28)

1 This is the good news about Jesus Christ, the Son of God.*ᵃ* ²It began just as God had said in the book written by Isaiah the prophet,

ᵃthe Son of God: These words are not in some manuscripts.

A Gospel is good news
(1) As we read the stories about Jesus' life we may wonder why Matthew, Mark, Luke, and John wrote these things. These writers wanted everyone to know that God has made a way of release from the actions

"I am sending my messenger
to get the way ready
for you.
3In the desert
someone is shouting,
'Get the road ready
for the Lord!
Make a straight path
for him.' "

4So John the Baptist showed up in the desert and told everyone, "Turn back to God and be baptized! Then your sins will be forgiven."

5From all Judea and Jerusalem crowds of people went to John. They told how sorry they were for their sins, and he baptized them in the Jordan River.

6John wore clothes made of camel's hair. He had a leather strap around his waist and ate grasshoppers and wild honey.

7John also told the people, "Someone more powerful is going to come. And I am not good enough even to stoop down and untie his sandals.*b* 8I baptize you with water, but he will baptize you with the Holy Spirit!"

The Baptism of Jesus
(Matthew 3.13–17; Luke 3.21, 22)

9About that time Jesus came from Nazareth in Galilee, and John baptized him in the Jordan River. 10As soon as Jesus came out of the water, he saw the sky open and the Holy Spirit coming down to him like a dove. 11A voice from heaven said, "You are my own dear Son, and I am pleased with you."

Jesus and Satan
(Matthew 4.1–11; Luke 4.1–13)

12Right away God's Spirit made Jesus go into the desert. 13He stayed there for forty days while Satan tested him. Jesus was with the wild animals, but angels took care of him.

buntie his sandals: This was the duty of a slave.

and attitudes that prevent us from knowing him. Jesus is that way of release. He sets us free from the power and blindness of sin.

The devil is a real person
(13) It suits the devil, or Satan, very well to know that most people don't believe in him. Then he can more easily undo the work of God in our lives. Jesus knew all about Satan. He knew he would have to defeat Satan and show everyone that God's work cannot be stopped by the king of evil and his kingdom. That's part of the good news about Jesus.

Jesus Begins His Work
(Matthew 4.12–17; Luke 4.14, 15)

¹⁴After John was arrested, Jesus went to Galilee and told the good news that comes from God.^c ¹⁵He said, "The time has come! God's kingdom will soon be here.^d Turn back to God and believe the good news!"

Jesus Chooses Four Fishermen
(Matthew 4.18–22; Luke 5.1–11)

¹⁶As Jesus was walking along the shore of Lake Galilee, he saw Simon and his brother Andrew. They were fishermen and were casting their nets into the lake. ¹⁷Jesus said to them, "Come with me! I will teach you how to bring in people instead of fish." ¹⁸Right then the two brothers dropped their nets and went with him.

¹⁹Jesus walked on and soon saw James

^c*that comes from God*: Or "that is about God."   ^d*will soon be here*: Or "is already here."

God's kingdom is coming
(15) More surely than the rising of the sun, the kingdom of God is coming. The King himself has come and has established his claims in the world. Neither devils nor men can now hold back the oncoming kingdom of God. There may be dark nights of waiting, but the sunrise of Jesus' return is always just at hand.

Are you a fisherman?
(17) Have you ever gone fishing? Then you'll know the work and patience needed to catch fish. But Jesus' disciples, like you, need to work and have patience to catch people for Jesus. Of course we don't actually catch people with real nets. Our net is the

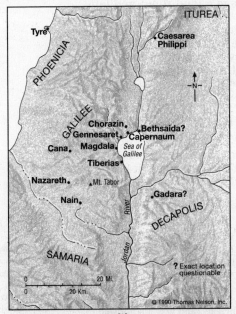

Galilee

and John, the sons of Zebedee. They were in a boat, mending their nets. 20At once Jesus asked them to come with him. They left their father in the boat with the hired workers and went with him.

A Man with an Evil Spirit
(Luke 4.31–37)

21Jesus and his disciples went to the town of Capernaum. Then on the next Sabbath he went into the Jewish meeting place and started teaching. 22Everyone was amazed at his teaching. He taught with authority, and not like the teachers of the Law of Moses. 23Suddenly a man with an evil spirite in him entered the meeting place and yelled, 24"Jesus from Nazareth, what do you want with us? Have you come to destroy us? I know who you are! You are God's Holy One."

25Jesus told the evil spirit, "Be quiet and come out of the man!" 26The spirit shook him. Then it gave a loud shout and left.

27Everyone was completely surprised and kept saying to each other, "What is this? It must be some new kind of powerful teaching! Even the evil spirits obey him." 28News about Jesus quickly spread all over that part of Galilee.

Jesus Heals Many People
(Matthew 8.14–17; Luke 4.38–41)

29As soon as Jesus left the meeting place with James and John, they went home with Simon and Andrew. 30When they got there, Jesus was told that Simon's mother-in-law was sick in bed with fever. 31Jesus went to her. He took hold of her hand and helped her up. The fever left her, and she served them a meal.

32That evening after sunset,f all who were

---

eevil spirit: A Jewish person who had an evil spirit was considered "unclean" and was not allowed to eat or worship with other Jewish people. fafter sunset: The Sabbath was over, and a new day began at sunset.

---

good news about Jesus the Savior. If we keep putting out that net we will bring people to know Jesus.

Evil spirits obey Jesus
(23) Not all problems in the world have natural causes. Sometimes problems are caused by invisible, spiritual enemies of God. But we must never imagine that God lacks the ability to put an end to these enemies. A word from Jesus, and the evil spirits are gone. Jesus is Lord of all creation, and all things must obey his commands.

Jesus is the great Healer
(32) Jesus is Lord of our bodies as well as our minds and spirits. One day we will join the crowd of those who have felt his healing touch. In that day our bodies will be renewed like his. Never

sick or had demons in them were brought to Jesus. 33In fact, the whole town gathered around the door of the house. 34Jesus healed all kinds of terrible diseases and forced out a lot of demons. But the demons knew who he was, and he did not let them speak.

35Very early the next morning Jesus got up and went to a place where he could be alone and pray. 36Simon and the others started looking for him. 37And when they found him, they said, "Everyone is looking for you!"

38Jesus replied, "We must go to the nearby towns, so that I can tell the good news to those people. This is why I have come." 39Then Jesus went to Jewish meeting places everywhere in Galilee, where he preached and forced out demons.

Jesus Heals a Man
(Matthew 8.1–4; Luke 5.12–16)

40A man with leprosyg came to Jesus and kneeled down.h He begged, "You have the power to make me well, if only you wanted to."

41Jesus felt sorry fori the man. So he put his hand on him and said, "I want to! Now you are well." 42At once the man's leprosy disappeared, and he was well.

43After Jesus strictly warned the man, he sent him on his way. 44He said, "Don't tell anyone about this. Just go and show the priest that you are well. Then take a gift to the temple as Moses commanded, and everyone will know that you have been healed."j

45The man talked about it so much and

again will we know sickness, or pain, or death. That was what God had in mind all along when he created us for himself.

"Don't tell anyone"
(44) Jesus didn't want to become known just as a miracle worker, because there was a lot more to it than just that. He wanted to keep his fame as a healer from spreading too fast. But people talked anyway.

---

gleprosy: In biblical times the word "leprosy" was used for many different kinds of skin diseases. hand kneeled down: These words are not in some manuscripts. ifelt sorry for: Some manuscripts have "was angry with." jeveryone will know that you have been healed: People with leprosy had to be examined by a priest and told that they were well (that is "clean") before they could once again live a normal life in the Jewish community. The gift that Moses commanded was the sacrifice of some lambs together with flour mixed with olive oil.

told so many people, that Jesus could no longer go openly into a town. He had to stay away from the towns, but people still came to him from everywhere.

Jesus Heals a Crippled Man
(Matthew 9.1–8; Luke 5.17–26)

2 Jesus went back to Capernaum, and a few days later people heard that he was at home.^k 2Then so many of them came to the house that there was not even standing room left in front of the door.

Jesus was still teaching 3when four people came up, carrying a crippled man on a mat. 4But because of the crowd, they could not get him to Jesus. So they made a hole in the roof^l above him and let the man down in front of everyone.

5When Jesus saw how much faith they had, he said to the crippled man, "My friend, your sins are forgiven."

6Some of the teachers of the Law of Moses were sitting there. They started wondering, 7"Why would he say such a thing? He must think he is God! Only God can forgive sins."

8Right away Jesus knew what they were thinking, and he said to them, "Why are you thinking such things? 9Is it easier for me to tell this crippled man that his sins are forgiven or to tell him to get up and pick up his mat and go on home? 10I will show you that the Son of Man has the right to forgive sins here on earth." So Jesus said to the man, 11"Get up! Pick up your mat and go on home."

12The man got right up. He picked up his mat and went out while everyone watched in amazement. They praised God and said, "We have never seen anything like this!"

One person's faith blessed another

(5) Notice here that Jesus rewarded the faith of the ones who *carried* the crippled man. We can bring the needs of others to the Lord in prayer, and he will answer because of our own faith.

---

^k*at home*: Or "in the house" (perhaps Simon Peter's home). ^l*roof*: In Palestine the houses usually had a flat roof. Stairs on the outside led up to the roof that was made of beams and boards covered with packed earth.

Jesus Chooses Levi
(Matthew 9.9–13; Luke 5.27–32)

13Once again Jesus went to the shore of Lake Galilee. A large crowd gathered around him, and he taught them. 14As he walked along, he saw Levi, the son of Alphaeus. Levi was sitting at the place for paying taxes, and Jesus said to him, "Come with me!" So he got up and went with Jesus.

15Later, Jesus and his disciples were having dinner at Levi's house.m Many tax collectorsn and other sinners had become followers of Jesus, and they were also guests at the dinner.

16Some of the teachers of the Law of Moses were Pharisees, and they saw that Jesus was eating with sinners and tax collectors. So they asked his disciples, "Why does he eat with tax collectors and sinners?"

17Jesus heard them and answered, "Healthy people don't need a doctor, but sick people do. I didn't come to invite good people to be my followers. I came to invite sinners."

Jesus loved sinners
(14) Levi was another name for Matthew, who was a tax collector. Tax collectors were hated by everybody because they served the government of the Roman tyrants, and their pay was based on how much they collected. But Jesus loved this tax collector. In fact Jesus loved a lot of unpopular people, and he even ate dinner with them. Thinking we're better than other people is very dangerous. God may decide we're not as wonderful as we like to think we are.

People Ask about Going without Eating
(Matthew 9.14–17; Luke 5.33–39)

18The followers of John the Baptist and the Pharisees often went without eating.o Some people came and asked Jesus, "Why do the followers of John and those of the Pharisees often go without eating, while your disciples never do?"

19Jesus answered:

The friends of a bridegroom don't go without eating while he is still with them. 20But the time will come when he will be taken from them. Then they will go without eating.

21No one patches old clothes by sew-

Why did people go without eating?
(18) Jesus told his disciples that the Pharisees went without eating to show off their religion. This practice is called "fasting" when it is done for religious reasons. It wasn't so much that Jesus was against fasting, since he sometimes advised it (see Matthew 6.17). But he was against worshiping in any way that would be meant to show off to others.

---

mLevi's house: Or "Jesus' house." ntax collectors: These were usually Jewish people who paid the Romans for the right to collect taxes. They were hated by other Jews who thought of them as traitors to their country and to their religion. owithout eating: The Jewish people sometimes went without eating (also called "fasting") to show their love for God and to become better followers.

ing on a piece of new cloth. The new piece would shrink and tear a bigger hole.

22No one pours new wine into old wineskins. The wine would swell and burst the old skins.p Then the wine would be lost, and the skins would be ruined. New wine must be put into new wineskins.

A Question about the Sabbath
(Matthew 12.1–8; Luke 6.1–5)

23One Sabbath Jesus and his disciples were walking through some wheat fields. His disciples were picking grains of wheat as they went along.q 24Some Pharisees asked Jesus, "Why are your disciples picking grain on the Sabbath? They are not supposed to do that!"

25Jesus answered, "Haven't you read what David did when he and his followers were hungry and in need? 26It was during the time of Abiathar the high priest. David went into the house of God and ate the sacred loaves of bread that only priests are allowed to eat. He also gave some to his followers."

27Jesus finished by saying, "People were not made for the good of the Sabbath. The Sabbath was made for the good of people. 28So the Son of Man is Lord over the Sabbath."

A Man with a Crippled Hand
(Matthew 12.9–14; Luke 6.6–11)

3 The next time that Jesus went into the meeting place, a man with a crippled hand was there. 2The Phariseesr wanted to accuse Jesus of doing something wrong, and they kept watching to see if Jesus would heal him on the Sabbath.

pswell and burst the old skins: While the juice from grapes was becoming wine, it would swell and stretch the skins in which it had been stored. If the skins were old and stiff, they would burst. qwent along: It was the custom to let hungry travelers pick grains of wheat. rPharisees: The Greek text has "they," but see verse 6.

Don't be a faultfinder
(24) The Pharisees didn't have much use for Jesus because he didn't seem to respect their special customs. So when they saw Jesus' disciples picking and eating grain on the Sabbath, they found fault. But Jesus used their remarks as an occasion to teach. God created the Sabbath as a day for blessing people. The disciples weren't working for profit. They were doing a harmless thing on their day off. It's sad when someone's religion becomes a means of finding fault with others.

Old opinions die hard
(2) Again, Jesus got in trouble for healing someone on the Sabbath. The Jewish leaders had set up detailed rules about the Sabbath, making sure no one did the least work on that day of the week. They were very angry at Jesus for questioning them. They weren't about to change their opinions. They took Jesus' actions as a personal insult, even though he was only trying to help someone.

³Jesus told the man to stand up where everyone could see him. ⁴Then he asked, "On the Sabbath should we do good deeds or evil deeds? Should we save someone's life or destroy it?" But no one said a word.

⁵Jesus was angry as he looked around at the people. Yet he felt sorry for them because they were so stubborn. Then he told the man, "Stretch out your hand." He did, and his bad hand was healed.

⁶The Pharisees left. And right away they started making plans with Herod's followers to kill Jesus.

Large Crowds Come to Jesus

⁷Jesus led his disciples down to the shore of the lake. Large crowds followed him from Galilee, Judea, ⁸and Jerusalem. People came from Idumea, as well as other places east of the Jordan River. They also came from the region around the cities of Tyre and Sidon. All of these crowds came because they had heard what Jesus was doing. ⁹He even had to tell his disciples to get a boat ready to keep him from being crushed by the crowds.

¹⁰After Jesus had healed many people, all the other sick people begged him to let them touch him. ¹¹And whenever any evil spirits saw Jesus, they would fall to the ground and shout, "You are the Son of God!" ¹²But Jesus warned the spirits not to tell who he was.

Jesus Chooses His Twelve Apostles
(Matthew 10.1–4; Luke 6.12–16)

¹³Jesus decided to ask some of his disciples to go up on a mountain with him, and they went. ¹⁴Then he chose twelve of them to be his apostles,ᵗ so that they could be with him. He also wanted to send them out to preach ¹⁵and to force out demons. ¹⁶Simon was one of the twelve, and Jesus

ˢ*Herod's followers*: People who were political followers of the family of Herod the Great and his son Herod Antipas. ᵗ*to be his apostles*: These words are not in some manuscripts.

What does it cost to be popular?
(8) Popularity means a lot to some people. How about you? Jesus was popular during the early part of his three-and-a-half-year ministry. But he always knew his popularity wouldn't last. The people were glad when he healed their sicknesses. Then he told them they would have to follow him and give up their old ways. So Jesus lost his popularity. We must not give up the truth to be popular.

Twelve special students
(14) Jesus chose twelve men to be with him day by day, special students who could learn by sharing Jesus' life with him—eating, sleeping, and traveling where he did. He wanted them to be able to go out and tell the good news on their own. Today, too, a major purpose for our learning about Jesus is to go tell others about him.

named him Peter. [17]There were also James and John, the two sons of Zebedee. Jesus called them Boanerges, which means "Thunderbolts." [18]Andrew, Philip, Bartholomew, Matthew, Thomas, James son of Alphaeus, and Thaddaeus were also apostles. The others were Simon, known as the Eager One,[u] [19]and Judas Iscariot,[v] who later betrayed Jesus.

Jesus and the Ruler of Demons
(Matthew 12.22–32; Luke 11.14–23; 12.10)

[20]Jesus went back home,[w] and once again such a large crowd gathered that there was no chance even to eat. [21]When Jesus' family heard what he was doing, they thought he was crazy and went to get him under control.

[22]Some teachers of the Law of Moses came from Jerusalem and said, "This man is under the power of Beelzebul, the ruler of demons! He is even forcing out demons with the help of Beelzebul."

[23]Jesus told the people to gather around him. Then he spoke to them in riddles and said:

How can Satan force himself out? [24]A nation whose people fight each other won't last very long. [25]And a family that fights won't last long either. [26]So if Satan fights against himself, that will be the end of him.

[27]How can anyone break into the house of a strong man and steal his things, unless he first ties up the strong man? Then he can take everything.

[28]I promise you that any of the sinful things you say or do can be forgiven, no matter how terrible those things are.

The teachers of the Law made a bad mistake
(22) Those jealous teachers of the Law who called the Spirit of God an evil spirit were doing an awful thing. Opposing the Holy Spirit would keep them from having faith in Jesus, and that would keep them lost.

[u]*known as the Eager One*: The Greek text has "Cananaean," which probably comes from a Hebrew word meaning "zealous" (see Luke 6.15). "Zealot" was the name later given to the members of a Jewish group which resisted and fought against the Romans.   [v]*Iscariot*: This may mean "a man from Kerioth" (a place in Judea). But more probably it means "a man who was a liar" or "a man who was a betrayer."   [w]*went back home*: Or "entered a house" (perhaps the home of Simon Peter).

29But if you speak against the Holy Spirit, you can never be forgiven. That sin will be held against you forever. 30Jesus said this because the people were saying that he had an evil spirit in him.

Jesus' Mother and Brothers
(Matthew 12.46–50; Luke 8.19–21)

31Jesus' mother and brothers came and stood outside. Then they sent someone with a message for him to come out to them. 32The crowd that was sitting around Jesus told him, "Your mother and your brothers and sistersˣ are outside and want to see you."

33Jesus asked, "Who is my mother and who are my brothers?" 34Then he looked at the people sitting around him and said, "Here are my mother and my brothers. 35Anyone who obeys God is my brother or sister or mother."

What about our families?
(31) Jesus had always obeyed and respected his parents. But a time came when he had to leave home and carry out the work his heavenly Father gave him to do. We should not neglect those who are closest to us, but God also calls us to serve in a world that needs us.

A Story about a Farmer
(Matthew 13.1–9; Luke 8.4–8)

4 The next time Jesus taught beside Lake Galilee, a big crowd gathered. It was so large that he had to sit in a boat out on the lake, while the people stood on the shore. 2He used stories to teach them many things, and this is part of what he taught:

3Now listen! A farmer went out to scatter seed in a field. 4While the farmer was scattering the seed, some of it fell along the road and was eaten by birds. 5Other seeds fell on thin, rocky ground and quickly started growing because the soil was not very deep. 6But when the sun came up, the plants were scorched and dried up, because they did not have enough roots. 7Some other seeds fell where thorn bushes grew up and choked out the plants. So they did not produce any grain. 8But a few seeds did fall on good ground where the plants grew and produced thirty or sixty or

---

ˣ*and sisters*: These words are not in some manuscripts.

even a hundred times as much as was scattered.

9Then Jesus said, "If you have ears, pay attention."

Why Jesus Used Stories
(Matthew 13.10–17; Luke 8.9, 10)

10When Jesus was alone with the twelve apostles and some others, they asked him about these stories. 11He answered:

I have explained the secrets about God's kingdom to you, but for others I can use only stories. 12The reason is,

"These people will look
and look, but never see.
They will listen and listen,
but never understand.
If they did,
they would turn to God,
and he would forgive them."

Jesus Explains the Story about the Farmer
(Matthew 13.18–23; Luke 8.11–15)

13Jesus told them:

If you don't understand this story, you won't understand any others. 14What the farmer is spreading is really the message about the kingdom. 15The seeds that fell along the road are the people who hear the message. But Satan soon comes and snatches it away from them. 16The seeds that fell on rocky ground are the people who gladly hear the message and accept it right away. 17But they don't have any roots, and they don't last very long. As soon as life gets hard or the message gets them in trouble, they give up.

18The seeds that fell among the thorn bushes are also people who hear the message. 19But they start worrying about the needs of this life. They are fooled by the desire to get rich and to have all kinds of other things. So the message gets choked out, and they never produce anything. 20The seeds that fell on good ground are the people

Keep a good attitude about Jesus' teaching
(11) Even though Jesus used simple stories to explain his message, still people did not understand. But the reason was that they had the wrong attitude. They never wanted Jesus to say things that made them feel uncomfortable. But sometimes he told the people their lives had to change toward God. So many of them didn't listen to Jesus. They didn't want to change.

What kind of ground are you?
(14) Attitude is very important. It can keep the truth of God from taking root in our hearts. If we are slow to believe, or quick to give up, or if we are worriers, these are all poor attitudes. Like poor ground, they cause faith to fail. A good attitude is like rich, moist ground that is good for growing.

who hear and welcome the message.
They produce thirty or sixty or even a
hundred times as much as was planted.

Light
(Luke 8.16–18)

21Jesus also said:

You don't light a lamp and put it under a clay pot or under a bed. Don't
you put a lamp on a lampstand? 22There
is nothing hidden that will not be made
public. There is no secret that will not
be well known. 23If you have ears, pay
attention!

24Listen carefully to what you hear!
The way you treat others will be the
way you will be treated. 25Everyone
who has something will be given more.
But people who don't have anything will
lose what little they have.

Let your light shine
(21) In God's sight the
world is a dark place be-
cause so many people have
turned their backs on the
light of his truth. Jesus tells
us that we must let the truth
shine in the world. If we
know God's word and live
by it, then the world can see
our light and be helped by
it.

Another Story about Seeds

26Again Jesus said:

God's kingdom is like what happens
when a farmer scatters seed in a field.
27The farmer sleeps at night and is up
and around during the day. Yet the
seeds keep sprouting and growing, and
he doesn't understand how. 28It is the
ground that makes the seeds sprout and
grow into plants that produce grain.
29Then when harvest season comes and
the grain is ripe, the farmer cuts it with
a sickle.*y*

Harvest time is coming
(26) After the growing season, when the grain is all
ripe, the crop is gathered in.
If we have done a good job
of planting God's truth in the
world, our work will multiply
and grow. Then God will
come to all in whom the seed
of his truth has grown, and
he will gather them into his
everlasting kingdom.

A Mustard Seed
(Matthew 13.31, 32; Luke 13.18, 19)

30Finally, Jesus said:

What is God's kingdom like? What
story can I use to explain it? 31It is like
what happens when a mustard seed is
planted in the ground. It is the smallest
seed in all the world. 32But once it is

*The news of God's
kingdom spreads*
(30) Jesus didn't begin his
great work in a big way. He
chose one of the smallest
countries in the world and
called a few ordinary men
to be his teachers. From
their small work the whole
world has been hearing the
good news about the king-
dom of God.

---

y sickle: A knife with a long curved blade, used to cut
grain and other crops.

planted, it grows larger than any garden plant. It even puts out branches that are big enough for birds to rest in its shade.

The Reason for Teaching with Stories
(Matthew 13.34, 35)

33Jesus used many other stories when he spoke to the people, and he taught them as much as they could understand. 34He did not tell them anything without using stories. But when he was alone with his disciples, he explained everything to them.

A Storm
(Matthew 8.23–27; Luke 8.22–25)

35That evening Jesus said to his disciples, "Let's cross to the east side." 36So they left the crowd, and his disciples started across the lake with him in the boat. Some other boats followed along. 37Suddenly a windstorm struck the lake. Waves started splashing into the boat, and it was about to sink.

38Jesus was in the back of the boat with his head on a pillow, and he was asleep. His disciples woke him and said, "Teacher, don't you care that we're about to drown?"

39Jesus got up and ordered the wind and the waves to be quiet. The wind stopped, and everything was calm.

40Jesus asked his disciples, "Why were you afraid? Don't you have any faith?"

41Now they were more afraid than ever and said to each other, "Who is this? Even the wind and the waves obey him!"

A Man with Evil Spirits
(Matthew 8.28–34; Luke 8.26–39)

5 Jesus and his disciples crossed Lake Galilee and came to shore near the town of Gerasa.z 2When he was getting out of the boat, a man with an evil spirit quickly

Can you sleep in storms of life?

(35) A man was flying from Chicago to Philadelphia. The plane was being bounced around the sky by a violent thunderstorm, but the man lay asleep across his seat and the one next to him. Later the stewardess came by and asked him how he could sleep. He told her that the God of storms was in charge of the plane. He was right—no matter how rough life gets, the God of storms is in control.

---

zGerasa: Some manuscripts have "Gadara," and others have "Gergesa."

ran to him ³from the graveyard*ᵃ* where he
had been living. No one was able to tie the
man up anymore, not even with a chain.
⁴He had often been put in chains and leg
irons, but he broke the chains and smashed
the leg irons. No one could control him.
⁵Night and day he was in the graveyard
or on the hills, yelling and cutting himself
with stones.

⁶When the man saw Jesus in the distance,
he ran up to him and kneeled down. ⁷He
shouted, "Jesus, Son of God in heaven, what
do you want with me? Promise me in God's
name that you won't torture me!" ⁸The man
said this because Jesus had already told the
evil spirit to come out of him.

⁹Jesus asked him, "What is your name?"
The man answered, "My name is Lots,
because I have 'lots' of evil spirits." ¹⁰He
then begged Jesus not to send them away.

¹¹Over on the hillside a large herd of pigs
was feeding. ¹²So the evil spirits begged
Jesus, "Send us into those pigs! Let us go
into them." ¹³Jesus let them go, and they
went out of the man and into the pigs. The
whole herd of about two thousand pigs
rushed down the steep bank into the lake
and drowned.

¹⁴The men taking care of the pigs ran
to the town and the farms to spread the
news. Then the people came out to see what
had happened. ¹⁵When they came to Jesus,
they saw the man who had once been full
of demons. He was sitting there with his
clothes on and in his right mind, and they
were terrified.

¹⁶Everyone who had seen what had happened told about the man and the pigs.
¹⁷Then the people started begging Jesus to
leave their part of the country.

¹⁸When Jesus was getting into the boat,
the man begged to go with him. ¹⁹But Jesus
would not let him. Instead, he said, "Go
home to your family and tell them how much
the Lord has done for you and how good
he has been to you."

**Jesus brings peace to
troubled lives**
(13) The man who lived in
the graveyard was miser-
able. He was controlled by
a spirit of terror and vio-
lence. In fact, many spirits
lived in him. But "Jesus let
them go." When the spirits
were gone, the man was
calm and in his right mind.
Jesus brings this calm to all
who seek him.

ᵃgraveyard: It was thought that demons and evil spirits
lived in graveyards.

20The man went away into the region near the ten cities known as Decapolis[b] and began telling everyone how much Jesus had done for him. Everyone who heard what happened was amazed.

A Dying Girl and a Sick Woman
(Matthew 9.18–26; Luke 8.40–56)

21Once again Jesus got into the boat and crossed Lake Galilee.[c] Then as he stood on the shore, a large crowd gathered around him. 22The person in charge of the Jewish meeting place was also there. His name was Jairus, and when he saw Jesus, he went over to him. He kneeled at Jesus' feet 23and started begging him for help. He said, "My daughter is about to die! Please come and touch her, so she will get well and live." 24Jesus went with Jairus. Many people followed along and kept crowding around.

25In the crowd was a woman who had been bleeding for twelve years. 26She had gone to many doctors, and they had not done anything except cause her a lot of pain. She had paid them all the money she had. But instead of getting better, she only got worse.

27The woman had heard about Jesus, so she came up behind him in the crowd and barely touched his clothes. 28She had said to herself, "If I can just touch his clothes, I will get well." 29As soon as she touched them, her bleeding stopped, and she knew she was well.

30At that moment Jesus felt power go out from him. He turned to the crowd and asked, "Who touched my clothes?"

31His disciples said to him, "Look at all these people crowding around you! How can you ask who touched you?" 32But Jesus turned to see who had touched him.

33The woman knew what had happened to her. She came shaking with fear and

Tell others what the Lord has done for you
(20) It's no surprise that the man who had the spirits in him couldn't keep quiet after what Jesus did for him. He was telling everybody he could find. Of course all were amazed at him, because they had known what kind of man he was, but he was in his right mind. Let's never get tired of telling people how much Jesus has done for us.

Trusting Jesus is a rewarding adventure
(28) The sick woman knew one thing clearly. If she could just touch Jesus she would be well. It was worth standing in the crowd just for the chance to touch his clothes. The woman spoke of her faith in Jesus and her need was met instantly. Like the woman, we have to care enough to come to Jesus. Our prayer of faith brings us near to him.

[b]*the ten cities known as Decapolis*: A group of ten cities east of Samaria and Galilee, where the people followed the Greek way of life. [c]*crossed Lake Galilee*: To the west side.

kneeled down in front of Jesus. Then she told him the whole story.

34Jesus said to the woman, "You are now well because of your faith. May God give you peace! You are healed, and you will no longer be in pain."

35While Jesus was still speaking, some men came from Jairus' home and said, "Your daughter has died! Why bother the teacher anymore?"

36Jesus heardd what they said, and he said to Jairus, "Don't worry. Just have faith!"

37Jesus did not let anyone go with him except Peter and the two brothers, James and John. 38They went home with Jairus and saw the people crying and making a lot of noise.e 39Then Jesus went inside and said to them, "Why are you crying and carrying on like this? The child is not dead. She is just asleep." 40But the people laughed at him.

After Jesus had sent them all out of the house, he took the girl's father and mother and his three disciples and went to where she was. 41-42He took the twelve-year-old girl by the hand and said, "Talitha, koum!"f which means, "Little girl, get up!" The girl got right up and started walking around. Everyone was greatly surprised. 43But Jesus ordered them not to tell anyone what had happened. Then he said, "Give her something to eat."

The People of Nazareth Turn against Jesus
(Matthew 13.53–58; Luke 4.16–30)

6 Jesus left and returned to his hometowng with his disciples. 2The next Sabbath he taught in the Jewish meeting place. Many of the people who heard him were amazed and asked, "How can he do all this? Where did he get such wisdom and the power to work these miracles? 3Isn't he the

---

dheard: Or "ignored." *ecrying and making a lot of noise*: The Jewish people often hired mourners for funerals. *fTalitha, koum*: These words are in Aramaic, a language spoken in Palestine during the time of Jesus. *ghometown*: Nazareth.

God rules over life and death
(39) We often think death is the end, and that's final. But to God, death is no more final than sleep. That's why Jesus said the little girl was "just asleep." God is far greater than anything that can happen to us—yes, even greater than death and the grave.

Jesus' familiar friends rejected him
(3) We only have to look around our world to see that Jesus isn't loved everywhere. Many people resent him, just as he was resented in his hometown years ago. The world hasn't changed much since then. Sometimes the people who know the

carpenter,[h] the son of Mary? Aren't James, Joseph, Judas, and Simon his brothers? Don't his sisters still live here in our town?" The people were very unhappy because of what he was doing.

[4]But Jesus said, "Prophets are honored by everyone, except the people of their hometown and their relatives and their own family." [5]Jesus could not work any miracles there, except to heal a few sick people by placing his hands on them. [6]He was surprised that the people did not have any faith.

most about Jesus love him the least. Some of the Lord's worst enemies live in places like North America and Europe, where the name of Jesus has been very well known for centuries.

Instructions for the Twelve Apostles
(Matthew 10.5–15; Luke 9.1–6)

Jesus taught in every town and village. [7]Then he called together his twelve apostles and sent them out two by two with power over evil spirits. [8]He told them, "You may take along a walking stick. But don't carry food or a traveling bag or any money. [9]It's all right to wear sandals, but don't take along a change of clothes. [10]When you are welcomed into a home, stay there until you leave that town. [11]If any place won't welcome you or listen to your message, leave and shake the dust from your feet[i] as a warning to them."

[12]The apostles left and started telling everyone to turn to God. [13]They forced out many demons and healed a lot of sick people by putting olive oil[j] on them.

Let us continue the work of Jesus
(7) The twelve apostles may have been surprised when Jesus sent them out to do his work without him. This was just a "trial run," because the day would come when he would not be with the apostles and they would have to continue alone. Jesus expects us to do his work by winning people to faith all over the world. But let's remember that although in one way Jesus isn't here, in another way he is very much with us at all times.

The Death of John the Baptist
(Matthew 14.1–12; Luke 9.7–9)

[14]Jesus became so well-known that Herod the ruler[k] heard about him. Some people thought he was John the Baptist, who had come back to life with the power

---

[h]*carpenter*: The Greek word may also mean someone who builds or works with stone or brick. [i]*shake the dust from your feet*: This was a way of showing rejection. [j]*olive oil*: The Jewish people used olive oil as a way of healing people. Sometimes olive oil is a symbol for healing by means of a miracle (see James 5.14). [k]*Herod the ruler*: Herod Antipas, the son of Herod the Great.

to work miracles. [15]Others thought he was Elijah[l] or some other prophet who had lived long ago. [16]But when Herod heard about Jesus, he said, "This must be John! I had his head cut off, and now he has come back to life."

[17-18]Herod had earlier married Herodias, the wife of his brother Philip. But John had told him, "It isn't right for you to take your brother's wife!" So, in order to please Herodias, Herod arrested John and put him in prison.

[19]Herodias had a grudge against John and wanted to kill him. But she could not do it [20]because Herod was afraid of John and protected him. He knew that John was a good and holy man. Even though Herod was confused by what John said,[m] he was glad to listen to him. And he often did.

[21]Finally, Herodias got her chance when Herod gave a great birthday celebration for himself and invited his officials, his army officers, and the leaders of Galilee. [22]The daughter of Herodias[n] came in and danced for Herod and his guests. She pleased them so much that Herod said, "Ask for anything, and it's yours! [23]I swear that I will give you as much as half of my kingdom, if you want it."

[24]The girl left and asked her mother, "What do you think I should ask for?"

Her mother answered, "The head of John the Baptist!"

[25]The girl hurried back and told Herod, "Right now on a platter I want the head of John the Baptist!"

[26]The king was very sorry for what he had said. But he did not want to break the promise he had made in front of his guests. [27]At once he ordered a guard to cut off John's head there in prison. [28]The guard put the head on a platter and took it to the girl. Then she gave it to her mother.

Obeying God will cost your life
(16) You might not be put to death like John the Baptist, but being a Christian will mean devoting your life to Jesus. In fact, you won't even *want* to live for yourself anymore when you give your life to him. Whether believers live or die, they are the Lord's to use in any way he wants.

Lust brings more evil
(22) Not only was the lust of Herod for his dancing stepdaughter evil, but as lust often does, it brought about more evil—the murder of an innocent man, a prophet sent from God. It's like what James writes about in his letter (James 1.14): "We are tempted by our own desires that drag us off and trap us." Herod's lust trapped him into committing an awful crime against God.

---

[l]*Elijah*: Many of the Jewish people expected the prophet Elijah to come and prepare the way for the Messiah.
[m]*was confused by what John said*: Some manuscripts have "did many things because of what John said."
[n]*Herodias*: Some manuscripts have "Herod."

29When John's followers learned that he had been killed, they took his body and put it in a tomb.

Jesus Feeds Five Thousand
(Matthew 14.13–21; Luke 9.10–17; John 6.1–14)

30After the apostles returned to Jesus,o they told him everything they had done and taught. 31But so many people were coming and going that Jesus and the apostles did not even have a chance to eat. Then Jesus said, "Let's go to a placep where we can be alone and get some rest." 32They left in a boat for a place where they could be alone. 33But many people saw them leave and figured out where they were going. So people from every town ran on ahead and got there first.

34When Jesus got out of the boat, he saw the large crowd that was like sheep without a shepherd. He felt sorry for the people and started teaching them many things.

35That evening the disciples came to Jesus and said, "This place is like a desert, and it is already late. 36Let the crowds leave, so they can go to the farms and villages near here and buy something to eat."

37Jesus replied, "You give them something to eat."

But they asked him, "Don't you know that it would take almost a year's wagesq to buy all of these people something to eat?"

38Then Jesus said, "How much bread do you have? Go and see!"

They found out and answered, "We have five small loaves of breadr and two fish." 39Jesus told his disciples to have the people sit down on the green grass. 40They sat down in groups of a hundred and groups of fifty.

Jesus makes much from our little

(36) The disciples were anxious about the hungry crowds who followed Jesus. They proposed an ordinary solution: sending the crowds away to buy food. But Jesus solved the problem himself. Sometimes, in ways we may not notice, God uses our few things to do great works. As Lord of heaven and earth, he can use little for much. He made the universe from nothing at all.

othe apostles returned to Jesus: From the mission on which he had sent them (see 6.7,12,13). pa place: This was probably northeast of Lake Galilee (see verse 45). qalmost a year's wages: The Greek text has "two hundred silver coins." Each coin was the average day's wage for a worker. rsmall loaves of bread: These would have been flat and round or in the shape of a bun.

41Jesus took the five loaves and the two fish. He looked up toward heaven and blessed the food. Then he broke the bread and handed it to his disciples to give to the people. He also divided the two fish, so that everyone could have some.

42After everyone had eaten all they wanted, 43Jesus' disciples picked up twelve large baskets of leftover bread and fish.

44There were five thousand men who ate the food.

Jesus Walks on the Water
(Matthew 14.22–33; John 6.15–21)

45Right away Jesus made his disciples get into the boat and start back across to Bethsaida. But he stayed until he had sent the crowds away. 46Then he told them goodby and went up on the side of a mountain to pray.

47Later that evening he was still there by himself, and the boat was somewhere in the middle of the lake. 48He could see that the disciples were struggling hard, because they were rowing against the wind. Not long before morning, Jesus came toward them. He was walking on the water and was about to pass the boat.

49When the disciples saw Jesus walking on the water, they thought he was a ghost, and they started screaming. 50All of them saw him and were terrified. But at that same time he said, "Don't worry! I am Jesus. Don't be afraid." 51He then got into the boat with them, and the wind died down. The disciples were completely confused. 52Their minds were closed, and they could not understand the true meaning of the loaves of bread.

Jesus Heals Sick People in Gennesaret
(Matthew 14.34–36)

53Jesus and his disciples crossed the lake and brought the boat to shore near the town of Gennesaret. 54As soon as they got out of the boat, the people recognized Jesus. 55So they ran all over that part of the country

"The boat was in the middle of the lake"
(47) This was Lake Galilee, about 70 miles north of Jerusalem. It is most often called "the *Sea* of Galilee," but it is smaller than many lakes, so "lake" is probably more accurate for a name. Its water is clear and drinkable, and people still fish there. The Jordan River flows through it. It was also called "Gennesaret" in Jesus' day, and many years earlier it had been called "Chinnereth." One of the Herod kings named it "the Sea of Tiberias" to honor a Roman emperor. That's a lot of names for one lake—but it was an important lake.

The power of God never runs out
(55) All who touched Jesus' clothes were healed. By touching his clothing, people showed their faith. The real power was not in the

to bring their sick people to him on mats. They brought them to him each time they heard where he was. [56]In every village or farm or market place where Jesus went, the people brought their sick to him. They begged him to let them just touch his clothes, and everyone who did was healed.

clothing, but in the wearer of the clothing. *All* were healed, not just some. There is no limit to what God can do to bless those who reach out to him.

The Teaching of the Ancestors
(Matthew 15.1–9)

7 Some Pharisees and several teachers of the Law of Moses from Jerusalem came and gathered around Jesus. [2]They noticed that some of his disciples ate without first washing their hands.s

[3]The Pharisees and all other Jewish people obey the teachings of their ancestors. They always wash their hands in the proper wayt before eating. [4]None of them will eat anything they buy in the market until it is washed. They also follow a lot of other teachings, such as washing cups, pitchers, and bowls.u

[5]The Pharisees and teachers asked Jesus, "Why don't your disciples obey what our ancestors taught us to do? Why do they eat without washing their hands?"

[6]Jesus replied:

You are nothing but showoffs! The prophet Isaiah was right when he wrote that God had said,

"All of you praise me
　　with your words,
but you never really
　　think about me.
[7]It is useless for you
　　to worship me,
when you teach rules
　　made up by humans."

[8]You disobey God's commands in order to obey what humans have taught.

First things first
(4) The Pharisees and teachers were "majoring on minors," observing strict rules about washing bowls and other fussy matters. They were forgetting about the really important parts of God's Law—the parts that had to do with how we treat other people. Love is the main point. Let's not lose sight of it.

---

swithout first washing their hands: The Jewish people had strict laws about washing their hands before eating, especially if they had been out in public. t in the proper way: The Greek text has "with the fist," but the exact meaning is not clear. It could mean "to the wrist" or "to the elbow." ubowls: Some manuscripts add "and sleeping mats."

9You are good at rejecting God's commands so that you can follow your own teachings! 10Didn't Moses command you to respect your father and mother? Didn't he tell you to put to death all who curse their parents? 11But you let people get by without helping their parents when they should. You let them say that what they own has been offered to God.v 12You won't let those people help their parents. 13And you ignore God's commands in order to follow your own teaching. You do a lot of other things that are just as bad.

What Really Makes People Unclean
(Matthew 15.10–20)

14Jesus called the crowd together again and said, "Pay attention and try to understand what I mean. 15-16The food that you put into your mouth does not make you unclean and unfit to worship God. The bad words that come out of your mouth are what make you unclean."w

17After Jesus and his disciples had left the crowd and had gone into the house, they asked him what these sayings meant. 18He answered, "Don't you know what I am talking about by now? Surely you know that the food you put into your mouth cannot make you unclean. 19It does not go into your heart, but into your stomach, and then out of your body." By saying this, Jesus meant that all foods were fit to eat.

20Then Jesus said:

What comes from your heart is what makes you unclean. 21Out of your heart come evil thoughts, vulgar deeds, stealing, murder, 22unfaithfulness in marriage, greed, meanness, deceit, indecency, envy, insults, pride, and foolishness. 23All of these come from

What is really unclean
(15) We are kept from being "clean" by what we do more than by what we eat or touch. Let's make sure there is no "dirt" coming out of our hearts, but that the world is a cleaner place because we are in it.

vhas been offered to God: According to Jewish custom, when anything was offered to God, it could not be used for anyone else, not even for a person's parents. wunclean: Some manuscripts add, "If you have ears, pay attention."

your heart, and they are what make you
unfit to worship God.

A Woman's Faith
(Matthew 15.21–28)

24Jesus left and went to the region near
the city of Tyre, where he stayed in someone's home. He did not want people to know
he was there, but they found out anyway.
25A woman whose daughter had an evil
spirit in her heard where Jesus was. And
right away she came and kneeled down at
his feet. 26The woman was Greek and had
been born in the part of Syria known as
Phoenicia. She begged Jesus to force the
demon out of her daughter. 27But Jesus said,
"The children must first be fed! It isn't right
to take away their food and feed it to dogs." x

28The woman replied, "Lord, even dogs
eat the crumbs that children drop from the
table."

29Jesus answered, "That's true! You may
go now. The demon has left your daughter."
30When the woman got back home, she
found her child lying on the bed. The demon
had gone.

Blessing came to a Gentile
(27) The Greek woman
from Syria would have been
considered "unclean" by
the strict Jews of Jesus' time.
Jesus referred to this opinion in his remark about
"dogs." But he rewarded
the woman's faith by healing her daughter. Jesus had
come to bless more than just
one race of people.

Jesus Heals a Man Who Was Deaf and Could Hardly Talk

31Jesus left the region around Tyre and
went by way of Sidon toward Lake Galilee.
He went through the land near the ten cities
known as Decapolis.y 32Some people
brought to him a man who was deaf and
could hardly talk. They begged Jesus just
to touch him.

33After Jesus had taken him aside from
the crowd, he stuck his fingers in the man's
ears. Then he spit and put it on the man's
tongue. 34Jesus looked up toward heaven,
and with a groan he said, "Effatha!"z which
means "Open up!" 35At once the man could

*Hearing and speaking are
also God's gifts*
(32) Animals can hear and
be taught to answer certain
sounds. But they can't
speak. This is a special gift
for those created in God's
likeness. We are also given
the ability to hear and understand. It was no trouble
for Christ, the Creator of
these gifts, to give them
back to a man who had lost
them.

---

xfeed it to dogs: The Jewish people often referred to
Gentiles as dogs.   ythe ten cities known as Decapolis:
See the note at 5.20.   zEffatha: This word is in Aramaic,
a language spoken in Palestine during the time of Jesus.

hear, and he had no more trouble talking clearly.

36Jesus told the people not to say anything about what he had done. But the more he told them, the more they talked about it. **37**They were completely amazed and said, "Everything he does is good! He even heals people who cannot hear or talk."

Jesus Feeds Four Thousand
(Matthew 15.32–39)

8 One day another large crowd gathered around Jesus. They had not brought along anything to eat. So Jesus called his disciples together and said, **2**"I feel sorry for these people. They have been with me for three days, and they don't have anything to eat. **3**Some of them live a long way from here. If I send them away hungry, they might faint on their way home."

4The disciples said, "This place is like a desert. Where can we find enough food to feed such a crowd?"

5Jesus asked them how much food they had. They replied, "Seven small loaves of bread."*a*

6After Jesus told the crowd to sit down, he took the seven loaves and blessed them. He then broke the loaves and handed them to his disciples, who passed them out to the crowd. **7**They also had a few little fish, and after Jesus had blessed these, he told the disciples to pass them around.

8-9 The crowd of about four thousand people ate all they wanted, and the leftovers filled seven large baskets.

As soon as Jesus had sent the people away, **10**he got into the boat with the disciples and crossed to the territory near Dalmanutha.*b*

A Sign from Heaven
(Matthew 16.1–4)

11The Pharisees came out and started an argument with Jesus. They wanted to test

The hungry were fed
(6) The four thousand people were fed all they wanted, and there was more left over. No matter what we lack, God has that and more. Through this miracle and the feeding of the five thousand told of in chapter 6, Jesus showed that he is the master of creation and that he has the power to supply all of our needs.

Signs from heaven don't create faith
(11) Many people think that if they could just see a miracle they would believe in God. But you need to believe in God first before you can see his miracles. God

---

asmall loaves of bread: See the note at 6.38.   *bDalmanutha*: The place is unknown.

him by asking for a sign from heaven. 12Jesus groaned and said, "Why are you always looking for a sign? I can promise you that you will not be given one!" 13Then he left them. He again got into a boat and crossed over to the west side of the lake.

The Yeast of the Pharisees and of Herod
(Matthew 16.5–12)

14The disciples had forgotten to bring any bread, and they had only one loaf with them in the boat. 15Jesus warned them, "Watch out! Guard against the yeast of the Pharisees and of Herod."c

16The disciples talked this over and said to each other, "He must be saying this because we don't have any bread."

17Jesus knew what they were thinking and asked, "Why are you talking about not having any bread? Don't you understand? Are your minds still closed? 18Are your eyes blind and your ears deaf? Don't you remember 19how many baskets of leftovers you picked up when I fed those five thousand people?"

"Yes," the disciples answered. "There were twelve baskets."

20Jesus then asked, "And how many baskets of leftovers did you pick up when I broke bread for those four thousand people?"

"Seven," they answered.

21"Don't you know what I am talking about by now?" Jesus asked.

Jesus Heals a Blind Man at Bethsaida

22As Jesus and his disciples were going into Bethsaida, some people brought a blind man to him and begged him to touch the man. 23Jesus took him by the hand and led him out of the village, where he spit into the man's eyes. He placed his hands on the blind man and asked him if he could see anything. 24The man looked up and said,

has done many miracles, but our problem is that we close our eyes to them. Even if someone came back from the dead, many would not believe. In fact, Jesus did come back to life, but many still didn't trust him.

Unbelief causes blindness
(18) Lack of faith brings about not physical blindness, but blindness to God's work. The disciples hadn't fully realized how Jesus fed the crowds. He had done it so simply and easily that they missed the lesson about the mighty power of God. Just like the Pharisees who wanted a sign, the disciples had not understood what their own eyes should have told them.

cHerod: Herod Antipas, the son of Herod the Great.

"I see people, but they look like trees walking around."

25Once again Jesus placed his hands on the man's eyes, and this time the man stared. His eyes were healed, and he saw everything clearly. 26Jesus said to the man, "You may return home now, but don't go into the village."

Who Is Jesus?
(Matthew 16.13–20; Luke 9.18–21)

27Jesus and his disciples went to the villages near the town of Caesarea Philippi. As they were walking along, he asked them, "What do people say about me?"

28The disciples answered, "Some say you are John the Baptist or maybe Elijah.d Others say you are one of the prophets."

29Then Jesus asked them, "But who do you say I am?"

"You are the Messiah!" Peter replied.

30Jesus warned the disciples not to tell anyone about him.

Jesus Speaks about His Suffering and Death
(Matthew 16.21–28; Luke 9.22–27)

31Jesus began telling his disciples what would happen to him. He said, "The nation's leaders, the chief priests, and the teachers of the Law of Moses will make the Son of Man suffer terribly. He will be rejected and killed, but three days later he will rise to life." 32Then Jesus explained clearly what he meant.

Peter took Jesus aside and told him to stop talking like that. 33But when Jesus turned and saw the disciples, he corrected Peter. He said to him, "Satan, get away from me! You are thinking like everyone else and not like God."

34Jesus then told the crowd and the disciples to come closer, and he said:

If any of you want to be my followers, you must forget about yourself. You must take up your cross and follow me.

dElijah: See the note at 6.15.

Do we really understand?
(29) Remember that puzzle you just couldn't solve no matter how hard you tried, then it suddenly came together? The disciples finally understood what their eyes and their ears had been telling them about Jesus. He really was the Messiah, the One sent from God. But they still did not understand his reason for coming.

What is a disciple?
(34) Is a disciple only someone two thousand years ago who walked around the Holy Land in a robe with a long walking stick? No, a disciple is anyone who follows Jesus in any place or time. To follow Jesus we

35If you want to save your life,e you will destroy it. But if you give up your life for me and for the good news, you will save it. 36What will you gain, if you own the whole world but destroy yourself? 37What could you give to get back your soul?

38Don't be ashamed of me and my message among these unfaithful and sinful people! If you are, the Son of Man will be ashamed of you when he comes in the glory of his Father with the holy angels.

9 I promise you that some of the people standing here will not die before they see God's kingdom come with power.

The True Glory of Jesus
(Matthew 17.1 13, Luke 9.28–36)

2Six days later Jesus took Peter, James, and John with him. They went up on a high mountain, where they could be alone. There in front of the disciples, Jesus was completely changed. 3And his clothes became much whiter than any bleach on earth could make them. 4Then Moses and Elijah were there talking with Jesus.

5Peter said to Jesus, "Teacher it is good for us to be here! Let us make three shelters, one for you, one for Moses, and one for Elijah." 6But Peter and the others were terribly frightened, and he did not know what he was talking about.

7The shadow of a cloud passed over and covered them. From the cloud a voice said, "This is my Son, and I love him. Listen to what he says!" 8At once the disciples looked around, but they saw only Jesus.

9As Jesus and his disciples were coming down the mountain, he told them not to say a word about what they had seen, until the Son of Man had been raised from death. 10So they kept it to themselves. But they wondered what he meant by the words "raised from death."

---

elife: In verses 35-37 the same Greek word is translated "life," "yourself," and "soul."

must leave our old cares behind and begin to care about the things Jesus cares about. Let's not be ashamed to be Christians. Let's be glad we have found Jesus, the greatest treasure of life. Then we can be his disciples too.

Has God's kingdom come?
(1) When you first set foot on some land you bought to build a house on, you say "this is my land," even though you need to go away for a while before you are ready to return there to live. When Jesus came to earth he showed in many ways that the ground he walked on was his own, and that he is the King of kings. The church is here as "the body of Christ," and in that sense the kingdom is here now. Then when Jesus returns, his kingdom will be set up fully, with the King here for all to see.

What does Jesus look like?
(8) When Jesus came in a human body he kept hidden most of what he is really like. On the mountain Jesus showed some of his real glory. In that moment the

11The disciples asked Jesus, "Don't the teachers of the Law of Moses say that Elijah must come before the Messiah does?"

12Jesus answered:

Elijah certainly will come*f* to get everything ready. But don't the Scriptures also say that the Son of Man must suffer terribly and be rejected? 13I promise you that Elijah has already come. And people treated him just as they wanted to, as the Scriptures say they would.

Jesus Heals a Boy
(Matthew 17.14–20; Luke 9.37–43a)

14When Jesus and his three disciples came back down, they saw a large crowd around the other disciples. The teachers of the Law of Moses were arguing with them.

15The crowd was really surprised to see Jesus, and everyone hurried over to greet him.

16Jesus asked, "What are you arguing about?"

17Someone from the crowd answered, "Teacher, I brought my son to you. A demon keeps him from talking. 18Whenever the demon attacks my son, it throws him to the ground and makes him foam at the mouth and grit his teeth in pain. Then he becomes stiff. I asked your disciples to force out the demon, but they couldn't do it."

19Jesus said, "You people don't have any faith! How much longer must I be with you? Why do I have to put up with you? Bring the boy to me."

20They brought the boy, and as soon as the demon saw Jesus, it made the boy shake all over. He fell down and began rolling on the ground and foaming at the mouth.*g*

21Jesus asked the boy's father, "How long has he been like this?"

The man answered, "Ever since he was a child. 22The demon has often tried to kill

disciples saw the King in his beauty, and they began to see something of the king-dom of God that Jesus had spoken about in verse 1.

---

f Elijah certainly will come: See the note at 6.15.   *g foaming at the mouth*: These symptoms are very much like what is today called epilepsy.

him by throwing him into a fire or into water. Please have pity and help us if you can!"

23Jesus replied, "Why do you say 'if you can'? Anything is possible for someone who has faith!"

24Right away the boy's father shouted, "I do have faith! Please help me to have even more."

25When Jesus saw that a crowd was gathering fast, he spoke sternly to the evil spirit that had kept the boy from speaking or hearing. He said, "I order you to come out of the boy! Don't ever bother him again."

26The spirit screamed and made the boy shake all over. Then it went out of him. The boy looked dead, and almost everyone said he was. 27But Jesus took hold of his hand and helped him stand up.

28After Jesus and the disciples had gone back home and were alone, they asked him, "Why couldn't we force out that demon?"

29Jesus answered, "Only prayer can force out that kind of demon."

Jesus Again Speaks about His Death
(Matthew 17.22, 23; Luke 9.43b–45)

30Jesus left with his disciples and started through Galilee. He did not want anyone to know about it, 31because he was teaching the disciples that the Son of Man would be handed over to people who would kill him. But three days later he would rise to life. 32The disciples did not understand what Jesus meant, and they were afraid to ask.

Who Is the Greatest
(Matthew 18.1–5; Luke 9.46–48)

33Jesus and his disciples went to his home in Capernaum. After they were inside the house, Jesus asked them, "What were you arguing about along the way?" 34They had been arguing about which one of them was the greatest, and so they did not answer.

35After Jesus sat down and told the twelve disciples to gather around him, he said, "If you want the place of honor, you must become a slave and serve others!"

Prayer drives out demons
(23) Not everyone can cope with demons, and science doesn't have the answer to all such problems. Jesus said that our greatest problem is that we don't have the faith we should. People of faith have proven that Jesus' promise doesn't fail. The steady prayer of faith will even drive out demons.

Slow to understand
(31) Jesus warned his disciples several times that he would be killed and then would rise again. But they would not understand until much later when they actually saw the risen Jesus. We wonder how the disciples could have been so slow to catch on. But we, too, are slow to really believe what the Bible tells us about Jesus.

What is real greatness?
(35) Some of the disciples were concerned about which of them would be the greatest when Jesus came to his throne as King. They missed the whole point. Jesus spoke of slaves and children—humble people. He was trying to show us how to be humble. That's what real greatness is.

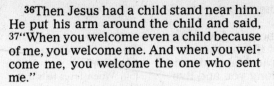

36Then Jesus had a child stand near him. He put his arm around the child and said, 37"When you welcome even a child because of me, you welcome me. And when you welcome me, you welcome the one who sent me."

For or against Jesus
(Luke 9.49, 50)

38John said, "Teacher, we saw a man using your name to force demons out of people. But he was not one of us, and we told him to stop."

39Jesus said to his disciples:
Don't stop him! No one who works miracles in my name will soon turn and say something bad about me. 40Anyone who is not against us is for us. 41And anyone who gives you a cup of water in my name, just because you belong to me, will surely be rewarded.

Temptations to Sin
(Matthew 18.6–9; Luke 17.1, 2)

42It will be terrible for people who cause even one of my little followers to sin. Those people would be better off thrown into the ocean with a heavy stone tied around the neck. 43-44So if your hand causes you to sin, cut it off! You would be better off to go into life crippled than to have two hands and be thrown into the fires of hell that never go out.h 45-46If your foot causes you to sin, chop it off. You would be better off to go into life lame than to have two feet and be thrown into hell.i 47If your eye causes you to sin, get rid of it. You would be better off to go into God's kingdom with only one eye than to have two eyes and be thrown into hell. 48The

"Not one of us"
(38) Over the years, Christians have often sinned by dividing the church. Although we probably can't start over with one church for all, we can pray not to be separated from one another in spirit. Jesus had other disciples who were working for him. He told his followers to be thankful for them also. We ought to do the same today, thanking God for all who truly seek to follow Jesus.

Be a good example to others
(42) If we aren't good examples, we're probably bad ones. That is the way we tempt people to do wrong. We always have to be aware of how others around us see our actions. If anything we do sends a message that sin is "okay," we're in danger of causing a lot of sorrow to others.

hnever go out: Some manuscripts add, "The worms there never die, and the fire never stops burning."
ithrown into hell: Some manuscripts add, "The worms there never die, and the fire never stops burning."

worms there never die, and the fire
never stops burning.
  [49]Everyone must be salted with fire.[j]
  [50]Salt is good. But if it no longer
tastes like salt, how can it be made salty
again? Have salt among you and live
at peace with each other.[k]

Teaching about Divorce
(Matthew 19.1–12; Luke 16.18)

10 After Jesus left, he went to Judea and
then on to the other side of the Jordan
River. Once again large crowds came to
him, and as usual, he taught them.

  [2]Some Pharisees wanted to test Jesus.
So they came up to him and asked if it was
right for a man to divorce his wife. [3]Jesus
asked them, "What does the Law of Moses
say about that?"

  [4]They answered, "Moses allows a man
to write out divorce papers and send his
wife away."

  [5]Jesus replied, "Moses gave you this law
because you are so heartless. [6]But in the
beginning God made a man and a woman.
[7]That's why a man leaves his father and
mother and gets married. [8]He becomes like
one person with his wife. Then they are no
longer two people, but one. [9]And no one
should separate a couple that God has
joined together."

  [10]When Jesus and his disciples were back
in the house, they asked him about what
he had said. [11]He told them, "A man who
divorces his wife and marries someone else
is unfaithful to his wife. [12]A woman who
divorces her husband[l] and marries again
is also unfaithful."

*Do you taste like a
Christian?*
(50) When Jesus tells us to
"have salt," we are re-
minded that some foods
without salt are not very
tasty. A sad Christian with
a long face isn't a very good
advertisement for Jesus. We
all get "down in the dumps"
sometimes, but let's remember our blessings. Then we'll
have a smile and an encouraging word for others.

*Our marriage promises
are sacred*
(8) Sometimes people enter
marriage with a wrong attitude. We easily think only
of the fun side of married
life. There are also sickness,
pain, suffering, and sorrow,
and often these experiences
in marriage are lifelong.
Then the reality of Christian
love is tested, and love either blossoms or dies.

[j]*salted with fire*: Some manuscripts add "and every
sacrifice will be seasoned with salt." The verse may
mean that Christ's followers must suffer because of
their faith. [k]*Have salt among you and live at peace
with each other*: This may mean that when Christ's
followers have to suffer because of their faith, they
must still try to live at peace with each other. [l]*A
woman who divorces her husband*: Roman law let a
woman divorce her husband, but Jewish law did not
let a woman do this.

Jesus Blesses Little Children
(Matthew 19.13–15; Luke 18.15–17)

13Some people brought their children to Jesus so that he could bless them by placing his hands on them. But his disciples told the people to stop bothering him.

14When Jesus saw this, he became angry and said, "Let the children come to me! Don't try to stop them. People who are like these little children belong to the kingdom of God.*m* 15I promise you that you cannot get into God's kingdom, unless you accept it the way a child does." 16Then Jesus took the children in his arms and blessed them by placing his hands on them.

A Rich Man
(Matthew 19.16–30; Luke 18.18–30)

17As Jesus was walking down a road, a man ran up to him. He kneeled down, and asked, "Good teacher, what can I do to have eternal life?"

18Jesus replied, "Why do you call me good? Only God is good. 19You know the commandments. 'Do not murder. Be faithful in marriage. Do not steal. Do not tell lies about others. Do not cheat. Respect your father and mother.'"

20The man answered, "Teacher, I have obeyed all these commandments since I was a young man."

21Jesus looked closely at the man. He liked him and said, "There's one thing you still need to do. Go sell everything you own. Give the money to the poor, and you will have riches in heaven. Then come with me."

22When the man heard Jesus say this, he went away gloomy and sad because he was very rich.

23Jesus looked around and said to his disciples, "It's hard for rich people to get into God's kingdom!" 24The disciples were

Children can come to Jesus

(13) We live too much in an adult world. Children belong to God, too, and this fact makes children important. Today's children are tomorrow's adults. Jesus wants them to come early to him. And then we need to keep a simple, trusting, childlike faith in God no matter how old we get.

---

*m*People who are like these little children belong to the kingdom of God: Or "The kingdom of God belongs to people who are like these little children."

shocked to hear this. So Jesus told them again, "It's terribly hard[n] to get into God's kingdom! 25In fact, it's easier for a camel to go through the eye of a needle than for a rich person to get into God's kingdom."

26Jesus' disciples were even more amazed. They asked each other, "How can anyone ever be saved?"

27Jesus looked at them and said, "There are some things that people cannot do, but God can do anything."

28Peter replied, "Remember, we left everything to be your followers!"

29Jesus told him:

You can be sure that anyone who gives up home or brothers or sisters or mother or father or children or land for me and for the good news 30will be rewarded. In this world they will be given a hundred times as many houses and brothers and sisters and mothers and children and pieces of land, though they will also be mistreated. And in the world to come, they will have eternal life. 31But many who are now first will be last, and many who are now last will be first.

Jesus Again Tells about His Death
(Matthew 20.17–19; Luke 18.31–34)

32The disciples were confused as Jesus led them toward Jerusalem, and his other followers were afraid. Once again Jesus took the twelve disciples aside and told them what was going to happen to him. He said:

33We are now on our way to Jerusalem where the Son of Man will be handed over to the chief priests and the teachers of the Law of Moses. They will sentence him to death and hand him over to foreigners,[o] 34who will make fun of him and spit on him. They will beat

God does impossible things
(27) We often meet people who we say are "creative." They're very good at thinking of better ways to make or do things. But God is the great Creator who does "impossible" things. In the beginning he created the universe from just nothing at all. The same God can also remake a sinner into a new person who loves and obeys him.

Staying alive is not our main purpose
(33) "The will to live" is one of our strongest instincts. Jesus also enjoyed living, but he knew that living was not his main purpose. There was something important to *die* for and he alone could do it. Our lives belong to God who gave them. It is our highest good to give back our lives when he asks us to.

---

[n]*hard*: Some manuscripts add "for people who trust in their wealth." Others add "for the rich."
[o]*foreigners*: The Romans who ruled Judea at this time.

him and kill him. But three days later he will rise to life.

The Request of James and John
(Matthew 20.20–28)

35James and John, the sons of Zebedee, came up to Jesus and asked, "Teacher, will you do us a favor?"
36Jesus asked them what they wanted, 37and they answered, "When you come into your glory, please let one of us sit at your right side and the other at your left."*p*
38Jesus told them, "You don't really know what you're asking! Are you able to drink from the cup*q* that I must soon drink from or be baptized as I must be baptized?"*r*
39"Yes, we are!" James and John answered.

Then Jesus replied, "You certainly will drink from the cup from which I must drink. And you will be baptized just as I must! 40But it is not for me to say who will sit at my right side and at my left. That is for God to decide."

41When the ten other disciples heard this, they were angry with James and John. 42But Jesus called the disciples together and said:

> You know that those foreigners who call themselves kings like to order their people around. And their great leaders have full power over the people they rule. 43But don't act like them. If you want to be great, you must be the servant of all the others. 44And if you want to be first, you must be everyone's slave. 45The Son of Man did not come to be a slave master, but a slave who will give his life to rescue*s* many people.

What does it mean to be important?
(42) The most important man in Jesus' time was the emperor at Rome. He thought he had more power than anybody in the world. He ruled most of Europe and parts of western Asia and northern Africa. Who could resist his authority? But Jesus said it is more important to serve than to rule, and the outcome of the Savior's life on earth showed us that.

---

pright side . . . left: The most powerful people in a kingdom sat at the right and left side of the king. *qdrink from the cup*: In the Scriptures a "cup" is sometimes used as a symbol of suffering. To "drink from the cup" would be to suffer. *ras I must be baptized*: Baptism is used with the same meaning that "cup" has in this verse. *srescue*: The Greek word often, though not always, means the payment of a price to free a slave or a prisoner.

Jesus Heals Blind Bartimaeus
(Matthew 20.29–34; Luke 18.35–43)

46Jesus and his disciples went to Jericho. And as they were leaving, they were followed by a large crowd. A blind beggar by the name of Bartimaeus son of Timaeus was sitting beside the road. 47When he heard that it was Jesus from Nazareth, he shouted, "Jesus, Son of David,*t* have pity on me!" 48Many people told the man to stop, but he shouted even louder, "Son of David, have pity on me!"

49Jesus stopped and said, "Call him over!"

They called out to the blind man and said, "Don't be afraid! Come on! He is calling for you." 50The man threw off his coat as he jumped up and ran to Jesus.

51Jesus asked, "What do you want me to do for you?"

The blind man answered, "Master,*u* I want to see!"

52Jesus told him, "You may go. Your eyes are healed because of your faith."

Right away the man could see, and he went down the road with Jesus.

Little people are important

(49) Jesus showed the truth of what he had just been saying by the way he treated a poor blind man. The man was pleading for Jesus to help him. But everybody tried to shut the man up. It was then that Jesus proved his point about who is important. The others must have been ashamed when they saw Jesus stop to heal the blind man.

Jesus Enters Jerusalem
(Matthew 21.1–11; Luke 19.28–40; John 12.12–19)

11 Jesus and his disciples reached Bethphage and Bethany near the Mount of Olives. When they were getting close to Jerusalem, Jesus sent two of them on ahead. 2He told them, "Go into the next village. As soon as you enter it, you will find a young donkey that has never been ridden. Untie the donkey and bring it here. 3If anyone asks why you are doing that, say, 'The Lord*v* needs it and will soon bring it back.' "

4The disciples left and found the donkey tied near a door that faced the street. While they were untying it, 5some of the people

---

tSon of David: The Jewish people expected the Messiah to be from the family of King David, and for this reason the Messiah was often called the "Son of David." *uMaster*: A Hebrew word that may also mean "Teacher." *vThe Lord*: Or "The master of the donkey."

standing there asked, "Why are you untying the donkey?" [6]They told them what Jesus had said, and the men let them take it.

[7]The disciples led the donkey to Jesus. They put some of their clothes on its back, and Jesus got on. [8]Many people spread clothes on the road, while others went to cut branches from the fields.w

[9]In front of Jesus and behind him, people went along shouting,

"Hooray!x
God bless the one who comes
in the name of the Lord!
[10]God bless the coming kingdom
of our ancestor David.
Hooray for God
in heaven above!"

[11]After Jesus had gone to Jerusalem, he went into the temple and looked around at everything. But since it was already late in the day, he went back to Bethany with the twelve disciples.

Jesus Puts a Curse on a Fig Tree
(Matthew 21.18, 19)

[12]When Jesus and his disciples left Bethany the next morning, he was hungry. [13]From a distance Jesus saw a fig tree covered with leaves, and he went to see if there were any figs on the tree. But there were not any, because it was not the season for figs. [14]So Jesus said to the tree, "Never again will anyone eat fruit from this tree!" The disciples heard him say this.

Jesus in the Temple
(Matthew 21.12–17; Luke 19.45–48;
John 2.13–22)

[15]After Jesus and his disciples reached Jerusalem, he went into the temple and began chasing out everyone who was selling and buying. He turned over the tables of

wspread . . . branches from the fields: This was one way that the Jewish people welcomed a famous person.
xHooray: This translates a word that can mean "please save us." But it is most often used as a shout of praise to God.

A lot of noise proves nothing
(9) A loud car may not mean a powerful engine. More often it means the car needs a new muffler. The noise of the crowd that met Jesus coming into Jerusalem didn't mean they really loved Jesus at all. Later the same crowd would cry out, "Nail him to a cross."

The fig tree stood for something
(13) We wonder why Jesus would curse a fig tree. It was to teach a lesson. The tree stood for something else: Israel. Jesus was showing that the Jewish people of his time—because of bad leaders—were not bearing the fruit that someone would expect from people who had been chosen, blessed, and guided by God. Are we bearing the right fruit today?

What happened in the temple?
(15) Did Jesus have the right to act the way he did? Maybe we think he should have been more polite, saying, "Would you please take your shops out of the temple?" But Jesus was Lord of

the moneychangers and the benches of those who were selling doves. 16Jesus would not let anyone carry things through the temple. 17Then he taught the people and said, "The Scriptures say, 'My house should be called a place of worship for all nations.' But you have made it a place where robbers hide!"

18The chief priests and the teachers of the Law of Moses heard what Jesus said, and they started looking for a way to kill him. They were afraid of him, because the crowds were completely amazed at his teaching.

19That evening Jesus and the disciples went outside the city.

A Lesson from the Fig Tree
(Matthew 21.20–22)

20As the disciples walked past the fig tree the next morning, they noticed that it was completely dried up, roots and all. 21Peter remembered what Jesus had said to the tree. Then Peter said, "Teacher, look! The tree you put a curse on has dried up."

22Jesus told his disciples:

Have faith in God! 23If you have faith in God and don't doubt, you can tell this mountain to get up and jump into the sea, and it will. 24Everything you ask for in prayer will be yours, if you only have faith.

25-26Whenever you stand up to pray, you must forgive what others have done to you. Then your Father in heaven will forgive your sins.*y*

A Question about Jesus' Authority
(Matthew 21.23–27; Luke 20.1–8)

27Jesus and his disciples returned to Jerusalem. And as he was walking through the temple, the chief priests, the nation's leaders, and the teachers of the Law of Moses came over to him. 28They asked, "What

the temple, and the merchants had no business there—except to meet God. They were using the house of God for their own selfish purposes, so Jesus chased them out.

Jesus sometimes used pictures to teach a lesson (23) Often Jesus used a kind of speech called hyperbole (pronounced hy-PUR-bo-lee), which is a clear overstatement—like when we say, "I could eat a horse," meaning we're very hungry. So, when Jesus wanted to teach the power of prayer, he could say, "You can tell this mountain to jump into the sea." Jesus was a master at using figures of speech like these to teach spiritual lessons.

---

yyour sins: Some manuscripts add, "But if you do not forgive others, God will not forgive you."

right do you have to do these things? Who gave you this authority?"

29Jesus answered, "I have just one question to ask you. If you answer it, I will tell you where I got the right to do these things. 30Who gave John the right to baptize? Was it God in heaven or merely some human being?"

31They thought it over and said to each other, "We can't say that God gave John this right. Jesus will ask us why we didn't believe John. 32On the other hand, these people think that John was a prophet. So we can't say that it was merely some human who gave John the right to baptize."

They were afraid of the crowd 33and told Jesus, "We don't know."

Jesus replied, "Then I won't tell you who gave me the right to do what I do."

Renters of a Vineyard
(Matthew 21.33–46; Luke 20.9–19)

12 This is one of the stories Jesus used when he spoke to the people:

A farmer once planted a vineyard. He built a wall around it and dug a pit to crush the grapes in. He also built a lookout tower. Then he rented out his vineyard and left the country.

2When it was harvest time, he sent a servant to get his share of the grapes. 3The renters grabbed the servant. They beat him up and sent him away without a thing.

4The owner sent another servant, but the renters beat him on the head and insulted him terribly. 5Then the man sent another servant, and they killed him. He kept sending servant after servant. They beat some of them and killed others.

6The owner had a son he loved very much. Finally, he sent his son to the renters because he thought they would respect him. 7But they said to themselves, "Someday he will own this vineyard. Let's kill him! That way we can have it all for ourselves." 8So they

They were afraid of the crowd
(29) Jesus knew that his question would make the leaders fearful. Those who don't care about God live in fear of people. That was the state of the temple leaders in Jesus' time. They had their power only as long as the people supported them. But Jesus' authority came from his Father in heaven. Where do we get our feeling of security—from God or from people?

Another story about Israel
(1) Again, Jesus taught about Israel with a story. The farmer is God. The servants are the prophets. The son is Jesus. The Jewish leaders had often mistreated the people God sent to them. Soon they would lose their country to Roman invaders.

grabbed the owner's son and killed him. Then they threw his body out of the vineyard.

9Jesus asked, "What do you think the owner of the vineyard will do? I'll tell you what he will do. He will come and kill those renters and let someone else have his vineyard. 10Surely you know that the Scriptures say,

> 'The stone that the builders
>   tossed aside
> is now the most important
>   stone of all.
> 11This is something
>   the Lord has done,
>   and it is amazing to us.' "

12The leaders knew that Jesus was really talking about them, and they wanted to arrest him. But because they were afraid of the crowd, they let him alone and left.

Paying Taxes
(Matthew 22.15–22; Luke 20.20–26)

13The Pharisees got together with Herod's followers.z Then they sent some men to trick Jesus into saying something wrong. 14They went to him and said, "Teacher, we know that you are honest. You treat everyone with the same respect, no matter who they are. And you teach the truth about what God wants people to do. Tell us, should we pay taxes to the Emperor or not?"

15Jesus knew what they were up to, and he said, "Why are you trying to test me? Show me a coin!"

16They brought him a silver coin, and he asked, "Whose picture and name are on it?"

"The Emperor's," they answered.

17Then Jesus told them, "Give the Emperor what belongs to him and give God what belongs to God." The men were amazed at Jesus.

Jesus is the greatest stone in God's temple
(10) God has a "building" not made of stones—it's made of people who trust Jesus as their Lord and Savior. In a stone building, the most important stone is called the "cornerstone." All the other stones are anchored to that stone, and its position determines the way the whole building sits. Christians are anchored to Jesus, like a living cornerstone.

Giving to the Emperor
(14) A follower of Jesus still needs to respect the government. It is one of the gifts God has given to us. If we owe taxes we should pay them. Good Christians are good citizens. We pay God what he has a right to ask for, and the government what it has a right to ask for.

zHerod's followers: People who were political followers of the family of Herod the Great and his son Herod Antipas.

Life in the Future World
(Matthew 22.23–33; Luke 20.27–40)

18The Sadducees did not believe that people would rise to life after death. So some of them came to Jesus and said:

19Teacher, Moses wrote that if a married man dies and has no children, his brother should marry the widow. Their first son would then be thought of as the son of the dead brother. 20There were once seven brothers. The first one married, but died without having any children. 21The second brother married his brother's widow, and he also died without having children. The same thing happened to the third brother, 22and finally to all seven brothers. At last the woman died. 23When God raises people from death, whose wife will this woman be? After all, she had been married to all seven brothers.

24Jesus answered:

You are completely wrong! You don't know what the Scriptures teach. And you don't know anything about the power of God. 25When God raises people to life, they won't marry. They will be like the angels in heaven. 26You surely know about people being raised to life. You know that in the story about Moses and the burning bush, God said, "I am the God worshiped by Abraham, Isaac, and Jacob."a 27He is not the God of the dead, but of the living. You Sadducees are all wrong.

The Most Important Commandment
(Matthew 22.34–40; Luke 10.25–28)

28One of the teachers of the Law of Moses came up while Jesus and the Sadducees were arguing. When he heard Jesus give a

The worst lies are the ones we tell to ourselves

(18) The Sadducees were not men of truth. They even deceived themselves. They thought they were true believers in God, but they ignored God's word. Jesus showed them their lie. Let's be honest with God. Then we'll be honest with ourselves and others.

---

a"*I am the God worshiped by Abraham, Isaac, and Jacob*": Jesus argues that if God is worshiped by these three, they must still be alive, because he is the God of the living.

good answer, he asked him, "What is the most important commandment?"

29Jesus answered, "The most important one says: 'People of Israel, you have only one Lord and God. 30You must love him with all your heart, soul, mind, and strength.' 31The second most important commandment says: 'Love others as much as you love yourself.' No other commandment is more important than these."

32The man replied, "Teacher, you are certainly right to say there is only one God. 33It is also true that we must love God with all our heart, mind, and strength, and that we must love others as much as we love ourselves. These commandments are more important than all the sacrifices and offerings that we could possibly make."

34When Jesus saw that the man had given a sensible answer, he told him, "You are not far from God's kingdom." After this, no one dared ask Jesus any more questions.

About David's Son
(Matthew 22.41–46; Luke 20.41–44)

35As Jesus was teaching in the temple, he said, "How can the teachers of the Law of Moses say that the Messiah will come from the family of King David? 36The Holy Spirit had David say,

'The Lord said to my Lord:
　Sit at my right side[b]
until I make your enemies
　into a footstool for you.'
37If David called the Messiah his Lord, how can the Messiah be his son?"[c]

The large crowd enjoyed listening to Jesus teach.

Jesus Condemns the Pharisees and the Teachers of the Law of Moses
(Matthew 23.1–36; Luke 20.45–47)

38As Jesus was teaching, he said:
　Guard against the teachers of the

Love is the greatest
(29) If we know God we will love him and all that he loves. Right from the start, this has been the main rule. Religion that is worth the name is really love that comes from God and lives in us. Love is God's greatest gift and the first thing he expects to see in his worshipers—love toward him and toward all people.

Don't be fooled by showoffs
(38) A building may be beautiful and admired by everybody. Then one day that building falls into rubbish in a moment: the building was infested with termites that ate out its insides. The teachers of Jesus' time

---

[b]right side: The place of power and honor.　[c]David . . . his son: See the note at 10.47.

Law of Moses! They love to walk around in long robes and be greeted in the market. 39They like the front seats in the meeting places and the best seats at banquets. 40But they cheat widows out of their homes and pray long prayers just to show off. They will be punished most of all.

A Widow's Offering
(Luke 21.1–4)

41Jesus was sitting in the temple near the offering box and watching people put in their gifts. He noticed that many rich people were giving a lot of money. 42Finally, a poor widow came up and put in two coins that were worth only a few pennies. 43Jesus told his disciples to gather around him. Then he said:

I tell you that this poor widow has put in more than all the others.
44Everyone else gave what they didn't need. But she is very poor and gave everything she had. Now she doesn't have a cent to live on.

The Temple Will Be Destroyed
(Matthew 24.1, 2; Luke 21.5, 6)

13 As Jesus was leaving the temple, one of his disciples said to him, "Teacher, look at these beautiful stones and wonderful buildings!"

2Jesus replied, "Do you see these huge buildings? They will certainly be torn down! Not one stone will be left in place."

Warning about Trouble
(Matthew 24.3–14; Luke 21.7–19)

3Later, as Jesus was sitting on the Mount of Olives across from the temple, Peter, James, John, and Andrew came to him in private. 4They asked, "When will these things happen? What will be the sign that they are about to take place?"
5Jesus answered:
Watch out and don't let anyone fool

were like that—all they had was an outward show. When they came before God they would fall into ruin.

Give your best to Jesus
(41) It's a cheap religion that allows us to give only a "tip" to God. By doing so we may tell ourselves we're good people. But God knows our hearts. Everything we have comes from him, and we owe it all to him. Our very lives belong to him. So let's not try to hold back what God has lent to us for only a short while anyway.

Place your hope in things that last
(1) Many in Jesus' day placed their hope in the temple. To serve in the temple was the greatest good they could think of. But Jesus pointed out what they should have known—the temple wouldn't last. Nothing that people build will last forever. But the things that God builds can never be destroyed.

you! 6Many will come and claim to be me. They will use my name and fool many people.

7When you hear about wars and threats of wars, don't be afraid. These things will have to happen first, but that is not the end. 8Nations and kingdoms will go to war against each other. There will be earthquakes in many places, and people will starve to death. But this is just the beginning of troubles.

9Be on your guard! You will be taken to courts and beaten with whips in their meeting places. And because of me, you will have to stand before rulers and kings to tell about your faith. 10But before the end comes, the good news must be preached to all nations.

11When you are arrested, don't worry about what you will say. You will be given the right words when the time comes. But you will not really be the ones speaking. Your words will come from the Holy Spirit.

12Brothers and sisters will betray each other and have each other put to death. Parents will betray their own children, and children will turn against their parents and have them killed. 13Everyone will hate you because of me. But if you keep on being faithful right to the end, you will be saved.

The Horrible Thing
(Matthew 24.15–21; Luke 21.20–24)

14Someday you will see that "Horrible Thing" where it should not be.d Everyone who reads this must try to understand! If you are living in Judea at that time, run to the mountains. 15If you are on the roofe of your house, don't go inside to get anything. 16If you are out in the field, don't go back for your coat. 17It will be an awful time for women who are expecting babies or

Don't be fooled
(5) Some people believe everything they're told. They even believe that all the fun of this world will never end, and so they live without thinking about God. We can believe God when he says that all the treasures of this world will come to an end. When we're in our right mind we must know that. Let's seek what will last forever.

Hard times are coming
(14) Several times in history foreign conquerors destroyed the temple at Jerusalem and even worshiped false gods that they set up there. The Romans took over Jerusalem in the year 70. But Jesus was pointing to a time when false christs will come and deceive many at the end of the age we are living in.

dwhere it should not be: Probably the holy place in the temple. eroof: See the note at 2.4.

nursing young children. [18]Pray that it won't happen in winter.[f] [19]This will be the worst time of suffering since God created the world, and nothing this terrible will ever happen again. [20]If the Lord doesn't make the time shorter, no one will be left alive. But because of his chosen and special ones, he will make the time shorter.

[21]If someone should say, "Here is the Messiah!" or "There he is!" don't believe it. [22]False messiahs and false prophets will come and work miracles and signs. They will even try to fool God's chosen ones. [23]But be on your guard! That's why I am telling you these things now.

When the Son of Man Appears
(Matthew 24.29–31; Luke 21.25–28)

[24]In those days, right after that time of suffering,

> "The sun will become dark,
>   and the moon
>   will no longer shine.
> [25]The stars will fall,
>   and the powers in the sky[g]
>   will be shaken."

[26]Then the Son of Man will be seen coming in the clouds with great power and glory. [27]He will send his angels to gather his chosen ones from all over the earth.

A Lesson from a Fig Tree
(Matthew 24.32–35; Luke 21.29–33)

[28]Learn a lesson from a fig tree. When its branches sprout and start putting out leaves, you know summer is near. [29]So when you see all these things happening, you will know that the time has almost come.[h] [30]You can be sure

This world will pass away
(24) We are used to seeing the sun rise every day and the moon at night. The stars all keep their special places in the skies. But God says even these things will fail at the end of this time we are living in. This should make us think about the things that cannot fail. The promises of God about life everlasting with him are absolutely sure.

[f]*in winter*: In Palestine the winters are cold and rainy and make travel difficult.   [g]*the powers in the sky*: In ancient times people thought that the stars were spiritual powers.   [h]*the time has almost come*: Or "he (that is, the Son of Man) will soon be here."

that some of the people living today will still be alive when all this happens. [31]The sky and the earth will not last forever, but my words will.

No One Knows the Day or Time
(Matthew 24.36–44)

[32]No one knows the day or the time. The angels in heaven don't know, and the Son himself doesn't know. Only the Father knows. [33]So watch out and be ready! You don't know when the time will come. [34]It is like what happens when a man goes away for a while and places his servants in charge of everything. He tells each of them what to do, and he orders the watchmen to be on their guard. [35]So be on your guard! You don't know when the master of the house will come back. It could be in the evening or at midnight or before dawn or in the morning. [36]But if he comes suddenly, don't let him find you asleep. [37]I tell everyone just what I have told you. Be on your guard!

Be ready always
(32) Some people try to forecast the date Jesus will return. But Jesus himself warned us not to. The important thing is for us to be watchful and ready *whenever* Jesus might return for us.

A Plot to Kill Jesus
(Matthew 26.1–5; Luke 22.1, 2; John 11.45–53)

14 It was now two days before Passover and the Feast of Thin Bread. The chief priests and the teachers of the Law of Moses were planning how they could sneak around and have Jesus arrested and put to death. [2]They were saying, "We must not do it during the feast, because the people will riot."

At Bethany
(Matthew 26.6–13; John 12.1–8)

[3]Jesus was eating in Bethany at the home of Simon, who once had leprosy,[i] when a woman came in with a very expensive bottle of sweet-smelling perfume.[j] After breaking

---

[i]*leprosy*: In biblical times the word "leprosy" was used for many different skin diseases. [j]*sweet-smelling perfume*: The Greek text has "perfume made of pure spiknard," a plant used to make perfume.

it open, she poured the perfume on Jesus' head. [4]This made some of the guests angry, and they said, "Why such a waste? [5]We could have sold this perfume for more than three hundred silver coins and given the money to the poor!" So they started saying cruel things to the woman.

[6]But Jesus said:

Leave her alone! Why are you bothering her? She has done a beautiful thing for me. [7]You will always have the poor with you. And whenever you want to, you can give to them. But you will not always have me here with you. [8]She has done all she could by pouring perfume on my body to prepare it for burial. [9]You may be sure that wherever the good news is told all over the world, people will remember what she has done. And they will tell others.

Judas and the Chief Priests
(Matthew 26.14–16; Luke 22.3–6)

[10]Judas Iscariot[k] was one of the twelve disciples. He went to the chief priests and offered to help them arrest Jesus. [11]They were glad to hear this, and they promised to pay him. So Judas started looking for a good chance to betray Jesus.

Jesus Eats with His Disciples
(Matthew 26.17–25; Luke 22.7–14, 21–23; John 13.21–30)

[12]It was the first day of the Feast of Thin Bread, and the Passover lambs were being killed. Jesus' disciples asked him, "Where do you want us to prepare the Passover meal?"

[13]Jesus said to two of the disciples, "Go into the city, where you will meet a man carrying a jar of water.[l] Follow him, [14]and when he goes into a house, say to the owner, 'Our teacher wants to know if you have a

Do beautiful things for Jesus
(6) We should love our neighbors. That's a good rule and God himself said so. But he also said we should love him *first*. In a simple way the woman at Bethany was doing just that when she poured the expensive perfume on Jesus. Her love for him was greater than anything else in her life.

---

[k]*Iscariot*: See the note at 3.19.   [l]*a man carrying a jar of water*: A male slave carrying water could mean that the family was rich.

room where he can eat the Passover meal with his disciples.' 15The owner will take you upstairs and show you a large room furnished and ready for you to use. Prepare the meal there."

16The two disciples went into the city and found everything just as Jesus had told them. So they prepared the Passover meal.

17-18While Jesus and the twelve disciples were eating together that evening, he said, "The one who will betray me is now eating with me."

19This made the disciples sad, and one after another they said to Jesus, "Surely you don't mean me!"

20He answered, "It is one of you twelve men who is eating from this dish with me. 21The Son of Man will die, just as the Scriptures say. But it is going to be terrible for the one who betrays me. That man would be better off if he had never been born."

The Lord's Supper
(Matthew 26.26–30; Luke 22.14–23; 1 Corinthians 11.23–25)

22During the meal Jesus took some bread in his hands. He blessed the bread and broke it. Then he gave it to his disciples and said, "Take this. It is my body."

23Jesus picked up a cup of wine and gave thanks to God. He then gave it to his disciples and said, "Drink it!" So they all drank some. 24Then he said, "This is my blood, which is poured out for many people, and with it God makes his agreement. 25From now on I will not drink any wine, until I drink new wine in God's kingdom." 26Then they sang a hymn and went out to the Mount of Olives.

Peter's Promise
(Matthew 26.31–35; Luke 22.31–34; John 13.36–38)

27Jesus said to his disciples, "All of you will reject me, as the Scriptures say,
'I will strike down
the shepherd,

"The one who will betray me"
(17) Imagine: one of the twelve disciples—the followers who were closest to Jesus—would betray him to his killers. How could anyone do such a thing? But believers today betray Jesus all the time. Many times we treat him as if he were unimportant, and we sin as if we didn't care about him. In many ways we aren't much better than Judas was.

They sang a hymn
(26) On their last night together before Jesus' death, he and his disciples sang a hymn. Religious singing isn't just something people have "added on" in recent years. It has always been important.

and the sheep
will be scattered.'
²⁸But after I am raised to life, I will go ahead
of you to Galilee."

²⁹Peter spoke up, "Even if all the others
reject you, I never will!"

³⁰Jesus replied, "This very night before
a rooster crows twice, you will say three
times that you don't know me."

³¹But Peter was so sure of himself that
he said, "Even if I have to die with you, I
will never say that I don't know you!"

All the others said the same thing.

Jesus Prays
(Matthew 26.36–46; Luke 22.39–46)

³²Jesus went with his disciples to a place
called Gethsemane, and he told them, "Sit
here while I pray."

³³Jesus took along Peter, James, and
John. He was sad and troubled and ³⁴told
them, "I am so sad that I feel as if I am
dying. Stay here and keep awake with me."

³⁵⁻³⁶Jesus walked on a little way. Then
he kneeled down on the ground and prayed,
"Father,*m* if it is possible, don't let this happen to me! Father, you can do anything.
Don't make me suffer by having me drink
from this cup.*n* But do what you want, and
not what I want."

³⁷When Jesus came back and found the
disciples sleeping, he said to Simon Peter,
"Are you asleep? Can't you stay awake for
just one hour? ³⁸Stay awake and pray that
you will not be tested. You want to do what
is right, but you are weak."

³⁹Jesus went back and prayed the same
prayer. ⁴⁰But when he returned to the disciples, he found them sleeping again. They
simply could not keep their eyes open, and
they did not know what to say.

⁴¹When Jesus returned to the disciples
the third time, he said, "Are you still sleep-

Peter was human
(31) Peter had good inten-
tions. He promised Jesus he
would never let him down,
but he did. Still, Peter was
forgiven. It's good to know
that we can be forgiven too.
When we're human and we
slip up, Jesus is ready to
take us back when we ask
him to.

Death is not nice
(35) Sometimes we try to
make death look beautiful.
Jesus didn't think it is. He
knew that death is the penalty for sin. He was a young
man, and he didn't want to
die. But he knew it was the
only way to finish the work
he came to do so we could
be saved. For that reason
he accepted a cruel death
on a cross, taking the punishment for our sins onto
himself.

---

m Father: The Greek text has "Abba," which is an Aramaic word meaning "father." *n by making me drink
from this cup*: See the note at 10.38.

ing and resting?o Enough of that! The time has come for the Son of Man to be handed over to sinners. 42Get up! Let's go. The one who will betray me is already here."

Jesus Is Arrested
(Matthew 26.47–56; Luke 22.47–53;
John 18.3–12)

43Jesus was still speaking, when Judas the betrayer came up. He was one of the twelve disciples, and a mob of men armed with swords and clubs were with him. They had been sent by the chief priests, the nation's leaders, and the teachers of the Law of Moses. 44Judas had told them ahead of time, "Arrest the man I greet with a kiss.p Tie him up tight and lead him away."

45Judas walked right up to Jesus and said, "Teacher!" Then Judas kissed him, 46and the men grabbed Jesus and arrested him.

47Someone standing there pulled out a sword. He struck the servant of the high priest and cut off his ear.

48Jesus said to the mob, "Why do you come with swords and clubs to arrest me like a criminal? 49Day after day I was with you and taught in the temple, and you didn't arrest me. But what the Scriptures say must come true."

50All of Jesus' disciples ran off and left him. 51One of them was a young man who was wearing only a linen cloth. And when the men grabbed him, 52he left the cloth behind and ran away naked.

Jesus Is Questioned by the Jewish Council
(Matthew 26.57–68; Luke 22.54, 55, 63–71;
John 18.13, 14, 19–24)

53Jesus was led off to the high priest. Then the chief priests, the nation's leaders, and

Why was Jesus arrested?
(46) The religious leaders and the mob had convinced themselves that Jesus was a criminal. That was their excuse. The leaders, of course, felt threatened by him. But Jesus said he was arrested so that what the Scriptures say could come true. Long years before this the Hebrew prophets had predicted Jesus' arrest.

---

oAre you still sleeping and resting?: Or "You may as well keep on sleeping and resting."   pgreet with a kiss: It was the custom for people to greet each other with a kiss on the cheek.

the teachers of the Law of Moses all met together. 54Peter had followed at a distance. And when he reached the courtyard of the high priest's house, he sat down with the guards to warm himself beside a fire.

55The chief priests and the whole council tried to find someone to accuse Jesus of a crime, so they could put him to death. But they could not find anyone to accuse him. 56Many people did tell lies against Jesus, but they did not agree on what they said. 57Finally, some men stood up and lied about him. They said, 58"We heard him say he would tear down this temple that we built. He also claimed that in three days he would build another one without any help." 59But even then they did not agree on what they said.

60The high priest stood up in the council and asked Jesus, "Why don't you say something in your own defense? Don't you hear the charges they are making against you?" 61But Jesus kept quiet and did not say a word. The high priest asked him another question, "Are you the Messiah, the Son of the glorious God?"q

62"Yes, I am!" Jesus answered.

"Soon you will see
     the Son of Man
  sitting at the right sider
  of God All-Powerful,
and coming with the clouds
  of heaven."

63At once the high priest ripped his robe apart and shouted, "Why do we need more witnesses? 64You heard him claim to be God! What is your decision?" They all agreed that he should be put to death.

65Some of the people started spitting on Jesus. They blindfolded him, hit him with their fists, and said, "Tell us who hit you!" Then the guards took charge of Jesus and beat him.

Jesus is the Messiah
(61) Who is "the Messiah"? Jesus, the eternal Son of God who had always lived in heaven with his Father, came to earth. He came to save us from our sins, our disobedience toward God. But when Jesus said that he is the Son of God, the Messiah, the authorities hated him even more. They couldn't get over their pride, like many people today who reject the Messiah and find that putting their faith in Jesus is hard for them to do.

---

qSon of the glorious God: "Son of God" was one of the titles used for the kings of Israel.   rright side: See the note at 12.36.

Peter Says He Does Not Know Jesus
*(Matthew 26.69–75; Luke 22.56–62;
John 18.15–18, 25–27)*

66While Peter was still in the courtyard, a servant girl of the high priest came up 67and saw Peter warming himself by the fire. She stared at him and said, "You were with Jesus from Nazareth!"

68Peter replied, "That's not true! I don't know what you're talking about. I don't have any idea what you mean." He went out to the gate, and a rooster crowed.[s]

69The servant girl saw Peter again and said to the people standing there, "This man is one of them!"

70"No, I'm not!" Peter replied.

A little while later some of the people said to Peter, "You certainly are one of them. You're a Galilean!"

71This time Peter began to curse and swear, "I don't even know the man you're talking about!"

72Right away the rooster crowed a second time. Then Peter remembered that Jesus had told him, "Before a rooster crows twice, you will say three times that you don't know me." So Peter started crying.

Peter was sorry
(72) Poor Peter did exactly what he promised Jesus he would never do. He realized it right away and he was heartbroken. That's the key. Peter was sorry he sinned. It would not be hard for Jesus to forgive him.

Pilate Questions Jesus
*(Matthew 27.1, 2, 11–14; Luke 23.1–5;
John 18.28–38)*

15 Early the next morning the chief priests, the nation's leaders, and the teachers of the Law of Moses met together with the whole Jewish council. They tied up Jesus and led him off to Pilate.

2He asked Jesus, "Are you the king of the Jews?"

"Those are your words," Jesus answered.

3The chief priests brought many charges against Jesus. 4Then Pilate questioned him again, "Don't you have anything to say? Don't you hear what crimes they say you have done?" 5But Jesus did not answer, and Pilate was amazed.

[s]*a rooster crowed:* These words are not in some manuscripts.

The Death Sentence
(Matthew 27.15–26; Luke 23.13–25; John 18.39—19.16)

⁶During Passover, Pilate always freed one prisoner chosen by the people. ⁷And at that time there was a prisoner named Barabbas. He and some others had been arrested for murder during a riot. ⁸The Jewish people now came and asked Pilate to set a prisoner free, just as he usually did.

⁹Pilate asked them, "Do you want me to free the king of the Jews?" ¹⁰Pilate knew that the chief priests had brought Jesus to him because they were jealous.

¹¹But the chief priests told the crowd to ask Pilate to free Barabbas. ¹²Again Pilate asked the crowd, "Do you want me to free this man you say isᵗ the king of the Jews?"

¹³They yelled, "Nail him to a cross!"

¹⁴Pilate asked, "But what crime has he done?"

"Nail him to a cross!" they yelled even louder.

¹⁵Pilate wanted to please the crowd. So he set Barabbas free. Then he ordered his soldiers to beat Jesus with a whip and nail him to a cross.

Soldiers Make Fun of Jesus
(Matthew 27.27–30; John 19.2, 3)

¹⁶The soldiers led Jesus inside the courtyard of the fortressᵘ and called together the rest of the troops. ¹⁷They put a purple robeᵛ on him, and on his head they placed a crown that they had made out of thorn branches. ¹⁸They made fun of Jesus and shouted, "Hey, you king of the Jews!" ¹⁹Then they beat him on the head with a stick. They spit on him and kneeled down and pretended to worship him.

Obey your conscience
(15) Pilate didn't do what his conscience told him to. He suspected that Jesus was telling the truth about himself. But Pilate was afraid to go against the will of the mob. Besides, he was afraid that the authorities at Rome might think he was allowing disloyalty against the emperor. We need to pray that we will always he guided by the truth, whether or not it pleases someone else.

ᵗ*this man you say is*: These words are not in some manuscripts. ᵘ*fortress*: The place where the Roman governor stayed. It was probably at Herod's palace west of Jerusalem, though it may have been Fortress Antonio, north of the temple, where the Roman troops were stationed. ᵛ*purple robe*: This was probably a Roman soldier's robe.

20When the soldiers had finished making fun of Jesus, they took off the purple robe. They put his own clothes back on him and led him off to be nailed to a cross. 21Simon from Cyrene happened to be coming in from a farm, and they forced him to carry Jesus' cross. Simon was the father of Alexander and Rufus.

Jesus Is Nailed to a Cross
(Matthew 27.31–44; Luke 23.27–43; John 19.17–27)

22The soldiers took Jesus to Golgotha, which means "Place of a Skull."w 23There they gave him some wine mixed with a drug to ease the pain, but he refused to drink it.

24They nailed Jesus to a cross and gambled to see who would get his clothes. 25It was about nine o'clock in the morning when they nailed him to the cross. 26On it was a sign that told why he was nailed there. It read, "This is the King of the Jews." 27-28The soldiers also nailed two criminals on crosses, one to the right of Jesus and the other to his left.x

29People who passed by said terrible things about Jesus. They shook their heads and shouted, "Ha! So you're the one who claimed you could tear down the temple and build it again in three days. 30Save yourself and come down from the cross!"

31The chief priests and the teachers of the Law of Moses also made fun of Jesus. They said to each other, "He saved others, but he can't save himself. 32If he is the Messiah, the king of Israel, let him come down from the cross! Then we will see and believe." The two criminals also said cruel things to Jesus.

The Son of God nailed to a cross
(24) They nailed Jesus to a cross, the way criminals were put to death. It's called *crucifixion,* a painful death in which nails were driven through the hands and into a plank. The plank was then placed across an upright beam. When the victim's feet were nailed to the beam, the cross was lifted up with the criminal nailed to it. Then the foot of the cross was dropped into a hole to keep the cross upright. They did this to the Son of God.

---

w*"Place of a Skull"*: The place was probably given this name because it was near a large rock in the shape of a human skull.   x*left*: Some manuscripts add, "So the Scriptures came true which say, 'He was accused of being a criminal.'"

The Death of Jesus
*(Matthew 27.45–56; Luke 23.44–49;
John 19.28–30)*

33About noon the sky turned dark and stayed that way until around three o'clock. 34Then about that time Jesus shouted, "Eloi, Eloi, lema sabachthani?"*y* which means, "My God, my God, why have you deserted me?"

35Some of the people standing there heard Jesus and said, "He is calling for Elijah."*z* 36One of them ran and grabbed a sponge. After he had soaked it in wine, he put it on a stick and held it up to Jesus. He said, "Let's wait and see if Elijah will come*a* and take him down!" 37Jesus shouted and then died.

yEloi . . . sabachthani: These words are in Aramaic, a language spoken in Palestine during the time of Jesus. *zElijah*: The name "Elijah" sounds something like "Eloi," which means "my God." *asee if Elijah will come*: See the note at 6.15.

Languages of the Bible

Hebrew	The original language of most of the Old Testament
Aramaic	The language Jesus used in everyday speech
	The original language of parts of the Old Testament books of Ezra and Daniel
	Sometimes called Chaldee
Greek	The original language of the New Testament
	The language of an Old Testament translation called the Septuagint, used by the early church
	The common language used throughout the Roman empire
Latin	The language of Rome itself, used for official business

38At once the curtain in the temple[b] tore in two from top to bottom.

39A Roman army officer was standing in front of Jesus. When the officer saw how Jesus died, he said, "This man really was the Son of God!"

40-41 Some women were looking on from a distance. They had come with Jesus to Jerusalem. But even before this they had been his followers and had helped him while he was in Galilee. Mary Magdalene and Mary the mother of the younger James and of Joseph were two of these women. Salome was also one of them.

Jesus Is Buried
(Matthew 27.57–61; Luke 23.50–56; John 19.38–42)

42It was now the evening before the Sabbath, and the Jewish people were getting ready for that sacred day. **43**A man named Joseph from Arimathea was brave enough to ask Pilate for the body of Jesus. Joseph was a highly respected member of the Jewish council, and he was also waiting for God's kingdom to come.

44Pilate was surprised to hear that Jesus was already dead, and he called in the army officer to find out if Jesus had been dead very long. **45**After the officer told him, Pilate let Joseph have Jesus' body.

46Joseph bought a linen cloth and took the body down from the cross. He had it wrapped in the cloth, and he put it in a tomb that had been cut into solid rock. Then he rolled a big stone against the entrance to the tomb.

47Mary Magdalene and Mary the mother of Joseph were watching and saw where the body was placed.

Why was the curtain torn?
(38) That seems like an unimportant event for Mark to mention during such dreadful happenings. But the torn curtain was very important. The curtain in the temple separated the holiest place of all from everyone but the high priest. The torn curtain meant that everyone could come to God because Jesus had opened the way for us by his death.

Joseph from Arimathea
(43) Joseph from Arimathea was an important man, but he loved Jesus too. It took courage for him to go and ask for the body of Jesus and take charge of its burial. Most men in his position would not have wanted to risk their reputation. What about us? Are we afraid to be associated with Jesus because of what our unbelieving friends might think?

[b]*curtain in the temple*: There were two curtains in the temple. One was at the entrance, and the other separated the holy place from the most holy place that the Jewish people thought of as God's home on earth. The second curtain is probably the one which is meant.

Jesus Is Alive
(Matthew 28.1–8; Luke 24.1–12; John 20.1–10)

16 After the Sabbath, Mary Magdalene, Salome, and Mary the mother of James bought some spices to put on Jesus' body. ²Very early on Sunday morning, just as the sun was coming up, they went to the tomb. ³On their way, they were asking one another, "Who will roll the stone away from the entrance for us?" ⁴But when they looked, they saw that the stone had already been rolled away. And it was a huge stone!

⁵The women went into the tomb, and on the right side they saw a young man in a white robe sitting there. They were alarmed. ⁶The man said, "Don't be alarmed! You are looking for Jesus from Nazareth, who was nailed to a cross. God has raised him to life, and he is not here. You can see the place where they put his body. ⁷Now go and tell his disciples, and especially Peter, that he will go ahead of you to Galilee. You will see him there, just as he told you."

⁸When the women ran from the tomb, they were confused and shaking all over. They were too afraid to tell anyone what had happened.

The stone was rolled away (4) Can you imagine the noise of that heavy stone being rolled back from the door of Jesus' tomb? If anybody had tried to steal Jesus' body, the guards at the tomb would have caught them at once. But no one was taken prisoner because God himself rolled back the stone, the guards ran away, and Jesus walked out of the tomb alive.

Jesus Appears to Mary Magdalene^c
(Matthew 28.9, 10; John 20.11–18)

⁹Very early on the first day of the week, after Jesus had risen to life, he appeared to Mary Magdalene. Earlier he had forced seven demons out of her. ¹⁰She left and told his friends, who were crying and mourning. ¹¹Even though they heard that Jesus was alive and that Mary had seen him, they would not believe it.

Jesus Appears to Two Disciples
(Luke 24.13–35)

¹²Later, Jesus appeared in another form to two disciples, as they were on their way out of the city. ¹³But when these disciples

---

^c*Jesus Appears to Mary Magdalene:* Mark 16.9-20 is not in most manuscripts.

told what had happened, the others would not believe.

What Jesus' Followers Must Do
*(Matthew 28.16–20; Luke 24.36–49;
John 20.19–23; Acts 1.6–8)*

14Afterwards, Jesus appeared to his eleven disciples as they were eating. He scolded them because they were too stubborn to believe the ones who had seen him after he had been raised to life. 15Then he told them:

Go and preach the good news to everyone in the world. 16Anyone who believes me and is baptized will be saved. But anyone who refuses to believe me will be condemned. 17Everyone who believes me will be able to do wonderful things. By using my name they will force out demons, and they will speak new languages. 18They will handle snakes and will drink poison and not be hurt. They will also heal sick people by placing their hands on them.

The early disciples were not easy believers
(14) The disciples were not ready to believe that Jesus was risen from death. To them, as to us, death seemed very final. They were discouraged and downhearted. But they couldn't deny what their own eyes told them at last. They saw Jesus alive, and only then were they ready to spend their whole lives telling others about Jesus.

Jesus Returns to Heaven
(Luke 24.50–53; Acts 1.9–11)

19After the Lord Jesus had said these things to the disciples, he was taken back up to heaven where he sat down at the right side*d* of God. 20Then the disciples left and preached everywhere. The Lord was with them, and the miracles they worked proved that their message was true.

ANOTHER OLD ENDING TO MARK'S GOSPEL*e*

9-10The women quickly told Peter and his friends what had happened. Later, Jesus sent the disciples to the east and to the west with his sacred and everlasting message of how people can be saved forever.

Where is Jesus now?
(19) Jesus had come from heaven in the beginning. He was the eternal Son of God, who was born with a human body and lived and died among us. Now he is alive forevermore. Jesus is our living Savior in heaven, from which he will return.

---

*d*right side: See the note at 12.36.　*e*Another Old Ending to Mark's Gospel: Some manuscripts and early translations have both this shorter ending and the longer one (verses 9-20).

LUKE TELLS THE GOOD NEWS

ABOUT THIS BOOK

God's love is for everyone! Jesus came into the world to be the Savior of all people! These are two of the main thoughts in this book. Several of the best known stories that Jesus used for teaching about God's love are found only in Luke's Gospel: The Good Samaritan (10.25–37), A Lost Sheep (15.1–7), and A Lost Son (15.11–32). Only Luke tells how Jesus visited in the home of a hated tax collector (19.1–10) and promised life in paradise to a dying criminal (23.39–43).

Luke mentions God's Spirit more than any of the other New Testament writers. For example, the power of the Spirit was with John the Baptist from the time he was born (1.15). And the angel promised Mary, "The Holy Spirit will come down to you . . . So your child will be the holy Son of God" (1.35). Jesus followed the Spirit (4.1,14,18; 10.21) and taught that the Spirit is God's greatest gift (11.13).

Luke shows how important prayer was to Jesus. Jesus prayed often: after being baptized (3.21), before choosing the disciples (6.12), before asking his disciples who they thought he was (9.18), and before giving up his life on the cross (23.34,46). From Luke we learn of three stories that Jesus told to teach about prayer (11.5–9; 18.1–8, 9–14).

An important part of Luke's story is the way in which he shows the concern of Jesus for the poor: the good news is preached to them (4.18; 7.22), they receive God's blessings (6.20), they are invited to the great feast (14.13,21), the poor man Lazarus is taken to heaven by angels (16.20,22), and Jesus commands his disciples to sell what they have and give the money to the poor (12.33).

To make sure that readers would understand that Jesus was raised physically from death, Luke reports that the risen Jesus ate a piece of fish (24.42,43). There could be no mistake about the risen Jesus: he was not a ghost. His being raised from death was real and not someone's imagination. Luke also wrote another book—the Acts of the Apostles—to show what happened to Jesus' followers after he was raised from death and taken up to heaven. No other Gospel has a second volume that continues the story.

Luke closes this first book that he wrote by telling that Jesus returned to heaven. But right before Jesus leaves, he tells his disciples:

The Scriptures say that the Messiah must suffer, then three days later he will rise from death. They also say that all people of every nation must be told in my name to turn to God, in order to be forgiven. So beginning in Jerusalem, you must tell everything that has happened. (24.46–48)

A QUICK LOOK AT THIS BOOK

1 Many people have tried to tell the story of what God has done among us. 2They wrote what we had been told by the ones who were there in the beginning and saw what happened. 3So I made a careful study*a* of everything and then decided to write and tell you exactly what took place. Honorable Theophilus, 4I have done this to let you know if what you have heard is true.

An Angel Tells about the Birth of John

5When Herod was king of Judea, there was a priest by the name of Zechariah from the priestly group of Abijah. His wife Elizabeth was from the family of Aaron.*b* 6Both of them were good people and pleased the Lord God by obeying all that he had commanded. 7But they did not have children. Elizabeth could not have any, and both Zechariah and Elizabeth were already old.

8One day Zechariah's group of priests were on duty, and he was serving God as a priest. 9According to the custom of the priests, he had been chosen to go into the Lord's temple that day and to burn incense,*c* 10while the people stood outside praying.

11All at once an angel from the Lord came and appeared to Zechariah at the right side of the altar. 12Zechariah was confused and afraid when he saw the angel. 13But the angel told him:

Don't be afraid, Zechariah! God has heard your prayers. Your wife Elizabeth will have a son, and you must name him John. 14His birth will make you very happy, and many people will be glad. 15Your son will be a great servant of the Lord. He must never drink wine or beer, and the power of the Holy Spirit will be with him from the time he is born.

Luke was a careful student
(3) Luke writes that he "made a careful study." He was different from other biblical writers because he was a Gentile, a non-Jew. He was also a medical doctor. Like a good doctor, Luke paid a lot of attention to details in his writings (this book and the Acts of the Apostles). Notice his detailed interest in the events surrounding the birth of Jesus.

What are angels?
(11) The word "angel" means messenger, and is usually a messenger from heaven. Angels were especially created by God, and they are not the same as humans. The angel who spoke to Zechariah was Gabriel, whose name means "God is great." Gabriel is a special messenger whom we see doing important tasks for God all through the Bible.

---

a a careful study: Or "a study from the beginning."
b Abijah . . . Aaron: The Jewish priests were divided into two groups, and one of these groups was named after Abijah. Each group served in the temple once a year for two weeks at a time. Aaron, the brother of Moses, was the first priest. *c burn incense:* This was done twice a day, once in the morning and again in the late afternoon.

16John will lead many people in Israel
to turn back to the Lord their God.
17He will go ahead of the Lord with the
same power and spirit that Elijah[d] had.
Because of John, parents will be more
thoughtful of their children. And people
who now disobey God will begin to
think as they ought to. That is how John
will get people ready for the Lord.

18Zechariah said to the angel, "How will
I know this is going to happen? My wife
and I are both very old."

19The angel answered, "I am Gabriel,
God's servant, and I was sent to tell you
this good news. 20You have not believed
what I have said. So you will not be able
to say a thing until all this happens. But
everything will take place when it is supposed to."

21The crowd was waiting for Zechariah
and kept wondering why he was staying
so long in the temple. 22When he did come
out, he could not speak, and they knew he
had seen a vision. He motioned to them with
his hands, but did not say a thing.

23When Zechariah's time of service in the
temple was over, he went home. 24Soon after that, his wife was expecting a baby, and
for five months she did not leave the house.
She said to herself, 25"What the Lord has
done for me will keep people from looking
down on me."[e]

An Angel Tells about the Birth of Jesus

26One month later God sent the angel Gabriel to the town of Nazareth in Galilee
27with a message for a virgin named Mary.
She was engaged to Joseph from the family
of King David. 28The angel greeted Mary
and said, "You are truly blessed! The Lord
is with you."

29Mary was confused by the angel's
words and wondered what they meant.

**Believing God's message
is our greatest need**
(20) Zechariah, the father
of John the Baptist, couldn't
believe the angel's mes-
sage. He was thinking about
his and his wife's lack of natural ability to have children.
Our most important need is
to believe God for all of life.
He is the God of nature, and
nature obeys his commands.

---

[d]Elijah: The prophet Elijah was known for his power
to work miracles. [e]keep people from looking down
on me: When a married woman could not have children,
it was thought that the Lord was punishing her.

30Then the angel told Mary, "Don't be afraid! God is pleased with you, 31and you will have a son. His name will be Jesus. 32He will be great and will be called the Son of God. The Lord God will make him king, as his ancestor David was. 33He will rule the people of Israel forever, and his kingdom will never end."

34Mary asked the angel, "How can this happen? I am not married!"

35The angel answered, "The Holy Spirit will come down to you, and God's power will come over you. So your child will be called the holy Son of God. 36Your relative Elizabeth is also going to have a son, even though she is old. No one thought she could ever have a baby, but in three months she will have a son. 37Nothing is impossible for God!"

38Mary said, "I am the Lord's servant! Let it happen as you have said." And the angel left her.

Mary Visits Elizabeth

39A short time later Mary hurried to a town in the hill country of Judea. 40She went into Zechariah's home, where she greeted Elizabeth. 41When Elizabeth heard Mary's greeting, her baby moved within her.

The Holy Spirit came upon Elizabeth. 42Then in a loud voice she said to Mary:

God has blessed you more than any other woman! He has also blessed the child you will have. 43Why should the mother of my Lord come to me? 44As soon as I heard your greeting, my baby became happy and moved within me. 45The Lord has blessed you because you believed that he will keep his promise.

Mary's Song of Praise

46Mary said:
47With all my heart
    I praise the Lord,
and I am glad
    because of God my Savior.

Why was Jesus born to a virgin?
(34) God might have chosen to let his Son be born in a natural way. But he didn't. Over and over again in the Bible we come across happenings that are not "natural"—they're *supernatural*. God wants us to understand that he is in charge of this world, and our being saved depends on his divine work, not on what we do for ourselves.

Can unborn babies be happy?
(41) The unborn John the Baptist was happy. The word translated "moved" also means "leaped." The unborn baby John was joyful in the presence of his unborn cousin Jesus. This passage shows us that unborn babies are people even when they are still inside their mothers.

Let's sing to God
(47) God's people have always been a singing people. We sing with joy, just as Mary sang, because God has saved us from our sins. If we have something to sing

⁴⁸He cares for me,
   his humble servant.
From now on,
all people will say
   God has blessed me.
⁴⁹God All-Powerful has done
   great things for me,
   and his name is holy.
⁵⁰He always shows mercy
  to everyone
   who worships him.
⁵¹The Lord has used
  his powerful arm
to scatter those
  who are proud.
⁵²He drags strong rulers
  from their thrones
and puts humble people
  in places of power.
⁵³He gives the hungry
  good things to eat,
and he sends the rich away
  with nothing in their hands.
⁵⁴He helps his servant Israel
  and is always merciful
   to his people.
⁵⁵He made this promise
  to our ancestors,
to Abraham and his family
  forever!

⁵⁶Mary stayed with Elizabeth about three months. Then she went back home.

The Birth of John the Baptist

⁵⁷When Elizabeth's son was born, ⁵⁸her neighbors and relatives heard how kind the Lord had been to her, and they too were glad.

⁵⁹Eight days later they did for the child what the Law of Moses commands.ᶠ They were going to name him Zechariah, after his father. ⁶⁰But Elizabeth said, "No! His name is John."

ᶠwhat the Law of Moses commands: This refers to circumcision. It is the cutting off of skin from the private part of Jewish boys eight days after birth to show that they belong to the Lord. See Word List: Circumcise.

about we will sing, and such singing will usually be happy. But sometimes our songs are rightly sad because our sins caused our Savior's suffering on the cross. We also sing because of our thanksgiving for what God has done for us.

"His name is John"

(60) The name John means "God has been kind." It would be John the Baptist's job to announce the coming of the Messiah. Even John's name announces God's kindness in sending his Son to save us from our sins.

⁶¹The people argued, "No one in your family has ever been named John." ⁶²So they motioned to Zechariah to find out what he wanted to name his son.

⁶³Zechariah asked for a writing tablet. Then he wrote, "His name is John." Everyone was amazed. ⁶⁴Right away Zechariah started speaking and praising God.

⁶⁵All the neighbors were frightened because of what had happened, and everywhere in the hill country people kept talking about these things. ⁶⁶Everyone who heard about this wondered what this child would grow up to be. They knew that the Lord was with him.

Zechariah Praises the Lord

⁶⁷The Holy Spirit came upon Zechariah, and he began to speak:
⁶⁸Praise the Lord,
      the God of Israel!
   He has come
      to save his people.
⁶⁹Our God has given us
      a mighty Savior[g]
   from the family
      of David his servant.
⁷⁰Long ago the Lord promised
   by the words
      of his holy prophets
⁷¹to save us from our enemies
   and from everyone
      who hates us.
⁷²God said he would be kind
   to our people and keep
      his sacred promise.
⁷³He told our ancestor Abraham
⁷⁴that he would rescue us
      from our enemies.
   Then we could serve him
      without fear,
⁷⁵by being holy and good
      as long as we live.

God's plan to save us is very old
(70) Zechariah praised God for his saving work. He said that God long ago planned to send a Savior and that John the Baptist would tell of the Savior's coming. It is important to realize that our being saved was not just a wonderful, unplanned happening in history. It has been God's great plan since ages past.

ᵍ*a mighty Savior*: The Greek text has "a horn of salvation." In the Scriptures animal horns are often a symbol of great strength.

76You, my son, will be called
a prophet of God
in heaven above.
You will go ahead of the Lord
to get everything ready
for him.
77You will tell his people
that they can be saved
when their sins
are forgiven.
78God's love and kindness
will shine upon us
like the sun that rises
in the sky.[h]
79On us who live
in the dark shadow
of death
this light will shine
to guide us
into a life of peace.

80As John grew up, God's Spirit gave him great power. John lived in the desert until the time he was sent to the people of Israel.

The Birth of Jesus
(Matthew 1.18–25)

2 About that time Emperor Augustus gave orders for the names of all the people to be listed in record books.[i] 2These first records were made when Quirinius was governor of Syria.[j]

3Everyone had to go to their own hometown to be listed. 4So Joseph had to leave Nazareth in Galilee and go to Bethlehem in Judea. Long ago Bethlehem had been King David's hometown, and Joseph went there because he was from David's family.

5Mary was engaged to Joseph and traveled with him to Bethlehem. She was soon going to have a baby, 6and while they were

Who was Emperor Augustus?
(1) Augustus was the ruler of the Roman empire, of which Palestine was a small part. He reigned for 45 years, from before the birth of Jesus until several years after. "Augustus" was a title meaning "sacred."

Joseph was from David's family
(4) Bethlehem was the town where David was born. Its name means "house of bread." This was an interesting name because Jesus called himself "the bread of life." The town of Bethlehem is still there today.

hlike the sun that rises in the sky: Or "like the Messiah coming from heaven." inames . . . listed in record books: This was done so that everyone could be made to pay taxes to the Emperor. jQuirinius was governor of Syria: It is known that Quirinius made a record of the people in A.D. 6 or 7. But the exact date of the record taking that Luke mentions is not known.

there, [7]she gave birth to her first-born[k] son.
She dressed him in baby clothes[l] and laid
him in a feed box, because there was no
room for them in the inn.

The Shepherds

[8]That night in the fields near Bethlehem
some shepherds were guarding their sheep.
[9]All at once an angel came down to them
from the Lord, and the brightness of the
Lord's glory flashed around them. The shepherds were frightened. [10]But the angel said,
"Don't be afraid! I have good news for you,
which will make everyone happy. [11]This
very day in King David's hometown a
Savior was born for you. He is Christ the
Lord. [12]You will know who he is, because
you will find him dressed in baby clothes
and lying in a feed box."

[13]Suddenly many other angels came
down from heaven and joined in praising
God. They said:
    [14]"Praise God in heaven!
    Peace on earth to everyone
      who pleases God."

[15]After the angels had left and gone back
to heaven, the shepherds said to each other,
"Let's go to Bethlehem and see what the
Lord has told us about." [16]They hurried off
and found Mary and Joseph, and they saw
the baby lying in the feed box.

[17]When the shepherds saw Jesus, they
told his parents what the angel had said
about him. [18]Everyone listened and was surprised. [19]But Mary kept thinking about all
this and wondering what it meant.

[20]As the shepherds returned to their
sheep, they were praising God and saying
wonderful things about him. Everything
they had seen and heard was just as the
angel had said.

[21]Eight days later Jesus' parents did for

Why the shepherds?
(9) Wouldn't the Messiah's
birth be announced first to
the emperor at Rome, or at
least to the high priest of the
temple in Jerusalem? No—
the humble shepherds were
told first. It makes us wonder
about what people think is
important—and what God
thinks.

[k]*first-born*: The Jewish people said that the first-born
son in each of their families belonged to the Lord.
[l]*dressed him in baby clothes*: The Greek text has
"wrapped him in wide strips of cloth," which was how
young babies were dressed.

him what the Law of Moses commands.^m
And they named him Jesus, just as the angel
had told Mary when he promised she would
have a baby.

Simeon Praises the Lord

22The time came for Mary and Joseph
to do what the Law of Moses says a mother
is supposed to do after her baby is born.^n
They took Jesus to the temple in Jerusalem and presented him to the Lord, 23just
as the Law of the Lord says, "Each first-
born^o baby boy belongs to the Lord."
24The Law of the Lord also says that parents
have to offer a sacrifice, giving at least a
pair of doves or two young pigeons. So that
is what Mary and Joseph did.

25At this time a man named Simeon was
living in Jerusalem. Simeon was a good
man. He loved God and was waiting for
God to save the people of Israel. God's Spirit
came to him 26and told him that he would
not die until he had seen Christ the Lord.

27When Mary and Joseph brought Jesus
to the temple to do what the Law of Moses
says should be done for a new baby, the
Spirit told Simeon to go into the temple.
28Simeon took the baby Jesus in his arms
and praised God,

29"Lord, I am your servant,
    and now I can die in peace,
  because you have kept
    your promise to me.
30With my own eyes I have seen
  what you have done
    to save your people,
31and foreign nations
    will also see this.
32Your mighty power is a light
    for all nations,

Simeon saw his Lord
(25) Once again God
picked an ordinary man.
Simeon recognized the
baby Jesus as the Savior
who he knew was to come.
Simeon said that God had
kept his promise, and that
Jews and non-Jews would
be blessed by the Messiah's
coming. Even Mary and
Joseph were surprised by
Simeon's words.

---

^mwhat the Law of Moses commands: See note at 1.59.
^nafter her baby is born: After a Jewish mother gave
birth to a son, she was considered "unclean" and had
to stay home until he was circumcised (see the note
at 1.59). Then she had to stay home for another 33
days, before offering a sacrifice to the Lord.   ^ofirst-
born: See the note at 2.7.

and it will bring honor
to your people Israel."

33Jesus' parents were surprised at what
Simeon had said. 34Then he blessed them
and told Mary, "This child of yours will
cause many people in Israel to fall and others to stand. The child will be like a warning
sign. Many people will reject him, 35and you,
Mary, will suffer as though you had been
stabbed by a dagger. But all this will show
what people are really thinking."

Anna Speaks about the Child Jesus

36The prophet Anna was also there in
the temple. She was the daughter of Phanuel
from the tribe of Asher, and she was very
old. In her youth she had been married for
seven years, but her husband died. 37And
now she was eighty-four years old.p Night
and day she served God in the temple by
praying and often going without eating.q

38At that time Anna came in and praised
God. She spoke about the child Jesus to
everyone who hoped for Jerusalem to be
set free.

Anna told the people about Jesus

(36) Anna was a prophet-
ess, someone who told others the word of God. She
did what we should always
be seeking to do—telling
others about Jesus. All true
believers in Jesus are
prophets in this way.

The Return to Nazareth

39After Joseph and Mary had done everything that the Law of the Lord commands,
they returned home to Nazareth in Galilee.
40The child Jesus grew. He became strong
and wise, and God blessed him.

The Boy Jesus in the Temple

41Every year Jesus' parents went to Jerusalem for Passover. 42And when Jesus was
twelve years old, they all went there as usual
for the celebration. 43After Passover his parents left, but they did not know that Jesus
had stayed on in the city. 44They thought
he was traveling with some other people,

Jesus grew up like other children

(40) During his life on earth,
Jesus was God in human
form. But being truly human,
he had to grow up in the
same way we all do. So
Jesus had the experience of
growing and learning. But
his unusual ability to grow
in wisdom surprised everyone. He understood a lot
more about the things of
God than any twelve-year-
old they had ever met.

pAnd now she was eighty-four years old: Or "And now
she had been a widow for eighty-four years." qwithout
eating: The Jewish people sometimes went without eating (also called "fasting") to show their love for God
and to become better followers.

and they went a whole day before they started looking for him. ⁴⁵When they could not find him with their relatives and friends, they went back to Jerusalem and started looking for him there.

⁴⁶Three days later they found Jesus sitting in the temple, listening to the teachers and asking them questions. ⁴⁷Everyone who heard him was surprised at how much he knew and at the questions he asked.

⁴⁸When his parents found him, they were amazed. His mother said, "Son, why have you done this to us? Your father and I have been very worried, and we have been searching for you!"

⁴⁹Jesus answered, "Why did you have to look for me? Didn't you know that I would be in my Father's house?"ʳ ⁵⁰But they did not understand what he meant.

⁵¹Jesus went back to Nazareth with his parents and obeyed them. His mother kept on thinking about all that had happened.

⁵²Jesus became wise, and he grew strong. God was pleased with him and so were the people.

The Preaching of John the Baptist
(Matthew 3.1–12; Mark 1.1–8; John 1.19–28)

3 For fifteen yearsˢ Emperor Tiberius had ruled that part of the world. Pontius Pilate was governor of Judea, and Herodᵗ was the ruler of Galilee. Herod's brother, Philip, was the ruler in the countries of Iturea and Trachonitis, and Lysanias was the ruler of Abilene. ²Annas and Caiaphas were the Jewish high priests.ᵘ

At that time God spoke to Zechariah's son John, who was living in the desert. ³So John went along the Jordan Valley, telling the people, "Turn back to God and be baptized! Then your sins will be forgiven."

Who ruled the Roman world in Jesus' day?
(1) Tiberius, the adopted son of Augustus, was emperor of Rome at the time of Jesus' ministry and death. He reigned during the years 14 through 37. The Herod brothers ruled in Palestine with the permission of Tiberius. Strange to say, the Herods were not even Jews, but Idumeans. The Idumeans were longtime enemies of the Jews. The high priests, not kings, had been the true rulers of the Jews for over five hundred years before the time of Christ.

ʳin my Father's house: Or "doing my Father's work." ˢFor fifteen years: This was either A.D. 28 or 29, and Jesus was about thirty years old (see 3.23). ᵗHerod: Herod Antipas, the son of Herod the Great. ᵘAnnas and Caiaphas . . . high priests: Annas was high priest from A.D. 6 until 15. His son-in-law Caiaphas was high priest from A.D. 18 until 37.

4Isaiah the prophet wrote about John when he said,

> "In the desert
>   someone is shouting,
> 'Get the road ready
>   for the Lord!
> Make a straight path
>   for him.
> 5Fill up every valley
>   and level every mountain
>   and hill.
> Straighten the crooked paths
>   and smooth out
>   the rough roads.
> 6Then everyone will see
>   the saving power of God.' "

7Crowds of people came out to be baptized, but John said to them, "You bunch of snakes! Who warned you to run from the coming judgment? 8Do something to show that you really have given up your sins. Don't start saying that you belong to Abraham's family. God can turn these stones into children for Abraham.ᵛ 9An ax is ready to cut the trees down at their roots. Any tree that does not produce good fruit will be cut down and thrown into a fire."

10The crowds asked John, "What should we do?"

11John told them, "If you have two coats, give one to someone who doesn't have any. If you have food, share it with someone else."

12When tax collectorsʷ came to be baptized, they asked John, "Teacher, what should we do?"

13John told them, "Don't make people pay more than they owe."

14Some soldiers asked him, "And what about us? What do we have to do?"

John told them, "Don't force people to

ᵛchildren for Abraham: The Jewish people thought they were God's chosen people because of God's promises to their ancestor Abraham. ʷtax collectors: These were usually Jewish people who paid the Romans for the right to collect taxes. They were hated by other Jews who thought of them as traitors to their country and to their religion.

pay money to make you leave them alone. Be satisfied with your pay."

15Everyone became excited and wondered, "Could John be the Messiah?"

16John said, "I am just baptizing with water. But someone more powerful is going to come, and I am not good enough even to untie his sandals.x He will baptize you with the Holy Spirit and with fire. 17His threshing forky is in his hand, and he is ready to separate the wheat from the husks. He will store the wheat in his barn and burn the husks with a fire that never goes out."

18In many different ways John preached the good news to the people. 19But to Herod the ruler, he said, "It was wrong for you to take Herodias, your brother's wife." John also said that Herod had done many other bad things. 20Finally, Herod put John in jail, and this was the worst thing he had done.

The Baptism of Jesus
(Matthew 3.13–17; Mark 1.9–11)

21After everyone else had been baptized, Jesus himself was baptized. Then as he prayed, the sky opened up, 22and the Holy Spirit came down upon him in the form of a dove. A voice from heaven said, "You are my own dear Son, and I am pleased with you."

The Ancestors of Jesus
(Matthew 1.1–17)

23When Jesus began to preach, he was about thirty years old. Everyone thought he was the son of Joseph. But his family went back through Heli, 24Matthat, Levi, Melchi, Jannai, Joseph, 25Mattathias, Amos, Nahum, Esli, Naggai, 26Maath, Mattathias, Semein, Josech, Joda;

27Joanan, Rhesa, Zerubbabel, Shealtiel,

John baptized with water
(16) John was telling the people that being baptized with water was not the main thing. John was showing by water baptism that baptism by the Spirit of God is the important thing. Water baptism is only a sign of baptism by the Spirit.

John wasn't always nice
(19) Sometimes it's hard to tell people the truth they need to hear. When we do, we can get into trouble. Some think we should never say things that make people angry or upset. Do you think John should have told Herod he was wrong to marry his brother's wife?

Two lists of ancestors
(23) This list is quite different from the one in Matthew's Gospel. A lot of scholars think the reason is that this list traces the ancestors of Jesus through his mother Mary. Notice that it doesn't actually call Heli the father of Joseph.

---

xuntie his sandals: This was the duty of a slave.
ythreshing fork: After Jewish farmers had trampled out the grain, they used a large fork to pitch the grain and the husks into the air. Wind would blow away the light husks, and the grain would fall back to the ground, where it could be gathered up.

Neri, 28Melchi, Addi, Cosam, Elmadam, Er,
29Joshua, Eliezer, Jorim, Matthat, Levi;

30Simeon, Judah, Joseph, Jonam, Eli-
akim, 31Melea, Menna, Mattatha, Nathan,
David, 32Jesse, Obed, Boaz, Salmon,
Nahshon;

33Amminadab, Admin, Arni, Hezron,
Perez, Judah, 34Jacob, Isaac, Abraham,
Terah, Nahor, 35Serug, Reu, Peleg, Eber,
Shelah;

36Cainan, Arphaxad, Shem, Noah, La-
mech, 37Methuselah, Enoch, Jared, Mahala-
leel, Kenan, 38Enosh, and Seth.

The family of Jesus went all the way back
to Adam and then to God.

Jesus and the Devil
(Matthew 4.1–11; Mark 1.12, 13)

4 When Jesus returned from the Jordan
River, the power of the Holy Spirit was
with him, and the Spirit led him into the
desert. 2For forty days Jesus was tested by
the devil, and during that time he went without eating.z When it was all over, he was
hungry.

3The devil said to Jesus, "If you are God's
Son, tell this stone to turn into bread."

4Jesus answered, "The Scriptures say,
'No one can live only on food.' "

5Then the devil led Jesus up to a high
place and quickly showed him all the nations on earth. 6The devil said, "I will give
all this power and glory to you. It has been
given to me, and I can give it to anyone I
want to. 7Just worship me, and you can have
it all."

8Jesus answered, "The Scriptures say:
'Worship the Lord your God
and serve only him!' "

9Finally, the devil took Jesus to Jerusalem and had him stand on top of the temple.
The devil said, "If you are God's Son, jump
off. 10-11The Scriptures say:
'God will tell his angels
to take care of you.

What is the devil's work?
(2) The devil's personal
name is Satan. "Devil"
means accuser or deceiver,
and "Satan" means enemy.
From his names we can see
that the devil's work is to deceive and attack. He began
by attacking God's authority, and he tries to deceive
people with clever lies. His
effort to deceive Jesus
failed. All lies have their beginning with Satan, whom
Jesus called "the father of
lies."

zwent without eating: See the note at 2.37.

They will catch you
in their arms,
and you will not hurt
your feet on the stones.' "
12Jesus answered, "The Scriptures also
say, 'Don't try to test the Lord your God!' "
13After the devil had finished testing
Jesus in every way possible, he left him for
a while.

Jesus Begins His Work
(Matthew 4.12–17; Mark 1.14, 15)

14Jesus returned to Galilee with the
power of the Spirit. News about him spread
everywhere. 15He taught in the Jewish meeting places, and everyone praised him.

The People of Nazareth Turn against Jesus
(Matthew 13.53–58; Mark 6.1–6)

16Jesus went back to Nazareth, where he
had been brought up, and as usual he went
to the meeting place on the Sabbath. When
he stood up to read from the Scriptures,
17he was given the book of Isaiah the
prophet. He opened it and read,
18"The Lord's Spirit
has come to me,
because he has chosen me
to tell the good news
to the poor.
The Lord has sent me
to announce freedom
for prisoners,
to give sight to the blind,
to free everyone
who suffers,
19and to say, 'This is the year
the Lord has chosen.' "
20Jesus closed the book, then handed it
back to the man in charge and sat down.
Everyone in the meeting place looked
straight at Jesus.
21Then Jesus said to them, "What you
have just heard me read has come true
today."
22All the people started talking about
Jesus and were amazed at the wonderful

*Jesus went to the meeting
place*
(16) The temple was in Jerusalem, many miles away
from places like Nazareth.
So the people met in their
little halls for worship. Be
careful to notice that Jesus
was not against this custom
of the people. He was Lord
of the Jewish meeting
places, too, and he attended
them on the Sabbath day
along with everyone else.

things he said. They kept on asking, "Isn't he Joseph's son?"

23Jesus answered:

You will certainly want to tell me this saying, "Doctor, first make yourself well." You will tell me to do the same things here in my own hometown that you heard I did in Capernaum. 24But you can be sure that no prophets are liked by the people of their own hometown.

25Once during the time of Elijah there was no rain for three and a half years, and people everywhere were starving. There were many widows in Israel, 26but Elijah was sent only to a widow in the town of Zarephath near the city of Sidon. 27During the time of the prophet Elisha, many men in Israel had leprosy.*a* But no one was healed, except Naaman who lived in Syria.

28When the people in the meeting place heard Jesus say this, they became so angry 29that they got up and threw him out of town. They dragged him to the edge of the cliff on which the town was built, because they wanted to throw him down from there. 30But Jesus slipped through the crowd and got away.

Jesus told the truth
(25) The people in Nazareth were slow to believe that this young man who had grown up among them was the one who would make Isaiah's prophecies come true. But Jesus told them that people outside of Israel would be blessed by having faith in him. The people were so angry they wanted to throw him off a cliff. It wasn't what they wanted to hear, but Jesus told them the truth.

A Man with an Evil Spirit
(Mark 1.21–28)

31Jesus went to the city of Capernaum in Galilee and taught the people on the Sabbath. 32His teaching amazed them because he spoke with power. 33There in the Jewish meeting place was a man with an evil spirit. He yelled out, 34"Hey, Jesus of Nazareth, what do you want with us? Are you here to get rid of us? I know who you are! You are God's Holy One."

35Jesus ordered the evil spirit to be quiet and come out. The demon threw the man to the ground in front of everyone and left without harming him.

There was power in Jesus
(32) Jesus spoke with power, and he had power over evil spirits. He was an amazing teacher. Usually, Jewish religious teachers would depend on the opinions of experts, who depended on experts before them. Jesus, the Son of God, got his power to teach and to heal directly from God.

*a*leprosy: In biblical times the word "leprosy" was used for many different kinds of skin diseases.

36They all were amazed and kept saying to each other, "What kind of teaching is this? He has power to order evil spirits out of people!" 37News about Jesus spread all over that part of the country.

Jesus Heals Many People
(Matthew 8.14–17; Mark 1.29–34)

38Jesus left the meeting place and went to Simon's home. When Jesus got there, he was told that Simon's mother-in-law was sick with a high fever. 39So Jesus went over to her and ordered the fever to go away. Right then she was able to get up and serve them.

40After the sun had set, people with all kinds of diseases were brought to Jesus. He put his hands on each one of them and healed them. 41Demons went out of many people and shouted, "You are the Son of God!" But Jesus ordered the demons not to speak because they knew he was the Messiah.

42The next morning Jesus went out to a place where he could be alone, and crowds came looking for him. When they found him, they tried to stop him from leaving. 43But Jesus said, "People in other towns must hear the good news about God's kingdom. That's why I was sent." 44So he kept on preaching in the Jewish meeting places in Judea.*b*

Jesus Chooses His First Disciples
(Matthew 4.18–22; Mark 1.16–20)

5 Jesus was standing on the shore of Lake Gennesaret, teaching the people as they crowded around him to hear God's message. 2Near the shore he saw two boats left there by some fishermen who had gone to wash their nets. 3Jesus got into the boat that belonged to Simon and asked him to row it out a little way from the shore. Then

Jesus loved his enemies
(40) Jesus went around healing the very people who would turn against him at last. He knew they would hate him, but he loved them and cared for their needs anyway. As we think about this, we should be glad to receive Jesus as our own Lord. The Son of God was kind to us when we didn't deserve it. He loved us before we loved him.

Jesus shared the good news
(43) As we read about his life and work, we realize that Jesus was a man of action. He seems to be always on the move. He intended for everyone to hear the good news about the kingdom of God. So Jesus became our example in this way. He not only did kind things, but he shared the truth about his kingdom with everyone he met.

bJudea: Some manuscripts have "Galilee."

Jesus sat down[c] in the boat to teach the crowd.

4When Jesus had finished speaking, he told Simon, "Row the boat out into the deep water and let your nets down to catch some fish."

5"Master," Simon answered, "we have worked hard all night long and have not caught a thing. But if you tell me to, I will let the nets down." 6They did it and caught so many fish that their nets began ripping apart. 7Then they signaled for their partners in the other boat to come and help them. The men came, and together they filled the two boats so full that they both began to sink.

8When Simon Peter saw this happen, he kneeled down in front of Jesus and said, "Lord, don't come near me! I am a sinner." 9Peter and everyone with him were completely surprised at all the fish they had caught. 10His partners James and John, the sons of Zebedee, were surprised too.

Jesus told Simon, "Don't be afraid! From now on you will bring in people instead of fish." 11The men pulled their boats up on the shore. Then they left everything and went with Jesus.

Jesus Heals a Man
(Matthew 8.1–4; Mark 1.40–45)

12Jesus came to a town where there was a man who had leprosy.[d] When the man saw Jesus, he kneeled down to the ground in front of Jesus and begged, "Lord, you have the power to make me well, if only you wanted to."

13Jesus put his hand on him and said, "I do want to! Now you are well." At once the man's leprosy disappeared. 14Jesus told him, "Don't tell anyone about this, but go and show yourself to the priest. Then take a gift to the temple, just as Moses com-

Obedience brings success
(5) Simon could have laughed at Jesus' idea to let the fishing nets down once again. But Simon did as Jesus commanded him, and the nets were overloaded with fish. Too often we follow our own ideas and end up disappointed. But listening to Jesus will result in greater success than we dreamed.

Does Jesus want to help us?
(12) The man with leprosy may have been unsure of Jesus. He believed Jesus could heal him, but he had to learn that Jesus really wanted to heal him. How happy is the day when we find out that Jesus really wants the very best for us, and he will give what is best when we ask him.

[c]sat down: Teachers in the ancient world, including Jewish teachers, usually sat down when they taught.
[d]leprosy: See the note at 4.27.

manded, and everyone will know that you have been healed."[e]

15News about Jesus kept spreading. Large crowds came to listen to him teach and to be healed of their diseases. 16But Jesus would often go to some place where he could be alone and pray.

Jesus Heals a Crippled Man
(Matthew 9.1–8; Mark 2.1–12)

17One day some Pharisees and experts in the Law of Moses sat listening to Jesus teach. They had come from every village in Galilee and Judea and from Jerusalem. God had given Jesus the power to heal the sick, 18and some people came carrying a crippled man on a mat. They tried to take him inside the house and put him in front of Jesus. 19But because of the crowd, they could not get him to Jesus. So they went up on the roof,[f] where they removed some tiles and let the mat down in the middle of the room.

20When Jesus saw how much faith they had, he said to the crippled man, "My friend, your sins are forgiven."

21The Pharisees and the experts began arguing, "Jesus must think he is God! Only God can forgive sins."

22Jesus knew what they were thinking, and he said, "Why are you thinking that? 23Is it easier for me to tell this crippled man that his sins are forgiven or to tell him to get up and walk? 24But now you will see that the Son of Man has the right to forgive sins here on earth." Jesus then said to the man, "Get up! Pick up your mat and walk home."

How does faith work?
(20) Jesus knew that the people who brought the crippled man had faith. How did he know that? They were *determined* to come to him. They even went up on the roof and tore it open so they could let their crippled friend down at Jesus' feet. Real faith will not be discouraged.

[e]*everyone will know that you have been healed*: People with leprosy had to be examined by a priest and told that they were well (that is "clean") before they could once again live a normal life in the Jewish community. The gift that Moses commanded was the sacrifice of some lambs together with flour mixed with olive oil.
[f]*roof*: In Palestine the houses usually had a flat roof. Stairs on the outside led up to the roof, which was made of beams and boards covered with packed earth. Luke says that the roof was made of (clay) tiles, which were also used for making roofs in New Testament times.

25At once the man stood up in front of everyone. He picked up his mat and went home, giving thanks to God. 26Everyone was amazed and praised God. What they saw surprised them, and they said, "We have seen a great miracle today!"

Jesus Chooses Levi
(Matthew 9.9–13; Mark 2.13–17)

27Later, Jesus went out and saw a tax collectorg named Levi sitting at the place for paying taxes. Jesus said to him, "Come with me." 28Levi left everything and went with Jesus.

29In his home Levi gave a big dinner for Jesus. Many tax collectors and other guests were also there.

30The Pharisees and some of their teachers of the Law of Moses grumbled to Jesus' disciples, "Why do you eat and drink with those tax collectors and other sinners?"

31Jesus answered, "Healthy people don't need a doctor, but sick people do. 32I didn't come to invite good people to turn to God. I came to invite sinners."

People Ask about Going without Eating
(Matthew 9.14–17; Mark 2.18–22)

33Some people said to Jesus, "John's followers often pray and go without eating,h and so do the followers of the Pharisees. But your disciples never go without eating or drinking."

34Jesus told them, "The friends of a bridegroom don't go without eating while he is still with them. 35But the time will come when he will be taken from them. Then they will go without eating."

36Jesus then told them these sayings:

No one uses a new piece of cloth to patch old clothes. The patch would shrink and make the hole even bigger.

37No one pours new wine into old wineskins. The new wine would swell

Who are the sinners?
(30) Jesus says he came to invite sinners to turn to God. Does that mean some of us aren't sinners and don't need God? Not at all. Jesus was saying that people who *confess* their sins are welcome. People who think they're already good enough cannot come into God's kingdom.

Old and new don't mix well
(36) Some people try to "tack Jesus on," thinking that faith can be mixed with unbelieving ways. But you can't build a Christian life on old habits any more than you can put new wine in old wineskins without bursting them, or put a new patch on old cloth without tearing it. We begin life all over again when we become followers of Jesus.

gtax collector: See the note at 3.12.   hwithout eating: See the note at 2.37.

and burst the old skins.[i] Then the wine would be lost, and the skins would be ruined. 38New wine must be put only into new wineskins.

39No one wants new wine after drinking old wine. They say, "The old wine is better."

A Question about the Sabbath
(Matthew 12.1–8; Mark 2.23–28)

6 One Sabbath when Jesus and his disciples were walking through some wheat fields,[j] the disciples picked some wheat. They rubbed the husks off with their hands and started eating the grain.

2Some Pharisees said, "Why are you picking grain on the Sabbath? You're not supposed to do that!"

3Jesus answered, "You surely have read what David did when he and his followers were hungry. 4He went into the house of God and took the sacred loaves of bread that only priests were supposed to eat. He not only ate some himself, but even gave some to his followers."

5Jesus finished by saying, "The Son of Man is Lord over the Sabbath."

A Man with a Crippled Hand
(Matthew 12.9–14; Mark 3.1–6)

6On another Sabbath[k] Jesus was teaching in a Jewish meeting place, and a man with a crippled right hand was there. 7Some Pharisees and teachers of the Law of Moses kept watching Jesus to see if he would heal the man. They did this because they wanted to accuse Jesus of doing something wrong.

8Jesus knew what they were thinking.

The Sabbath was a day for doing good
(5) A lot of what Jesus wanted the Jews to know about the Sabbath (Saturday) can be applied to the Lord's day (Sunday) for Christians. It's a special day on which most of us have the privilege of serving God in greater ways than we can on other days. There are people in need everywhere. Many have not known the love and mercy of Jesus. We can take his love to them on the Lord's day.

[i]swell and burst the old skins: While the juice from grapes was becoming wine, it would swell and stretch the skins in which it had been stored. If the skins were old and stiff, they would burst.   [j]walking through some wheat fields: It was the custom to let hungry travelers pick grains of wheat.   [k]On another Sabbath: Some manuscripts have a reading which may mean "the Sabbath after the next."

So he told the man to stand up where everyone could see him. And the man stood up. 9Then Jesus asked the people, "On the Sabbath should we do good deeds or evil deeds? Should we save someone's life or destroy it?"

10After he had looked around at everyone, he told the man, "Stretch out your hand." He did, and his bad hand became completely well.

11The teachers and the Pharisees were furious and started saying to each other, "What can we do about Jesus?"

Jesus Chooses His Twelve Apostles
(Matthew 10.1–4; Mark 3.13–19)

12About that time Jesus went off to a mountain to pray, and he spent the whole night there. 13The next morning he called his disciples together and chose twelve of them to be his apostles. 14One was Simon, and Jesus named him Peter. Another was Andrew, Peter's brother. There were also James, John, Philip, Bartholomew, 15Matthew, Thomas, and James the son of Alphaeus. The rest of the apostles were Simon, known as the Eager One,*l* 16Jude, who was the son of James, and Judas Iscariot,*m* who later betrayed Jesus.

Jesus Teaches, Preaches, and Heals
(Matthew 4.23–25)

17Jesus and his apostles went down from the mountain and came to some flat, level ground. Many other disciples were there to meet him. Large crowds of people from all over Judea, Jerusalem, and the coastal cities of Tyre and Sidon were there too. 18These people had come to listen to Jesus and to be healed of their diseases. All who were troubled by evil spirits were also healed.

*l*known as the Eager One: The word "eager" translates the Greek word "zealot," which was a name later given to the members of a Jewish group that resisted and fought against the Romans. *m*Iscariot: This may mean "a man from Kerioth" (a place in Judea). But more probably it means "a man who was a liar" or "a man who was a betrayer."

What kind of disciple are you?
(13) Jesus called twelve close disciples (apostles) and most of them remained faithful until the day of their death. But one—Judas— was unfaithful. The Bible shows us that we don't live in a perfect world. Even among those who are called Christians there are those who are not true to Jesus, who betray him by their actions and thoughts. This is a warning to each of us, to be honest with God every day.

How could Jesus heal people?
(18) Jesus was not a magician. We cannot "learn the art" of healing people in the way Jesus did. Jesus is the Lord from heaven, and he has God's power over nature. He used this power to do good to people and to reveal his heavenly Father's glory.

19Everyone was trying to touch Jesus, because power was going out from him and healing them all.

Blessings and Troubles
(Matthew 5.1–12)

20Jesus looked at his disciples and said:
    God will bless you people
        who are poor.
        His kingdom belongs to you!
    21God will bless
        you hungry people.
    You will have plenty
        to eat!
    God will bless you people
        who are crying.
        You will laugh!
22God will bless you when others hate you and won't have anything to do with you. God will bless you when people insult you and say cruel things about you, all because you are a follower of the Son of Man! 23Long ago your own people did these same things to the prophets. So when this happens to you, be happy and jump for joy! You will have a great reward in heaven.
    24But you rich people
        are in for trouble.
    You have already had
        an easy life!
    25You well-fed people
    are in for trouble.
        You will go hungry!
    You people
    who are laughing now
        are in for trouble.
    You are going to cry
        and weep!
26You are in for trouble when everyone says good things about you. That is what your own people said about those prophets who told lies.

Love for Enemies
(Matthew 5.38–48; 7.12a)

27This is what I say to all who will listen to me:

Jesus made great promises

(20) God's kingdom will belong to poor people. Hungry people will be fed. Sad people will be happy. Jesus was not promising things the people would have *right now*. For instance, in Matthew 5, verse 6, Jesus speaks about being hungry for *righteousness*. When we desire the *right things*, God will finally supply all of our other needs too.

Whom should you love?

(27) Everybody loves his or her friends. But Jesus tells us to love our enemies too. How is that possible? First, it doesn't mean we approve

Love your enemies, and be good to everyone who hates you. [28]Ask God to bless anyone who curses you, and pray for everyone who is cruel to you. [29]If someone slaps you on one cheek, don't stop that person from slapping you on the other cheek. If someone wants to take your coat, don't try to keep back your shirt. [30]Give to everyone who asks and don't ask people to return what they have taken from you. [31]Treat others just as you want to be treated.

[32]If you love only someone who loves you, will God praise you for that? Even sinners love people who love them. [33]If you are kind only to someone who is kind to you, will God be pleased with you for that? Even sinners are kind to people who are kind to them. [34]If you lend money only to someone you think will pay you back, will God be pleased with you for that? Even sinners lend to sinners because they think they will get it all back.

[35]But love your enemies and be good to them. Lend without expecting to be paid back.[n] Then you will get a great reward, and you will be the true children of God in heaven. He is good even to people who are unthankful and cruel. [36]Have pity on others, just as your Father has pity on you.

Judging Others
(Matthew 7.1–5)

[37]Jesus said:

Don't judge others, and God will not judge you. Don't be hard on others, and God will not be hard on you. Forgive others, and God will forgive you. [38]If you give to others, you will be given a full amount in return. It will be packed down, shaken together, and spilling over into your lap. The way you treat others is the way you will be treated.

[n]*without expecting to be paid back*: Some manuscripts have "without giving up on anyone."

of what our enemies may be doing. It does mean that we see all people as God's special creations. Because our enemies are created by God they are to be treated with respect and kindness whenever we have the chance to do so.

God doesn't ask us to be judges

(37) We can't know all about another person the way God does. So we have to be careful what we think about people. God "sees the heart." This means that God understands everything about all of us. What we see is only a small part of another person's life. We ought to be glad we aren't called to be judges. A judge has a terrible responsibility, and most of us don't do a very good job of judging.

39Jesus also used some sayings as he spoke to the people. He said:

Can one blind person lead another blind person? Won't they both fall into a ditch? **40**Are students better than their teacher? But when they are fully trained, they will be like their teacher.

41You can see the speck in your friend's eye. But you don't notice the log in your own eye. **42**How can you say, "My friend, let me take the speck out of your eye," when you don't see the log in your own eye? You showoffs! First, get the log out of your own eye. Then you can see how to take the speck out of your friend's eye.

A Tree and Its Fruit
(Matthew 7.17–20; 12.34b, 35)

43A good tree cannot produce bad fruit, and a bad tree cannot produce good fruit. **44**You can tell what a tree is like by the fruit it produces. You cannot pick figs or grapes from thorn bushes. **45**Good people do good things because of the good in their hearts. Bad people do bad things because of the evil in their hearts. Your words show what is in your hearts.

Let's inspect our fruit
(43) All believers should be "fruit inspectors." That is to say, we ought to inspect our own lives to make sure that the "fruit" we bear is good because it comes from the right kind of "tree."

Two Builders
(Matthew 7.24–27)

46Why do you keep on saying that I am your Lord, when you refuse to do what I say? **47**Anyone who comes and listens to me and obeys me **48**is like someone who dug down deep and built a house on solid rock. When the flood came and the river rushed against the house, it was built so well that it didn't even shake. **49**But anyone who hears what I say and doesn't obey me is like someone whose house was not built on solid rock. As soon as the river rushed against that house, it was smashed to pieces!

Build on solid rock
(46) No one with any sense would build a house on a swamp. And sand is no better—even though it might seem solid enough before the rain comes. But as you look around your world, where do you find a true foundation to build your life on? Ideas come and go, and they turn out to be poor foundations for many unhappy people. Jesus is like a rock that can never fail us. He's the one to build on.

Jesus Heals an Army Officer's Servant
(Matthew 8.5–13; John 4.43–54)

7 After Jesus had finished teaching the people, he went to Capernaum. 2In that town an army officer's servant was sick and about to die. The officer liked this servant very much. 3And when he heard about Jesus, he sent some Jewish leaders to ask him to come and heal the servant.

4The leaders went to Jesus and begged him to do something. They said, "This man deserves your help! 5He loves our nation and even built us a meeting place." 6So Jesus went with them.

When Jesus was not far from the house, the officer sent some friends to tell him, "Lord, don't go to any trouble for me! I am not good enough for you to come into my house. 7And I am certainly not worthy to come to you. Just say the word, and my servant will get well. 8I have officers who give orders to me, and I have soldiers who take orders from me. I can say to one of them, 'Go!' and he goes. I can say to another, 'Come!' and he comes. I can say to my servant, 'Do this!' and he will do it."

9When Jesus heard this, he was so surprised that he turned and said to the crowd following him, "In all of Israel I've never found anyone with this much faith!"

10The officer's friends returned and found the servant well.

Know where you stand with Jesus
(8) The army officer in this passage knew where he stood with Jesus. The officer understood the meaning of authority because he lived by giving and taking orders. He recognized Jesus as his great "commanding officer"—the one who could give an order and it would be done. Jesus honored that man's faith. Do we have faith like this, or do we doubt Jesus' authority?

A Widow's Son

11Soon Jesus and his disciples were on their way to the town of Nain, and a big crowd was going along with them. 12As they came near the gate of the town, they saw people carrying out the body of a widow's only son. Many people from the town were walking along with her.

13When the Lord saw the woman, he felt sorry for her and said, "Don't cry!"

14Jesus went over and touched the stretcher on which the people were carrying the dead boy. They stopped, and Jesus said, "Young man, get up!" 15The man sat up and began to speak. Jesus then gave him back to his mother.

16Everyone was frightened and praised God. They said, "A great prophet is here with us! God has come to his people."

17News about Jesus spread all over Judea and everywhere else in that part of the country.

John the Baptist
(Matthew 11.1–19)

18-19John's followers told John everything that was being said about Jesus. So he sent two of them to ask the Lord, "Are you the one we should be looking for? Or must we wait for someone else?"

20When these messengers came to Jesus, they said, "John the Baptist sent us to ask, 'Are you the one we should be looking for? Or are we supposed to wait for someone else?'"

21At that time Jesus was healing many people who were sick or in pain or were troubled by evil spirits, and he was giving sight to a lot of blind people. 22Jesus said to the messengers sent by John, "Go and tell John what you have seen and heard. Blind people are now able to see, and the lame can walk. People who have leprosyo are being healed, and the deaf can now hear. The dead are raised to life, and the poor are hearing the good news. 23God will bless everyone who does not reject me because of what I do."

24After John's messengers had gone, Jesus began speaking to the crowds about John:

What kind of person did you go out to the desert to see? Was he like tall grass blown about by the wind? 25What kind of man did you really go out to see? Was he someone dressed in fine clothes? People who wear expensive clothes and live in luxury are in the king's palace. 26What then did you go out to see? Was he a prophet? He cer-

Who can raise the dead?
(16) The crowd that saw the widow's son raised to life by a simple command said that Jesus was a prophet. That was true as far as it went. But Jesus was much more than a prophet. He is the Lord of life and death. When we realize this, we also trust him with our own lives—and our own death.

Who was John the Baptist?
(24) We know from what we have read so far that he was the son of Zechariah and Elizabeth, and that he was the man who baptized Jesus. But he was also the living link between the Old Testament and the New Testament. He was a faithful Old Testament kind of prophet. But there were things about God's plan that John did not yet understand. There were things that Jesus came to reveal about God's kingdom that John did not know.

---

oleprosy: See the note at 4.27.

tainly was! I tell you that he was more
than a prophet. 27In the Scriptures, God
calls John his messenger and says, "I
am sending my messenger ahead of you
to get things ready for you." 28No one
ever born on this earth is greater than
John. But whoever is least important
in God's kingdom is greater than John.
29Everyone had been listening to John.
Even the tax collectors[p] had obeyed God
and had done what was right by letting John
baptize them. 30But the Pharisees and the
experts in the Law of Moses refused to obey
God and be baptized by John.
31Jesus went on to say:
What are you people like? What kind
of people are you? 32You are like children sitting in the market and shouting
to each other,

"We played the flute,
but you would not dance!
We sang a funeral song,
but you would not cry!"

33John the Baptist did not go around
eating and drinking, and you said,
"John has a demon in him!" 34But because the Son of Man goes around eating and drinking, you say, "Jesus eats
and drinks too much! He is even a friend
of tax collectors and sinners." 35Yet
Wisdom is shown to be right by what
its followers do.

Let's not be too hard to please

(31) Elsewhere we read that Jesus said believers should come to him like children. Here's a way *not* to be like children. Sometimes a child is hard to satisfy, like the people who criticized John the Baptist and Jesus for opposite things. We ought to be *childlike,* but not *childish.*

Simon the Pharisee

36A Pharisee invited Jesus to have dinner
with him. So Jesus went to the Pharisee's
home and got ready to eat.[q]
37When a sinful woman in that town
found out that Jesus was there, she bought
an expensive bottle of perfume. 38Then she
came and stood behind Jesus. She cried and

[p] *tax collectors*: See the note at 3.12. [q] *got ready to eat*: On special occasions the Jewish people often followed the Greek and Roman custom of lying down on their left side and leaning on their left elbow, while eating with their right hand. This is how the woman could come up behind Jesus and wash his feet (see verse 38).

started washing his feet with her tears and drying them with her hair. The woman kissed his feet and poured the perfume on them.

³⁹The Pharisee who had invited Jesus saw this and said to himself, "If this man really were a prophet, he would know what kind of woman is touching him! He would know that she is a sinner."

⁴⁰Jesus said to the Pharisee, "Simon, I have something to say to you."

"Teacher, what is it?" Simon replied.

⁴¹Jesus told him, "Two people were in debt to a moneylender. One of them owed him five hundred silver coins, and the other owed him fifty. ⁴²Since neither of them could pay him back, the moneylender said that they didn't have to pay him anything. Which one of them will like him more?"

⁴³Simon answered, "I suppose it would be the one who had owed more and didn't have to pay it back."

"You are right," Jesus said.

⁴⁴He turned toward the woman and said to Simon, "Have you noticed this woman? When I came into your home, you didn't give me any water so I could wash my feet. But she has washed my feet with her tears and dried them with her hair. ⁴⁵You didn't greet me with a kiss, but from the time I came in, she has not stopped kissing my feet. ⁴⁶You didn't even pour olive oil on my head,^r but she has poured expensive perfume on my feet. ⁴⁷So I tell you that all her sins are forgiven, and that is why she has shown great love. But anyone who has been forgiven only a little will show only a little love."

⁴⁸Then Jesus said to the woman, "Your sins are forgiven."

⁴⁹Some other guests started saying to one

How much do we owe God?

(41) The story about forgiveness was aimed at Simon, Jesus' host at dinner. Simon the Pharisee thought he was better than the woman that Jesus forgave. If only Simon could have known how much he also needed forgiveness, then he would have loved Jesus as much as the woman did. But Simon didn't seem to understand how much he really needed Jesus' forgiveness.

^r*washed my feet . . . greet me with a kiss . . . pour olive oil on my head*: Guests in a home were usually offered water so they could wash their feet, because most people either went barefoot or wore sandals and would come in the house with very dusty feet. Guests were also greeted with a kiss on the cheek, and special ones often had sweet-smelling olive oil poured on their head.

another, "Who is this who dares to forgive sins?"

50But Jesus told the woman, "Because of your faith, you are now saved.s May God give you peace!"

Women Who Helped Jesus

8 Soon after this, Jesus was going through towns and villages, telling the good news about God's kingdom. His twelve apostles were with him, 2and so were some women who had been healed of evil spirits and all sorts of diseases. One of the women was Mary Magdalene,t who once had seven demons in her. 3Joanna, Susanna, and many others had also used what they owned to help Jesusu and his disciples. Joanna's husband Chuza was one of Herod's officials.v

A Story about a Farmer
(Matthew 13.1–9; Mark 4.1–9)

4When a large crowd from several towns had gathered around Jesus, he told them this story:

5A farmer went out to scatter seed in a field. While the farmer was doing it, some of the seeds fell along the road and were stepped on or eaten by birds. 6Other seeds fell on rocky ground and started growing. But the plants did not have enough water and soon dried up. 7Some other seeds fell where thorn bushes grew up and choked the plants. 8The rest of the seeds fell on good ground where they grew and produced a hundred times as many seeds.

When Jesus had finished speaking, he said, "If you have ears, pay attention!"

Everyone can be a servant
(2) Many of us want to be bosses, but Jesus honors us just by letting us be his servants. This was the way it was with the men and women who traveled with Jesus. Notice also that Chuza, one of Herod's officials, is mentioned in the list. The greatest of us can also be great servants.

---

ssaved: Or "healed." The Greek word may have either meaning. tMagdalene: Meaning "from Magdala," a small town on the western shore of Lake Galilee. There is no hint that she is the sinful woman in 7.36-50. uused what they owned to help Jesus: Women often helped Jewish teachers by giving them money. vHerod's officials: Herod Antipas, the son of Herod the Great.

Why Jesus Used Stories
(Matthew 13.10–17; Mark 4.10–12)

9Jesus' disciples asked him what the story meant. 10So he answered:

I have explained the secrets about God's kingdom to you, but for others I can only use stories. These people look, but they don't see, and they hear, but they don't understand.

Jesus Explains the Story about the Farmer
(Matthew 13.18–23; Mark 4.13–20)

11This is what the story means: The seed is God's message, 12and the seeds that fell along the road are the people who hear the message. But the devil comes and snatches the message out of their hearts, so that they will not believe and be saved. 13The seeds that fell on rocky ground are the people who gladly hear the message and accept it. But they don't have deep roots, and they believe only for a little while. As soon as life gets hard, they give up. 14The seeds that fell among the thorn bushes are also people who hear the message. But they are so eager for riches and pleasures that they never produce anything. 15Those seeds that fell on good ground are the people who listen to the message and keep it in good and honest hearts. They last and produce a harvest.

Light
(Mark 4.21–25)

16No one lights a lamp and puts it under a bowl or under a bed. A lamp is always put on a lampstand, so that people who come into a house will see the light. 17There is nothing hidden that will not be found. There is no secret that will not be well known. 18Pay attention to how you listen! Everyone who has something will be given more, but people who have nothing will lose what little they think they have.

Which kind of soil are you?
(9) Crops can't grow just anywhere. They must have good soil. The seeds of God's great message can't grow just anywhere either. Those seeds grow in people who have an attitude of obedience to Jesus. In such people, the secrets of God's kingdom grow and blossom, and they also touch other lives and help them to grow in the knowledge of God.

What you are will shine
(16) A light can't be hidden. So, when all is said and done, what we truly are will be seen at last. It makes a great deal of sense to make sure our light is the truth of Jesus. This is the light that God and everyone can see when we live for Jesus in the world.

Jesus' Mother and Brothers
(Matthew 12.46–50; Mark 3.31–35)

19Jesus' mother and brothers went to see him, but because of the crowd they could not get near him. 20Someone told Jesus, "Your mother and brothers are standing outside and want to see you."

21Jesus answered, "My mother and my brothers are those people who hear and obey God's message."

A Storm
(Matthew 8.23–27; Mark 4.35–41)

22One day Jesus and his disciples got into a boat, and he said, "Let's cross the lake."w They started out, 23and while they were sailing across, he went to sleep.

Suddenly a windstorm struck the lake, and the boat started sinking. They were in danger. 24So they went to Jesus and woke him up, "Master, Master! We are about to drown!"

Jesus got up and ordered the wind and waves to stop. They obeyed, and everything was calm. 25Then Jesus asked the disciples, "Don't you have any faith?"

But they were frightened and amazed. They said to each other, "Who is this? He can give orders to the wind and the waves, and they obey him!"

A Man with Demons in Him
(Matthew 8.28–34; Mark 5.1–20)

26Jesus and his disciples sailed across Lake Galilee and came to shore near the town of Gerasa.x 27As Jesus was getting out of the boat, he was met by a man from that town. The man had demons in him. He had gone naked for a long time and no longer lived in a house, but in the graveyard.y

28The man saw Jesus and screamed. He

Who is this Lord of storms?
(24) It almost seems comical that the disciples had such a hard time believing in Jesus. After all, he was right there with them, and they had seen his other miracles. We have a great advantage: we know the whole of Jesus' life, while they didn't. But many times we are just as slow to believe as the first disciples were. Getting to really know Jesus takes time.

---

wcross the lake: To the eastern shore of Lake Galilee, where most of the people were not Jewish.   xGerasa: Some manuscripts have "Gergesa."   ygraveyard: It was thought that demons and evil spirits lived in graveyards.

kneeled down in front of him and shouted,
"Jesus, Son of God in heaven, what do you
want with me? I beg you not to torture me!"
[29]He said this because Jesus had already
told the evil spirit to go out of him.

The man had often been attacked by the
demon. And even though he had been bound
with chains and leg irons and kept under
guard, he smashed whatever bound him.
Then the demon would force him out into
lonely places.

[30]Jesus asked the man, "What is your
name?"

He answered, "My name is Lots." He said
this because there were 'lots' of demons in
him. [31]They begged Jesus not to send them
to the deep pit,[z] where they would be
punished.

[32]On a hillside not far from there a large
herd of pigs was feeding. So the demons
begged Jesus to let them go into the pigs,
and Jesus let them go. [33]Then the demons
left the man and went into the pigs. The
whole herd rushed down the steep bank into
the lake and drowned.

[34]When the men taking care of the pigs
saw this, they ran to spread the news in
the town and on the farms. [35]The people
went out to see what had happened, and
when they came to Jesus, they also found
the man. The demons had gone out of him,
and he was sitting there at the feet of Jesus.
He had clothes on and was in his right mind.
But the people were terrified.

[36]Then all who had seen the man healed
told about it. [37]Everyone from around Gerasa[a] begged Jesus to leave, because they
were so frightened.

When Jesus got into the boat to start
back, [38]the man who had been healed
begged to go with him. But Jesus sent him off
and said, [39]"Go back home and tell everyone how much God has done for you." The
man then went all over town, telling everything that Jesus had done for him.

**Who makes the best
witness for Jesus?**
(38) The man who had the
demons sent out of him had
a lot to tell—and he did. If
you met a great doctor who
could treat your serious disease, you would tell everyone. But Jesus is the greatest
of doctors who heals our
disease of sin. That should
give us a lot to tell others
about.

---

[z]*deep pit*: The place where evil spirits are kept and
punished.   [a]*Gerasa*: See the note at 8.26.

A Dying Girl and a Sick Woman
(Matthew 9.18–26; Mark 5.21–43)

40Everyone had been waiting for Jesus, and when he came back, a crowd was there to welcome him. 41Just then the man in charge of the Jewish meeting place came and kneeled down in front of Jesus. His name was Jairus, and he begged Jesus to come to his home 42because his twelve-year-old child was dying. She was his only daughter.

While Jesus was on his way, people were crowding all around him. 43In the crowd was a woman who had been bleeding for twelve years. She had spent everything she had on doctors,b but none of them could make her well.

44As soon as she came up behind Jesus and barely touched his clothes, her bleeding stopped.

45"Who touched me?" Jesus asked.

While everyone was denying it, Peter said, "Master, people are crowding all around and pushing you from every side."c

46But Jesus answered, "Someone touched me, because I felt power going out from me." 47The woman knew that she could not hide, so she came trembling and kneeled down in front of Jesus. She told everyone why she had touched him and that she had been healed right away.

48Jesus said to the woman, "You are now well because of your faith. May God give you peace!"

49While Jesus was speaking, someone came from Jairus' home and said, "Your daughter has died! Why bother the teacher anymore?"

50When Jesus heard this, he told Jairus, "Don't worry! Have faith, and your daughter will get well."

51Jesus went into the house, but he did not let anyone else go with him, except Peter, John, James, and the girl's father and

Jesus notices all who seek him

(48) The Lord was on his way to the house of Jairus, whose little daughter was dying. Just then a sick woman reached out and touched him. We might think Jesus would have been too busy just then to be bothered with her problem. But Jesus cared about her and healed her. We can be sure that Jesus cares about everyone who comes to him.

bShe had spent everything she had on doctors: Some manuscripts do not have these words. cfrom every side: Some manuscripts add "and you ask, 'Who touched me?'"

mother. 52Everyone was crying and weeping for the girl. But Jesus said, "The child is not dead. She is just asleep." 53The people laughed at him because they knew she was dead.

54Jesus took hold of the girl's hand and said, "Child, get up!" 55She came back to life and got right up. Jesus told them to give her something to eat. 56Her parents were surprised, but Jesus ordered them not to tell anyone what had happened.

Instructions for the Twelve Apostles
(Matthew 10.5–15; Mark 6.7–13)

9 Jesus called together his twelve apostles and gave them complete power over all demons and diseases. 2Then he sent them to tell about God's kingdom and to heal the sick. 3He told them, "Don't take anything with you! Don't take a walking stick or a traveling bag or food or money or even a change of clothes. 4When you are welcomed into a home, stay there until you leave that town. 5If people won't welcome you, leave the town and shake the dust from your feet*d* as a warning to them."

6The apostles left and went from village to village, telling the good news and healing people everywhere.

Herod Is Worried
(Matthew 14.1–12; Mark 6.14–29)

7Herod*e* the ruler heard about all that was happening, and he was worried. Some people were saying that John the Baptist had come back to life. 8Others were saying that Elijah had come*f* or that one of the prophets from long ago had come back to life. 9But Herod said, "I had John's head cut off! Who is this I hear so much about?" Herod was eager to meet Jesus.

---

dshake the dust from your feet: This was a way of showing rejection. *eHerod*: Herod Antipas, the son of Herod the Great. *fElijah had come*: Many of the Jewish people expected the prophet Elijah to come and prepare the way for the Messiah.

The apostles traveled light
(3) The twelve apostles didn't have much to carry as they went from village to village. That may sound bad, but it's good not to have a lot to haul around. How about us? Are we carrying any "baggage" that keeps us from serving Jesus the way we should?

Sin causes fear
(7) This is Herod Antipas, son of King Herod the Great who had tried to murder the baby Jesus (see Matthew 2). The Herod family were not the lawful rulers of the Jews, but the Roman government made them kings anyway. Herod Antipas was afraid because his own sins and the sins of his father were on his conscience. He wanted to learn about Jesus, but it was like someone wanting to learn about a threat. It's too bad he couldn't trust Jesus to take his sins away. Let's not make the same mistake Herod did.

Jesus Feeds Five Thousand
(Matthew 14.13–21; Mark 6.30–44; John 6.1–14)

10The apostles came back and told Jesus everything they had done. He then took them with him to the village of Bethsaida, where they could be alone. 11But a lot of people found out about this and followed him. Jesus welcomed them. He spoke to them about God's kingdom and healed everyone who was sick.

12Late in the afternoon the twelve apostles came to Jesus and said, "Send the crowd to the villages and farms around here. They need to find a place to stay and something to eat. There is nothing in this place. It is like a desert!"

13Jesus answered, "You give them something to eat."

But they replied, "We have only five small loaves of bread^g and two fish. If we are going to feed all these people, we will have to go and buy food." 14There were about five thousand men in the crowd.

Jesus said to his disciples, "Have the people sit in groups of fifty." 15They did this, and all the people sat down. 16Jesus took the five loaves and the two fish. He looked up toward heaven and blessed the food. Then he broke the bread and fish and handed them to his disciples to give to the people.

17Everyone ate all they wanted. What was left over filled twelve baskets.

Where do we look?
(12) When the five thousand needed feeding, the apostles looked for a natural way to get the job done. Jesus looked to the power of God, who can do things there is no natural way to do. Do we remember to give God a chance to help us?

Who Is Jesus?
(Matthew 16.13–19; Mark 8.27–29)

18When Jesus was alone praying, his disciples came to him, and he asked them, "What do people say about me?"

19They answered, "Some say that you are John the Baptist or Elijah^h or a prophet from long ago who has come back to life."

20Jesus then asked them, "But who do you say I am?"

Who do you say Jesus is?
(18) This was the question Jesus asked his disciples. But each of us needs to answer that question. If we each can say sincerely that Jesus is the Son of God and our Savior, then we are truly Christians. For Peter, saying Jesus is the Messiah was a first great step of faith.

---

^g*small loaves of bread*: These would have been flat and round or in the shape of a bun.   ^h*Elijah*: See the note at 9.8.

Peter answered, "You are the Messiah sent from God."

21Jesus strictly warned his disciples not to tell anyone what had happened.

Jesus Speaks about His Suffering and Death
(Matthew 16.20–28; Mark 8.30—9.1)

22Jesus told his disciples, "The nation's leaders, the chief priests, and the teachers of the Law of Moses will make the Son of Man suffer terribly. They will reject him and kill him, but three days later he will rise to life."

23Then Jesus said to all the people:

If any of you want to be my followers, you must forget about yourself. You must take up your cross each day and follow me. 24If you want to save your life,*i* you will destroy it. But if you give up your life for me, you will save it. 25What will you gain, if you own the whole world but destroy yourself or waste your life? 26If you are ashamed of me and my message, the Son of Man will be ashamed of you when he comes in his glory and in the glory of his Father and the holy angels. 27You can be sure that some of the people standing here will not die before they see God's kingdom.

We, too, have a cross
(23) We can't carry the cross that Jesus carried. Only he could die for our sins. But we have our own crosses that he asks us to carry for him. These crosses are the daily decisions we make to live for Jesus, which include loving and caring for those around us. But sometimes when we follow Jesus others won't like it. Sometimes others will say and do mean things to us, just because we want to be like Jesus. But we should remember that Jesus suffered greatly for us, and certainly we can suffer a little for him.

The True Glory of Jesus
(Matthew 17.1–8; Mark 9.2–8)

28About eight days later Jesus took Peter, John, and James with him and went up on a mountain to pray. 29While he was praying, his face changed, and his clothes became shining white. 30Suddenly Moses and Elijah were there speaking with him. 31They appeared in heavenly glory and talked about all that Jesus' death*j* in Jerusalem would mean.

32Peter and the other two disciples had

ilife: In verses 24,25 a Greek word which often means "soul" is translated "life" and "yourself." *jJesus' death*: In Greek this is "his departure," which probably includes his rising to life and his return to heaven.

been sound asleep. All at once they woke up and saw how glorious Jesus was. They also saw the two men who were with him.

33Moses and Elijah were about to leave, when Peter said to Jesus, "Master, it is good for us to be here! Let us make three shelters, one for you, one for Moses, and one for Elijah." But Peter did not know what he was talking about.

34While Peter was still speaking, a shadow from a cloud passed over them, and they were frightened as the cloud covered them. 35From the cloud a voice spoke, "This is my chosen Son. Listen to what he says!"

36After the voice had spoken, Peter, John, and James saw only Jesus. For some time they kept quiet and did not say anything about what they had seen.

There is a time to be quiet
(33) Peter liked to talk. But this time God made him be quiet. The reason? Peter should be listening to Jesus. Our first duty to Jesus is to *listen* to him speaking in his word. We learn as we listen to Jesus, and then we can obey by having faith in him, doing his works and speaking his words.

Jesus Heals a Boy
(Matthew 17.14–18; Mark 9.14–27)

37The next day Jesus and his three disciples came down from the mountain and were met by a large crowd. 38Just then someone in the crowd shouted, "Teacher, please do something for my son! He is my only child! 39A demon often attacks him and makes him scream. It shakes him until he foams at the mouth, and it won't leave him until it has completely worn the boy out.k 40I begged your disciples to force out the demon, but they couldn't do it."

41Jesus said to them, "You people are stubborn and don't have any faith! How much longer must I be with you? Why do I have to put up with you?"

Then Jesus said to the man, "Bring your son to me." 42While the boy was being brought, the demon attacked him and made him shake all over. Jesus ordered the demon to stop. Then he healed the boy and gave him back to his father. 43Everyone was amazed at God's great power.

Stubbornness gets in faith's way
(41) Here we see Jesus scolding people who were stubborn and didn't have faith in God's great power. Do we stubbornly cling to ways of thinking that don't give God enough credit?

---

kshakes him . . . foams at the mouth . . . completely worn the boy out: These symptoms are very much like what is today called epilepsy.

Jesus Again Speaks about His Death
(Matthew 17.22, 23; Mark 9.30–32)

While everyone was still amazed at what Jesus was doing, he said to his disciples, [44]"Pay close attention to what I am telling you! The Son of Man will be handed over to his enemies." [45]But the disciples did not know what he meant. The meaning was hidden from them. They could not understand it, and they were afraid to ask.

Who Is the Greatest?
(Matthew 18.1–5; Mark 9.33–37)

[46]Jesus' disciples were arguing about which one of them was the greatest. [47]Jesus knew what they were thinking, and he had a child stand there beside him. [48]Then he said to his disciples, "When you welcome even a child because of me, you welcome me. And when you welcome me, you welcome the one who sent me. Whichever one of you is the most humble is the greatest."

For or against Jesus
(Mark 9.38–40)

[49]John said, "Master, we saw a man using your name to force demons out of people. But we told him to stop, because he is not one of us."

[50]"Don't stop him!" Jesus said. "Anyone who is not against you is for you."

A Samaritan Village Refuses to Receive Jesus

[51]Not long before it was time for Jesus to be taken up to heaven, he made up his mind to go to Jerusalem. [52]He sent some messengers on ahead to a Samaritan village to get things ready for him. [53]But he was on his way to Jerusalem, so the people there refused to welcome him. [54]When the disciples James and John saw what was happening, they asked, "Lord, do you want us to call down fire from heaven to destroy these people?"[l]

You can be a great person (46) Everybody should want to count for something in the world. But sometimes we make the mistake of thinking we have to push ahead of other people in order to be noticed. Have you heard about Mother Teresa of India? She didn't want fame, but she became famous by being a servant of others. Pleasing God is what makes us count for something.

[l]*to destroy these people:* Some manuscripts add "as Elijah did."

55But Jesus turned and corrected them for what they had said.m 56Then they all went on to another village.

Three People Who Wanted to Be Followers
(Matthew 8.19–22)

57Along the way someone said to Jesus, "I'll go anywhere with you!"

58Jesus said, "Foxes have dens, and birds have nests, but the Son of Man doesn't have a place to call his own."

59Jesus told someone else to come with him. But the man said, "Lord, let me wait until I bury my father."n

60Jesus answered, "Let the dead take care of the dead, while you go and tell about God's kingdom."

61Then someone said to Jesus, "I want to go with you, Lord, but first let me go back and take care of things at home."

62Jesus answered, "Anyone who starts plowing and keeps looking back isn't worth a thing in God's kingdom!"

The Work of the Seventy-two Followers

10 Later the Lord chose seventy-twoo other followers and sent them out two by two to every town and village where he was about to go. 2He said to them:

A large crop is in the fields, but there are only a few workers. Ask the Lord in charge of the harvest to send out workers to bring it in. 3Now go, but remember, I am sending you like lambs into a pack of wolves. 4Don't take along a moneybag or a traveling bag or san-

Punishment isn't God's first choice
(55) Sometimes we want to see people punished for not doing what we want them to do. But in the Bible we notice that God often waits a very long time before he punishes people. God's way is to teach by example and word so that people will trust and obey him. He gives us every chance to follow him. We need to learn God's kind of patience.

Let's decide what is important
(61) The three people Jesus spoke to each had an excuse for not following him. As we think about them, the excuses seem pretty good. But they weren't good enough. *Nothing* is as important as doing what Jesus commands us to do.

---

mwhat they had said: Some manuscripts add, "and said, 'Don't you know what spirit you belong to? The Son of Man did not come to destroy people's lives, but to save them.'" nbury my father: The Jewish people taught that giving someone a proper burial was even more important than helping the poor. oseventy-two: Some manuscripts have "seventy." According to the book of Genesis, there were seventy nations on earth. But the ancient Greek translation of the Old Testament has "seventy-two" in place of "seventy." Jesus probably chose this number of followers to show that his message was for everyone in the world.

dals. And don't waste time greeting people on the road.^{p} 5As soon as you enter a home, say, "God bless this home with peace." 6If the people living there are peace-loving, your prayer for peace will bless them. But if they are not peace-loving, your prayer will return to you. 7Stay with the same family, eating and drinking whatever they give you, because workers are worth what they earn. Don't move around from house to house.

8If the people of a town welcome you, eat whatever they offer you. 9Heal their sick and say, "God's kingdom will soon be here!"^{q}

10But if the people of a town refuse to welcome you, go out into the street and say, 11"We are shaking the dust from our feet^r as a warning to you. You can be sure that God's kingdom will soon be here!"^{s} 12I tell you that on the day of judgment the people of Sodom will get off easier than the people of that town!

The Unbelieving Towns
(Matthew 11.20–24)

13You people of Chorazin are in for trouble! You people of Bethsaida are also in for trouble! If the miracles that took place in your towns had happened in Tyre and Sidon, the people there would have turned to God long ago. They would have dressed in sackcloth and put ashes on their heads.^{t} 14On the day of judgment the people of Tyre and Sidon will get off easier than you will. 15People of Capernaum, do you think you will be honored in heaven? Well, you will go down to hell!

Not everyone is God's friend
(10) Jesus told the seventy-two followers they would meet some in their journey who would be friendly to God's message. But others would not be so friendly. So we should not be disappointed when everybody isn't friendly to us. Not everyone was friendly to Jesus and his earliest followers, either. In fact, if we're popular with *everyone,* maybe something is wrong.

Where does your town stand?
(14) Notice here that Jesus spoke to whole towns. What kind of town is yours? What would Jesus have to say to it? We ought to pray for our towns, and try to share the good news in them. At times whole towns have been known to come to faith in Jesus.

^{p}*waste time greeting people on the road*: In those days a polite greeting could take a long time. ^{q}*will soon be here*: Or "is already here." ^{r}*shaking the dust from our feet*: This was a way of showing rejection. ^{s}*will soon be here*: Or "is already here." ^{t}*dressed in sackcloth . . . ashes on their heads*: This was one way that people showed how sorry they were for their sins.

16My followers, whoever listens to you is listening to me. Anyone who says "No" to you is saying "No" to me. And anyone who says "No" to me is really saying "No" to the one who sent me.

The Return of the Seventy-two

17When the seventy-twou followers returned, they were excited and said, "Lord, even the demons obeyed when we spoke in your name!"

18Jesus told them:

I saw Satan fall from heaven like a flash of lightning. 19I have given you the power to trample on snakes and scorpions and to defeat the power of your enemy Satan. Nothing can harm you. 20But don't be happy because evil spirits obey you. Be happy that your names are written in heaven!

Satan is a real person
(18) Satan would rather we didn't believe he is real. Then he could more easily do his evil and deceitful work. Jesus believed Satan was real. But he also saw that Satan was his defeated enemy. If we have trusted our lives to Jesus, then God will keep us from Satan's harm.

Jesus Thanks His Father
(Matthew 11.25–27; 13.16, 17)

21At that same time Jesus felt the joy that comes from the Holy Spirit,v and he said:

My Father, Lord of heaven and earth, I am grateful that you hid all this from wise and educated people and showed it to ordinary people. Yes, Father, that is what pleased you.

22My Father has given me everything, and he is the only one who knows the Son. The only one who really knows the Father is the Son. But the Son wants to tell others about the Father, so that they can know him too.

23Jesus then turned to his disciples and said to them in private, "You are really blessed to see what you see! 24Many prophets and kings were eager to see what you see and to hear what you hear. But I tell you that they did not see or hear."

Who are God's people?
(21) Jesus says that his people aren't necessarily the smartest people in the world. In fact, an overactive brain can keep people from realizing the plainest facts of life. It's not what we *know* that helps us to live; it's how we *use* what we know. That's wisdom. Sometimes it's the ordinary people who have the most wisdom to believe the good news about Jesus.

---

useventy-two: See the note at 10.1. vthe Holy Spirit: Some manuscripts have "his spirit."

The Good Samaritan

25An expert in the Law of Moses stood up and asked Jesus a question to see what he would say. "Teacher," he asked, "What must I do to have eternal life?"

26Jesus answered, "What is written in the Scriptures? How do you understand them?"

27The man replied, "The Scriptures say, 'Love the Lord your God with all your heart, soul, strength, and mind.' They also say, 'Love your neighbors as much as you love yourself.' "

28Jesus said, "You have given the right answer. If you do this, you will have eternal life."

29But the man wanted to show that he knew what he was talking about. So he asked Jesus, "Who are my neighbors?"

30Jesus replied:

As a man was going down from Jerusalem to Jericho, robbers attacked him and grabbed everything he had. They beat him up and ran off, leaving him half dead.

31A priest happened to be going down the same road. But when he saw the man, he walked by on the other side. **32**Later a temple helper[w] came to the same place. But when he saw the man who had been beaten up, he also went by on the other side.

33A man from Samaria then came traveling along that road. When he saw the man, he felt sorry for him **34**and went over to him. He treated his wounds with olive oil and wine[x] and bandaged them. Then he put him on his own donkey and took him to an inn, where he took care of him. **35**The next morning he gave the innkeeper two silver coins and said, "Please take care of the man. If you spend more than this on him, I will pay you when I return."

Who is your neighbor?
(30) The story of the good Samaritan was hard for the legal expert to take. Most Jews didn't believe there were any "good" Samaritans. But that's why Jesus told the legal expert this story—so that the man could see he needed to love even his Samaritan neighbors.

---

[w]*temple helper*: A man from the tribe of Levi, whose job it was to work around the temple. [x]*olive oil and wine*: In New Testament times these were used as medicine. Sometimes olive oil is a symbol for healing by means of a miracle (James 5.14).

³⁶Then Jesus asked, "Which one of these three people was a real neighbor to the man who was beaten up by robbers?"

³⁷The teacher answered, "The one who showed pity."

Jesus said, "Go and do the same!"

Martha and Mary

³⁸The Lord and his disciples were traveling along and came to a village. When they got there, a woman named Martha welcomed him into her home. ³⁹She had a sister named Mary, who sat down in front of the Lord and was listening to what he said. ⁴⁰Martha was worried about all that had to be done. Finally, she went to Jesus and said, "Lord, doesn't it bother you that my sister has left me to do all the work by myself? Tell her to come and help me!"

⁴¹The Lord answered, "Martha, Martha! You are worried and upset about so many things, ⁴²but only one thing is necessary. Mary has chosen what is best, and it will not be taken away from her."

What comes first— hearing or doing?
(38) Martha was a great doer, and that was fine. But Mary was a great listener, and that was better. Of course, listening without learning and doing is useless. But before we can know what really pleases God, we must first pay close attention to what he says. Then we will know what to do.

Prayer
(Matthew 6.9–13; 7.7–11)

11 When Jesus had finished praying, one of his disciples said to him, "Lord, teach us to pray, just as John taught his followers to pray."

²So Jesus told them, "Pray in this way:
'Father, help us
    to honor your name.
Come and set up
    your kingdom.
³Give us each day
    the food we need.ʸ
⁴Forgive our sins,
    as we forgive everyone
        who has done wrong to us.
And keep us
    from being tempted.' "

⁵Then Jesus went on to say:

Jesus teaches us to pray
(2) We shouldn't just ramble on when we pray. But also, let's not just ask God for things that please us in a selfish way. God knows and cares about our needs, and we should bring them to him. But we ought to study Jesus' prayer so we can learn to ask for those things that please God.

ʸ*the food we need*: Or "food for today" or "food for the coming day."

Suppose one of you goes to a friend in the middle of the night and says, "Let me borrow three loaves of bread. 6A friend of mine has dropped in, and I don't have a thing for him to eat." 7And suppose your friend answers, "Don't bother me! The door is bolted, and my children and I are in bed. I cannot get up to give you something."

8He may not get up and give you the bread, just because you are his friend. But he will get up and give you as much as you need, simply because you are not ashamed to keep on asking.

9So I tell you to ask and you will receive, search and you will find, knock and the door will be opened for you. 10Everyone who asks will receive, everyone who searches will find, and the door will be opened for everyone who knocks. 11Which one of you fathers would give your hungry child a snake if the child asked for a fish? 12Which one of you would give your child a scorpion if the child asked for an egg? 13As bad as you are, you still know how to give good gifts to your children. But your heavenly Father is even more ready to give the Holy Spirit to anyone who asks.

Keep on asking
(9) Don't give up if your prayers aren't all answered right away. Keep on asking. God is much more generous than people. If our requests aren't right, he'll show us how to change them.

Jesus and the Ruler of Demons
(Matthew 12.22–30; Mark 3.20–27)

14Jesus forced a demon out of a man who could not talk. After the demon had gone out, the man started speaking, and the crowds were amazed. 15But some people said, "He forces out demons by the power of Beelzebul, the ruler of the demons!"

16Others wanted to put Jesus to the test. So they asked him to show them a sign from God. 17Jesus knew what they were thinking, and he said:

A kingdom where people fight each other will end up in ruin. And a family that fights will break up. 18If Satan fights against himself, how can his kingdom last? Yet you say that I force out

demons by the power of Beelzebul.
19If I use his power to force out demons,
whose power do your own followers use
to force them out? They are the ones
who will judge you. 20But if I use God's
power to force out demons, it proves
that God's kingdom has already come
to you.

21When a strong man arms himself
and guards his home, everything he
owns is safe. 22But if a stronger man
comes and defeats him, he will carry
off the weapons in which the strong man
trusted. Then he will divide with others
what he has taken. 23If you are not on
my side, you are against me. If you don't
gather in the crop with me, you scatter it.

Return of an Evil Spirit
(Matthew 12.43–45)

24When an evil spirit leaves a person,
it travels through the desert, looking for
a place to rest. But when it doesn't find
a place, it says, "I will go back to the
home I left." 25When it gets there and
finds the place clean and fixed up, 26it
goes off and finds seven other evil spirits
even worse than itself. They all come
and make their home there, and that
person ends up in worse shape than
before.

Being Really Blessed

27While Jesus was still talking, a woman
in the crowd spoke up, "The woman who
gave birth to you and nursed you is
blessed!"

28Jesus replied, "That's true, but the people who are really blessed are the ones who
hear and obey God's message!"z

Fill your life with good things
(24) Like the man who got
rid of his evil spirit, we're
sometimes satisfied just to
get rid of our sins. Being forgiven is great, but God also
wants us to be filled with the
Holy Spirit. By doing so, we
will also replace our old
bad habits with new good
ones. Then there will be no
room for the evil habits to
return.

---

z"That's true, but the people who are really blessed
. . . message": Or " 'That's not true, the people who
are blessed . . . message.' "

A Sign from God
(Matthew 12.38–42; Mark 8.12)

29As crowds were gathering around Jesus, he said:

You people of today are evil! You keep looking for a sign from God. But what happened to Jonah*a* is the only sign you will be given. 30Just as Jonah was a sign to the people of Nineveh, the Son of Man will be a sign to the people of today. 31When the judgment comes, the Queen of the South*b* will stand there with you and condemn you. She traveled a long way to hear Solomon's wisdom, and yet here is something far greater than Solomon. 32The people of Nineveh will also stand there with you and condemn you. They turned to God when Jonah preached, and yet here is something far greater than Jonah.

Light
(Matthew 5.15; 6.22, 23)

33No one lights a lamp and then hides it or puts it under a clay pot. A lamp is put on a lampstand, so that everyone who comes into the house can see the light. 34Your eyes are the lamp for your body. When your eyes are good, you have all the light you need. But when your eyes are bad, everything is dark. 35So be sure that your light is not darkness. 36If you have light, and nothing is dark, then light will be everywhere, as when a lamp shines brightly on you.

Jesus Condemns the Pharisees and Teachers of the Law of Moses
(Matthew 23.1–36; Mark 12.38–40; Luke 20.45–47)

37When Jesus finished speaking, a Pharisee invited him home for a meal. Jesus went

Seeing Jesus
(29) Today we wish we could have been there when Jesus walked among the people. We long for a chance to see him. But the people of his day saw Jesus, and most still didn't appreciate who he was. The Son of God was right there in front of them, but they missed it. It is better for us who believe without seeing, than for those who saw and did not believe.

awhat happened to Jonah: Jonah was in the stomach of a big fish for three days and nights. See Matthew 12.40. *bQueen of the South*: Sheba, probably a country in southern Arabia.

and sat down to eat.*c* 38The Pharisee was surprised that he did not wash his hands*d* before eating. 39So the Lord said to him:

You Pharisees clean the outside of cups and dishes, but on the inside you are greedy and evil. 40You fools! Didn't God make both the outside and the inside?*e* 41If you would only give what you have to the poor, everything you do would please God.

42You Pharisees are in for trouble! You give God a tenth of the spices from your gardens, such as mint and rue. But you cheat people, and you don't love God. You should be fair and kind to others and still give a tenth to God.

43You Pharisees are in for trouble! You love the front seats in the meeting places, and you like to be greeted with honor in the market. 44But you are in for trouble! You are like unmarked graves*f* that people walk on without even knowing it.

45A teacher of the Law of Moses spoke up, "Teacher, you said cruel things about us."

46Jesus replied:

You teachers are also in for trouble! You load people down with heavy burdens, but you won't lift a finger to help them carry the loads. 47Yes, you are really in for trouble. You build monuments to honor the prophets your own people murdered long ago. 48You must think that was the right thing for your people to do, or else you would not have built monuments for the prophets they murdered.

49Because of your evil deeds, the Wisdom of God said, "I will send prophets

Let's not fool ourselves
(39) Have you heard the tale about "The Emperor Who Had No Clothes"? A certain emperor fooled himself by believing he was dressed in beautiful clothes. The truth was that he was wearing no clothes at all. Even though nearly everyone bowed before the emperor, a small boy spoke up and said, "Look—the emperor has no clothes." That was like the Pharisees who pretended to be holy. Jesus said they were really unholy in their inner lives. Let's not just pretend to be Christians.

---

csat down to eat: See the note at 7.36. *ddid not wash his hands*: The Jewish people had strict laws about washing their hands before eating, especially if they had been out in public. *edidn't God make both the outside and the inside?*: Or "doesn't the person who washes the outside always wash the inside too?" *funmarked graves*: Tombs were whitewashed to keep anyone from accidentally touching them. A person who touched a dead body or a tomb was considered unclean and could not worship with other Jewish people.

and apostles to you. But you will murder some and mistreat others." 50You people living today will be punished for all the prophets who have been murdered since the beginning of the world. 51This includes every prophet from the time of Abel to the time of Zechariah,g who was murdered between the altar and the temple. You people will certainly be punished for all of this.

52You teachers of the Law of Moses are really in for trouble! You carry the keys to the door of knowledge about God. But you never go in, and you keep others from going in.

53Jesus was about to leave, but the teachers and the Pharisees wanted to get even with him. They tried to make him say what he thought about other things, 54so that they could catch him saying something wrong.

Warnings

12 As thousands of people crowded around Jesus and were stepping on each other, he told his disciples:

Be sure to guard against the dishonest teachingh of the Pharisees! It is their way of fooling people. 2Everything that is hidden will be found out, and every secret will be known. 3Whatever you say in the dark will be heard when it is day. Whatever you whisper in a closed room will be shouted from the housetops.

The One to Fear
(Matthew 10.28–31)

4My friends, don't be afraid of people. They can kill you, but after that, there is nothing else they can do. 5God is the

gfrom the time of Abel . . . Zechariah: Genesis is the first book in the Jewish Scriptures, and it tells that Abel was the first person to be murdered. Second Chronicles is the last book in the Jewish Scriptures, and the last murder that it tells about is that of Zechariah. hdishonest teaching: The Greek text has "yeast," which is used here of a teaching that is not true. See Matthew 16.6,12.

Keys are for opening
(52) Jesus was unhappy with teachers who kept others from the truth. Their "keys to the door of knowledge" were supposed to be for opening the door, not closing it. It was bad enough that they turned away from God's truth, but it was worse that they stood in the way of others. Are we doing everything we can to encourage those who want to know more about Jesus?

Jesus warned about quacks
(1) "Quacks" are what we call people who pretend to be doctors but really aren't. There are religious quacks, too. Sometimes these people make themselves very rich by peddling their false teaching. Jesus also had to deal with quacks. They cheated people in his time, too. But he warned that their lies would be found out. They can't keep secrets from God.

Fear is a great enemy
(4) President Franklin Roosevelt said, "The only thing we have to fear is fear itself." In this passage we see bad fear and good fear. Bad fear is the kind Roosevelt was talking about, the kind that is always afraid of things that can harm us in this world. Good fear is the fear that comes from respect for the power of God. Let's be sure we're on his side.

one you must fear. Not only can he take your life, but he can throw you into hell. God is certainly the one you should fear!

6Five sparrows are sold for just two pennies, but God does not forget a one of them. 7Even the hairs on your head are counted. So don't be afraid! You are worth much more than many sparrows.

Telling Others about Christ
(Matthew 10.32, 33; 12.32; 10.19, 20)

8If you tell others that you belong to me, the Son of Man will tell God's angels that you are my followers. 9But if you reject me, you will be rejected in front of them. 10If you speak against the Son of Man, you can be forgiven, but if you speak against the Holy Spirit, you cannot be forgiven.

11When you are brought to trial in the Jewish meeting places or before rulers or officials, don't worry about how you will defend yourselves or what you will say. 12At that time the Holy Spirit will tell you what to say.

A Rich Fool

13A man in a crowd said to Jesus, "Teacher, tell my brother to give me my share of what our father left us when he died."

14Jesus answered, "Who gave me the right to settle arguments between you and your brother?"

15Then he said to the crowd, "Don't be greedy! Owning a lot of things won't make your life safe."

16So Jesus told them this story:

A rich man's farm produced a big crop, 17and he said to himself, "What can I do? I don't have a place large enough to store everything."

18Later, he said, "Now I know what I'll do. I'll tear down my barns and build bigger ones, where I can store all my

The Holy Spirit helps us
(11) God never leaves us completely alone. He is always there when we need him. This is especially true when we have to answer people about our faith. The Spirit of God himself makes us able to show others that the good news about Jesus is true. In Acts 7, for example, you can read about how the Holy Spirit helped Stephen speak for Christ.

"You can't take it with you"
(18) Rich and poor alike have to die some day. How foolish it is to hoard money as if we could take it with us when we die. God blesses us with goods in this world so we can use them to benefit others.

grain and other goods. 19Then I'll say to myself, 'You have stored up enough good things to last for years to come. Live it up! Eat, drink, and enjoy yourself.' "

20But God said to him, "You fool! Tonight you will die. Then who will get what you have stored up?"

21"This is what happens to people who store up everything for themselves, but are poor in the sight of God."

Worry
(Matthew 6.25–34)

22Jesus said to his disciples:

I tell you not to worry about your life! Don't worry about having something to eat or wear. 23Life is more than food or clothing. 24Look at the crows! They don't plant or harvest, and they don't have storehouses or barns. But God takes care of them. You are much more important than any birds. 25Can worry make you live longer?*i* 26If you don't have power over small things, why worry about everything else?

27Look how the wild flowers grow! They don't work hard to make their clothes. But I tell you that Solomon with all his wealth*j* was not as well clothed as one of these flowers. 28God gives such beauty to everything that grows in the fields, even though it is here today and thrown into a fire tomorrow. Won't he do even more for you? You have such little faith!

29Don't keep worrying about having something to eat or drink. 30Only people who don't know God are always worrying about such things. Your Father knows what you need. 31But put God's work first, and these things will be yours as well.

How much are you worth?
(22) Jesus said we are worth more than birds. And we are certainly worth more than flowers in a field. But are we worth more than all the things we can ever own? Yes—it is a great shame when we value our lives by money or property. Those things pass away, but our souls last forever. The lasting things are important to God, and they should be important to us.

---

ilive longer: Or "grow taller." *jSolomon with all his wealth*: The Jewish people thought that Solomon was the richest person who had ever lived.

Treasures in Heaven
(Matthew 6.19–21)

32My little group of disciples, don't be afraid! Your Father wants to give you the kingdom. 33Sell what you have and give the money to the poor. Make yourselves moneybags that never wear out. Make your treasure safe in heaven, where thieves cannot steal it and moths cannot destroy it. 34Your heart will always be where your treasure is.

Faithful and Unfaithful Servants
(Matthew 24.45–51)

35Be ready and keep your lamps burning just 36like those servants who wait up for their master to return from a wedding feast. As soon as he comes and knocks, they open the door for him. 37Servants are fortunate if their master finds them awake and ready when he comes! I promise you that he will get ready and have his servants sit down so he can serve them. 38Those servants are really fortunate if their master finds them ready, even though he comes late at night or early in the morning. 39You would surely not let a thief break into your home, if you knew when the thief was coming. 40So always be ready! You don't know when the Son of Man will come.

41Peter asked Jesus, "Did you say this just for us or for everyone?"

42The Lord answered:

Who are faithful and wise servants? Who are the ones the master will put in charge of giving the other servants their food supplies at the proper time? 43Servants are fortunate if their master comes and finds them doing their job. 44A servant who is always faithful will surely be put in charge of everything the master owns.

45But suppose one of the servants thinks that the master will not return until late. Suppose that servant starts

Will you let go?
(32) Jesus had some hard words to say about the things of this world. We are in danger of becoming too attached to our material goods. He wants us to let them go, if necessary, for the sake of doing his work.

Always be ready for the master
(42) Jesus may return for us at any moment. Let's not be like the servants who decided their master would not be returning any time soon. Let's live each day as if it were the day Jesus is coming back to take us to be with him. It just might be. Have you been putting off sharing the good news about Jesus with someone? We might not be here tomorrow.

beating all the other servants and eats and drinks and gets drunk. 46If that happens, the master will surely come on a day and at a time when the servant least expects him. That servant will then be punished and thrown out with the servants who cannot be trusted.

47If servants are not ready or willing to do what their master wants them to do, they will be beaten hard. 48But servants who don't know what their master wants them to do will not be beaten so hard for doing wrong. If God has been generous with you, he will expect you to serve him well. But if he has been more than generous, he will expect you to serve him even better.

Not Peace, But Trouble
(Matthew 10.34–36)

49I came to set fire to the earth, and I surely wish it were already on fire! 50I am going to be put to a hard test. And I will have to suffer a lot of pain until it is over. 51Do you think that I came to bring peace to earth? No indeed! I came to make people choose sides. 52A family of five will be divided, with two of them against the other three. 53Fathers and sons will turn against one another, and mothers and daughters will do the same. Mothers-in-law and daughters-in-law will also turn against each other.

Knowing What to Do
(Matthew 16.2, 3; 5.25, 26)

54Jesus said to all the people:

As soon as you see a cloud coming up in the west, you say, "It's going to rain," and it does. 55When the south wind blows, you say, "It's going to get hot," and it does. 56Are you trying to fool someone? You can predict the weather by looking at the earth and sky, but you don't really know what's going on right now. 57Why don't you under-

A divider of families
(49) Jesus says we may be surprised by those who become our enemies because of our faith in him. Jesus wants us to have good relationships in our families, but sometimes even a believer's closest relatives will turn into enemies because of that person's faith.

Understand your times
(56) Jesus knew his death was near. He also knew that the Jewish nation would be destroyed by invaders from Rome not many years later. God was going to punish the people for rejecting his kingdom. We live in uncertain times, too. Now is the time to find peace with God, because tomorrow might be too late.

stand the right thing to do? 58When someone accuses you of something, try to settle things before you are taken to court. If you don't, you will be dragged before the judge. Then the judge will hand you over to the jailer, and you will be locked up. 59You won't get out until you have paid the last cent you owe.

Turn Back to God

13 About this same time Jesus was told that Pilate had given orders for some people from Galilee to be killed while they were offering sacrifices. 2Jesus replied:

Do you think that these people were worse sinners than everyone else in Galilee just because of what happened to them? 3Not at all! But you can be sure that if you don't turn back to God, every one of you will also be killed. 4What about those eighteen people who died when the tower in Siloam fell on them? Do you think they were worse than everyone else in Jerusalem? 5Not at all! But you can be sure that if you don't turn back to God, every one of you will also die.

A Story about a Fig Tree

6Jesus then told them this story:

A man had a fig tree growing in his vineyard. One day he went out to pick some figs, but he didn't find any. 7So he said to the gardener, "For three years I have come looking for figs on this tree, and I haven't found any yet. Chop it down! Why should it take up space?"

8The gardener answered, "Master, leave it for another year. I'll dig around it and put some manure on it to make it grow. 9Maybe it will have figs on it next year. If it doesn't, you can have it cut down."

Healing a Woman on the Sabbath

10One Sabbath Jesus was teaching in a Jewish meeting place, 11and a woman was

Death is our payment for sin

(1) Of course, we don't like to think about death and dying. It's the most dreadful thing we face in this world. But death, however it may happen, is our fair payment for sin. When we hear about someone's death, that is when we should look into our own souls. Then we should ask God to forgive our sins and make us fit for heaven, because of what Jesus did when he died in our place, paying our sin debt himself.

Be a good gardener

(6) The fault was not in the fig tree. The gardener hadn't been doing his job. But the owner gave the gardener another chance. God doesn't like to punish us, so he is always giving us new chances to be useful to him. Are we making the best of the chances God gives us every day? Let's plan to have lots of good fruit in our lives when Jesus comes.

there who had been crippled by an evil spirit for eighteen years. She was completely bent over and could not straighten up. 12When Jesus saw the woman, he called her over and said, "You are now well." 13He placed his hands on her, and right away she stood up straight and praised God.

14The man in charge of the meeting place was angry because Jesus had healed someone on the Sabbath. So he said to the people, "Each week has six days when we can work. Come and be healed on one of those days, but not on the Sabbath."

15The Lord replied, "Are you trying to fool someone? Won't any one of you untie your ox or donkey and lead it out to drink on a Sabbath? 16This woman belongs to the family of Abraham, but Satan has kept her bound for eighteen years. Isn't it right to set her free on the Sabbath?" 17Jesus' words made all his enemies ashamed. But everyone else in the crowd was happy about the wonderful things he was doing.

A Mustard Seed and Yeast
(Matthew 13.31–33; Mark 4.30–32)

18Jesus said, "What is God's kingdom like? What can I compare it with? 19It is like what happens when someone plants a mustard seed in a garden. The seed grows as big as a tree, and birds nest in its branches."

20Then Jesus said, "What can I compare God's kingdom with? 21It is like what happens when a woman mixes yeast into three batches of flour. Finally, all the dough rises."

The Narrow Door
(Matthew 7.13, 14, 21–23)

22As Jesus was on his way to Jerusalem, he taught the people in the towns and villages. 23Someone asked him, "Lord, are only a few people going to be saved?"

Jesus answered:

24Do all you can to go in by the narrow door! A lot of people will try to

God's laws make good sense

(14) When Jesus healed a woman on the Sabbath, the man in charge of the meeting place was angry because he thought Jesus was "working" on God's special day. The man knew something in his head about the Law of God, but he didn't understand the Law's purpose. The Sabbath was supposed to be a day for honoring God. What better way is there to honor God on his day than by doing a kind thing for someone?

The news of God's kingdom spreads

(19) What Jesus said about the mustard seed two thousand years ago has actually come true. The good news of the kingdom of God began as a very small thing in a very small country. But the news of that kingdom has grown into a tree which has spread all over the world. The church has gone into every nation, with amazing effects on the lives of many millions of people.

Don't be left out

(24) The door to God stands open for all who wish to go through it. Jesus himself is that door. He himself is the way to heaven. By receiving him and turning

get in, but will not be able to. ²⁵Once
the owner of the house gets up and locks
the door, you will be left standing outside. You will knock on the door and
say, "Sir, open the door for us!"

But the owner will answer, "I don't
know a thing about you!"

²⁶Then you will start saying, "We
dined with you, and you taught in our
streets."

²⁷But he will say, "I really don't know
who you are! Get away from me, all
you evil people!"

²⁸Then when you have been thrown
outside, you will weep and grit your
teeth because you will see Abraham and
Isaac and all the prophets in God's kingdom. ²⁹People will come from all directions and sit down to feast in God's kingdom. ³⁰There the ones who are now
least important will be the most important, and those who are now most important will be least important.

Jesus and Herod

³¹At that time some Pharisees came to
Jesus and said, "You had better get away
from here! Herodᵏ wants to kill you."

³²Jesus said to them:

Go tell that fox, "I am going to force
out demons and heal people today and
tomorrow, and three days later I'll be
through." ³³But I am going on my way
today and tomorrow and the next day.
After all, Jerusalem is the place where
prophets are killed.

Jesus Loves Jerusalem
(Matthew 23.37–39)

³⁴Jerusalem, Jerusalem! Your people
have killed the prophets and have
stoned the messengers who were sent
to you. I have often wanted to gather
your people, as a hen gathers her chicks

ᵏHerod: Herod Antipas, the son of Herod the Great.

away from our selfish lives,
we have eternal life. The
door is narrow, and we can
just squeeze through if we
are willing to leave the baggage of our sins behind.

Poor Jerusalem
(34) Over the centuries, the
city of Jerusalem has been
destroyed more than once.
But the city keeps rising up
again. The nation of Israel
is the only ancient society
that has been destroyed
only to be set up again in
modern times. God used the
United Nations to begin re-
storing the land of Israel in
1948. Jesus predicted that
Israel will welcome him the
second time he appears, instead of rejecting him as
they did the first time.

under her wings. But you wouldn't let me. [35]Now your temple will be deserted. You will not see me again until the time when you say,

> "Blessed is the one who comes
> in the name of the Lord."

Jesus Heals a Sick Man

14 One Sabbath Jesus was having dinner in the home of an important Pharisee, and everyone was carefully watching Jesus. [2]All of a sudden a man with swollen legs stood up in front of him. [3]Jesus turned and asked the Pharisees and the teachers of the Law of Moses, "Is it right to heal on the Sabbath?" [4]But they did not say a word.

Jesus took hold of the man. Then he healed him and sent him away. [5]Afterwards, Jesus asked the people, "If your son or ox falls into a well, wouldn't you pull him out right away, even on the Sabbath?" [6]There was nothing they could say.

How to Be a Guest

[7]Jesus saw how the guests had tried to take the best seats. So he told them:

[8]When you are invited to a wedding feast, don't sit in the best place. Someone more important may have been invited. [9]Then the one who invited you will come and say, "Give your place to this other guest!" You will be embarrassed and will have to sit in the worst place.

[10]When you are invited to be a guest, go and sit in the worst place. Then the one who invited you may come and say, "My friend, take a better seat!" You will then be honored in front of all the other guests. [11]If you put yourself above others, you will be put down. But if you humble yourself, you will be honored.

[12]Then Jesus said to the man who had invited him:

Honoring God on his day
(1) At present the Lord's special day is Sunday, not the Sabbath (Saturday) as it was when Jesus was here. The point is the same: the Lord's Day is a day for honoring God, and we honor God when we do acts of kindness and mercy for others.

Jesus invites us to be losers
(10) Being a loser doesn't seem very exciting. But it was Jesus' own way to *lose* in order to *win*. Our way is just the opposite. We all want to be winners. But Jesus puzzles us by saying we can't win by pushing other people around, or by using other people just to gain our own advantage. The real way to get ahead in God's plan is to use our own lives to help others along the path of life.

When you give a dinner or a banquet, don't invite your friends and family and relatives and rich neighbors. If you do, they will invite you in return, and you will be paid back. 13When you give a feast, invite the poor, the crippled, the lame, and the blind. 14They cannot pay you back. But God will bless you and reward you when his people rise from death.

The Great Banquet
(Matthew 22.1–10)

15After Jesus had finished speaking, one of the guests said, "The greatest blessing of all is to be at the banquet in God's kingdom!"

16Jesus told him:

A man once gave a great banquet and invited a lot of guests. 17When the banquet was ready, he sent a servant to tell the guests, "Everything is ready! Please come."

18One guest after another started making excuses. The first one said, "I bought some land, and I've got to look it over. Please excuse me."

19Another guest said, "I bought five teams of oxen, and I need to try them out. Please excuse me."

20Still another guest said, "I have just gotten married, and I can't be there."

21The servant told his master what happened, and the master became so angry that he said, "Go as fast as you can to every street and alley in town! Bring in everyone who is poor or crippled or blind or lame."

22When the servant returned, he said, "Master, I've done what you told me, and there is still plenty room for more people."

23His master then told him, "Go out along the back roads and fence rows and make people come in, so that my house will be full. 24Not one of the guests

We can be replaced

(18) The invited guests were too busy to come to the banquet. All right, then—the host just sent out and brought in the most unimportant people he could find. Those guests who were first invited were probably very disappointed to find out they could be so easily replaced. If we don't accept God's kindness, he can easily find others who will.

I first invited will get even a bite of my food!"

Being a Disciple
(Matthew 10.37, 38)

25Large crowds were walking along with Jesus, when he turned and said:

26You cannot be my disciple, unless you love me more than you love your father and mother, your wife and children, and your brothers and sisters. You cannot come with me unless you love me more than you love your own life.

27You cannot be my disciple unless you carry your own cross and come with me.

28Suppose one of you wants to build a tower. What is the first thing you will do? Won't you sit down and figure out how much it will cost and if you have enough money to pay for it? 29Otherwise, you will start building the tower, but not be able to finish. Then everyone who sees what is happening will laugh at you. 30They will say, "You started building, but could not finish the job."

31What will a king do if he has only ten thousand soldiers to defend himself against a king who is about to attack him with twenty thousand soldiers? Before he goes out to battle, won't he first sit down and decide if he can win? 32If he thinks he won't be able to defend himself, he will send messengers and ask for peace while the other king is still a long way off. 33So then, you cannot be my disciple unless you give away everything you own.

Salt and Light
(Matthew 5.13; Mark 9.50)

34Salt is good, but if it no longer tastes like salt, how can it be made to taste salty again? 35It is no longer good for the soil or even for the manure pile. People simply throw it out. If you have ears, pay attention!

"How much will it cost?"
(28) You will usually ask this question before you buy something that might be expensive. Before you decide to follow Jesus you should also ask, "What will it cost me to be a disciple?" If you're doing it right, it will cost everything you are and all you have. But if you say "Yes" to Jesus and then try to hold back, you might end up worse off than before.

What flavor is a Christian?
(34) Jesus says a Christian should be "salty." He means that our lives should not be dull and lifeless, but exciting and alive. Christians have eternal life—a good reason to be joyful and encouraging to those around them. Salt was also used to preserve food. "Salty" Christians preserve others from "rotting" by showing them the good news about being saved through the Lord Jesus.

One Sheep
(Matthew 18.12–14)

15 Tax collectors[1] and sinners were all crowding around to listen to Jesus. [2]So the Pharisees and the teachers of the Law of Moses started grumbling, "This man is friendly with sinners. He even eats with them."

[3]Then Jesus told them this story:

[4]If any of you has a hundred sheep, and one of them gets lost, what will you do? Won't you leave the ninety-nine in the field and go look for the lost sheep until you find it? [5]And when you find it, you will be so glad that you will put it on your shoulder [6]and carry it home. Then you will call in your friends and neighbors and say, "Let's celebrate! I've found my lost sheep."

[7]Jesus said, "In the same way there is more happiness in heaven because of one sinner who turns to God than over ninety-nine good people who don't need to."

How valuable is one person?

(4) With today's growing population, individual persons seem to get lost and forgotten in the crowd. The stories about the one sheep and the one coin tell us that God knows and cares about each one of us. God doesn't just think about people in groups, but he thinks about them all *one by one*. So there is great happiness in heaven when one person comes to Jesus.

One Coin

[8]Jesus told the people another story:

What will a woman do if she has ten silver coins and loses one of them? Won't she light a lamp, sweep the floor, and look carefully until she finds it? [9]Then she will call in her friends and neighbors and say, "Let's celebrate! I've found the coin I lost."

[10]Jesus said, "In the same way God's angels are happy when even one person turns to him."

Two Sons

[11]Jesus also told them another story:

Once a man had two sons. [12]The younger son said to his father, "Give me my share of the property." So the father divided his property between his two sons.

---

[1]*Tax collectors*: See the note at 3.12.

13Not long after that, the younger son packed up everything he owned and left for a foreign country, where he wasted all his money in wild living. 14He had spent everything, when a bad famine spread through that whole land. Soon he had nothing to eat.

15He went to work for a man in that country, and the man sent him out to take care of his pigs.*m* 16He would have been glad to eat what the pigs were eating,*n* but no one gave him a thing.

17Finally, he came to his senses and said, "My father's workers have plenty to eat, and here I am, starving to death! 18I will leave and go to my father and say to him, 'Father, I have sinned against God in heaven and against you. 19I am no longer good enough to be called your son. Treat me like one of your workers.' "

20The younger son got up and started back to his father. But when he was still a long way off, his father saw him and felt sorry for him. He ran to his son and hugged and kissed him.

21The son said, "Father, I have sinned against God in heaven and against you. I am no longer good enough to be called your son."

22But his father said to the servants, "Hurry and bring the best clothes and put them on him. Give him a ring for his finger and sandals*o* for his feet. 23Get the best calf and prepare it, so we can eat and celebrate. 24This son of mine was dead, but has now come back to life. He was lost and has now been found." And they began to celebrate.

Who was the lost son?
(21) We might say that the younger son was the lost son. But wait—that lost son was *found*. At the end of the story, we aren't told what happened to the older son. The last time we saw him, he was pouting because his father loved the younger son. Let's hope that the older son did not become the lost son, shutting himself out of his father's family. He should have joined the party, glad to see his younger brother home again. Likewise, we ought to be glad when lost people come home to Jesus.

m pigs: The Jewish religion taught that pigs were not fit to eat or even to touch. A Jewish man would have felt terribly insulted if he had to feed pigs, much less eat with them. *n what the pigs were eating*: The Greek text has "(bean) pods," which came from a tree in Palestine. These were used to feed animals. Poor people sometimes ate them too. *o ring . . . sandals*: These show that the young man's father fully accepted him as his son. A ring was a sign of high position in the family. Sandals showed that he was a son instead of a slave, since slaves did not usually wear sandals.

25The older son had been out in the field. But when he came near the house, he heard the music and dancing. 26So he called one of the servants over and asked, "What's going on here?"

27The servant answered, "Your brother has come home safe and sound, and your father ordered us to kill the best calf." 28The older brother got so mad that he would not even go into the house.

His father came out and begged him to go in. 29But he said to his father, "For years I have worked for you like a slave and have always obeyed you. But you have never even given me a little goat, so that I could give a dinner for my friends. 30This other son of yours wasted your money on bad women. And now that he has come home, you ordered the best calf to be killed for a feast."

31His father replied, "My son, you are always with me, and everything I have is yours. 32But we should be glad and celebrate! Your brother was dead, but he is now alive. He was lost and has now been found."

A Dishonest Manager

16 Jesus said to his disciples:
A rich man once had a manager to take care of his business. But he was told that his manager was wasting money. 2So the rich man called him in and said, "What is this I hear about you? Tell me what you have done! You are no longer going to work for me."

3The manager said to himself, "What shall I do now that my master is going to fire me? I can't dig ditches, and I'm ashamed to beg. 4I know what I'll do, so that people will welcome me into their homes after I've lost my job."

5Then one by one he called in the people who were in debt to his master. He asked the first one, "How much do you owe my master?"

6"A hundred barrels of olive oil," the man answered.

So the manager said, "Take your bill and sit down and quickly write 'fifty'."

7The manager asked someone else who was in debt to his master, "How much do you owe?"

"A thousand bushels^p of wheat," the man replied.

The manager said, "Take your bill and write 'eight hundred'."

8The master praised his dishonest manager for looking out for himself so well. That's how it is! The people of this world look out for themselves better than the people who belong to the light.

9My disciples, I tell you to use wicked wealth to make friends for yourselves. Then when it is gone, you will be welcomed into an eternal home. 10Anyone who can be trusted in little matters can also be trusted in important matters. But anyone who is dishonest in little matters will be dishonest in important matters. 11If you cannot be trusted with this wicked wealth, who will trust you with true wealth? 12And if you cannot be trusted with what belongs to someone else, who will give you something that will be your own? 13You cannot be the slave of two masters. You will like one more than the other or be more loyal to one than to the other. You cannot serve God and money.

Some Sayings of Jesus
(Matthew 11.12, 13; 5.31, 32; Mark 10.11, 12)

14The Pharisees really loved money. So when they heard what Jesus said, they made fun of him. 15But Jesus told them:

You are always making yourselves look good, but God sees what is in your heart. The things that most people think are important are worthless as far as God is concerned.

^p*a thousand bushels*: The Greek text has "a hundred measures," and each measure is about ten or twelve bushels.

What shall we spend our lives for?
(8) The dishonest manager spent his employer's wealth to make himself rich. We all have a certain amount of this world's goods and abilities, and these all come from God. How do we spend the wealth God gives us? Do we use the gifts of God to fatten ourselves? Or do we use them for the sake of God's heavenly kingdom?

God is not a means to an end
(14) The Pharisees really loved money. For the worst of them, that was their chief interest in life. They didn't care about pleasing God, or even about keeping the Law they were always talking about. This meant that their outward service to God was just a show by which they made themselves rich. It's horrible to think there are people who believe they can use God as a way to get wealthy.

16Until the time of John the Baptist, people had to obey the Law of Moses and the Books of the Prophets.q But since God's kingdom has been preached, everyone is trying hard to get in. 17Heaven and earth will disappear before the smallest letter of the Law does.

18It is a terrible sinr for a man to divorce his wife and marry another woman. It is also a terrible sin for a man to marry a divorced woman.

Lazarus and the Rich Man

19There was once a rich man who wore expensive clothes and every day ate the best food. 20But a poor beggar named Lazarus was brought to the gate of the rich man's house. 21He was happy just to eat the scraps that fell from the rich man's table. His body was covered with sores, and dogs kept coming up to lick them. 22The poor man died, and angels took him to the place of honor next to Abraham.s

The rich man also died and was buried. 23He went to hellt and was suffering terribly. When he looked up and saw Abraham far off and Lazarus at his side, 24he said to Abraham, "Have pity on me! Send Lazarus to dip his finger in water and touch my tongue. I'm suffering terribly in this fire."

25Abraham answered, "My friend, remember that while you lived, you had everything good, and Lazarus had everything bad. Now he is happy, and you are in pain. 26And besides, there

The Law matters to God
(17) We shouldn't get the idea that God doesn't care about how we live, but only about how we believe. That's a false idea. Jesus made it clear that every part of the Law was important. In this passage, Jesus was aiming his words about divorce mainly at the Pharisees. The truth was that the Pharisees didn't really care about the Law, even though they were always teaching it. In fact they were breaking the Law very badly.

What happens when we die?
(22) Some people say death is the end of everything. But Jesus tells us that we will continue to live either in heaven or in hell. Heaven is a happy place with God, and hell is a place of great misery. Why did the rich man in this story go to hell? It wasn't because he was rich, but because he would not turn to God. Make no mistake—hell is real, and Jesus spoke of hell more than anybody else in the Bible did. We need to face the hard fact of hell, and make sure we're headed for heaven.

qthe Law of Moses and the Books of the Prophets: The Jewish Scriptures, that is, the Old Testament. ra terrible sin: The Greek text uses a word that means the sin of being unfaithful in marriage. sthe place of honor next to Abraham: The Jewish people thought that heaven would be a banquet that God would give for them. Abraham would be the most important person there, and the guest of honor would sit next to him. thell: The Greek text has "hades," which the Jewish people often thought of as the place where the dead wait for the final judgment.

is a deep ditch between us, and no one from either side can cross over."

27But the rich man said, "Abraham, then please send Lazarus to my father's home. 28Let him warn my five brothers, so they won't come to this horrible place."

29Abraham answered, "Your brothers can read what Moses and the prophetsu wrote. They should pay attention to that."

30Then the rich man said, "No, that's not enough! If only someone from the dead would go to them, they would listen and turn to God."

31So Abraham said, "If they won't pay attention to Moses and the prophets, they won't listen even to someone who comes back from the dead."

Faith and Service
(Matthew 18.6, 7, 21, 22; Mark 9.42)

17 Jesus said to his disciples:
There will always be something that causes people to sin. But anyone who causes them to sin is in for trouble. A person who causes even one of my little followers to sin 2would be better off thrown into the ocean with a heavy stone tied around the neck. 3So be careful what you do.

Correct any followersv of mine who sin, and forgive the ones who say they are sorry. 4Even if one of them mistreats you seven times in one day and says, "I am sorry," you should still forgive that person.

5The apostles said to the Lord, "Make our faith stronger!"

6Jesus replied:
If you had faith no bigger than a tiny mustard seed, you could tell this mulberry tree to pull itself up, roots and

Make our faith stronger
(5) It seems that Jesus was answering the disciples' request for stronger faith when he told them the story about the servant. We really have faith when we don't think we're great just because we do what God tells us. Obeying God is only what we're supposed to do. We're great only because God loved us and forgave us as his free gift. Our good deeds are only our way of saying "thank you" to God.

---

uMoses and the prophets: The Jewish Scriptures, that is, the Old Testament.   vfollowers: The Greek text has "brothers," which is often used in the New Testament for followers of Jesus.

all, and to plant itself in the ocean. And it would!

7If your servant comes in from plowing or from taking care of the sheep, would you say, "Welcome! Come on in and have something to eat?" 8No, you wouldn't say that. You would say, "Fix me something to eat. Get ready to serve me, so I can have my meal. Then later on you can eat and drink." 9Servants don't deserve special thanks for doing what they are supposed to do. 10And that's how it should be with you. When you've done all you should, then say, "We are merely servants, and we have simply done our duty."

Ten Men with Leprosy

11On his way to Jerusalem, Jesus went along the border between Samaria and Galilee. 12As he was going into a village, ten

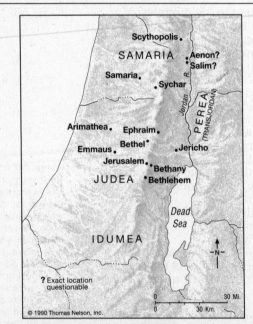

Judea and Samaria

men with leprosy[w] came toward him. They stood at a distance [13]and shouted, "Jesus, Master, have pity on us!"

[14]Jesus looked at them and said, "Go show yourselves to the priests."[x]

On their way they were healed. [15]When one of them discovered that he was healed, he came back, shouting praises to God. [16]He bowed down at the feet of Jesus and thanked him. The man was from the country of Samaria.

[17]Jesus asked, "Weren't ten men healed? Where are the other nine? [18]Why was this foreigner the only one who came back to thank God?" [19]Then Jesus told the man, "You may get up and go. Your faith has made you well."

Let's be thankful

(15) It's always a joy to do things for thankful people. But if we're ungrateful, it isn't easy for God or humans to do kind things for us. We send the message to others that we don't appreciate kindness and we would rather just be left alone. Usually we get our wish. We just end up being alone in the world.

God's Kingdom
(Matthew 24.23–28, 37–41)

[20]Some Pharisees asked Jesus when God's kingdom would come. He answered, "God's kingdom is not something you can see. [21]There is no use saying, 'Look! Here it is' or 'Look! There it is.' God's kingdom is here with you."[y]

[22]Jesus said to his disciples:

The time will come when you will long to see one of the days of the Son of Man, but you will not. [23]When people say to you, "Look there," or "Look here," don't go looking for him. [24]The day of the Son of Man will be like lightning flashing across the sky. [25]But first he must suffer terribly and be rejected by the people of today. [26]When the Son of Man comes, things will be just as they were when Noah lived. [27]People were eating, drinking, and getting married right up to the day when Noah went into the big boat. Then the flood came and drowned everyone on earth.

What is God's kingdom?

(20) Jesus answered the Pharisees in a puzzling way. They couldn't see the kingdom of God because they weren't ready for the kingdom. This was plain because they didn't recognize the King himself—Jesus. If they couldn't see the King, how could they know anything about God's kingdom?

---

[w]leprosy: See the note at 4.27.   [x]show yourselves to the priests: See the note at 5.14.   [y]here with you: Or "in your hearts."

28When Lotz lived, people were also eating and drinking. They were buying, selling, planting, and building. 29But on the very day Lot left Sodom, fiery flames poured down from the sky and killed everyone. 30The same will happen on the day when the Son of Man appears.

31At that time no one on a rooftopa should go down into the house to get anything. No one in a field should go back to the house for anything. 32Remember what happened to Lot's wife.b

33People who try to save their lives will lose them, and those who lose their lives will save them. 34On that night two people will be sleeping in the same bed, but only one will be taken. The other will be left. 35-36Two women will be together grinding wheat, but only one will be taken. The other will be left.c

37Then Jesus' disciples spoke up, "But where will this happen, Lord?"

Jesus said, "Where there is a corpse, there will always be buzzards."d

God's kingdom will come
(30) King Jesus *has* come, *is* coming, and *will* come. The kingdom of God was with us when Jesus was here. The kingdom is also with us in the good news that we have today about Jesus, and among those who truly love him. And the kingdom of God will also come in a powerful and final way at a time that is still in the future, when King Jesus returns to earth.

A Widow and a Judge

18 Jesus told his disciples a story about how they should keep on praying and never give up:

2In a town there was once a judge who didn't fear God or care about people. 3In that same town there was a widow who kept going to the judge and

God is listening, and he cares
(2) Some people don't return our phone calls because they don't care about us. But God sometimes delays answering our prayers to teach us important lessons. God isn't a vending machine that gives us a candy bar for the right change. God is interested in what is best for us, and he has a best time for meeting our needs. God will answer our prayers when he's ready. But it's good for us to keep asking while we're waiting, because God himself is worth the time we spend talking to him.

zNoah . . . Lot: When God destroyed the earth by a flood, he saved Noah and his family. And when God destroyed the cities of Sodom and Gomorrah and the evil people who lived there, he rescued Lot and his family. arooftop: See the note at 5.19. bwhat happened to Lot's wife: She turned to a block of salt when she disobeyed God. cwill be left: Some manuscripts add, "Two men will be in the same field, but only one will be taken. The other will be left." dWhere there is a corpse, there will always be buzzards: This saying may mean that when anything important happens, people soon know about it. Or the saying may mean that whenever something bad happens, curious people gather around and stare. But the word translated "buzzard" also means "eagle" and may refer to the Roman army, which had an eagle as its symbol.

saying, "Make sure that I get fair treatment in court."

⁴For a while the judge refused to do anything. Finally, he said to himself, "Even though I don't fear God or care about people, ⁵I will help this widow because she keeps on bothering me. If I don't help her, she will wear me out."

⁶The Lord said:

Think about what that crooked judge said. ⁷Won't God protect his chosen ones who pray to him day and night? Won't he be concerned for them? ⁸He will surely hurry and help them. But when the Son of Man comes, will he find on this earth anyone with faith?

A Pharisee and a Tax Collector

⁹Jesus told a story to some people who thought they were better than others and who looked down on everyone else:

¹⁰Two men went into the temple to pray.ᵉ One was a Pharisee and the other a tax collector.ᶠ ¹¹The Pharisee stood over by himself and prayed,ᵍ "God, I thank you that I am not greedy, dishonest, and unfaithful in marriage like other people. And I am really glad that I am not like that tax collector over there. ¹²I go without eatingʰ for two days a week, and I give you one tenth of all I earn."

¹³The tax collector stood off at a distance and did not think he was good enough even to look up toward heaven. He was so sorry for what he had done that he pounded his chest and prayed, "God, have pity on me! I am such a sinner."

¹⁴Then Jesus said, "When the two men went home, it was the tax collector and not the Pharisee who was pleasing to God. If

Pride separates us from God

(11) The Pharisee in Jesus' story knew more about his religion than the tax collector did. The Pharisee was even a "good man" by our way of measuring goodness. But he wasn't humble enough to see himself as a needy sinner. Everybody is a sinner. So the Pharisee's pride separated him from God. But the lowly tax collector saw the truth about himself, so God accepted him.

ᵉ*into the temple to pray:* Jewish people usually prayed there early in the morning and late in the afternoon. ᶠ*tax collector:* See the note at 3.12. ᵍ*stood over by himself and prayed:* Some manuscripts have "stood up and prayed to himself." ʰ*without eating:* See the note at 2.37.

you put yourself above others, you will be put down. But if you humble yourself, you will be honored."

Jesus Blesses Little Children
(Matthew 19.13–15; Mark 10.13–16)

15Some people brought their little children for Jesus to bless. But when his disciples saw them doing this, they told the people to stop bothering him. 16So Jesus called the children over to him and said, "Let the children come to me! Don't try to stop them. People who are like these children belong to God's kingdom.i 17You will never get into God's kingdom unless you enter it like a child!"

God cares about the small
(15) We shouldn't let ourselves get too big and important. Jesus cared about the children people brought to him. He was never too busy. He loved the honest, simple faith he saw in children, and wished people of all ages could be more like children in this way.

A Rich and Important Man
(Matthew 19.16–30; Mark 10.17–31)

18An important man asked Jesus, "Good Teacher, what must I do to have eternal life?"

19Jesus said, "Why do you call me good? Only God is good. 20You know the commandments: 'Be faithful in marriage. Do not murder. Do not steal. Do not tell lies about others. Respect your father and mother.'"

21He told Jesus, "I have obeyed all these commandments since I was a young man."

22When Jesus heard this, he said, "There is one thing you still need to do. Go and sell everything you own! Give the money to the poor, and you will have riches in heaven. Then come and be my follower." 23When the man heard this, he was sad, because he was very rich.

24Jesus saw how sad the man was. So he said, "It's terribly hard for rich people to get into God's kingdom! 25In fact, it's easier for a camel to go through the eye of a needle than for a rich person to get into God's kingdom."

26When the people heard this, they asked, "How can anyone ever be saved?"

Only God is good
(19) This fits what we just saw about the Pharisee and the tax collector. As soon as we begin to think we're "good," we start to cut ourselves off from God. The important man in this passage thought he had been good all his life. But his property was too important to him, and he went away sad. God has no equals.

iPeople who are like these children belong to God's kingdom: Or "God's kingdom belongs to people who are like these children."

27Jesus replied, "There are some things that people cannot do, but God can do anything."

28Peter said, "Remember, we left everything to be your followers!"

29Jesus answered, "You can be sure that anyone who gives up home or wife or brothers or family or children because of God's kingdom 30will be given much more in this life. And in the future world they will have eternal life."

Jesus Again Tells about His Death
(Matthew 20.17–19; Mark 10.32–34)

31Jesus took the twelve apostles aside and said:

We are now on our way to Jerusalem. Everything that the prophets wrote about the Son of Man will happen there. 32He will be handed over to foreigners,*j* who will make fun of him, mistreat him, and spit on him. 33They will beat him and kill him, but three days later he will rise to life.

34The apostles did not understand what Jesus was talking about. They could not understand, because the meaning of what he said was hidden from them.

Jesus Heals a Blind Beggar
(Matthew 20.29–34; Mark 10.46–52)

35When Jesus was coming close to Jericho, a blind man sat begging beside the road. 36The man heard the crowd walking by and asked what was happening. 37Some people told him that Jesus from Nazareth was passing by. 38So the blind man shouted, "Jesus, Son of David,*k* have pity on me!" 39The people who were going along with Jesus told the man to be quiet. But he shouted even louder, "Son of David, have pity on me!"

Jesus paid our debt

(31) We miss the whole plan of God if we think Jesus came just to teach us a lot of good rules for living. Jesus came to die in our place. We owed God a very great debt because of our sins. Jesus paid that debt.

Thank God

(35) The no-longer-blind beggar went with Jesus and thanked God. These were two good things to do. When we think of what Jesus has done for us, do we walk with him? Do we thank God in a way others can see? The beggar was a good example for others: soon the crowds were praising God too.

jforeigners: The Romans, who ruled Judea at this time.
kSon of David: The Jewish people expected the Messiah to be from the family of King David, and for this reason the Messiah was often called the "Son of David."

40Jesus stopped and told some people to bring the blind man over to him. When the blind man was getting near, Jesus asked, 41"What do you want me to do for you?"

"Lord, I want to see!" he answered.

42Jesus replied, "Look and you will see! Your eyes are healed because of your faith." 43Right away the man could see, and he went with Jesus and started thanking God. When the crowds saw what happened, they praised God.

Zacchaeus

19 Jesus was going through Jericho, 2where a man named Zacchaeus lived. He was in charge of collecting taxes[l] and was very rich. 3-4Jesus was heading his way, and Zacchaeus wanted to see what he was like. But Zacchaeus was a short man and could not see over the crowd. So he ran ahead and climbed up into a sycamore tree.

5When Jesus got there, he looked up and said, "Zacchaeus, hurry down! I want to stay with you today." 6Zacchaeus hurried down and gladly welcomed Jesus.

7Everyone who saw this started grumbling, "This man Zacchaeus is a sinner! And Jesus is going home to eat with him."

8Later that day Zacchaeus stood up and said to the Lord, "I will give half of my property to the poor. And I will now pay back four times as much[m] to everyone I have ever cheated."

9Jesus said to Zacchaeus, "Today you and your family have been saved,[n] because you are a true son of Abraham.[o] 10The Son of Man came to look for and to save people who are lost."

A mean man becomes kind

(6) Zacchaeus probably became rich by cheating people, something tax collectors were known for in those days. But Zacchaeus had a change of heart. He saw Jesus the Master, and he became a new man. The crowd didn't like it. They needed new hearts, too, but they couldn't stand the idea. Only people who know they're lost and need to do something about it—like Zacchaeus—can be saved.

[l]*in charge of collecting taxes*: See the note at 3.12. [m]*pay back four times as much*: Both Jewish and Roman law said that a person must pay back four times the amount that was taken. [n]*saved*: Zacchaeus was Jewish, but it is only now that he is rescued from sin and placed under God's care. [o]*son of Abraham*: As used in this verse, the words mean that Zacchaeus is truly one of God's special people.

A Story about Ten Servants
(Matthew 25.14–30)

11The people were still listening to Jesus as he was getting close to Jerusalem. Many of them thought that God's kingdom would soon appear, 12and Jesus told them this story:

A prince once went to a foreign country to be crowned king and then to return. 13But before leaving, he called in ten servants and gave each of them some money. He told them, "Use this to earn more money until I get back."

14But the people of his country hated him, and they sent messengers to the foreign country to say, "We don't want this man to be our king."

15After the prince had been made king, he returned and called in his servants. He asked them how much they had earned with the money they had been given.

16The first servant came and said, "Sir, with the money you gave me I have earned ten times as much."

17"That's fine, my good servant!" the king said. "Since you have shown that you can be trusted with a small amount, you will be given ten cities to rule."

18The second one came and said, "Sir, with the money you gave me, I have earned five times as much."

19The king said, "You will be given five cities."

20Another servant came and said, "Sir, here is your money. I kept it safe in a handkerchief. 21You are a hard man, and I was afraid of you. You take what is not yours, and you harvest crops you didn't plant."

22"You worthless servant!" the king told him. "You have condemned yourself by what you have just said. You knew that I am a hard man, taking what is not mine and harvesting what I've not planted. 23Why didn't you put my money in the bank? On my return, I

What does God expect from us?
(20) Some people think it's smart to "play it safe." But God doesn't want that from us. He wants the kind of people who can be a help to his kingdom. The man who hid the money in his handkerchief had done no good for anyone—and least of all for the prince in Jesus' story. By giving ourselves and our time to carry God's blessing to others we are good servants for Jesus our King.

could have had the money together with interest."

24Then he said to some other servants standing there, "Take the money away from him and give it to the servant who earned ten times as much."

25But they said, "Sir, he already has ten times as much!"

26The king replied, "Those who have something will be given more. But everything will be taken away from those who don't have anything. 27Now bring me the enemies who didn't want me to be their king. Kill them while I watch!"

Jesus Enters Jerusalem
(Matthew 21.1–11; Mark 11.1–11; John 12.12–19)

28When Jesus had finished saying all this, he went on toward Jerusalem. 29As he was getting near to Bethphage and Bethany on the Mount of Olives, he sent two of his disciples on ahead. 30He told them, "Go into the next village, where you will find a young donkey that has never been ridden. Untie the donkey and bring it here. 31If anyone asks why you are doing that, just say, 'The Lordp needs it.'"

32They went off and found everything just as Jesus had said. 33While they were untying the donkey, its owners asked, "Why are you doing that?"

34They answered, "The Lordp needs it."

35Then they led the donkey to Jesus. They put some of their clothes on its back and helped Jesus get on. 36And as he rode along, the people spread clothes on the roadq in front of him. 37When Jesus was starting down the Mount of Olives, his large crowd of disciples were happy and praised God because of all the miracles they had seen. 38They shouted,

> "Blessed is the king who comes
> in the name of the Lord!

Jesus knows

(32) Even when he was on earth in human form, Jesus showed at times that he had knowledge about things that he had not learned in an ordinary way. It is much more so today, now that Jesus has risen from the dead and has been taken up to heaven. Jesus knows all things and all people perfectly. Not a thing can be hidden from him.

---

pThe Lord: Or "The master of the donkey." qspread clothes on the road: This was one way that the Jewish people welcomed a famous person.

Peace in heaven
and glory to God."

39Some Pharisees in the crowd said to Jesus, "Teacher, make your disciples stop shouting!"

40But Jesus answered, "If they keep quiet, these stones will start shouting."

41When Jesus came closer and could see Jerusalem, he cried **42**and said:

It is too bad that today your people don't know what will bring them peace! Now it is hidden from them. **43**Jerusalem, the time will come when your enemies will build walls around you to attack you. Armies will surround you and close in on you from every side. **44**They will level you to the ground and kill your people. Not one stone in your buildings will be left on top of another. This will happen because you did not see that God had come to save you.*r*

Jesus in the Temple
*(Matthew 21.12–17; Mark 11.15–19;
John 2.13–22)*

45When Jesus entered the temple, he started chasing out the people who were selling things. **46**He told them, "The Scriptures say, 'My house should be a place of worship.' But you have made it a place where robbers hide!"

47Each day Jesus kept on teaching in the temple. So the chief priests, the teachers of the Law of Moses, and some other important people tried to have him killed. **48**But they could not find a way to do it, because everyone else was eager to listen to him.

A Question about Jesus' Authority
(Matthew 21.23–27; Mark 11.27–33)

20 One day Jesus was teaching in the temple and telling the good news. So the chief priests, the teachers, and the na-

Jesus foretold the future
(43) Jesus exactly described the destruction of Jerusalem. Forty years after Jesus spoke these words, a Roman army under General Titus built a wall around the city. No one in Jerusalem could get out, and no food could get in. Many starved to death. The temple and other parts of the city were destroyed. If the people had accepted Jesus when they had a chance, the city could have been spared from Rome's attack.

Why did they want to kill Jesus?
(45) Jesus did the most dangerous thing he could do by showing what the Jewish religious leaders were really like. For years they had gotten away with pretending to be holy men when they were actually taking bribes from merchants in the temple. It was as if Jesus threw ice water on those men. They would make him pay for his words.

*r*that God had come to save you: The Jewish people looked for the time when God would come and rescue them from their enemies. But when Jesus came, many of them refused to obey him.

tion's leaders ²asked him, "What right do you have to do these things? Who gave you this authority?"

³Jesus replied, "I want to ask you a question. ⁴Who gave John the right to baptize? Was it God in heaven or merely some human being?"

⁵They talked this over and said to each other, "We can't say that God gave John this right. Jesus will ask us why we didn't believe John. ⁶And we can't say that it was merely some human who gave John the right to baptize. The crowd will stone us to death, because they think John was a prophet."

⁷So they told Jesus, "We don't know who gave John the right to baptize."

⁸Jesus replied, "Then I won't tell you who gave me the right to do what I do."

Not much honesty here
(3) Jesus turned the Jewish leaders' question back on them. They were so concerned about their well-being that they couldn't say what was on their minds. They didn't want to risk upsetting the crowd. Maybe some of them suspected John's right to baptize was from God, but couldn't admit it to themselves. It's sad when people can't stand to be honest.

Renters of a Vineyard
(Matthew 21.33–46; Mark 12.1–12)

⁹Jesus told the people this story:

A man once planted a vineyard and rented it out. Then he left the country for a long time. ¹⁰When it was time to harvest the crop, he sent a servant to ask the renters for his share of the grapes. But they beat up the servant and sent him away without anything. ¹¹So the owner sent another servant. The renters also beat him up. They insulted him terribly and sent him away without a thing. ¹²The owner sent a third servant. He was also beaten terribly and thrown out of the vineyard.

¹³The owner then said to himself, "What am I going to do? I know what. I'll send my son, the one I love so much. They will surely respect him!"

¹⁴When the renters saw the owner's son, they said to one another, "Someday he will own the vineyard. Let's kill him! Then we can have it all for ourselves." ¹⁵So they threw him out of the vineyard and killed him.

Jesus asked, "What do you think the owner of the vineyard will do? ¹⁶I'll tell you what he will do! He will come and kill those renters and let someone else have his vineyard."

When the people heard this, they said, "This must never happen!"

17But Jesus looked straight at them and said, "Then what do the Scriptures mean when they say, 'The stone that the builders tossed aside is now the most important stone of all'? 18Anyone who stumbles over this stone will get hurt, and anyone it falls on will be smashed to pieces."

19The chief priests and the teachers of the Law of Moses knew that Jesus was talking about them when he was telling this story. They wanted to arrest him right then, but they were afraid of the people.

Paying Taxes
(Matthew 22.15–22; Mark 12.13–17)

20Jesus' enemies kept watching him closely, because they wanted to hand him over to the Roman governor. So they sent some men who pretended to be good. But they were really spies trying to catch Jesus saying something wrong. 21The spies said to him, "Teacher, we know that you teach the truth about what God wants people to do. And you treat everyone with the same respect, no matter who they are. 22Tell us, should we pay taxes to the Emperor or not?"

23Jesus knew that they were trying to trick him. So he told them, 24"Show me a coin." Then he asked, "Whose picture and name are on it?"

"The Emperor's," they answered.

25Then he told them, "Give the Emperor what belongs to him and give God what belongs to God." 26Jesus' enemies could not catch him saying anything wrong there in front of the people. They were amazed at his answer and kept quiet.

Life in the Future World
(Matthew 22.23–33; Mark 12.18–27)

27The Sadducees did not believe that people would rise to life after death. So some of them came to Jesus 28and said:

Who will get the vineyard?
(16) Jesus had come to offer himself to Israel as their King. But he taught that because of Israel's coldness toward him, their special blessing would be given to other people. A lesson we can learn is that if we don't accept God's love, then he will bless other people who will appreciate him and his Son.

How deceitful we can be
(20) Think of it: the spies were actually using their religion to trick Jesus. Then they would be able to have him arrested. A great prophet once said that the human heart is more deceitful than anything—so deceitful that we can even use God's word as a way to do evil. May the Lord keep us from ever being so hardhearted.

Teacher, Moses wrote that if a married man dies and has no children, his brother should marry the widow. Their first son would then be thought of as the son of the dead brother.

29There were once seven brothers. The first one married, but died without having any children. 30The second one married his brother's widow, and he also died without having any children. 31The same thing happened to the third one. Finally, all seven brothers married that woman and died without having any children. 32At last the woman died. 33When God raises people from death, whose wife will this woman be? All seven brothers had married her. 34Jesus answered:

The people in this world get married. 35But in the future world no one who is worthy to rise from death will either marry 36or die. They will be like the angels and will be God's children, because they have been raised to life.

37In the story about the burning bush, Moses clearly shows that people will live again. He said, "The Lord is the God worshiped by Abraham, Isaac, and Jacob."s 38So the Lord is not the God of the dead, but of the living. This means that everyone is alive as far as God is concerned.

39Some of the teachers of the Law of Moses said, "Teacher, you have given a good answer!" 40From then on, no one dared to ask Jesus any questions.

About David's Son
(Matthew 22.41–46; Mark 12.35–37)

41Jesus asked, "Why do people say that the Messiah will be the son of King David?t 42In the book of Psalms, David himself says,

Don't ask foolish questions
(29) That's what the Sadducees were doing when they asked about the dead man's widow. The worst of it was that they even *knew* the question was foolish. But they asked it anyway, hoping to put Jesus on the spot. Later on, a famous apostle named Paul warned about asking useless questions (see 1 Timothy 6.4, 5).

A tough question
(41) Jesus' enemies were asking "tough questions," so he tried one on them. Because Jesus is the Son of God, his ancestor David called him "my Lord." It was right there in the book of Psalms, but the enemies of Jesus didn't want to see it.

s"The Lord is the God worshiped by Abraham, Isaac, and Jacob": Jesus argues that if God is worshiped by these three, they must be alive, because he is the God of the living. tthe son of King David: See the note at 18.38.

'The Lord said to my Lord,
Sit at my right side^u
⁴³until I make your enemies
into a footstool for you.'
⁴⁴David spoke of the Messiah as his Lord,
so how can the Messiah be his son?"

Jesus and the Teachers of the Law of Moses
*(Matthew 23.1–36; Mark 12.38–40;
Luke 11.37–54)*

⁴⁵While everyone was listening to Jesus,
he said to his disciples:

⁴⁶Guard against the teachers of the
Law of Moses! They love to walk around
in long robes, and they like to be greeted
in the market. They want the front seats
in the meeting places and the best seats
at banquets. ⁴⁷But they cheat widows
out of their homes and then pray long
prayers just to show off. These teachers
will be punished most of all.

A Widow's Offering
(Mark 12.41–44)

21 Jesus looked up and saw some rich
people tossing their gifts into the offering box. ²He also saw a poor widow putting in two pennies. ³And he said, "I tell
you that this poor woman has put in more
than all the others. ⁴Everyone else gave
what they didn't need. But she is very poor
and gave everything she had."

The Temple Will Be Destroyed
(Matthew 24.1, 2; Mark 13.1, 2)

⁵Some people were talking about the
beautiful stones used to build the temple
and about the gifts that had been placed
in it. Jesus said, ⁶"Do you see these stones?
The time is coming when not one of them
will be left in place. They will all be knocked
down."

^{u}*right side*: The place of power and honor.

Love God for his own sake
(45) The "teachers of the
Law of Moses" liked to be
well thought of by everyone.
It's not wrong to be well
thought of, but these men
made a career out of being
popular. The truth didn't
matter—as long as the
teachers stayed rich and
powerful. Neither was there
anything wrong with the Law
they taught—but they didn't
obey it. Jesus said that these
showoffs would receive
more punishment. Let that
be a warning to us.

*What shall we give to
God?*
(1) We should never insult
God by giving him what
costs us nothing. God gave
his very own Son for us. We
owe him our very lives and
all we have. As the famous
hymn writer Isaac Watts put
it, "Love so amazing, so divine, demands my soul, my
life, my all."

All buildings pass away
(5) We enjoy beauty of all
kinds, and so we enjoy
beautiful buildings. Jesus
was probably sad when he
announced that the beautiful temple would be de-
stroyed—as indeed it was in
the year 70. Let's not forget
that even the most lasting
things of this world will pass
away some day. In his
church Jesus is building
something that will never
pass away.

Warning about Trouble
(Matthew 24.3–14; Mark 13.3–13)

7Some people asked, "Teacher, when will all this happen? How can we know when these things are about to take place?"

8Jesus replied:

Don't be fooled by all those who will come and claim to be me. They will say, "I am Christ!" and "Now is the time!" But don't follow them. 9When you hear about wars and riots, don't be afraid. These things will have to happen first, but that is not the end.

10Nations will go to war against one another, and kingdoms will attack each other. 11There will be great earthquakes, and in many places people will starve to death and suffer terrible diseases. All sorts of frightening things will be seen in the sky.

12Before all this happens, you will be arrested and punished. You will be tried in the Jewish meeting places and put in jail. Because of me you will be placed on trial before kings and governors. 13But this will be your chance to tell about your faith.

14Don't worry about what you will say to defend yourselves. 15I will give you the wisdom to know what to say. None of your enemies will be able to oppose you or to say that you are wrong. 16You will be betrayed by your own parents, brothers, family, and friends. Some of you will even be killed. 17Because of me you will be hated by everyone. 18But don't worry!v 19You will be saved by being faithful to me.

Jerusalem Will Be Destroyed
(Matthew 24.15–21; Mark 13.14–19)

20When you see Jerusalem surrounded by soldiers, you will know that it will soon be destroyed. 21If you are

vBut don't worry: The Greek text has "Not a hair of your head will be lost," which means, "There's no need to worry."

Believers are saved at last
(12) Many Christians would have to go through hard times before seeing Jesus. Even those closest to them might hate them. Many of them would be killed. That was hard. Who would want to follow such a faith? Today believers still suffer for Jesus, but they come through it for three reasons: (1) Jesus suffered for us first; (2) we have his real friendship now; (3) we want to see him face to face.

Jerusalem would be destroyed
(20) Some of the people listening to Jesus would be alive forty years later when everything he told about would happen. How did Jesus know those things in such great detail? It was because Jesus is who the Bible says he is—the Son of God from heaven. He is in charge of the past, the present, and the future.

living in Judea at that time, run to the mountains. If you are in the city, leave it. And if you are out in the country, don't go back into the city. 22This time of punishment is what is written about in the Scriptures. 23It will be an awful time for women who are expecting babies or nursing young children! Everywhere in the land people will suffer horribly and be punished. 24Some of them will be killed by swords. Others will be carried off to foreign countries. Jerusalem will be overrun by foreign nations until their time comes to an end.

When the Son of Man Appears
(Matthew 24.29–31; Mark 13.24–27)

25Strange things will happen to the sun, moon, and stars. The nations on earth will be afraid of the roaring sea and tides, and they won't know what to do. 26People will be so frightened that they will faint because of what is happening to the world. Every power in the sky will be shaken.w 27Then the Son of Man will be seen, coming in a cloud with great power and glory. 28When all of this starts happening, stand up straight and be brave. You will soon be set free.

Nature will be shaken
(25) We may imagine that the sun, moon, stars, and all of nature will go on and on without end. But nothing in the material universe has to last forever. Things last only as long as their Creator keeps them all in place. Some day he will shake it all like a tree of ripe fruit, and all will come crashing down. Through it all, believers will be kept safe. Then Jesus will come, and God will make all things new.

A Lesson from a Fig Tree
(Matthew 24.32–35; Mark 13.28–31)

29Then Jesus told them a story:
When you see a fig tree or any other tree 30putting out leaves, you know that summer will soon come. 31So, when you see these things happening, you know that God's kingdom will soon be here. 32You can be sure that some of the people living today will still be alive when all of this takes place. 33The sky and the earth won't last forever, but my words will.

wEvery power in the sky will be shaken: In ancient times people thought that the stars were spiritual powers.

A Warning

34Don't spend all of your time thinking about eating or drinking or worrying about life. If you do, the final day will suddenly catch you 35like a trap. That day will surprise everyone on earth. 36Watch out and keep praying that you can escape all that is going to happen and that the Son of Man will be pleased with you.

37Jesus taught in the temple each day, and he spent each night on the Mount of Olives. 38Everyone got up early and came to the temple to hear him teach.

A Plot to Kill Jesus
(Matthew 26.1–5, 14, 16; Mark 14.1, 2, 10, 11; John 11.45–53)

22 The Feast of Thin Bread, also called Passover, was near. 2The chief priests and the teachers of the Law of Moses were looking for a way to get rid of Jesus, because they were afraid of what the people might do. 3Then Satan entered the heart of Judas Iscariot,x who was one of the twelve apostles.

4Judas went to talk with the chief priests and the officers of the temple police about how he could help them arrest Jesus. 5They were very pleased and offered to pay Judas some money. 6He agreed and started looking for a good chance to betray Jesus when the crowds were not around.

Jesus Eats with His Disciples
(Matthew 26.17–25; Mark 14.12–21; John 13.21–30)

7The day had come for the Feast of Thin Bread, and it was time to kill the Passover lambs. 8So Jesus said to Peter and John, "Go and prepare the Passover meal for us to eat."

9But they asked, "Where do you want us to prepare it?"

10Jesus told them, "As you go into the

We are not deathless
(34) Are you living as if this were the day of your death? Death brings the end of all chances to get our lives in line with God. Thinking only about things like eating, drinking, jobs, houses, cars, and clothing is therefore a waste of time. It would be better to make our time spent worrying into time spent praying. Each day, each hour, may be our last on earth. Are we ready to meet God?

Why was Jesus on the mountain?
(37) Surely Jesus could have found a place to stay besides that mountain. But he needed time to be alone so he could pray to his Father, and a good place for that was on a mountain. In this way, too, Jesus is our example of how to live. We see that he spent a lot of time in public, but he also needed lots of time alone for prayer. So do we.

Look out for Satan's work
(3) Judas had allowed himself to think thoughts about Jesus that weren't true. As he turned these evil thoughts over in his mind, Satan took control of his life. We dare not imagine that Satan cannot attack us. He tries to deceive us at every turn in life. But we pray, as Jesus taught us, to be protected from "the evil one" (see the footnote at Matthew 6.13). And we will be protected.

xIscariot: See the note at 6.16.

city, you will meet a man carrying a jar of water.^y Follow him into the house ¹¹and say to the owner, 'Our teacher wants to know where he can eat the Passover meal with his disciples.' ¹²The owner will take you upstairs and show you a large room ready for you to use. Prepare the meal there."

¹³Peter and John left. They found everything just as Jesus had told them, and they prepared the Passover meal.

Time for the lambs to die
(13) The time to kill the Passover lambs would also be the time for Jesus, the perfect Lamb of God, to die for the sins of the world.

The Lord's Supper
(Matthew 26.26–30; Mark 14.22–26;
1 Corinthians 11.23–25)

¹⁴When the time came for Jesus and the apostles to eat, ¹⁵he said to them, "I have very much wanted to eat this Passover meal with you before I suffer. ¹⁶I tell you that I

^y*a man carrying a jar of water:* A male slave carrying water would probably mean that the family was rich.

The Twelve Apostles

1. Simon Peter, son of Jonah; from Bethsaida, then Capernaum

2. Andrew; brother of no. 1; both were fishermen

3. James, "the older," son of Zebedee; from Bethsaida

4. John; Gospel writer; brother of no. 3; both were fishermen

5. James, "the younger," son of Alphaeus; from Galilee

6. Thaddaeus (or Jude or Lebbaeus); brother of no. 5

7. Philip; from Bethsaida; not the same as the Philip in Acts 8

8. Bartholomew (or Nathaniel); from Cana in Galilee

9. Matthew (or Levi); Gospel writer; from Capernaum; tax collector

10. Thomas ("the twin"); from Galilee; "doubting Thomas"

11. Simon ("the Cananaean" or "the Eager One"); from Galilee

12. Judas Iscariot; betrayed Jesus; replaced by Matthias (Acts 1)

will not eat another Passover meal until it
is finally eaten in God's kingdom."

17Jesus took a cup of wine in his hands
and gave thanks to God. Then he told the
apostles, "Take this wine and share it with
each other. 18I tell you that I will not drink
any more wine until God's kingdom comes."

19Jesus took some bread in his hands and
gave thanks for it. He broke the bread and
handed it to his apostles. Then he said, "This
is my body, which is given for you. Eat this
as a way of remembering me!"

20After the meal he took another cup of
wine in his hands. Then he said, "This is
my blood. It is poured out for you, and with
it God makes his new agreement. 21The one
who will betray me is here at the table with
me! 22The Son of Man will die in the way
that has been decided for him, but it will
be terrible for the one who betrays him!"

23Then the apostles started arguing about
who would ever do such a thing.

An Argument about Greatness

24The apostles got into an argument
about which one of them was the greatest.
25So Jesus told them:

Foreign kings order their people
around, and powerful rulers call themselves everyone's friends.z 26But don't
be like them. The most important one
of you should be like the least important, and your leader should be like a
servant. 27Who do people think is the
greatest, a person who is served or one
who serves? Isn't it the one who is
served? But I have been with you as a
servant.

28You have stayed with me in all my
troubles. 29So I will give you the right
to rule as kings, just as my Father has
given me the right to rule as a king.
30You will eat and drink with me in my
kingdom, and you will each sit on a

What does the Lord's Supper mean?

(17) It has been said that the Lord's Supper is "the good news without words." Jesus commands us to eat and drink the supper at which we remember his death. He said, "This is my body," and, "This is my blood." The bread and the wine are not actually his body and blood, but they are a real picture of Christ's death for us. The idea is that we are to be filled with Jesus' life by his spirit working in us.

We are great by serving

(24) At a time like this, with Jesus about to die, the apostles argued about which of them was greatest. Jesus could see a day when they would be great in his king-dom, but for the time being they would have to be ser-vants. We are great when we "lay down our lives" for others in service. That makes us like Jesus.

zeveryone's friends: This translates a Greek word that
rulers sometimes used as a title for themselves or for
special friends.

throne to judge the twelve tribes of
Israel.

Jesus' Disciples Will Be Tested
(Matthew 26.31–35; Mark 14.27–31;
John 13.36–38)

³¹Jesus said, "Simon, listen to me! Satan
has demanded the right to test each one
of you, as a farmer does when he separates
wheat from the husks.ᵃ ³²But Simon, I have
prayed that your faith will be strong. And
when you have come back to me, help the
others."

³³Peter said, "Lord, I am ready to go with
you to jail and even to die with you."

³⁴Jesus replied, "Peter, I tell you that before a rooster crows tomorrow morning,
you will say three times that you don't know
me."

Why was Simon tested?
(31) Why are any of us
tested? We take tests to see
whether we can do a certain
job. If we aren't tested we
become weak, but testing
proves how strong or weak
we are. Simon Peter later
discovered how weak he
was when he denied Jesus.
But that was good in the long
run, because Simon Peter
learned to trust God rather
than his own ability.

Moneybags, Traveling Bags, and Swords

³⁵Jesus asked his disciples, "When I sent
you out without a moneybag or a traveling
bag or sandals, did you need anything?"

"No!" they answered.

³⁶Jesus told them, "But now, if you have
a moneybag, take it with you. Also take a
traveling bag, and if you don't have a
sword,ᵇ sell some of your clothes and buy
one. ³⁷Do this because the Scriptures say,
'He was considered a criminal.' This was
written about me, and it will soon come
true."

³⁸The disciples said, "Lord, here are two
swords!"

"Enough of that!" Jesus replied.

Be ready to travel
(35) When Jesus sent out the
apostles the first time, they
traveled only in Palestine.
But this time Jesus was going
to leave them, and they
would be scattered across
the whole world. So he told
them to be ready for a
longer journey than the first
time—to take money,
clothes, and even a sword.

Jesus Prays
(Matthew 26.36–46; Mark 14.32–42)

³⁹Jesus went out to the Mount of Olives,
as he often did, and his disciples went with

ᵃ*separates wheat from the husks:* See the note at 3.17.
ᵇ*moneybag . . . traveling bag . . . sword:* These were
things that someone would take on a dangerous journey. Jesus was telling his disciples to be ready for anything that might happen. They seem to have understood
what he meant (see 22.49-51).

him. 40When they got there, he told them, "Pray that you will not be tested."

41Jesus walked on a little way before he kneeled down and prayed, 42"Father, if you will, please don't make me suffer by having me drink from this cup.c But do what you want, and not what I want."

43Then an angel from heaven came to help him. 44Jesus was in great pain and prayed so sincerely that his sweat fell to the ground like drops of blood.d

45Jesus got up from praying and went over to his disciples. They were asleep and worn out from being so sad. 46He said to them, "Why are you asleep? Wake up and pray that you will not be tested."

Jesus Is Arrested
(Matthew 26.47–56; Mark 14.43–50; John 18.3–11)

47While Jesus was still speaking, a crowd came up. It was led by Judas, one of the twelve apostles. He went over to Jesus and greeted him with a kiss.e

48Jesus asked Judas, "Are you betraying the Son of Man with a kiss?"

49When Jesus' disciples saw what was about to happen, they asked, "Lord, should we attack them with a sword?" 50One of the disciples even struck at the high priest's servant with his sword and cut off the servant's right ear.

51"Enough of that!" Jesus said. Then he touched the servant's ear and healed it.

52Jesus spoke to the chief priests, the temple police, and the leaders who had come to arrest him. He said, "Why do you come out with swords and clubs and treat me like a criminal? 53I was with you everyday in the temple, and you didn't arrest me. But this is your time, and darknessf is in control."

Why do we have to pray?
(40) As Jesus prayed, the disciples fell asleep because they were tired. They didn't realize the danger they were in, and that Jesus would soon be arrested. If they had known these things, they would not have been able to sleep. We need to be aware—but not fearful—of the dangers we always face in the world. The answer to danger is prayer.

Jesus healed the high priest's servant
(51) Not only did Jesus not fight to keep himself from being arrested, but he even healed the ear of the high priest's servant. Jesus had such love that even when he was about to be taken to his death, he had mercy on a man who was his enemy. Do we have love like that?

---

cmake me drink from this cup: In the Scriptures "to drink from a cup" sometimes means to suffer. dThen an angel . . . like drops of blood: Verses 43,44 are not in some manuscripts. egreeted him with a kiss: It was the custom for people to greet each other with a kiss on the cheek. fdarkness: Darkness stands for the power of the devil.

Peter Says He Does Not Know Jesus
*(Matthew 26.57, 58, 67–75; Mark 14.53, 54,
66–72; John 18.12–18, 25–27)*

54Jesus was arrested and led away to the house of the high priest, while Peter followed at a distance. 55Some people built a fire in the middle of the courtyard and were sitting around it. Peter sat there with them, 56and a servant girl saw him. Then after she had looked at him carefully, she said, "This man was with Jesus!"

57Peter said, "Woman, I don't even know that man!"

58A little later someone else saw Peter and said, "You surely are one of them!"

"No, I'm not!" Peter replied.

59About an hour later another man insisted, "This man must have been with Jesus. They both come from Galilee."

60Peter replied, "I don't know what you are talking about!" Right then, while Peter was still speaking, a rooster crowed. 61The Lord turned and looked at Peter. And Peter remembered that the Lord had said, "Before a rooster crows tomorrow morning, you will say three times that you don't know me." 62Then Peter went out and cried hard.

63The men who were guarding Jesus made fun of him and beat him. 64They put a blindfold on him and said, "Tell us who struck you!" 65They kept on insulting Jesus in many other ways.

Fear is a strong enemy
(57) Peter was so afraid, he wouldn't even admit to a servant girl that he knew Jesus. We see here that fear can make cowards out of even the strongest people. Peter was sorry when he realized what he had done. It's a good thing God can forgive us when fear overcomes us and we fail him like Peter did.

Jesus Is Questioned by the Jewish Council
*(Matthew 26.59–66; Mark 14.55–64;
John 18.19–24)*

66At daybreak the nation's leaders, the chief priests, and the teachers of the Law of Moses got together and brought Jesus before their council. 67They said, "Tell us! Are you the Messiah?"

Jesus replied, "If I said so, you wouldn't believe me. 68And if I asked you a question, you wouldn't answer. 69But from now on, the Son of Man will be seated at the right side of God All-Powerful."

Who was Jesus?
(67) Both the Jewish council and Pilate the governor asked just about the same question. Jesus knew the words "Son of God" and "Messiah" could not mean to them what the words meant to him. So he let them answer their own question. Of course he was the Son of God. As Jesus once said, it is never right to give pearls to pigs (see Matthew 7.6).

70Then they asked, "Are you the Son of God?"*g*

Jesus answered, "You say I am!"*h*

71They replied, "Why do we need more witnesses? He said it himself!"

Pilate Questions Jesus
(Matthew 27.1, 2, 11–14; Mark 15.1–5; John 18.28–38)

23 Everyone in the council got up and led Jesus off to Pilate. **2**They started accusing him and said, "We caught this man trying to get our people to riot and to stop paying taxes to the Emperor. He also claims that he is the Messiah, our king."

3Pilate asked Jesus, "Are you the king of the Jews?"

"Those are your words," Jesus answered.

4Pilate told the chief priests and the crowd, "I don't find him guilty of anything."

5But they all kept on saying, "He has been teaching and causing trouble all over Judea. He started in Galilee and has now come all the way here."

Jesus Is Brought before Herod

6When Pilate heard this, he asked, "Is this man from Galilee?" **7**After Pilate learned that Jesus came from the region ruled by Herod,*i* he sent him to Herod, who was in Jerusalem at that time.

8For a long time Herod had wanted to see Jesus and was very happy because he finally had this chance. He had heard many things about Jesus and hoped to see him work a miracle.

9Herod asked him a lot of questions, but Jesus did not answer. **10**Then the chief priests and the teachers of the Law of Moses stood up and accused him of all kinds of bad things.

11Herod and his soldiers made fun of Jesus and insulted him. They put a fine robe

The council lied about Jesus
(2) Jesus certainly had not been trying to get the people to riot and stop paying taxes. He taught just the opposite. The council was accusing Jesus falsely. But notice that Jesus did not leap to his own defense the way most of us would. He quietly took the sins of others against him, because he knew the will of God was for him to give up his life on the cross.

Herod was curious
(8) Curiosity is the cause of all the interest some people have in religious things. Herod was curious about miracles and wanted to see the new miracle doer. Many people, just like Herod, think it would be "fun" to see a miracle. But miracles are not for fun; they are God's works that show how he creates and saves.

gSon of God: This was one of the titles used for the kings of Israel. *hYou say I am*: Or "That's what you say." *iHerod*: Herod Antipas, the son of Herod the Great.

on him and sent him back to Pilate. 12That same day Herod and Pilate became friends, even though they had been enemies before this.

The Death Sentence
(Matthew 27.15–26; Mark 15.6–15; John 18.39—19.16)

13Pilate called together the chief priests, the leaders, and the people. 14He told them, "You brought Jesus to me and said he was a troublemaker. But I have questioned him here in front of you, and I have not found him guilty of anything that you say he has done. 15Herod didn't find him guilty either and sent him back. This man doesn't deserve to be put to death! 16-17I will just have him beaten with a whip and set free."*j*

18But the whole crowd shouted, "Kill Jesus! Give us Barabbas!" 19Now Barabbas was in jail because he had started a riot in the city and had murdered someone.

20Pilate wanted to set Jesus free, so he spoke again to the crowds. 21But they kept shouting, "Nail him to a cross! Nail him to a cross!"

22Pilate spoke to them a third time, "But what crime has he done? I have not found him guilty of anything for which he should be put to death. I will have him beaten with a whip and set free."

23The people kept on shouting as loud as they could for Jesus to be put to death. 24Finally, Pilate gave in. 25He freed the man who was in jail for rioting and murder, because he was the one the crowd wanted to be set free. Then Pilate handed Jesus over for them to do what they wanted with him.

Jesus Is Nailed to a Cross
(Matthew 27.31–44; Mark 15.21–32; John 19.17–27)

26As Jesus was being led away, some soldiers grabbed hold of a man from Cyrene

---

*j*set free: Some manuscripts add, "Pilate said this, because at every Passover he was supposed to set one prisoner free for the Jewish people."

Evil enemies agreed
(12) Pilate was afraid of Jesus, and it seems that Herod thought Jesus was a joke. But both Pilate and Herod agreed about one thing—Jesus had to die. Evil people can agree to do wrong even if they are not friends. The world is filled with people who don't agree on many things—but they agree that they don't want God to run their lives.

The worst injustice ever
(24) Pilate's job was to enforce Roman justice in Judea. But he knew he had to keep the Roman emperor as his friend. If he didn't, Pilate could get fired. He knew there would be trouble if he offended the Jewish leaders and got them stirred up against Rome. So, even though he knew Jesus was not guilty, Pilate allowed the mob to have the Son of God nailed to a cross. The great Law of the Romans was not great this time. This was the worst day in the history of human justice.

named Simon. He was coming in from the fields, but they put the cross on him and made him carry it behind Jesus.

27A large crowd was following Jesus, and in the crowd a lot of women were crying and weeping for him. 28Jesus turned to the women and said:

Women of Jerusalem, don't cry for me! Cry for yourselves and for your children. 29Someday people will say, "Women who never had children are really fortunate!" 30At that time everyone will say to the mountains, "Fall on us!" They will say to the hills, "Hide us!" 31If this can happen when the wood is green, what do you think will happen when it is dry?k

32Two criminals were led out to be put to death with Jesus. 33When the soldiers came to the place called "The Skull,"l they nailed Jesus to a cross. They also nailed the two criminals to crosses, one on each side of Jesus.

34-35Jesus said, "Father, forgive these people! They don't know what they're doing."m

While the crowd stood there watching Jesus, the soldiers gambled for his clothes. The leaders insulted him by saying, "He saved others. Now he should save himself, if he really is God's chosen Messiah!"

36The soldiers made fun of Jesus and brought him some wine. 37They said, "If you are the king of the Jews, save yourself!"

38Above him was a sign that said, "This is the King of the Jews."

39One of the criminals hanging there also insulted Jesus by saying, "Aren't you the Messiah? Save yourself and save us!"

40But the other criminal told the first one off, "Don't you fear God? Aren't you getting

Jesus prayed for us

(34) Our sins caused Jesus to be nailed to the cross. It isn't true that we would have done better than others if we had been there. But the Lord Jesus knows we don't understand how wicked we are. So he prays for us in our ignorance—"Father, forgive them." It should grieve us to think that Jesus loved us enough to pray for us even while he was dying because of our sins.

kIf this can happen when the wood is green, what do you think will happen when it is dry?: This saying probably means, "If this can happen to an innocent person, what do you think will happen to one who is guilty?" l"The Skull": The place was probably given this name because it was near a large rock in the shape of a human skull. mJesus said, "Father, forgive these people! They don't know what they're doing.": These words are not in some manuscripts.

the same punishment as this man? 41We got what was coming to us, but he didn't do anything wrong." 42Then he said to Jesus, "Remember me when you come into power!"

43Jesus replied, "I promise that today you will be with me in paradise."n

The Death of Jesus
(Matthew 27.45–56; Mark 15.33–41; John 19.28–30)

44Around noon the sky turned dark and stayed that way until the middle of the afternoon. 45The sun stopped shining, and the curtain in the templeo split down the middle. 46Jesus shouted, "Father, I put myself in your hands!" Then he died.

47When the Roman officer saw what had happened, he praised God and said, "Jesus must really have been a good man!"

48A crowd had gathered to see the terrible sight. After they saw it, they felt brokenhearted and went home. 49All of Jesus' close friends and the women who had come with him from Galilee stood at a distance and watched.

Jesus Is Buried
(Matthew 27.57–61; Mark 15.42–47; John 19.38–42)

50-51There was a man named Joseph, who was from Arimathea in Judea. Joseph was a good and honest man, and he was eager for God's kingdom to come. He was also a member of the Jewish council, but he did not agree with what they had decided.

52Joseph went to Pilate and asked for Jesus' body. 53He took the body down from

A criminal was saved on the cross

(43) This is a beautiful picture. Here was a criminal at the end of his wicked life. He was being put to death for his crimes. But Jesus, in his own suffering, heard the man's prayer to be saved. Notice that the man didn't use a lot of words—just a dying man's last prayer. Then Jesus told the man that he would be in paradise with him that very day. There is no better example of how willing Jesus is to save us from our sins.

True friends

(49) The friends and the women who had come with Jesus from Galilee stuck by him until his death and took care of the body afterward. Their love for Jesus overcame whatever fear they might have felt. How strong is our love for Jesus? How much are we willing to stand for his sake?

nparadise: In the Greek translation of the Old Testament, this word is used for the Garden of Eden. In New Testament times it was sometimes used for the place where God's people are happy and at rest, as they wait for the final judgment. ocurtain in the temple: There were two curtains in the temple. One was at the entrance, and the other separated the holy place from the most holy place that the Jewish people thought of as God's home on earth. The second curtain is probably the one which is meant.

the cross and wrapped it in fine cloth. Then he put it in a tomb that had been cut out of solid rock and had never been used. [54]It was Friday, and the Sabbath was about to begin.[p]

[55]The women who had come with Jesus from Galilee followed Joseph and watched how Jesus' body was placed in the tomb. [56]Then they went to prepare some sweet-smelling spices for his burial. But on the Sabbath they rested, as the Law of Moses commands.

Jesus Is Alive
(Matthew 28.1–10; Mark 16.1–8; John 20.1–10)

24 Very early on Sunday morning the women went to the tomb, carrying the spices that they had prepared. [2]When they found the stone rolled away from the entrance, [3]they went in. But they did not find the body of the Lord[q] Jesus, [4]and they did not know what to think.

Suddenly two men in shining white clothes stood beside them. [5]The women were afraid and bowed to the ground. But the men said, "Why are you looking in the place of the dead for someone who is alive? [6]Jesus is not here! He has been raised from death. Remember that while he was still in Galilee, he told you, [7]'The Son of Man will be handed over to sinners who will nail him to a cross. But three days later he will rise to life.' " [8]Then they remembered what Jesus had said.

[9-10]Mary Magdalene, Joanna, Mary the mother of James, and some other women were the ones who had gone to the tomb. When they returned, they told the eleven apostles and the others what had happened. [11]The apostles thought it was all nonsense, and they would not believe.

[12]But Peter ran to the tomb. And when he stooped down and looked in, he saw only

They thought it was nonsense

(11) Some people think that having faith was easier for people in Jesus' time than it is now. It wasn't easier at all, and here is an example. The apostles didn't believe the report that Jesus was alive, even though he had predicted more than once that he would rise again. Now that it had happened, they thought the idea was nonsense. People then were no different than people now. Faith can happen only when God makes it possible in the heart of each person.

---

[p]*the Sabbath was about to begin*: The Sabbath begins at sunset on Friday. [q]*the Lord*: These words are not in some manuscripts.

the burial clothes. Then he returned, wondering what had happened.r

Jesus Appears to Two Disciples
(Mark 16.12, 13)

13That same day two of Jesus' disciples were going to the village of Emmaus, which was about seven miles from Jerusalem. 14As they were talking and thinking about what had happened, 15Jesus came near and started walking along beside them. 16But they did not know who he was.

17Jesus asked them, "What were you talking about as you walked along?"

The two of them stood there looking sad and gloomy. 18Then the one named Cleopas asked Jesus, "Are you the only person from Jerusalem who didn't know what was happening there these last few days?"

19"What do you mean?" Jesus asked. They answered:

Those things that happened to Jesus from Nazareth. By what he did and said he showed that he was a powerful prophet, who pleased God and all the people. 20Then the chief priests and our leaders had him arrested and sentenced to die on a cross. 21We had hoped that he would be the one to set Israel free! But it has already been three days since all this happened.

22Some women in our group surprised us. They had gone to the tomb early in the morning, 23but did not find the body of Jesus. They came back, saying that they had seen a vision of angels who told them that he is alive. 24Some men from our group went to the tomb and found it just as the women had said. But they didn't see Jesus either.

25Then Jesus asked the two disciples, "Why can't you understand? How can you be so slow to believe all that the prophets said? 26Didn't you know that the Messiah would have to suffer before he was given

Jesus walked with his friends

(15) Here is one of the most beautiful events in the New Testament—Jesus walking and talking with two of his disciples after he came back from death. At first they didn't recognize him. But later, as he broke bread, they remembered how he broke bread with them before. It was then that the two disciples knew who he was. Jesus still walks with us today, and we know him when we share the bread at the Lord's Supper.

---

rwhat had happened: Verse 12 is not in some manuscripts.

his glory?" 27Jesus then explained everything written about himself in the Scriptures, beginning with the Law of Moses and the Books of the Prophets.s

28When the two of them came near the village where they were going, Jesus seemed to be going farther. 29They begged him, "Stay with us! It's already late, and the sun is going down." So Jesus went into the house to stay with them.

30After Jesus sat down to eat, he took some bread. He blessed it and broke it. Then he gave it to them. 31At once they knew who he was, but he disappeared. 32They said to each other, "When he talked with us along the road and explained the Scriptures to us, didn't it warm our hearts?" 33So they got right up and returned to Jerusalem.

The two disciples found the eleven apostles and the others gathered together. 34And they learned from the group that the Lord was really alive and had appeared to Peter. 35Then the disciples from Emmaus told what happened on the road and how they knew he was the Lord when he broke the bread.

What Jesus' Followers Must Do
(Matthew 28.16–20; Mark 16.14–18;
John 20.19–23; Acts 1.6–8)

36While Jesus' disciples were talking about what had happened, Jesus appeared to them and said, "May God give you peace!" 37They were frightened and terrified because they thought they were seeing a ghost.

38But Jesus said, "Why are you so frightened? Why do you doubt? 39Look at my hands and my feet and see who I am! Touch me and find out for yourselves. Ghosts don't have flesh and bones as you see I have."

40After Jesus said this, he showed them his hands and his feet. 41The disciples were so glad and amazed that they could not believe it. Jesus then asked them, "Do you

Jesus arose in a real body
(36) The risen Jesus was quick to remind his disciples that he was no ghost. He was a complete person with both body and spirit. He also reminded them that his death and rising again carried out the promises of the Jewish Scriptures (the Old Testament) about him.

---

sthe Law of Moses and the Books of the Prophets: The Jewish Scriptures, that is, the Old Testament.

have something to eat?" [42]They gave him a piece of baked fish. [43]He took it and ate it as they watched.

[44]Jesus said to them, "While I was still with you, I told you that everything written about me in the Law of Moses, the Books of the Prophets, and in the Psalms[t] had to happen."

[45]Then he helped them understand the Scriptures. [46]He told them:

The Scriptures say that the Messiah must suffer, then three days later he will rise from death. [47]They also say that all people of every nation must be told in my name to turn to God, in order to be forgiven. So beginning in Jerusalem, [48]you must tell everything that has happened. [49]I will send you the one my Father has promised,[u] but you must stay in the city until you are given power from heaven.

Jesus Returns to Heaven
(Mark 16.19, 20; Acts 1.9–11)

[50]Jesus led his disciples out to Bethany, where he raised his hands and blessed them. [51]As he was doing this, he left and was taken up to heaven.[v] [52]After his disciples had worshiped him,[w] they returned to Jerusalem and were very happy. [53]They spent their time in the temple, praising God.

Jesus was God's answer to our sins

(45) God had a plan all along to save us from our sins. Jesus was sent to carry out that plan. He was not just a great and good teacher. Jesus was God's sacrifice for our sins—a sacrifice that we owed but could never pay.

[t]*Psalms*: The Jewish Scriptures were made up of three parts: (1) the Law of Moses, (2) the Books of the Prophets, (3) and the Writings, which included the Psalms. Sometimes the Scriptures were just called the Law or the Law (of Moses) and the Books of the Prophets. [u]*the one my Father has promised*: Jesus means the Holy Spirit. [v]*and was taken up to heaven*: These words are not in some manuscripts. [w]*After his disciples had worshiped him*: These words are not in some manuscripts.

JOHN TELLS THE GOOD NEWS

ABOUT THIS BOOK

Who is Jesus Christ? John answers this question in the first chapter of his Gospel. Using the words of an early Christian hymn, he calls Jesus the "Word" by which God created everything and by which he gave life to everyone (1.3,4). He shows how John the Baptist announced Jesus' coming, "Here is the Lamb of God who takes away the sin of the world" (1.29). When Philip met Jesus he knew Jesus was "the one that Moses and the Prophets wrote about" (1.45). And, in the words of Nathanael, Jesus is "the Son of God and the King of Israel" (1.49).

In John's Gospel we learn a lot about who Jesus is by observing what he said and did when he was with other people. These include a Samaritan woman who received Jesus' offer of life-giving water, a woman who had been caught in sin, his friend Lazarus who was brought back to life by Jesus, and his follower Thomas who doubted that Jesus was raised from death. Jesus also refers to himself as "I am", a phrase which translates the most holy name for God in the Hebrew Scriptures. He uses this name for himself when he makes his claim to be the life-giving bread, the light of the world, the good shepherd, and the true vine.

Jesus performs seven miracles that are more than miracles. Each of them is a "sign" that tells us something about Jesus as the Son of God. For example, by healing a lame man (5.1–8), Jesus shows that he is just like his Father, who never stops working (5.17). This sign also teaches that the Son does only what he sees his Father doing (5.19), and that like the Father "the Son gives life to anyone he wants to" (5.21).

The way John tells the story of Jesus is quite different from the other three gospels. Here, Jesus has long conversations with people about who he is and what God sent him to do. In these conversations he teaches many important things—for example, that he is the way, the truth and the life.

Why did John write? John himself tells us, "So that you will put your faith in Jesus as the Messiah and the Son of God" (20.31). How is this possible? Jesus answers that question in his words to Nicodemus:

God loved the people of this world so much that he gave his only Son, so that everyone who has faith in him will have eternal life and never die. (3.16)

A QUICK LOOK AT THIS BOOK

The Word of Life

1 In the beginning was the one
who is called the Word.
The Word was with God
and was truly God.

Christ came into the world
(1) Unlike Matthew and Luke, John didn't offer any details of Jesus' birth in his

2From the very beginning
   the Word was with God.

3And with this Word,
   God created all things.
Nothing was made
   without the Word.
Everything that was created
4   received its life from him,
and his life gave light
   to everyone.
5The light keeps shining
   in the dark,
and darkness has never
   put it out.*a*
6God sent a man named John,
7who came to tell
   about the light
and to lead all people
   to have faith.
8John wasn't that light.
He came only to tell
   about the light.

9The true light that shines
on everyone
   was coming into the world.
10The Word was in the world,
   but no one knew him,
though God had made the world
   with his Word.
11He came into his own world,
   but his own nation
   did not welcome him.
12Yet some people accepted him
   and put their faith in him.
So he gave them the right
   to be the children of God.
13They were not God's children
by nature or because
   of any human desires.
God himself was the one
   who made them his children.

14The Word became a human being
   and lived here with us.
We saw his true glory,

Gospel. John wanted us to
understand that Jesus Christ
is the Word of God from
heaven. And that Word is
really God himself—God
the Son of God the Father,
who has always been and
always will be.

**Jesus Christ is the true
light of the world**
(5) Light chases away the
darkness; darkness cannot
overcome light. That is why
all the darkness of evil can
never put out the greatest
light of all—Jesus Christ
himself.

**Jesus Christ is the light of
God's children**
(9) We become God's children when we accept Jesus
the Son of God as our
Savior. Jesus, the light of the
world, has shone on everyone, but he enters the lives
of those who trust him. By
faith we become members
of the family of God.

aput it out: Or "understood it."

the glory of the only Son
 of the Father.
From him all the kindness
and all the truth of God
 have come down to us.

15John spoke about him and shouted, "This is the one I told you would come! He is greater than I am, because he was alive before I was born."

16Because of all that the Son is, we have been given one blessing after another.b 17The Law was given by Moses, but Jesus Christ brought us God's kindness and truth. 18No one has ever seen God. The only Son, who is truly God and is closest to the Father, has shown us what God is like.

John the Baptist Tells about Jesus
(Matthew 3.1–12; Mark 1.1–8; Luke 3.15–17)

19-20The Jewish leaders in Jerusalem sent priests and temple helpers to ask John who he was. He told them plainly, "I am not the Messiah." 21Then when they asked him if he were Elijah, he said, "No, I am not!" And when they asked if he were the Prophet,c he also said "No!"

22Finally, they said, "Who are you then? We have to give an answer to the ones who sent us. Tell us who you are!"

23John answered in the words of the prophet Isaiah, "I am only someone shouting in the desert, 'Get the road ready for the Lord!'"

24Some Pharisees had also been sent to John. 25They asked him, "Why are you baptizing people, if you are not the Messiah or Elijah or the Prophet?"

26John told them, "I use water to baptize people. But here with you is someone you don't know. 27Even though I came first, I am not good enough to untie his sandals."

John the Baptist announced Christ's coming

(15) Who was this man John? He said that he was not the Messiah, and that he had come just as the Old Testament prophet Isaiah foretold. You might say John was an announcer. Believers today also can announce the Savior to a darkened world. Jesus the true light has come. When we announce him, he shines into people's lives, and they can become new people by receiving him.

---

bone blessing after another: Or "one blessing in place of another." cthe Prophet: Many of the Jewish people expected God to send them a prophet who would be like Moses, but with even greater power. See Deuteronomy 18.15,18.

28John said this as he was baptizing east of the Jordan River in Bethany.*d*

The Lamb of God

29The next day John saw Jesus coming toward him and said:

Here is the Lamb of God who takes away the sin of the world! 30He is the one I told you about when I said, "Someone else will come. He is greater than I am, because he was alive before I was born." 31I didn't know who he was. But I came to baptize you with water, so that everyone in Israel would see him.

32I was there and saw the Spirit come down on him like a dove from heaven. And the Spirit stayed on him. 33Before this I didn't know who he was. But the one who sent me to baptize with water had told me, "You will see the Spirit come down and stay on someone. Then you will know that he is the one who will baptize with the Holy Spirit." 34I saw this happen, and I tell you that he is the Son of God.

The First Disciples of Jesus

35The next day John was there again, and two of his followers were with him. 36When he saw Jesus walking by, he said, "Here is the Lamb of God!" 37John's two followers heard him, and they went with Jesus.

38When Jesus turned and saw them, he asked, "What do you want?"

They answered, "Rabbi, where do you live?" The Hebrew word "Rabbi" means "Teacher."

39Jesus replied, "Come and see!" It was already about four o'clock in the afternoon when they went with him and saw where he lived. So they stayed on for the rest of the day.

40One of the two men who had heard John and had gone with Jesus was Andrew,

Jesus is the Lamb of God
(29) Jesus has many titles, but this may seem the strangest one. In Old Testament times, God commanded a spotless lamb to be sacrificed often for the sins of the people. The people didn't understand it all then, but they were doing something that foretold the coming of the Savior. Jesus would let himself be sacrificed as the true and final offering for sins—a "spotless" lamb, without sin. That is why John used the title "Lamb of God" for Jesus.

---

*d*Bethany: An unknown village east of the Jordan with the same name as the village near Jerusalem.

the brother of Simon Peter. [41]The first thing Andrew did was to find his brother and tell him, "We have found the Messiah!" The Hebrew word "Messiah" means the same as the Greek word "Christ."

[42]Andrew brought his brother to Jesus. And when Jesus saw him, he said, "Simon son of John, you will be called Cephas." This name can be translated as "Peter."[e]

Jesus Chooses Philip and Nathanael

[43-44]The next day Jesus decided to go to Galilee. There he met Philip, who was from Bethsaida, the hometown of Andrew and Peter. Jesus said to Philip, "Come with me."

[45]Philip then found Nathanael and said, "We have found the one that Moses and the Prophets[f] wrote about. He is Jesus, the son of Joseph from Nazareth."

[46]Nathanael asked, "Can anything good come from Nazareth?"

Philip answered, "Come and see."

[47]When Jesus saw Nathanael coming toward him, he said, "Here is a true descendant of our ancestor Israel. And he is not deceitful."[g]

[48]"How do you know me?" Nathanael asked.

Jesus answered, "Before Philip called you, I saw you under the fig tree."

[49]Nathanael said, "Rabbi, you are the Son of God and the King of Israel!"

[50]Jesus answered, "Did you believe me just because I said that I saw you under the fig tree? You will see something even greater. [51]I tell you for certain that you will see heaven open and God's angels going up and coming down on the Son of Man."[h]

---

[e]*Peter*: The Aramaic name "Cephas" and the Greek name "Peter" each mean "rock." [f]*Moses and the Prophets*: The Jewish Scriptures, that is, the Old Testament. [g]*Israel . . . not deceitful*: Israel (meaning "a man who wrestled with God" or "a prince of God") was the name that the Lord gave to Jacob (meaning "cheater" or "deceiver"), the famous ancestor of the Jewish people. [h]*going up and coming down on the Son of Man*: When Jacob (see the note at verse 47) was running from his brother Esau, he had a dream in which he saw angels going up and down on a ladder from earth to heaven. See Genesis 32.22-32.

Tell somebody

(41) When Andrew found Jesus and went with him, the first thing he did was tell his brother about the good news—he had found the long-awaited Messiah. His brother turned out to be the apostle Peter. We ought to be bursting to tell someone the news about what we've found in Jesus. Think of the good it will do our friend or loved one—and the good that person might do someday.

Nazareth of all places

(46) Nathanael wasn't expecting the Messiah, the King of Israel, to come from a "hick town" like Nazareth. But it was right for Jesus to be a humble, poor person from a simple, working family. God planned it that way, so Jesus and the common people could understand each other.

Jesus at a Wedding in Cana

2 Three days later Mary, the mother of Jesus, was at a wedding feast in the village of Cana in Galilee. ²Jesus and his disciples had also been invited and were there.

³When the wine was all gone, Mary said to Jesus, "They don't have any more wine."

⁴Jesus replied, "Mother, my time has not yet come!ⁱ You must not tell me what to do."

⁵Mary then said to the servants, "Do whatever Jesus tells you to do."

⁶At the feast there were six stone water jars that were used by the people for washing themselves in the way that their religion said they must. Each jar held about twenty or thirty gallons. ⁷Jesus told the servants to fill them to the top with water. Then after the jars had been filled, ⁸he said, "Now take some water and give it to the man in charge of the feast."

The servants did as Jesus told them, ⁹and the man in charge drank some of the water that had now turned into wine. He did not know where the wine had come from, but the servants did. He called the bridegroom over ¹⁰and said, "The best wine is always served first. Then after the guests have had plenty, the other wine is served. But you have kept the best until last!"

¹¹This was Jesus' first miracle,ʲ and he did it in the village of Cana in Galilee. There Jesus showed his glory, and his disciples put their faith in him. ¹²After this, he went with his mother, his brothers, and his disciples to the town of Capernaum, where they stayed for a few days.

ⁱ*my time has not yet come!*: The time when the true glory of Jesus would be seen, and he would be recognized as God's Son. See 12.23. ʲ*miracle*: The Greek text has "sign." In the Gospel of John the word "sign" is used for the miracle itself and as a way of pointing to Jesus as the Son of God.

Jesus went to parties
(1) Jesus enjoyed happy gatherings of people. This may surprise us when we think about the serious work Jesus came to do. But Jesus wanted to be where he could talk to people and get them interested in the kingdom of God. He didn't preach at the wedding reception, but he added to its joy by supplying more wine. His act must have made a lasting impression on some of those who were there.

Jesus had a higher duty
(12) After Jesus' childhood we never hear again about Joseph, Mary's husband, the man who was an earthly father to Jesus. But we continue to meet Mary, Jesus' mother, in a number of places. In this chapter we see that Mary was beginning to understand that Jesus was much more than her own Son. She would take her place among the other disciples and witnesses of his work as Savior and Lord.

Jesus in the Temple
*(Matthew 21.12, 13; Mark 11.15–17;
Luke 19.45, 46)*

13Not long before the Jewish festival of Passover, Jesus went to Jerusalem. 14There he found people selling cattle, sheep, and doves in the temple. He also saw money-changers sitting at their tables. 15So he took some rope and made a whip. Then he chased everyone out of the temple, together with their sheep and cattle. He turned over the tables of the moneychangers and scattered their coins.

16Jesus said to the people who had been selling doves, "Get those doves out of here! Don't make my Father's house a market-place."

17The disciples then remembered that the Scriptures say, "My love for your house burns in me like a fire."

18The Jewish leaders asked Jesus, "What miracle*ʲ* will you work to show us why you have done this?"

19"Destroy this temple," Jesus answered, "and in three days I will build it again!"

20The leaders replied, "It took forty-six years to build this temple. What makes you think you can rebuild it in three days?"

21But Jesus was talking about his body as a temple. 22And when he was raised from death, his disciples remembered what he had told them. Then they believed the Scriptures and the words of Jesus.

Jesus Knows What People Are Like

23In Jerusalem during Passover many people put their faith in Jesus, because they saw him work miracles.*ʲ* 24But Jesus knew what was in their hearts, and he would not let them have power over him. 25No one had to tell him what people were like. He already knew.

Jesus and Nicodemus

3 1-2There was a man named Nicodemus who was a Pharisee and a Jewish leader.

ʲmiracles: See the note at 2.11.

Jesus puzzled his hearers
(19) He said he could raise up the temple again in three days. Even if he had explained to the leaders what he meant, they wouldn't have understood. They would have been more puzzled than ever. Later they accused him of saying that he, himself, would destroy the temple (see Matthew 27.40). So we see that people of Jesus' day were just as confused by their own wickedness as people are today.

What are people like?
(23) Jesus saw us as we really are, not as we like to think we are. As sinners, we don't love the things God loves, and we love ourselves too much. We are not sincere about what we say. Many people decided to "put their faith" in Jesus because they thought he would grant their selfish wishes. But they didn't want him as their Savior from sin.

One night he went to Jesus and said, "Sir, we know that God has sent you to teach us. You could not work these miracles, unless God were with you."

3Jesus replied, "I tell you for certain that you must be born from above[k] before you can see God's kingdom!"

4Nicodemus asked, "How can a grown man ever be born a second time?"

5Jesus answered:

I tell you for certain that before you can get into God's kingdom, you must be born not only by water, but by the Spirit. 6Humans give life to their children. Yet only God's Spirit can change you into a child of God. 7Don't be surprised when I say that you must be born from above. 8Only God's Spirit gives new life. The Spirit is like the wind that blows wherever it wants to. You can hear the wind, but you don't know where it comes from or where it is going. 9"How can this be?" Nicodemus asked.

10Jesus replied:

How can you be a teacher of Israel and not know these things? 11I tell you for certain that we know what we are talking about because we have seen it ourselves. But none of you will accept what we say. 12If you don't believe when I talk to you about things on earth, how can you possibly believe if I talk to you about things in heaven?

13No one has gone up to heaven except the Son of Man, who came down from there. 14And the Son of Man must be lifted up, just as that metal snake was lifted up by Moses in the desert.[l] 15Then everyone who has faith in the Son of Man will have eternal life.

16God loved the people of this world so much that he gave his only Son, so

What do people really need?

(3) We have just shown how Jesus sees us as we really are, not as we imagine ourselves to be. So what is needed? Jesus' talk with Nicodemus tells us our greatest need. We must be "born from above." Our old inner self must give way to a new inner self that God gives us. Then we are able to please God, because we then love the things he loves. Then we appreciate Jesus for who he really is—our Savior from heaven. We must ask God to create us all over again in this way.

What did the metal snake mean?

(14) The metal snake that Moses made and placed on a pole stood for what Jesus would do. The people who were being bitten by snakes in the desert in Moses' time could be healed just by looking at that metal snake. By looking to Jesus who was nailed up on a cross, we can be healed from the poison of sin. In this case, it's a kind of healing that lasts forever.

kfrom above: Or "in a new way." The same Greek word is used in verses 7,31.   ljust as that metal snake was lifted up by Moses in the desert: When the Lord punished the people of Israel by sending snakes to bite them, he told Moses to hold a metal snake up on a pole. Everyone who looked at the snake was cured of the snake bites. See Numbers 21.4-9.

that everyone who has faith in him will
have eternal life and never die. 17God
did not send his Son into the world to
condemn its people. He sent him to save
them! 18No one who has faith in God's
Son will be condemned. But everyone
who does not have faith in him has already been condemned for not having
faith in God's only Son.

19The light has come into the world,
and people who do evil things are
judged guilty because they love the dark
more than the light. 20People who do
evil hate the light and won't come to
the light, because it clearly shows what
they have done. 21But everyone who
lives by the truth will come to the light,
because they want others to know that
God is really the one doing what they
do.

The light shows all
(19) Jesus is the light that
shows all the things in the
world, whether they are
good or evil. The people
who come to the light are
doing so because they love
God, who sent the light.
Those who don't love Jesus
hate the light and would
rather live in the darkness
of sin.

Jesus and John the Baptist

22Later, Jesus and his disciples went to
Judea, where he stayed with them for a
while and was baptizing people.

23-24John had not yet been put in jail. He
was at Aenon near Salim, where there was
a lot of water, and people were coming there
for John to baptize them.

25John's followers got into an argument
with a Jewish man*m* about a ceremony of
washing.*n* 26They went to John and said,
"Rabbi, you spoke about a man when you
were with him east of the Jordan. He is now
baptizing people, and everyone is going to
him."

27John replied:
No one can do anything unless God
in heaven allows it. 28Surely you remember how I told you that I am not
the Messiah. I am only the one sent
ahead of him.

29At a wedding the groom is the one

---

m a Jewish man: Some manuscripts have "some Jewish
men." *n about a ceremony of washing*: The Jewish people had many rules about washing themselves and their
dishes, in order to make themselves fit to worship God.

who gets married. The best man is glad just to be there and to hear the groom's voice. That's why I am so glad. 30Jesus must become more important, while I become less important.

The One Who Comes from Heaven

31God's Son comes from heaven and is above all others. Everyone who comes from the earth belongs to the earth and speaks about earthly things. The one who comes from heaven is above all others. 32He speaks about what he has seen and heard, and yet no one believes him. 33But everyone who does believe him has shown that God is truthful. 34The Son was sent to speak God's message, and he has been given the full power of God's Spirit.

35The Father loves the Son and has given him everything. 36Everyone who has faith in the Son has eternal life. But no one who rejects him will ever share in that life, and God will be angry with them forever.

4 Jesus knew that the Pharisees had heard that he was winning and baptizing more followers than John was. 2But Jesus' disciples were really the ones doing the baptizing, and not Jesus himself.

Jesus and the Samaritan Woman

3Jesus left Judea and started for Galilee again. 4This time he had to go through Samaria, 5and on his way he came to the town of Sychar. It was near the field that Jacob had long ago given to his son Joseph. 6-8The well that Jacob had dug was still there, and Jesus sat down beside it because he was tired from traveling. It was noon, and after Jesus' disciples had gone into town to buy some food, a Samaritan woman came to draw water from the well.

Jesus asked her, "Would you please give me a drink of water?"

9"You are a Jew," she replied, "and I am a Samaritan woman. How can you ask me

Put Jesus first

(30) John the Baptist knew who Jesus was, and John knew that Jesus had to take first place. Jesus is the Messiah, the Son of God. John thought that it was an honor just to be Christ's servant. We should learn from John that Jesus belongs in first place in our lives.

Eternal life right now

(36) Notice that this passage says that everyone who has faith in Jesus *has* eternal life. Not *will* have, but *has.* If you have faith in Jesus, life forever with him is yours *right now,* just as surely as if you were already in heaven. That is a joyful thing to realize.

for a drink of water when Jews and Samaritans won't have anything to do with each other?"ᵒ

¹⁰Jesus answered, "You don't know what God wants to give you, and you don't know who is asking you for a drink. If you did, you would ask him for the water that gives life."

¹¹"Sir," the woman said, "you don't even have a bucket, and the well is deep. Where are you going to get this life-giving water? ¹²Our ancestor Jacob dug this well for us, and his family and animals got water from it. Are you greater than Jacob?"

¹³Jesus answered, "Everyone who drinks this water will get thirsty again. ¹⁴But no one who drinks the water I give will ever be thirsty again. The water I give is like a flowing fountain that gives eternal life."

¹⁵The woman replied, "Sir, please give me a drink of that water! Then I won't have to come to this well again."

¹⁶Jesus told her, "Go and bring your husband."

¹⁷⁻¹⁸The woman answered, "I don't have a husband."

"That's right," Jesus replied, "you're telling the truth. You don't have a husband. You have already been married five times, and the man you are now living with is not your husband."

¹⁹The woman said, "Sir, I can see that you are a prophet. ²⁰My ancestors worshiped on this mountain,ᵖ but you Jews say Jerusalem is the only place to worship."

²¹Jesus said to her:

Believe me, the time is coming when you won't worship God either on this mountain or in Jerusalem. ²²You Samaritans don't really know the one you worship. But we Jews do know the God we worship, and by using us God will save the world. ²³But a time is coming,

Jesus is like living water

(10) In the Old Testament times of Moses the great leader of Israel, God supplied a living rock that provided water for the people in the desert. Many years later Paul the apostle said that the rock stood for Christ (1 Corinthians 10.4). Jesus told a woman that he would give her living water, and then she would have eternal life. When we come to Jesus, it is like someone dying of thirst coming to a cool spring of water. Jesus satisfies our deep need to live forever with him.

Jesus knows and understands us

(17) The woman at the well was living in a sinful way, and Jesus knew all about her. But he wasn't angry with her. Instead, he invited her to come and drink the water of everlasting life. The woman was surprised because she thought Jesus would condemn her. If we only knew how much Jesus loves us, we wouldn't be afraid to come to him about the things we know are wrong in our lives.

ᵒ*won't have anything to do with each other*: Or "won't use the same cups." The Samaritans lived in the land between Judea and Galilee. They worshiped God differently from the Jews and did not get along with them. ᵖ*this mountain*: Mount Gerizim, near the city of Shechem.

and it is already here! Even now the true worshipers are being led by the Spirit to worship the Father according to the truth. These are the ones the Father is seeking to worship him. 24God is Spirit, and those who worship God must be led by the Spirit to worship him according to the truth.

25The woman said, "I know that the Messiah will come. He is the one we call Christ. When he comes, he will explain everything to us."

26"I am that one," Jesus told her, "and I am speaking to you now."

27The disciples returned about this time and were surprised to find Jesus talking with a woman. But none of them asked him what he wanted or why he was talking with her.

28The woman left her water jar and ran back into town. She said to the people, 29"Come and see a man who told me everything I have ever done! Could he be the Messiah?" 30Everyone in town went out to see Jesus.

31While this was happening, Jesus' disciples were saying to him, "Teacher, please eat something."

32But Jesus told them, "I have food that you don't know anything about."

33His disciples started asking each other, "Has someone brought him something to eat?"

34Jesus said:

My food is to do what God wants! He is the one who sent me, and I must finish the work that he gave me to do. 35You may say that there are still four months until harvest time. But I tell you to look, and you will see that the fields are ripe and ready to harvest.

36Even now the harvest workers are receiving their reward by gathering a harvest that brings eternal life. Then everyone who planted the seed and everyone who harvests the crop will celebrate together. 37So the saying proves true, "Some plant the seed, and others harvest the crop." 38I am sending you

We can tell only what we know about Jesus

(28) First the people of Samaria heard *about* Jesus, then they heard him themselves. Only then were they able to tell about him. We can't tell others what we don't know personally. We must first "meet" Jesus ourselves. We can meet him because the Spirit of God reveals Jesus to our minds. Then we know him and can tell others about him and how he saved us from our sins.

Eat the food that God gives

(34) What really satisfies us? Some of us overeat because we aren't satisfied inside ourselves about life. So we try to fill our emptiness with food, or pleasures, or drugs, or other things that harm us. We can never be satisfied without God. We need to enjoy the invisible, special food that God gives to those who ask him.

to harvest crops in fields where others have done all the hard work.

39A lot of Samaritans in that town put their faith in Jesus because the woman had said, "This man told me everything I have ever done." **40**They came and asked him to stay in their town, and he stayed on for two days.

41Many more Samaritans put their faith in Jesus because of what they heard him say. **42**They told the woman, "We no longer have faith in Jesus just because of what you told us. We have heard him ourselves, and we are certain that he is the Savior of the world!"

Jesus Heals an Official's Son
(Matthew 8.5–13; Luke 7.1–10)

43-44 Jesus had said, "Prophets are honored everywhere, except in their own country." Then two days later he left **45**and went to Galilee. The people there welcomed him, because they had gone to the festival in Jerusalem and had seen everything he had done.

46While Jesus was in Galilee, he returned to the village of Cana, where he had turned the water into wine. There was an official in Capernaum whose son was sick. **47**And when the man heard that Jesus had come from Judea, he went and begged him to keep his son from dying.

48Jesus told the official, "You won't have faith unless you see miracles and wonders!"

49The man replied, "Lord, please come before my son dies!"

50Jesus then said, "Your son will live. Go on home to him." The man believed Jesus and started back home.

51Some of the official's servants met him along the road and told him, "Your son is better!" **52**He asked them when the boy got better, and they answered, "The fever left him yesterday at one o'clock."

53The boy's father realized that at one o'clock the day before Jesus had told him, "Your son will live!" So the man and everyone in his family put their faith in Jesus.

What do you put your faith in?

(48) You've heard that "seeing is believing." This is often a sour way of saying, "I'll believe when I see it with my own eyes." But there are lots of things we believe without seeing— what science says about atoms, for example. We can be confident about putting our faith in Jesus even if he doesn't first perform a miracle. The miracle comes *after* we trust him, not before.

54This was the second miracle*q* that Jesus worked after he left Judea and went to Galilee.

Jesus Heals a Sick Man

5 Later, Jesus went to Jerusalem for another Jewish festival.*r* **2**In the city near the sheep gate was a pool with five porches, and its name in Hebrew was Bethzatha.*s*

3-4 Many sick, blind, lame, and crippled people were lying close to the pool.*t*

5Beside the pool was a man who had been sick for thirty-eight years. **6**When Jesus saw the man and realized that he had been crippled for a long time, he asked him, "Do you want to be healed?"

7The man answered, "Lord, I don't have anyone to put me in the pool when the water is stirred up. I try to get in, but someone else always gets there first."

8Jesus told him, "Pick up your mat and walk!" **9**Right then the man was healed. He picked up his mat and started walking around. The day on which this happened was a Sabbath.

10When the Jewish leaders saw the man carrying his mat, they said to him, "This is the Sabbath! No one is allowed to carry a mat on the Sabbath."

11But he replied, "The man who healed me told me to pick up my mat and walk."

12They asked him, "Who is this man that told you to pick up your mat and walk?" **13**But he did not know who Jesus was, and Jesus had left because of the crowd.

14Later, Jesus met the man in the temple and told him, "You are now well. But don't sin anymore or something worse might happen to you." **15**The man left and told the leaders that Jesus was the one who had

What healed the sick man?
(9) The pool had been there a long time, and it's still there today. But neither the water from that pool, nor any other water, had ever healed anyone. Water has no magical power. But Jesus is the Lord from heaven, God the creator in human form. Only he has authority to command us to be healed, as this man found out for himself.

Who is this Jesus?
(12) Jesus did miracles. But that is not the main thing that makes him great. Jesus is the everlasting Son of the everlasting Father. Just as God the Father gives life, so also God the everlasting Son gives life. It shouldn't puzzle us that the Author of life gives life when he pleases and how he pleases. He always has and always will have life for everyone who comes to him.

*q*miracle: See the note at 2.11. *r*another Jewish festival: Either the Festival of Shelters or Passover. *s*Bethzatha: Some manuscripts have "Bethesda" and others have "Bethsaida." *t*pool: Some manuscripts add, "They were waiting for the water to be stirred, because an angel from the Lord would sometimes come down and stir it. The first person to get into the pool after that would be healed."

healed him. [16]They started making a lot of trouble for Jesus because he did things like this on the Sabbath.

[17]But Jesus said, "My Father has never stopped working, and that is why I keep on working." [18]Now the leaders wanted to kill Jesus for two reasons. First, he had broken the law of the Sabbath. But even worse, he had said that God was his Father, which made him equal with God.

The Son's Authority

[19]Jesus told the people:

I tell you for certain that the Son cannot do anything on his own. He can do only what he sees the Father doing, and he does exactly what he sees the Father do. [20]The Father loves the Son and has shown him everything he does. The Father will show him even greater things, and you will be amazed. [21]Just as the Father raises the dead and gives life, so the Son gives life to anyone he wants to.

[22]The Father doesn't judge anyone, but he has made his Son the judge of everyone. [23]The Father wants all people to honor the Son as much as they honor him. When anyone refuses to honor the Son, that is the same as refusing to honor the Father who sent him. [24]I tell you for certain that everyone who hears my message and has faith in the one who sent me has eternal life and will never be condemned. They have already gone from death to life.

[25]I tell you for certain that the time will come, and it is already here, when all of the dead will hear the voice of the Son of God. And those who listen to it will live! [26]The Father has the power to give life, and he has given that same power to the Son. [27]And he has given his Son the right to judge everyone, because he is the Son of Man.

[28]Don't be surprised! The time will come when all of the dead will hear the voice of the Son of Man, [29]and they will

We can trust Jesus because of what he does (21) The world knows that Jesus was a one-of-a-kind person, that he even rose from the dead. That alone ought to lead us to trust him. But to really find out the truth about Jesus, we must come to him ourselves. He never turns anyone away. When he gives us his eternal life, then we have the proof of who Jesus really is, in our own lives.

come out of their graves. Everyone who has done good things will rise to life, but everyone who has done evil things will rise and be condemned.

30I cannot do anything on my own. The Father sent me, and he is the one who told me how to judge. I judge with fairness, because I obey him, and I don't just try to please myself.

Witnesses to Jesus

31If I speak for myself, there is no way to prove I am telling the truth. 32But there is someone else who speaks for me, and I know what he says is true. 33You sent messengers to John, and he told them the truth. 34I don't depend on what people say about me, but I tell you these things so that you may be saved. 35John was a lamp that gave a lot of light, and you were glad to enjoy his light for a while.

36But something more important than John speaks for me. I mean the things that the Father has given me to do! All of these speak for me and say that the Father sent me.

37The Father who sent me also speaks for me, but you have never heard his voice or seen him face to face. 38You have not believed his message, because you refused to have faith in the one he sent.

39You search the Scriptures, because you think you will find eternal life in them. The Scriptures tell about me, 40but you refuse to come to me for eternal life.

41I don't care about human praise, 42but I do know that none of you love God. 43I have come with my Father's authority, and you have not welcomed me. But you will welcome people who come on their own. 44How could you possibly believe? You like to have your friends praise you, and you don't care about praise that the only God can give! 45Don't think that I will be the one

The Bible itself cannot give eternal life

(39) The Bible is entirely the word of God. But the Bible is just "words on a page" to us until we surrender our lives to the Author of the words. The book alone can't save us from our sins any more than waving a wand can cure disease. It is God himself who gives eternal life.

to accuse you to the Father. You have put your hope in Moses, yet he is the very one who will accuse you. 46Moses wrote about me, and if you had believed Moses, you would have believed me. 47But if you don't believe what Moses wrote, how can you believe what I say?

Feeding Five Thousand
(Matthew 14.13–21; Mark 6.30–44; Luke 9.10–17)

6 Jesus crossed Lake Galilee, which was also known as Lake Tiberias. 2A large crowd had seen him work miracles to heal the sick, and those people went with him. 3-4It was almost time for the Jewish festival of Passover, and Jesus went up on a mountain with his disciples and sat down.u

5When Jesus saw the large crowd coming toward him, he asked Philip, "Where will we get enough food to feed all these people?" 6He said this to test Philip, since he already knew what he was going to do.

7Philip answered, "Don't you know that it would take almost a year's wagesv just to buy only a little bread for each of these people?"

8Andrew, the brother of Simon Peter, was one of the disciples. He spoke up and said, 9"There is a boy here who has five small loavesw of barley bread and two fish. But what good is that with all these people?"

10The ground was covered with grass, and Jesus told his disciples to have everyone sit down. About five thousand men were in the crowd. 11Jesus took the bread in his hands and gave thanks to God. Then he passed the bread to the people, and he did the same with the fish, until everyone had plenty to eat.

12The people ate all they wanted, and Jesus told his disciples to gather up the left-

---

usat down: Possibly to teach. Teachers in the ancient world, including Jewish teachers, usually sat down to teach. valmost a year's wages: The Greek text has "two hundred silver coins." Each coin was worth the average day's wages for a worker. wsmall loaves: These would have been flat and round or in the shape of a bun.

Moses wrote about Jesus
(46) We must not imagine that the Bible contains two separate religions—the Old Testament religion and the New Testament religion. Someone has written that the New Testament is enclosed in the Old Testament, and the Old Testament is opened up by the New Testament. Both testaments lead us to Jesus Christ. Moses knew that the Messiah, Jesus, would come some day. Many other prophets wrote about the King who would come to Israel.

The Lord of creation fed the crowd
(11) Only this miracle is told of in all four Gospels. It teaches us something important: that Jesus is the Lord of creation. He could take a few scraps of food and make enough to feed thousands. The crowd got "carried away," however, and wanted to make Jesus an earthly king. The people meant well, but they didn't fully understand who Jesus was and what he came to do, so he had to get away from them.

overs, so that nothing would be wasted.
13The disciples gathered them up and filled
twelve large baskets with what was left over
from the five barley loaves.

14After the people had seen Jesus work
this miracle,x they began saying, "This must
be the Prophety who is to come into the
world!" 15Jesus realized that they would try
to force him to be their king. So he went
up on a mountain, where he could be alone.

Jesus Walks on the Water
(Matthew 14.22–27; Mark 6.45–52)

16That evening Jesus' disciples went
down to the lake. 17They got into a boat
and started across for Capernaum. Later
that evening Jesus had still not come to
them, 18and a strong wind was making the
water rough.

19When the disciples had rowed for three
or four miles, they saw Jesus walking on
the water. He kept coming closer to the boat,
and they were terrified. 20But he said, "I
am Jesus!z Don't be afraid!" 21The disciples
wanted to take him into the boat, but suddenly the boat reached the shore where they
were headed.

The Bread That Gives Life

22The people who had stayed on the east
side of the lake knew that only one boat
had been there. They also knew that Jesus
had not left in it with his disciples. But the
next day 23some boats from Tiberias sailed
near the place where the crowd had eaten
the bread for which the Lord had given
thanks. 24They saw that Jesus and his disciples had left. Then they got into the boats
and went to Capernaum to look for Jesus.
25They found him on the west side of the
lake and asked, "Rabbi, when did you get
here?"

26Jesus answered, "I tell you for certain
that you are not looking for me because

*Fear of the Savior doesn't
make sense*
(19) The disciples were in
the middle of a storm on the
lake when Jesus came walking toward them on the water. They were afraid, thinking they saw a ghost (see
Matthew 14). Imagine—the
disciples were afraid of
Jesus, the one who could
calm the winds and the
waves. They weren't thinking straight in this storm. We
have stormy times in our
lives, too. Let's not be afraid
of Jesus, the one who can
lead us out of our times of
trouble.

---

xmiracle: See the note at 2.11.   ythe Prophet: See the
note at 1.21.   zI am Jesus: The Greek text has "I am."
See the note at 8.24.

you saw the miracles,*a* but because you ate all the food you wanted. 27Don't work for food that spoils. Work for food that gives eternal life. The Son of Man will give you this food, because God the Father has given him the right to do so."

28"What exactly does God want us to do?" the people asked.

29Jesus answered, "God wants you to have faith in the one he sent."

30They replied, "What miracle will you work, so that we can have faith in you? What will you do? 31For example, when our ancestors were in the desert, they were given manna*b* to eat. It happened just as the Scriptures say, 'God gave them bread from heaven to eat.'"

32Jesus then told them, "I tell you for certain that Moses was not the one who gave you bread from heaven. My Father is the one who gives you the true bread from heaven. 33And the bread that God gives is the one who came down from heaven to give life to the world."

34The people said, "Lord, give us this bread and don't ever stop!"

35Jesus replied:

I am the bread that gives life! No one who comes to me will ever be hungry. No one who has faith in me will ever be thirsty. 36I have told you already that you have seen me and still do not have faith in me. 37Everything and everyone that the Father has given me will come to me, and I won't turn any of them away.

38I didn't come from heaven to do what I want! I came to do what the Father wants me to do. He sent me, 39and he wants to make certain that none of the ones he has given me will be lost. Instead, he wants me to raise

Eat the bread that gives life

(32) You know that the bread you buy in the grocery store gives life. But that bread doesn't last. Jesus said he can give us bread that is everlasting. He himself is that bread. We feed on Jesus by taking him into our lives—not through our mouths, but through trusting him. When we do that Jesus himself becomes our very life.

---

amiracles: The Greek text has "signs" here and "sign" in verse 30. See the note at 2.11.   *bmanna*: When the people of Israel were wandering through the desert, the Lord gave them a special kind of food to eat. It tasted like a wafer and was called "manna," which in Hebrew means, "What is this?"

them to life on the last day.c 40My Father wants everyone who sees the Son to have faith in him and to have eternal life. Then I will raise them to life on the last day.

41The people started grumbling because Jesus had said he was the bread that had come down from heaven. 42They were asking each other, "Isn't he Jesus, the son of Joseph? Don't we know his father and mother? How can he say that he has come down from heaven?"

43Jesus told them:

Stop grumbling! 44No one can come to me, unless the Father who sent me makes them want to come. But if they do come, I will raise them to life on the last day. 45One of the prophets wrote, "God will teach all of them." And so everyone who listens to the Father and learns from him will come to me.

46The only one who has seen the Father is the one who has come from him. No one else has ever seen the Father. 47I tell you for certain that everyone who has faith in me has eternal life.

48I am the bread that gives life! 49Your ancestors ate mannad in the desert, and later they died. 50But the bread from heaven has come down, so that no one who eats it will ever die. 51I am that bread from heaven! Everyone who eats it will live forever. My flesh is the life-giving bread that I give to the people of this world.

52They started arguing with each other and asked, "How can he give us his flesh to eat?"

53Jesus answered:

I tell you for certain that you won't live unless you eat the flesh and drink the blood of the Son of Man. 54But if you do eat my flesh and drink my blood, you will have eternal life, and I will raise

Don't excuse your lack of trust

(42) The people who were listening to Jesus found an excuse not to trust him. He was just their own fellow citizen, the son of Joseph (or so they thought). Familiarity often causes distrust. If Jesus had come from a far country, they would have listened to him just because he was new and different. Jesus is well known among us. There are churches in every town. So many just pass Jesus off as a worn-out old story, and that is very sad.

Jesus is life to us

(54) By "eat my flesh and drink my blood," Jesus was talking about having faith in him and then taking part in the Lord's Supper to show that we are united with him. The wine or grape juice stands for his blood and the bread stands for his body. When we eat and drink the Lord's Supper, we show that we are part of the church, "the body of Christ," and that we have eternal life from him.

cthe last day: When God will judge all people.
dmanna: See the note at 6.31.

you to life on the last day. 55My flesh is the true food, and my blood is the true drink. 56If you eat my flesh and drink my blood, you are one with me, and I am one with you.

57The living Father sent me, and I have life because of him. Now everyone who eats my flesh will live because of me. 58The bread that comes down from heaven is not like what your ancestors ate. They died, but whoever eats this bread will live forever.

59Jesus was teaching in a Jewish place of worship in Capernaum when he said these things.

The Words of Eternal Life

60Many of Jesus' disciples heard him and said, "This is too hard for anyone to understand."

61Jesus knew that his disciples were grumbling. So he asked, "Does this bother you? 62What if you should see the Son of Man go up to heaven where he came from? 63The Spirit is the one who gives life! Human strength can do nothing. The words that I have spoken to you are from that life-giving Spirit. 64But some of you refuse to have faith in me." Jesus said this, because from the beginning he knew who would have faith in him. He also knew which one would betray him.

65Then Jesus said, "You cannot come to me, unless the Father makes you want to come. That is why I have told these things to all of you."

66Because of what Jesus said, many of his disciples turned their backs on him and stopped following him. 67Jesus then asked his twelve disciples if they were going to leave him. 68Simon Peter answered, "Lord, there is no one else that we can go to! Your words give eternal life. 69We have faith in you, and we are sure that you are God's Holy One."

70Jesus told his disciples, "I chose all twelve of you, but one of you is a demon!" 71Jesus was talking about Judas, the son

There is no one else to go to

(68) Peter told the truth. Sometimes people may imagine that there are lots of religions in the world, so what's so great about Jesus? But you soon see that people who say such things haven't trusted the other religions either. They've just decided not to seek the truth at all, so they never find it. If they truly looked for the truth, they would come to Jesus, because he alone has the words that give eternal life.

of Simon Iscariot.*e* He would later betray Jesus, even though he was one of the twelve disciples.

Jesus' Brothers Don't Have Faith in Him

7 Jesus decided to leave Judea and to start going through Galilee because the Jewish leaders wanted to kill him. ²It was almost time for the Festival of Shelters, ³and Jesus' brothers said to him, "Why don't you go to Judea? Then your disciples can see what you are doing. ⁴No one does anything in secret, if they want others to know about them. So let the world know what you are doing!" ⁵Even Jesus' own brothers had not yet become his followers.

⁶Jesus answered, "My time hasn't yet come,*f* but your time is always here. ⁷The people of this world cannot hate you. They hate me, because I tell them that they do evil things. ⁸Go on to the festival. My time hasn't yet come, and I am not going." ⁹Jesus said this and stayed on in Galilee.

Jesus at the Festival of Shelters

¹⁰After Jesus' brothers had gone to the festival, he decided to go, and he went secretly, without telling anyone.

¹¹During the festival the Jewish leaders looked for Jesus and asked, "Where is he?" ¹²The crowds even got into an argument about him. Some were saying, "Jesus is a good man," while others were saying, "He is lying to everyone." ¹³But the people were afraid of their leaders, and none of them talked in public about him.

¹⁴When the festival was about half over, Jesus stood up and started teaching in the temple. ¹⁵The leaders were surprised and said, "How does this man know so much? He has never been taught!"

¹⁶Jesus replied:

I am not teaching something that I thought up. What I teach comes from

Why didn't Jesus' brothers believe?
(5) At first the brothers of Jesus turned away from him. Growing up with him may have caused them to resent or envy him. No doubt he had been the favorite son because Mary and Joseph knew about who he was. But this case ended well. After Jesus rose from death his brothers believed in him. Some of them became leaders in the early church.

What was the Festival of Shelters?
(11) Many centuries before Jesus the Israelites escaped from slavery in Egypt, with Moses as their leader. Then for forty years they lived in tents (shelters) in the Sinai desert. The Festival of Shelters was held in memory of that time in Israel's history, when God freed them and kept them safe.

---

eIscariot: See the note at 12.4.   *fMy time has not yet come*: See the note at 2.4.

the one who sent me. [17]If you really want to obey God, you will know if what I teach comes from God or from me. [18]If I wanted to bring honor to myself, I would speak for myself. But I want to honor the one who sent me. That is why I tell the truth and not a lie. [19]Didn't Moses give you the Law? Yet none of you obey it! So why do you want to kill me?

[20]The crowd replied, "You're crazy! What makes you think someone wants to kill you?"

[21]Jesus answered:

I worked one miracle,[g] and it amazed you. [22]Moses commanded you to circumcise your sons. But it wasn't really Moses who gave you this command. It was your ancestors, and even on the Sabbath you circumcise your sons [23]in order to obey the Law of Moses. Why are you angry with me for making someone completely well on the Sabbath? [24]Don't judge by appearances. Judge by what is right.

[25]Some of the people from Jerusalem were saying, "Isn't this the man they want to kill? [26]Yet here he is, speaking for everyone to hear. And no one is arguing with him. Do you suppose the authorities know that he is the Messiah? [27]But how could that be? No one knows where the Messiah will come from, but we know where this man comes from."

[28]As Jesus was teaching in the temple, he shouted, "Do you really think you know me and where I came from? I didn't come on my own! The one who sent me is truthful, and you don't know him. [29]But I know the one who sent me, because I came from him."

[30]Some of the people wanted to arrest Jesus right then. But no one even laid a hand on him, because his time had not yet come.[h] [31]A lot of people in the crowd put their faith in him and said, "When the

Jesus didn't invent his teaching

(16) Jesus didn't just think up what he said. He received it from God the Father. Over the centuries many religious leaders have become famous because of teachings that were their own original work. Jesus made no such claim. He taught only what he was given in heaven. We don't need a new teaching. We need to listen to the teaching that comes from God.

---

[g]one miracle: The healing of the lame man (5.1-18). See the note at 2.11.   [h]his time had not yet come: See the note at 2.4.

Messiah comes, he surely won't perform more miracles[i] than this man has done!"

Officers Sent to Arrest Jesus

32When the Pharisees heard the crowd arguing about Jesus, they got together with the chief priests and sent some temple police to arrest him. 33But Jesus told them, "I will be with you a little while longer, and then I will return to the one who sent me. 34You will look for me, but you won't find me. You cannot go where I am going."

35The Jewish leaders asked each other, "Where can he go to keep us from finding him? Is he going to some foreign country where our people live? Is he going there to teach the Greeks?[j] 36What did he mean by saying that we will look for him, but won't find him? Why can't we go where he is going?"

Streams of Life-Giving Water

37On the last and most important day of the festival, Jesus stood up and shouted, "If you are thirsty, come to me and drink! 38Have faith in me, and you will have life-giving water flowing from deep inside you, just as the Scriptures say." 39Jesus was talking about the Holy Spirit, who would be given to everyone that had faith in him. The Spirit had not yet been given to anyone, since Jesus had not yet been given his full glory.[k]

The People Take Sides

40When the crowd heard Jesus say this, some of them said, "He must be the Prophet!"[l] 41Others said, "He is the Messiah!" Others even said, "Can the Mes-

Why didn't the leaders understand Jesus?
(34) Jesus said, "You cannot go where I am going." Of course, he meant that he was going back to heaven. The leaders couldn't understand this because they were so earth-minded. They had read the Scriptures in the Old Testament about Jesus. But they were so determined to have power on earth that they cared nothing for the true Messiah from God or for the heaven he talked about.

The Holy Spirit was coming
(39) Without the Holy Spirit, also called the Spirit of God, we can't fully understand the Scriptures or Jesus. But when we have faith and the Holy Spirit comes to us, he gives us ability to appreciate Jesus and to accept his words.

[i]*miracles*: See the note at 2.11. [j]*Greeks*: Perhaps Gentiles or Jews who followed Greek customs. [k]*had not yet been given his full glory*: In the Gospel of John, Jesus is given his full glory both when he is nailed to the cross and when he is raised from death to sit beside his Father in heaven. [l]*the Prophet*: See the note at 1.21.

siah come from Galilee? 42The Scriptures say that the Messiah will come from the family of King David. Doesn't this mean that he will be born in David's hometown of Bethlehem?" 43The people started taking sides against each other because of Jesus. 44Some of them wanted to arrest him, but no one laid a hand on him.

The Jewish Leaders Refuse to Have Faith in Jesus

45When the temple police returned to the chief priests and Pharisees, they were asked, "Why didn't you bring Jesus here?"
46They answered, "No one has ever spoken like that man!"
47The Pharisees said to them, "Have you also been fooled? 48Not one of the chief priests or the Pharisees has faith in him. 49And these people who don't know the Law are under God's curse anyway."
50Nicodemus was there at the time. He was the same one who had earlier come to see Jesus.m Nicodemus was a member of the Jewish council and said, 51"Our Law doesn't let us condemn people before we hear what they have to say. We cannot judge them before we know what they have done."
52Then they said, "Nicodemus, you must be from Galilee! Read the Scriptures, and you will find that no prophet is to come from Galilee."

A Woman Caught in Sin

8 53Everyone else went home, 1but Jesus walked out to the Mount of Olives. 2Then early the next morning he went to the temple. The people came to him, and he sat downn and started teaching them.
3The Pharisees and the teachers of the Law of Moses brought in a woman who had been caught in bed with a man who was not her husband. They made her stand in the middle of the crowd. 4Then they said,

Jesus caused division
(43) Jesus promised he would be the cause of arguments. Even today people still take sides for or against Jesus. Sometimes we get tired of the endless debate and lies about him. But when Jesus comes again all of the arguments will stop forever. Which side will you be on?

Beware of pride
(49) The chief priests and Pharisees thought they were better than the common people. They said the common people were ignorant and didn't know the Scriptures. That may have been true. But the leaders were worse. Their sin was their pride that blinded them about Jesus. They didn't even know their Messiah when they saw him—even though they knew the Old Testament Scriptures that spoke about him.

mwho had earlier come to see Jesus: See 3.1-21.   nsat down: See the note at 6.3, 4.

"Teacher, this woman was caught sleeping with a man who is not her husband. 5The Law of Moses teaches that a woman like this should be stoned to death! What do you say?"

6They asked Jesus this question, because they wanted to test him and bring some charge against him. But Jesus simply bent over and started writing on the ground with his finger.

7They kept on asking Jesus about the woman. Finally, he stood up and said, "If any of you have never sinned, then go ahead and throw the first stone at her!" 8Once again he bent over and began writing on the ground. 9The people left one by one, beginning with the oldest one in the crowd. Finally, Jesus and the woman were there alone.

10Jesus stood up and asked her, "Where is everyone? Isn't there anyone left to accuse you?"

11"No sir," the woman answered.

Then Jesus told her, "I am not going to accuse you either. You may go now, but don't sin anymore."*o*

Jesus Is the Light for the World

12Once again Jesus spoke to the people. This time he said, "I am the light for the world! Follow me, and you won't be walking in the dark. You will have the light that gives life."

13The Pharisees objected, "You are the only one speaking for yourself, and what you say isn't true!"

14Jesus replied:

Even if I do speak for myself, what I say is true! I know where I came from and where I am going. But you don't know where I am from or where I am going. 15You judge in the same way that everyone else does, but I don't judge

Jesus forgives sinners

(5) We like to feel we have good morals as long as we think we can point to someone worse than ourselves. That's how we make ourselves feel that we are good in God's eyes. That is also the way the teachers of the Law felt when they caught a woman in her sin. But Jesus saw their real attitude, and he made them understand their self-deceit. But he forgave the woman with a warning.

Why is Jesus a light?

(12) The passage about the woman caught in sin gives the answer. Jesus shows us what we are—sinners. But his light drives away the darkness of our sins. This is shown by the way he dealt with the sins of the woman. Jesus didn't come to make people feel guilty. His great work is to forgive—to take away sin and the guilt that it causes.

odon't sin anymore: Verses 1-11 are not in some manuscripts. In other manuscripts these verses are placed after 7.36 or after 21.25 or after Luke 21.38, with some differences in the text.

anyone. [16]If I did judge, I would judge
fairly, because I would not be doing it
alone. The Father who sent me is here
with me. [17]Your Law requires two witnesses to prove that something is true.
[18]I am one of my witnesses, and the
Father who sent me is the other one.

[19]"Where is your Father?" they asked
Jesus.

"You don't know me or my Father!" Jesus
answered. "If you knew me, you would
know my Father."

[20]Jesus said this while he was still teaching in the place where the temple treasures
were stored. But no one arrested him, because his time had not yet come.[p]

You Cannot Go Where I Am Going

[21]Jesus also told them, "I am going away,
and you will look for me. But you cannot
go where I am going, and you will die with
your sins unforgiven."

[22]The Jewish leaders asked, "Does he intend to kill himself? Is that what he means
by saying we cannot go where he is going?"

[23]Jesus answered, "You are from below,
but I am from above. You belong to this
world, but I don't. [24]That is why I said you
will die with your sins unforgiven. If you
don't have faith in me for who I am,[q] you
will die, and your sins will not be forgiven."

[25]"Who are you?" they asked Jesus.

Jesus answered, "I am exactly who I told
you at the beginning. [26]I have a lot more
to say about you, especially about all the
evil you have done. The one who sent me
is truthful, and I tell the people of this world
only what I have heard from him."

[27]No one understood that Jesus was talking to them about the Father.

[28]Jesus went on to say, "When you have
lifted up the Son of Man,[r] you will know
who I am. You will also know that I don't

Who are you?
(25) Jesus' words about
himself were well under-
stood by the Jewish leaders.
They knew he was saying
that he is the Messiah. But
their hearts were cold to
him. They decided they
didn't want Jesus for their
Messiah—because that
would mean giving up their
wealth and power.

[p]his time had not yet come: See the note at 2.4.   [q]I
am: For the Jewish people the most holy name of God
is "Yahweh," which may be translated "I am." In the
Gospel of John "I am" is sometimes used by Jesus to
show that he is that one.   [r]lifted up the Son of Man:
See the note at 7.39.

do anything on my own. I say only what my Father taught me. 29The one who sent me is with me. I always do what pleases him, and he will never leave me."

30After Jesus said this, many of the people put their faith in him.

The Truth Will Set You Free

31Jesus told the people who had faith in him, "If you keep on obeying what I have said, you truly are my disciples. 32You will know the truth, and the truth will set you free."

33They answered, "We are Abraham's children! We have never been anyone's slaves. How can you say we will be set free?"

34Jesus replied:

I tell you for certain that anyone who sins is a slave of sin! 35And slaves don't stay in the family forever, though the Son will always remain in the family. 36If the Son gives you freedom, you are free! 37I know that you are from Abraham's family. Yet you want to kill me, because my message is not really in your hearts. 38I am telling you what my Father has shown me, just as you are doing what your father has taught you.

Your Father Is the Devil

39The people said to Jesus, "Abraham is our father!"

Jesus replied, "If you were Abraham's children, you would do what Abraham did. 40Instead, you want to kill me for telling you the truth that God gave me. Abraham never did anything like that. 41But you are doing exactly what your father does."

"Don't accuse us of having someone else as our father!" they said. "We just have one father, and he is God."

42Jesus answered:

If God were your Father, you would love me, because I came from God and only from him. He sent me. I did not come on my own. 43Why can't you understand what I am talking about? Can't

What does it mean to be free?
(32) Over the entrance to a famous college are the words, "The truth shall make you free." But most people who go in there don't know where the words come from. The Jews didn't even remember they once had been slaves in Egypt. Jesus had come to them as the living Truth who alone sets people free from the slavery of sin.

you stand to hear what I am saying?
44Your father is the devil, and you do exactly what he wants. He has always been a murderer and a liar. There is nothing truthful about him. He speaks on his own, and everything he says is a lie. Not only is he a liar himself, but he is also the father of all lies.

45Everything I have told you is true, and you still refuse to have faith in me. 46Can any of you accuse me of sin? If you cannot, why won't you have faith in me? After all, I am telling you the truth. 47Anyone who belongs to God will listen to his message. But you refuse to listen, because you don't belong to God.

Who is your father?

(44) In one way, God is the Father of all people because he is the Creator. But sin broke the relationship. God can't be our Father again until the relationship is put back together somehow. That happens when we believe in Jesus. But until then, God will have to deny we are his children. Until we have faith, we are lost in sin, and we are the children of the devil.

Jesus and Abraham

48The people told Jesus, "We were right to say that you are a Samaritan*s* and that you have a demon in you!"

49Jesus answered, "I don't have a demon in me. I honor my Father, and you refuse to honor me. 50I don't want honor for myself. But there is one who wants me to be honored, and he is also the one who judges. 51I tell you for certain that if you obey my words, you will never die."

52Then the people said, "Now we are sure that you have a demon. Abraham is dead, and so are the prophets. How can you say that no one who obeys your words will ever die? 53Are you greater than our father Abraham? He died, and so did the prophets. Who do you think you are?"

54Jesus replied, "If I honored myself, it would mean nothing. My Father is the one who honors me. You claim that he is your God, 55even though you don't really know him. If I said I didn't know him, I would be a liar, just like all of you. But I know him, and I do what he says. 56Your father Abraham was really glad to see me."

57"You are not even fifty years old!" they said. "How could you have seen Abraham?"

*s*Samaritan: See 4.9 and the note there.

58Jesus answered, "I tell you for certain that even before Abraham was, I was, and I am."*t* 59The people picked up stones to kill Jesus, but he hid and left the temple.

Jesus Heals a Man Born Blind

9 As Jesus walked along, he saw a man who had been blind since birth. 2Jesus' disciples asked, "Teacher, why was this man born blind? Was it because he or his parents sinned?"

3"No, it wasn't!" Jesus answered. "But because of this, you will see God work a miracle for him. 4As long as it is day, we must do what the one who sent me wants me to do. When night comes, no one can work. 5While I am in the world, I am the light for the world."

6After Jesus said this, he spit on the ground. He made some mud and smeared it on the man's eyes. 7Then he said, "Go and wash off the mud in Siloam Pool." The man went and washed in Siloam, which means "One Who Is Sent." When he had washed off the mud, he could see.

8The man's neighbors and the people who had seen him begging wondered if he really could be the same man. 9Some of them said he was the same beggar, while others said he only looked like him. But he told them, "I am that man."

10"Then how can you see?" they asked.

11He answered, "Someone named Jesus made some mud and smeared it on my eyes. He told me to go and wash it off in Siloam Pool. When I did, I could see."

12"Where is he now?" they asked.

"I don't know," he answered.

The Pharisees Try to Find Out What Happened

13-14The day when Jesus made the mud and healed the man was a Sabbath. So the people took the man to the Pharisees. 15They asked him how he was able to see, and he answered, "Jesus made some mud

These were Jesus' most shocking words
(58) Here Jesus tells the people that he lived—and always had lived—before Abraham, who was born some two thousand years earlier. We are glad Jesus said this when we personally know him as our Savior. But if we don't know him this way, these words don't make sense to us. They sound like something it would take a lot of nerve to say. But Jesus really is the God-Man who has lived forever.

Why did Jesus heal the blind man?
(3) Jesus wanted his disciples to know he came to heal all kinds of people. The disciples thought the man was cursed with blindness because of somebody's bad deeds, and so he probably couldn't be healed. But it didn't matter what the cause of the blindness was—Jesus would heal him. Jesus also wants to open our eyes to the truth.

t I am: See the note at 8.24.

and smeared it on my eyes. Then after I washed off the mud, I could see."

16Some of the Pharisees said, "This man Jesus does not come from God. If he did, he would not break the law of the Sabbath."

Others asked, "How could someone who is a sinner work such a miracle?"u

Since the Pharisees could not agree among themselves, 17they asked the man, "What do you say about this one who healed your eyes?"

"He is a prophet!" the man told them.

18But the Jewish leaders would not believe that the man had once been blind. They sent for his parents 19and asked them, "Is this the son that you said was born blind? How can he now see?"

20The man's parents answered, "We are certain that he is our son, and we know that he was born blind. 21But we don't know how he got his sight or who gave it to him. Ask him! He is old enough to speak for himself."

22-23The man's parents said this because they were afraid of the Jewish leaders. The leaders had already agreed that no one was to have anything to do with anyone who said Jesus was the Messiah.

24The leaders called the man back and said, "Swear by God to tell the truth! We know that Jesus is a sinner."

25The man replied, "I don't know if he is a sinner or not. All I know is that I used to be blind, but now I can see!"

26"What did he do to you?" the Jewish leaders asked. "How did he heal your eyes?"

27The man answered, "I have already told you once, and you refused to listen. Why do you want me to tell you again? Do you also want to become his disciples?"

28The leaders insulted the man and said, "You are his follower! We are followers of Moses. 29We are sure that God spoke to Moses, but we don't even know where Jesus comes from."

30The man replied, "How strange! He

What was the Pharisees' problem?

(25) The Pharisees knew the man could see. But they didn't want to believe what had happened. Their hatred of Jesus blinded them to the clear truth. In spite of the Pharisees' arguing, the man who was blind could see. So they took out their spite on the man who had been blind. Sin makes people unreasonable and blind in their hearts.

umiracle: See the note at 2.11.

healed my eyes, and yet you don't know where he comes from. 31We know that God listens only to people who love and obey him. God doesn't listen to sinners. 32And this is the first time in history that anyone has ever given sight to someone born blind. 33Jesus could not do anything unless he came from God."

34The leaders told the man, "You have been a sinner since the day you were born! Do you think you can teach us anything?" Then they said, "You can never come back into any of our meeting places!"

35When Jesus heard what had happened, he went and found the man. Then Jesus asked, "Do you have faith in the Son of Man?"

36He replied, "Sir, if you will tell me who he is, I will put my faith in him."

37"You have already seen him," Jesus answered, "and right now he is talking with you."

38The man said, "Lord, I put my faith in you!" Then he worshiped Jesus.

39Jesus told him, "I came to judge the people of this world. I am here to give sight to the blind and to make blind everyone who sees."

40When the Pharisees heard Jesus say this, they asked, "Are we blind?"

41Jesus answered, "If you were blind, you would not be guilty. But now that you claim to see, you will keep on being guilty."

A Story about Sheep

10 Jesus said:
I tell you for certain that only thieves and robbers climb over the fence instead of going in through the gate to the sheep pen. 2-3But the gatekeeper opens the gate for the shepherd, and he goes in through it. The sheep know their shepherd's voice. He calls each of them by name and leads them out.

4When he has led out all of his sheep, he walks in front of them, and they follow, because they know his voice. 5The sheep will not follow strangers. They

Jesus shows us himself
(35) The poor man didn't even know who had healed him of his blindness. Jesus hadn't demanded that the man must understand it all. Afterwards, Jesus showed himself to the man. Then the man trusted him. Jesus shows himself to us in these pages. Can we trust him too?

Did Jesus make people blind?
(39) He says he did. Jesus means he won't help people who are satisfied with themselves. Jesus came to help people who have no hope and know it. A doctor can't help dying people who say they are well, and Jesus can't help people who say they have no sin and no need of him.

Sheep know their shepherd
(2) In the land where Jesus lived—even today—shepherds call their sheep by name. Also, if you mix two flocks of sheep, and each shepherd calls to his own sheep, then each flock will go to its own shepherd. Jesus knows his people by name, and they won't follow anyone but him.

don't recognize a stranger's voice, and they run away.

6Jesus told the people this story. But they did not understand what he was talking about.

Jesus Is the Good Shepherd

7Jesus said:

I tell you for certain that I am the gate for the sheep. 8Everyone who came before me was a thief or a robber, and the sheep did not listen to any of them. 9I am the gate. All who come in through me will be saved. Through me they will come and go and find pasture.

10A thief comes only to rob, kill, and destroy. I came so that everyone would have life, and have it in its fullest. 11I am the good shepherd, and the good shepherd gives up his life for his sheep. 12Hired workers are not like the shepherd. They don't own the sheep, and when they see a wolf coming, they run off and leave the sheep. Then the wolf attacks and scatters the flock. 13Hired workers run away because they don't care about the sheep.

14I am the good shepherd. I know my sheep, and they know me. 15Just as the Father knows me, I know the Father, and I give up my life for my sheep. 16I have other sheep that are not in this sheep pen. I must bring them together too, when they hear my voice. Then there will be one flock of sheep and one shepherd.

17The Father loves me, because I give up my life, so that I may receive it back again. 18No one takes my life from me. I give it up willingly! I have the power to give it up and the power to receive it back again, just as my Father commanded me to do.

19The Jews took sides because of what Jesus had told them. 20Many of them said, "He has a demon in him! He is crazy! Why listen to him?"

21But others said, "How could anyone

Who were the thieves and robbers?

(10) The thieves and robbers were the false shepherds, the false teachers. God wanted leaders for the people who were chosen and guided by his own will. The leaders in Jesus' time didn't care much about the people. They were using the people to make themselves rich and important.

They said Jesus was crazy

(20) We could imagine people today saying Jesus was out of his mind. Some modern people think they know too much to have faith in prophets or messengers from God. In Jesus' time they didn't know about all of today's excuses for not believing. But they were like people are now—they didn't want to have faith in Jesus because their lives were not right with God.

with a demon in him say these things? No one like that could give sight to a blind person!"

Jesus Is Rejected

22That winter Jesus was in Jerusalem for the Temple Festival. 23One day he was walking in that part of the temple known as Solomon's Porch,v 24and the people gathered all around him. They said, "How long are you going to keep us guessing? If you are the Messiah, tell us plainly!"

25Jesus answered:

I have told you, and you refused to believe me. The things I do by my Father's authority show who I am. 26But since you are not my sheep, you don't believe me. 27My sheep know my voice, and I know them. They follow me, 28and I give them eternal life, so that they will never be lost. No one can snatch them out of my hand. 29My Father gave them to me, and he is greater than all others.w No one can snatch them from his hands, 30and I am one with the Father.

31Once again the Jewish leaders picked up stones in order to kill Jesus. 32But he said, "I have shown you many good things that my Father sent me to do. Which one are you going to stone me for?"

33They answered, "We are not stoning you because of any good thing you did. We are stoning you because you did a terrible thing. You are just a man, and here you are claiming to be God!"

34Jesus replied:

In your Scriptures doesn't God say, "You are gods?" 35The Scriptures cannot be destroyed, and God spoke to those people and called them gods. 36So why do you accuse me of a terrible sin for saying that I am the Son of God?

Jesus keeps his people safe
(28) Jesus says about his sheep (believers), "No one can snatch them out of my hand." It comforts us to know that Jesus will keep us forever when we give our lives to him. He was not just a good man. He is the Son of God, and we can never be lost if we are in his hands.

Why did they want to stone Jesus?
(33) Killing people by throwing stones at them was a legal method of putting criminals to death. In the minds of the leaders Jesus was the worst kind of criminal—he had said he was God. But the Old Testament prophets also said this about him. It is hard to understand how the leaders of Jesus' day knew so little about their own Scriptures.

vSolomon's Porch: A public place with tall columns along the east side of the temple. whe is greater than all others: Some manuscripts have "they are greater than all others."

After all, it is the Father who prepared me for this work. He is also the one who sent me into the world. 37If I don't do as my Father does, you should not believe me. 38But if I do what my Father does, you should believe because of that, even if you don't have faith in me. Then you will know for certain that the Father is one with me, and I am one with the Father.

39Again they wanted to arrest Jesus. But he escaped 40and crossed the Jordan to the place where John had earlier been baptizing. While Jesus was there, 41many people came to him. They were saying, "John didn't work any miracles, but everything he said about Jesus is true." 42A lot of those people also put their faith in Jesus.

The Death of Lazarus

11 1-2A man by the name of Lazarus was sick in the village of Bethany. He had two sisters, Mary and Martha. This was the same Mary who later poured perfume on the Lord's head and wiped his feet with her hair. 3The sisters sent a message to the Lord and told him that his good friend Lazarus was sick.

4When Jesus heard this, he said, "His sickness won't end in death. It will bring glory to God and his Son."

5Jesus loved Martha and her sister and brother. 6But he stayed where he was for two more days. 7Then he said to his disciples, "Now we'll go back to Judea."

8"Teacher," they said, "the people there want to stone you to death! Why do you want to go back?"

9Jesus answered, "Aren't there twelve hours in each day? If you walk during the day, you will have light from the sun, and you won't stumble. 10But if you walk during the night, you will stumble, because there isn't any light inside you." 11Then he told them, "Our friend Lazarus is asleep, and I am going there to wake him up."

12They replied, "Lord, if he is asleep, he will get better." 13Jesus really meant that

Many people came to Jesus
(41) In spite of everything the Jewish leaders could say or do, crowds of people flocked to hear Jesus and to be healed. They had better understanding than their leaders. They could see the sense in everything Jesus said and did. But most of the leaders were blinded by jealousy and religious hate.

Lazarus was dead, but they thought he was talking only about sleep.

14Then Jesus told them plainly, "Lazarus is dead! 15I am glad that I wasn't there, because now you will have a chance to put your faith in me. Let's go to him."

16Thomas, whose nickname was "Twin," said to the other disciples, "Come on. Let's go so we can die with him."

Jesus Brings Lazarus to Life

17When Jesus got to Bethany, he found that Lazarus had already been in the tomb four days. 18Bethany was only about two miles from Jerusalem, 19and many people had come from the city to comfort Martha and Mary because their brother had died.

20When Martha heard that Jesus had arrived, she went out to meet him, but Mary stayed in the house. 21Martha said to Jesus, "Lord, if you had been here, my brother would not have died. 22Yet even now I know that God will do anything you ask."

23Jesus told her, "Your brother will live again!"

24Martha answered, "I know that he will be raised to life on the last day,ˣ when all the dead are raised."

25Jesus then said, "I am the one who raises the dead to life! Everyone who has faith in me will live, even if they die. 26And everyone who lives because of faith in me will never die. Do you believe this?"

27"Yes, Lord!" she replied. "I believe that you are Christ, the Son of God. You are the one we hoped would come into the world."

28After Martha said this, she went and privately said to her sister Mary, "The Teacher is here, and he wants to see you." 29As soon as Mary heard this, she got up and went out to Jesus. 30He was still outside the village where Martha had gone to meet him. 31Many people had come to comfort Mary, and when they saw her quickly leave

Our faith sometimes fails
(16) Jesus told his disciples that he was going to "wake up" Lazarus from death. But they didn't believe him. We talk a lot about our faith. But often we find that our faith doesn't go very far, as the disciples' didn't in this case. The only thing that keeps us going sometimes is the fact that Jesus is always faithful toward us, even when our faith in him is weak.

A great promise
(26) There is encouragement here as Jesus says, "Everyone who lives because of faith in me will never die." If we have been at the bedside of a dying Christian, we may have seen for ourselves how true these words are. Those who trust in Jesus don't die—they go out with joy to meet him.

ˣthe last day: When God will judge all people.

the house, they thought she was going out to the tomb to cry. So they followed her.

32Mary went to where Jesus was. Then as soon as she saw him, she kneeled at his feet and said, "Lord, if you had been here, my brother would not have died."

33When Jesus saw that Mary and the people with her were crying, he was terribly upset 34and asked, "Where have you put his body?"

They replied, "Lord, come and you will see."

35Jesus started crying, 36and the people said, "See how much he loved Lazarus."

37Some of them said, "He gives sight to the blind. Why couldn't he have kept Lazarus from dying?"

38Jesus was still terribly upset. So he went to the tomb, which was a cave with a stone rolled against the entrance. 39Then he told the people to roll the stone away. But Martha said, "Lord, you know that Lazarus has been dead four days, and there will be a bad smell."

40Jesus replied, "Didn't I tell you that if you had faith, you would see the glory of God?"

41After the stone had been rolled aside, Jesus looked up toward heaven and prayed, "Father, I thank you for answering my prayer. 42I know that you always answer my prayers. But I said this, so that the people here would believe that you sent me."

43When Jesus had finished praying, he shouted, "Lazarus, come out!" 44The man who had been dead came out. His hands and feet were wrapped with strips of burial cloth, and a cloth covered his face.

Jesus then told the people, "Untie him and let him go."

The Plot to Kill Jesus
(Matthew 26.1–5; Mark 14.1, 2; Luke 22.1, 2)

45Many of the people who had come to visit Mary saw the things that Jesus did, and they put their faith in him. 46Others went to the Pharisees and told what Jesus had done. 47Then the chief priests and the

Why did Jesus cry?
(35) Was Jesus crying because he had lost his friend in death? No, Jesus knew what he was going to do. But he saw the others crying, and saw how death was their great enemy. Jesus was crying for the others whom the thought of death had defeated.

Pharisees called the council together and said, "What should we do? This man is working a lot of miracles.*y* *48*If we don't stop him now, everyone will put their faith in him. Then the Romans will come and destroy our temple and our nation."*z*

*49*One of the council members was Caiaphas, who was also high priest that year. He spoke up and said, "You people don't have any sense at all! *50*Don't you know it is better for one person to die for the people than for the whole nation to be destroyed?" *51*Caiaphas did not say this on his own. As high priest that year, he was prophesying that Jesus would die for the nation. *52*Yet Jesus would not die just for the Jewish nation. He would die to bring together all of God's scattered people. *53*From that day on, the council started making plans to put Jesus to death.

*54*Because of this plot against him, Jesus stopped going around in public. He went to the town of Ephraim, which was near the desert, and he stayed there with his disciples.

*55*It was almost time for Passover. Many of the Jewish people who lived out in the country had come to Jerusalem to get themselves ready*a* for the festival. *56*They looked around for Jesus. Then when they were in the temple, they asked each other, "You don't think he will come here for Passover, do you?"

*57*The chief priests and the Pharisees told the people to let them know if any of them saw Jesus. That is how they hoped to arrest him.

At Bethany
(Matthew 26.6–13; Mark 14.3–9)

12 Six days before Passover Jesus went back to Bethany, where he had raised

Caiaphas said a mouthful
(50) "It is better for one person to die for the people." That was exactly what would happen. Jesus would die for his people. But the high priest said more than he understood, because he was only thinking about sacrificing Jesus to please the Romans. Notice also that Jesus died not only for the Jews but for all of God's people everywhere.

Why did Jesus stay away?
(54) Jesus was not afraid of the Jewish leaders. But he knew there was a right time for his arrest, his trial, and his death. That time would be at the Jewish Passover: the feast when a lamb was killed, when Jews remembered how they were saved from slavery in Egypt. Jesus the Lamb of God would save us by his own sacrifice from our slavery to sin and death.

ymiracles: See the note at 2.11. *zdestroy our temple and our nation*: The Jewish leaders were afraid that Jesus would lead his followers to rebel against Rome and that the Roman army would then destroy their nation. *aget themselves ready*: The Jewish people had to do certain things to prepare themselves to worship God.

Lazarus from death. 2A meal had been prepared for Jesus. Martha was doing the serving, and Lazarus himself was there.

3Mary took a very expensive bottle of perfume[b] and poured it on Jesus' feet. She wiped them with her hair, and the sweet smell of the perfume filled the house.

4A disciple named Judas Iscariot[c] was there. He was the one who was going to betray Jesus, and he asked, 5"Why wasn't this perfume sold for three hundred silver coins and the money given to the poor?" 6Judas did not really care about the poor. He asked this because he carried the money-bag and sometimes would steal from it.

7Jesus replied, "Leave her alone! She has kept this perfume for the day of my burial. 8You will always have the poor with you, but you won't always have me."

A Plot to Kill Lazarus

9A lot of people came when they heard that Jesus was there. They also wanted to see Lazarus, because Jesus had raised him from death. 10So the chief priests made plans to kill Lazarus. 11He was the reason that many of the Jewish people were turning from them and putting their faith in Jesus.

Jesus Enters Jerusalem
(Matthew 21.1–11; Mark 11.1–11; Luke 19.28–40)

12The next day a large crowd was in Jerusalem for Passover. When they heard that Jesus was coming for the festival, 13they took palm branches and went out to greet him.[d] They shouted,
"Hooray![e]

Jesus accepted Mary's gift
(7) Maybe we think Jesus should have agreed with Judas. The money from the perfume could have been given to the poor. But it was Mary's loving act for Jesus. He always accepts our works of love, even when they don't make sense to other people. The Son of God deserves our best. Besides, Judas was only pretending. He was a thief and he didn't care what Mary did.

Trying to kill the truth
(10) It's hard to imagine such stubbornness. The chief priests knew that Jesus had raised a man to life. But instead of believing in Jesus, they tried to kill the man. It shows how far some people will go who don't want to accept Jesus.

---

[b]*very expensive bottle of perfume*: The Greek text has "expensive perfume made of pure spikenard," a plant used to make perfume. [c]*Iscariot*: This may mean "a man from Kerioth" (a place in Judea). But more probably it means "a man who was a liar" or "a man who was a betrayer." [d]*took palm branches and went out to greet him*: This was one way that the Jewish people welcomed a famous person. [e]*Hooray*: This translates a word that can mean "please save us." But it is most often used as a shout of praise to God.

God bless the one who comes
   in the name of the Lord!
God bless the King
   of Israel!''

14Jesus found a donkey and rode on it, just as the Scriptures say,

15"People of Jerusalem,
   don't be afraid!
Your King is now coming,
   and he is riding
     on a donkey."

16At first, Jesus' disciples did not understand. But after he had been given his glory,f they remembered all this. Everything had happened exactly as the Scriptures said it would.

17-18A crowd had come to meet Jesus because they had seen him call Lazarus out of the tomb. They kept talking about him and this miracle.g 19But the Pharisees said to each other, "There is nothing that can be done! Everyone in the world is following Jesus."

Some Greeks Want to Meet Jesus

20Some Greeksh had gone to Jerusalem to worship during Passover. 21Philip from Bethsaida in Galilee was there too. So they went to him and said, "Sir, we would like to meet Jesus." 22Philip told Andrew. Then the two of them went to Jesus and told him.

The Son of Man Must Be Lifted Up

23Jesus said:

The time has come for the Son of Man to be given his glory.i 24I tell you for certain that a grain of wheat that falls on the ground will never be more than one grain unless it dies. But if it dies, it will produce lots of wheat. 25If you love your life, you will lose it. If you give it up in this world, you will be given eternal life. 26If you serve me,

The Old Testament had told about this day
(14) Jesus would ride a donkey into Jerusalem, carrying out a prophecy from the Scriptures. It is very important to see that Jesus was following the great plan of God. In ages past God had planned to send his Son to be our Savior. Prophets had been telling about this for many hundreds of years.

Other nations worshiped Jesus
(21) Already we see here that the good news about Jesus was reaching the Gentile peoples. Some of them were coming to Jesus at Passover time. It was at this time that Jesus announced that he would have to suffer and die.

---

fhad been given his glory: See the note at 7.39.   gmiracle: See the note at 2.11.   hGreeks: Perhaps Gentiles who worshiped with the Jews. See the note at 7.35.
ibe given his glory: See the note at 7.39.

you must go with me. My servants will be with me wherever I am. If you serve me, my Father will honor you.

27Now I am deeply troubled, and I don't know what to say. But I must not ask my Father to keep me from this time of suffering. In fact, I came into the world to suffer. 28So Father, bring glory to yourself.

A voice from heaven then said, "I have already brought glory to myself, and I will do it again!" 29When the crowd heard the voice, some of them thought it was thunder. Others thought an angel had spoken to Jesus.

30Then Jesus told the crowd, "That voice spoke to help you, not me. 31This world's people are now being judged, and the ruler of this worldj is already being thrown out! 32If I am lifted up above the earth, I will make everyone want to come to me." 33Jesus was talking about the way he would be put to death.

34The crowd said to Jesus, "The Scriptures teach that the Messiah will live forever. How can you say that the Son of Man must be lifted up? Who is this Son of Man?"

35Jesus answered, "The light will be with you for only a little longer. Walk in the light while you can. Then you won't be caught walking blindly in the dark. 36Have faith in the light while it is with you, and you will be children of the light."

The People Refuse to Have Faith in Jesus

After Jesus had said these things, he left and went into hiding. 37He had worked a lot of miraclesk among the people, but they were still not willing to have faith in him. 38This happened so that what the prophet Isaiah had said would come true,

"Lord, who has believed
our message?

Jesus would be lifted up
(32) This was another way of saying Jesus would be crucified or nailed to a cross. The crowd didn't understand that the Messiah, who is the Son of God, cannot truly die. They couldn't understand that the Messiah had to pass through death and rise again in order to give life to us.

The miracles made no difference
(37) The crowds were amazed by the wonderful things Jesus did—even bringing Lazarus back from the dead. But they still did not understand or accept Jesus as their Messiah. We're all like that. We may live for Jesus one day, but the next day we may fail him. Let's pray for courage to be loyal to Jesus at all times.

jworld: In the Gospel of John "world" sometimes refers to the people who live in this world and to the evil forces that control their lives.   kmiracles: See the note at 2.11.

> And who has seen
> your mighty strength?"

39The people could not have faith in Jesus, because Isaiah had also said,

> 40"The Lord has blinded
> the eyes of the people,
> and he has made
> the people stubborn.
> He did this so that they
> could not see
> or understand,
> and so that they
> would not turn to the Lord
> and be healed."

41Isaiah said this, because he saw the glory of Jesus and spoke about him.*l* 42Even then, many of the leaders put their faith in Jesus, but they did not tell anyone about it. The Pharisees had already given orders for the people not to have anything to do with anyone who had faith in Jesus. 43And besides, the leaders liked praise from others more than they liked praise from God.

Jesus Came to Save the World

44In a loud voice Jesus said:

Everyone who has faith in me also has faith in the one who sent me. 45And everyone who has seen me has seen the one who sent me. 46I am the light that has come into the world. No one who has faith in me will stay in the dark.

47I am not the one who will judge those who refuse to obey my teachings. I came to save the people of this world, not to be their judge. 48But everyone who rejects me and my teachings will be judged on the last day*m* by what I have said. 49I don't speak on my own. I say only what the Father who sent me has told me to say. 50I know that his commands will bring eternal life. That is why I tell you exactly what the Father has told me.

To believe in Jesus is to believe in God

(44) That's the important thing. Many people are willing to see Jesus as one of the world's great teachers. But they don't understand that our problem is not lack of teachers. There are many to tell us how we should live. What we need is someone to save us from our sins. That is why Jesus is different—he saves us from the sins that keep us away from God.

l he saw the glory of Jesus and spoke about him: Or "he saw the glory of God and spoke about Jesus."
m the last day: When God will judge all people.

Jesus Washes the Feet of His Disciples

13 It was before Passover, and Jesus knew that the time had come for him to leave this world and to return to the Father. He had always loved his followers in this world, and he loved them to the very end.

²Even before the evening meal started, the devil had made Judas, the son of Simon Iscariot,[n] decide to betray Jesus.

³Jesus knew that he had come from God and would go back to God. He also knew that the Father had given him complete power. ⁴So during the meal Jesus got up, removed his outer garment, and wrapped a towel around his waist. ⁵He put some water into a large bowl. Then he began washing his disciples' feet and drying them with the towel he was wearing.

⁶But when he came to Simon Peter, that disciple asked, "Lord, are you going to wash my feet?"

⁷Jesus answered, "You don't really know what I am doing, but later you will understand."

⁸"You will never wash my feet!" Peter replied.

"If I don't wash you," Jesus told him, "you don't really belong to me."

⁹Peter said, "Lord, don't wash just my feet. Wash my hands and my head."

¹⁰Jesus answered, "People who have bathed and are clean all over need to wash just their feet. And you, my disciples, are clean, except for one of you." ¹¹Jesus knew who would betray him. That is why he said, "except for one of you."

¹²After Jesus had washed his disciples' feet and had put his outer garment back on, he sat down again.[o] Then he said:

Do you understand what I have done?
¹³You call me your teacher and Lord, and you should, because that is who I

Jesus "washes our feet"
(5) Jesus showed us how to be a servant. When guests came to someone's home in Jesus' time, their feet would be hot and covered with dust from the road. The host's slave (or the host if there were no slave) would wash the guests' feet. Jesus put on the clothing of a slave and did this for his disciples. He is showing us that he took the lowest place—by becoming a man and dying a shameful death—because he loves us. We also should love by serving one another.

---

[n]*Iscariot:* See the note at 12.4.　[o]*sat down again:* On special occasions the Jewish people followed the Greek and Roman custom of lying down on their left side and leaning on their left elbow, while eating with their right hand.

am. 14And if your Lord and teacher has washed your feet, you should do the same for each other. 15I have set the example, and you should do for each other exactly what I have done for you. 16I tell you for certain that servants are not greater than their master, and messengers are not greater than the one who sent them. 17You know these things, and God will bless you, if you do them.

18I am not talking about all of you. I know the ones I have chosen. But what the Scriptures say must come true. And they say, "The man who ate with me has turned against me!" 19I am telling you this before it all happens. Then when it does happen, you will believe who I am.p 20I tell you for certain that anyone who welcomes my messengers also welcomes me, and anyone who welcomes me welcomes the one who sent me.

Jesus Tells What Will Happen to Him
(Matthew 26.20–25; Mark 14.17–21; Luke 22.21–23)

21After Jesus had said these things, he was deeply troubled and told his disciples, "I tell you for certain that one of you will betray me." 22They were confused about what he meant. And they just stared at each other.

23Jesus' favorite disciple was sitting next to him at the meal, 24and Simon motioned for that disciple to find out which one Jesus meant. 25So the disciple leaned toward Jesus and asked, "Lord, which one of us are you talking about?"

26Jesus answered, "I will dip this piece of bread in the sauce and give it to the one I was talking about."

Then Jesus dipped the bread and gave it to Judas, the son of Simon Iscariot.q 27Right then Satan took control of Judas.

Jesus knew what was going to happen
(23) Judas would sell his Master to the Jewish leaders. Jesus told this to John, the one who wrote this Gospel. But the others didn't realize what Judas was going to do. John tells us that Satan, the great spiritual enemy of God, was by that time in control of Judas' life.

pI am: See the note at 8.24.   qIscariot: See the note at 12.4.

Jesus said, "Judas, go quickly and do what you have to do." 28No one at the meal understood what Jesus meant. 29But because Judas was in charge of the money, some of them thought that Jesus had told him to buy something they needed for the festival. Others thought that Jesus had told him to give some money to the poor. 30Judas took the piece of bread and went out.

It was already night.

The New Command

31After Judas had gone, Jesus said:
Now the Son of Man will be given glory, and he will bring glory to God. 32Then, after God is given glory because of him, God will bring glory to him, and God will do it very soon.

33My children, I will be with you for a little while longer. Then you will look for me, but you won't find me. I tell you just as I told the people, "You cannot go where I am going." 34But I am giving you a new command. You must love each other, just as I have loved you. 35If you love each other, everyone will know that you are my disciples.

Peter's Promise
(Matthew 26.31–35; Mark 14.27–31; Luke 22.31–34)

36Simon Peter asked, "Lord, where are you going?"

Jesus answered, "You can't go with me now, but later on you will."

37Peter asked, "Lord, why can't I go with you now? I would die for you!"

38"Would you really die for me?" Jesus asked. "I tell you for certain that before a rooster crows, you will say three times that you don't even know me."

Jesus Is the Way to the Father

14 Jesus said to his disciples, "Don't be worried! Have faith in God and have

Jesus gives us a new commandment
(34) Ever since Old Testament times God has told us we should love our neighbors as we love ourselves. Jesus went further—we should love others just as Jesus loved us. He laid down his life for us. Our lives also belong to each other. People know we're Christians by the kind of love we have—the kind that says "My life is for you."

Peter meant well
(37) Peter really wanted to belong to Jesus, so much that he had asked Jesus to wash him from head to toe (verse 9). Peter said he would even die for Jesus. But Jesus knew that Peter's own strength would fail him. We might mean to do well, too, but in our own strength we fail Jesus again and again. But he will forgive us the way he did Peter, and then the Holy Spirit will work through us to please God.

faith in me.*r* 2There are many rooms in my Father's house. I wouldn't tell you this, unless it was true. I am going there to prepare a place for each of you. 3After I have done this, I will come back and take you with me. Then we will be together. 4You know the way to where I am going."

5Thomas said, "Lord, we don't even know where you are going! How can we know the way?"

6"I am the way, the truth, and the life!" Jesus answered. "Without me, no one can go to the Father. 7If you had known me, you would have known the Father. But from now on, you do know him, and you have seen him."

8Philip said, "Lord, show us the Father. That is all we need."

9Jesus replied:

Philip, I have been with you for a long time. Don't you know who I am? If you have seen me, you have seen the Father. How can you ask me to show you the Father? 10Don't you believe that I am one with the Father and that the Father is one with me? What I say is not said on my own. The Father who lives in me does these things.

11Have faith in me when I say that the Father is one with me and that I am one with the Father. Or else have faith in me simply because of the things I do. 12I tell you for certain that if you have faith in me, you will do the same things that I am doing. You will do even greater things, now that I am going back to the Father. 13Ask me, and I will do whatever you ask. This way the Son will bring honor to the Father. 14I will do whatever you ask me to do.

The Holy Spirit Is Promised

15Jesus said to his disciples:

If you love me, you will do as I command. 16Then I will ask the Father to

A place for each of us
(2) This passage has always been a great source of comfort to believers. No matter what happens to us in this world, if we believe in Jesus, we know that he has a special place ready for each of us when we leave here. That's how much Jesus loves us and cares about us.

What does God look like?
(8) Even though no one has seen what God the Father looks like, no one needs to. He sent his Son to be a human being in this world and to be seen. What does God look like? He looks like Jesus.

---

rHave faith in God and have faith in me: Or "You have faith in God, so have faith in me."

send you the Holy Spirit who will help[s] you and always be with you. [17]The Spirit will show you what is true. The people of this world cannot accept the Spirit, because they don't see or know him. But you know the Spirit, who is with you and will keep on living in you.

[18]I won't leave you like orphans. I will come back to you. [19]In a little while the people of this world won't be able to see me, but you will see me. And because I live, you will live. [20]Then you will know that I am one with the Father. You will know that you are one with me, and I am one with you. [21]If you love me, you will do what I have said, and my Father will love you. I will also love you and show you what I am like.

[22]The other Judas, not Judas Iscariot,[t] then spoke up and asked, "Lord, what do you mean by saying that you will show us what you are like, but you will not show the people of this world?"

[23]Jesus replied:

If anyone loves me, they will obey me. Then my Father will love them, and we will come to them and live in them. [24]But anyone who doesn't love me, won't obey me. What they have heard me say doesn't really come from me, but from the Father who sent me.

[25]I have told you these things while I am still with you. [26]But the Holy Spirit will come and help[u] you, because the Father will send the Spirit to take my place. The Spirit will teach you everything and will remind you of what I said while I was with you.

[27]I give you peace, the kind of peace that only I can give. It is not like the peace that this world can give. So don't be worried or afraid.

[28]You have already heard me say that I am going and that I will also come back to you. If you really love me, you

We need the Holy Spirit

(16) All the words in the Bible will not help us if we don't first have the Holy Spirit. The Holy Spirit is an invisible person—the third person in the being we call God. God the Father and God the Son send the Holy Spirit to help us understand the things God has said in the Bible, including the things Jesus said. When the Holy Spirit lives in us, it's just as if Christ himself were living in us. Then we have God with us as our friend at all times.

We have peace from Jesus

(27) This peace is different and greater than any other peace we can ever know. It is the peace of God. One of the apostles said this peace is greater than we can completely understand (Philippians 4.7). This is the peace we have when the Holy Spirit comes to live in us.

[s]help: The Greek word may mean "comfort," "encourage," or "defend." [t]Iscariot: See the note at 12.4. [u]help: See the note at verse 16.

should be glad that I am going back to the Father, because he is greater than I am.

29I am telling you this before I leave, so that when it does happen, you will have faith in me. 30I cannot speak with you much longer, because the ruler of this world is coming. But he has no power over me. 31I obey my Father, so that everyone in the world might know that I love him.

It is time for us to go now.

Jesus Is the True Vine

15 Jesus said to his disciples:
I am the true vine, and my Father is the gardener. 2He cuts away every branch of mine that does not produce fruit. But he trims clean every branch that does produce fruit, so that it will produce even more fruit. 3You are already clean because of what I have said to you.

4Stay joined to me, and I will stay joined to you. Just as a branch cannot produce fruit unless it stays joined to the vine, you cannot produce fruit unless you stay joined to me. 5I am the vine, and you are the branches. If you stay joined to me, and I stay joined to you, then you will produce lots of fruit. But you cannot do anything without me. 6If you don't stay joined to me, you will be thrown away. You will be like dry branches that are gathered up and burned in a fire.

7Stay joined to me and let my teachings become part of you. Then you can pray for whatever you want, and your prayer will be answered. 8When you become fruitful disciples of mine, my Father will be honored. 9I have loved you, just as my Father has loved me. So make sure that I keep on loving you. 10If you obey me, I will keep loving me, because I have obeyed him.

11I have told you this to make you

Be a branch in the true vine
(5) Christians know they have no life of their own. Their life comes from Jesus himself. He is like a grapevine, and we are like branches that grow out of him. Then our lives show good results, like rich grapes on the vine. But those results can only grow if we stay joined to Christ so that his life can flow through us.

as completely happy as I am. 12Now I tell you to love each other, as I have loved you. 13The greatest way to show love for friends is to die for them. 14And you are my friends, if you obey me. 15Servants don't know what their master is doing, and so I don't speak to you as my servants. I speak to you as my friends, and I have told you everything that my Father has told me.

16You did not choose me. I chose you and sent you out to produce fruit, the kind of fruit that will last. Then my Father will give you whatever you ask for in my name.v 17So I command you to love each other.

The World's Hatred

18If the people of this worldw hate you, just remember that they hated me first. 19If you belonged to the world, its people would love you. But you don't belong to the world. I have chosen you to leave the world behind, and that is why its people hate you. 20Remember how I told you that servants are not greater than their master. So if people mistreat me, they will mistreat you. If they do what I say, they will do what you say.

21People will do to you exactly what they did to me. They will do it because you belong to me, and they don't know the one who sent me. 22If I had not come and spoken to them, they would not be guilty of sin. But now they have no excuse for their sin. 23Everyone who hates me also hates my Father. 24I have done things that no one else has ever done. If they had not seen me do these things, they would not be guilty. But they did see me do these things, and they still hate me and my Father too. 25That is why the Scriptures

How much did Jesus love us?

(12) In chapter 13 of John's Gospel we saw that Jesus became a servant so we could see his love for us. But remember—Jesus is also the Son of God. It was a long way from the throne of heaven to the floor of that room where he kneeled to wash his disciples' feet. But it was a much longer way from that great throne to the cross on which the God of heaven and earth died. That's how much Jesus loved us.

Be ready for hatred

(18) Christians should not feel that they're being picked on because some people hate them. It has to be that way because not everybody knows and loves God. Therefore they don't understand God's people either. We ought to feel sorry for people who hate us. They're unhappy, and they need to be saved from their sins. Remember, Jesus said, "Father, forgive these people. They don't know what they're doing" (Luke 23.34).

vin my name: Or "because you are my followers."
wworld: See the note at 12.31.

are true when they say, "People hated me for no reason."

26I will send you the Spirit who comes from the Father and shows what is true. The Spirit will help[x] you and will tell you about me. 27Then you will also tell others about me, because you have been with me from the beginning.

16 I am telling you this to keep you from being afraid. 2You will be chased out of the Jewish meeting places. The time will come when people will kill you and think they are doing God a favor. 3They will do all these things because they don't know either the Father or me. 4I am saying this to you now, so that when the time comes, you will remember what I have said.

The Work of the Holy Spirit

I was with you at the first, and so I didn't tell you these things. 5But now I am going back to the Father who sent me, and none of you asks me where I am going. 6You are very sad from hearing all of this. 7But I tell you that I am going to do what is best for you. That is why I am going away. The Holy Spirit cannot come to help[x] you until I leave. But after I am gone, I will send the Spirit to you.

8The Spirit will come and show the people of this world the truth about sin and God's justice and the judgment. 9The Spirit will show them that they are wrong about sin, because they didn't have faith in me. 10They are wrong about God's justice, because I am going to the Father, and you won't see me again. 11And they are wrong about the judgment, because God has already judged the ruler of this world.

12I have much more to say to you, but right now it would be more than you could understand. 13The Spirit

Jesus was to return to his Father
(5) Jesus Christ, the Son of God, did not begin his life as a baby at Bethlehem. He had been in heaven forever. He was God the Son, and God the Father was another person in the one Being the Bible calls God. God the Son became human in order to save us from our sins. Then he went back to heaven, which had been his home all along.

Who is the Holy Spirit?
(7) We have just spoken about the one God who consists of God the Father and God the Son. But there is a third person in the Being of God. That is the person the Bible calls the Holy Spirit. Jesus promised to send the Holy Spirit to be with us after Jesus went back to heaven.

---

[x]help: See the note at 14.16.

shows what is true and will come and guide you into the full truth. The Spirit does not speak on his own. He will tell you only what he has heard from me, and he will let you know what is going to happen. 14The Spirit will bring glory to me by taking my message and telling it to you. 15Everything that the Father has is mine. That is why I have said that the Spirit takes my message and tells it to you.

Sorrow Will Turn into Joy

16Jesus told his disciples, "You will see me for a little while, and then for a little while you won't see me."

17They said to each other, "What does Jesus mean by saying that we will see him for a little while, and then we won't see him for a little while? What does he mean by saying that he is going to the Father? 18What is this 'little while' that he is talking about? We don't know what he means."

19Jesus knew that they had some questions, so he said:

You are wondering what I meant when I said that you will see me for a little while, and then in a little while you won't see me. 20I tell you for certain that you will cry and be sad, but the world will be happy. You will be sad, but later you will be happy.

21When a woman is about to give birth, she is in great pain. But after it is all over, she is happy, because she has brought a child into the world. 22You are now very sad. But later I will see you, and you will be so happy that no one will be able to change the way you feel. 23When that time comes, you won't have to ask me about anything. I tell you for certain that the Father will give you whatever you ask for in my name. 24You have not asked for anything in this way before, but now you must ask in my name.y Then it will be

yin my name . . . in my name: Or "as my disciples . . . as my disciples."

What does the Holy Spirit do for us?
(15) Sometimes the Holy Spirit is called the Comforter or Helper. He is the invisible presence of God who helps us to be happy in the world. He reminds us that Jesus is alive as our Savior. He also helps us to understand God's word, and he gives us the power to do things for God that will last forever.

Sometimes we are sad
(22) Jesus warned us that life would not always be "a bed of roses." Sometimes Christians are alone and mistreated in the world. But one day Jesus will come back, and all of our sadness will be gone forever. The disciples came to know what Jesus meant by this when he rose from death and proved to them that he is stronger than the grave. He overcomes all of the evil forces in the world.

given to you, so that you will be completely happy.

25I have used examples to explain to you what I have been talking about. But the time will come when I will speak to you plainly about the Father and will no longer use examples like these. 26You will ask the Father in my name,z and I won't have to ask him for you. 27God the Father loves you because you love me, and you believe that I have come from him. 28I came from the Father into the world, but I am leaving the world and returning to the Father.

29The disciples said, "Now you are speaking plainly to us! You are not using examples. 30At last we know that you understand everything, and we don't have any more questions. Now we believe that you truly have come from God."

31Jesus replied:

Do you really believe me? 32The time will come and is already here when all of you will be scattered. Each of you will go back home and leave me by myself. But the Father will be with me, and I won't be alone. 33I have told you this, so that you might have peace in your hearts because of me. While you are in the world, you will have to suffer. But cheer up! I have defeated the world.a

Jesus Prays

17 After Jesus had finished speaking to his disciples, he looked up toward heaven and prayed:

Father, the time has come for you to bring glory to your Son, in order that he may bring glory to you. 2And you gave him power over all people, so that he would give eternal life to everyone you give him. 3Eternal life is to know you, the only true God, and to know Jesus Christ, the one you sent. 4I have

What is eternal life?
(2) Usually we think of eternal life as life that goes on forever and ever. And it is. But eternal life is much more than endless time. It is a *kind* of life that is only in God. That's why Jesus says that eternal life is to know God. When we know God as he means for us to know him— when we love him—we have eternal life right now.

---

zin my name: Or "because you are my followers."
aworld: See the note at 12.31.

brought glory to you here on earth by
doing everything you gave me to do.
5Now, Father, give me back the glory
that I had with you before the world
was created.

6You have given me some followers
from this world, and I have shown them
what you are like. They were yours, but
you gave them to me, and they have
obeyed you. 7They know that you gave
me everything I have. 8I told my followers what you told me, and they accepted
it. They know that I came from you,
and they believe that you are the one
who sent me. 9I am praying for them,
but not for those who belong to this
world.a My followers belong to you, and
I am praying for them. 10All that I have
is yours, and all that you have is mine,
and they will bring glory to me.

11Holy Father, I am no longer in the
world. I am coming to you, but my followers are still in the world. So keep
them safe by the power of the name
that you have given me. Then they will
be one with each other, just as you and
I are one. 12While I was with them, I
kept them safe by the power you have
given me. I guarded them, and not one
of them was lost, except the one who
had to be lost. This happened so that
what the Scriptures say would come
true.

13Father, I am on my way to you. But
I say these things while I am still in
the world, so that my followers will have
the same complete joy that I do. 14I have
told them your message. But the people
of this world hate them, because they
don't belong to this world, just as I don't.

15Father, I don't ask you to take my
followers out of the world, but keep
them safe from the evil one. 16They
don't belong to this world, and neither
do I. 17Your word is the truth. So let
this truth make them completely yours.
18I am sending them into the world, just

Jesus prayed for believers
(9) Jesus says he doesn't
pray for those who belong
to the world. He prays for
the people that his Father
gave him from the world.
They are the ones who really
love God and obey him. You
can be one of the gifts that
the Father gave to his Son
if only you confess your sins
and ask him to accept you.

*How does Jesus' Father
keep you safe?*
(15) God is in charge of the
world, and nothing can happen to you without his permission. Even if you are put
to death because you love
Jesus, his Father will rescue
the part of you that can
never die. Most of all he will
protect you from Satan, the
Evil One, who is the enemy
of God and the enemy of
God's people.

aworld: See the note at 12.31.

as you sent me. 19I have given myself completely for their sake, so that they may belong completely to the truth.

20Father, I am not praying just for these followers. I am also praying for everyone else who will have faith because of what my followers will say about me. 21I want all of them to be one with each other, just as I am one with you and you are one with me. I also want them to be one with us. Then the people of this world will believe that you sent me.

22I have honored my followers in the same way that you honored me, in order that they may be one with each other, just as we are one. 23I am one with them, and you are one with me, so that they may become completely one. Then this world's people will know that you sent me. They will know that you love my followers as much as you love me.

24Father, I want everyone you have given me to be with me, wherever I am. Then they will see the glory that you have given me, because you loved me before the world was created. 25Good Father, the people of this world don't know you. But I know you, and my followers know that you sent me. 26I told them what you are like, and I will tell them even more. Then the love that you have for me will become part of them, and I will be one with them.

Jesus Is Betrayed and Arrested
(Matthew 26.47–56; Mark 14.43–50; Luke 22.47–53)

18 When Jesus had finished praying, he and his disciples crossed the Kidron Valley and went into a garden.*b* 2Jesus had often met there with his disciples, and Judas knew where the place was.

3-5Judas had promised to betray Jesus. So he went to the garden with some Roman

bgarden: The Greek word is usually translated "garden," but probably referred to an olive orchard.

Why did Judas betray Jesus?
(3) Most people have "good" reasons for doing their evil deeds. Judas might have convinced himself that Jesus was the enemy of Israel. He might have thought he was doing his country good by selling out his Master to the authorities. On the other hand, some think Judas wanted to give Jesus a "push" by arranging his arrest, hoping he would defend himself more openly. Either way, Judas was on the wrong track. The devil is in the business of deceiving people as he did Judas.

soldiers and temple police, who had been
sent by the chief priests and the Pharisees.
They carried torches, lanterns, and weapons. When Jesus saw them, he knew why
they had come, and he asked, "Who are
you looking for?"

They answered, "We are looking for
Jesus from Nazareth!"

Jesus told them, "I am Jesus!"c 6At once
they all backed away and fell to the ground.

7Jesus again asked, "Who are you looking for?"

"We are looking for Jesus from Nazareth," they answered.

8This time Jesus replied, "I have already
told you that I am Jesus. If I am the one
you are looking for, let these others go.
9Then everything will happen, just as the
Scriptures say, 'I did not lose anyone you
gave me.' "

10Simon Peter had brought along a
sword. He now pulled it out and struck at
the servant of the high priest. The servant's
name was Malchus, and Peter cut off his
right ear. 11Jesus told Peter, "Put your
sword away. I must drink from the cupd
that the Father has given me."

Jesus Is Brought to Annas
(Matthew 26.57, 58; Mark 14.53, 54; Luke 22.54)

12The Roman officer and his men, together with the temple police, arrested Jesus
and tied him up. 13They took him first to
Annas, who was the father-in-law of Caiaphas, the high priest that year. 14This was
the same Caiaphas who had told the Jewish
leaders, "It is better if one person dies for
the people."

Peter Says He Does Not Know Jesus
*(Matthew 26.69, 70; Mark 14.66–68;
Luke 22.55–57)*

15Simon Peter and another disciple followed Jesus. That disciple knew the high

**Peter attacked one of the
officers with a sword**

(10) It was a natural thing
to fight back. Peter had to
learn, like the others, that
God's kingdom doesn't
come because we force it
on others. We overcome the
world by loving our ene-
mies. This doesn't mean we
stop enforcing the laws of
our earthly countries. It
means that God rules in this
world when people let him
have his way in their lives.

Who was the high priest?

(13) We have here the
names of the high priest and
of his father-in-law who was
high priest before him. For
hundreds of years the Jews
had been ruled by their high
priests because there was
no king after 587 B.C. Even
though the Herod family
ruled as kings at that time,
they were not lawful kings.
They were placed in that position by the Romans. So
Jesus was taken first to the
high priest.

cI am Jesus: The Greek text has "I am." See the note
at 8.24.   ddrink from the cup: In the Scriptures a cup
is sometimes used as a symbol of suffering. To "drink
from the cup" is to suffer.

priest, and he followed Jesus into the courtyard of the high priest's house. 16Peter stayed outside near the gate. But the other disciple came back out and spoke to the girl at the gate. She let Peter go in, 17but asked him, "Aren't you one of that man's followers?"

"No, I am not!" Peter answered.

18It was cold, and the servants and temple police had made a charcoal fire. They were warming themselves around it, when Peter went over and stood near the fire to warm himself.

Jesus Is Questioned by the High Priest
(Matthew 26.59–66; Mark 14.55–64;
Luke 22.66–71)

19The high priest questioned Jesus about his followers and his teaching. 20But Jesus told him, "I have spoken freely in front of everyone. And I have always taught in our meeting places and in the temple, where all of our people come together. I have not said anything in secret. 21Why are you questioning me? Why don't you ask the people who heard me? They know what I have said."

22As soon as Jesus said this, one of the temple police hit him and said, "That's no way to talk to the high priest!"

23Jesus answered, "If I have done something wrong, say so. But if not, why did you hit me?" 24Jesus was still tied up, and Annas sent him to Caiaphas the high priest.

Peter Again Denies that He Knows Jesus
(Matthew 26.71–75; Mark 14.69–72;
Luke 22.58–62)

25While Simon Peter was standing there warming himself, someone asked him, "Aren't you one of Jesus' followers?"

Again Peter denied it and said, "No, I am not!"

26One of the high priest's servants was there. He was a relative of the servant whose ear Peter had cut off, and he asked, "Didn't I see you in the garden with that man?"

We are all cowards by nature
(17) We guard our earthly lives more than anything. In order not to place ourselves in danger, we often deny that we know the truth. That's what Peter did. But later, by the power of the Holy Spirit, Jesus' disciples would become bold. Over the years, untold numbers of Jesus' followers have died rather than deny their Master before cruel earthly powers. History tells us that as an older man, Peter himself was crucified for Jesus' sake.

27Once more Peter denied it, and right then a rooster crowed.

Jesus Is Tried by Pilate
(Matthew 27.1, 2, 11–14; Mark 15.1–5;
Luke 23.1–5)

28It was early in the morning when Jesus was taken from Caiaphas to the building where the Roman governor stayed. But the Jewish crowd waited outside. Any of them who had gone inside would have become unclean and would not be allowed to eat the Passover meal.e

29Pilate came out and asked, "What charges are you bringing against this man?"

30They answered, "He is a criminal! That's why we brought him to you."

31Pilate told them, "Take him and judge him by your own laws."

The crowd replied, "We are not allowed to put anyone to death." 32And so what Jesus said about his deathf would soon come true.

33Pilate then went back inside. He called Jesus over and asked, "Are you the king of the Jews?"

34Jesus answered, "Are you asking this on your own or did someone tell you about me?"

35"You know I'm not a Jew!" Pilate said. "Your own people and the chief priests brought you to me. What have you done?"

36Jesus answered, "My kingdom does not belong to this world. If it did, my followers would have fought to keep the Jewish leaders from handing me over to you. No, my kingdom does not belong to this world."

37"So you are a king." Pilate replied.

"You are saying that I am a king." Jesus told him. "I was born into this world to tell

The crowd deserted Jesus
(28) The same crowd that had cheered as Jesus entered Jerusalem on a donkey was screaming for his blood. They were careful not to go into Pilate's headquarters and make themselves "unclean" according to their beliefs. But they were willing to nail the Son of God to a cross.

---

ewould have become unclean and would not be allowed to eat the Passover meal: Jewish people who came in close contact with foreigners right before Passover were not allowed to eat the Passover meal. fabout his death: Jesus had said that he would die by being "lifted up," which meant that he would die on a cross. The Romans killed criminals by nailing them on a cross, but they did not let the Jews kill anyone in this way.

about the truth. And everyone who belongs to the truth knows my voice."

³⁸Pilate asked Jesus, "What is truth?"

Jesus Is Sentenced to Death
(Matthew 27.15–31; Mark 15.6–20;
Luke 23.13–25)

Pilate went back out to the Jewish crowd and said, "I don't find this man guilty of anything! ³⁹And since I usually set a prisoner free for you at Passover, would you like for me to set free the king of the Jews?"

⁴⁰They all shouted, "No, not him! We want Barabbas." Now Barabbas was a terrorist.^g

19 Pilate gave orders for Jesus to be beaten with a whip. ²The soldiers made a crown out of thorn branches and put it on Jesus. Then they put a purple robe on him. ³They came up to him and said, "Hey, you king of the Jews!" They also hit him with their fists.

⁴Once again Pilate went out to the crowd. This time he said, "I will have Jesus brought out to you again. Then you can see for yourselves that I have not found him guilty."

⁵Jesus came out, wearing the crown of thorns and the purple robe. Pilate said, "Here is the man!"^h

⁶When the chief priests and the temple police saw him, they yelled, "Nail him to a cross! Nail him to a cross!"

Pilate told them, "You take him and nail him to a cross! I don't find him guilty of anything."

⁷The crowd replied, "He claimed to be the Son of God! Our Jewish law says that he must be put to death."

⁸When Pilate heard this, he was terrified. ⁹He went back inside and asked Jesus, "Where are you from?" But Jesus did not answer.

¹⁰"Why won't you answer my question?" Pilate asked. "Don't you know that I have

What is truth?
(38) This may be the greatest question in the Bible— perhaps even in the history of mankind. But notice that Pilate didn't wait for the answer to his question, but he went back out to listen again to the demands of Jesus' enemies. It was quite a tragedy for Pilate. Maybe he later realized the answer to his question. He had wanted to set Jesus free—but wasn't brave enough to disappoint the crowd.

God's plan happened
(6) Pilate wanted to let Jesus go, but the crowd made him afraid to. So he passed the death sentence. But remember—God knew this would happen. It was his plan that Jesus would shed his blood on a cross, dying in the place of sinners. Even though this was a terrible thing, for the innocent Jesus to be killed like a criminal, God allowed it. It was why Jesus came here.

^g*terrorist*: Someone who stirred up trouble against the Romans in the hope of gaining freedom for the Jewish people.   ^h*"Here is the man!"*: Or "Look at the man!"

the power to let you go free or to nail you to a cross?"

11Jesus replied, "If God had not given you the power, you couldn't do anything at all to me. But the one who handed me over to you did something even worse."

12Then Pilate wanted to set Jesus free. But the Jewish crowd again yelled, "If you set this man free, you are no friend of the Emperor! Anyone who claims to be a king is an enemy of the Emperor."

13When Pilate heard this, he brought Jesus out. Then he sat down on the judge's bench at the place known as "The Stone Pavement." In Aramaic this pavement is called "Gabbatha." 14It was about noon on the day before Passover, and Pilate said to the crowd, "Look at your king!"

15"Kill him! Kill him!" they yelled. "Nail him to a cross!"

"So you want me to nail your king to a cross?" Pilate asked.

The chief priests replied, "The Emperor is our king!" 16Then Pilate handed Jesus over to be nailed to a cross.

Jesus Is Nailed to a Cross
(Matthew 27.32–44; Mark 15.21–32;
Luke 23.26–43)

Jesus was taken away, 17and he carried his cross to a place known as "The Skull."[i] In Aramaic this place is called "Golgotha." 18There Jesus was nailed to the cross, and on each side of him a man was also nailed to a cross.

19Pilate ordered the charge against Jesus to be written on a board and put above the cross. It read, "Jesus of Nazareth, King of the Jews." 20The words were written in Hebrew, Latin, and Greek.

The place where Jesus was taken was not far from the city, and many of the Jewish people read the charge against him. 21So the chief priests went to Pilate and said, "Why did you write that he is King of the

---

[i]"The Skull": The place was probably given this name because it was near a large rock in the shape of a human skull.

Pilate wrote the truth
(19) "Jesus of Nazareth, King of the Jews," said the sign above the head of Jesus. The priests wanted Pilate to change the wording, but he wouldn't. Jesus died not only for his friends, but even for his enemies. Pilate, too, could be saved if he would later turn to God in faith and ask to be forgiven because of the sacrifice of the crucified King. But we don't know whether Pilate ever did that.

Jews? You should have written, 'He claimed to be King of the Jews.' "

22But Pilate told them, "What is written will not be changed!"

23After the soldiers had nailed Jesus to the cross, they divided up his clothes into four parts, one for each of them. But his outer garment was made from a single piece of cloth, and it did not have any seams. 24The soldiers said to each other, "Let's not rip it apart. We'll gamble to see who gets it." This happened so that the Scriptures would come true, which say,

> "They divided up my clothes
> and gambled
>   for my garments."

The soldiers then did what they had decided.

25Jesus' mother stood beside his cross with her sister and Mary the wife of Clopas. Mary Magdalene was standing there too.*j* 26When Jesus saw his mother and his favorite disciple with her, he said to his mother, "This man is now your son." 27Then he said to the disciple, "She is now your mother." From then on, that disciple took her into his own home.

The Death of Jesus
(Matthew 27.45–56; Mark 15.33–41; Luke 23.44–49)

28Jesus knew that he had now finished his work. And in order to make the Scriptures come true, he said, "I am thirsty!" 29A jar of cheap wine was there. Someone then soaked a sponge with the wine and held it up to Jesus' mouth on the stem of a hyssop plant. 30After Jesus drank the wine, he said, "Everything is done!" He bowed his head and died.

jJesus' mother stood beside his cross with her sister and Mary the wife of Clopas. Mary Magdalene was standing there too: The Greek text may also be understood to include only three women ("Jesus' mother stood beside the cross with her sister, Mary the mother of Clopas. Mary Magdalene was standing there too.") or merely two women ("Jesus' mother was standing there with her sister Mary of Clopas, that is Mary Magdalene."). "Of Clopas" may mean "daughter of" or "mother of."

Jesus remembered his mother
(26) Even in his suffering Jesus was thinking of others. Notice that he began at home with concern for his mother. God created families, and our first duty on earth is to the people in our families. Some of us don't have families, but we can ask God to give us love for those who gave us life and for those we might bring into the world.

"Everything is done"
(30) This is what Jesus said as he died. What did he mean? Jesus came into the world to do just what he did on the cross—to die for the very sinners who nailed him there. Let's try to understand that *our* sins also nailed Jesus to the cross. He finished the work of saving us from our sins by laying down his life for us.

A Spear Is Stuck in Jesus' Side

31The next day would be both a Sabbath and the Passover. It was a special day for the Jewish people,k and they did not want Jesus' body to stay on the cross during that day. So they asked Pilate to break the men's legsl and take their bodies down. 32The soldiers first broke the legs of the other two men who were nailed there. 33But when they came to Jesus, they saw that he was already dead, and they did not break his legs.

34One of the soldiers stuck his spear into Jesus' side, and blood and water came out. 35We know this is true, because it was told by someone who saw it happen. Now you can have faith too. 36All this happened so that the Scriptures would come true, which say, "No bone of his body will be broken" 37and, "They will see the one in whose side they stuck a spear."

Jesus Is Buried
(Matthew 27.57–61; Mark 15.42–47;
Luke 23.50–56)

38Joseph from Arimathea was one of Jesus' disciples. He had kept it secret though, because he was afraid of the Jewish leaders. But now he asked Pilate to let him have Jesus' body. Pilate gave him permission, and Joseph took it down from the cross.

39Nicodemus also came with about seventy-five pounds of spices made from myrrh and aloes. This was the same Nicodemus who had visited Jesus one night.m 40The two men wrapped the body in a linen cloth, together with the spices, which was how the Jewish people buried their dead. 41In the place where Jesus had been nailed to a cross, there was a garden with a tomb that had never been used. 42The tomb was

Remember Nicodemus?
(39) Nicodemus, the man who had come during the night to see Jesus, came back to help Joseph from Arimathea bury the Savior's body. Nicodemus had been looking for the truth when he made his visit in the dark to question Jesus. Here it looks like Nicodemus has become a believer. Like Nicodemus, we can come to Jesus and find the new birth he offers (see John 3.3).

ka special day for the Jewish people: Passover could be any day of the week. But according to the Gospel of John, Passover was on a Sabbath in the year that Jesus was nailed to a cross. lbreak their legs: This was the way that the Romans sometimes speeded up the death of a person who had been nailed to a cross. mNicodemus who had visited Jesus one night: See 3.1-21.

nearby, and since it was the time to prepare for the Sabbath, they were in a hurry to put Jesus' body there.

Jesus Is Alive
(Matthew 28.1–10; Mark 16.1–8; Luke 24.1–12)

20 On Sunday morning while it was still dark, Mary Magdalene went to the tomb and saw that the stone had been rolled away from the entrance. ²She ran to Simon Peter and to Jesus' favorite disciple and said, "They have taken the Lord from the tomb! We don't know where they have put him."

³Peter and the other disciple started for the tomb. ⁴They ran side by side, until the other disciple ran faster than Peter and got there first. ⁵He bent over and saw the strips of linen cloth lying inside the tomb, but he did not go in.

⁶When Simon Peter got there, he went into the tomb and saw the strips of cloth. ⁷He also saw the piece of cloth that had

The Risen Jesus Appears

been used to cover Jesus' face. It was rolled up and in a place by itself. 8The disciple who got there first then went into the tomb, and when he saw it, he believed. 9At that time Peter and the other disciple did not know that the Scriptures said Jesus would rise to life. 10So the two of them went back to the other disciples.

Jesus Appears to Mary Magdalene
(Mark 16.9–11)

11Mary Magdalene stood crying outside the tomb. She was still weeping, when she stooped down 12and saw two angels inside. They were dressed in white and were sitting where Jesus' body had been. One was at the head and the other was at the foot. 13The angels asked Mary, "Why are you crying?"

She answered, "They have taken away my Lord's body! I don't know where they have put him."

14As soon as Mary said this, she turned around and saw Jesus standing there. But she did not know who he was. 15Jesus asked her, "Why are you crying? Who are you looking for?"

She thought he was the gardener and said, "Sir, if you have taken his body away, please tell me, so I can go and get him."

16Then Jesus said to her, "Mary!"

She turned and said to him, "Rabboni." The Aramaic word "Rabboni" means "Teacher."

17Jesus told her, "Don't hold on to me! I have not yet gone to the Father. But tell my disciples that I am going to the one who is my Father and my God, as well as your Father and your God." 18Mary Magdalene then went and told the disciples that she had seen the Lord. She also told them what he had said to her.

Jesus Appears to His Disciples
(Matthew 28.16–20; Mark 16.14–18; Luke 24.36–49)

19The disciples were afraid of the Jewish leaders, and on the evening of that same Sunday they locked themselves in a room.

The disciples were not quick to believe
(9) Sometimes we may think it's harder to put faith in Jesus now than when he walked the earth. Perhaps we think it was just natural for people of Jesus' day to be what we call "religious." But look at Mary Magdalene and the other disciples. Jesus had told them he would rise again on the third day. But they still didn't understand why his tomb was empty.

"Don't hold on to me"
(17) We learn two things from this scene outside Jesus' tomb. First, it must have been dark in the early morning of that Sunday when Mary arrived. She couldn't recognize Jesus at first. Second, he was no ghost. He had a real body which Mary could hold on to. Paul taught that some day believers too will have bodies like Jesus' body—better than the bodies we have now, but bodies that are solid and can be touched and seen (see 1 Corinthians 15).

Suddenly, Jesus appeared in the middle of the group. He greeted them [20]and showed them his hands and his side. When the disciples saw the Lord, they became very happy.

[21]After Jesus had greeted them again, he said, "I am sending you, just as the Father has sent me." [22]Then he breathed on them and said, "Receive the Holy Spirit. [23]If you forgive anyone's sins, they will be forgiven. But if you don't forgive their sins, they will not be forgiven."

Jesus and Thomas

[24]Although Thomas the Twin was one of the twelve disciples, he was not with the others when Jesus appeared to them. [25]So they told him, "We have seen the Lord!"

But Thomas said, "First, I must see the nail scars in his hands and touch them with my finger. I must put my hand where the spear went into his side. I won't believe unless I do this!"

[26]A week later the disciples were together again. This time Thomas was with them. Jesus came in while the doors were still locked and stood in the middle of the group. He greeted his disciples [27]and said to Thomas, "Put your finger here and look at my hands! Put your hand into my side. Stop doubting and have faith!"

[28]Thomas replied, "You are my Lord and my God!"

[29]Jesus said, "Thomas, do you have faith because you have seen me? The people who have faith in me without seeing me are the ones who are really blessed!"

Why John Wrote His Book

[30]Jesus worked many other miracles[n] for his disciples, and not all of them are written in this book. [31]But these are written so that you will put your faith in Jesus as the

He showed them his wounds
(20) It would be natural to suspect that the person who came to the disciples was not the same Jesus who was nailed to a cross. But he showed them his hands and his side where the wounds of his death were. There could be no mistake. Jesus was alive, and the disciples lived and died telling others this great news for all the world.

The disciples were doubters
(25) Are you a doubter? That's natural. So were all the disciples, but especially Thomas. Of course, he was not there when Jesus appeared the first time. But even Thomas lost his doubts when he saw the Lord alive.

John's book is for you
(31) "So that you will put your faith in Jesus." John didn't write his book to tell us everything Jesus did. But he wrote enough to show us that faith in Jesus makes a great deal of sense. As we read John's book we are convinced that it is true.

---

[n]*miracles:* See the note at 2.11.

Messiah and the Son of God. If you have faith in⁰ him, you will have true life.

Jesus Appears to Seven Disciples

21 Jesus later appeared to his disciples along the shore of Lake Tiberias. 2Simon Peter, Thomas the Twin, Nathanael from Cana in Galilee, and the two sons of Zebedee,ᵖ were there, together with two other disciples. 3Simon Peter said, "I'm going fishing!"

The others said, "We'll go with you." They went out in their boat. But they didn't catch a thing that night.

4Early the next morning Jesus stood on the shore, but the disciples did not realize who he was. 5Jesus shouted, "Friends, have you caught anything?"

"No!" they answered.

6So he told them, "Let your net down on the right side of your boat, and you will catch some fish."

They did, and the net was so full of fish that they could not drag it up into the boat.

7Jesus' favorite disciple told Peter, "It's the Lord!" When Simon heard that it was the Lord, he put on the clothes that he had taken off while he was working. Then he jumped into the water. 8The boat was only about a hundred yards from shore. So the other disciples stayed in the boat and dragged in the net full of fish.

9When the disciples got out of the boat, they saw some bread and a charcoal fire with fish on it. 10Jesus told his disciples, "Bring some of the fish you just caught." 11Simon Peter got back into the boat and dragged the net to shore. In it were one hundred fifty-three large fish, but still the net did not rip.

12Jesus said, "Come and eat!" But none of the disciples dared ask who he was. They knew he was the Lord. 13Jesus took the bread in his hands and gave some of it to

The disciples caught no fish
(6) There was no catch of fish at first. Then Jesus came and told the disciples what to do, and their net was full of fish. But after all, Jesus didn't need the disciples to go fishing for fish. He already had fish on the fire for breakfast. He needed the disciples to go fishing for *people.*

⁰*put your faith in . . . have faith in:* Some manuscripts have "keep on having faith in . . . keep on having faith in." ᵖ*the two sons of Zebedee:* James and John.

his disciples. He did the same with the fish.
14This was the third time that Jesus appeared to his disciples after he was raised
from death.

Jesus and Peter

15When Jesus and his disciples had finished eating, he asked, "Simon son of John,
do you love me more than the others do?"[q]
Simon Peter answered, "Yes, Lord, you
know I do!"
"Then feed my lambs," Jesus said.
16Jesus asked a second time, "Simon son
of John, do you love me?"
Peter answered, "Yes, Lord, you know
I love you!"
"Then take care of my sheep," Jesus told
him.
17Jesus asked a third time, "Simon son
of John, do you love me?"
Peter was hurt because Jesus had asked
him three times if he loved him. So he told
Jesus, "Lord, you know everything. You
know I love you."
Jesus replied, "Feed my sheep. 18I tell
you for certain that when you were a young
man, you dressed yourself and went wherever you wanted to go. But when you are
old, you will hold out your hands. Then others will wrap your belt around you and lead
you where you don't want to go."
19Jesus said this to tell how Peter would
die and bring honor to God. Then he said
to Peter, "Follow me!"

Do you love Jesus?
(15) Like Peter, we may be ashamed to say, "Yes, Lord, you know I do." Peter had denied the Lord three times. Three times Peter was asked to confess that he loved Jesus. Sometimes we feel that we fail our Lord—and we're right. But he keeps calling us back to the important question—"Do you honestly love me?" What is your answer?

Jesus and His Favorite Disciple

20Peter turned and saw Jesus' favorite
disciple following them. He was the same
one who had sat next to Jesus at the meal
and had asked, "Lord, who is going to betray you?" 21When Peter saw that disciple,
he asked Jesus, "Lord, what about him?"
22Jesus answered, "What is it to you, if
I want him to live until I return? You must

[q]*more than the others do?*: Or "more than you love these things?"

What about John?
(21) There is envy even among those who put their faith in Jesus. Peter envied John. Peter always thought he should be first, but he probably felt guilty here because he had denied the Lord—and John had not. Jesus simply told Peter that John's work was John's business, not Peter's. Peter was to follow Jesus. And so

follow me." 23So the rumor spread among the other disciples that this disciple would not die. But Jesus did not say he would not die. He simply said, "What is it to you, if I want him to live until I return?"

24This disciple is the one who told all of this. He wrote it, and we know he is telling the truth.

25Jesus did many other things. If they were all written in books, I don't suppose there would be room enough in the whole world for all the books.

must we all. (History says that John was the only disciple who died of old age, when he was about a hundred years old. All of the other apostles were put to death for their preaching.)

Events in the Time of the New Testament

(Very few events in the Bible can be dated exactly, but these dates are probably close.)

B.C. 5   Jesus is born in Bethlehem

A.D. 8   Mary and Joseph visit the temple with 12-year-old Jesus

27   Jesus is baptized and starts teaching and healing

30   Jesus dies, rises again, and goes up to heaven; the Holy Spirit fills the apostles at Pentecost

33   Stephen is killed by stoning; Paul is saved

36   Paul visits Jerusalem

40   Peter starts telling Gentiles the good news

44   Herod Agrippa I kills James

47   Paul's first trip begins

50   The meeting at Jerusalem; Paul's second trip begins

54   Paul's third trip begins

58   Paul is arrested in Jerusalem and put in jail

60   Paul is sent to Rome

(Paul was kept a prisoner in Rome for at least two years. That is where the history in the book of Acts ends. Paul may have been set free for a while, then arrested again by the Romans. Some say that Paul and Peter were both killed by the Romans, about the year 67.)

70   Jerusalem is destroyed by the Romans

95   John is exiled on the island of Patmos

THE ACTS OF THE APOSTLES

ABOUT THIS BOOK

This is the second book written by Luke. His first one is commonly known as the Gospel of Luke. In it he told "all that Jesus did and taught from the very first until he was taken up to heaven" (1.1,2). In this book Luke continues the story by describing some of the struggles the disciples faced as they tried to obey the command of Jesus: "You will tell everyone about me in Jerusalem, in all Judea, in Samaria, and everywhere in the world" (1.8).

So many different countries are mentioned in Acts that the book may seem to have been written only to tell about the spread of the Christian message. But that is only part of the story. After Jesus was taken up to heaven, one of the big problems for his followers was deciding who could belong to God's people. And since Jesus and his first followers were Jews, it was only natural for many of them to think that his message was only for Jews. But in Acts the Spirit is always present to show that Jesus came to save both Jews and Gentiles, and that God wants followers from every nation and race to be part of his people.

The first conflict between Christians and Jews took place when some of the Jewish religious leaders rejected the message about Jesus (4.1–31; 7.1–50). But the most serious problems for the early church happened because the disciples at first failed to understand that anyone could become a follower of Jesus without first becoming a Jew. This began to change when Philip dared to take the message to the Samaritans (8.7–25), and when Peter went to the home of Cornelius, a captain in the Roman army (10.1–48).

Finally, Peter reported to the church in Jerusalem (11.1–18) and a meeting was held there (15.3–35) to discuss the question of who could become followers of Christ. Before the meeting was over, everyone agreed that the Spirit of God was leading them to reach out to Gentiles as well as Jews with the good news of Jesus.

The one who did the most for the spread of the faith was a man named Paul, and much of the book tells about his preaching among the Gentiles. Finally, he took the message to Rome, the world's most important city at that time (28.16–31). One of Luke's main reasons for writing was to show that nothing could keep the Christian message from spreading everywhere:

For two years Paul stayed in a rented house and welcomed everyone who came to see him. He bravely preached about God's kingdom and taught about the Lord Jesus Christ, and no one tried to stop him. (28.30,31)

A QUICK LOOK AT THIS BOOK

1 Theophilus, I first wrote to you[a] about all that Jesus did and taught from the very first 2until he was taken up to heaven. But before he was taken up, he gave orders to the apostles he had chosen with the help of the Holy Spirit.

3For forty days after Jesus had suffered and died, he proved in many ways that he had been raised from death. He appeared to his apostles and spoke to them about God's kingdom. 4While he was still with them, he said:

Don't leave Jerusalem yet. Wait here for the Father to give you the Holy Spirit, just as I told you he has promised to do. 5John baptized with water, but in a few days you will be baptized with the Holy Spirit.

Jesus Is Taken to Heaven

6While the apostles were still with Jesus, they asked him, "Lord, are you now going to give Israel its own king again?"[b]

7Jesus said to them, "You don't need to know the time of those events that only the Father controls. 8But the Holy Spirit will come upon you and give you power. Then you will tell everyone about me in Jerusalem, in all Judea, in Samaria, and everywhere in the world." 9After Jesus had said this and while they were watching, he was taken up into a cloud. They could not see him, 10but as he went up, they kept looking up into the sky.

Suddenly two men dressed in white clothes were standing there beside them. 11They said, "Why are you men from Galilee standing here and looking up into the sky? Jesus has been taken to heaven. But he will come back in the same way that you have seen him go."

Theophilus honored again
(1) Acts continues the history Luke began in his Gospel. Like Luke's Gospel, the book of Acts is addressed to his friend, Theophilus. The name means "lover of God." He may have been an important Gentile citizen of that time. As an educated Gentile himself, Luke wanted to present to his people the message of Christ in a complete and accurate way.

Jesus returned to heaven
(9) Again in Acts, Luke reviews this happening that he also covered at the end of his Gospel. Jesus' return to heaven was an important final event in his earthly life. The presence of Christ before God now stands as a guarantee that his saving work for us on earth cannot be canceled. Jesus is our representative in heaven.

Jesus will come back to earth
(11) Jesus didn't die and rise from death only so we could go to heaven. He will return again and set up his rule on earth. A new day is coming, long foretold by the ancient prophets. Then this present world system will pass away, and Christ himself will govern a new world of righteousness.

---

[a]*I first wrote to you*: The Gospel of Luke.   [b]*are you now going to give Israel its own king again?*: Or "Are you now going to rule Israel as its king?"

Someone to Take the Place of Judas

12-13The Mount of Olives was about half a mile from Jerusalem. The apostles who had gone there were Peter, John, James, Andrew, Philip, Thomas, Bartholomew, Matthew, James the son of Alphaeus, Simon, known as the Eager One,c and Judas the son of James.

After the apostles returned to the city, they went upstairs to the room where they had been staying.

14The apostles often met together and prayed with a single purpose in mind.d The women and Mary the mother of Jesus would meet with them, and so would his brothers. 15One day there were about a hundred and twenty of the Lord's followers meeting together, and Peter stood up to speak to them. 16-17He said:

My friends, long ago by the power of the Holy Spirit, David said something about Judas, and what he said has now happened. Judas was one of us and had worked with us, but he brought the mob to arrest Jesus. 18Then Judas bought some land with the money he was given for doing that evil thing. He fell head-first into the field. His body burst open, and all his insides came out. 19When the people of Jerusalem found out about this, they called the place Akeldama, which in the local language means "Field of Blood."

20In the book of Psalms David said,
"Leave his house empty,
   and don't let anyone
      live there."
It also says,
"Let someone else
   have his job."
21-22So we need someone else to help

The Lord's followers met for prayer
(14) Right away after Jesus was taken to heaven, his followers began meeting together for prayer. It is important for the Lord's followers to pray together. That's how we get wisdom and guidance from God. Remember what Jesus said (Matthew 18.20): "Whenever two or three of you come together in my name, I am there with you."

Seeking the right replacement
(21) Jesus' followers needed to replace Judas Iscariot with someone who could tell about Jesus as a witness who had been with him. Today we have the New Testament as an accurate witness to Jesus. At that

cknown as the Eager One: The Greek text has "Cananaean," which probably comes from a Hebrew word meaning "zealous" (see Luke 6.15). "Zealot" was the name later given to the members of a Jewish group which resisted and fought against the Romans. dmet together and prayed with a single purpose in mind: Or "met together in a special place for prayer."

us tell others that Jesus has been raised from death. He must also be one of the men who was with us from the very beginning. He must have been with us from the time the Lord Jesus was baptized by John until the day he was taken to heaven.

23Two men were suggested: One of them was Joseph Barsabbas, known as Justus, and the other was Matthias. 24Then they all prayed, "Lord, you know what everyone is like! Show us the one you have chosen 25to be an apostle and to serve in place of Judas, who got what he deserved." 26They drew names, and Matthias was chosen to join the group of the eleven apostles.

The Coming of the Holy Spirit

2 On the day of Pentecost^e all the Lord's followers were together in one place. 2Suddenly there was a noise from heaven like the sound of a mighty wind! It filled the house where they were meeting. 3Then they saw what looked like fiery tongues moving in all directions, and a tongue came and settled on each person there. 4The Holy Spirit took control of everyone, and they began speaking whatever languages the Spirit let them speak.

5Many religious Jews from every country in the world were living in Jerusalem. 6And when they heard this noise, a crowd gathered. But they were surprised, because they were hearing everything in their own languages. 7They were excited and amazed, and said:

Don't all these who are speaking come from Galilee? 8Then why do we hear them speaking our very own languages? 9Some of us are from Parthia, Media, and Elam. Others are from Mesopotamia, Judea, Cappadocia, Pontus, Asia, 10Phrygia, Pamphylia, Egypt,

time it was very important for someone who was preaching to be able to say, "I was there and I saw it with my own eyes."

---

^ePentecost: A Jewish festival that came fifty days after Passover and celebrated the wheat harvest. Jews later celebrated Pentecost as the time when they were given the Law of Moses.

parts of Libya near Cyrene, Rome, 11-12Crete, and Arabia. Some of us were born Jews, and others of us have chosen to be Jews. Yet we all hear them using our own languages to tell the wonderful things God has done.

Everyone was excited and confused. Some of them even kept asking each other, "What does all this mean?"

13Others made fun of the Lord's followers and said, "They are drunk."

Peter Speaks to the Crowd

14Peter stood with the eleven apostles and spoke in a loud and clear voice to the crowd:

Friends and everyone else living in Jerusalem, listen carefully to what I have to say! 15You are wrong to think that these people are drunk. After all, it is only nine o'clock in the morning.

"What does all this mean?"
(12) This was the question people asked when the Holy Spirit of God came. Jesus had returned to heaven. But he had promised that he and his Father would send the Holy Spirit to be the constant Helper and Companion of believers on earth. The Holy Spirit makes Jesus real to us and gives us power to live for God.

Nations of Pentecost

16But this is what God had the prophet
Joel say,

17"When the last days come,
I will give my Spirit
to everyone.
Your sons and daughters
will prophesy.
Your young men
will see visions,
and your old men
will have dreams.
18In those days I will give
my Spirit to my servants,
both men and women,
and they will prophesy.

19I will work miracles
in the sky above
and wonders
on the earth below.
There will be blood and fire
and clouds of smoke.
20The sun will turn dark,
and the moon
will be as red as blood
before the great
and wonderful day
of the Lord appears.
21Then the Lord
will save everyone
who asks for his help."

22Now, listen to what I have to say
about Jesus from Nazareth. God proved
that he sent Jesus to you by having him
work miracles, wonders, and signs. All
of you know this. 23God had already
planned and decided that Jesus would
be handed over to you. So you took him
and had evil men put him to death on
a cross. 24But God set him free from
death and raised him to life. Death could
not hold him in its power. 25What David
said are really the words of Jesus,

"I always see the Lord
near me,
and I will not be afraid
with him at my right side.
26Because of this,
my heart will be glad,

Peter told the history of God's promise

(17) The coming of the Holy
Spirit, who is God himself,
was a planned event that
had been talked about for
centuries. The prophets had
predicted years before
about this great happening,
which was like the great
birthday of Christianity. On
this day, it was clear that
God's word would be
spread in a powerful way,
because the Holy Spirit
would give power to the
preaching of that word.

King David had told about Christ

(25) David was a great king
of the Jews who lived a thousand years before Jesus was
born. In fact, David was a
great ancestor of Jesus. It's
exciting to see how David
knew that his great descendant, Jesus, would rise from
death a thousand years
later. David knew this because God showed it to him.

my words will be joyful,
    and I will live in hope.
27The Lord won't leave me
    in the grave.
I am his holy one,
    and he won't let
    my body decay.
28He has shown me
    the path to life,
and he makes me glad
    by being near me."

29My friends, it is right for me to speak to you about our ancestor David. He died and was buried, and his tomb is still here. 30But David was a prophet, and he knew that God had made a promise he would not break. He had told David that someone from his own family would someday be king.

31David knew this would happen, and so he told us that Christ would be raised to life. He said that God would not leave him in the grave or let his body decay. 32All of us can tell you that God has raised Jesus to life!

33Jesus was taken up to sit at the right side*f* of God, and he was given the Holy Spirit, just as the Father had promised. Jesus is also the one who has given the Spirit to us, and that is what you are now seeing and hearing.

34David didn't go up to heaven. So he wasn't talking about himself when he said, "The Lord told my Lord to sit at his right side, 35until he made my Lord's enemies into a footstool for him." 36Everyone in Israel should then know for certain that God has made Jesus both Lord and Christ, even though you put him to death on a cross.

37When the people heard this, they were very upset. They asked Peter and the other apostles, "Friends, what shall we do?"

38Peter said, "Turn back to God! Be baptized in the name of Jesus Christ, so that your sins will be forgiven. Then you will be given the Holy Spirit. 39This promise is

f right side: The place of honor and power.

Why did Peter preach?
(38) Was Peter just trying to amaze the crowd? No, Peter told the people that Christ had died and risen to save them from their sins. So he taught them to turn back to God, and their sins would be forgiven. Then they too would receive the Holy Spirit. This is the reason for all Christian preaching and witnessing: to get listeners to answer with faith toward God.

for you and your children. It is for everyone our Lord God will choose, no matter where they live."

40Peter told them many other things as well. Then he said, "I beg you to save yourselves from what will happen to all these evil people." 41On that day about three thousand believed his message and were baptized. 42They spent their time learning from the apostles, and they were like family to each other. They also broke bread^g and prayed together.

Life among the Lord's Followers

43Everyone was amazed by the many miracles and wonders that the apostles worked. 44All the Lord's followers often met together, and they shared everything they had. 45They would sell their property and possessions and give the money to whoever needed it. 46Day after day they met together in the temple. They broke bread^g together in different homes and shared their food happily and freely, 47while praising God. Everyone liked them, and each day the Lord added to their group others who were being saved.

Peter and John Heal a Lame Man

3 The time of prayer^h was about three o'clock in the afternoon, and Peter and John were going into the temple. 2A man who had been born lame was being carried to the temple door. Each day he was placed beside this door, known as the Beautiful Gate. He sat there and begged from the people who were going in.

3The man saw Peter and John entering the temple, and he asked them for money. 4But they looked straight at him and said, "Look up at us!"

How should Christians behave?
(44) Notice how the Holy Spirit changed the lives of those who believed Peter's preaching. Luke tells us they were eager to learn about God, and they treated each other like family members. They shared their money and food, and they were a happy people. This is the kind of behavior that spreads the good news about Jesus by *showing* as well as by talking.

^g*broke bread*: They ate together and celebrated the Lord's Supper.   ^h*The time of prayer*: Many of the Jewish people prayed in their homes at regular times each day (see Daniel 6.11), and on special occasions they prayed in the temple.

5The man stared at them and thought he was going to get something. 6But Peter said, "I don't have any silver or gold! But I will give you what I do have. In the name of Jesus Christ from Nazareth, get up and start walking." 7Peter then took him by the right hand and helped him up.

At once the man's feet and ankles became strong, 8and he jumped up and started walking. He went with Peter and John into the temple, walking and jumping and praising God. 9Everyone saw him walking around and praising God. 10They knew that he was the beggar who had been lying beside the Beautiful Gate, and they were completely surprised. They could not imagine what had happened to the man.

Jesus' works continue

(7) Jesus didn't stop working because he had gone up to heaven. By the Holy Spirit he continued his work on earth through the apostles, like Peter. So we shouldn't be surprised at Peter's command to the lame man. Peter believed that Jesus still lived, and that Jesus would heal the man.

Peter Speaks in the Temple

11While the man kept holding on to Peter and John, the whole crowd ran to them in amazement at the place known as Solomon's Porch.[i] 12Peter saw that a crowd had gathered, and he said:

Friends, why are you surprised at what has happened? Why are you staring at us? Do you think we have some power of our own? Do you think we were able to make this man walk because we are so religious? 13The God that Abraham, Isaac, Jacob, and our other ancestors worshiped has brought honor to his Servant[j] Jesus. He is the one you betrayed. You turned against him when he was being tried by Pilate, even though Pilate wanted to set him free.

14You rejected Jesus, who was holy and good. You asked for a murderer to be set free, 15and you killed the one who leads people to life. But God raised him from death, and all of us can tell you what he has done. 16You see this man, and you know him. He put his faith

What is the good news?

(12) Peter gave us an example of preaching the good news about Jesus as he spoke in the temple. He explained to his hearers that Jesus was not just a good man who simply came and helped them with their problems, and then died like other men. Jesus was the one foretold by the prophets and great leaders that people knew from reading the Old Testament: he was the Messiah, who would save his people from their sins.

[i] *Solomon's Porch*: A public place with tall columns along the east side of the temple. [j] *Servant*: Or "Son."

in the name of Jesus and was made strong. Faith in Jesus made this man completely well while everyone was watching.

17My friends, I am sure that you and your leaders didn't know what you were doing. 18But God had his prophets tell that his Messiah would suffer, and now he has kept that promise. 19So turn to God! Give up your sins, and you will be forgiven. 20Then that time will come when the Lord will give you fresh strength. He will send you Jesus, his chosen Messiah. 21But Jesus must stay in heaven until God makes all things new, just as his holy prophets promised long ago.

22Moses said, "The Lord your God will choose one of your own people to be a prophet, just as he chose me. Listen to everything he tells you. 23No one who disobeys that prophet will be one of God's people any longer."

24Samuel and all the other prophets who came later also spoke about what is now happening. 25You are really the ones God told his prophets to speak to. And you were given the promise that God made to your ancestors. He said to Abraham, "All nations on earth will be blessed because of someone from your family." 26God sent his chosen Sonk to you first, because God wanted to bless you and make each one of you turn away from your sins.

Peter and John Are Brought in Front of the Council

4 The apostles were still talking to the people, when some priests, the captain of the temple guard, and some Sadducees arrived. 2These men were angry because the apostles were teaching the people that the dead would be raised from death, just as Jesus had been raised from death. 3By now it was already late in the afternoon,

kSon: Or "Servant."

It's not over yet
(21) We must see that the coming of Jesus was in the great plan of God from eternal ages past. The coming of Jesus will also make a great difference for the eternal future. Jesus is the King of heaven who will bring his everlasting kingdom to a new world. He is raising up a new people, his church, by their faith in him. They will serve someday in his kingdom.

Christians are often mistreated
(3) It doesn't take a negative attitude to realize that Christians often suffer unjustly. Even some news items by non-Christian reporters have noted this fact. The wonder is that the mistreatment happens even though there is no true reason for being unkind to Christians. But sometimes people just feel threatened because Christians are different. Such people sometimes strike out against what they don't understand.

and they arrested Peter and John and put them in jail for the night. 4But a lot of people who had heard the message believed it. So by now there were about five thousand followers of the Lord.

5The next morning the leaders, the elders, and the teachers of the Law of Moses met in Jerusalem. 6The high priest Annas was there, as well as Caiaphas, John, Alexander, and other members of the high priest's family. 7They brought in Peter and John and made them stand in the middle while they questioned them. They asked, "By what power and in whose name have you done this?"

8Peter was filled with the Holy Spirit and told the nation's leaders and the elders:

9You are questioning us today about a kind deed in which a crippled man was healed. 10But there is something we must tell you and everyone else in Israel. This man is standing here completely well because of the power of Jesus from Nazareth. You put Jesus to death on a cross, but God raised him to life. 11He is the stone that you builders thought was worthless, and now he is the most important stone of all. 12Only Jesus has the power to save! His name is the only one in all the world that can save anyone.

13The officials were amazed to see how brave Peter and John were, and they knew that these two apostles were only ordinary men and not well educated. The officials were certain that these men had been with Jesus. 14But they could not deny what had happened. The man who had been healed was standing there with the apostles.

15The officials commanded them to leave the council room. Then the officials said to each other, 16"What can we do with these men? Everyone in Jerusalem knows about this miracle, and we cannot say it didn't happen. 17But to keep this thing from spreading, we will warn them never again to speak to anyone about the name of Jesus." 18So they called the two apostles back in and told them that they must never,

How do Christians answer their accusers?
(8) The Holy Spirit helped Peter with his answer, and the same Holy Spirit helps us. Peter reminded his accusers that they were angry because he did a kind deed. That should have caused them shame. But then Peter told them straight out that they had crucified the Son of God, who is now alive and saves people from their sins. Again, Peter showed his hearers that they would have to decide about Jesus.

The truth stops evil
(18) Those who arrested Peter and John were confused and didn't know what to do. Peter had stopped them in their tracks when he reminded them that he had only done a kind deed. So the officials just ordered the apostles to be quiet and let them go. (Of course, there would be no way to keep them quiet.) In the end, we'll never be sorry for being bold about Jesus.

for any reason, teach anything about the name of Jesus.

19Peter and John answered, "Do you think God wants us to obey you or to obey him? 20We cannot keep quiet about what we have seen and heard."

21-22The officials could not find any reason to punish Peter and John. So they threatened them and let them go. The man who was healed by this miracle was more than forty years old, and everyone was praising God for what had happened.

Peter and Others Pray for Courage

23As soon as Peter and John had been set free, they went back and told the others everything that the chief priests and the leaders had said to them. 24When the rest of the Lord's followers heard this, they prayed together and said:

Master, you created heaven and earth, the sea, and everything in them. 25And by the Holy Spirit you spoke to our ancestor David. He was your servant, and you told him to say:

"Why are all the Gentiles
   so furious?
Why do people
   make foolish plans?
26The kings of earth
   prepare for war,
and the rulers
   join together
against the Lord
   and his Messiah."

27Here in Jerusalem, Herod*l* and Pontius Pilate got together with the Gentiles and the people of Israel. Then they turned against your holy Servant*m* Jesus, your chosen Messiah. 28They did what you in your power and wisdom had already decided would happen.

29Lord, listen to their threats! We are your servants. So make us brave enough to speak your message. 30Show your

Prayer is the key
(24) When Peter and John were freed they didn't start preaching again right away. They and the other Christians met to pray. Prayer brings power for serving God. God answered the believers' prayers by giving them power to witness for Jesus. He will also give us power (for his glory) when we seek him first.

---

lHerod: Herod Antipas, the son of Herod the Great.
mServant: See the note at 3.13.

mighty power, as we heal people and work miracles and wonders in the name of your holy Servant[m] Jesus.

31After they had prayed, the meeting place shook. They were all filled with the Holy Spirit and bravely spoke God's message.

Sharing Possessions

32The group of followers all felt the same way about everything. None of them claimed that their belongings were their own, and they shared everything they had with each other. 33In a powerful way the apostles told everyone that the Lord Jesus was now alive. God greatly blessed his followers,[n] 34and no one went in need of anything. Everyone who owned land or houses would sell them and bring the money 35to the apostles. Then they would give the money to anyone who needed it.

36-37Joseph was one of the followers who had sold a piece of property and brought the money to the apostles. He was a Levite from Cyprus, and the apostles called him Barnabas, which means, "one who encourages others."

Peter Condemns Ananias and Sapphira

5 Ananias and his wife Sapphira also sold a piece of property. 2But they agreed to cheat and keep some of the money for themselves.

So when Ananias took the rest of the money to the apostles, 3Peter said, "Why has Satan made you keep back some of the money from the sale of the property? Why have you lied to the Holy Spirit? 4The property was yours before you sold it, and even after you sold it, the money was still yours. What made you do such a thing? You didn't lie to people. You lied to God!"

5As soon as Ananias heard this, he

Christians are willing sharers
(32) Was this combining of property some sort of communism? Not really. The Christians were not forced to give up their property. They were sharing it with each other willingly. They were putting their property together because of their faith in Christ, and they could decide for themselves whether to do so.

Tell God the truth
(4) Wealthy people among the Christians sold land and gave the money to the apostles so they could help the poor. But two people described in this chapter, Ananias and Sapphira, were only putting on a show of being kind. Their fate is a warning to us about trying to deceive God. Sooner or later, lying results in punishment.

[m]*Servant:* See the note at 3.13.   [n]*God greatly blessed his followers:* Or "Everyone highly respected his followers."

dropped dead, and everyone who heard about it was frightened. 6Some young men came in and wrapped up his body. Then they took it out and buried it.

7Three hours later Sapphira came in, but she did not know what had happened to her husband. 8Peter asked her, "Tell me, did you sell the property for this amount?"

"Yes," she answered, "that's the amount."

9Then Peter said, "Why did the two of you agree to test the Lord's Spirit? The men who buried Ananias are by the door, and they will carry you out!" 10At once she fell at Peter's feet and died.

When the young men came back in, they found Sapphira lying there dead. So they carried her out and buried her beside her husband. 11All the church members were afraid, and so was everyone else who heard what had happened.

Peter's Unusual Power

12The apostles worked many miracles and wonders among the people. All of the Lord's followers often met in the part of the temple known as Solomon's Porch.o 13No one outside their group dared join them, even though everyone liked them very much.

14Many men and women started having faith in the Lord. 15Then sick people were brought out to the road and placed on cots and mats. It was hoped that Peter would walk by, and his shadow would fall on them and heal them. 16A lot of people living in the towns near Jerusalem brought those who were sick or troubled by evil spirits, and they were all healed.

The Jewish Leaders Make Trouble for the Apostles

17The high priest and all the other Sadducees who were with him became jealous. 18They arrested the apostles and put them

True divine healing honors God
(15) Sadly, some people have falsely pretended to be great miracle healers. God wants to heal us when he can be honored by the work, but not to bring wealth or honor to a human celebrity. Peter was able to heal because of the power of the Holy Spirit in him. But those who thought it was Peter's shadow that had the power to heal them had the wrong idea.

oSolomon's Porch: See the note at 3.11.

in the city jail. [19]But that night an angel
from the Lord opened the doors of the jail
and led the apostles out. The angel said,
[20]"Go to the temple and tell the people
everything about this new life." [21]So they
went into the temple before sunrise and
started teaching.

The high priest and his men called together their council, which included all of
Israel's leaders. Then they ordered the apostles to be brought to them from the jail.
[22]The servants who were sent to the jail
did not find the apostles. They returned and
said, [23]"We found the jail locked tight and
the guards standing at the doors. But when
we opened the doors and went in, we didn't
find anyone there." [24]The captain of the
temple guard and the chief priests listened
to their report, but they did not know what
to think about it.

[25]Just then someone came in and said,
"Right now those men you put in jail are
in the temple, teaching the people!" [26]The
captain of the temple police went with some
of his servants and brought the apostles
back. But they did not use force. They were
afraid that the people might start throwing
stones at them.

[27]When the apostles were brought before
the council, the high priest said to them,
[28]"We told you plainly not to teach in the
name of Jesus. But look what you have
done! You have been teaching all over Jerusalem, and you are trying to blame us for
his death."

[29]Peter and the apostles replied:

We don't obey people. We obey God.
[30]You killed Jesus by nailing him to a
cross. But the God our ancestors worshiped raised him to life [31]and made
him our Leader and Savior. Then God
gave him a place at his right side,[p] so
that the people of Israel would turn back
to him and be forgiven. [32]We are here
to tell you about all this, and so is the
Holy Spirit, who is God's gift to everyone who obeys God.

What was wrong with the leaders?

(27) The apostles were released from prison by a miracle, and they were teaching in the temple. But the
temple leaders were jeal-
ous. Why? They too might
have enjoyed the good
things the apostles were
preaching about. But the
leaders refused, because
they loved their important
place in society more than
they loved God. These were
unhappy people.

[p]*right side:* See the note at 2.33.

33When the council members heard this, they became so angry that they wanted to kill the apostles. 34But one of them was the Pharisee Gamaliel, a highly respected teacher. He ordered the apostles to be taken out of the room for a little while. 35Then he said to the council:

Men of Israel, be careful what you do with these two men. 36Not long ago Theudas claimed to be someone important, and about four hundred men joined him. But he was killed. All his followers were scattered, and that was the end of that.

37Later, when the people of our nation were being counted, Judas from Galilee showed up. A lot of people followed him, but he was killed, and all his followers were scattered.

38So I advise you to stay away from these men. Leave them alone. If what they are planning is something of their own doing, it will fail. 39But if God is behind it, you cannot stop it anyway, unless you want to fight against God.

The council members agreed with what he said, 40and they called the apostles back in. They had them beaten with a whip and warned them not to speak in the name of Jesus. Then they let them go.

41The apostles left the council and were happy, because God had considered them worthy to suffer for the sake of Jesus. 42Every day they spent time in the temple and in one home after another. They never stopped teaching and telling the good news that Jesus is the Messiah.

Seven Leaders for the Church

6 A lot of people were now becoming followers of the Lord. But some of the ones who spoke Greek started complaining about the ones who spoke Aramaic. They complained that the Greek-speaking widows were not given their share when the food supplies were handed out each day.

2The twelve apostles called the whole group of followers together and said, "We

You can't have it both ways
(38) Poor Gamaliel—he was afraid to see the apostles killed, but he also wanted to please the temple leaders. We don't read that Gamaliel objected to the whipping of the apostles. He hoped to keep peace with God and with an evil society as well. That's a sad spot to be in, but it's the spot Gamaliel chose for himself.

We are one family of God
(1) Some Jews had been living for a long time among Gentiles. So these Jews took on Greek language and ways. Other Jews had been living in Palestine. So their language and ways were different from the Greek-speaking Jews. That caused a division among the Christians. In that division we see the beginning of cracks in the happy Christian unity we saw in Acts 2.

should not give up preaching God's message in order to serve at tables.q 3My friends, choose seven men who are respected and wise and filled with God's Spirit. We will put them in charge of these things. 4We can spend our time praying and serving God by preaching."

5This suggestion pleased everyone, and they began by choosing Stephen. He had great faith and was filled with the Holy Spirit. Then they chose Philip, Prochorus, Nicanor, Timon, Parmenas, and also Nicolaus, who worshiped with the Jewish peopler in Antioch. 6These men were brought to the apostles. Then the apostles prayed and placed their hands on the men to show that they had been chosen to do this work. 7God's message spread, and many more people in Jerusalem became followers. Even a large number of priests put their faith in the Lord.

God needs different kinds of workers

(4) The apostles were burdened with preaching the good news. But somebody had to care for the needy. So they appointed special helpers for that work. Some think this was the beginning of the work of *deacons*. The word "deacon" comes from a Greek word meaning servant. Many churches still have deacons today.

Stephen Is Arrested

8God gave Stephen the power to work great miracles and wonders among the people. 9But some Jews from Cyrene and Alexandria were members of a group who called themselves "Free Men."s They started arguing with Stephen. Some others from Cilicia and Asia also argued with him. 10But they were no match for Stephen, who spoke with the great wisdom that the Spirit gave him. 11So they talked some men into saying, "We heard Stephen say terrible things against Moses and God!"

12They turned the people and their leaders and the teachers of the Law of Moses against Stephen. Then they all grabbed Ste-

What was Stephen's work?

(8) Stephen was one of the chosen servants, but his work wasn't only collecting and caring for the poor. Stephen was able to work miracles. He also was a power-filled debater. Not only that, but he preached a mighty sermon, as we shall see. The Christ who has gone to heaven gives power to his servants.

---

qto serve at tables: This may mean either that they were in charge of handing out food to the widows or that they were in charge of the money, since the Greek word "table" may also mean "bank." rworshiped with the Jewish people: This translates the Greek word "proselyte" that means a Gentile who had accepted the Jewish religion. s"Free Men": A group of Jewish men who had once been slaves, but had been freed.

phen and dragged him in front of the council. 13Some men agreed to tell lies about Stephen, and they said, "This man keeps on saying terrible things about this holy temple and the Law of Moses. 14We have heard him claim that Jesus from Nazareth will destroy this place and change the customs that Moses gave us." 15Then all the council members stared at Stephen. They saw that his face looked like the face of an angel.

Stephen's Speech

7 The high priest asked Stephen, "Are they telling the truth about you?" 2Stephen answered:

Friends, listen to me. Our glorious God appeared to our ancestor Abraham while he was still in Mesopotamia, before he had moved to Haran. 3God told him, "Leave your country and your relatives and go to a land that I will show you." 4Then Abraham left the land of the Chaldeans and settled in Haran.

After his father died, Abraham came and settled in this land where you now live. 5God didn't give him any part of it, not even a square foot. But God did promise to give it to him and his family forever, even though Abraham didn't have any children. 6God said that Abraham's descendants would live for a while in a foreign land. There they would be slaves and would be mistreated four hundred years. 7But he also said, "I will punish the nation that makes them slaves. Then later they will come and worship me in this place."

8God said to Abraham, "Every son in each family must be circumcised to show that you have kept your agreement with me." So when Isaac was eight days old, Abraham circumcised him. Later, Isaac circumcised his son Jacob, and Jacob circumcised his twelve sons. 9 These men were our ancestors.

Joseph was also one of our famous ancestors. His brothers were jealous of

Stephen told about Abraham
(2) Abraham was the great ancestor of the Jews who lived two thousand years before Christ. Stephen reminded his listeners of God's promise that Abraham would be the father of a great people. Because Abraham believed God, he was called the father of the faithful. His name means "father of many people."

Stephen told about Joseph
(9) Joseph was another great man in Jewish history. He was a great-grandson of Abraham, and he became a great leader in Egypt. Because of his position of power and influence, Joseph was used by God to save his people the Israelites from starvation. We see from this that God can see our needs years in advance, and is able to provide answers.

him and sold him as a slave to be taken to Egypt. But God was with him [10]and rescued him from all his troubles. God made him so wise that the Egyptian king Pharaoh thought highly of him. Pharaoh even made Joseph governor over Egypt and put him in charge of everything he owned.

[11]Everywhere in Egypt and Canaan the grain crops failed. There was terrible suffering, and our ancestors could not find enough to eat. [12]But when Jacob heard that there was grain in Egypt, he sent our ancestors there for the first time. [13]It was on their second trip that Joseph told his brothers who he was, and Pharaoh learned about Joseph's family.

[14]Joseph sent for his father and his relatives. In all, there were seventy-five of them. [15]His father went to Egypt and died there, just as our ancestors did. [16]Later their bodies were taken back to Shechem and placed in the tomb that Abraham had bought from the sons of Hamor.

[17]Finally, the time came for God to do what he had promised Abraham. By then the number of our people in Egypt had greatly increased. [18]Another king was ruling Egypt, and he didn't know anything about Joseph. [19]He tricked our ancestors and was cruel to them. He even made them leave their babies outside, so they would die.

[20]During this time Moses was born. He was a very beautiful child, and for three months his parents took care of him in their home. [21]Then when they were forced to leave him outside, the king's daughter found him and raised him as her own son. [22]Moses was given the best education in Egypt. He was a strong man and a powerful speaker.

[23]When Moses was forty years old, he wanted to help the Israelites because they were his own people. [24]One day he saw an Egyptian mistreating one of them. So he rescued the man and killed

Stephen told about Moses
(20) Moses was the Jews' great lawgiver who lived about fifteen hundred years before Christ. Moses was God's man to lead the Jews out of Egypt after four hundred years of slavery. Then Moses was given the Ten Commandments and all the other laws that the Jews lived by. Moses was like Jesus, who leads us out of the slavery of sin.

the Egyptian. 25Moses thought the rest of his people would realize that God was going to use him to set them free. But they didn't understand.

26The next day Moses saw two of his own people fighting, and he tried to make them stop. He said, "Men, you are both Israelites. Why are you so cruel to each other?"

27But the man who had started the fight pushed Moses aside and asked, "Who made you our ruler and judge? 28Are you going to kill me, just as you killed that Egyptian yesterday?" 29When Moses heard this, he ran away to live in the country of Midian. His two sons were born there.

30Forty years later, an angel appeared to Moses from a burning bush in the desert near Mount Sinai. 31Moses was surprised by what he saw. He went closer to get a better look, and the Lord said, 32"I am the God who was worshiped by your ancestors, Abraham, Isaac, and Jacob." Moses started shaking all over and didn't dare to look at the bush.

33The Lord said to him, "Take off your sandals. The place where you are standing is holy. 34With my own eyes I have seen the suffering of my people in Egypt. I have heard their groans and have come down to rescue them. Now I am sending you back to Egypt."

35This was the same Moses that the people rejected by saying, "Who made you our leader and judge?" God's angel had spoken to Moses from the bush. And God had even sent the angel to help Moses rescue the people and be their leader.

36In Egypt and at the Red Sea and in the desert, Moses rescued the people by working miracles and wonders for forty years. 37Moses is the one who told the people of Israel, "God will choose one of your people to be a prophet, just as he chose me." 38Moses brought our people together in the desert, and the

angel spoke to him on Mount Sinai.
There he was given these life-giving
words to pass on to us. 39But our ancestors refused to obey Moses. They rejected him and wanted to go back to
Egypt.

40The people said to Aaron, "Make
some gods to lead us! Moses led us out
of Egypt, but we don't know what's happened to him now." 41Then they made
an idol in the shape of a calf. They
offered sacrifices to the idol and were
pleased with what they had done.

42God turned his back on his people
and left them. Then they worshiped the
stars in the sky, just as it says in the
Book of the Prophets, "People of Israel,
you didn't offer sacrifices and offerings
to me during those forty years in the
desert. 43Instead, you carried the tent
where the god Molech is worshiped, and
you took along the star of your god
Rephan. You made those idols and
worshiped them. So now I will have
you carried off beyond Babylonia."

44The tent where our ancestors worshiped God was with them in the desert.
This was the same tent that God had
commanded Moses to make. And it was
made like the model that Moses had
seen. 45Later it was given to our ancestors, and they took it with them when
they went with Joshua. They carried the
tent along as they took over the land
from those people that God had chased
out for them. Our ancestors used this
tent until the time of King David.46 He
pleased God and asked him if he could
build a house of worship for the peoplet
of Israel. 47And it was finally King Solomon who built a house for God.u

48But the Most High God does not
live in houses made by humans. It is
just as the prophet said, when he spoke
for the Lord,
    49"Heaven is my throne,

People wouldn't let God bless them

(39) God himself had given
Moses his Law on Mount Sinai, but the people kept re-
belling. All through Israel's
history, the people kept
turning from God in spite of
the many ways he had
shown his love to them. Right
up to the day Stephen spoke,
most of the Jewish people
and their leaders were refusing to see what God had
done for them. That's "human nature," not wanting to
trust God and live for him.

---

tthe people: Some manuscripts have "God." uGod:
Or "the people."

and the earth
  is my footstool.
What kind of house
  will you build for me?
In what place will I rest?
  50   I have made everything."
51You stubborn and hardheaded people! You are always fighting against the Holy Spirit, just as your ancestors did. 52Is there one prophet that your ancestors didn't mistreat? They killed the prophets who told about the coming of the One Who Obeys God.v And now you have turned against him and killed him. 53Angels gave you God's Law, but you still don't obey it.

Stephen Is Stoned to Death

54When the council members heard Stephen's speech, they were angry and furious. 55But Stephen was filled with the Holy Spirit. He looked toward heaven, where he saw our glorious God and Jesus standing at his right side.w 56Then Stephen said, "I see heaven open and the Son of Man standing at the right side of God!"

57The council members shouted and covered their ears. At once they all attacked Stephen 58and dragged him out of the city. Then they started throwing stones at him. The men who had brought charges against him put their coats at the feet of a young man named Saul.x

59As Stephen was being stoned to death, he called out, "Lord Jesus, please welcome me!" 60He kneeled down and shouted, "Lord, don't blame them for what they have done." Then he died.

8 1-2Saul approved the stoning of Stephen. Some faithful followers of the Lord buried Stephen and mourned very much for him.

---

vOne Who Obeys God: That is, Jesus. wstanding at his right side: The "right side" is the place of honor and power. "Standing" may mean that Jesus is welcoming Stephen (see verse 59). xSaul: Better known as Paul, who became a famous follower of Jesus.

Why was Stephen murdered?
(54) Stephen's speech proved to his hearers that they had been disobedient to God. This made them feel guilty and angry. So the mob killed Stephen. Even today some people will get angry when they are told they have rejected God's message. They like to feel that their sins are their own business. But we owe our very lives to God, and he expects us to do his will.

Who was Saul?
(1) We are going to read much more about this young man Saul. He was a leading Pharisee, a smart student and teacher of the Law. (Later, his name would be changed to Paul after he became a Christian.) At first Saul was the greatest single enemy of Christ, so his later faith in Christ would be a great miracle and a source of wonder to those in the church. We will see by this that no one is so awful that they are beyond being saved.

Saul Makes Trouble for the Church

At that time the church in Jerusalem suffered terribly. All of the Lord's followers, except the apostles, were scattered everywhere in Judea and Samaria. ³Saul started making a lot of trouble for the church. He went from house to house, arresting men and women and putting them in jail.

The Good News Is Preached in Samaria

⁴The Lord's followers who had been scattered went from place to place, telling the good news. ⁵Philip went to the town of Samaria and told the people about Christ. ⁶They crowded around Philip because they were eager to hear what he was saying and to see him work miracles. ⁷Many people with evil spirits were healed, and the spirits went out of them with a shout. A lot of crippled and lame people were also healed. ⁸Everyone in that city was very glad because of what was happening.

⁹For some time a man named Simon had lived in the city of Samaria and had amazed the people. He practiced witchcraft and claimed to be somebody great. ¹⁰Everyone, rich and poor, crowded around him. They said, "This man is the power of God called 'The Great Power.'"

¹¹For a long time Simon had used witchcraft to amaze the people, and they kept crowding around him. ¹²But when they believed what Philip was saying about God's kingdom and about the name of Jesus Christ, they were all baptized. ¹³Even Simon believed and was baptized. He stayed close to Philip, because he marveled at all the miracles and wonders.

¹⁴When the apostles in Jerusalem heard that some people in Samaria had accepted God's message, they sent Peter and John. ¹⁵When the two apostles arrived, they prayed that the people would be given the Holy Spirit. ¹⁶Before this, the Holy Spirit had not been given to anyone in Samaria though some of them had been baptized in the name of the Lord Jesus. ¹⁷Peter and John

Who was Philip?
(5) Philip was one of the men we met in chapter 6 who were appointed to help the poor. Stephen was also one of those men. But we see that Philip, like Stephen, was also used by God as a great preacher of the good news about the Lord Jesus.

Who was Simon?
(11) Don't confuse this man with the apostle, Simon Peter. The Simon we meet here practiced witchcraft. We would say today that he practiced the occult. You could imagine someone like that today being called "The Great Power" (verse 10). Such practices come from the devil. Simon tried to "buy his way in," thinking he could get the power of the Holy Spirit with money. Peter scolded him for such foolishness.

then placed their hands on everyone who had faith in the Lord, and they were given the Holy Spirit.

18Simon noticed that the Spirit was given only when the apostles placed their hands on the people. So he brought money 19and said to Peter and John, "Let me have this power too! Then anyone I place my hands on will also be given the Holy Spirit."

20Peter said to him, "You and your money will both end up in hell if you think you can buy God's gift! 21You don't have any part in this, and God sees that your heart is not right. 22Get rid of these evil thoughts and ask God to forgive you. 23I can see that you are jealous and bound by your evil ways."

24Simon said, "Please pray to the Lord, so that what you said won't happen to me."

25After Peter and John had preached about the Lord, they returned to Jerusalem. On their way they told the good news in many villages of Samaria.

Philip and an Ethiopian Official

26The Lord's angel said to Philip, "Go south*y* along the desert road that leads from Jerusalem to Gaza."*z* 27So Philip left.

An important Ethiopian official happened to be going along that road in his chariot. He was the chief treasurer for Candace, the Queen of Ethiopia. The official had gone to Jerusalem to worship 28and was now on his way home. He was sitting in his chariot, reading the book of the prophet Isaiah.

29The Spirit told Philip to catch up with the chariot. 30Philip ran up close and heard the man reading aloud from the book of Isaiah. Philip asked him, "Do you understand what you are reading?"

31The official answered, "How can I understand unless someone helps me?" He

Philip explained about Jesus
(27) The man Philip met was from Ethiopia, a country in Africa. The man was reading in a place in the Old Testament that tells how Jesus would die for our sins. But the man from Ethiopia didn't know who the Old Testament prophet was talking about. So Philip told the man about Jesus. We must use every chance we get to explain Jesus to people.

yGo south: Or "About noon go." *z the desert road that leads from Jerusalem to Gaza*: Or "the road that leads from Jerusalem to Gaza in the desert."

then invited Philip to come up and sit beside him.

32The man was reading the passage that said,

> "He was led like a sheep
>   on its way to be killed.
> He was silent as a lamb,
>   whose wool
>   is being cut off,
> and he did not say
>   a word.
> **33**He was treated like a nobody
>   and did not receive
>   a fair trial.
> How can he have children,
>   if his life
>   is snatched away?"

34The official said to Philip, "Tell me, was the prophet talking about himself or about someone else?" **35**So Philip began at this place in the Scriptures and explained the good news about Jesus.

36-37 As they were going along the road, they came to a place where there was some water. The official said, "Look! Here is some water. Why can't I be baptized?"*a* **38**He ordered the chariot to stop. Then they both went down into the water, and Philip baptized him.

39After they had come out of the water, the Lord's Spirit took Philip away. The official never saw him again, but he was very happy as he went on his way.

40Philip later appeared in Azotus. He went from town to town, all the way to Caesarea, telling people about Jesus.

Saul Becomes a Follower of the Lord
(Acts 22.6–16; 26.12–18)

9 Saul kept on threatening to kill the Lord's followers. He even went to the high priest **2**and asked for letters to the Jewish leaders in Damascus. He did this be-

---

"Why can't I be baptized?"

(37) As soon as the official believed in Jesus, he wanted to be baptized as Jesus taught. That's the sign of an obedient heart. Sometimes when people decide to have faith in Jesus, they are embarrassed about being baptized. Surely this official wasn't embarrassed—he couldn't wait.

---

aWhy can't I be baptized: Some manuscripts add, "Philip replied, 'You can, if you believe with all your heart.' "The official answered, 'I believe that Jesus Christ is the Son of God.'"

cause he wanted to arrest and take to Jerusalem any man or woman who had accepted the Lord's Way.*b* ³When Saul had almost reached Damascus, a bright light from heaven suddenly flashed around him. ⁴He fell to the ground and heard a voice that said, "Saul! Saul! Why are you so cruel to me?"

⁵"Who are you?" Saul asked.

"I am Jesus," the Lord answered. "I am the one you are so cruel to. ⁶Now get up and go into the city, where you will be told what to do."

⁷The men with Saul stood there speechless. They had heard the voice, but they had not seen anyone. ⁸Saul got up from the ground, and when he opened his eyes, he could not see a thing. Someone then led him by the hand to Damascus, ⁹and for three days he was blind and did not eat or drink.

¹⁰A follower named Ananias lived in Damascus, and the Lord spoke to him in a vision. Ananias answered, "Lord, here I am."

¹¹The Lord said to him, "Get up and go to the house of Judas on Straight Street. When you get there, you will find a man named Saul from the city of Tarsus. Saul is praying, ¹²and he has seen a vision. He saw a man named Ananias coming to him and putting his hands on him, so that he could see again."

¹³Ananias replied, "Lord, a lot of people have told me about the terrible things this man has done to your followers in Jerusalem. ¹⁴Now the chief priests have given him the power to come here and arrest anyone who worships in your name."

¹⁵The Lord said to Ananias, "Go! I have chosen him to tell foreigners, kings, and the people of Israel about me. ¹⁶I will show him how much he must suffer for worshiping in my name."

¹⁷Ananias left and went into the house where Saul was staying. Ananias placed his hands on him and said, "Saul, the Lord

baccepted the Lord's Way: In the book of Acts, this means to become a follower of the Lord Jesus.

Saul met his master

(5) Saul the Pharisee was very eager to destroy the followers of Jesus. But Saul got a surprise. Jesus was alive from the dead, and he met Saul who was on his way to arrest the Christians in Damascus. The risen Christ changed Saul's mind, and he became the most powerful apostle of all. As Paul, he would write thirteen books of the New Testament. Not even the worst enemy of the Lord Jesus can resist him when he is ready to work in that person's life.

Saul received his sight

(17) Saul had been blinded by the bright appearance of the risen Savior. Then Saul was filled with the Holy Spirit and he got back his sight. When the Holy Spirit fills our lives, we too receive new sight. As Jesus said, when you are born from above, you can see (or understand) the kingdom of God (John 3.3).

Jesus has sent me. He is the same one who appeared to you along the road. He wants you to be able to see and to be filled with the Holy Spirit."

18Suddenly something like fish scales fell from Saul's eyes, and he could see. He got up and was baptized. 19Then he ate and felt much better.

Saul Preaches in Damascus

For several days Saul stayed with the Lord's followers in Damascus. 20Soon he went to the Jewish meeting places and started telling people that Jesus is the Son of God. 21Everyone who heard Saul was amazed and said, "Isn't this the man who caused so much trouble for those people in Jerusalem who worship in the name of Jesus? Didn't he come here to arrest them and take them to the chief priests?"

22Saul preached with such power that he completely confused the Jewish people in Damascus, as he tried to show them that Jesus is the Messiah.

23Later some of them made plans to kill Saul, 24but he found out about it. He learned that they were guarding the gates of the city day and night in order to kill him. 25Then one night his followers let him down over the city wall in a large basket.

Saul in Jerusalem

26When Saul arrived in Jerusalem, he tried to join the followers. But they were all afraid of him, because they did not believe he was a true follower. 27Then Barnabas helped him by taking him to the apostles. He explained how on the road to Damascus, Saul had seen the Lord and how the Lord had spoken to Saul. Barnabas also said that when Saul was in Damascus, he had spoken bravely in the name of Jesus.

28Saul moved about freely with the followers in Jerusalem and told everyone about the Lord. 29He was always arguing with the Jews who spoke Greek, and so they tried to kill him. 30But the followers found

Saul told about Jesus right away

(20) Saul, the former Pharisee, couldn't wait to tell people about Jesus. At first the Christians were surprised at Saul because he had persecuted them. They thought maybe this was some sort of trick. But Saul was filled with the Holy Spirit and had to share about it. When Jesus changes our lives, we want to bring others to know him, too.

God made a way of escape

(25) Poor Saul was faced with a trap at Damascus. The gates were being watched so he could be arrested when he tried to leave. But the Christians in the city "used their heads" and let Saul down over the wall in a basket. When enemies of Christ tried to kill Saul in Jerusalem, he went back to Tarsus where he grew up. God had a plan for Saul, and would not let anyone else prevent it from being carried out. God has a plan for every person who believes in him, and he provides for us in dangerous times.

thing to do with other people. But God has shown me that he doesn't think anyone is unclean or unfit. 29I agreed to come here, but I want to know why you sent for me."

30Cornelius answered:

Four days ago at about three o'clock in the afternoon I was praying at home. Suddenly a man in bright clothes stood in front of me. 31He said, "Cornelius, God has heard your prayers, and he knows about your gifts to the poor. 32Now send to Joppa for Simon Peter. He is visiting in the home of Simon the leather maker, who lives near the sea."

33I sent for you right away, and you have been good enough to come. All of us are here in the presence of the Lord God, so that we can hear what he has to say.

34Peter then said:

Now I am certain that God treats all people alike. 35God is pleased with everyone who worships him and does right, no matter what nation they come from. 36This is the same message that God gave to the people of Israel, when he sent Jesus Christ, the Lord of all, to offer peace to them.

37You surely know what happened[h] everywhere in Judea. It all began in Galilee after John had told everyone to be baptized. 38God gave the Holy Spirit and power to Jesus from Nazareth. He was with Jesus, as he went around doing good and healing everyone who was under the power of the devil. 39We all saw what Jesus did both in Israel and in the city of Jerusalem.

Jesus was put to death on a cross. 40But three days later, God raised him to life and let him be seen. 41Not everyone saw him. He was seen only by us, who ate and drank with him after he was raised from death. We were the ones God chose to tell others about him.

42God told us to announce clearly to the people that Jesus is the one he has

Peter changed his mind about Gentiles
(35) At first Peter imagined that the Messiah had come only for the Jews. God had to shake Peter up about this opinion. Even from Old Testament times, God's prophets had been telling about his great plan to bless the Gentile nations. This began to happen in a big way at this point. The result is that today the church includes not only Jews but Gentiles too, mostly Gentiles.

[h]what happened: Or "the message that went."

out about this and took Saul to Caesarea. From there they sent him to the city of Tarsus.

31The church in Judea, Galilee, and Samaria now had a time of peace and kept on worshiping the Lord. The church became stronger, as the Holy Spirit encouraged it and helped it grow.

Peter Heals Aeneas

32While Peter was traveling from place to place, he visited the Lord's followers who lived in the town of Lydda. 33There he met a man named Aeneas, who for eight years had been sick in bed and could not move. 34Peter said to Aeneas, "Jesus Christ has healed you! Get up and make up your bed."[c] Right away he stood up.

35Many people in the towns of Lydda and Sharon saw Aeneas and became followers of the Lord.

Peter Brings Dorcas Back to Life

36In Joppa there was a follower named Tabitha. Her Greek name was Dorcas, which means "deer." She was always doing good things for people and had given much to the poor. 37But she got sick and died, and her body was washed and placed in an upstairs room. 38Joppa was not far from Lydda, and the followers heard that Peter was there. They sent two men to say to him, "Please come with us as quickly as you can!" 39Right away Peter went with them.

The men took Peter upstairs into the room. Many widows were there crying. They showed him the coats and clothes that Dorcas had made while she was still alive.

40After Peter had sent everyone out of the room, he kneeled down and prayed. Then he turned to the body of Dorcas and said, "Tabitha, get up!" The woman opened her eyes, and when she saw Peter, she sat up. 41He took her by the hand and helped her to her feet.

Jesus continues his work
(34) Notice that Peter didn't say *he* healed Aeneas. He said Jesus did. Remember, Jesus is not a dead hero; he is a living Savior. We are his body in the world today. Like Peter, all believers are in a position to do the work of Jesus. Are you a worker for the living Lord?

Could Peter raise people from death?
(40) If he were here, Peter would tell us he could do nothing except what Jesus did through him, including the raising up of Dorcas. We ought to think and pray constantly about how our Lord would wish to use us in his continuing work. Jesus Christ can do great things by his power working through us.

[c]and make up your bed: Or "and fix something to eat."

Peter called in the widows and the other followers and showed them that Dorcas had been raised from death. [42]Everyone in Joppa heard what had happened, and many of them put their faith in the Lord. [43]Peter stayed on for a while in Joppa in the house of a man named Simon, who made leather.

Peter and Cornelius

10 In Caesarea there was a man named Cornelius, who was the captain of a group of soldiers called "The Italian Unit." [2]Cornelius was a very religious man. He worshiped God, and so did everyone else who lived in his house. He had given a lot of money to the poor and was always praying to God.

[3]One afternoon at about three o'clock,[d] Cornelius had a vision. He saw an angel from God coming to him and calling him by name. [4]Cornelius was surprised and stared at the angel. Then he asked, "What is this all about?"

The angel answered, "God has heard your prayers and knows about your gifts to the poor. [5]Now send some men to Joppa for a man named Simon Peter. [6]He is visiting with Simon the leather maker, who lives in a house near the sea." [7]After saying this, the angel left.

Cornelius called in two of his servants and one of his soldiers who worshiped God. [8]He explained everything to them and sent them off to Joppa.

[9]The next day about noon these men were coming near to Joppa. Peter went up on the roof[e] of the house to pray [10]and became very hungry. While the food was being prepared, he fell sound asleep and had a vision. [11]He saw heaven open, and something came down like a huge sheet held up by its four corners. [12]In it were all kinds of animals,

God came to a Roman soldier

(3) God is in the business of saving all kinds of people, not only Jewish fishermen like Peter. Cornelius was an officer in the Roman army, and the Lord wanted to save him. The Gentile, non-Jewish world was being brought into the church. Cornelius was the beginning of this work.

---

[d]*at about three o'clock*: Probably while he was praying. See 3.1 and the note there.   [e]*roof*: In Palestine the houses usually had a flat roof. Stairs on the outside led up to the roof, which was made of beams and boards covered with packed earth.

snakes, and birds. [13]A voice said to him, "Peter, get up! Kill these and eat them."

[14]But Peter said, "Lord, I can't do that! I've never eaten anything that is unclean and not fit to eat."[f]

[15]The voice spoke to him again, "When God says that something can be used for food, don't say it isn't fit to eat."

[16]This happened three times before the sheet was suddenly taken back to heaven.

[17]Peter was still wondering what all of this meant, when the men sent by Cornelius came and stood at the gate. They had found their way to Simon's house [18]and were asking if Simon Peter was staying there.

[19]While Peter was still thinking about the vision, the Holy Spirit said to him, "Three[g] men are here looking for you. [20]Hurry down and go with them. Don't worry, I sent them."

[21]Peter went down and said to the men, "I am the one you are looking for. Why have you come?"

[22]They answered, "Captain Cornelius sent us. He is a good man and worships God. All the Jewish people like him. One of God's holy angels told Cornelius to send for you, so he could hear what you have to say." [23]Peter invited them to spend the night.

The next morning Peter and some of the Lord's followers in Joppa left with the men who had come from Cornelius. [24]The next day they all arrived in Caesarea where Cornelius was waiting for them. He had also invited his relatives and close friends.

[25]When Peter arrived, Cornelius greeted him. Then he kneeled at Peter's feet and started worshiping him. [26]But Peter took hold of him and said, "Stand up! I am nothing more than a human."

[27]As Peter entered the house, he was still talking with Cornelius. Many people were there, [28]and Peter said to them, "You know that we Jews are not allowed to have any-

Cornelius was a true follower of God

(22) Even before Peter came to him, Cornelius ha[d] worshiped God. The Jews had earlier spread all ov[er] the Roman Empire and ha[d] taken the Old Testament with them. Through the Je[ws] many Gentiles became wh[at] were called "God-fearers[.]" They didn't know about Jesus yet, but they worshiped God according to [what] they knew from the Old Te[s]tament.

Why did the Jews have such strict rules?

(28) Under the Law that God gave them, Jews we[re] not allowed to eat with Ge[n]tiles or have them as frien[ds.] This was God's way of keeping his people pure u[n]til Jesus came. If the Jews had not obeyed these rul[es,] they would have been mix[ed] in with the Gentiles, and th[ere] would no longer have bee[n] a separate race for Jesus th[e] Son of David to be born [into,] the Scriptures predicted.

---

[f]*unclean and not fit to eat*: The Law of Moses taught that some foods were not fit to eat.   [g]*Three*: Some manuscripts have "two;" one manuscript has "some."

chosen to judge the living and the dead. 43Every one of the prophets has said that all who have faith in Jesus will have their sins forgiven in his name.

44While Peter was still speaking, the Holy Spirit took control of everyone who was listening. 45Some Jewish followers of the Lord had come with Peter, and they were surprised that the Holy Spirit had been given to Gentiles. 46Now they were hearing Gentiles speaking unknown languages and praising God.

Peter said, 47"These Gentiles have been given the Holy Spirit, just as we have! I am certain that no one would dare stop us from baptizing them." 48Peter ordered them to be baptized in the name of Jesus Christ, and they asked him to stay on for a few days.

Peter Reports to the Church in Jerusalem

11 The apostles and the followers in Judea heard that Gentiles had accepted God's message. 2So when Peter came to Jerusalem, some of the Jewish leaders started arguing with him. They wanted Gentile followers to be circumcised, and 3they said, "You stayed in the homes of Gentiles, and you even ate with them!"

4Then Peter told them exactly what had happened:

5I was in the town of Joppa and was praying when I fell sound asleep and had a vision. I saw heaven open, and something like a huge sheet held by its four corners came down to me. 6When I looked in it, I saw animals, wild beasts, snakes, and birds. 7I heard a voice saying to me, "Peter, get up! Kill these and eat them."

8But I said, "Lord, I can't do that! I've never taken a bite of anything that is unclean and not fit to eat."*i*

9The voice from heaven spoke to me again, "When God says that something can be used for food, don't say it isn't

The Holy Spirit made the difference

(44) Until Peter came and preached the good news about Jesus to Cornelius, all the Gentile God-fearers had was the Law and the Old Testament. Peter said the old differences between Jews and Gentiles don't matter anymore. The Holy Spirit came into the lives of Cornelius and the other Gentiles. The Jewish Christians could see that they were all one family of God along with the Gentile believers.

The Church believed Peter

(4) Peter told the church at Jerusalem all that had happened to the Gentile believers. He shared the whole exciting story with the Christians at Jerusalem. Peter was not starting a new Gentile religion. The truths believed by Cornelius and the Gentiles had to be the same as those that were given to the Jewish Christians. No group of Christians is an item unto itself. We believers are all one family in God's eyes.

iunclean and not fit to eat: See the note at 10.14.

fit to eat." 10This happened three times before it was all taken back into heaven.

11Suddenly three men from Caesarea stood in front of the house where I was staying. 12The Holy Spirit told me to go with them and not to worry. Then six of the Lord's followers went with me to the home of a man 13who told us that an angel had appeared to him. The angel had ordered him to send to Joppa for someone named Simon Peter. 14Then Peter would tell him how he and everyone in his house could be saved.

15After I started speaking, the Holy Spirit was given to them, just as the Spirit had been given to us at the beginning. 16I remembered that the Lord had said, "John baptized with water, but you will be baptized with the Holy Spirit." 17God gave those Gentiles the same gift that he gave us when we put our faith in the Lord Jesus Christ. So how could I have gone against God?

18When the Jewish leaders heard Peter say this, they stopped arguing and started praising God. They said, "God has now let Gentiles turn to him, and he has given life to them!"

The Church in Antioch

19Some of the Lord's followers had been scattered because of the terrible trouble that started when Stephen was killed. They went as far as Phoenicia, Cyprus, and Antioch, but they told the message only to the Jews.

20Some of the followers from Cyprus and Cyrene went to Antioch and started telling Gentiles*j* the good news about the Lord Jesus. 21The Lord's power was with them, and many people turned to the Lord and put their faith in him. 22News of what was happening reached the church in Jerusa-

jGentiles: This translates a Greek word that may mean "people who speak Greek" or "people who live as Greeks do." Here the word seems to mean "people who are not Jews." Some manuscripts have "Greeks," which also seems to mean "people who are not Jews."

Trouble spreads the good news

(19) It had been a sad day for the Christians in Jerusalem when Stephen was put to death (see chapter 7). But God used this tragedy to spread the good news. Many Christians decided to leave Jerusalem and go up to live in Antioch, which was then a city in the country of Syria. There the Christians told the people of Syria about Christ, and many of them became Christians. Today, too, God often uses the bad times in our lives to bring about good.

Who was Barnabas?

(22) His name means "son of comfort," and he was a great comfort to Christians everywhere. When he saw how the Christians at Antioch believed, he could see that God was doing the same work there as he did

lem. Then they sent Barnabas to Antioch.
23When Barnabas got there and saw what
God had been kind enough to do for them,
he was very glad. So he begged them to
remain faithful to the Lord with all their
hearts. 24Barnabas was a good man of great
faith, and he was filled with the Holy Spirit.
Many more people turned to the Lord.

25Barnabas went to Tarsus to look for
Saul. 26He found Saul and brought him to
Antioch, where they met with the church
for a whole year and taught many of its
people. There in Antioch the Lord's followers were first called Christians.

27During this time some prophets from
Jerusalem came to Antioch. 28One of them
was Agabus. Then with the help of the
Spirit, he told that there would be a terrible
famine everywhere in the world. And it
happened when Claudius was Emperor.k
29The followers in Antioch decided to send
whatever help they could to the followers
in Judea. 30So they had Barnabas and Saul
take their gifts to the church leaders in
Jerusalem.

Herod Causes Trouble for the Church

12 At that time King Herodl caused terrible suffering for some members of
the church. 2He ordered soldiers to cut off
the head of James, the brother of John.
3When Herod saw that this pleased the Jewish people, he had Peter arrested during the
Feast of Thin Bread. 4He put Peter in jail
and ordered four squads of soldiers to guard
him. Herod planned to put him on trial in
public after the feast.

5While Peter was being kept in jail, the
church never stopped praying to God for
him.

Peter Is Rescued

6The night before Peter was to be put
on trial, he was asleep and bound by two

kwhen Claudius was Emperor: A.D. 41-54. lHerod:
Herod Agrippa I, the grandson of Herod the Great.

in Jerusalem. We can all be
"sons of comfort" by en-
couraging our brothers and
sisters in Christ about the
great work God is doing
through them wherever they
might be.

Saul was accepted at Antioch

(26) You will remember that
Saul (Paul) had gone back
to Tarsus to live. This city
was in an area called Cilicia, not far from Antioch.
Some time later, Barnabas
got Saul and brought him to
Antioch, which was by then
the headquarters of the
Christian church. The leaders at Antioch accepted Saul
as a Christian worker, and
he was sent with Barnabas
to help in Jerusalem. We see
how Saul had to "bide his
time" before God was
ready to use him. It must
have taken patience, but
Saul was able to prepare
during his time of waiting.
Sometimes God has us wait
like that. Are we patient? Do
we make good use of the
time?

Christians are not always tolerated

(2) King Herod Agrippa
killed the apostle James,
brother of the John who
wrote John's Gospel, and
jailed other church leaders.
He figured it would make
him popular. We may won-
der why Christians, a peace-
loving people, are often
hated by the world. The reason is that the world doesn't
love God and therefore
doesn't love God's people
either. Evil can't stand good.

chains. A soldier was guarding him on each side, and two other soldiers were guarding the entrance to the jail. 7Suddenly an angel from the Lord appeared, and light flashed around in the cell. The angel poked Peter in the side and woke him up. Then he said, "Quick! Get up!"

The chains fell off his hands, 8and the angel said, "Get dressed and put on your sandals." Peter did what he was told. Then the angel said, "Now put on your coat and follow me." 9Peter left with the angel, but he thought everything was only a dream. 10They went past the two groups of soldiers, and when they came to the iron gate to the city, it opened by itself. They went out and were going along the street, when all at once the angel disappeared.

11Peter now realized what had happened, and he said, "I am certain that the Lord sent his angel to rescue me from Herod and from everything the Jewish leaders planned to do to me." 12Then Peter went to the house of Mary the mother of John whose other name was Mark. Many of the Lord's followers had come together there and were praying.

13Peter knocked on the gate, and a servant named Rhoda came to the door. 14When she heard Peter's voice, she was too excited to open the gate. She ran back into the house and said that Peter was standing there.

15Everyone told her, "You are crazy!" But she kept saying that it was Peter. Then they said, "It must be his angel."m 16But Peter kept on knocking, until finally they opened the gate. They saw him and were completely amazed.

17Peter motioned for them to keep quiet. Then he told how the Lord had led him out of jail. He also said, "Tell James and the others what has happened." After that, he left and went somewhere else.

18The next morning the soldiers who had been on guard were terribly worried and wondered what had happened to Peter.

How was Peter rescued?
(7) To answer this question we must believe that God is able and willing to do what he did for Peter. A person who did not believe in God would be very puzzled by this. That person would have to explain Peter's escape in some other way. Non-believers have to explain a lot of things. It makes more sense to let God have the credit for what he has done.

Rhoda wasn't crazy
(14) The Christians were praying at the home of John Mark, author of Mark's Gospel. They were probably praying for Peter's release from prison. But when it happened, they didn't believe it. They thought Rhoda was crazy because she said Peter was at the door. Many times Christians are that way today—we have faith enough to pray, but not enough faith to expect an answer.

mhis angel: Probably meaning "his guardian angel."

[19]Herod ordered his own soldiers to search for him, but they could not find him. Then he questioned the guards and had them put to death. After this, Herod left Judea to stay in Caesarea for a while.

Herod Dies

[20]Herod and the people of Tyre and Sidon were very angry with each other. But their country got its food supply from the region that he ruled. So a group of them went to see Blastus, who was one of Herod's high officials. They convinced Blastus that they wanted to make peace between their cities and Herod, [21]and a day was set for them to meet with him.

Herod came dressed in his royal robes. He sat down on his throne and made a speech. [22]The people shouted, "You speak more like a god than a man!" [23]At once an angel from the Lord struck him down because he took the honor that belonged to God. Later, Herod was eaten by worms and died.

[24]God's message kept spreading. [25]And after Barnabas and Saul had done the work they were sent to do, they went back to Jerusalem[n] with John, whose other name was Mark.

Barnabas and Saul Are Chosen and Sent

13 The church at Antioch had several prophets and teachers. They were Barnabas, Simeon, also called Niger, Lucius from Cyrene, Manaen, who was Herod's[o] close friend, and Saul. [2]While they were worshiping the Lord and going without eating,[p] the Holy Spirit told them, "Appoint Barnabas and Saul to do the work for which I have chosen them." [3]Everyone prayed and went without eating for a while longer.

Human power comes to an end
(20) Herod Agrippa, who is the first Herod we read of in the book of Acts, was a cruel and brutal man. He was like the two Herods before him, written about in the Gospels. This Herod killed the soldiers who had guarded Peter before his escape. Then he pretended to be equal with God. But his power ended when he died of a terrible disease. Proud human power comes to a bad end.

God chose his servants
(2) Notice that the church at Antioch didn't decide to send Barnabas and Saul. God himself made the decision, while the people prayed and fasted (went without eating). The people were fasting not for health reasons or to punish themselves, but so they could concentrate more on praying. Meals take a lot of attention, and there are times when not having meals is helpful.

---

[n]*went back to Jerusalem*: Some manuscripts have "left Jerusalem," and others have "went to Antioch."   [o]*Herod's*: Herod Antipas, the son of Herod the Great.   [p]*going without eating*: The Jews often went without eating as a way of showing how much they loved God. This is also called "fasting."

Next, they placed their hands on Barnabas and Saul to show that they had been appointed to do this work. Then everyone sent them on their way.

Barnabas and Saul in Cyprus

⁴After Barnabas and Saul had been sent by the Holy Spirit, they went to Seleucia. From there they sailed to the island of Cyprus. ⁵They arrived at Salamis and began to preach God's message in the Jewish meeting places. They also had John*q* as a helper.

⁶They went all the way to the city of Paphos on the other end of the island, where they met a Jewish man named Bar-Jesus. He practiced witchcraft and was a false prophet. ⁷He also worked for Sergius Paul-

---

qJohn: Whose other name was Mark (12.12,25).

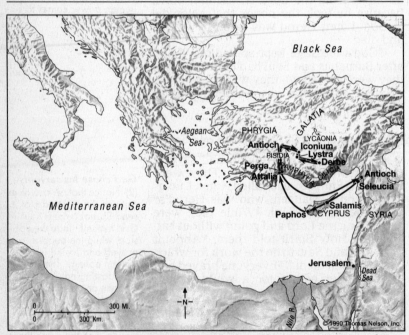

Paul's First Missionary Trip

us, who was very smart and was the governor of the island. Sergius Paulus wanted to hear God's message, and he sent for Barnabas and Saul. 8But Bar-Jesus, whose other name was Elymas, was against them. He even tried to keep the governor from having faith in the Lord.

9Then Saul, better known as Paul, was filled with the Holy Spirit. He looked straight at Elymas 10and said, "You son of the devil! You are a liar, a crook, and an enemy of everything that is right. When will you stop speaking against the true ways of the Lord? 11The Lord is going to punish you by making you completely blind for a while."

Suddenly the man's eyes were covered by a dark mist, and he went around trying to get someone to lead him by the hand. 12When the governor saw what had happened, he was amazed at this teaching about the Lord. So he put his faith in the Lord.

Paul and Barnabas in Antioch of Pisidia

13Paul and the others left Paphos and sailed to Perga in Pamphylia. But John*q* left them and went back to Jerusalem. 14The rest of them went on from Perga to Antioch in Pisidia. Then on the Sabbath they went to the Jewish meeting place and sat down.

15After the reading of the Law and the Prophets,*r* the leaders sent someone over to tell Paul and Barnabas, "Friends, if you have anything to say that will help the people, please say it."

16Paul got up. He motioned with his hand and said:

People of Israel, and everyone else who worships God, listen! 17The God of Israel chose our ancestors, and he let our people prosper while they were living in Egypt. Then with his mighty power he led them out, 18and for about

Introducing: Paul
(9) We see Saul and Barnabas going out as missionaries from Antioch to the lands that lay before them to the west. At this point we notice that Saul's name has been changed to Paul. Sometimes Christians changed their names as a way of reminding themselves that they were new people who were "born again." Saul means "asked for," and Paul means "little," which may tell us that Paul was sort of small physically. Or maybe it was Paul's way of being humble instead of proud like the old Saul.

The traveling good news
(14) Until this time, the good news about Jesus had been heard only in Israel and Syria. Then Cyprus heard it. Then Paul and Barnabas brought the good news to the regions of Pamphylia and Pisidia in Turkey. (In those days part of Turkey was called "Asia." Turkey is just a tiny part of the huge continent we call Asia today.)

---

qJohn: Whose other name was Mark (12.12,25). *rthe Law and the Prophets*: The Jewish Scriptures, that is, the Old Testament.

forty years he took care of[s] them in the desert. 19He destroyed seven nations in the land of Canaan and gave their land to our people. 20All this happened in about 450 years.

Then God gave our people judges until the time of the prophet Samuel, 21but the people demanded a king. So for forty years God gave them King Saul, the son of Kish from the tribe of Benjamin. 22Later, God removed Saul and let David rule in his place. God said about him, "David the son of Jesse is the kind of person who pleases me most! He does everything I want him to do."

23God promised that someone from David's family would come to save the people of Israel, and Jesus is that one. 24But before Jesus came, John was telling everyone in Israel to turn back to God and be baptized. 25Then, when John's work was almost done, he said, "Who do you people think I am? Do you think I am the Promised One? He will come later, and I am not good enough to untie his sandals."

26Now listen, you descendants of Abraham! Pay attention, all of you Gentiles who are here to worship God! Listen to this message about how to be saved, because it is for everyone. 27The people of Jerusalem and their leaders didn't realize who Jesus was. And they didn't understand the words of the prophets that they read each Sabbath. So they condemned Jesus just as the prophets had said.

28-29They did exactly what the Scriptures said they would. Even though they couldn't find any reason to put Jesus to death, they still asked Pilate to have him killed.

After Jesus had been put to death, he was taken down from the cross[t] and put in a tomb. 30But God raised him from

Paul preached about the Son of David

(23) In Pisidia there was another town called Antioch (not to be confused with the town of the same name in Syria). Paul and Barnabas stayed in this Antioch many days, and Paul preached a great sermon. He showed how God's old promise to save both Jews and Gentiles was fulfilled in the work of Jesus Christ the Lord, the Son of David. Many people in Antioch believed the good news and came back the following week to hear more.

---

[s]took care of: Some manuscripts have "put up with."
[t]cross: This translates a Greek word that means "wood," "pole," or "tree."

death! 31Then for many days Jesus appeared to his followers who had gone with him from Galilee to Jerusalem. Now they are telling our people about him.

32God made a promise to our ancestors. And we are here to tell you the good news 33that he has kept this promise to us. It is just as the second Psalm says about Jesus,

"You are my son because today
I have become your Father."

34God raised Jesus from death and will never let his body decay. It is just as God said,

"I will make to you
the same holy promise
that I made to David."

35And in another psalm it says, "God will never let the body of his Holy One decay."

36When David was alive, he obeyed God. Then after he died, he was buried in the family grave, and his body decayed. 37But God raised Jesus from death, and his body did not decay.

38My friends, the message is that Jesus can forgive your sins! The Law of Moses could not set you free from all your sins. 39But everyone who has faith in Jesus is set free. 40Make sure that what the prophets have said doesn't happen to you. They said,

41"Look, you people
who make fun of God!
Be amazed
and disappear.
I will do something today
that you won't believe,
even if someone
tells you about it!"

42As Paul and Barnabas were leaving the meeting, the people begged them to say more about these same things on the next Sabbath. 43After the service, many Jews and a lot of Gentiles who worshiped God went with them. Paul and Barnabas begged them all to remain faithful to God, who had been so kind to them.

The Jewish Scriptures point to Jesus

(33) As we saw earlier in the preaching of Peter and Stephen, and as we see in Paul's speech here, the early Christians were very clear that the news about Jesus was not a new thing. The history of Israel, as told in the Scriptures, had been leading up to him for centuries. A Jew who believed the word of God should have believed in the Messiah whom God predicted he would send.

⁴⁴The next Sabbath almost everyone in town came to hear the message about the Lord.ᵘ ⁴⁵When the Jewish people saw the crowds, they were very jealous. They insulted Paul and spoke against everything he said.

⁴⁶But Paul and Barnabas bravely said:

We had to tell God's message to you before we told it to anyone else. But you rejected the message! This proves that you don't deserve eternal life. Now we are going to the Gentiles. ⁴⁷The Lord has given us this command,

"I have placed you here
as a light
for the Gentiles.
You are to take
the saving power of God
to people everywhere
on earth."

⁴⁸This message made the Gentiles glad, and they praised what they had heard about the Lord.ᵘ Everyone who had been chosen for eternal life then put their faith in the Lord.

⁴⁹The message about the Lord spread all over that region. ⁵⁰But the Jewish leaders went to some of the important men in the town and to some respected women who were religious. They turned them against Paul and Barnabas and started making trouble for them. They even chased them out of that part of the country.

⁵¹Paul and Barnabas shook the dust from that place off their feetᵛ and went on to the city of Iconium.

⁵²But the Lord's followers in Antioch were very happy and were filled with the Holy Spirit.

Paul and Barnabas in Iconium

14 Paul and Barnabas spoke in the Jewish meeting place in Iconium, just as

Jews rejected the message and Gentiles accepted it
(46) Here is an amazing thing. The Jews had been the ones who gave us the promise of the coming Messiah. But now that he had come, most Jews rejected him. On the other hand, the Gentiles had been outsiders to what God had done for the Jews. But here it is Gentiles we see welcoming the good news. God is always reaching out to people who will listen to his word.

The apostles kept moving
(1) Paul and Barnabas didn't wait around to be killed in Antioch. The believers there would carry on the work. But the apostles went on to the next city, Iconium. There they preached the good news again, and again some believed. But others wanted to kill the apostles. Christians must realize that everybody is not on God's side. The good news will please some and anger others.

ᵘ*the Lord*: Some manuscripts have "God." ᵛ*shook the dust from that place off their feet*: This was a way of showing rejection.

they had done at Antioch, and many Jews and Gentiles[w] put their faith in the Lord. [2]But the Jews who did not have faith in him made the other Gentiles angry and turned them against the Lord's followers.

[3]Paul and Barnabas stayed there for a while, having faith in the Lord and bravely speaking his message. The Lord gave them the power to work miracles and wonders, and he showed that their message about his great kindness was true.

[4]The people of Iconium did not know what to think. Some of them believed the Jewish group, and others believed the apostles. [5]Finally, some Gentiles and Jews, together with their leaders, decided to make trouble for Paul and Barnabas and to kill them by throwing stones at them.

[6-7]But when the two apostles found out what was happening, they escaped to the region of Lycaonia. They preached the good news there in the towns of Lystra and Derbe and in the nearby countryside.

Paul and Barnabas in Lystra

[8]In Lystra there was a man who had been born with crippled feet and had never been able to walk. [9]The man was listening to Paul speak, when Paul saw that he had faith in Jesus and could be healed. So he looked straight at the man [10]and shouted, "Stand up!" The man jumped up and started walking around.

[11]When the crowd saw what Paul had done, they yelled out in the language of Lycaonia, "The gods have turned into humans and have come down to us!" [12]They gave Barnabas the name Zeus, and they gave Paul the name Hermes,[x] because he did the talking.

[13]The temple of Zeus was near the entrance to the city. Its priest and the crowds

Can people be gods?
(11) Of course people cannot be gods, only children of the one true God. The people of Lystra wanted to believe that Barnabas and Paul were gods. The two apostles "tore their clothes"—a Jewish way of expressing grief—and pleaded with the people not to worship them. One basic problem humans have is that they want to "hero worship" other humans. But God said, "You shall have no other gods."

---

[w]*Gentiles*: The Greek text has "Greeks," which probably means people who were not Jews. But it may mean Gentiles who worshiped with the Jews.   [x]*Hermes*: The Greeks thought of Hermes as the messenger of the other gods, especially of Zeus, their chief god.

wanted to offer a sacrifice to Barnabas and Paul. So the priest brought some bulls and flowers to the city gates. 14When the two apostles found out about this, they tore their clothes in horror and ran to the crowd, shouting:

15Why are you doing this? We are humans just like you. Please give up all this foolishness. Turn to the living God, who made the sky, the earth, the sea, and everything in them. 16In times past, God let each nation go its own way. 17But he showed that he was there by the good things he did. God sends rain from heaven and makes your crops grow. He gives food to you and makes your hearts glad.

18Even after Paul and Barnabas had said all this, they could hardly keep the people from offering a sacrifice to them.

19Some Jewish leaders from Antioch and Iconium came and turned the crowds against Paul. They hit him with stones and dragged him out of the city, thinking he was dead. 20But when the Lord's followers gathered around Paul, he stood up and went back into the city. The next day he and Barnabas went to Derbe.

Paul and Barnabas Return to Antioch in Syria

21Paul and Barnabas preached the good news in Derbe and won some people to the Lord. Then they went back to Lystra, Iconium, and Antioch in Pisidia. 22They encouraged the followers and begged them to remain faithful. They told them, "We have to suffer a lot before we can get into God's kingdom." 23Paul and Barnabas chose some of those who had faith in the Lord to be leaders for each of the churches. Then they went without eatingʸ and prayed that the Lord would take good care of these leaders.

24Paul and Barnabas went on through Pisidia to Pamphylia, 25where they preached in the town of Perga. Then they went down

Why did they want to kill Paul?

(19) It's not easy to explain human spite—resentment of something new, jealousy, fear of what we don't understand. All of these things cause people to act the way they did toward Paul. Christians are not fanatics—we have no need to strike out in anger against our enemies. God takes care of us and defends us. God defended Paul, too.

Paul and Barnabas retraced their steps

(21) The two apostles went back through the towns they had visited. This gave them a chance to see people there who had believed in Jesus. That's a good policy: to "follow up" on the people with whom we have shared the good news, to make sure they are growing well in their faith.

ʸwent without eating: See the note at 13.2.

to Attalia [26]and sailed to Antioch in Syria. It was there that they had been placed in God's care for the work they had now completed.[z]

[27]After arriving in Antioch, they called the church together. They told the people what God had helped them do and how he had made it possible for the Gentiles to believe. [28]Then they stayed there with the followers for a long time.

15 Some people came from Judea and started teaching the Lord's followers that they could not be saved, unless they were circumcised as Moses had taught. [2]This caused trouble, and Paul and Barnabas argued with them about this teaching. So it was decided to send Paul and Barnabas and a few others to Jerusalem to discuss this problem with the apostles and the church leaders.

The Church Leaders Meet in Jerusalem

[3]The men who were sent by the church went through Phoenicia and Samaria and told how the Gentiles had turned to God. This news made the Lord's followers very happy. [4]When the men arrived in Jerusalem, they were welcomed by all the church, including the apostles and the leaders. They told them everything that God had helped them do. [5]But some Pharisees had become followers of the Lord. They stood up and said, "Gentiles who have faith in the Lord must be circumcised and told to obey the Law of Moses."

[6]The apostles and church leaders met to discuss this problem about Gentiles. [7]They had talked it over for a long time, when Peter got up and said:

My friends, you know that God decided long ago to let me be the one from your group to preach the good news to the Gentiles. God did this so that they would hear and obey him. [8]He knows what is in everyone's heart. And he showed that he had chosen the Gentiles,

What was the meeting about?
(6) Paul and Barnabas had just finished the first great Christian missionary journey to the Gentiles. While they were gone, some of the Jewish Christians were upset because Paul and Barnabas didn't make Gentile Christians obey the strict Jewish laws. So the Christian leaders met in Jerusalem to decide what to do.

[z]*the work they had now completed:* See 13.1-3.

when he gave them the Holy Spirit, just as he had given his Spirit to us. 9God treated them in the same way that he treated us. They put their faith in him, and he made their hearts pure.

10Now why are you trying to make God angry by placing a heavy burden on these followers? This burden was too heavy for us or our ancestors. 11But our Lord Jesus was kind to us Jews, and we are saved by faith in him, just as the Gentiles are.

12Everyone kept quiet and listened as Barnabas and Paul told how God had given them the power to work a lot of miracles and wonders for the Gentiles.

13After they had finished speaking, James*a* said:

My friends, listen to me! 14Simon Peter*b* has told how God first came to the Gentiles and made some of them his own people. 15This agrees with what the prophets wrote,

16"I, the Lord, will return
and rebuild
   David's fallen house.
I will build it from its ruins
   and set it up again.
17Then other nations
   will turn to me
   and be my chosen ones.
I, the Lord, say this.
18   I promised it long ago."

19And so, my friends, I don't think we should place burdens on the Gentiles who are turning to God. 20We should simply write and tell them not to eat anything that has been offered to idols. They should be told not to eat the meat of any animal that has been strangled or that still has blood in it. They must also not commit any terrible sexual sins.*c*

What was decided at the Jerusalem meeting?

(13) Peter made it clear that both Jews and Gentiles are saved through faith in Jesus, and not by following Jewish customs. Gentile Christians should not have been asked to live exactly like the Jews. James, the leader at Jerusalem, agreed and said that the Gentiles must obey laws having to do with morality and offerings to idols, but not the special Jewish religious customs.

aJames: The Lord's brother. *bSimon Peter*: The Greek text has "Simeon," which is another form of the name "Simon." The apostle Peter is meant. *cnot commit any terrible sexual sins*: This probably refers to the laws about the wrong kind of marriages that are forbidden in Leviticus 18.6-18 or to some serious sexual sin.

21We must remember that the Law of Moses has been preached in city after city for many years, and every Sabbath it is read when we Jews meet.

A Letter to Gentiles Who Had Faith in the Lord

22The apostles, the leaders, and all the church members decided to send some men to Antioch along with Paul and Barnabas. They chose Silas and Judas Barsabbas,d who were two leaders of the Lord's followers. 23They wrote a letter that said:

We apostles and leaders send friendly greetings to all of you Gentiles who are followers of the Lord in Antioch, Syria, and Cilicia.

24We have heard that some people from here have terribly upset you by what they said. But we did not send them! 25So we met together and decided to choose some men and to send them to you along with our good friends Barnabas and Paul. 26These men have risked their lives for our Lord Jesus Christ. 27We are also sending Judas and Silas, who will tell you in person the same things that we are writing.

28The Holy Spirit has shown us that we should not place any extra burden on you. 29But you should not eat anything offered to idols. You should not eat any meat that still has the blood in it or any meat of any animal that has been strangled. You must also not commit any terrible sexual sins. If you follow these instructions, you will do well.

We send our best wishes.

30The four men left Jerusalem and went to Antioch. Then they called all the church members together and gave them the letter. 31When the letter was read, it made everyone glad and gave them lots of encouragement. 32Judas and Silas were prophets, and

How bad was the "Gentile problem"?

(23) Many things were not yet clear about the new faith. Just how did God expect the Gentile Christians to live? This question caused bad feeling against Paul, because some Jewish Christians thought he was too easy on the Gentiles. Some accused him of being a false apostle because he didn't make the Gentiles keep the Jewish customs. The letter from Jerusalem helped to calm the Jewish believers, but that was not the end of arguments in the church. Groups of Christians continue to make trouble about issues that aren't very important in God's eyes.

---

dJudas Barsabbas: He may have been a brother of Joseph Barsabbas (see 1.23), but the name "Barsabbas" was often used by the Jewish people.

they spoke a long time, encouraging and helping the Lord's followers.

³³The men from Jerusalem stayed on in Antioch for a while. And when they left to return to the ones who had sent them, the followers wished them well. ³⁴⁻³⁵But Silas, Paul, and Barnabas stayed on in Antioch, where they and many others taught and preached about the Lord.^e

Paul and Barnabas Go Their Separate Ways

³⁶Sometime later Paul said to Barnabas, "Let's go back and visit the Lord's followers in all the cities where we preached his message. Then we will know how they are doing." ³⁷Barnabas wanted to take along John, whose other name was Mark. ³⁸But Paul did not want to, because Mark had left them in Pamphylia and had stopped working with them.

³⁹Paul and Barnabas argued, then each of them went his own way. Barnabas took Mark and sailed to Cyprus, ⁴⁰but Paul took Silas and left after the followers had placed them in God's care. ⁴¹They traveled through Syria and Cilicia, encouraging the churches.

Timothy Works with Paul and Silas

16 Paul and Silas went back to Derbe and Lystra, where there was a follower named Timothy. His mother was also a follower. She was Jewish, and his father was Greek. ²The Lord's followers in Lystra and Iconium said good things about Timothy, ³and Paul wanted him to go with them. But Paul first had him circumcised, because all the Jewish people around there knew that Timothy's father was Greek.^f

⁴As Paul and the others went from city to city, they told the followers what the apostles and leaders in Jerusalem had de-

---

^eVerse 34, which says that Silas decided to stay on in Antioch, is not in some manuscripts. ^fhad him circumcised . . . Timothy's father was Greek: Timothy would not have been acceptable to the Jews unless he had been circumcised, and Greeks did not circumcise their sons.

Christians sometimes disagree
(37) You sometimes have to be tough-minded to be an effective Christian. We see this in the argument between Paul and Barnabas about John Mark. This young man was Barnabas' nephew, and he had left the apostles on their first trip. So Paul said "No" to John on the second trip. But later in life Paul praised John Mark as a useful young friend in the Lord (see 2 Timothy 4.11).

A young helper taken on
(1) We will hear more about this young man. Paul wrote two letters to him, 1 and 2 Timothy. Notice that Paul wasn't totally against the Jewish practice of circumcision. By granting circumcision to Timothy, Paul avoided a useless quarrel with the Jews, many of whom would have welcomed such an excuse to reject the message Paul was bringing.

cided, and they urged them to follow these instructions. ⁵The churches became stronger in their faith, and each day more people put their faith in the Lord.

Paul's Vision in Troas

⁶Paul and his friends went through Phrygia and Galatia, but the Holy Spirit would not let them preach in Asia. ⁷After they arrived in Mysia, they tried to go into Bithynia, but the Spirit of Jesus would not let them. ⁸So they went on through Mysia until they came to Troas.

⁹During the night, Paul had a vision of someone from Macedonia who was standing there and begging him, "Come over to Macedonia and help us!" ¹⁰After Paul had seen the vision, we began looking for a way

Paul called to Europe
(6) Up to this point, the good news had gone only as far west as Asia Minor (present-day Turkey). Paul's dream told him that God was about to send the good news further westward to Europe. So Paul set out for Macedonia in northern Greece.

Luke was an eyewitness
(10) The last few chapters have been mostly about Paul, Barnabas, and then Silas. So far the author has used the "they" pronoun. Here the writer begins to use

Paul's Second Missionary Trip

to go to Macedonia. We were sure that God had called us to preach the good news there.

Lydia Becomes a Follower of the Lord

¹¹We sailed from Troas and went straight to Samothrace. The next day we arrived in Neapolis. ¹²From there we went to Philippi, which is a Roman colony in the first district of Macedonia.ᵍ

We spent several days in Philippi. ¹³Then on the Sabbath we went outside the city gate to a place by the river, where we thought there would be a Jewish meeting place for prayer. We sat down and talked with the women who came. ¹⁴One of them was Lydia, who was from the city of Thyatira and sold expensive purple cloth. She was a worshiper of the Lord God, and he made her willing to accept what Paul was saying. ¹⁵Then after she and her family were baptized, she kept on begging us, "If you think I really do have faith in the Lord, come stay in my home." Finally, we accepted her invitation.

Paul and Silas Are Put in Jail

¹⁶One day on our way to the place of prayer, we were met by a slave girl. She had a spirit in her that gave her the power to tell the future. By doing this she made a lot of money for her owners. ¹⁷The girl followed Paul and the rest of us and kept yelling, "These men are servants of the Most High God! They are telling you how to be saved."

¹⁸This went on for several days. Finally, Paul got so upset that he turned and said to the spirit, "In the name of Jesus Christ, I order you to leave this girl alone!" At once the evil spirit left her.

¹⁹When the girl's owners realized that they had lost all chances for making more money, they grabbed Paul and Silas and dragged them into court. ²⁰They told the

ᵍ*in the first district of Macedonia*: Some manuscripts have "and the leading city of Macedonia."

the word "we," which shows he had just joined the group. Luke, the author of Acts, accompanied Paul, Silas, and Timothy on their journey into Greece.

A great Christian lady
(14) Lydia was a wealthy merchant. As a leader in her community she must have had great influence for the Christian faith. We are impressed by her kindness to the apostles. Kind hearts and kind deeds make the good news hard to resist.

Evil takes many forms
(18) Here was a young female slave who was inspired by Satan to say all the right things in the wrong way. She told everybody in a loud voice what the apostles were doing. But people were being scared off by this loud-mouthed young woman. So Paul drove out the evil spirit that was causing her behavior.

officials, "These Jews are upsetting our city! 21They are telling us to do things we Romans are not allowed to do."

22The crowd joined in the attack on Paul and Silas. Then the officials tore the clothes off the two men and ordered them to be beaten with a whip. 23After they had been badly beaten, they were put in jail, and the jailer was told to guard them carefully. 24The jailer did as he was told. He put them deep inside the jail and chained their feet to heavy blocks of wood.

25About midnight Paul and Silas were praying and singing praises to God, while the other prisoners listened. 26Suddenly a strong earthquake shook the jail to its foundations. The doors opened, and the chains fell from all the prisoners.

27When the jailer woke up and saw that the doors were open, he thought that the prisoners had escaped. He pulled out his sword and was about to kill himself. 28But Paul shouted, "Don't harm yourself! No one has escaped."

29The jailer asked for a torch and went into the jail. He was shaking all over as he kneeled down in front of Paul and Silas. 30After he had led them out of the jail, he asked, "What must I do to be saved?"

31They replied, "Have faith in the Lord Jesus and you will be saved! This is also true for everyone who lives in your home."

32Then Paul and Silas told him and everyone else in his house about the Lord. 33While it was still night, the jailer took them to a place where he could wash their cuts and bruises. Then he and everyone in his home were baptized. 34They were very glad that they had put their faith in God. After this, the jailer took Paul and Silas to his home and gave them something to eat.

35The next morning the officials sent some police with orders for the jailer to let Paul and Silas go. 36The jailer told Paul, "The officials have ordered me to set you free. Now you can leave in peace."

37But Paul told the police, "We are Ro-

Satan never gives up
(23) The slave girl was free, but this made Satan's servants angry at Paul and Silas. The men who owned her had made money from her fortune telling. Now they had lost their income from her. So they got even with the apostles by having them thrown in jail. Don't be surprised if everything seems to go wrong in your life just when you have done a great work for God.

Our bad times can be God's good times
(26) God uses the hard times in our lives to make good things happen. Many people would have given up hope, but Paul and Silas were singing in jail. Then God acted, and they were free.

A jailer came to Christ
(31) This is one of the great missionary passages in the New Testament. "What must I do to be saved?" has its answer: "Have faith in the Lord Jesus." This is the answer to everyone who has been defeated in life. The jailer trusted in Jesus. Then he and his family were saved. There must have been quite a celebration at that jailer's home.

man citizens,[h] and the Roman officials had us beaten in public without giving us a trial. They threw us into jail. Now do they think they can secretly send us away? No, they cannot! They will have to come here themselves and let us out."

[38]When the police told the officials that Paul and Silas were Roman citizens, the officials were afraid. [39]So they came and apologized. They led them out of the jail and asked them to please leave town. [40]But Paul and Silas went straight to the home of Lydia, where they saw the Lord's followers and encouraged them. Then they left.

Trouble in Thessalonica

17 After Paul and his friends had traveled through Amphipolis and Apollonia, they went on to Thessalonica. A Jewish meeting place was in that city. [2]So as usual, Paul went there to worship, and on three Sabbaths he spoke to the people. He used the Scriptures [3]to show them that the Messiah had to suffer, but that he would rise from death. Paul also told them that Jesus is the Messiah he was preaching about. [4]Some of the Jews believed what Paul had said, and they became followers with Paul and Silas. Some Gentiles[i] and many important women also believed the message.

[5]The Jewish leaders were jealous and got some worthless bums who hung around the marketplace to start a riot in the city. They wanted to drag Paul and Silas out to the mob, and so they went straight to Jason's home. [6]But when they did not find them there, they dragged out Jason and some of the Lord's followers. They took them to the city authorities and shouted, "Paul and Silas have been upsetting things everywhere. Now they have come here, [7]and Jason has welcomed them into his home. All of them break the laws of the Roman Emperor by

More struggle

(2) Others besides the local Jewish leaders were allowed to speak at meeting places on the Sabbath. So Paul was able to use the meeting places wherever he went, to preach the good news about the Messiah for whom the Jews had been waiting. But the authorities at Thessalonica were jealous of Paul's success, so they caused a riot. Then Paul and Silas were arrested again.

Does the good news bring peace?

(6) We've heard it said that the good news about Jesus brings peace, and so the Bible says. But what about Paul and Silas? It seems that trouble followed them everywhere. We *do* have peace within, but Jesus said that the message about him would cause trouble with those who do not know him (see John 16.2, 3).

[h]*Roman citizens:* Only a small number of the people living in the Roman Empire were citizens, and they had special rights and privileges. [i]*Gentiles:* See the note at 14.1.

claiming that someone named Jesus is king."

⁸The officials and all the people were upset when they heard this. ⁹So they made Jason and the other followers pay bail before they would let them go.

People in Berea Welcome the Message

¹⁰That same night the Lord's followers sent Paul and Silas on to Berea, and after they arrived, they went to the Jewish meeting place. ¹¹The people in Berea were much nicer than those in Thessalonica, and they gladly accepted the message. Day after day they studied the Scriptures to see if these things were true. ¹²Many of them put their faith in the Lord, including some important Greek women and several men.

¹³When the Jewish leaders in Thessalonica heard that Paul had been preaching God's message in Berea, they went there and caused trouble by turning the crowds against Paul.

¹⁴Right away the followers sent Paul down to the coast, but Silas and Timothy stayed in Thessalonica. ¹⁵Some men went with Paul as far as Athens. They returned with instructions for Silas and Timothy to join him as soon as possible.

Paul in Athens

¹⁶While Paul was waiting in Athens, he was upset to see all the idols in the city. ¹⁷He went to the Jewish meeting place to speak to the Jews and to anyone who worshiped with them. Day after day he also spoke to everyone he met in the market. ¹⁸Some of them were Epicureans*ʲ* and some were Stoics,*ᵏ* and they started arguing with him.

People were asking, "What is this know-it-all trying to say?"

Sometimes we are encouraged

(11) Paul and Silas were welcomed at Berea. The people at the Jewish meeting place were eager to hear and read about Jesus the Messiah. Then many put their trust in Christ. But once again there was trouble—the Jewish leaders followed the apostles to Berea and made life hard for them.

ʲEpicureans: People who followed the teaching of a man named Epicurus, who taught that happiness should be the main goal in life.   *ᵏStoics*: Followers of a man named Zeno, who taught that people should learn self-control and be guided by their consciences.

Some even said, "Paul must be preaching about foreign gods! That's what he means when he talks about Jesus and about people rising from death."[l]

19They brought Paul before a council called the Areopagus, and said, "Tell us what your new teaching is all about. 20We have heard you say some strange things, and we want to know what it means."

21More than anything else the people of Athens and the foreigners living there loved to hear and to talk about anything new. 22So Paul stood up in front of the council and said:

People of Athens, I see that you are very religious. 23As I was going through your city and looking at the things you worship, I found an altar with the words, "To an Unknown God." You worship this God, but you don't really know him. So I want to tell you about him. 24This God made the world and everything in it. He is Lord of heaven and earth, and he doesn't live in temples built by human hands. 25He doesn't need help from anyone. He gives life, breath, and everything else to all people. 26From one person God made all nations who live on earth, and he decided when and where every nation would be.

27God has done all this, so that we will look for him and reach out and find him. He is not far from any of us, 28and he gives us the power to live, to move, and to be who we are. "We are his children," just as some of your poets have said.

29Since we are God's children, we must not think that he is like an idol made out of gold or silver or stone. He is not like anything that humans have thought up and made. 30In the past God forgave all this because people did not know what they were doing. But now he says that everyone everywhere must turn to him. 31He has set a day when

[l]*people rising from death*: Or "a goddess named 'Rising from Death.'"

"Wisdom" at Athens

(21) Athens was the cultural center of the world in Paul's day. Here the great leaders in human wisdom had taught for years—men like Socrates, Plato, and Aristotle. The people of Athens were very proud of their great thinkers. But the good news sounded like nonsense to most of the citizens. The idea of a risen Savior seemed impossible to them—as it does to many wise heads today.

Paul's learning

(28) Paul had been more than just a Jewish teacher who knew only the Scriptures, as good as that would have been. He had grown up in Tarsus of Cilicia, second only to Athens for its learning. A great university and brilliant teachers were there. So Paul knew the wisdom of the Greeks, and he was able to speak to them about their beliefs. But most Athenians were not interested in Paul's message. They were satisfied with themselves.

he will judge all the world's people with fairness. And he has chosen the man Jesus to do the judging for him. God has given proof of this to all of us by raising Jesus from death.

32As soon as the people heard Paul say that a man had been raised from death, some of them started laughing. Others said, "We'll hear you talk about this some other time." 33When Paul left the council meeting, 34some of the men put their faith in the Lord and went with Paul. One of them was a council member named Dionysius. A woman named Damaris and several others also put their faith in the Lord.

Paul in Corinth

18 Paul left Athens and went to Corinth, 2where he met Aquila, a Jewish man from Pontus. Not long before this, Aquila had come from Italy with his wife Priscilla, because Emperor Claudius had ordered all the Jewish people to leave Rome.m Paul went to see Aquila and Priscilla 3and found out that they were tent makers. Paul was a tent maker too. So he stayed with them, and they worked together.

4Every Sabbath Paul went to the Jewish meeting place. He spoke to Jews and Gentilesn and tried to win them over. 5But after Silas and Timothy came from Macedonia, he spent all his time preaching to the Jews about Jesus the Messiah. 6Finally, they turned against him and insulted him. So he shook the dust from his clotheso and told them, "Whatever happens to you will be your own fault! I am not to blame. From now on I am going to preach to the Gentiles."

7Paul then moved into the house of a man named Titius Justus, who worshiped God and lived next door to the Jewish meeting

Corinth needed the news
(1) Corinth was an important city near the southern tip of Greece. Paul spent about eighteen months there preaching and setting up a Christian church. He had more success in Corinth than at Athens, even though Corinth was a very immoral city. But the most undesirable people in the world are often the people God is seeking. Corinth is where Paul met Aquila and Priscilla, a couple who helped him very much in his ministry.

---

mEmperor Claudius had ordered all the Jewish people to leave Rome: Probably A.D. 49, though it may have been A.D. 41. nGentiles: Here the word is "Greeks." But see the note at 14.1. oshook the dust from his clothes: This means the same as shaking dust from the feet. See the note at 13.51.

place. 8Crispus was the leader of the meeting place. He and everyone in his family put their faith in the Lord. Many others in Corinth also heard the message, and all the people who had faith in the Lord were baptized.

9One night Paul had a vision, and in it the Lord said, "Don't be afraid to keep on preaching. Don't stop! 10I am with you, and you won't be harmed. Many people in this city belong to me." 11Paul stayed on in Corinth for a year and a half, teaching God's message to the people.

12While Gallio was governor of Achaia, some of the Jewish leaders got together and grabbed Paul. They brought him into court 13and said, "This man is trying to make our people worship God in a way that is against our Law!"

14Even before Paul could speak, Gallio said, "If you were charging this man with a crime or some other wrong, I would have to listen to you. 15But since this concerns only words, names, and your own law, you will have to take care of it. I refuse to judge such matters." 16Then he sent them all out of the court. 17The crowd grabbed Sosthenes, the Jewish leader, and beat him up in front of the court. But none of this mattered to Gallio.

Paul Returns to Antioch in Syria

18After Paul had stayed for a while with the Lord's followers in Corinth, he told them good-by and sailed on to Syria with Aquila and Priscilla. But before he left, he had his head shavedp at Cenchreae because he had made a promise to God.

19The three of them arrived in Ephesus, where Paul left Priscilla and Aquila. He then went into the Jewish meeting place to talk with the people there. 20They asked him to

The Lord protects us
(9) Just as elsewhere, the Jewish leaders at Corinth rejected the good news about Christ. So Paul began preaching to the Gentiles. But surprisingly, Justus and the leader of the Jewish meeting place accepted Paul's message. Then, however, some of the community's leading Jews had Paul arrested. But see how God caused the Roman governor to let Paul go. The Lord is in charge of our lives, and harm cannot come to us without his permission.

The end of Paul's second mission
(18) This is the second time Paul had gone out from Antioch in Syria, the Christian headquarters, to preach the good news to the Gentiles of the Western world. On this second trip Paul had gone beyond Asia Minor to Macedonia and Greece. He returned to Antioch by way of Ephesus.

phe had his head shaved: Paul had promised to be a "Nazarite" for a while. This meant that for the time of the promise, he could not cut his hair or drink wine. When the time was over, he would have to cut his hair and offer a sacrifice to God.

stay longer, but he refused. 21He told them good-by and said, "If God lets me, I will come back."

22Paul sailed to Caesarea, where he greeted the church. Then he went on to Antioch. 23After staying there for a while, he left and visited several places in Galatia and Phrygia. He helped all the followers there to become stronger in their faith.

Apollos in Ephesus

24A Jewish man named Apollos came to Ephesus. Apollos had been born in the city of Alexandria. He was a very good speaker and knew a lot about the Scriptures. 25He also knew much about the Lord's Way,q and he spoke about it with great excitement. What he taught about Jesus was right, but

The beginning of Paul's third journey
(23) This was Paul's last real missionary trip. He went back to Asia Minor and there visited the Roman provinces of Galatia and Phrygia. He had been there before and had started new churches. Now Paul was encouraging these young churches. He cared deeply about the people he had led to faith in Jesus.

qthe Lord's Way: See the note at 9.2.

Paul's Third Missionary Trip

all he knew was John's message about baptism.

26Apollos started speaking bravely in the Jewish meeting place. But when Priscilla and Aquila heard him, they took him to their home and helped him understand God's Way even better.

27Apollos decided to travel through Achaia. So the Lord's followers wrote letters and encouraged the followers there to welcome him. After Apollos arrived in Achaia, he was a great help to everyone who had put their faith in the Lord Jesus because of God's kindness. 28He got into fierce arguments with the Jewish people, and in public he used the Scriptures to prove that Jesus is the Messiah.

We have to grow up in our Christian faith
(26) Apollos seems to have been a bright young man. But he had a lot to learn. He can be thankful that Paul's friends, Priscilla and Aquila, were on hand to help Apollos understand the full meaning of the good news. We are all on our way to God's eternal city, and we need one another's help along the road. Like Apollos, let's be good learners as we go.

Paul in Ephesus

19 While Apollos was in Corinth, Paul traveled across the hill country to Ephesus, where he met some of the Lord's followers. 2He asked them, "When you put your faith in Jesus, were you given the Holy Spirit?"

"No!" they answered. "We have never even heard of the Holy Spirit."

3"Then why were you baptized?" Paul asked.

They answered, "Because of what John taught."*r*

4Paul replied, "John baptized people so that they would turn to God. But he also told them that someone else was coming, and that they should put their faith in him. Jesus is the one that John was talking about." 5After the people heard Paul say this, they were baptized in the name of the Lord Jesus. 6Then Paul placed his hands on them. The Holy Spirit was given to them, and they spoke unknown languages and prophesied. 7There were about twelve men in this group.

Ephesus reached for Christ
(1) Ephesus was an important Roman city on the western coast of Asia Minor. There again Paul was opposed by many of the Jews. But he stayed in Ephesus for about three years, preaching and teaching. To really reach people for Jesus, the church should be a place where Christians are taught the word of God in detail.

*r*Then why were you baptized? . . . Because of what John taught: Or "In whose name were you baptized? . . . We were baptized in John's name."

8For three months Paul went to the Jewish meeting place and talked bravely with the Jewish people about God's kingdom. He tried to win them over, 9but some of them were stubborn and refused to believe. In front of everyone they said terrible things about God's Way. Paul left and took the followers with him to the lecture hall of Tyrannus. He spoke there every day 10for two years, until every Jew and Gentile^s in Asia had heard the Lord's message.

The Sons of Sceva

11God gave Paul the power to work great miracles. 12People even took handkerchiefs and aprons that had touched Paul's body, and they carried them to everyone who was sick. All of the sick people were healed, and the evil spirits went out.

13Some Jewish men started going around trying to force out evil spirits by using the name of the Lord Jesus. They said to the spirits, "Come out in the name of that same Jesus that Paul preaches about!"

14Seven sons of a Jewish high priest named Sceva were doing this, 15when an evil spirit said to them, "I know Jesus! And I have heard about Paul. But who are you?" 16Then the man with the evil spirit jumped on them and beat them up. They ran out of the house, naked and bruised.

17All the Jews and Gentiles^s in Ephesus heard about this. They were so frightened that they praised the name of the Lord Jesus. 18Many who were followers now started telling everyone about the evil things they had been doing. 19Some who had been practicing witchcraft even brought their books and burned them in public. These books were worth about fifty thousand silver coins. 20So the Lord's message spread and became even more powerful.

Fakes really exist
(13) Loving everybody doesn't mean accepting everybody's teaching. We have to know the difference between truth and falsehood. There are people who go around offering themselves as messengers of truth, but like the sons of Sceva they are really out for personal power. False teachers are often showy and self-important. Many times just common sense will track down a fake. And the Bible is always the test of truth.

^sGentile(s): The text has "Greek(s)" (see the note at 14.1).

The Riot in Ephesus

21After all of this had happened, Paul decided[t] to visit Macedonia and Achaia on his way to Jerusalem. Paul had said, "From there I will go on to Rome." 22So he sent his two helpers, Timothy and Erastus, to Macedonia. But he stayed on in Asia for a while.

23At that time there was serious trouble because of the Lord's Way.[u] 24A silversmith named Demetrius had a business that made silver models of the temple of the goddess Artemis. Those who worked for him earned a lot of money. 25Demetrius brought together everyone who was in the same business and said:

Friends, you know that we make a good living at this. 26But you have surely seen and heard how this man Paul is upsetting a lot of people, not only in Ephesus, but almost everywhere in Asia. He claims that the gods we humans make are not really gods at all. 27Everyone will start saying terrible things about our business. They will stop respecting the temple of the goddess Artemis, who is worshiped in Asia and all over the world. Our great goddess will be forgotten!

28When the workers heard this, they got angry and started shouting, "Great is Artemis, the goddess of the Ephesians!" 29Soon the whole city was in a riot, and some men grabbed Gaius and Aristarchus, who had come from Macedonia with Paul. Then everyone in the crowd rushed to the place where the town meetings were held.

30Paul wanted to go out and speak to the people, but the Lord's followers would not let him. 31A few of the local officials were friendly to Paul, and they sent someone to warn him not to go.

32Some of the people in the meeting were shouting one thing, and others were shouting something else. Everyone was com-

A riot about idols

(23) Many Ephesians worshiped a statue named Artemis, which people claimed fell from heaven. Paul's message about the one true God hurt the business of metalworkers who made idols, so they started a riot. Paul's message was brave, clear, and direct. It left no doubt that the idol dealers were not in keeping with God's truth.

---

[t]*Paul decided*: Or "Paul was led by the Holy Spirit."
[u]*the Lord's Way*: See the note at 9.2.

pletely confused, and most of them did not even know why they were there.

³³Several of the Jewish leaders pushed a man named Alexander to the front of the crowd and started telling him what to say. He motioned with his hand and tried to explain what was going on. ³⁴But when the crowd saw that he was Jewish, they all shouted for two hours, "Great is Artemis, the goddess of the Ephesians!"

³⁵Finally, a town official made the crowd be quiet. Then he said:

People of Ephesus, who in the world does not know that our city is the center for worshiping the great goddess Artemis? Who does not know that her image which fell from heaven is right here? ³⁶No one can deny this, and so you should calm down and not do anything foolish. ³⁷You have brought men in here who have not robbed temples or spoken against our goddess.

³⁸If Demetrius and his workers have a case against these men, we have courts and judges. Let them take their complaints there. ³⁹But if you want to do more than that, the matter will have to be brought before the city council. ⁴⁰We could easily be accused of starting a riot today. There is no excuse for it! We cannot even give a reason for this uproar.

⁴¹After saying this, he told the people to leave.

The truth wins in the end
(35) There is still a lot of common sense in the world, and the town official had lots of it. We don't know what his personal faith was, but he had the ability to see right and wrong, and he soon cooled the rioters down. God has people everywhere who will not let lies go unchecked. Let's be thankful for all kinds of helpers along the way.

Paul Goes Through Macedonia and Greece

20 When the riot was over, Paul sent for the followers and encouraged them. He then told them good-by and left for Macedonia. ²As he traveled from place to place, he encouraged the followers with many messages. Finally, he went to Greeceᵛ ³and stayed there for three months.

Paul was about to sail to Syria. But some of the Jewish leaders plotted against him, so he decided to return by way of Macedo-

ᵛGreece: Probably Corinth.

nia. 4With him were Sopater, son of Pyrrhus from Berea, and Aristarchus and Secundus from Thessalonica. Gaius from Derbe was also with him, and so were Timothy and the two Asians, Tychicus and Trophimus. 5They went on ahead to Troas and waited for us there. 6After the Festival of Thin Bread, we sailed from Philippi. Five days later we met them in Troas and stayed there for a week.

Paul's Last Visit to Troas

7On the first day of the weekw we met to worship and to break bread together.x Paul spoke to the people until midnight because he was leaving the next morning. 8In the upstairs room where we were meeting, there were a lot of lamps. 9A young man by the name of Eutychus was sitting on a window sill. While Paul was speaking, the young man got very sleepy. Finally, he went to sleep and fell three floors all the way down to the ground. When they picked him up, he was dead.

10Paul went down and bent over Eutychus. He took him in his arms and said, "Don't worry! He's alive." 11After Paul had gone back upstairs, he broke bread, and ate with us. He then spoke until dawn and left. 12Then the followers took the young man home alive and were very happy.

The Voyage from Troas to Miletus

13Paul decided to travel by land to Assos. The rest of us went on ahead by ship, and we were to take him aboard there. 14When he met us in Assos, he came aboard, and we sailed on to Mitylene. 15The next day we came to a place near Chios, and the following day we reached Samos. The day after that we sailed to Miletus. 16Paul had decided to sail on past Ephesus, because he did not want to spend too much time in Asia.

wOn the first day of the week: Since the Jewish day began at sunset, the meeting would have begun in the evening.   xbreak bread together: See the note at 2.42.

The festival of thin bread
(6) About 3,500 years ago, God led the ancient Jews out of slavery in Egypt. This was called "the Passover," which was celebrated in the early spring. The "festival of thin bread" was celebrated for seven days after Passover started. "Thin bread" means bread that is not mixed with leaven, or yeast, to make the bread rise. This festival was the way the Jews remembered that they had no time to wait for bread to rise when they were escaping from Egypt.

Stay awake
(9) Eutychus (pronounced YOU-ti-kus) must not have been very excited by Paul's preaching. Paul himself said he was not a great speaker. Let's be attentive to God's word at all times, even if we have to force ourselves to stay awake. Preachers may not always be fascinating, but the truth is always important.

Being a Christian is work
(15) Christians don't just sit around reading the Bible and praying, as necessary as these activities are. There is also work to do for God, and sometimes the work is hard. Paul's travels were hard work, but it was worth it in order to get the good news about Jesus to people.

He was in a hurry and wanted to be in Jerusalem in time for Pentecost.ʸ

Paul Says Good-by to the Church Leaders of Ephesus

¹⁷From Miletus Paul sent a message for the church leaders at Ephesus to come and meet with him. ¹⁸When they got there, he said:

You know everything I did during the time I was with you when I first came to Asia. ¹⁹Some of the Jews plotted against me and caused me a lot of sorrow and trouble. But I served the Lord and was humble. ²⁰When I preached in public or taught in your homes, I didn't hold back from telling anything that would help you. ²¹I told Jews and Gentiles to turn to God and have faith in our Lord Jesus.

²²I don't know what will happen to me in Jerusalem, but I must obey God's Spirit and go there. ²³In every city that I visit, the Holy Spirit tells me I will be put in jail and will be in trouble in Jerusalem. ²⁴But I don't care what happens to me, as long as I finish the work that the Lord Jesus gave me to do. And that work is to tell the good news about God's great kindness.

²⁵I have gone from place to place, preaching to you about God's kingdom, but now I know that none of you will ever see me again. ²⁶I tell you today that I am no longer responsible for any of you! ²⁷I have told you everything that God wants you to know. ²⁸Look after yourselves and everyone the Holy Spirit has placed in your care. Be like shepherds to God's church. It is the flock that he bought with the blood of his own Son.ᶻ

²⁹I know that after I am gone, others will come like fierce wolves to attack

A Christian understands the real world
(24) Paul didn't kid himself. He knew that the world was against his message. But he was prepared to obey God because he also knew the good news would win in the long run. Christians must look beyond the present to the future—and the goal of helping people to know Jesus as Savior.

ʸ*in time for Pentecost:* The Jewish people liked to be in Jerusalem for this festival. See the note at 2.1.   ᶻ*the blood of his own Son:* Or "his own blood."

you. 30Some of your own people will tell lies to win over the Lord's followers. 31Be on your guard! Remember how day and night for three years I kept warning you with tears in my eyes.

32I now place you in God's care. Remember the message about his great kindness! This message can help you and give you what belongs to you as God's people. 33I have never wanted anyone's money or clothes. 34You know how I have worked with my own hands to make a living for myself and my friends. 35By everything I did, I showed how you should work to help everyone who is weak. Remember that our Lord Jesus said, "More blessings come from giving than from receiving."

36After Paul had finished speaking, he kneeled down with all of them and prayed. 37Everyone cried and hugged and kissed him. 38They were especially sad because Paul had told them, "You will never see me again."

Then they went with him to the ship.

Paul Goes to Jerusalem

21 After saying good-by, we sailed straight to Cos. The next day we reached Rhodes and from there sailed on to Patara. 2We found a ship going to Phoenicia, so we got on board and sailed off.

3We came within sight of Cyprus and then sailed south of it on to the port of Tyre in Syria. The ship was going to unload its cargo there. 4We looked up the Lord's followers and stayed with them for a week. The Holy Spirit had told them to warn Paul not to go on to Jerusalem. 5But when the week was over, we started on our way again. All the men, together with their wives and children, walked with us from the town to the seashore. We kneeled on the beach and prayed. 6Then after saying good-by to each other, we got into the ship, and they went back home.

7We sailed from Tyre to Ptolemais, where we greeted the followers and stayed with

Christians are not freeloaders

(34) A freeloader is able to work, but lives by the work of others. Paul was willing to work with his own hands to make a living. Whatever your calling may be in the world, be sure you aren't just loafing. Be sure you are producing something that will give glory to God and be of real benefit to mankind.

A Christian lives in hope

(5) We might wonder what kept Paul going. He couldn't see, as we do, the centuries ahead when his work would have such great results. But he lived and worked in the confidence that God's way must win at last. As we trust God to help us, we also have Paul's confidence that our work for God will not be useless.

them for a day. 8The next day we went to Caesarea and stayed with Philip, the preacher. He was one of the seven men who helped the apostles, 9and he had four unmarried*a* daughters who prophesied.

10We had been in Caesarea for several days, when the prophet Agabus came to us from Judea. 11He took Paul's belt, and with it he tied up his own hands and feet. Then he told us, "The Holy Spirit says that some of the Jewish leaders in Jerusalem will tie up the man who owns this belt. They will also hand him over to the Gentiles." 12After Agabus said this, we and the followers living there begged Paul not to go to Jerusalem.

13But Paul answered, "Why are you crying and breaking my heart? I am not only willing to be put in jail for the Lord Jesus. I am even willing to die for him in Jerusalem!"

14Since we could not get Paul to change his mind, we gave up and said, "Lord, please make us willing to do what you want."

15Then we got ready to go to Jerusalem. 16Some of the followers from Caesarea went with us and took us to stay in the home of Mnason. He was from Cyprus and had been a follower from the beginning.

Paul Visits James

17When we arrived in Jerusalem, the Lord's followers gladly welcomed us. 18Paul went with us to see James*b* the next day, and all the church leaders were present. 19Paul greeted them and told how God had used him to help the Gentiles. 20Everyone who heard this praised God and said to Paul:

My friend, you can see how many tens of thousands of the Jewish people have become followers! And all of them are eager to obey the Law of Moses. 21But they have been told that you are teaching those who live among the Gentiles to disobey this Law. They claim

Was Paul a fanatic?
(13) Paul was willing to die for Christ—and eventually he did. The term "fanatic" is usually a way of describing an overexcited or overzealous person. So we ask the question, was Paul an overzealous fanatic? No. The difference here is that Christ is truly worth dying for.

James
(18) We see that Paul visited "James" in Jerusalem. We saw this James earlier in Acts 15, when he made a speech stating the decision of the council at Jerusalem. This James was a leader of the Jerusalem church. He was also a younger brother of Jesus. James came to believe in Jesus after his brother rose from death. (This is not the James written about in Acts 12.2, who was the brother of John the apostle.)

---

aunmarried: Or "virgin."   *bJames*: The Lord's brother.

that you are telling them not to circumcise their sons or to follow Jewish customs.

22What should we do now that our people have heard that you are here? 23Please do what we ask, because four of our men have made special promises to God. 24Join with them and prepare yourself for the ceremony that goes with the promises. Pay the cost for their heads to be shaved. Then everyone will learn that the reports about you are not true. They will know that you do obey the Law of Moses.

25Some while ago we told the Gentile followers what we think they should do. We instructed them not to eat anything offered to idols. They were told not to eat any meat with blood still in it or the meat of an animal that has been strangled. They were also told not to commit any terrible sexual sins.c

26The next day Paul took the four men with him and got himself ready at the same time they did. Then he went into the temple and told them when the final ceremony would take place and when an offering would be made for each of them.

Paul Is Arrested

27When the period of seven days for the ceremony was almost over, some of the Jewish people from Asia saw Paul in the temple. They got a large crowd together and started attacking him. 28They were shouting, "Friends, help us! This man goes around everywhere, saying bad things about our nation and about the Law of Moses and about this temple. He has even brought shame to this holy temple by bringing in Gentiles." 29Some of them thought that Paul had brought Trophimus from Ephesus into the temple, because they had seen them together in the city.

30The whole city was in an uproar, and

cnot to commit any terrible sexual sins: See the note at 15.20.

Don't let your faith become bigotry

(30) The Jews at Jerusalem had a great heritage. God had given them great promises. But they turned bitter because Jewish Christians had been associating with Gentiles. Many Jews wanted to put a stop to this and have Paul killed. It was an act of bigotry—wanting to harm someone for religious reasons. We ought to learn from this ugly scene and avoid bigotry in our own hearts.

the people turned into a mob. They grabbed
Paul and dragged him out of the temple.
Then suddenly the doors were shut. 31The
people were about to kill Paul when the Roman army commander heard that all Jerusalem was starting to riot. 32So he quickly
took some soldiers and officers and ran to
where the crowd had gathered.

As soon as the mob saw the commander
and soldiers, they stopped beating Paul.
33The army commander went over and arrested him and had him bound with two
chains. Then he tried to find out who Paul
was and what he had done. 34Part of the
crowd shouted one thing, and part of them
shouted something else. But they were making so much noise that the commander
could not find out a thing. Then he ordered
Paul to be taken into the fortress. 35As they
reached the steps, the crowd became so wild
that the soldiers had to lift Paul up and carry
him. 36The crowd followed and kept shouting, "Kill him! Kill him!"

Paul Speaks to the Crowd

37When Paul was about to be taken into
the fortress, he asked the commander, "Can
I say something to you?"

"How do you know Greek?" the commander asked. 38"Aren't you that Egyptian
who started a riot not long ago and led four
thousand terrorists into the desert?"

39"No!" Paul replied. "I am a Jew from
Tarsus, an important city in Cilicia. Please
let me speak to the crowd."

40The commander told him he could
speak, so Paul stood on the steps and motioned to the people. When they were quiet,
he spoke to them in Aramaic:

22 "My friends and leaders of our nation, listen as I explain what happened!" 2When the crowd heard Paul speak
to them in Aramaic, they became even
quieter. Then Paul said:

3I am a Jew, born and raised in the
city of Tarsus in Cilicia. I was a student
of Gamaliel and was taught to follow
every single law of our ancestors. In

*Thank God for good
government*
(34) No human government
is perfect, but God expects
us to obey the just laws of
our government. If it had not
been for the Roman com-
mander, the Jews would
have murdered Paul. It's
pretty sad that a pagan government was more merciful
than God's chosen people
were at that time.

fact, I was just as eager to obey God as any of you are today.

⁴I made trouble for everyone who followed the Lord's Way,ᵈ and I even had some of them killed. I had others arrested and put in jail. I didn't care if they were men or women. ⁵The high priest and all the council members can tell you that this is true. They even gave me letters to the Jewish leaders in Damascus, so that I could arrest people there and bring them to Jerusalem to be punished.

⁶One day about noon I was getting close to Damascus, when a bright light from heaven suddenly flashed around. ⁷I fell to the ground and heard a voice asking me, "Saul, Saul, why are you so cruel to me?"

⁸"Who are you?" I answered.

The Lord replied, "I am Jesus from Nazareth! I am the one you are so cruel to." ⁹The men who were traveling with me saw the light, but did not hear the voice.

¹⁰I asked, "Lord, what do you want me to do?"

Then he told me, "Get up and go to Damascus. When you get there, you will be told what to do." ¹¹The light had been so bright that I couldn't see. And the other men had to lead me by the hand to Damascus.

¹²In that city there was a man named Ananias, who faithfully obeyed the Law of Moses and was well liked by all the Jewish people living there. ¹³He came to me and said, "Saul, my friend, you can now see again!"

At once I could see. ¹⁴Then Ananias told me, "The God that our ancestors worshiped has chosen you to know what he wants done. He has chosen you to see the One Who Obeys Godᵉ and to hear his voice. ¹⁵You must tell everyone what you have seen and heard.

Do you have a story to tell?

(3) Christians should be ready to tell others about how they came to Christ. Not all of us will have a dramatic message like Paul's, but it will be a good story if it's real. Maybe you found Christ as a child at home— or maybe in a prison—but it's always a great story regardless.

ᵈfollowed the Lord's Way: See the note at 9.2.   ᵉOne Who Obeys God: That is, Jesus.

16What are you waiting for? Get up! Be baptized, and wash away your sins by praying to the Lord."

17After this I returned to Jerusalem and went to the temple to pray. There I had a vision 18of the Lord who said to me, "Hurry and leave Jerusalem! The people will not listen to what you say about me."

19I replied, "Lord, they know that in many of our meeting places I arrested and beat people who had faith in you. 20Stephen was killed because he spoke for you, and I stood there and cheered them on. I even guarded the clothes of the men who murdered him."

21But the Lord told me to go, and he promised to send me far away to the Gentiles.

22The crowd listened until Paul said this. Then they started shouting, "Get rid of this man! He doesn't deserve to live." 23They kept shouting. They even tore their clothes and threw dust into the air.

Paul and the Roman Army Commander

24The Roman commander ordered Paul to be taken into the fortress and beaten with a whip. He did this to find out why the people were screaming at Paul.

25While the soldiers were tying Paul up to be beaten, he asked the officer standing there, "Is it legal to beat a Roman citizen before he has been tried in court?"

26When the officer heard this, he went to the commander and said, "What are you doing? This man is a Roman citizen!"

27The commander went to Paul and asked, "Tell me, are you a Roman citizen?"

"Yes," Paul answered.

28The commander then said, "I paid a lot of money to become a Roman citizen."*f*

But Paul replied, "I was born a Roman citizen."

29The men who were about to beat and question Paul quickly backed off. And the

Paul "hit a nerve"
(22) The crowd was willing to listen to Paul's detailed story of how he came to know the Lord Jesus—until Paul "hit a nerve" by mentioning that he would take the good news to the Gentiles too. The Jerusalem crowd would not believe that God's blessings could go outside of Israel. Sadly, even today people still have such wrong attitudes about race, language, or place of birth.

fRoman citizen: See the note at 16.37.

commander himself was frightened when he realized that he had put a Roman citizen in chains.

Paul Is Tried by the Council

30The next day the commander wanted to know the real reason why the Jewish leaders had brought charges against Paul. So he had Paul's chains removed, and he ordered the chief priests and the whole council to meet. Then he had Paul led in and made him stand in front of them.

23 Paul looked straight at the council members and said, "My friends, to this day I have served God with a clear conscience!"

2Then Ananias the high priest ordered the men standing beside Paul to hit him on the mouth. 3Paul turned to the high priest and said, "You whitewashed wall!g God will hit you. You sit there to judge me by the Law of Moses. But at the same time you order men to break the Law by hitting me."

4The men standing beside Paul asked, "Don't you know you are insulting God's high priest?"

5Paul replied, "Oh! I didn't know he was the high priest. The Scriptures do tell us not to speak evil about a leader of our people."

6When Paul saw that some of the council members were Sadducees and others were Pharisees, he shouted, "My friends, I am a Pharisee and the son of a Pharisee. I am on trial simply because I believe that the dead will be raised to life."

7As soon as Paul said this, the Pharisees and the Sadducees got into a big argument, and the council members started taking sides. 8The Sadducees do not believe in angels or spirits or that the dead will rise to life. But the Pharisees believe in all of these, 9and so there was a lot of shouting. Some of the teachers of the Law of Moses were Pharisees. Finally, they became angry and

It pays to be wise
(1) Paul finally had to stand before the council. Quickly he turned the tables by showing that it was the high priest who was the law-breaker. Then he got the Pharisees and Sadducees into an argument between themselves. So the Roman commander had to take Paul safely away from danger. Paul had used his wits very well, and we should too.

gwhitewashed wall: Someone who pretends to be good, but really isn't.

said, "We don't find anything wrong with this man. Maybe a spirit or an angel really did speak to him."

10The argument became fierce, and the commander was afraid that Paul would be pulled apart. So he ordered the soldiers to go in and rescue Paul. Then they took him back into the fortress.

11That night the Lord stood beside Paul and said, "Don't worry! Just as you have told others about me in Jerusalem, you must also tell about me in Rome."

A Plot to Kill Paul

12-13The next morning more than forty Jewish men got together and vowed that they would not eat or drink anything until they had killed Paul. 14Then some of them went to the chief priests and the nation's leaders and said, "We have promised God that we would not eat a thing until we have killed Paul. 15You and everyone in the council must go to the commander and pretend that you want to find out more about the charges against Paul. Ask for him to be brought before your court. Meanwhile, we will be waiting to kill him before he gets there."

16When Paul's nephew heard about the plot, he went to the fortress and told Paul about it. 17So Paul said to one of the army officers, "Take this young man to the commander. He has something to tell him."

18The officer took the young man to the commander and said, "The prisoner named Paul asked me to bring this young man to you, because he has something to tell you."

19The commander took the young man aside and asked him in private, "What do you want to tell me?"

20He answered, "Some men are planning to ask you to bring Paul down to the Jewish council tomorrow. They will claim that they want to find out more about him. 21But please don't do what they say. More than forty men are going to attack Paul. They have made a vow not to eat or drink any-

God is near us in trouble (11) After the uproar between the Pharisees and Sadducees, the Lord visited Paul and promised to be with him. In the darkest night of your trouble God will comfort you, too. The Lord is not a faraway God, but a God who is always near, a God who makes himself known to us when we need him.

thing until they have killed him. Even now they are waiting to hear what you decide."

22The commander sent the young man away after saying to him, "Don't let anyone know that you told me this."

Paul Is Sent to Felix the Governor

23The commander called in two of his officers and told them, "By nine o'clock tonight have two hundred soldiers ready to go to Caesarea. Take along seventy men on horseback and two hundred foot soldiers with spears. 24Get a horse ready for Paul and make sure that he gets safely through to Felix the governor."

25The commander wrote a letter that said:

26Greetings from Claudius Lysias to the Honorable Governor Felix:

27Some Jews grabbed this man and were about to kill him. But when I found out that he was a Roman citizen, I took some soldiers and rescued him.

28I wanted to find out what they had against him. So I brought him before their council 29and learned that the charges concern only their Jewish laws. This man is not guilty of anything for which he should die or even be put in jail.

30As soon as I learned that there was a plot against him, I sent him to you and told their leaders to bring charges against him in your court.

31The soldiers obeyed the commander's orders, and that same night they took Paul to the city of Antipatris. 32The next day the foot soldiers returned to the fortress and let the soldiers on horseback take him the rest of the way. 33When they came to Caesarea, they gave the letter to the governor and handed Paul over to him.

34The governor read the letter. Then he asked Paul and found out that he was from Cilicia. 35The governor said, "I will listen to your case as soon as the people come to bring their charges against you." After

A continuing struggle
(23) The Jews were not satisfied that Paul was arrested, but they wanted to murder him. So they plotted against him. Once again, God had a way to save Paul from his enemies. Even the Romans seemed to be sympathetic to Paul. So the commander sent Paul to the governor's city under heavy guard.

Use the tools you have
(27) Paul was not wealthy, and he didn't have a lot of friends in the Roman world. Many people wanted him dead. But Paul was a Roman citizen. It's almost funny at times how Paul was able to use his rights as a citizen to escape harm. Eventually he even got a free sea trip to Rome. Don't be afraid to use every good tool you have to get God's work done.

saying this, he gave orders for Paul to be
kept as a prisoner in Herod's palace.*h*

Paul Is Accused in the Court of Felix

24 Five days later Ananias the high
priest, together with the Jewish leaders and a lawyer named Tertullus, went to
the governor to present their case against
Paul. 2So Paul was called in, and Tertullus
stated the case against him:*i*

Honorable Felix, you have brought
our people a long period of peace, and
because of your concern our nation is
much better off. 3All of us are always
grateful for what you have done. 4I don't
want to bother you, but please be patient
with us and listen to me for just a few
minutes.

5This man has been found to be a
real pest and troublemaker for Jews all
over the world. He is also a leader of
a group called Nazarenes. 6-8When he
tried to disgrace the temple, we arrested
him.*j* If you question him, you will find
out for yourself that all our charges are
true.

9The Jewish crowd spoke up and
agreed with what Tertullus had said.

Paul Defends Himself

10The governor motioned for Paul to
speak, and he began:

I know that you have judged the people of our nation for many years, and
I am glad to defend myself in your court.
11It was no more than twelve days
ago that I went to worship in Jerusalem.
You can find this out easily enough.

Was Paul a pest?
(5) No doubt the Jews
thought Paul was a pest, and
his preaching greatly irri-
tated them. This was probably a tough burden for Paul
to carry—to be hated so by
his own people. But he had
to make the choice between
the friendship of his people
and the friendship of God.
Every Christian has to make
this choice at some time.

---

hHerod's palace: The palace built by Herod the Great
and used by the Roman governors of Palestine. *iPaul
was called in, and Tertullus stated the case against
him*: Or "Tertullus was called in and stated the case
against Paul." *jwe arrested him*: Some manuscripts
add, "We wanted to judge him by our own laws. But
Lysias the commander took him away from us by force.
Then Lysias ordered us to bring our charges against
this man in your court."

12Never once did the Jews find me arguing with anyone in the temple. I didn't cause trouble in the Jewish meeting places or in the city itself. 13There is no way that they can prove these charges that they are now bringing against me.

14I admit that the Jewish leaders think that the Lord's Way^k which I follow is based on wrong beliefs. But I still worship the same God that my ancestors worshiped. And I believe everything written in the Law of Moses and in the Prophets.^l 15I am just as sure as these people are that God will raise from death everyone who is good or evil. 16And because I am sure, I try my best to have a clear conscience in whatever I do for God or for people.

17After being away for several years, I returned here to bring gifts for the poor people of my nation and to offer sacrifices. 18This is what I was doing when I was found going through a ceremony in the temple. I was not with a crowd, and there was no uproar.

19Some Jews from Asia were there at that time, and if they have anything to say against me, they should be here now. 20Or ask the ones who are here. They can tell you that they didn't find me guilty of anything when I was tried by their own council. 21The only charge they can bring against me is what I shouted out in court, when I said, "I am on trial today because I believe that the dead will be raised to life!"

22Felix knew a lot about the Lord's Way.^m But he brought the trial to an end and said, "I will make my decision after Lysias the commander arrives." 23He then ordered the army officer to keep Paul under guard, but not to lock him up or to stop his friends from helping him.

God's peace gives us clear minds

(16) Paul knew he had done no wrong—to God or to his people. But he was accused of disturbing the peace. All the same, Paul had God's peace, as always when he testified for Christ. So Paul was able to show that the charges against him were nonsense. When we have peace with God we can think straight.

---

^kthe Lord's Way: See the note at 9.2. ^lLaw of Moses . . . the Prophets: The Jewish Scriptures, that is, the Old Testament. ^mthe Lord's Way: See the note at 9.2.

Paul Is Kept Under Guard

24Several days later Felix and his wife Drusilla, who was Jewish, went to the place where Paul was kept under guard. They sent for Paul and listened while he spoke to them about having faith in Christ Jesus. 25But Felix was frightened when Paul started talking to them about doing right, about self-control, and about the coming judgment. So he said to Paul, "That's enough for now. You may go. But when I have time I will send for you." 26After this, Felix often sent for Paul and talked with him, because he hoped that Paul would offer him a bribe.

27Two years later Porcius Festus became governor in place of Felix. But since Felix wanted to do the Jewish leaders a favor, he kept Paul in jail.

Paul Asks to Be Tried by the Roman Emperor

25 Three days after Festus had become governor, he went from Caesarea to Jerusalem. 2There the chief priests and the Jewish leaders told him about their charges against Paul. They also asked Festus 3if he would be willing to bring Paul to Jerusalem. They begged him to do this because they were planning to attack and kill Paul on the way. 4But Festus told them, "Paul will be kept in Caesarea, and I am soon going there myself. 5If he has done anything wrong, let your leaders go with me and bring charges against him there."

6Festus stayed in Jerusalem for eight or ten more days before going to Caesarea. Then the next day he took his place as judge and had Paul brought into court. 7As soon as Paul came in, the Jewish leaders from Jerusalem crowded around him and said he was guilty of many serious crimes. But they could not prove anything. 8Then Paul spoke in his own defense, "I have not broken the Law of my people. And I have not done anything against either the temple or the Emperor."

9Festus wanted to please the Jewish leaders. So he asked Paul, "Are you willing to

Felix wanted a bribe
(26) Even today in many countries, you can hardly get civil servants to do anything for you unless you bribe them. Paul ran into this problem with Felix. Paul probably had no money and would not have bribed Felix if he had. So he stayed in jail for two years.

go to Jerusalem and be tried by me on these charges?"

10Paul replied, "I am on trial in the Emperor's court, and that's where I should be tried. You know very well that I have not done anything to harm the Jewish nation. 11If I had done something deserving death, I would not ask to escape the death penalty. But I am not guilty of any of these crimes, and no one has the right to hand me over to these Jews. I now ask to be tried by the Emperor himself."

12After Festus had talked this over with members of his council, he told Paul, "You have asked to be tried by the Emperor, and to the Emperor you will go!"

Paul Speaks to Agrippa and Bernice

13A few days later King Agrippa and Bernice came to Caesarea to visit Festus. 14They had been there for several days, when Festus told the king about the charges against Paul. He said:

Felix left a man here in jail, 15and when I went to Jerusalem, the chief priests and the Jewish leaders came and asked me to find him guilty. 16I told them that it is not the Roman custom to hand a man over to people who are bringing charges against him. He must first have the chance to meet them face to face and to defend himself against their charges.

17So when they came here with me, I wasted no time. On the very next day I took my place on the judge's bench and ordered him to be brought in. 18But when the men stood up to make their charges against him, they did not accuse him of any of the crimes that I thought they would. 19Instead, they argued with him about some of their Jewish beliefs and about a dead man named Jesus, who Paul said was alive.

20Since I did not know how to find out the truth about all this, I asked Paul if he would be willing to go to Jerusalem and be put on trial there. 21But Paul

Paul's appeal to Rome
(10) Whatever we think of the ancient Romans, they were famous for their system of laws. We see an example of this in Paul's appeal to Rome. He couldn't get a fair trial in Palestine because the Jews hated him so much. But the law allowed Paul, a citizen of Rome, to be taken there for trial. So the governor had to let Paul take a sea trip to Rome to be tried.

Another King Agrippa
(13) This was King Agrippa the Second, the son of the King Agrippa who had put James the apostle to death (Acts 12). Agrippa the Second was less than thirty years old at the time of the events in Acts 25. Years later, he returned to Rome after Jerusalem was destroyed, and he died in the year 100.

asked to be kept in jail until the Emperor could decide his case. So I ordered him to be kept here until I could send him to the Emperor.

22Then Agrippa said to Festus, "I would also like to hear what this man has to say."

Festus answered, "You can hear him tomorrow."

23The next day Agrippa and Bernice made a big show as they came into the meeting room. High ranking army officers and leading citizens of the town were also there. Festus then ordered Paul to be brought in 24and said:

King Agrippa and other guests, look at this man! Every Jew from Jerusalem and Caesarea has come to me, demanding for him to be put to death. 25I have not found him guilty of any crime deserving death. But because he has asked to be judged by the Emperor, I have decided to send him to Rome.

26I have to write some facts about this man to the Emperor. So I have brought him before all of you, but especially before you, King Agrippa. After we have talked about his case, I will then have something to write. 27It makes no sense to send a prisoner to the Emperor without stating the charges against him.

Paul's Defense before Agrippa

26 Agrippa told Paul, "You may now speak for yourself."

Paul stretched out his hand and said:

2King Agrippa, I am glad for this chance to defend myself before you today on all these charges that my own people have brought against me. 3You know a lot about our Jewish customs and the beliefs that divide us. So I ask you to listen patiently to me.

4-5All the Jews have known me since I was a child. They know what kind of life I have lived in my own country and in Jerusalem. If they were willing, they could tell you that I was a Pharisee, a

First-century politics
(23) Quite a show was put on here in Caesarea at this "summit conference" between the Roman governor and King Agrippa. Paul was brought out and questioned, but we get the impression that this was mostly for the sake of political relations between Festus and Agrippa, not because of a desire to do Paul justice. But God used it just the same.

King Agrippa heard the good news
(2) Once again Paul seized the chance to tell how he became a Christian. Governor Festus and King Agrippa were much upset by what they heard. It seems as though Agrippa would almost have been willing to be a Christian if only he had more time to think about it. So far as we know, however,

member of a group that is more strict than any other. 6Now I am on trial because I believe the promise that God made to our people long ago.

7Day and night our twelve tribes have earnestly served God, waiting for his promised blessings. King Agrippa, because of this hope, the Jewish leaders have brought charges against me. 8Why should any of you doubt that God raises the dead to life?

9I once thought that I should do everything I could to oppose Jesus from Nazareth. 10I did this first in Jerusalem, and with the authority of the chief priests I put many of God's people in jail. I even voted for them to be killed. 11I often had them punished in our meeting places, and I tried to make them give up their faith. In fact, I was so angry with them, that I went looking for them in foreign cities.

12King Agrippa, one day I was on my way to Damascus with the authority and permission of the chief priests. 13About noon I saw a light brighter than the sun. It flashed from heaven on me and on everyone traveling with me. 14We all fell to the ground. Then I heard a voice say to me in Aramaic, "Saul, Saul, why are you so cruel to me? It's foolish to fight against me!"

15"Who are you?" I asked.

Then the Lord answered, "I am Jesus! I am the one you are so cruel to. 16Now stand up. I have appeared to you, because I have chosen you to be my servant. You are to tell others what you have learned about me and what I will show you later."

17The Lord also said, "I will protect you from the Jews and from the Gentiles that I am sending you to. 18I want you to open their eyes, so that they will turn from darkness to light and from the power of Satan to God. Then their sins will be forgiven, and by faith in me they will become part of God's holy people."

Agrippa never turned to Christ. As Paul would later write, God has not called many mighty men. But he does call some. God seeks all kinds of people.

19King Agrippa, I obeyed this vision from heaven. 20First I preached to the people in Damascus, and then I went to Jerusalem and all over Judea. Finally, I went to the Gentiles and said, "Stop sinning and turn to God! Then prove what you have done by the way you live."

21That is why the Jews grabbed me in the temple and tried to kill me. 22But all this time God has helped me, and I have preached both to the rich and to the poor. I have told them only what the prophets and Moses said would happen. 23I told them how the Messiah would suffer and be the first to be raised from death, so that he could bring light to his own people and to the Gentiles.

24Before Paul finished defending himself, Festus shouted, "Paul, you're crazy! Too much learning has driven you out of your mind."

25But Paul replied, "Honorable Festus, I am not crazy. What I am saying is true, and it makes sense. 26None of these things happened off in a corner somewhere. I am sure that King Agrippa knows what I am talking about. That's why I can speak so plainly to him."

27Then Paul said to Agrippa, "Do you believe what the prophets said? I know you do."

28Agrippa asked Paul, "In such a short time do you think you can talk me into being a Christian?"

29Paul answered, "Whether it takes a short time or a long time, I wish you and everyone else who hears me today would become just like me! Except, of course, for these chains."

30Then King Agrippa, Governor Festus, Bernice, and everyone who was with them got up. 31But before they left, they said, "This man is not guilty of anything. He doesn't deserve to die or to be put in jail."

32Agrippa told Festus, "Paul could have been set free, if he had not asked to be tried by the Roman Emperor."

Paul could have been free (32) Think of that—Paul chose to go to Rome, although he could have been set free at his trial before Agrippa. Why did Paul do this? Jesus had called Paul to go to the Gentiles, and this trip to Rome was Paul's big chance to carry out his work. All things were working together to get Paul to Rome where he would continue his ministry for several years.

Paul Is Taken to Rome

27 When it was time for us to sail to Rome, Captain Julius from the Emperor's special troops was put in charge of Paul and the other prisoners. ²We went aboard a ship from Adramyttium that was about to sail to some ports along the coast of Asia. Aristarchus from Thessalonica in Macedonia sailed on the ship with us.

³The next day we came to shore at Sidon. Captain Julius was very kind to Paul. He even let him visit his friends, so they could give him whatever he needed. ⁴When we left Sidon, the winds were blowing against us, and we sailed close to the island of Cyprus to be safe from the wind. ⁵Then we sailed south of Cilicia and Pamphylia until we came to the port of Myra in Lycia. ⁶There the army captain found a ship from

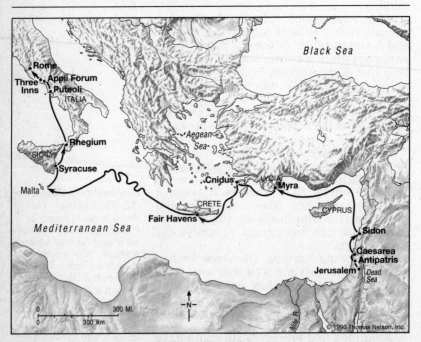

Paul Is Taken to Rome

Alexandria that was going to Italy. So he ordered us to board that ship.

7We sailed along slowly for several days and had a hard time reaching Cnidus. The wind would not let us go any farther in that direction, so we sailed past Cape Salmone, where the island of Crete would protect us from the wind. 8We went slowly along the coast and finally reached a place called Fair Havens, not far from the town of Lasea.

9By now we had already lost a lot of time, and sailing was no longer safe. In fact, even the Day of Atonement[n] was past. 10Then Paul spoke to the crew of the ship, "Men, listen to me! If we sail now, our ship and its cargo will be badly damaged, and many lives will be lost." 11But Julius listened to the captain of the ship and its owner, rather than to Paul.

12The harbor at Fair Havens was not a good place to spend the winter. Because of this, almost everyone agreed that we should at least try to sail along the coast of Crete as far as Phoenix. It had a harbor that opened toward the southwest and northwest,[o] and we could spend the winter there.

The Storm at Sea

13When a gentle wind from the south started blowing, the men thought it was a good time to do what they had planned. So they pulled up the anchor, and we sailed along the coast of Crete. 14But soon a strong wind called "The Northeaster" blew against us from the island. 15The wind struck the ship, and we could not sail against it. So we let the wind carry the ship.

16We went along the island of Cauda on the side that was protected from the wind. We had a hard time holding the lifeboat in place, 17but finally we got it where it belonged. Then the sailors wrapped ropes

Paul took charge

(10) A Roman army captain was in charge of Paul's ship to Rome. Sailing across the Mediterranean Sea, Paul warned the captain that there would be rough weather if they set out from the island of Crete after the middle of April. But he didn't listen to Paul. During the storm that followed, the crew and passengers were saved only when they took Paul's advice.

[n]*Day of Atonement*: This Jewish festival took place near the end of September. The sailing season was dangerous after the middle of September, and it was stopped completely between the middle of November and the middle of March. [o]*southwest and northwest*: Or "northeast and southeast."

around the ship to hold it together. They lowered the sail and let the ship drift along, because they were afraid it might hit the sandbanks in the gulf of Syrtis.

18The storm was so fierce that the next day they threw some of the ship's cargo overboard. 19Then on the third day, with their bare hands they threw overboard some of the ship's gear. 20For several days we could not see either the sun or the stars. A strong wind kept blowing, and we finally gave up all hope of being saved.

21Since none of us had eaten anything for a long time, Paul stood up and told the men:

You should have listened to me! If you had stayed on in Crete, you would not have had this damage and loss. 22But now I beg you to cheer up, because you will be safe. Only the ship will be lost.

23I belong to God, and I worship him. Last night he sent an angel 24to tell me, "Paul, don't be afraid! You will stand trial before the Emperor. And because of you, God will save the lives of everyone on the ship." 25Cheer up! I am sure that God will do exactly what he promised. 26But we will first be shipwrecked on some island.

27For fourteen days and nights we had been blown around over the Mediterranean Sea. But about midnight the sailors realized that we were getting near land. 28They measured and found that the water was about one hundred and twenty feet deep. A little later they measured again and found it was only about ninety feet. 29The sailors were afraid that we might hit some rocks, and they let down four anchors from the back of the ship. Then they prayed for daylight.

30The sailors wanted to escape from the ship. So they lowered the lifeboat into the water, pretending that they were letting down an anchor from the front of the ship. 31But Paul said to Captain Julius and the soldiers, "If the sailors don't stay on the ship, you won't have any chance to save your lives." 32The soldiers then cut the ropes that held the lifeboat and let it fall into the sea.

33Just before daylight Paul begged the people to eat something. He told them, "For fourteen days you have been so worried that you haven't eaten a thing. 34I beg you to eat something. Your lives depend on it. Do this and not one of you will be hurt."

35After Paul had said this, he took a piece of bread and gave thanks to God. Then in front of everyone, he broke the bread and ate some. 36They all felt encouraged, and each of them ate something. 37There were 276 people on the ship, 38and after everyone had eaten, they threw the cargo of wheat into the sea to make the ship lighter.

The Shipwreck

39Morning came, and the ship's crew saw a coast that they did not recognize. But they did see a cove with a beach. So they decided to try to run the ship aground on the beach. 40They cut the anchors loose and let them sink into the sea. At the same time they untied the ropes that were holding the rudders. Next, they raised the sail at the front of the ship and let the wind carry the ship toward the beach. 41But it ran aground on a sandbank. The front of the ship stuck firmly in the sand, and the rear was being smashed by the force of the waves.

42The soldiers decided to kill the prisoners to keep them from swimming away and escaping. 43But Captain Julius wanted to save Paul's life, and he did not let the soldiers do what they had planned. Instead, he ordered everyone who could swim to dive into the water and head for shore. 44Then he told the others to hold on to planks of wood or parts of the ship. At last, everyone safely reached shore.

On the Island of Malta

28 When we came ashore, we learned that the island was called Malta. 2The local people were very friendly, and

A witness for Jesus
(35) Even as they were being tossed around on the waves, Paul took advantage of an opportunity to witness about his faith. As he took bread in his hands and broke it, he gave thanks to God. The other people on the ship were encouraged and got their appetites back. Paul the prisoner was Paul the leader, by the power of the Holy Spirit.

Paul continued his work
(1) The island of Malta, in the central Mediterranean Sea, is a military base today. In Paul's time it was a Roman colony. While Paul was there he wonderfully survived a snake bite, just as Jesus had promised in Mark 16.18. Paul also healed the governor's sick father. Wherever Paul went, he used his time to spread the good news about Christ.

they welcomed us by building a fire, because
it was rainy and cold.

3After Paul had gathered some wood and
had put it on the fire, the heat caused a
snake to crawl out, and it bit him on the
hand. 4When the local people saw the snake
hanging from Paul's hand, they said to each
other, "This man must be a murderer! He
didn't drown in the sea, but the goddess
of justice will kill him anyway."

5Paul shook the snake off into the fire
and was not harmed. 6The people kept
thinking that Paul would either swell up
or suddenly drop dead. They watched him
for a long time, and when nothing happened
to him, they changed their minds and said,
"This man is a god."

7The governor of the island was named
Publius, and he owned some of the land
around there. Publius was very friendly and
welcomed us into his home for three days.
8His father was in bed, sick with fever and
stomach trouble, and Paul went to visit him.
Paul healed the man by praying and placing
his hands on him.

9After this happened, everyone on the
island brought their sick people to Paul, and
they were all healed. 10The people were very
respectful to us, and when we sailed, they
gave us everything we needed.

From Malta to Rome

11Three months later we sailed in a ship
that had been docked at Malta for the winter. The ship was from Alexandria in Egypt
and was known as "The Twin Gods."p
12We arrived in Syracuse and stayed for
three days. 13From there we sailed to Rhe-
gium. The next day a south wind began to
blow, and two days later we arrived in Pu-
teoli. 14There we found some of the Lord's
followers, who begged us to stay with them.
A week later we left for the city of Rome.
15Some of the followers in Rome heard

Paul went on to Rome
(11) Notice that Luke, the
author of the book of Acts,
had been with the group
since they left Palestine (see
in chapter 27 the many times
the word "we" appears).
Arriving at Italy, Paul and
his companions traveled to
Rome by the Appian Way,
a road still used today.

pknown as "The Twin Gods": Or "carried on its bow
a wooden carving of the Twin Gods." These gods were
Castor and Pollux, two of the favorite gods among sailors.

about us and came to meet us at the Market
of Appius and at the Three Inns. When Paul
saw them, he thanked God and was encouraged.

Paul in Rome

16We arrived in Rome, and Paul was allowed to live in a house by himself with a
soldier to guard him.

17Three days after we got there, Paul
called together some of the Jewish leaders
and said:

My friends, I have never done anything to hurt our people, and I have
never gone against the customs of our
ancestors. But in Jerusalem I was
handed over as a prisoner to the Romans. 18They looked into the charges
against me and wanted to release me.
They found that I had not done anything
deserving death. 19The Jewish leaders
disagreed, so I asked to be tried by the
Emperor.

But I don't have anything to say
against my own nation. 20I am bound
by these chains because of what we people of Israel hope for. That's why I have
called you here to talk about this hope
of ours.

21The Jewish leaders replied, "No one
from Judea has written us a letter about
you. And not one of them has come here
to report on you or to say anything against
you. 22But we would like to hear what you
have to say. We understand that people
everywhere are against this new group."

23They agreed on a time to meet with
Paul, and many of them came to his house.
From early morning until late in the afternoon, Paul talked to them about God's kingdom. He used the Law of Moses and the
Books of the Prophetsq to try to win them
over to Jesus.

24Some of the Jewish leaders agreed with
what Paul said, but others did not. 25Since

---

qLaw of Moses and the Books of the Prophets: The
Jewish Bible, that is, the Old Testament.

**Paul met with the Jews at
Rome**
(25) Again Paul defended
his ministry before the Jewish people living at Rome.
But once again many of the
Jewish leaders were against
Paul. So he had to continue
his ministry to the Gentiles.
We have to realize that
everybody in the world will
not agree with the good
news. But God calls us to
share that news as Paul did,
with everyone who will hear.

they could not agree among themselves, they started leaving. But Paul said, "The Holy Spirit said the right thing when he sent Isaiah the prophet 26to tell our ancestors,

> 'Go to these people
>   and tell them:
> You will listen and listen,
>   but never understand.
> You will look and look,
>   but never see.
> 27All of you
>   have stubborn hearts.
> Your ears are stopped up,
>   and your eyes are covered.
> You cannot see or hear
>   or understand.
> If you could,
> you would turn to me,
>   and I would heal you.' "

28-29Paul said, "You may be sure that God wants to save the Gentiles! And they will listen."r

30For two years Paul stayed in a rented house and welcomed everyone who came to see him. 31He bravely preached about God's kingdom and taught about the Lord Jesus Christ, and no one tried to stop him.

rAnd they will listen: Some manuscripts add, "After Paul said this, the people left, but they got into a fierce argument among themselves."

Paul rented his own house
(30) Fortunately, Paul did not have to go to prison while he awaited trial at Rome. He had his own rented home, and he seems to have been guarded by one soldier. There he enjoyed much freedom, and for two years was able to teach those who came to his house. After that he was probably released for a time and may have traveled as far as Spain. But he was arrested again and executed during Emperor Nero's reign, in about the year 67. (See Paul's Second Letter to Timothy, written just before the apostle's death.)

PAUL'S LETTER TO THE CHURCH IN ROME

ABOUT THIS LETTER

Paul wrote this letter to introduce himself and his message to the church at Rome. He had never been to this important city, although he knew the names of many Christians there and hoped to visit them soon (15.22—16.21). Paul tells them that he is an apostle, chosen to preach the good news (1.1). And the message he proclaims "is God's powerful way of saving all people who have faith, whether they are Jews or Gentiles" (1.16).

Paul reminds his readers, "All of us have sinned and fallen short of God's glory" (3.23). But how can we be made acceptable to God? This is the main question that Paul answers in this letter. He begins by showing how everyone has failed to do what God requires. The Jews have not obeyed the Law of Moses, and the Gentiles have refused even to think about God, although God has spoken to them in many different ways (1.18—3.20).

Now we see how God makes us acceptable to him (3.21):

God treats everyone alike. He accepts people only because they have faith in Jesus Christ . . . God is kind! Because of Jesus Christ, he freely accepts us and sets us free from our sins. (3.22—24)

God gave Christ to die for our sins, and he raised him to life, so that we would be acceptable to God. (4.25)

A QUICK LOOK AT THIS LETTER

1. Paul and His Message of Good News (1.1–17)
2. Everyone Is Guilty (1.18—3.20)
3. God's Way of Accepting People (3.21—4.25)
4. A New Life for God's People (5.1—8.39)
5. What about the People of Israel? (9.1—11.36)
6. How to Live the New Life of Love (12.1—15.13)
7. Paul's Plans and Personal Greetings (15.14—16.27)

1 From Paul, a servant of Christ Jesus.
    God chose me to be an apostle, and he appointed me to preach the good news ²that he promised long ago by what his prophets said in the holy Scriptures. ³⁻⁴This good news is about his Son, our Lord Jesus Christ! As a human, he was from the family of David. But the Holy Spirit[a] proved that Jesus is the powerful Son of God,[b] because he was raised from death.

⁵Jesus was kind to me and chose me to

Paul was a servant

(1) Paul had a greater ministry than all the other apostles put together. But still he called himself a servant. Paul obeyed the command of Jesus that the chief among his apostles should be the servant of all (Luke 22.26).

Paul's news is about a risen Savior

(4) Paul had something both old and new to tell about. By rising from the grave, the long-promised

---

[a]*the Holy Spirit*: Or "his own spirit of holiness." [b]*proved that Jesus is the powerful Son of God*: Or "proved in a powerful way that Jesus is the Son of God."

be an apostle,c so that people of all nations would obey and have faith. 6You are some of those people chosen by Jesus Christ.

7This letter is to all of you in Rome. God loves you and has chosen you to be his very own people.

I pray that God our Father and our Lord Jesus Christ will be kind to you and will bless you with peace!

A Prayer of Thanks

8First, I thank God in the name of Jesus Christ for all of you. I do this because people everywhere in the world are talking about your faith. 9God has seen how I never stop praying for you, while I serve him with all my heart and tell the good news about his Son.

10In all my prayers, I ask God to make it possible for me to visit you. 11I want to see you and share with you the same blessings that God's Spirit has given me. Then you will grow stronger in your faith. 12What I am saying is that we can encourage each other by the faith that is ours.

13My friends, I want you to know that I have often planned to come for a visit. But something has always kept me from doing it. I want to win followers to Christ in Rome, as I have done in many other places. 14-15It doesn't matter if people are civilized and educated or if they are uncivilized and uneducated. I must tell the good news to everyone. That's why I am eager to visit all of you in Rome.

The Power of the Good News

16I am proud of the good news! It is God's powerful way of saving all people who have faith, whether they are Jews or Gentiles. 17The good news tells how God accepts everyone who has faith, but only those who

---

cJesus was kind to me and chose me to be an apostle: Or "Jesus was kind to us and chose us to be his apostles."

Christ completed the eternal plan to save believers. This proved that Jesus is the Son of God, who could die for our sins. He is a living Savior.

Jesus chooses believers
(6) It insults human pride to think that Jesus chooses us, instead of our choosing him. Some day we will understand better what Paul writes here and in other places about that. For now, let's be humble enough to accept the idea that God has had us in mind for a very long time.

Let's pray for one another
(9) Paul prayed a lot, and so should we. God sees to it that our prayers for one another make a difference. Often the best thing we can do is pray for the needs of others, especially for things that we can't help ourselves. Only God can convince people that they need Christ. Our words alone won't do it, but prayer makes a difference.

The good news is for all kinds of people
(14) The news about Jesus is not only for the "civilized and educated," but for the "uncivilized and uneducated." The good news is for people regardless of their importance in the world. We must be careful not to make the good news hard for people to understand. Even small children should be able to come to Jesus and be saved.

Faith is the key
(17) Faith is trusting what God has said about his Son.

have faith.*d* It is just as the Scriptures say, "The people God accepts because of their faith will live."*e*

Everyone Is Guilty

18From heaven God shows how angry he is with all the wicked and evil things that sinful people do to crush the truth. 19They know everything that can be known about God, because God has shown it all to them. 20God's eternal power and character cannot be seen. But from the beginning of creation, God has shown what these are like by all he has made. That's why those people don't have any excuse. 21They know about God, but they don't honor him or even thank him. Their thoughts are useless, and their stupid minds are in the dark. 22They claim to be wise, but they are fools. 23They don't worship the glorious and eternal God. Instead, they worship idols that are made to look like humans who cannot live forever, and like birds, animals, and reptiles.

24So God let these people go their own way. They did what they wanted to do, and their filthy thoughts made them do shameful things with their bodies. 25They gave up the truth about God for a lie, and they worshiped God's creation instead of God, who will be praised forever. Amen.

26God let them follow their own evil desires. Women no longer wanted to have sex in a natural way, and they did things with each other that were not natural. 27Men behaved in the same way. They stopped wanting to have sex with women and had strong desires for sex with other men. They did shameful things with each other, and what has happened to them is punishment for their foolish deeds.

28Since these people refused even to think about God, he let their useless minds rule over them. That's why they do all sorts

Faith says, "I accept Jesus as my Savior and I ask him to take away my sins." When we have this kind of faith, Paul writes that we "will live." For the first time, we realize what real living is like—when God breathes his own life into us. Without faith, we live a life of sin, rebellion, and death.

What happens when we reject God

(28) When we reject God, everything else goes wrong, too. Paul lists the things that happen in our lives when we turn our backs on God. The picture of human behavior that Paul paints is an ugly one indeed. The tragedy is that it is all so needless. God calls us back from this "wrong turn" to enjoy friendship with him.

d but only those who have faith: Or "and faith is all that matters." *e The people God accepts because of their faith will live*: Or "The people God accepts will live because of their faith."

of indecent things. 29They are evil, wicked, and greedy, as well as mean in every possible way. They want what others have, and they murder, argue, cheat, and are hard to get along with. They gossip, 30say cruel things about others, and hate God. They are proud, conceited, and boastful, always thinking up new ways to do evil.

These people don't respect their parents. 31They are stupid, unreliable, and don't have any love or pity for others. 32They know God has said that anyone who acts this way deserves to die. But they keep on doing evil things, and they even encourage others to do them.

God's Judgment Is Fair

2 Some of you accuse others of doing wrong. But there is no excuse for what you do. When you judge others, you condemn yourselves, because you are guilty of doing the very same things. 2We know that God is right to judge everyone who behaves in this way. 3Do you really think God won't punish you, when you behave exactly like the people you accuse? 4You surely don't think much of God's wonderful goodness or of his patience and willingness to put up with you. Don't you know that the reason God is good to you is because he wants you to turn to him?

5But you are stubborn and refuse to turn to God. So you are making things even worse for yourselves on that day when he will show how angry he is and will judge the world with fairness. 6God will reward each of us for what we have done. 7He will give eternal life to everyone who has patiently done what is good in the hope of receiving glory, honor, and life that lasts forever. 8But he will show how angry and furious he can be with every selfish person who rejects the truth and wants to do evil. 9All who are wicked will be punished with trouble and suffering. It doesn't matter if they are Jews or Gentiles. 10But all who do right will be rewarded with glory, honor,

Be careful about judging
(1) We might make judgments correctly about others, but if God decided to find fault with us, we would be in bad shape. There's a saying: when you point your finger at someone, you have three more pointing back at you. Meaning: when you make judgments, remember that you too are a sinner.

and peace, whether they are Jews or Gentiles. [11]God doesn't have any favorites!

[12]Those people who don't know about God's Law will still be punished for what they do wrong. And the Law will be used to judge everyone who knows what it says. [13]God accepts those who obey his Law, but not those who simply hear it.

[14]Some people naturally obey the Law's commands, even though they don't have the Law. [15]This proves that the conscience is like a law written in the human heart. And it will show whether we are forgiven or condemned, [16]when God has Jesus Christ judge everyone's secret thoughts, just as my message says.

The Jews and the Law

[17]Some of you call yourselves Jews. You trust in the Law and take pride in God. [18]By reading the Scriptures you learn how God wants you to behave, and you discover what is right. [19]You are sure that you are a guide for the blind and a light for all who are in the dark. [20]And since there is knowledge and truth in God's Law, you think you can instruct fools and teach young people.

[21]But how can you teach others when you refuse to learn? You preach that it is wrong to steal. But do you steal? [22]You say people should be faithful in marriage. But are you faithful? You hate idols, yet you rob their temples. [23]You take pride in the Law, but you disobey the Law and bring shame to God. [24]It is just as the Scriptures tell us, "You have made foreigners say insulting things about God."

[25]Being circumcised is worthwhile, if you obey the Law. But if you don't obey the Law, you are no better off than people who are not circumcised. [26]In fact, if they obey the Law, they are as good as anyone who is circumcised. [27]So everyone who obeys the Law, but has never been circumcised, will condemn you. Even though you are circumcised and have the Law, you still don't obey its teachings.

[28]Just because you live like a Jew and

How God judges
(12) God judges by his Law. If God judges us according to what we deserve, then there is no hope for any of us. But read on—God offers another way for us to be accepted by him. Everyone has sinned, and the Law can only condemn us. But God has made it possible for us to come back to him and have our sins forgiven.

The Jews were an example of disobedience
(17) The Jews had the Scriptures and they knew the Law. They even became very proud of these facts. But they were really no better than other people. They too failed to keep God's Law. There is a danger that people can imagine that they are good just because they *know* what they should do. But they don't *do* what they should, so their knowledge does them no good.

Mere religion can't cover our sins
(25) The Jews had many religious ceremonies. But God couldn't accept their religious ceremonies without obedient lives. Today's Christians might count too much on ceremonies, too. Sometimes children enjoy playing church, but it's sad when grownups "play church" and aren't living and worshiping in a way that pleases God.

are circumcised does not make you a real Jew. 29To be a real Jew you must obey the Law. True circumcision is something that happens deep in your heart, not something done to your body. And besides, you should want praise from God and not from humans.

3 What good is it to be a Jew? What good is it to be circumcised? 2It is good in a lot of ways! First of all, God's messages were spoken to the Jews. 3It is true that some Jews did not believe the message. But does this mean that God cannot be trusted, just because they did not have faith? 4No, indeed! God tells the truth, even if everyone else is a liar. The Scriptures say about God,

"Your words
   will be proven true,
and in court
   you will win your case."

5If our evil deeds show how right God is, then what can we say? Is it wrong for God to become angry and punish us? What a foolish thing to ask. 6But the answer is, "No." Otherwise, how could God judge the world? 7Since your lies bring great honor to God by showing how truthful he is, you may ask why God still says you are a sinner. 8You might as well say, "Let's do something evil, so that something good will come of it!" Some people even claim that we are saying this. But God is fair and will judge them as well.

No One Is Good

9What does all this mean? Does it mean that we Jews are better off*f* than the Gentiles? No, it doesn't! Jews, as well as Gentiles, are ruled by sin, just as I have said. 10The Scriptures tell us,

"No one is acceptable to God!
11Not one of them understands
   or even searches for God.
12They have all turned away
   and are worthless.
There is not one person
   who does right.

f better off: Or "worse off."

Our disobedience doesn't mean God is wrong too
(3) Today, too, people blame their unhappiness and even their sins on God. It is our own actions that make us miserable. God always can be trusted to do right, to tell us the truth about himself and ourselves. It makes sense to listen to God and not be fooled by lies.

All of us are sinners
(10) Paul has been writing these hard things about us to show that we are all disobedient and that no one is excused. When we come before God, we have to admit the truth of all that Paul has written. This makes us feel very bad, because we know that it's no good to blame God or others for the way we are. Each of us falls short of what God rightly expects of people made in his image.

¹³Their words are like
   an open pit,
and their tongues are good
   only for telling lies.
Each word is as deadly
   as the fangs of a snake,
¹⁴and they say nothing
   but bitter curses.
¹⁵These people quickly
   become violent.
¹⁶Wherever they go,
   they leave ruin
   and destruction.
¹⁷They don't know how
   to live in peace.
¹⁸ They don't even fear God."

¹⁹We know that everything in the Law was written for those who are under its power. The Law says these things to stop anyone from making excuses and to let God show that the whole world is guilty. ²⁰God does not accept people simply because they obey the Law. No, indeed! All the Law does is to point out our sin.

God's Way of Accepting People

²¹Now we see how God does make us acceptable to him. The Law and the Prophets*g* tell how we become acceptable, and it isn't by obeying the Law of Moses. ²²God treats everyone alike. He accepts people only because they have faith in Jesus Christ. ²³All of us have sinned and fallen short of God's glory. ²⁴But God is really kind,*h* and because of Jesus Christ, he freely accepts us and sets us free from our sins. ²⁵⁻²⁶God sent Christ to be our sacrifice. Christ offered his life's blood, so that by faith in him we could come to God. And

Christ is the answer
(21) There's good news: God has provided the way of escape from the penalty of his Law. It's the way his Son Jesus provided by paying our debt, by dying on the cross in our place. There Jesus accepted all of God's judgment for our sins. When we receive Jesus as our sin-bearer, then God says we are "declared not guilty."

Someone took your place
(25) Imagine you have committed a bad crime. You are in court, and the judge is about to sentence you. Then he stops, and he calls someone from the back of the courtroom. It's the judge's own son. Speaking to you, the judge says, "You deserve to die for your crime, but my son has asked to die in your place. I have decided to let my very own son die for you." That is what Jesus did for you.

---

g The Law and the Prophets: The Jewish Scriptures, that is, the Old Testament. *h really kind*: The Greek word traditionally rendered "grace" (from gratia of the Latin Vulgate) is often translated in the CEV as "God's kindness" or "God's great kindness" or "God is kind" in order to express in a more contemporary way the overwhelming kindness of God, who treats us far better than we deserve.

God did this to show that in the past he was right to be patient and forgive sinners. This also shows that God is right when he accepts people who have faith in Jesus. 27What is left for us to brag about? Not a thing! Is it because we obeyed some law? No! It is because of faith. 28We see that people are acceptable to God because they have faith, and not because they obey the Law. 29Does God belong only to the Jews? Isn't he also the God of the Gentiles? Yes, he is! 30There is only one God, and he accepts Gentiles as well as Jews, simply because of their faith. 31Do we destroy the Law by our faith? Not at all! We make it even more powerful.

The Example of Abraham

4 Well then, what can we say about our ancestor Abraham? 2If he became acceptable to God because of what he did, then he would have something to brag about. But he would never be able to brag about it to God. 3The Scriptures say, "God accepted Abraham because Abraham had faith in him."

4Money paid to workers isn't a gift. It is something they earn by working. 5But you cannot make God accept you because of something you do. God accepts sinners only because they have faith in him. 6In the Scriptures David talks about the blessings that come to people who are acceptable to God, even though they don't do anything to deserve these blessings. David says,

7"God blesses people
    whose sins are forgiven
and whose evil deeds
    are forgotten.
8The Lord blesses people
    whose sins are erased
    from his book."

9Are these blessings meant for circumcised people or for those who are not circumcised? Well, the Scriptures say that God accepted Abraham because Abraham had faith in him. 10But when did this happen?

Does God destroy his Law?

(31) Through Jesus, God has made his Law work better than ever. Jesus carried the load of our sins as he hung on the cross. Now God gives us, as a free gift, the goodness of Jesus. He paid all that we owed. Now we belong to God forever, and we love to please the one who saved us.

You can't earn God's forgiveness

(1) Abraham is an example of God's free gift. We can't pay to be saved, but God himself could bless us as a gift. The gift wasn't really free, however. Jesus paid the price with his own blood. Like Abraham, we are accepted by God because of our faith.

King David knew about Jesus

(7) David sang in his Psalms about what Jesus would do. He said that God can wipe out our sins as though they never happened. Think about it—God is able to forget that we ever sinned against him.

Was it before or after Abraham was circumcised? Of course, it was before.

11Abraham let himself be circumcised to show that he had been accepted because of his faith even before he was circumcised. This makes Abraham the father of all who are acceptable to God because of their faith, even though they are not circumcised. 12This also makes Abraham the father of everyone who is circumcised and has faith in God, as Abraham did before he was circumcised.

The Promise Is for All Who Have Faith

13God promised Abraham and his descendants that he would give them the world. This promise was not made because Abraham had obeyed the Law, but because his faith in God made him acceptable. 14If Abraham and his descendants were given this promise because they had obeyed the Law, then faith would mean nothing, and the promise would be worthless.

15God becomes angry when his law is broken. But where there isn't a Law, it cannot be broken. 16Everything depends on having faith in God, so that God can keep his promise because he is kind. This promise is not only for Abraham's descendants who have the Law. It is for all who are Abraham's descendants because they have faith, just as he did. Abraham is the ancestor of us all. 17The Scriptures say that Abraham would become the ancestor of many nations. This promise was made to Abraham because he had faith in God, who raises the dead to life and creates new things.

18God promised Abraham a lot of descendants. And when it all seemed hopeless, Abraham still had faith in God and became the ancestor of many nations. 19Abraham's faith never became weak, not even when he was nearly a hundred years old. He knew that he was almost dead and that his wife Sarah could not have children. 20But Abraham never doubted or questioned God's promise. His faith made him strong, and he gave all the credit to God.

What circumcision was for
(12) Hospitals today often circumcise baby boys, Jew and Gentile, for health reasons. In Bible times, circumcision was for Jews only— a sign of membership in the family of God. But *faith* was the really important thing. Paul points out that Abraham had to be a believer in God before he was circumcised.

21Abraham was certain that God could do what he had promised. 22So God accepted him, 23just as we read in the Scriptures. But these words were not written only for Abraham. 24They were written for us, since we will also be accepted because of our faith in God, who raised our Lord Jesus Christ to life. 25God gave Christ to die for our sins, and he raised him to life, so that we would be made acceptable to God.

What It Means to Be Acceptable to God

5 By faith we have been made acceptable to God. And now, because of our Lord Jesus Christ, we live at peace[i] with God. 2Christ has also introduced us[j] to God's kindness on which we take our stand. So we are happy, as we look forward to sharing in the glory of God. 3But that's not all! We gladly suffer,[k] because we know that suffering helps us to endure. 4And endurance builds character, which gives us a hope 5that will never disappoint us. All of this happens because God has given us the Holy Spirit, who fills our hearts with his love.

6Christ died for us at a time when we were helpless and sinful. 7No one is really willing to die for an honest person, though someone might be willing to die for a truly good person. 8But God showed how much he loved us by having Christ die for us, even though we were sinful.

9But there is more! Now that God has accepted us because Christ sacrificed his life's blood, we will also be kept safe from God's anger. 10Even when we were God's enemies, he made peace with us, because his Son died for us. Yet something even greater than friendship is ours. Now that we are at peace with God, we will be saved by his Son's life. 11And in addition to everything else, we are happy because God sent

God promises eternal life to all believers
(24) Not only to Abraham and the Jews, but to all people, God offers to save those who trust God as Abraham did. This promise is as old as Abraham himself, because God promised him that his blessing would come to all nations. That includes you and me.

God can be trusted
(1) The first thing God wants us to do is have faith in him. If we're sick and go to a doctor, but don't have faith in his or her ability, we might as well stay home. Neither will God help us if we don't trust him.

The Holy Spirit helps us
(5) At one time our future was uncertain, but not any more. Even though people may reject us, we have the promise of God's friendship forever. We know this because God's Holy Spirit now lives in us and assures us that God loves us.

Now nothing separates us from God
(10) Only our own refusal to accept his kindness can separate us from God. Imagine you have long owed a lot of money to someone—so much you could never pay it. But then a rich friend pays off your debt for you. That is what Jesus did when he paid for your sins. So now you may be at peace with God.

---

[i]we live at peace: Some manuscripts have "let us live at peace." [j]introduced us: Some manuscripts add "by faith." [k]We gladly suffer: Or "Let us gladly suffer."

our Lord Jesus Christ to make peace with
us.

Adam and Christ

12Adam sinned, and that sin brought
death into the world. Now everyone has
sinned, and so everyone must die. 13Sin was
in the world before the Law came. But no
record of sin was kept, because there was
no Law. 14Yet death still had power over
all who lived from the time of Adam to the
time of Moses. This happened, though not
everyone disobeyed a direct command from
God, as Adam did.

In some ways Adam is like Christ who
came later. 15But the gift that God was kind
enough to give was very different from
Adam's sin. That one sin brought death to
many others. Yet in an even greater way,
Jesus Christ alone brought God's gift of
kindness to many people.

16There is a lot of difference between
Adam's sin and God's gift. That one sin led
to punishment. But God's gift made it possible for us to be acceptable to him, even
though we have sinned many times. 17Death
ruled like a king because Adam had sinned.
But that cannot compare with what Jesus
Christ has done. God has been so kind
to us, and he has accepted us because of
Jesus. And so we will live and rule like
kings.

18Everyone was going to be punished
because Adam sinned. But because of the
good thing that Christ has done, God accepts us and gives us the gift of life.
19Adam disobeyed God and caused many
others to be sinners. But Jesus obeyed him
and will make many people acceptable to
God.

20The Law came, so that the full power
of sin could be seen. Yet where sin was
powerful, God's kindness was even more
powerful. 21Sin ruled by means of death.
But God's kindness now rules, and God has
accepted us because of Jesus Christ our
Lord. This means that we will have eternal
life.

*We are sinful children
of Adam*

(16) We are all children of
our very first ancestor,
Adam, who passed on his
sinful nature to us. Sin
caused death. But God has
made a way to help us. Jesus
undid the harm that Adam
did by bringing sin into the
world. By sending Jesus to
die in our place God passed
on Jesus' godly nature to all
who accept him.

*What good did the Law
do?*

(20) If God had not given
us his Law, we would not
clearly know how great our
disobedience is. That was
the Law's purpose—to show
us our need to be saved
from our sins. We must not
think that God gave us his
Law because we can be
saved by keeping it. We
can't. But by his kindness
God has given the gift of his
Son, Jesus. When Jesus died
and rose again from death
he made it possible for us
to have our sins forgiven
and to have life forever with
him.

Dead to Sin but Alive because of Christ

6 What should we say? Should we keep on sinning, so that God's kindness will show up even better? 2No, we should not! If we are dead to sin, how can we go on sinning? 3Don't you know that all who share in Christ Jesus by being baptized also share in his death? 4When we were baptized, we died and were buried with Christ. We were baptized, so that we would live a new life, as Christ was raised to life by the glory of God the Father.

5If we shared in Jesus' death by being baptized, we will surely be raised to life with him. 6We know that the persons we used to be were nailed to the cross with Jesus. This was done, so that our sinful bodies would no longer be the slaves of sin. 7We know that sin does not have power over dead people.

8As surely as we died with Christ, we believe we will also live with him. 9We know that death no longer has any power over Christ. He died and was raised to life, never again to die. 10When Christ died, he died for sin once and for all. But now he is alive, and he lives only for God. 11In the same way, you must think of yourselves as dead to the power of sin. But Christ Jesus has given life to you, and you live for God.

12Don't let sin rule your body. After all, your body is bound to die, so don't obey its desires 13or let any part of it become a slave of evil. Give yourselves to God, as people who have been raised from death to life. Make every part of your body a slave that pleases God. 14Don't let sin keep ruling your lives. You are ruled by God's kindness and not by the Law.

Slaves Who Do What Pleases God

15What does all this mean? Does it mean we are free to sin, because we are ruled by God's kindness and not by the Law? Certainly not! 16Don't you know that you are slaves of anyone you obey? You can be

What do we do about our sins?

(1) We should not go on sinning just because God has forgiven us. If God has forgiven us, we will hate our sins. But we can't stop sinning by ourselves. If Christ lives in us then we have a new life from him because he rose from death. But he also put our sins to death when he died on the cross. So we claim his death as death for our sins. Our old selves are dead, and we are now new people because Christ lives in us.

Dead to sin

(7) When we really put our faith in Christ, we feel so close to him that it is as if we have experienced his death and new life. We are dead to sin and alive with Christ. He helps us live in a new way—his way—a way that leaves no room for sin.

Sin works through our bodies

(12) God created our bodies very good. But since Adam's time, our bodies have become the means by which sin works. We live in physical bodies, and our actions are carried out by our bodies. But Christ's death for us means that our bodies don't have to live for sin anymore.

slaves of sin and die, or you can be obedient slaves of God and be acceptable to him. 17You used to be slaves of sin. But I thank God that with all your heart you obeyed the teaching you received from me. 18Now you are set free from sin and are slaves who please God.

19I am using these everyday examples, because in some ways you are still weak. You used to let the different parts of your body be slaves of your evil thoughts. But now you must make every part of your body serve God, so that you will belong completely to him.

20When you were slaves of sin, you didn't have to please God. 21But what good did you receive from the things you did? All you have to show for them is your shame, and they lead to death. 22Now you have been set free from sin, and you are God's slaves. This will make you holy and will lead you to eternal life. 23Sin pays off with death. But God's gift is eternal life given by Jesus Christ our Lord.

An Example from Marriage

7 My friends, you surely understand enough about law to know that laws only have power over people who are alive. 2For example, the Law says that a man's wife must remain his wife as long as he lives. But once her husband is dead, she is free 3to marry someone else. However, if she goes off with another man while her husband is still alive, she is said to be unfaithful.

4That is how it is with you, my friends. You are now part of the body of Christ and are dead to the power of the Law. You are free to belong to Christ, who was raised to life so that we could serve God. 5When we thought only of ourselves, the Law made us have sinful desires. It made every part of our bodies into slaves who are doomed to die. 6But the Law no longer rules over us. We are like dead people, and it cannot have any power over us. Now we can serve God in a new way by obeying his Spirit,

The Law is not our master
(18) When we live in sin, we live in fear, because the Law reminds us of how sinful we are. But that fear caused by the Law only makes us sin more and more. When God gives us the new life of Jesus, his Son, then we don't fear the Law anymore. We want to obey God because we love him, not because we're afraid.

We aren't free to sin
(22) A criminal who has been in prison is set free. What does he do then? Does he go back to his old ways of crime? Not if he's smart. He has learned that crime doesn't pay. The Christian is like a criminal who has been set free by Christ. Now the Christian sees that obeying God is the true way of happiness and everlasting life.

Marriage is for life
(2) Many marriages fail because people don't realize at the start that marriage is for life. Paul uses marriage to show that we were once "married" to the Law. But we died with Jesus when he died on the cross. Now we are free from the old Law and we are "married" to Christ in his risen life. Marriage to Christ in this way is a happy marriage that lasts forever.

How the Law works
(5) Do you remember when someone told you when you were small, "Don't do that, or you'll be punished," but the command only made you want to do that thing even more? That is the way

and not in the old way by obeying the written Law.

The Battle with Sin

7Does this mean that the Law is sinful? Certainly not! But if it had not been for the Law, I would not have known what sin is really like. For example, I would not have known what it means to want something that belongs to someone else, unless the Law had told me not to do that. 8It was sin that used this command as a way of making me have all kinds of desires. But without the Law, sin is dead.

9Before I knew about the Law, I was alive. But as soon as I heard that command, sin came to life, 10and I died. The very command that was supposed to bring life to me, instead brought death. 11Sin used this command to trick me, and because of it I died. 12Still, the Law and its commands are holy and correct and good.

13Am I saying that something good caused my death? Certainly not! It was sin that killed me by using something good. Now we can see how terrible and evil sin really is. 14We know that the Law is spiritual. But I am merely a human, and I have been sold as a slave to sin. 15In fact, I don't understand why I act the way I do. I don't do what I know is right. I do the things I hate. 16Although I don't do what I know is right, I agree that the Law is good. 17So I am not the one doing these evil things. The sin that lives in me is what does them.

18I know that my selfish desires won't let me do anything that is good. Even when I want to do right, I cannot. 19Instead of doing what I know is right, I do wrong. 20And so, if I don't do what I know is right, I am no longer the one doing these evil things. The sin that lives in me is what does them.

21The Law has shown me that something in me keeps me from doing what I know is right. 22With my whole heart I agree with the Law of God. 23But in every part of me I discover something fighting against my

sin works through the Law. Sin becomes worse because without being saved, sinners want to disobey what is right.

The Law is good

(12) What Paul writes about the Law may lead someone to think the Law is an evil thing. Not so. Our sinful nature uses the Law to make us sin worse. Until we receive Christ into our lives we continue to live in wickedness. When Jesus comes in, our love of sin passes away, and we come to love goodness.

Christians are in a new war with sin

(18) Before Jesus becomes real to us as our Savior, our sins don't upset us very much. Then Jesus comes into our lives, so our old slavery to sin and its misery can be broken. But if we don't ask Jesus for his help, sin still tempts us and makes us unhappy. We can win when Jesus fights our war for us against sin.

mind, and it makes me a prisoner of sin that controls everything I do. 24What a miserable person I am. Who will rescue me from this body that is doomed to die? 25Thank God! Jesus Christ will rescue me.*l*

So with my mind I serve the Law of God, although my selfish desires make me serve the law of sin.

Living by the Power of God's Spirit

8 If you belong to Christ Jesus, you won't be punished. 2The Holy Spirit will give you life that comes from Christ Jesus and will set you*m* free from sin and death. 3The Law of Moses cannot do this, because our selfish desires make the Law weak. But God set you free when he sent his own Son to be like us sinners and to be a sacrifice for our sin. God used Christ's body to condemn sin. 4He did this, so that we would do what the Law commands by obeying the Spirit instead of our own desires.

5People who are ruled by their desires think only of themselves. Everyone who is ruled by the Holy Spirit thinks about spiritual things. 6If our minds are ruled by our desires, we will die. But if our minds are ruled by the Spirit, we will have life and peace. 7Our desires fight against God, because they do not and cannot obey God's laws. 8If we follow our desires, we cannot please God.

9You are no longer ruled by your desires, but by God's Spirit, who lives in you. People who don't have the Spirit of Christ in them don't belong to him. 10But Christ lives in you. So you are alive because God has accepted you, even though your bodies must die because of your sins. 11Yet God raised Jesus to life! God's Spirit now lives in you, and he will raise you to life by his Spirit.

12My dear friends, we must not live to satisfy our desires. 13If you do, you will die. But you will live, if by the help of God's Spirit you say "No" to your desires. 14Only those people who are led by God's Spirit

Jesus took our punishment
(1) Why did sin have to be punished? Why couldn't God just let everyone into heaven, sins and all? But how would you like to live in a heaven where sinful people keep getting worse and worse forever and ever? That's why Jesus, the Son of God, let himself be punished for our sins. Then God could take away our sins and let us live with him forever.

Be ruled by the Holy Spirit
(4) When we are ruled by God's Spirit, we love thoughts of God and goodness. This is a wonderful way to live, because we are then free from the desires that were killing us, even when we didn't know they were.

Don't give in to all your desires
(8) Think of the diseases and unhappiness that result from giving our bodies everything they want. We ought to feed our new spiritual nature on the things of the Holy Spirit. Then we will grow in our ability to love and enjoy God. This is exactly what we were created to do.

Believers will have new bodies someday
(11) When a seed is planted, it seems to die, but it grows up into a beautiful new plant. When Jesus died for us, he was buried, but he rose again in a more wonderful body. Believers in Jesus will have wonderful bodies like his when they rise from death.

---

*l*me: Or "us." *m*you: Some manuscripts have "me."

are his children. [15]God's Spirit doesn't make us slaves who are afraid of him. Instead, we become his children and call him our Father.[n] [16]God's Spirit makes us sure that we are his children. [17]His Spirit lets us know that together with Christ we will be given what God has promised. We will also share in the glory of Christ, because we have suffered with him.

A Wonderful Future for God's People

[18]I am sure that what we are suffering now cannot compare with the glory that will be shown to us. [19]In fact, all creation is eagerly waiting for God to show who his children are. [20]Meanwhile, creation is confused, but not because it wants to be confused. God made it this way in the hope [21]that creation would be set free from decay and would share in the glorious freedom of his children. [22]We know that all creation is still groaning and is in pain, like a woman about to give birth.

[23]The Spirit makes us sure about what we will be in the future. But now we groan silently, while we wait for God to show that we are his children.[o] This means that our bodies will also be set free. [24]And this hope is what saves us. But if we already have what we hope for, there is no need to keep on hoping. [25]However, we hope for something we have not yet seen, and we patiently wait for it.

[26]In certain ways we are weak, but the Spirit is here to help us. For example, when we don't know what to pray for, the Spirit prays for us in ways that cannot be put into words. [27]All of our thoughts are known to God. He can understand what is in the mind of the Spirit, as the Spirit prays for God's

Why does God's creation suffer?
(22) God has a plan to save his creation from the bad effects of sin. Now, our world is full of decay, unhappiness, and pain. But as a woman feels some pain when she is about to give birth to a baby, so too does the world feel pain now while it awaits the birth of a new and wonderful creation from God.

The Holy Spirit prays for us
(26) We may sometimes pray for things that aren't really good for us, or we might not know what to pray for. But the Holy Spirit steps in and prays for us. Then, more and more, we find ourselves praying for the things that will please God. And God is always arranging everything for our good—if we love him.

[n]*our Father*: The Greek text uses the Aramaic word "Abba" (meaning "father"), which shows the close relation between the children and their father.   [o]*to show that we are his children*: These words are not in some manuscripts. The translation of the remainder of the verse would then read, "while we wait for God to set our bodies free."

people. 28We know that God is always at work for the good of everyone who loves him.p They are the ones God has chosen for his purpose, 29and he has always known who his chosen ones would be. He had decided to let them become like his own Son, so that his Son would be the first of many children. 30God then accepted the people he had already decided to choose, and he has shared his glory with them.

God's Love

31What can we say about all this? If God is on our side, can anyone be against us? 32God did not keep back his own Son, but he gave him for us. If God did this, won't he freely give us everything else? 33If God says his chosen ones are acceptable to him, can anyone bring charges against them? 34Or can anyone condemn them? No indeed! Christ died and was raised to life, and now he is at God's right side,q speaking to him for us. 35Can anything separate us from the love of Christ? Can trouble, suffering, and hard times, or hunger and nakedness, or danger and death? 36It is exactly as the Scriptures say,

> "For you we face death
> all day long.
> We are like sheep
> on their way
> to the butcher."

37In everything we have won more than a victory because of Christ who loves us. 38I am sure that nothing can separate us from God's love—not life or death, not angels or spirits, not the present or the future, 39and not powers above or powers below. Nothing in all creation can separate us from God's love for us in Christ Jesus our Lord!

pGod is always at work for the good of everyone who loves him: Or "All things work for the good of everyone who loves God" or "God's Spirit always works for the good of everyone who loves God."   qright side: The place of power and honor.

God knows his children
(30) Here is a great mystery, but it's not so strange if you think about it. God has always known who his people would be. He has been planning a whole new human race with Jesus as the head instead of Adam. Whoever wants to be in God's family can be a member by accepting Jesus.

Is God on our side?
(38) Whether God is on our side depends on whether *we* are on *God's* side. If we are, nothing can stop us from doing and being all that God would like us to be. No one can accuse us or condemn us. God has accepted us. Nothing in heaven or earth or hell can separate us from Jesus. That's the greatest news in the world.

God's Choice of Israel

9 I am a follower of Christ, and the Holy Spirit is a witness to my conscience. So I tell the truth and I am not lying when I say [2]my heart is broken and I am in great sorrow. [3]I would gladly be placed under God's curse and be separated from Christ for the good of my own Jewish people. [4]They are the descendants of Israel, and they are also God's chosen people. God showed them his glory. He made agreements with them and gave them his Law. The temple is theirs and so are the promises that God made to them. [5]They have those famous ancestors, who were also the ancestors of Jesus Christ. I pray that God, who rules over all, will be praised forever![r] Amen.

[6]It cannot be said that God broke his promise. After all, not all of the people of Israel are the true people of God. [7-8]In fact, when God made the promise to Abraham, he meant only Abraham's descendants by his son Isaac. God was talking only about Isaac when he promised [9]Sarah, "At this time next year I will return, and you will already have a son."

[10]Don't forget what happened to the twin sons of Isaac and Rebecca. [11-12]Even before they were born or had done anything good or bad, the Lord told Rebecca that her older son would serve the younger one. The Lord said this to show that he makes his own choices and that it was not because of anything either of them had done. [13]That's why the Scriptures say that the Lord liked Jacob more than Esau.

[14]Are we saying that God is unfair? Certainly not! [15]The Lord told Moses that he has pity and mercy on anyone he wants to. [16]Everything then depends on God's mercy and not on what people want or do.

[r]*Christ. I pray that God, who rules over all, will be praised forever:* Or "Christ, who rules over all. I pray that God will be praised forever" or "Christ. And I pray that Christ, who is God and rules over all, will be praised forever."

Paul loved his people more than himself
(3) Most people seem to be interested in themselves. That's why we are sometimes called the "me" generation. It comes as a shock to us to find a truly unselfish person. This was Paul. He even said he would rather go to hell himself than see his people lost in sin. We should think about Paul's kind of love.

God is not unfair
(14) If God had been a human being he would be unfair for choosing some and not others. He has mercy on some, and not on others. But God is not a selfish man, and he has perfect reasons for the decisions he makes, even if we can't understand his reasons. An infant doesn't understand its parent either. But if we love God, we trust him to do everything as it should be done. Then we don't ask foolish questions, like the man Paul describes in verse 19.

17In the Scriptures the Lord says to Pharaoh, "I let you become king, so that I could show you my power and be praised by all people on earth." 18Everything depends on what God decides to do, and he can either have pity on people or make them stubborn.

God's Anger and Mercy

19Someone may ask, "How can God blame us, if he makes us behave in the way he wants us to?" 20But, my friend, I ask, "Who do you think you are to question God? Does the clay have the right to ask the potter why he shaped it the way he did? 21Doesn't a potter have the right to make a fancy bowl and a plain bowl out of the same lump of clay?"

22God wanted to show his anger and reveal his power against everyone who deserved to be destroyed. But instead, he patiently put up with them. 23He did this by showing how glorious he is when he has pity on the people he has chosen to share in his glory. 24Whether Jews or Gentiles, we are those chosen ones, 25just as the Lord says in the book of Hosea,

"Although they are not
my people,
    I will make them my people.
I will treat with love
those nations
    that have never been loved.
26"Once they were told,
    'You are not my people.'
But in that very place
they will be called
    children of the living God."

27And this is what the prophet Isaiah said about the people of Israel,

"The people of Israel
are as many
as the grains of sand
    along the beach.
But only a few who are left
    will be saved.
28The Lord will be quick
    and sure to do on earth

Why did God choose some people?

(23) God's mercy was the reason he chose to save some. He could have let us all go to hell, but in his kindness he decided to send his Son to die for people. Then, whoever really wanted to could be saved by choosing Christ. Which are you choosing today: your own way, or God's way? That choice tells the story of your future.

what he has warned
he will do."
29Isaiah also said,
"If the Lord All-Powerful
had not spared some
of our descendants,
we would have been destroyed
like the cities of Sodom
and Gomorrah."s

Israel and the Good News

30What does all of this mean? It means
that the Gentiles were not trying to be acceptable to God, but they found that he
would accept them if they had faith. 31It
also means that the people of Israel were
not acceptable to God. And why not? It was
because they were tryingt to be acceptable
by obeying the Law 32instead of by having
faith in God. The people of Israel fell over
the stone that makes people stumble,
33just as God says in the Scriptures,
"Look! I am placing in Zion
a stone to make people
stumble and fall.
But those who have faith
in that one will never
be disappointed."

10 Dear friends, my greatest wish and
my prayer to God is for the people
of Israel to be saved. 2I know they love God,
but they don't understand 3what makes people acceptable to him. So they refuse to trust
God, and they try to be acceptable by obeying the Law. 4But Christ makes the Law
no longer necessaryu for those who become
acceptable to God by faith.

Anyone Can Be Saved

5Moses said that a person could become
acceptable to God by obeying the Law. He

Don't stumble over Jesus
(30) God opened a way for
all to be saved, by faith. He
also put a stone in front of
those who would try to earn
their way into heaven. All
without faith would stumble
over that stone, which is
Jesus.

Faith gets us accepted
(3) The Law is for knowing
what God expects, but it
can't make people good.
The Law helps people realize they are sinners. Trying
to be accepted by keeping
the Law is a "dead-end
street." God accepts people
by faith in his Son Jesus.

sSodom and Gomorrah: During the time of Abraham
the Lord destroyed these two cities because their people
were so sinful.   tbecause they were trying: Or "while
they were trying" or "even though they were trying."
uBut Christ makes the Law no longer necessary: Or
"But Christ gives the full meaning to the Law."

did this when he wrote, "If you want to live, you must do all that the Law commands."

6But people whose faith makes them acceptable to God will never ask, "Who will go up to heaven to bring Christ down?" 7Neither will they ask, "Who will go down into the world of the dead to raise him to life?"

8All who are acceptable because of their faith simply say, "The message is as near as your mouth or your heart." And this is the same message we preach about faith. 9So you will be saved, if you say that God raised Jesus Christ from death, and if you believe this with all your heart. 10God will accept you and save you, if you truly believe this and tell it to others.

11The Scriptures say that no one who has faith will be disappointed, 12no matter if that person is a Jew or a Gentile. There is only one Lord, and he is generous to everyone who asks for his help. 13All who call out to the Lord will be saved.

14But how can people ask the Lord to save them, if they have never had faith in him? How can they hear about him unless someone tells them? 15And how can anyone tell them without being sent by the Lord? The Scriptures say it is a beautiful sight to see even the feet of someone coming to preach the good news. 16Yet not everyone has believed the message. For example, the prophet Isaiah asked, "Lord, has anyone believed what we said?"

17No one can have faith without hearing the message about Christ. 18But am I saying that the people of Israel did not hear? No, I am not! The Scriptures say,

"The message was told
everywhere on earth.
It was announced
all over the world."

19Did the people of Israel understand or not? Moses answered this question when he told that the Lord had said,

"I will make Israel jealous
of people
who are a nation
of nobodies.

Just ask God to save you

(9) Do you want to be saved? You don't have to know everything the religious experts know. You only have to know that God is waiting for you to come back to him. Then you will be safe forever with him. Everyone is saved who asks God for forgiveness because of Jesus who died and rose again.

Beautiful feet

(15) Here is a strange but good expression. God wants us to carry this good news about how to be saved all over the world, and many are doing this. The nations can't believe in Jesus if our feet don't carry the good news. Such feet are beautiful feet indeed.

The good news comes to the Gentiles

(18) The Jews heard the good news first, but many of them refused to put their faith in Jesus. So God continued with his plan. He used some of the Jewish believers to carry the good news to the people of other nations, and a great many of them trusted in Christ as their Savior.

I will make them angry
    at people
who don't understand
    a thing."

20Isaiah was fearless enough to tell that
the Lord had said,

"I was found by people
who were not looking
    for me.
I appeared to the ones
who were not asking
    about me."

21And Isaiah said about the people of Israel,

"All day long the Lord
    has reached out
to people who are stubborn
    and refuse to obey."

God Has Not Rejected His People

11 Am I saying that God has turned his back on his people? Certainly not! I am one of the people of Israel, and I myself am a descendant of Abraham from the tribe of Benjamin. 2God did not turn his back on his chosen people. Don't you remember reading in the Scriptures how Elijah complained to God about the people of Israel? 3He said, "Lord, they killed your prophets and destroyed your altars. I am the only one left, and now they want to kill me."

4But the Lord told Elijah, "I still have seven thousand followers who have not worshiped Baal." 5It is the same way now. God was kind to the people of Israel, and so a few of them are still his followers. 6This happened because of God's kindness and not because of anything they have done. It could not have happened except for God's kindness.

7This means that only a few of the people of Israel found what all of them were searching for. And the rest of them were stubborn, 8just as the Scriptures say,

"God made them so stupid
    that their eyes are blind,
and their ears
    are still deaf."

God has no spoiled children

(21) The Jews became spoiled because they thought God cared only about them. They even hated other nations, whom they treated as outsiders. God soon corrected that idea. He sent his word to the Gentiles, and many of them have believed the good news.

God keeps his promises

(2) At first it may seem that God has forgotten Israel because of their sins. But he hasn't. God used the Jews as a channel to reach the Gentiles with the good news. But the Gentiles must remember how much they owe the Jews for the message they have received. The Lord also will remember his chosen people, the Jews, when he brings them back into his kingdom.

9Then David said,
"Turn their meals
    into bait for a trap,
so that they will stumble
and be given
    what they deserve.
10Blindfold their eyes!
    Don't let them see.
Bend their backs
beneath a burden
    that will never be lifted."

Gentiles Will Be Saved

11Do I mean that the people of Israel fell, never to get up again? Certainly not! Their failure made it possible for the Gentiles to be saved, and this will make the people of Israel jealous. 12But if the rest of the world's people were helped so much by Israel's sin and loss, they will be helped even more by Israel's full return.

13I am now speaking to you Gentiles, and as long as I am an apostle to you, I will take pride in my work. 14I hope in this way to make some of my own people jealous enough to be saved. 15When Israel rejected God, the rest of the people in the world were able to turn to him. So when God makes friends with Israel, it will be like bringing the dead back to life. 16If part of a batch of dough is made holy by being offered to God, then all of the dough is holy. If the roots of a tree are holy, the rest of the tree is holy too.

17You Gentiles are like branches of a wild olive tree that were made to be part of a cultivated olive tree. You have taken the place of some branches that were cut away from it. And because of this, you enjoy the blessings that come from being part of that cultivated tree. 18But don't think you are better than the branches that were cut away. Just remember that you are not supporting the roots of that tree. Its roots are supporting you.

19Maybe you think those branches were cut away, so that you could be put in their place. 20That's true enough. But they were

We are like branches in a tree

(17) We can't be proud about being Christians. All that we are and have comes from God. Not only that, but we're like small branches in a bigger tree that God has planted. Abraham, the father of the Jews, was the original root of the tree. The early branches were the Jews. But Gentile believers are only the later branches put onto God's tree.

cut away because they did not have faith, and you are where you are because you do have faith. So don't be proud, but be afraid. 21If God cut away those natural branches, couldn't he do the same to you?

22Now you see both how kind and how hard God can be. He was hard on those who fell, but he was kind to you. And he will keep on being kind to you, if you keep on trusting in his kindness. Otherwise, you will be cut away too.

23If those other branches will start having faith, they will be made a part of that tree again. God has the power to put them back. 24After all, it was not natural for branches to be cut from a wild olive tree and to be made part of a cultivated olive tree. So it is much more likely that God will join the natural branches back to the cultivated olive tree.

The People of Israel Will Be Brought Back

25My friends, I don't want you Gentiles to be too proud of yourselves. So I will explain the mystery of what has happened to the people of Israel. Some of them have become stubborn, and they will stay like that until the complete number of you Gentiles has come in. 26In this way all of Israel will be saved, as the Scriptures say,

"From Zion someone will come
to rescue us.
Then Jacob's descendants
will stop being evil.
27This is what the Lord
has promised to do
when he forgives
their sins."

28The people of Israel are treated as God's enemies, so that the good news can come to you Gentiles. But they are still the chosen ones, and God loves them because of their famous ancestors. 29God does not take back the gifts he has given or forget about the people he has chosen.

30At one time you Gentiles rejected God. But now Israel has rejected God, and you

Watch out for pride
(25) We must be careful about being proud. God can save anyone he wishes. He has chosen to save all who have faith in Jesus, whether they are Jews or Gentiles. When we consider people who have not accepted Jesus, we should be humble, not proud. God has the right to save or not save anyone. It is his mercy, not our "smart move," that does the saving.

have been shown mercy. 31And because of the mercy shown to you, they will also be shown mercy. 32All people have disobeyed God, and that's why he treats them as prisoners. But he does this, so that he can have mercy on all of them.

33Who can measure the wealth and wisdom and knowledge of God? Who can understand his decisions or explain what he does?

> 34"Has anyone known
>   the thoughts of the Lord
>   or given him advice?
> 35Has anyone loaned
>   something to the Lord
>   that must be repaid?"

36Everything comes from the Lord. All things were made because of him and will return to him. Praise the Lord forever! Amen.

We can't figure out God's ways

(33) Our goal in life is to obey God, not to understand all that he is doing. We know that he does everything right and he does everything well. God is the Creator and Owner of all that we can and cannot see. All that we have comes from him. We just have to trust him for the things we can't understand.

Christ Brings New Life

12 Dear friends, God is good. So I beg you to offer your bodies to him as a living sacrifice, pure and pleasing. That's the most sensible way to serve God. 2Don't be like the people of this world, but let God change the way you think. Then you will know how to do everything that is good and pleasing to him.

3I realize how kind God has been to me, and so I tell each of you not to think you are better than you really are. Use good sense and measure yourself by the amount of faith God has given you. 4A body is made up of many parts, and each of them has its own use. 5That's how it is with us. There are many of us, but we each are part of the body of Christ, as well as part of one another.

6God has also given each of us different gifts to use. If we can prophesy, we should do it according to the amount of faith we have. 7If we can serve others, we should serve. If we can teach, we should teach. 8If we can encourage others, we should encourage them. If we can give, we should be generous. If we are leaders, we should

What you can give to God

(1) Since God owns everything anyway, you can't give him anything he doesn't already possess. But you can willingly give back your life to him as an act of thanksgiving. Jesus died for you, so surely you can live for him. Then let God change your mind. When you think God's thoughts your life will be happy, because you will then want to please God.

Do your job

(6) God has given us different jobs to do. We honor God and we reach our goals by doing well whatever he gives us to do in the world. What do you think God wants you to do for him?

do our best. If we are good to others, we should do it cheerfully.

Rules for Christian Living

⁹Be sincere in your love for others. Hate everything that is evil and hold tight to everything that is good. ¹⁰Love each other as brothers and sisters and honor others more than you do yourself. ¹¹Never give up. Eagerly follow the Holy Spirit and serve the Lord. ¹²Let your hope make you glad. Be patient in time of trouble and never stop praying. ¹³Take care of God's needy people and welcome strangers into your home.

¹⁴Ask God to bless everyone who mistreats you. Ask him to bless them and not to curse them. ¹⁵When others are happy, be happy with them, and when they are sad, be sad. ¹⁶Be friendly with everyone. Don't be proud and feel that you are smarter than others. Make friends with ordinary people.ᵛ ¹⁷Don't mistreat someone who has mistreated you. But try to earn the respect of others, ¹⁸and do your best to live at peace with everyone.

¹⁹Dear friends, don't try to get even. Let God take revenge. In the Scriptures the Lord says,

"I am the one to take revenge
and pay them back."

²⁰The Scriptures also say,

"If your enemies are hungry,
give them something to eat.
And if they are thirsty,
give them something
to drink.
This will be the same
as piling burning coals
on their heads."

²¹Don't let evil defeat you, but defeat evil with good.

Obey Rulers

13 Obey the rulers who have authority over you. Only God can give author-

ᵛ*Make friends with ordinary people*: Or "Do ordinary jobs."

Love is the great answer

(9) If we have the love of God in our hearts, then we will do all things in a way that pleases him. We can't do wrong to anyone if we are controlled by love. And we should have a special love for other believers, our brothers and sisters in the Lord.

Where hope comes from

(12) Hope looks for the best even when things are going wrong. And hope comes from having a healthy trust in God. We don't always understand what God plans to do, but we know he does everything just as it should be done. Then we are glad and have hope.

How do you treat enemies?

(19) You can't trust those who do you wrong, but hating them isn't the answer either. Feelings of hate destroy the hater more than the hated person. People who have a hateful spirit are actually ruining their health and taking years off their lives. It's better to be kind to our enemies as God was kind to us.

Human government is part of God's plan

(1) We shouldn't imagine that because we're Christians we don't have to obey laws. Some people in history have imagined that, and they have done a lot of harm to God's work in the world. Of course we can't obey laws that really cause us to disobey God. But in general, Christians are good

ity to anyone, and he puts these rulers in their places of power. 2People who oppose the authorities are opposing what God has done, and they will be punished. 3Rulers are a threat to evil people, not to good people. There is no need to be afraid of the authorities. Just do right, and they will praise you for it. 4After all, they are God's servants, and it is their duty to help you.

If you do something wrong, you ought to be afraid, because these rulers have the right to punish you. They are God's servants who punish criminals to show how angry God is. 5But you should obey the rulers because you know it is the right thing to do, and not just because of God's anger.

6You must also pay your taxes. The authorities are God's servants, and it is their duty to take care of these matters. 7Pay all that you owe, whether it is taxes and fees or respect and honor.

Love

8Let love be your only debt! If you love others, you have done all that the Law demands. 9In the Law there are many commands, such as, "Be faithful in marriage. Do not murder. Do not steal. Do not want what belongs to others." But all of these are summed up in the command that says, "Love others as much as you love yourself." 10No one who loves others will harm them. So love is all that the Law demands.

The Day When Christ Returns

11You know what sort of times we live in, and so you should live properly. It is time to wake up. You know that the day when we will be saved is nearer now than when we first put our faith in the Lord. 12Night is almost over, and day will soon appear. We must stop behaving as people do in the dark and be ready to live in the light. 13So behave properly, as people do in the day. Don't go to wild parties or get drunk or be vulgar or indecent. Don't quarrel or be jealous. 14Let the Lord Jesus Christ

citizens who pay their taxes and do what the law says.

Earthly rulers are also God's servants
(4) Rulers may not always mean to serve God, but God sees to it that they do. They carry out God's plan whether they wish to or not. So you don't need to be afraid of authorities, even cruel ones. God will take care of us just the same.

Love proves itself to be right
(8) Jesus summed up the Law of God by commanding us to love one another. Just as Paul says, when we love others we do them no wrong. But we do them a lot of good. The good news about Jesus would spread all over the world if Christians loved one another completely.

Jesus is coming soon
(12) Even in Paul's day the times were so evil that it seemed the Lord must come very soon. We live in days like that too. This world is passing away. Since we know the Lord is surely coming, we should spend our lives in ways that honor Christ and bless others.

be as near to you as the clothes you wear. Then you won't try to satisfy your selfish desires.

Don't Criticize Others

14 Welcome all the Lord's followers, even those whose faith is weak. Don't criticize them for having beliefs that are different from yours. ²Some think it is all right to eat anything, while those whose faith is weak will eat only vegetables. ³But you should not criticize others for eating or for not eating. After all, God welcomes everyone. ⁴What right do you have to criticize someone else's servants? Only their Lord can decide if they are doing right, and the Lord will make sure that they do right.

⁵Some of the Lord's followers think one day is more important than another. Others think all days are the same. But each of you should make up your own mind. ⁶Any followers who count one day more important than another day do it to honor their Lord. And any followers who eat meat give thanks to God, just like the ones who don't eat meat.

⁷Whether we live or die, it must be for God, rather than for ourselves. ⁸Whether we live or die, it must be for the Lord. Alive or dead, we still belong to the Lord. ⁹This is because Christ died and rose to life, so that he would be the Lord of the dead and of the living. ¹⁰Why do you criticize other followers of the Lord? Why do you look down on them? The day is coming when God will judge all of us. ¹¹In the Scriptures God says,

"I swear by my very life
　that everyone will kneel down
　　and praise my name!"

¹²And so, each of us must give an account to God for what we do.

Don't Cause Problems for Others

¹³We must stop judging others. We must also make up our minds not to upset anyone's faith. ¹⁴The Lord Jesus has made it

We're all different
(1) There are no two people alike. So we can't very well expect everybody to live like ourselves in every way. If we aren't careful, we can get into the habit of finding fault with little things that don't really matter. Of course, sin is always wrong, but when it comes to mere customs, let's give people room to be themselves.

Why do we live?
(7) It's important to know why we live. We quickly come to the end of our earthly lives, and we shouldn't waste the time God has given us. We won't get to live this life again. We want to be able to say, "I spent my time trying to honor God."

God will judge everyone
(10) We may have to judge others' abilities to decide what they are fit to do, but we can't decide what God thinks about people. He is the only judge of that. We may be surprised to find out that some people we turn away from now are people God will one day accept.

Consider others' feelings
(13) We might feel free to do certain things that another believer doesn't feel free to do. If so, we should not wave our freedom in the other believer's face. It might hurt that believer's conscience. Out of love, we sometimes need to choose not to use our freedom right in front of such a person.

clear to me that God considers all foods fit to eat. But if you think some foods are unfit to eat, then for you they are not fit.

15If you are hurting others by the foods you eat, you are not guided by love. Don't let your appetite destroy someone Christ died for. 16Don't let your right to eat bring shame to Christ. 17God's kingdom is not about eating and drinking. It is about pleasing God, about living in peace, and about true happiness. All this comes from the Holy Spirit. 18If you serve Christ in this way, you will please God and be respected by people. 19We should try^w to live at peace and help each other have a strong faith.

20Don't let your appetite destroy what God has done. All foods are fit to eat, but it is wrong to cause problems for others by what you eat. 21It is best not to eat meat or drink wine or do anything else that causes problems for other followers of the Lord. 22What you believe about these things should be kept between you and God. You are fortunate, if your actions don't make you have doubts. 23But if you do have doubts about what you eat, you are going against your beliefs. And you know that is wrong, because anything you do against your beliefs is sin.

If in doubt, don't
(22) If we doubt whether something is right or wrong, that makes it wrong for us. We ought to have a clear conscience. Better to *know* we're not sinning than to have to *hope* we aren't.

Please Others and Not Yourself

15 If our faith is strong, we should be patient with the Lord's followers whose faith is weak. We should try to please them instead of ourselves. 2We should think of their good and try to help them by doing what pleases them. 3Even Christ did not try to please himself. But as the Scriptures say, "The people who insulted you also insulted me." 4And the Scriptures were written to teach and encourage us by giving us hope. 5God is the one who makes us patient and cheerful. I pray that he will help you live at peace with each other, as you follow Christ. 6Then all of you together will praise God, the Father of our Lord Jesus Christ.

The importance of patience
(1) When you have friends who fall into sin, what do you do? Do you make sure they feel as guilty as they should? Or do you try to help them through their failure and show them you still love them? Patience doesn't quickly give up on people. Also, you sometimes might have to be patient with people who judge *you* harshly.

^w*We should try*: Some manuscripts have "We try."

The Good News Is for Jews and Gentiles

7Honor God by accepting each other, as Christ has accepted you. 8I tell you that Christ came as a servant of the Jews to show that God has kept the promises he made to their famous ancestors. Christ also came, 9so that the Gentiles would praise God for being kind to them. It is just as the Scriptures say,

"I will tell the nations
about you,
and I will sing praises
to your name."

10The Scriptures also say to the Gentiles, "Come and celebrate with God's people." 11Again the Scriptures say,

"Praise the Lord,
all you Gentiles.
All you nations, come
and worship him."

12Isaiah says,

"Someone from David's family
will come to power.
He will rule the nations,
and they will put their hope
in him."

13I pray that God, who gives hope, will bless you with complete happiness and peace because of your faith. And may the power of the Holy Spirit fill you with hope.

Accept each other
(7) In Paul's day, the problem was between Jews and Gentiles. In our time the problem is often between Christians with different beliefs. We must all try hard to learn the truth. But we have to be patient with differences and accept one another until we get to heaven. Let's not quarrel about words and teachings that no one understands perfectly.

Paul's Work as a Missionary

14My friends, I am sure that you are very good and that you have all the knowledge you need to teach each other. 15But I have spoken to you plainly and have tried to remind you of some things. God was so kind to me! 16He chose me to be a servant of Christ Jesus for the Gentiles and to do the work of a priest in the service of his good news. God did this so that the Holy Spirit could make the Gentiles into a holy offering, pleasing to him. That's why I have spoken to you so plainly and have tried to remind you of these few things.

17Because of Christ Jesus, I can take pride in my service for God. 18In fact, all I will

What is a missionary?
(14) A missionary is not just someone who carries the good news across the sea. We should do that, too. But a missionary is a Christian who always tries, as Paul did, to share the news about Jesus with all who have never heard or understood why Jesus came. Every Christian is called by God to be a missionary like that.

talk about is how Christ let me speak and work, so that the Gentiles would obey him. 19Indeed, I will tell how Christ worked miracles and wonders by the power of the Holy Spirit. I have preached the good news about him all the way from Jerusalem to Illyricum. 20But I have always tried to preach where people have never heard about Christ. I am like a builder who doesn't build on anyone else's foundation. 21It is just as the Scriptures say,

> "All who have not
> been told about him
>   will see him,
> and those who have not
> heard about him
>   will understand."

Paul's Plan to Visit Rome

22My work has always kept me from coming to see you. 23Now there is nothing left for me to do in this part of the world, and for years I have wanted to visit you. 24So I plan to stop off on my way to Spain. Then after a short, but refreshing, visit with you, I hope you will quickly send me on.

25-26I am now on my way to Jerusalem to deliver the money that the Lord's followers in Macedonia and Achaia collected for God's needy people. 27This is something they really wanted to do. But sharing their money with the Jews was also like paying back a debt, because the Jews had already shared their spiritual blessings with the Gentiles. 28After I have safely delivered this money, I will visit you and then go on to Spain. 29And when I do arrive in Rome, I know it will be with the full blessings of Christ.

30My friends, by the power of the Lord Jesus Christ and by the love that comes from the Holy Spirit, I beg you to pray sincerely with me and for me. 31Pray that God will protect me from the unbelievers in Judea, and that his people in Jerusalem will be pleased with what I am doing. 32Ask God to let me come to you and have a pleasant and refreshing visit. 33I pray that God,

How did the church at Rome get started?
(22) Notice that Paul hadn't been to Rome yet. So he is writing in his letter to a church that existed before he made the journey we read about at the end of the book of Acts. It may be that the Roman church was started by Roman Jews who were present at the Day of Pentecost told about in Acts 2.

Christians help one another
(26) Paul was carrying a gift from the Greeks to the believing Jews in Jerusalem. The Jewish Christians at Jerusalem were unable to earn a living because the other Jews rejected them. Here is a beautiful early example of the care Christians have for one another. Where there is true Christianity there is kindness.

Prayer helps
(30) Paul asked the Roman Christians to pray for his safety in Judea, where he was going. We know from the book of Acts that Paul had a hard time in Judea with unbelieving Jews. But God saved Paul from those who wanted to kill him there. God answers our prayers, but not always in the way we might expect.

who gives peace, will be with all of you. Amen.

Personal Greetings

16 I have good things to say about Phoebe, who is a leader in the church at Cenchreae. ²Welcome her in a way that is proper for someone who has faith in the Lord and is one of God's own people. Help her in any way you can. After all, she has proved to be a respected leader for many others, including me.

³Give my greetings to Priscilla and Aquila. They have not only served Christ Jesus together with me, ⁴but they have even risked their lives for me. I am grateful for them and so are all the Gentile churches. ⁵Greet the church that meets in their home.

Greet my dear friend Epaenetus, who was the first person in Asia to have faith in Christ.

⁶Greet Mary, who has worked so hard for you.

⁷Greet my relativesˣ Andronicus and Junias, who were in jail with me. They are highly respected by the apostles and were followers of Christ before I was.

⁸Greet Ampliatus, my dear friend whose faith is in the Lord.

⁹Greet Urbanus, who serves Christ along with us.

Greet my dear friend Stachys.

¹⁰Greet Apelles, a faithful servant of Christ.

Greet Aristobulus and his family.

¹¹Greet Herodion, who is a relativeˣ of mine.

Greet Narcissus and the others in his family, who have faith in the Lord.

¹²Greet Tryphaena and Tryphosa, who work hard for the Lord.

Greet my dear friend Persis. She also works hard for the Lord.

¹³Greet Rufus, that special servant of the

Paul had many to greet
(1) Rome was a crossroads that became home to many people who had been born elsewhere, a lot like New York City and Los Angeles are today. Some people would live in Rome for a while and then move on. Paul must have known many Roman Christians, even though he had never set foot there, and there were many he wanted to greet.

ˣ*relative(s):* Or "Jewish friend(s)."

Lord, and greet his mother, who has been like a mother to me.

¹⁴Greet Asyncritus, Phlegon, Hermes, Patrobas, and Hermas, as well as our friends who are with them.

¹⁵Greet Philologus, Julia, Nereus and his sister, and Olympas, and all of God's people who are with them.

¹⁶Be sure to give each other a warm greeting.

All of Christ's churches greet you.

¹⁷My friends, I beg you to watch out for anyone who causes trouble and divides the church by refusing to do what all of you were taught. Stay away from them! ¹⁸They want to serve themselves and not Christ the Lord. Their flattery and fancy talk fool people who don't know any better. ¹⁹I am glad that everyone knows how well you obey the Lord. But still, I want you to understand what is good and not have anything to do with evil. ²⁰Then God, who gives peace, will soon crush Satan under your feet. I pray that our Lord Jesus will be kind to you.

²¹Timothy, who works with me, sends his greetings, and so do my relatives,^x Lucius, Jason, and Sosipater.

²²I, Tertius, also send my greetings. I am a follower of the Lord, and I wrote this letter.^y

²³⁻²⁴Gaius welcomes me and the whole church into his home, and he sends his greetings.

Erastus, the city treasurer, and our dear friend Quartus send their greetings too.^z

Paul's Closing Prayer

²⁵Praise God! He can make you strong by means of my good news, which is the message about^a Jesus Christ. For ages and ages this message was kept secret, ²⁶but now at last it has been told. The eternal

Watch out for troublemakers

(17) Paul had taught the Roman Christians what they should believe and how they should live. But he wanted them to watch out for people who cause arguments and divide the church. Sadly, there are some like that today. Such troublemakers often deceive with smooth words and pretend to be something they really are not. We must follow God's word in all things.

Paul's prayer was answered

(25) Through the years Paul's great letter to the Romans has been a bright, guiding light to Christians. Those who hear their Master's voice through Paul's good words have been strengthened and kept in their faith. Only the good news about Jesus can save us from sin and give us eternal life with God.

---

^x*relative(s)*: Or "Jewish friend(s)."   ^y*I wrote this letter*: Paul probably dictated this letter to Tertius.   ^z*send their greetings, too*: Some manuscripts add, "I pray that our Lord Jesus Christ will always be kind to you. Amen."   ^a*about*: Or "from."

God commanded his prophets to write about the good news, so that all nations would obey and have faith. ²⁷And now, because of Jesus Christ, we can praise the only wise God forever! Amen.*b*

---

*b*Amen: Some manuscripts have verses 25-27 after 14.23. Others have the verses here and after 14.23, and one manuscript has them after 15.33.

PAUL'S FIRST LETTER TO THE CHURCH IN CORINTH

ABOUT THIS LETTER

Although this letter is called the First Letter to the Corinthians, it is not really the first one that Paul wrote to this church. We know this because he mentions in this letter that he had written one before (5.9). The Christians in Corinth had also written to him (7.1), and part of First Corinthians contains Paul's answers to questions they had asked.

Corinth is a large port city in southern Greece. Paul began his work there in a Jewish meeting place, but he had to move next door to the home of a Gentile who had become a follower of Jesus (Act 18.1–17). Most of the followers in Corinth were poor people (1 Corinthians 1.26–29), though some of them were wealthy (1 Corinthians 11.18–21), and one was even the city treasurer (Romans 16.23). While he was in Corinth, Paul worked as a tentmaker to earn a living (Acts 18.3; 1 Corinthians 4.12; 9.1–18).

Paul was especially concerned about the way the Corinthian Christians were always arguing and dividing themselves into groups (1.10–4.21) and about the way they treated one another (5.1—6.20). These are two of Paul's main concerns as he writes this letter. But he also wants to answer the questions they asked him about marriage (7.1–40) and food offered to idols (8.1–13). Paul encourages them to worship God the right way (10.1–14.40) and to be firm in their belief that God has given them victory over death (15.1–58).

Love, Paul tells them, is even more important than faith or hope. All of the problems in the church could be solved, if all the members would love one another, as Christians should:

> Love is kind and patient,
> never jealous, boastful,
>   proud, or rude.
> Love rejoices in the truth,
>   but not in evil.
> Love is always supportive,
> loyal, hopeful,
>   and trusting.
> Love never fails! (13.4,5,6–8)

A QUICK LOOK AT THIS LETTER

1 From Paul, chosen by God to be an apostle of Christ Jesus, and from Sosthenes, who is also a follower.

2To God's church in Corinth. Christ Jesus chose you to be his very own people, and you worship in his name, as we and all others do who call him Lord.

3My prayer is that God our Father and the Lord Jesus Christ will be kind to you and will bless you with peace!

4I never stop thanking my God for being kind enough to give you Christ Jesus, 5who helps you speak and understand so well. 6Now you are certain that everything we told you about our Lord Christ Jesus is true. 7You are not missing out on any blessings, as you wait for him to return. 8And until the day Christ does return, he will keep you completely innocent. 9God can be trusted, and he chose you to be partners with his Son, our Lord Jesus Christ.

Taking Sides

10My dear friends, as a follower of our Lord Jesus Christ, I beg you to get along with each other. Don't take sides. Always try to agree in what you think. 11Several people from Chloe's family*a* have already reported to me that you keep arguing with each other. 12They have said that some of you claim to follow me, while others claim to follow Apollos or Peter*b* or Christ.

13Has Christ been divided up? Was I nailed to a cross for you? Were you baptized in my name? 14I thank God*c* that I didn't baptize any of you except Crispus and Gaius. 15Not one of you can say that you were baptized in my name. 16I did baptize the family*d* of Stephanas, but I don't remember if I baptized anyone else. 17Christ did not send me to baptize. He sent me to tell the good news without using big words that

Paul was a good thanker

(4) Paul never stopped thanking God for giving Jesus to believers. We probably don't thank God as much as we should. Notice also how quickly Paul mentioned the return of the Lord Jesus. Do we expect Jesus as strongly today? We should. He could return at any time.

Christians are one family

(10) How easy it is to take our eyes off Jesus and become followers of some other leader. We revere the earthly teachers God sends to us, especially those who lead us to believe in Christ. But our true leader is Jesus himself. There ought to be no division in the family of God. We are the earthly body of Christ, and he is the head of that body.

---

afamily: Family members and possibly slaves and others who may have lived in the house. *bPeter*: The Greek text has "Cephas," which is an Aramaic name meaning "rock." Peter is the Greek name with the same meaning. *cI thank God*: Some manuscripts have "I thank my God." *dfamily*: See the note at 1.11.

would make the cross of Christ lose its power.

Christ Is God's Power and Wisdom

18The message about the cross doesn't make any sense to lost people. But for those of us who are being saved, it is God's power at work. 19As God says in the Scriptures,
"I will destroy the wisdom
of all who claim
to be wise.
I will confuse those
who think they know
so much."
20What happened to those wise people? What happened to those experts in the Scriptures? What happened to the ones who think they have all the answers? Didn't God show that the wisdom of this world is foolish? 21God was wise and decided not to let the people of this world use their wisdom to learn about him.

Instead, God chose to save only those who believe the foolish message we preach. 22Jews ask for miracles, and Greeks want something that sounds wise. 23But we preach that Christ was nailed to a cross. Most Jews have problems with this, and most Gentiles think it is foolish. 24Our message is God's power and wisdom for the Jews and the Greeks that he has chosen. 25Even when God is foolish, he is wiser than everyone else, and even when God is weak, he is stronger than everyone else.

26My dear friends, remember what you were when God chose you. The people of this world didn't think that many of you were wise. Only a few of you were in places of power, and not many of you came from important families. 27But God chose the foolish things of this world to put the wise to shame. He chose the weak things of this world to put the powerful to shame.

28What the world thinks is worthless, useless, and nothing at all is what God has used to destroy what the world considers important. 29God did all this to keep anyone from bragging to him. 30You are God's chil-

*God's foolishness
is wisdom*
(18) Paul didn't mean that God can really be foolish. Paul uses that language to show that the greatest human wisdom counts for nothing compared to God's simplest thoughts. Paul's remarks take away any pride we may have about how smart we are. What we must do is learn God's wisdom by thinking his thoughts. But God's thoughts are shown by the preaching of Christ nailed to the cross, which most people think is foolishness.

See how God chose
(26) Paul writes that God mainly chose humble, ordinary people to be believers, usually not the "VIP's." We should remember that when we share the good news today. All types of people are important in God's eyes, but especially the ones who are the least in the eyes of the world.

dren. He sent Christ Jesus to save us and to make us wise, acceptable, and holy. 31So if you want to brag, do what the Scriptures say and brag about the Lord.

Telling about Christ and the Cross

2 Friends, when I came and told you the mystery[e] that God had shared with us, I didn't use big words or try to sound wise. 2In fact, while I was with you, I made up my mind to speak only about Jesus Christ, who had been nailed to a cross.

3At first, I was weak and trembling with fear. 4When I talked with you or preached, I didn't try to prove anything by sounding wise. I simply let God's Spirit show his power. 5That way you would have faith because of God's power and not because of human wisdom.

6We do use wisdom when speaking to people who are mature in their faith. But it is not the wisdom of this world or of its rulers, who will soon disappear. 7We speak of God's hidden and mysterious wisdom that God decided to use for our glory long before the world began. 8The rulers of this world didn't know anything about this wisdom. If they had known about it, they would not have nailed the glorious Lord to a cross. 9But it is just as the Scriptures say,

"What God has planned
for people who love him
is more than eyes have seen
or ears have heard.
It has never even
entered our minds!"

10God's Spirit has shown you everything. His Spirit finds out everything, even what is deep in the mind of God. 11You are the only one who knows what is in your own mind, and God's Spirit is the only one who knows what is in God's mind. 12But God has given us his Spirit. That's why we don't think the same way that the people of this world think. That's also why we can recognize the blessings that God has given us.

emystery: Some manuscripts have "testimony."

Christians have one message
(2) The ancient Greeks were proud of their great schools of wisdom. Paul put all of that to shame by saying that God's wisdom is Christ nailed to the cross, not great human thoughts. Scholars often spend a lot of time, in today's places of learning, guessing about the meaning of life. God has told us life's meaning by sending his Son to die for our sins. That is the great wisdom of God that makes life worthwhile.

God's Spirit our teacher
(10) This is an important thing the Holy Spirit does for believers: he reveals the mind of God. It was the Spirit who inspired the writers of this letter and other Scriptures. And the same Spirit shows us God's truth as we read. God's wisdom is a wonderful treasure, ready to be revealed to us if we are open to the Holy Spirit.

13Every word we speak was taught to us by God's Spirit, not by human wisdom. And this same Spirit helps us teach spiritual things to spiritual people.*f* 14That's why only someone who has God's Spirit can understand spiritual blessings. Anyone who does not have God's Spirit thinks these blessings are foolish. 15People who are guided by the Spirit can make all kinds of judgments, but they cannot be judged by others. 16The Scriptures ask,

> "Has anyone ever known
> the thoughts of the Lord
> or given him advice?

But we understand what Christ is thinking.*g*

Working Together for God

3 My friends, you are acting like the people of this world. That's why I could not speak to you as spiritual people. You are like babies as far as your faith in Christ is concerned. 2So I had to treat you like babies and feed you milk. You could not take solid food, and you still cannot, 3because you are not yet spiritual. You are jealous and argue with each other. This proves that you are not spiritual and that you are acting like the people of this world.

4Some of you say that you follow me, and others claim to follow Apollos. Isn't that how ordinary people behave? 5Apollos and I are merely servants who helped you to have faith. It was the Lord who made it all happen. 6I planted the seeds, Apollos watered them, but God made them sprout and grow. 7What matters is not those who planted or watered, but God who made the plants grow. 8The one who plants is just as important as the one who waters. Each one will be paid for what they do. 9Apollos and I work together for God, and you are God's garden and God's building.

Grow up
(1) Have you ever been told to grow up? This is what Paul says to us when we argue about small things that don't matter. Truly grown-up Christians have learned to be at peace with God and with those around them. Otherwise they're still babies.

Planters and waterers
(6) Sometimes one Christian will "plant the seed" of the good news, but another will "water," and then it is God who makes it grow. When we share the message about Jesus, we should not always expect to see results right away. There is sometimes a lot more watering and growing that still has to happen. It might look like somebody is rejecting the message. But God and other Christians can help your seed grow.

---

f teach spiritual things to spiritual people: Or "compare spiritual things with spiritual things." *g we understand what Christ is thinking*: Or "we think as Christ does."

Only One Foundation

10God was kind and let me become an expert builder. I laid a foundation on which others have built. But we must each be careful how we build, 11because Christ is the only foundation. 12-13Whatever we build on that foundation will be tested by fire on the day of judgment. Then everyone will find out if we have used gold, silver, and precious stones, or wood, hay, and straw. 14We will be rewarded if our building is left standing. 15But if it is destroyed by the fire, we will lose everything. Yet we ourselves will be saved, like someone escaping from flames.

16All of you surely know that you are God's temple and that his Spirit lives in you. 17Together you are God's holy temple, and God will destroy anyone who destroys his temple.

18Don't fool yourselves! If any of you think you are wise in the things of this world, you will have to become foolish before you can be truly wise. 19This is because God considers the wisdom of this world to be foolish. It is just as the Scriptures say, "God catches the wise when they try to outsmart him." 20The Scriptures also say, "The Lord knows that the plans made by wise people are useless." 21-22So stop bragging about what anyone has done. Paul and Apollos and Peterh all belong to you. In fact, everything is yours, including the world, life, death, the present, and the future. Everything belongs to you, 23and you belong to Christ, and Christ belongs to God.

Build on a good foundation

(10) The secret of a building that lasts is its foundation. If we want to build a good life, we must build our lives on Jesus. Paul isn't against our being wise if Christ is the foundation of our wisdom. But we can't know any more about God than what he shows us in his word. Wisdom is what makes us able to use God's word to live well.

The Work of the Apostles

4 Think of us as servants of Christ who have been given the work of explaining God's mysterious ways. 2And since our first duty is to be faithful to the one we work for, 3it doesn't matter to me if I am judged by you or even by a court of law. In fact, I don't judge myself. 4I don't know of anything against me, but that doesn't prove that

Our judge is God

(4) We can look at this two ways. First, since God is our judge, we do what we ought to do for him, without trying to please all of the human "judges" who are looking on. Second, we ought to remember always that God is indeed the judge of all we think, say, and do. So we must always honor him and his word.

hPeter: See the note at 1.12.

I am right. The Lord is my judge. 5So don't judge anyone until the Lord comes. He will show what is hidden in the dark and what is in everyone's heart. Then God will be the one who praises each of us.

6Friends, I have used Apollos and myself as examples to teach you the meaning of the saying, "Follow the rules." I want you to stop saying that one of us is better than the other. 7What is so special about you? What do you have that you were not given? And if it was given to you, how can you brag? 8Are you already satisfied? Are you now rich? Have you become kings while we are still nobodies? I wish you were kings. Then we could have a share in your kingdom.

9It seems to me that God has put us apostles in the worst possible place. We are like prisoners on their way to death. Angels and the people of this world just laugh at us. 10Because of Christ we are thought of as fools, but Christ has made you wise. We are weak and hated, but you are powerful and respected. 11Even today we go hungry and thirsty and don't have anything to wear except rags. We are mistreated and don't have a place to live. 12We work hard with our own hands, and when people abuse us, we wish them well. When we suffer, we are patient. 13When someone curses us, we answer with kind words. Until now we are thought of as nothing more than the trash and garbage of this world.

14I am not writing to embarrass you. I want to help you, just as parents help their own dear children. 15Ten thousand people may teach you about Christ, but I am your only father. You became my children when I told you about Christ Jesus, 16and I want you to be like me. 17That's why I sent Timothy to you. I love him like a son, and he is a faithful servant of the Lord. Timothy will tell you what I do to follow Christ and how it agrees with what I always teach about Christ in every church.

18Some of you think I am not coming for a visit, and so you are bragging. 19But if the Lord lets me come, I will soon be there.

Riches don't count with God

(11) Jesus wasn't a rich man, and neither was Paul. In fact Paul said he had nothing to wear but rags. If we want to be leaders for Christ, let's not set our minds on being wealthy. If we do, we may forget Christ in our pursuit of riches. The desire to be rich is like quicksand: you can be swallowed by the very thing you hoped would hold you up.

Then I will find out if the ones who are doing all this bragging really have any power. 20God's kingdom is not just a lot of words. It is power. 21What do you want me to do when I arrive? Do you want me to be hard on you or to be kind and gentle?

Immoral Followers

5 I have heard terrible things about some of you. In fact, you are behaving worse than the Gentiles. A man is even sleeping with his own stepmother.*i* 2You are proud, when you ought to feel bad enough to chase away anyone who acts like that.

3-4I am with you only in my thoughts. But in the name of our Lord Jesus I have already judged this man, as though I were with you in person. So when you meet together and the power of the Lord Jesus is with you, I will be there too. 5You must then hand that man over to Satan. His body will be destroyed, but his spirit will be saved when the Lord Jesus returns.

6Stop being proud! Don't you know how a little yeast can spread through the whole batch of dough? 7Get rid of the old yeast! Then you will be like fresh bread made without yeast, and that is what you are. Our Passover lamb is Christ, who has already been sacrificed. 8So don't celebrate the festival by being evil and sinful, which is like serving bread made with yeast. Be pure and truthful and celebrate by using bread made without yeast.

9In my other letter*j* I told you not to have anything to do with immoral people. 10But I wasn't talking about the people of this world. You would have to leave this world to get away from everyone who is immoral or greedy or who cheats or worships idols. 11I was talking about your own people who are immoral or greedy or worship idols or curse others or get drunk or cheat. Don't

A Christian can't be immoral

(1) Make no mistake about it—oil and water can't mix, and Christ and immoral living can't mix. Either the immoral practice must go, or you will be in danger of losing the friendship of Christ. Too often we hear of foolish people who thought they could be Christians and follow the devil too. That's hopeless.

---

i is even sleeping with his own stepmother: Or "has even married his own stepmother." *j other letter:* An unknown letter that Paul wrote to the Christians at Corinth before he wrote this one.

even eat with them! 12Why should I judge outsiders? Aren't we supposed to judge only church members? 13God judges everyone else. The Scriptures say, "Chase away any of your own people who are evil."

Taking Each Other to Court

6 When one of you has a complaint against another, do you take your complaint to a court of sinners? Or do you take it to God's people? 2Don't you know that God's people will judge the world? And if you are going to judge the world, can't you settle small problems? 3Don't you know that we will judge angels? And if that is so, we can surely judge everyday matters. 4Why do you take everyday complaints to judges who are not respected by the church? 5I say this to your shame. Aren't any of you wise enough to act as a judge between one follower and another? 6Why should one of you take another to be tried by unbelievers?

7When one of you takes another to court, all of you lose. It would be better to let yourselves be cheated and robbed. 8But instead, you cheat and rob other followers.

9Don't you know that evil people won't have a share in the blessings of God's kingdom? Don't fool yourselves! No one who is immoral or worships idols or is unfaithful in marriage or is a pervert or behaves like a homosexual 10will share in God's kingdom. Neither will any thief or greedy person or drunkard or anyone who curses and cheats others. 11Some of you used to be like that. But now the name of our Lord Jesus Christ and the power of God's Spirit have washed you and made you holy and acceptable to God.

Honor God with Your Body

12Some of you say, "We can do anything we want to." But I tell you that not everything is good for us. So I refuse to let anything have power over me. 13You also say, "Food is meant for our bodies, and our bodies are meant for food." But I tell you that

Let Christians act like brothers and sisters
(1) Christians should be able to settle their own differences. If we can't agree in private, then we can always ask wiser brothers and sisters in Christ to help us with our disagreements. Our goal is not to get the best of one another, but to honor our Savior. And we should not mind losing if we are "dead with Christ."

Our bodies are Christ's property
(12) We belong to Jesus, who paid for us with his blood. The Holy Spirit lives inside us, and we are parts of the body of Christ, the church. So we should treat our bodies as the holy things they are, keeping them pure for Jesus' sake. This is especially important to remember in these days of widespread drug abuse and sexual sin.

God will destroy them both. We are not supposed to do indecent things with our bodies. We are to use them for the Lord who is in charge of our bodies. 14God will raise us from death by the same power that he used when he raised our Lord to life.

15Don't you know that your bodies are part of the body of Christ? Is it right for me to join part of the body of Christ to an immoral woman? No, it isn't! 16Don't you know that a man who does that becomes part of her body? The Scriptures say, "The two of them will be like one person." 17But anyone who is joined to the Lord is one in spirit with him.

18Don't be immoral in matters of sex. That is a sin against your own body in a way that no other sin is. 19Surely you know that your body is a temple where the Holy Spirit lives. The Spirit is in you and is a gift from God. You are no longer your own. 20God paid a great price for you. So use your body to honor God.

Questions about Marriage

7 Now I will answer the questions that you asked in your letter. You asked, "Is it best for people not to marry?"k 2Well, having your own husband or wife should keep you from doing something immoral. 3Husbands and wives should be fair with each other about having sex. 4A wife belongs to her husband instead of to herself, and a husband belongs to his wife instead of to himself. 5So don't refuse sex to each other, unless you agree not to have sex for a little while, in order to spend time in prayer. Then Satan won't be able to tempt you because of your lack of self-control. 6In my opinion that is what should be done, though I don't know of anything the Lord said about this matter. 7I wish that all of you were like me, but God has given different gifts to each of us.

8Here is my advice for people who have

Be loyal to the one you marry

(1) If we say we're Christians, and we say we love one another, but we don't love our wives or husbands, then where is the love? Loving your neighbor, as Jesus said, certainly must mean loving the one closest to you—your husband or your wife. For love's sake and for Christ's, we ought to learn to give and take in marriage. Not forgiving and carrying each other's burdens leads to misery and ruin.

kpeople not to marry: Or "married couples not to have sex."

never been married and for widows. You should stay single, just as I am. 9But if you don't have enough self-control, then go ahead and get married. After all, it is better to marry than to burn with desire.*l*

10I instruct married couples to stay together, and this is exactly what the Lord himself taught. A wife who leaves her husband 11should either stay single or go back to her husband. And a husband should not leave his wife.

12I don't know of anything else the Lord said about marriage. All I can do is to give you my own advice. If your wife is not a follower of the Lord, but is willing to stay with you, don't divorce her. 13If your husband is not a follower, but is willing to stay with you, don't divorce him. 14Your husband or wife who is not a follower is made holy by having you as a mate. This also makes your children holy and keeps them from being unclean in God's sight.

15If your husband or wife is not a follower of the Lord and decides to divorce you, then you should agree to it. You are no longer bound to that person. After all, God chose you and wants you to live at peace. 16And besides, how do you know if you will be able to save your husband or wife who is not a follower?

Obeying the Lord at All Times

17In every church I tell the people to stay as they were when the Lord Jesus chose them and God called them to be his own. Now I say the same thing to you. 18If you are already circumcised, don't try to change it. If you are not circumcised, don't get circumcised. 19Being circumcised or uncircumcised is not really what matters. The important thing is to obey God's commands. 20So don't try to change what you were when God chose you. 21Are you a slave? Don't let that bother you. But if you can win your freedom, you should. 22When the Lord chooses slaves, they become his free

Send down your roots
(17) It is said that tumbleweeds never send down roots—which means they never amount to anything. Christians need to appreciate the places where God plants them. Let's not always be looking for a new church, or a new job, or a new home. God sometimes might be leading a person someplace else, but every Christian should be thankful for the place God has given, and use it to grow strong as Christ's servant.

---

lwith desire: Or "in the flames of hell."

people. And when he chooses free people, they become slaves of Christ. 23God paid a great price for you. So don't become slaves of anyone else. 24Stay what you were when God chose you.

Unmarried People

25I don't know of anything that the Lord said about widows or people who have never been married.[m] But I will tell you what I think. And you can trust me, because the Lord has treated me with kindness. 26We are now going through hard times, and I think it is best for you to stay as you are. 27If you are married, stay married. If you are not married, don't try to get married. 28It isn't wrong to marry, even if you have never been married before. But those who marry will have a lot of trouble, and I want to protect you from that.

29My friends, what I mean is that the Lord will soon come,[n] and it won't matter if you are married or not. 30It will be all the same if you are crying or laughing, or if you are buying or are completely broke. 31It won't make any difference how much good you are getting from this world or how much you like it. This world as we know it is now passing away.

32I want all of you to be free from worry. An unmarried man worries about how to please the Lord. 33But a married man has more worries. He must worry about the things of this world, because he wants to please his wife. 34So he is pulled in two directions. Unmarried women and women who have never been married[o] worry only about pleasing the Lord, and they keep their bodies and minds pure. But a married woman worries about the things of this world, because she wants to please her husband. 35What I am saying is for your own

Marriage isn't the goal of life
(27) Too many young people rush into marriage without counting what it will cost them. Then the marriage often ends in ruin. It's far better not to marry at all than to make a marriage that can't be happy. Marriage may cost more self-sacrifice for your husband's or wife's sake than you plan on giving. Think it over seriously.

---

[m]*people who have never been married*: Or "virgins."
[n]*the Lord will soon come*: Or "There's not much time left" or "The time for decision comes quickly."
[o]*women who have never been married*: Or "virgins."

good. I want to help you to live right and to love the Lord above all else.

36But suppose you are engaged to someone old enough to be married, and you want her so much that all you can think about is getting married. Then go ahead and marry.p There is nothing wrong with that. 37But it is better to have self-control and to make up your mind not to marry. 38It is perfectly all right to marry, but it is better not to get married at all.

39A wife should stay married to her husband until he dies. Then she is free to marry again, but only to a man who is a follower of the Lord. 40However, I think I am obeying God's Spirit when I say she would be happier to stay single.

Food Offered to Idols

8 In your letter you asked me about food offered to idols. All of us know something about this subject. But knowledge makes us proud of ourselves, while love makes us helpful to others. 2In fact, people who think they know so much don't know anything at all. 3But God has no doubts about who loves him.

4Even though food is offered to idols, we know that none of the idols in this world are alive. After all, there is only one God. 5Many things in heaven and on earth are called gods and lords, but none of them really are gods or lords. 6We have only one God, and he is the Father. He created everything, and we live for him. Jesus Christ is our only Lord. Everything was made by him, and by him life was given to us.

7Not everyone knows these things. In fact, many people have grown up with the

Truth is what counts
(1) Christians in Corinth were concerned about eating food that might have been offered to some false idol in a temple. But Paul advised them not to worry about things they couldn't know for sure. After all, an idol is a false god, not a real one. A lesson for us here is that we should keep our eyes on the true God, and not worry so much about unknown dangers.

---

pBut suppose you are engaged . . . go ahead and marry: Verses 36-38 may also be translated: 36"If you feel that you are not treating your grown daughter right by keeping her from getting married, then let her marry. You won't be doing anything wrong. 37But it is better to have self-control and make up your mind not to let your daughter get married. 38It is all right for you to let her marry. But it is better if you don't let her marry at all."

belief that idols have life in them. So when they eat meat offered to idols, they are bothered by a weak conscience. 8But food doesn't bring us any closer to God. We are no worse off if we don't eat, and we are no better off if we do.

9Don't cause problems for someone with a weak conscience, just because you have the right to eat anything. 10You know all this, and so it doesn't bother you to eat in the temple of an idol. But suppose a person with a weak conscience sees you and decides to eat food that has been offered to idols. 11Then what you know has destroyed someone Christ died for. 12When you sin by hurting a follower with a weak conscience, you sin against Christ. 13So if I hurt one of the Lord's followers by what I eat, I will never eat meat as long as I live.

The Rights of an Apostle

9 I am free. I am an apostle. I have seen the Lord Jesus and have led you to have faith in him. 2Others may think that I am not an apostle, but you are proof that I am an apostle to you.

3When people question me, I tell them 4that Barnabas and I have the right to our food and drink. 5We each have the right to marry one of the Lord's followers and to take her along with us, just as the other apostles and the Lord's brothers and Peter*q* do. 6Are we the only ones who have to support ourselves by working at another job? 7Do soldiers pay their own salaries? Don't people who raise grapes eat some of what they grow? Don't shepherds get milk from their own goats?

8-9I am not saying this on my own authority. The Law of Moses tells us not to muzzle an ox when it is grinding grain. But was God concerned only about an ox? 10No, he wasn't! He was talking about us. This was written in the Scriptures so that all who

qPeter: See the note at 1.12.

Be willing to lose your rights
(9) "Getting my rights" is too important to many people. When we have Christ, we don't need to go around demanding our rights. This is especially true if using our right to do something means someone else will be offended by it. In a case like that, we should think about the other person's feelings more than our own rights.

Supporting the Lord's work
(7) A good worker doing good work deserves good pay. This is especially true of those who preach the good news and work to help churches. But all too often, Christians give pastors and other religious workers low pay, as if they weren't doing anything very important. Pastors certainly don't need to be rich, but let's not keep them poor while we live well. God is not honored by that.

plow and all who grind the grain will look forward to sharing in the harvest.

11When we told the message to you, it was like planting spiritual seed. So we have the right to accept material things as our harvest from you. 12If others have the right to do this, we have an even greater right. But we haven't used this right of ours. We are willing to put up with anything to keep from causing trouble for the message about Christ.

13Don't you know that people who work in the temple make their living from what is brought to the temple? Don't you know that a person who serves at the altar is given part of what is offered? 14In the same way, the Lord wants everyone who preaches the good news to make a living from preaching this message.

15But I have never used these privileges of mine, and I am not writing this because I want to start now. I would rather die than have someone rob me of the right to take pride in this. 16I don't have any reason to brag about preaching the good news. Preaching is something God told me to do, and if I don't do it, I am doomed. 17If I preach because I want to, I will be paid. But even if I don't want to, it is still something that God has sent me to do. 18What pay am I given? It is the chance to preach the good news free of charge and not to use the privileges that are mine because I am a preacher.

19I am not anyone's slave. But I have become a slave to everyone, so that I can win as many people as possible. 20When I am with the Jews, I live like a Jew to win Jews. They are ruled by the Law of Moses, and I am not. But I live by the Law to win them. 21And when I am with people who are not ruled by the Law, I forget about the Law to win them. Of course, I never really forget about the law of God. In fact, I am ruled by the law of Christ. 22When I am with people whose faith is weak, I live as they do to win them. I do everything I can to win everyone I possibly can. 23I do all this for the good news, because I want to share in its blessings.

Do what it takes to win people to Christ
(19) Missionaries need to live among the people they hope to bring to Jesus. This means taking on their customs, as much as someone can without sinning. Paul was willing to live like a Jew or like a Gentile. He would do whatever he was called to do for spreading the good news. Let's not be so "set in our ways" that we can't give up our personal desires in order to attract people to Jesus.

A Race and a Fight

24You know that many runners enter a race, and only one of them wins the prize. So run to win! 25Athletes work hard to win a crown that cannot last, but we do it for a crown that will last forever. 26I don't run without a goal. And I don't box by beating my fists in the air. 27I keep my body under control and make it my slave, so I won't lose out after telling the good news to others.

Don't Worship Idols

10 Friends, I want to remind you that all of our ancestors walked under the cloud and went through the sea. 2This was like being baptized and becoming followers of Moses. 3All of them also ate the same spiritual food 4and drank the same spiritual drink, which flowed from the spiritual rock that followed them. That rock was Christ. 5But most of them did not please God. So they died, and their bodies were scattered all over the desert.

6What happened to them is a warning to keep us from wanting to do the same evil things. 7They worshiped idols, just as the Scriptures say, "The people sat down to eat and drink. Then they got up to dance around." So don't worship idols. 8Some of those people did shameful things, and in a single day about twenty-three thousand of them died. Don't do shameful things as they did. 9And don't try to test Christ,r as some of them did and were later bitten by poisonous snakes. 10Don't even grumble, as some of them did and were killed by the destroying angel. 11These things happened to them as a warning to us. All this was written in the Scriptures to teach us who live in these last days.

12Even if you think you can stand up to temptation, be careful not to fall. 13You are tempted in the same way that everyone else is tempted. But God can be trusted not to let you be tempted too much, and he

We need self-control
(24) Professional athletes need to go without many luxuries if they're going to make the team. Keeping weight down and muscles toned requires work and discipline. The Christian is like such an athlete. We have decided to follow Jesus, and we're glad to leave behind the things that hold us back from spreading the good news about him. Can you play the game of life for Jesus?

Do we worship idols?
(6) We usually don't make statues of stone or wood and pray to them. But an idol is really anything besides God that comes first in our lives. An idol can be a career, a loved one, or something as trivial as a new car. God said, "You shall have no gods other than me." It only makes sense that God our Creator should be first in all of our thoughts.

rChrist: Some manuscripts have "the Lord."

will show you how to escape from your temptations.

14My friends, you must keep away from idols. 15I am speaking to you as people who have enough sense to know what I am talking about. 16When we drink from the cup that we ask God to bless, isn't that sharing in the blood of Christ? When we eat the bread that we break, isn't that sharing in the body of Christ? 17By sharing in the same loaf of bread, we become one body, even though there are many of us.

18Aren't the people of Israel sharing in the worship when they gather around the altar and eat the sacrifices offered there? 19Am I saying that either the idols or the food sacrificed to them is anything at all? 20No, I am not! That food is really sacrificed to demons and not to God. I don't want you to have anything to do with demons. 21You cannot drink from the cup of demons and still drink from the Lord's cup. You cannot eat at the table of demons and still eat at the Lord's table. 22We would make the Lord jealous if we did that. And we are not stronger than the Lord.

Always Honor God

23Some of you say, "We can do whatever we want to!" But I tell you that not everything we do is good or helpful. 24We should think about others and not about ourselves. 25However, when you buy meat in the market, go ahead and eat it. Keep your conscience clear by not asking where the meat came from. 26The Scriptures say, "The earth and everything in it belong to the Lord."

27If an unbeliever invites you to dinner, and you want to go, then go. Eat whatever you are served. Don't cause a problem for someone's conscience by asking where the food came from. 28-29But if you are told that it has been sacrificed to idols, don't cause a problem by eating it. I don't mean a problem for yourself, but for the one who told you. Why should my freedom be limited by someone else's conscience? 30If I give

Christians are free, but . . .

(23) Believers are not living under the Jewish system of laws. The law that really governs Christians is the law of love. But love doesn't allow us to live in a way that dishonors God. The difference between right and wrong is always the same. Love means, too, that we should do without things that may set a bad example for other people, even though those things don't hurt us personally.

thanks for what I eat, why should anyone accuse me of doing wrong? ³¹When you eat or drink or do anything else, always do it to honor God. ³²Don't cause problems for Jews or Greeks or anyone else who belongs to God's church. ³³I always try to please others instead of myself, in the hope that many of them will

11 be saved. ¹You must follow my example, as I follow the example of Christ.

Rules for Worship

²I am proud of you, because you always remember me and obey the teachings I gave you. ³Now I want you to know that Christ is the head over all men, and a man is the head over a woman. But God is the head over Christ. ⁴This means that any man who prays or prophesies with something on his head brings shame to his head.

⁵But any woman who prays or prophesies without something on her head brings shame to her head. In fact, she may as well shave her head.ˢ ⁶A woman should wear something on her head. It is a disgrace for a woman to shave her head or cut her hair. But if she refuses to wear something on her head, let her cut off her hair.

⁷Men were created to be like God and to bring honor to God. This means that a man should not wear anything on his head. Women were created to bring honor to men. ⁸It was the woman who was made from a man, and not the man who was made from a woman. ⁹He was not created for her. She was created for him. ¹⁰And so, because of this, and also because of the angels, a woman ought to wear something on her head. This will show that she is under someone's authority.

¹¹As far as the Lord is concerned, men and women need each other. ¹²It is true that

Be natural
(1) Paul writes here about customs of worship and personal grooming. Although it seems that some of these matters are minor, there is an important idea here: we should honor the social customs of others. If we break them just to prove we're superior, that's pride, which is a sin. We should not try to be "one up" on somebody else. In our life together our goal is not to force our opinions on people, but to accept each other's wishes as much as we can.

ˢ*she may as well shave her head*: A woman's hair was a mark of beauty, and it was shameful for a woman to cut her hair short or to shave her head, so that she looked like a man.

the first woman came from a man, but all other men have been given birth by women. Yet God is the one who created everything. 13Ask yourselves if it is proper for a woman to pray without something on her head. 14Isn't it unnatural and disgraceful for men to have long hair? 15But long hair is a beautiful way for a woman to cover her head. 16This is how things are done in all of God's churches,*t* and that's why none of you should argue about what I have said.

Rules for the Lord's Supper

17Your worship services do you more harm than good. I am certainly not going to praise you for this. 18I am told that you can't get along with each other when you worship, and I am sure that some of what I have heard is true. 19You are bound to argue with each other, but it is easy to see which of you have God's approval.

20When you meet together, you don't really celebrate the Lord's Supper. 21You even start eating before everyone gets to the meeting, and some of you go hungry, while others get drunk. 22Don't you have homes where you can eat and drink? Do you hate God's church? Do you want to embarrass people who don't have anything? What can I say to you? I certainly cannot praise you.

The Lord's Supper
(Matthew 26.26–29; Mark 14.22–25; Luke 22.14–20)

23I have already told you what the Lord Jesus did on the night he was betrayed. And it came from the Lord himself.

He took some bread in his hands. 24Then after he had given thanks, he broke it and said, "This is my body, which is given for you. Eat this and remember me."

Proper behavior at worship
(17) How awful it is when people sin even while they meet together for worship. We should honor God with our thoughts, words, and actions at all times, but especially when we meet to worship him. To truly worship God, we need to have him on the throne, not ourselves.

We love the Lord's Supper
(23) The Lord's Supper is the special time when we remember our Savior's death as a Christian group. Because Jesus died for our sins, we owe him our very lives. Remembering the Lord in this way draws us closer to him and reminds us of what his death means to us.

---

t This is how things are done in all of God's churches: Or "There is no set rule for this in any of God's churches."

25After the meal, Jesus took a cup of wine in his hands and said, "This is my blood, and with it God makes his new agreement with you. Drink this and remember me."

26The Lord meant that when you eat this bread and drink from this cup, you tell about his death until he comes.

27But if you eat the bread and drink the wine in a way that is not worthy of the Lord, you sin against his body and blood. 28That's why you must examine the way you eat and drink. 29If you fail to understand that you are the body of the Lord, you will condemn yourselves by the way you eat and drink. 30That's why many of you are sick and weak and why a lot of others have died. 31If we carefully judge ourselves, we won't be punished. 32But when the Lord judges and punishes us, he does it to keep us from being condemned with the rest of the world.

33My dear friends, you should wait until everyone gets there before you start eating. 34If you really are hungry, you can eat at home. Then you won't condemn yourselves when you meet together.

After I arrive, I will instruct you about the other matters.

Spiritual Gifts

12 My friends, you asked me about spiritual gifts. 2I want you to remember that before you became followers of the Lord, you were led in all the wrong ways by idols that cannot even talk. 3Now I want you to know that if you are led by God's Spirit, you will say that Jesus is Lord, and you will never curse Jesus.

4There are different kinds of spiritual gifts, but they all come from the same Spirit. 5There are different ways to serve the same Lord, 6and we can each do different things. Yet the same God works in all of us and helps us in everything we do.

7The Spirit has given each of us a special way of serving others. 8Some of us can speak with wisdom, while others can speak with knowledge, but these gifts come from

God gives us gifts for service

(1) The Holy Spirit gives at least one spiritual gift to each believer. The gift is not for showing off, but it is for serving in a way that builds up God's church. It's important that each of us is not just a watcher of how others use their gifts. But each must find out his or her gift and use it as God commands.

the same Spirit. 9To others the Spirit has given great faith or the power to heal the sick 10or the power to work mighty miracles. Some of us are prophets, and some of us recognize when God's Spirit is present. Others can speak different kinds of languages, and still others can tell what these languages mean. 11But it is the Spirit who does all this and decides which gifts to give to each of us.

One Body with Many Parts

12The body of Christ has many different parts, just as any other body does. 13Some of us are Jews, and others are Gentiles. Some of us are slaves, and others are free. But God's Spirit baptized each of us and made us part of the body of Christ. Now we each drink from that same Spirit.u

14Our bodies don't have just one part. They have many parts. 15Suppose a foot says, "I'm not a hand, and so I'm not part of the body." Wouldn't the foot still belong to the body? 16Or suppose an ear says, "I'm not an eye, and so I'm not part of the body." Wouldn't the ear still belong to the body? 17If our bodies were only an eye, we couldn't hear a thing. And if they were only an ear, we couldn't smell a thing. 18But God has put all parts of our body together in the way that he decided is best.

19A body is not really a body, unless there is more than one part. 20It takes many parts to make a single body. 21That's why the eyes cannot say they don't need the hands. That's also why the head cannot say it doesn't need the feet. 22In fact, we cannot get along without the parts of the body that seem to be the weakest. 23We take special care to dress up some parts of our bodies. We are modest about our personal parts,

Be a working part of Christ's body
(12) Jesus leaves us on earth to be his presence in the world. In a real sense, we all are parts of the present earthly body of Jesus. That's awesome, isn't it? Think of how necessary it is for you to do your part in the body. If you don't, then the body is crippled. Pray that God will help you every day to be what he wants you to be in the world.

uSome of us are Jews . . . that same Spirit: Verse 13 may also be translated, "God's Spirit is inside each of us, and all around us as well. So it doesn't matter that some of us are Jews and others are Gentiles and that some are slaves and others are free. Together we are one body."

24but we don't have to be modest about other parts.

God put our bodies together in such a way that even the parts that seem the least important are valuable. 25He did this to make all parts of the body work together smoothly, with each part caring about the others. 26If one part of our body hurts, we hurt all over. If one part of our body is honored, the rest of the body will be honored too.

27Together you are the body of Christ. Each one of you is part of his body. 28First, God chose some people to be apostles and prophets and teachers for the church. But he also chose some to work miracles or heal the sick or help others or be leaders or speak different kinds of languages. 29Not everyone is an apostle. Not everyone is a prophet. Not everyone is a teacher. Not everyone can work miracles. 30Not everyone can heal the sick. Not everyone can speak different kinds of languages. Not everyone can tell what these languages mean. 31I want you to desire the best gifts.v So I will show you a much better way.

Different people, different parts

(27) Imagine what it would be like if an actor in a play started saying lines that were not his, but another actor's. The play would be a mess. Likewise, not all people in the church have all of the gifts God has given. We ought to know the place where God wants us, and do our best for him there.

Love

13 What if I could speak
all languages of humans
and of angels?
If I did not love others,
I would be nothing more
than a noisy gong
or a clanging cymbal.
2What if I could prophesy
and understand all secrets
and all knowledge?
And what if I had faith
that moved mountains?
I would be nothing,
unless I loved others.
3What if I gave away all
that I owned

The greatest gift

(1) When Paul got through describing spiritual gifts, he wanted to show that one gift is greater than all others. That gift is love. As you read carefully the way this love works, ask yourself, "Am I like that?" We would all be ashamed to know how far short of real love we come at times. But God will help us. Our love should be for the world, especially for other believers, and particularly for those with whom we live closest.

vI want you to desire the best gifts: Or "You desire the best gifts."

and let myself
   be burned alive?[w]
I would gain nothing,
   unless I loved others.
4Love is kind and patient,
never jealous, boastful,
   proud, or 5rude.
Love isn't selfish
   or quick tempered.
It doesn't keep a record
   of wrongs that others do.
6Love rejoices in the truth,
   but not in evil.
7Love is always supportive,
loyal, hopeful,
   and trusting.
8Love never fails!

Everyone who prophesies
   will stop,
and unknown languages
will no longer
   be spoken.
All that we know
   will be forgotten.
9We don't know everything,
and our prophecies
   are not complete.
10But what is perfect
   will someday appear,
and what is not perfect
   will then disappear.

11When we were children,
we thought and reasoned,
   as children do.
But when we grew up,
   we quit our childish ways.
12Now all we can see of God
is like a cloudy picture
   in a mirror.
Later we will see him
   face to face.
We don't know everything,
   but then we will,

Someday we'll have
the answers

(9) In this world God has revealed a lot to us, but there is still a lot that we just don't understand. But when God takes us to himself someday, the rest of what there is to know will become very clear to us. What a time that will be, as God opens up the treasures of his knowledge to us.

[w]and let myself be burned alive: Some manuscripts have
"so that I could brag."

just as God completely
understands us.
13For now there are faith,
hope, and love.
But of these three,
the greatest is love.

Speaking Unknown Languages and Prophesying

14 Love should be your guide. Be eager to have the gifts that come from the Holy Spirit, especially the gift of prophecy. 2If you speak languages that others don't know, God will understand what you are saying, though no one else will know what you mean. You will be talking about mysteries that only the Spirit understands. 3But when you prophesy, you will be understood, and others will be helped. They will be encouraged and made to feel better.

4By speaking languages that others don't know, you help only yourself. But by prophesying you help everyone in the church. 5I am glad for you to speak unknown languages, although I had rather for you to prophesy. In fact, prophesying does much more good than speaking unknown languages, unless someone can help the church by explaining what you mean.

6My friends, what good would it do, if I came and spoke unknown languages to you and didn't explain what I meant? How would I help you, unless I told you what God had shown me or gave you some knowledge or prophecy or teaching? 7If all musical instruments sounded alike, how would you know the difference between a flute and a harp? 8If a bugle call isn't clear, how would you know to get ready for battle?

9That's how it is when you speak unknown languages. If no one can understand what you are talking about, you will only be talking to the wind. 10There are many different languages in this world, and all of them make sense. 11But if I don't understand the language that someone is using, we will be like foreigners to each other. 12If you really want spiritual gifts, choose

Always try to make good sense

(4) Let's be sure we speak of God's saving work in ways that make sense to those around us. Just because people have the ability to speak strange languages and puzzle others, that doesn't mean they're doing something wonderful and good. Prophecy is useful, writes Paul, because it is a message that makes good sense to everybody.

the ones that will be most helpful to the church.

¹³When we speak languages that others don't know, we should pray for the power to explain what we mean. ¹⁴For example, if I use an unknown language in my prayers, my spirit prays but my mind is useless. ¹⁵Then what should I do? There are times when I should pray with my spirit, and times when I should pray with my mind. Sometimes I should sing with my spirit, and at other times I should sing with my mind.

¹⁶Suppose some strangers are in your worship service, when you are praising God with your spirit. If they don't understand you, how will they know to say, "Amen"? ¹⁷You may be worshiping God in a wonderful way, but no one else will be helped. ¹⁸I thank God that I speak unknown languages more than any of you. ¹⁹But words that make sense can help the church. That's why in church I had rather speak five words that make sense than to speak ten thousand words in a language that others don't know.

²⁰My friends, stop thinking like children. Think like mature people and be as innocent as tiny babies. ²¹In the Scriptures the Lord says,

> "I will use strangers
> who speak unknown languages
>   to talk to my people.
> They will speak to them
>   in foreign languages,
> but still my people
>   won't listen to me."

²²Languages that others don't know may mean something to unbelievers, but not to the Lord's followers. Prophecy, on the other hand, is for followers, not for unbelievers. ²³Suppose everyone in your worship service started speaking unknown languages, and some outsiders or some unbelievers come in. Won't they think you are crazy? ²⁴But suppose all of you are prophesying when those unbelievers and outsiders come in. They will realize that they are sinners, and they will want to change their ways because

Be both young and old
(20) Paul's advice to the church at Corinth was for them to be both young and old. Christians should be innocent as little children, honest and trusting. But we should have the maturity of adults, behaving ourselves and not being selfish.

of what you are saying. 25They will tell what is hidden in their hearts. Then they will kneel down and say to God, "We are certain that you are with these people."

Worship Must Be Orderly

26My friends, when you meet to worship, you must do everything for the good of everyone there. That's how it should be when someone sings or teaches or tells what God has said or speaks an unknown language or explains what the language means. 27No more than two or three of you should speak unknown languages during the meeting. You must take turns, and someone should always be there to explain what you mean. 28If no one can explain, you must keep silent in church and speak only to yourself and to God.

29Two or three persons may prophesy, and everyone else must listen carefully. 30If someone sitting there receives a message from God, the speaker must stop and let the other person speak. 31Let only one person speak at a time, then all of you will learn something and be encouraged. 32A prophet should be willing to stop and let someone else speak. 33God wants everything to be done peacefully and in order.

When God's people meet in church, 34the women must not be allowed to speak. They must keep quiet and listen, as the Law of Moses teaches. 35If there is something they want to know, they can ask their husbands when they get home. It is disgraceful for women to speak in church. 36God's message did not start with you people, and you are not the only ones it has reached.

37If you think of yourself as a prophet or a spiritual person, you will know that I am writing only what the Lord has commanded. 38So don't pay attention to anyone who ignores what I am writing. 39My friends, be eager to prophesy and don't stop anyone from speaking languages that others don't know. 40But do everything properly and in order.

A church meeting isn't a riot

(26) It seems that some of the meetings at Corinth were almost riots. Everybody was talking at once, and there was a lot of noise and confusion. It takes self-control to be a good listener, so others can have a turn at speaking. God is the One we want to hear from, not our noisy selves.

Christ Was Raised to Life

15 My friends, I want you to remember the message that I preached and that you believed and trusted. 2You will be saved by this message, if you hold firmly to it. But if you don't, your faith was all for nothing.

3I told you the most important part of the message, and you believed it. That part is:

> Christ died for our sins,
>   as the Scriptures say.
> 4He was buried,
>   and three days later
> he was raised to life,
>   as the Scriptures say.
> 5Christ appeared to Peter,x
>   then to the twelve.
> 6After this, he appeared
> to more than five hundred
>   other followers.
> Most of them are still alive,
>   but some have died.
> 7He also appeared to James,
> and then to all
>   of the apostles.

8Finally, he appeared to me, even though I am like someone who was born at the wrong time.y

9I am the least important of all the apostles. In fact, I caused so much trouble for God's church that I don't even deserve to be called an apostle. 10But God was kind! He made me what I am, and his kindness was not wasted. I worked much harder than any of the other apostles, although it was really God's kindness at work and not me. 11But it doesn't matter if I preached or if they preached. All of you believed the message just the same.

God's People Will Be Raised to Life

12If we preach that Christ was raised from death, how can some of you say that the

What the good news is
(3) The good news is that Jesus didn't stay in his tomb. He rose up again on the third day, and he is alive now. If he lives in you by the Holy Spirit, you will be able to do his work now. Then other people will believe the good news about Jesus and live forever with him. Because he lives, we will live too.

---

xPeter: See the note at 1.12.   ywho was born at the wrong time: The meaning of these words in Greek is not clear.

dead will not be raised to life? 13If they won't be raised to life, Christ himself was not raised to life. 14And if Christ was not raised to life, our message is worthless, and so is your faith. 15If the dead won't be raised to life, we have told lies about God by saying that he raised Christ to life, when he really did not.

16So if the dead won't be raised to life, Christ was not raised to life. 17Unless Christ was raised to life, your faith is useless, and you are still living in your sins. 18And those people who died after putting their faith in him are completely lost. 19If our hope in Christ is good only for this life, we are worse off than anyone else.

20But Christ has been raised to life! And he makes us certain that others will also be raised to life. 21Just as we will die because of Adam, we will be raised to life because of Christ. 22Adam brought death to all of us, and Christ will bring life to all of us. 23But we must each wait our turn. Christ was the first to be raised to life, and his people will be raised to life when he returns. 24Then after Christ has destroyed all powers and forces, the end will come, and he will give the kingdom to God the Father.

25Christ will rule until he puts all his enemies under his power, 26and the last enemy he destroys will be death. 27When the Scriptures say that he will put everything under his power, they don't include God. It was God who put everything under the power of Christ. 28After everything is under the power of God's Son, he will put himself under the power of God, who put everything under his Son's power. Then God will mean everything to everyone.

29If the dead are not going to be raised to life, what will people do who are being baptized for them? Why are they being baptized for those dead people? 30And why do we always risk our lives 31and face death every day? The pride that I have in you because of Christ Jesus our Lord is what makes me say this. 32What do you think I gained by fighting wild animals in Ephesus? If the dead are not raised to life,

The risen Christ

(14) What Paul's whole message rests on is the fact that Jesus Christ was raised to life. Without a risen Christ, the good news could not help anyone. A dead Savior whose bones lie cold in a grave somewhere could not save anyone from sin. But praise God—the grave is empty. Jesus Christ is alive.

Christ will reign over all

(25) When Jesus came the first time, he mostly acted like a servant. He wanted us not to be afraid of him, but to trust him. And he needed to die to save us. But some day he will return, and then we will see what a great King he really is. No other king could ever be like him. He shall reign forever and ever. That will be a glad forever indeed.

"Let's eat and drink.
    Tomorrow we die."
33Don't fool yourselves. Bad friends will destroy you. 34Be sensible and stop sinning. You should be embarrassed that some people still don't know about God.

What Our Bodies Will Be Like

35Some of you have asked, "How will the dead be raised to life? What kind of bodies will they have?" 36Don't be foolish. A seed must die before it can sprout from the ground. 37Wheat seeds and all other seeds look different from the sprouts that come up. 38This is because God gives everything the kind of body he wants it to have. 39People, animals, birds, and fish are each made of flesh, but none of them are alike. 40Everything in the heavens has a body, and so does everything on earth. But each one is very different from all the others. 41The sun is not like the moon, the moon is not like the stars, and each star is different.

42That's how it will be when our bodies are raised to life. These bodies will die, but the bodies that are raised will live forever. 43These ugly and weak bodies will become beautiful and strong. 44As surely as there are physical bodies, there are spiritual bodies. And our physical bodies will be changed into spiritual bodies.

45The first man was named Adam, and the Scriptures tell us that he was a living person. But Jesus, who may be called the last Adam, is a life-giving spirit. 46We see that the one with a spiritual body did not come first. He came after the one who had a physical body. 47The first man was made from the dust of the earth, but the second man came from heaven. 48Everyone on earth has a body like the body of the one who was made from the dust of the earth. And everyone in heaven has a body like the body of the one who came from heaven. 49Just as we are like the one who was made out of earth, we will be like the one who came from heaven.

50My friends, I want you to know that

How will we live again?
(35) Jesus said that he came to give us life—a new kind of life, the life of God himself. When we have that life of God, we don't really die. If our bodies die before Jesus returns, we know that someday we will be raised to life with bodies that can never die. This is the kind of life God planned for us before sin came into the world and caused death.

our bodies of flesh and blood will decay. This means that they cannot share in God's kingdom, which lasts forever. 51I will explain a mystery to you. Not every one of us will die, but we will all be changed. 52It will happen suddenly, quicker than the blink of an eye. At the sound of the last trumpet the dead will be raised. We will all be changed, so that we will never die again. 53Our dead and decaying bodies will be changed into bodies that won't die or decay. 54The bodies we now have are weak and can die. But they will be changed into bodies that are eternal. Then the Scriptures will come true,

"Death has lost the battle!
55Where is its victory?
Where is its sting?"

56Sin is what gives death its sting, and the Law is the power behind sin. 57But thank God for letting our Lord Jesus Christ give us the victory!

58My dear friends, stand firm and don't be shaken. Always keep busy working for the Lord. You know that everything you do for him is worthwhile.

A Collection for God's People

16 When you collect money for God's people, I want you to do exactly what I told the churches in Galatia to do. 2That is, each Sunday each of you must put aside part of what you have earned. If you do this, you won't have to take up a collection when I come. 3Choose some followers to take the money to Jerusalem. I will send them on with the money and with letters which show that you approve of them. 4If you think I should go along, they can go with me.

Paul's Travel Plans

5After I have gone through Macedonia, I hope to see you 6and visit with you for a while. I may even stay all winter, so that you can help me on my way to wherever I will be going next. 7If the Lord lets me, I

Christ will return suddenly
(51) When Jesus returns, his living followers will be changed in that moment, and believers who have died will be raised. All weakness, sickness, and death that we have grown used to will be no more. We shall be new people with new and different bodies that experience only health, strength, and happiness. Believers who had died will be reunited with those they left behind, never to be separated again

What we do for God will never be lost
(58) Paul elsewhere describes work done for God as gold, silver, and precious stones (see 1 Corinthians 3.12). Anything not done for God will not last. That is a great privilege. We can work with God to do things that last forever. The people we win to Christ, and even the little things we do, like giving a cool drink of water for Christ, will be treasured forever by God.

Christians are friendly
(5) Notice this other side of Paul's character. Usually we think of him as being concerned only about high matters, perhaps even severe at times. But Paul's real per-

would rather come later for a longer visit than to stop off now for only a short visit. 8I will stay in Ephesus until Pentecost, 9because there is a wonderful opportunity for me to do some work here. But there are also many people who are against me.

10When Timothy arrives, give him a friendly welcome. He is doing the Lord's work, just as I am. 11Don't let anyone mistreat him. I am looking for him to return to me together with the other followers. So when he leaves, send him off with your blessings.

12I have tried hard to get our friend Apollos to visit you with the other followers. He doesn't want to come just now, but he will come when he can.

Personal Concerns and Greetings

13Keep alert. Be firm in your faith. Stay brave and strong. 14Show love in everything you do.

15You know that Stephanas and his family were the first in Achaia to have faith in the Lord. They have done all they can for God's people. My friends, I ask you 16to obey leaders like them and to do the same for all others who work hard with you.

17I was glad to see Stephanas and Fortunatus and Achaicus. Having them here was like having you. 18They made me feel much better, just as they made you feel better. You should appreciate people like them.

19Greetings from the churches in Asia.

Aquila and Priscilla, together with the church that meets in their house, send greetings in the name of the Lord.

20All of the Lord's followers send their greetings.

Give each other a warm greeting.

21I am signing this letter myself: PAUL.

22I pray that God will put a curse on everyone who does not love the Lord. And may the Lord come soon.

23I pray that the Lord Jesus will be kind to you.

24I love everyone who belongs to Christ Jesus. Amen.

sonality was tender and friendly. He enjoyed the friendship of God's people. This is a model for us. A stand-offish Christian just doesn't make sense.

Strength plus love
(13) Paul's advice here for Christians is to be firm, brave, and strong, *and* always to show love. That's quite a combination—to be tough and tender at the same time. But that's what it means to be like Jesus.

PAUL'S SECOND LETTER TO THE CHURCH IN CORINTH

ABOUT THIS LETTER

In the beginning of this letter Paul answers the concerns of the Christians in Corinth who accused him of not living up to his promise to visit them. Paul had changed his mind for a good reason. He had stayed away from Corinth so that he would not seem to be too hard and demanding (1.23). He also wanted to see if they would follow his instructions about forgiving and comforting people who had sinned (2.5–11).

Paul reminds the Corinthians that God is generous and wants them to be just as generous in their giving to help God's people in Jerusalem and Judea (8.1—9.15).

Paul is a servant of God's new agreement (3.1–17). He is faithful in trying to bring people to God, even if it means terrible suffering for himself (4.1—6.13; 10.1—12.10). And what has God done to make it possible for us to come to him? *God has done it all! He sent Christ to make peace between himself and us, and he has given us the work of making peace between himself and others. What we mean is that God was in Christ, offering peace and forgiveness to the people of this world. And he has given us the work of sharing his message about peace. (5.18,19)*

A QUICK LOOK AT THIS LETTER

1 From Paul, chosen by God to be an apostle of Jesus Christ, and from Timothy, who is also a follower.

To God's church in Corinth and to all of God's people in Achaia.

2I pray that God our Father and the Lord Jesus Christ will be kind to you and will bless you with peace!

Paul Gives Thanks

3Praise God, the Father of our Lord Jesus Christ! The Father is a merciful God, who always gives us comfort. 4He comforts us when we are in trouble, so that we can share that same comfort with others in trouble. 5We share in the terrible sufferings of Christ, but also in the wonderful comfort

Suffering should help us
(5) No one wants to suffer. But living in the world brings some suffering to everyone. For Christians, suffering is

he gives. 6We suffer in the hope that you will be comforted and saved. And because we are comforted, you will also be comforted, as you patiently endure suffering like ours. 7You never disappoint us. You suffered as much as we did, and we know that you will be comforted as we were.

8My friends, I want you to know what a hard time we had in Asia. Our sufferings were so horrible and so unbearable that death seemed certain. 9In fact, we felt sure that we were going to die. But this made us stop trusting in ourselves and start trusting God, who raises the dead to life. 10God saved us from the threat of death,ᵃ and we are sure that he will do it again and again. 11Please help us by praying for us. Then many people will give thanks for the blessings we receive in answer to all these prayers.

Paul's Change of Plans

12We can be proud of our clear conscience. We have always lived honestly and sincerely, especially when we were with you. And we were guided by God's kindness instead of by the wisdom of this world. 13I am not writing anything you cannot read and understand. I hope you will understand it completely, 14just as you already partly understand us. Then when our Lord Jesus returns, you can be as proud of us as we are of you.

15I was so sure of your pride in us that I had planned to visit you first of all. In this way you would have the blessing of two visits from me. 16Once on my way to Macedonia and again on my return from there. Then you could send me on to Judea. 17Do you think I couldn't make up my mind about what to do? Or do I seem like someone who says "Yes" or "No" simply to please others? 18God can be trusted, and so can I, when I say that our answer to you has

a means of drawing us into closer friendship with God. When we suffer, we remember that Jesus himself suffered for us. The Holy Spirit helps us even to be thankful for suffering. Times of suffering are times when God comes nearest to us and comforts us with his presence.

ᵃ*the threat of death*: Some manuscripts have "many threats of death."

always been "Yes" and never "No." [19]This
is because Jesus Christ the Son of God is
always "Yes" and never "No." And he is
the one that Silas,[b] Timothy, and I told you
about.

[20]Christ says "Yes" to all of God's promises. That's why we have Christ to say
"Amen"[c] for us to the glory of God. [21]And
so God makes it possible for you and us
to stand firmly together with Christ. God
is also the one who chose us [22]and put his
Spirit in our hearts to show that we belong
only to him.

[23]God is my witness that I stayed away
from Corinth, just to keep from being hard
on you. [24]We are not bosses who tell you
what to believe. We are working with you
to make you glad, because your faith is
strong.

2 I have decided not to make my next visit
with you so painful. [2]If I make you feel
bad, who would be left to cheer me up, except the people I had made to feel bad?
[3]The reason I want to be happy is to make
you happy. I wrote as I did because I didn't
want to visit you and be made to feel bad,
when you should make me feel happy.
[4]At the time I wrote, I was suffering terribly.
My eyes were full of tears, and my heart
was broken. But I didn't want to make you
feel bad. I only wanted to let you know how
much I cared for you.

Forgiveness

[5]I don't want to be hard on you. But if
one of you has made someone feel bad, I
am not really the one who has been made
to feel bad. Some of you are the ones.
[6]Most of you have already pointed out the
wrong that person did, and that is punishment enough for what was done.

[7]When people sin, you should forgive and
comfort them, so they won't give up in despair. [8]You should make them sure of your
love for them.

[b]*Silas*: The Greek text has "Silvanus," which is another
form of the name Silas.   [c]*Amen*: The word "amen" is
used here with the meaning of "yes."

Jesus says "yes"
(19) This means that the
Corinthians enjoyed the
good things God promised
to those who love his only
Son. If we love Jesus as
many of the Corinthians did,
then God is saying "yes" to
us, too. We say "yes" to
God's offer to save us because of Jesus and his death
on the cross. Then we have
God's "yes" in reply. He has
accepted us, and he will
never leave us.

*Mercy is better than
punishment*
(7) Being like Jesus means
wanting to forgive instead
of blame. It means wanting
to bring back sinners in-
stead of punishing them and
sending them away. This is
the way we should act to-
ward people in our churches
who have sinned. We should
do all we can to get them
to turn from their sins and
come back.

⁹I also wrote because I wanted to test you and find out if you would follow my instructions. ¹⁰I will forgive anyone you forgive. Yes, for your sake and with Christ as my witness, I have forgiven whatever needed to be forgiven. ¹¹I have done this to keep Satan from getting the better of us. We all know what goes on in his mind.

¹²When I went to Troas to preach the good news about Christ, I found that the Lord had already prepared the way. ¹³But I was worried when I didn't find my friend Titus there. So I left the other followers and went on to Macedonia.

¹⁴I am grateful that God always makes it possible for Christ to lead us to victory. God also helps us spread the knowledge about Christ everywhere, and this knowledge is like the smell of perfume. ¹⁵⁻¹⁶In fact, God thinks of us as a perfume that brings Christ to everyone. For people who are being saved, this perfume has a sweet smell and leads them to a better life. But for people who are lost, it has a bad smell and leads them to a horrible death.

No one really has what it takes to do this work. ¹⁷A lot of people try to get rich from preaching God's message. But we are God's sincere messengers, and by the power of Christ we speak our message with God as our witness.

God's New Agreement

3 Are we once again bragging about ourselves? Do we need letters to you or from you to tell others about us? Some people do need letters that tell about them. ²But you are our letter, and you are in our*d* hearts for everyone to read and understand. ³You are like a letter written by Christ and delivered by us. But you are not written with pen and ink or on tablets made of stone. You are written in our hearts by the Spirit of the living God.

⁴We are sure about all this. Christ makes us sure in the very presence of God. ⁵We

Does the good news smell sweet to you?
(14) This is an unusual statement. But it's a good way of saying that the news about Jesus really comes as happy, good news to many people. But, strangely, to others it comes as bad news. This "bad smell" is how the news about Jesus seems to people who don't want their lives to change. The news only makes them uncomfortable.

*d*our: Some manuscripts have "your."

don't have the right to claim that we have done anything on our own. God gives us what it takes to do all that we do. 6He makes us worthy to be the servants of his new agreement that comes from the Holy Spirit and not from a written Law. After all, the Law brings death, but the Spirit brings life.

7The Law of Moses brought only the promise of death, even though it was carved on stones and given in a wonderful way. Still the Law made Moses' face shine so brightly that the people of Israel could not look at it, even though it was a fading glory. 8So won't the agreement that the Spirit brings to us be even more wonderful? 9If something that brings the death sentence is glorious, won't something that makes us acceptable to God be even more glorious? 10In fact, the new agreement is so wonderful that the Law is no longer glorious at all. 11The Law was given with a glory that faded away. But the glory of the new agreement is much greater, because it will never fade away.

12This wonderful hope makes us feel like speaking freely. 13We are not like Moses. His face was shining, but he covered it to keep the people of Israel from seeing the brightness fade away. 14The people were stubborn, and something still keeps them from seeing the truth when the Law is read. Only Christ can take away the covering that keeps them from seeing.

15When the Law of Moses is read, the people of Israel have their minds covered over 16with a covering that is removed only for those who turn to the Lord. 17The Lord and the Spirit are one and the same, and the Lord's Spirit sets us free. 18So our faces are not covered. They show the bright glory of the Lord, as the Lord's Spirit makes us more and more like our glorious Lord.

Treasure in Clay Jars

4 God has been kind enough to trust us with this work. That's why we never give up. 2We don't do shameful things that

Jesus brings life
(6) The Old Testament was a part of God's plan that has passed away. The Law that it proclaimed was a good Law that brought death to those who refused to obey it. But the New Testament grows out of the Old Testament. Jesus Christ was the One promised by the Old Testament prophets. Jesus doesn't bring death, but life everlasting by the Holy Spirit.

Christ removes the covering
(14) Sometimes people can hear about the good news again and again, and they don't accept it. It's like their understanding is hidden under a covering. That's what sin does—it keeps people from seeing God's truth. But Jesus Christ can remove the covering, so even the worst sinner can see the truth. Do you know someone whose mind is still "covered"? Pray that Christ will take the covering away.

must be kept secret. And we don't try to fool anyone or twist God's message around. God is our witness that we speak only the truth, so others will be sure that we can be trusted. ³If there is anything hidden about our message, it is hidden only to someone who is lost.

⁴The god who rules this world has blinded the minds of unbelievers. They cannot see the light, which is the good news about our glorious Christ, who shows what God is like. ⁵We are not preaching about ourselves. Our message is that Jesus Christ is Lord. He also sent us to be your servants. ⁶The Scriptures say, "God commanded light to shine in the dark." Now God is shining in our hearts to let you know that his glory is seen in Jesus Christ.

⁷We are like clay jars in which this treasure is stored. The real power comes from God and not from us. ⁸We often suffer, but we are never crushed. Even when we don't know what to do, we never give up. ⁹In times of trouble, God is with us, and when we are knocked down, we get up again. ¹⁰⁻¹¹We face death every day because of Jesus. Our bodies show what his death was like, so that his life can also be seen in us. ¹²This means that death is working in us, but life is working in you.

¹³In the Scriptures it says, "I spoke because I had faith." We have that same kind of faith. So we speak ¹⁴because we know that God raised Jesus Christ to life. And just as God raised Jesus, he will also raise us to life. Then he will bring us into his presence together with you. ¹⁵All of this has been done for you, so that more and more people will know how kind God is and will praise and honor him.

Faith in the Lord

¹⁶We never give up. Our bodies are gradually dying, but we ourselves are being made stronger each day. ¹⁷These little troubles are getting us ready for an eternal glory that will make all our troubles seem like nothing. ¹⁸Things that are seen don't last

Christ lives in Christians
(7) When we are "born from above" (John 3.3), Jesus really comes to live inside us. We're new people after we're born again. In one way we remain the same persons we were, but in another way we're changed to be like Jesus. We can stand whatever trouble the world might send our way, not because of our strength, but on account of the strength of the Son of God, who was crucified and rose again.

forever, but things that are not seen are eternal. That's why we keep our minds on the

5 things that cannot be seen. ¹Our bodies are like tents that we live in here on earth. But when these tents are destroyed, we know that God will give each of us a place to live. These homes will not be buildings that someone has made, but they are in heaven and will last forever. ²While we are here on earth, we sigh because we want to live in that heavenly home. ³We want to put it on like clothes and not be naked.

⁴These tents we now live in are like a heavy burden, and we groan. But we don't do this just because we want to leave these bodies that will die. It is because we want to change them for bodies that will never die. ⁵God is the one who makes all of this possible. He has given us his Spirit to make us certain that he will do it. ⁶So always be cheerful!

As long as we are in these bodies, we are away from the Lord. ⁷But we live by faith, not by what we see. ⁸We should be cheerful, because we would rather leave these bodies and be at home with the Lord. ⁹But whether we are at home with the Lord or away from him, we still try our best to please him. ¹⁰After all, Christ will judge each of us for the good or the bad that we do while living in these bodies.

Bringing People to God

¹¹We know what it means to respect the Lord, and we encourage everyone to turn to him. God himself knows what we are like, and I hope you also know what kind of people we are. ¹²We are not trying once more to brag about ourselves. But we want you to be proud of us, when you are with those who are not sincere and brag about what others think of them.

¹³If we seem out of our minds, it is between God and us. But if we are in our right minds, it is for your good. ¹⁴We are ruled by Christ's love for us. We are certain that if one person died for everyone else, then

Our bodies are like tents
(1) A tent is a place to live in for just a short time. Likewise, we live for a short time in our bodies. Sometimes our bodies give us trouble. But we are happy as we realize what a great and everlasting treasure we carry inside ourselves since God made us new people. The old life that we lived for the body is passing away. We will live forever the new life that we live for God.

How Christ will judge Christians
(10) When Paul writes that Christ will judge us according to the good we have done in our bodies, we should not confuse this judgment with being saved. We are saved by having faith in Jesus Christ, who suffered in our place on the cross, died, and then rose again. When Christ judges the good we have done, he will be judging believers who are already saved. This judgment determines the *rewards* each saved person will receive.

all of us have died. 15And Christ did die for all of us. He died so we would no longer live for ourselves, but for the one who died and was raised to life for us.

16We are careful not to judge people by what they seem to be, though we once judged Christ in that way. 17Anyone who belongs to Christ is a new person. The past is forgotten, and everything is new. 18God has done it all! He sent Christ to make peace between himself and us, and he has given us the work of making peace between himself and others.

19What we mean is that God was in Christ, offering peace and forgiveness to the people of this world. And he has given us the work of sharing his message about peace. 20We were sent to speak for Christ, and God is begging you to listen to our message. We speak for Christ and sincerely ask you to make peace with God. 21Christ never sinned! But God treated him as a sinner, so that Christ could make us acceptable to God.

6 We work together with God, and we beg you to make good use of God's kindness to you. 2In the Scriptures God says,
    "When the time came,
        I listened to you,
    and when you needed help,
        I came to save you."
That time has come. This is the day for you to be saved.

3We don't want anyone to find fault with our work, and so we try hard not to cause problems. 4But in everything and in every way we show that we truly are God's servants. We have always been patient, though we have had a lot of trouble, suffering, and hard times. 5We have been beaten, put in jail, and hurt in riots. We have worked hard and have gone without sleep or food. 6But we have kept ourselves pure and have been understanding, patient, and kind. The Holy Spirit has been with us, and our love has been real. 7We have spoken the truth, and God's power has worked in us. In all our struggles we have said and done only what is right.

Jesus took the place of sinners

(21) Not only did God treat Jesus as a sinner, but as he hung there on the cross, Jesus actually took upon himself the punishment for all of our sins. Our sin became his to carry, and his goodness became ours.

Today is the day

(2) Paul was writing to a church, but it could be that some of the people there still needed to put their trust in Jesus and be saved. There is no time like the present. Who can be sure that they will have more time to "play games" with God? Death could come at any time, and so could the Lord's return.

8Whether we were honored or dishonored or praised or cursed, we always told the truth about ourselves. But some people said we did not. 9We are unknown to others, but well known to you. We seem to be dying, and yet we are still alive. We have been punished, but never killed, 10and we are always happy, even in times of suffering. Although we are poor, we have made many people rich. And though we own nothing, everything is ours.

11Friends in Corinth, we are telling the truth when we say that there is room in our hearts for you. 12We are not holding back on our love for you, but you are holding back on your love for us. 13I speak to you as I would speak to my own children. Please make room in your hearts for us.

The Temple of the Living God

14Stay away from people who are not followers of the Lord! Can someone who is good get along with someone who is evil? Are light and darkness the same? 15Is Christ a friend of Satan?*e* Can people who follow the Lord have anything in common with those who don't? 16Do idols belong in the temple of God? We are the temple of the living God, as God himself says,

"I will live with these people
    and walk among them.
I will be their God,
    and they will be my people."
17The Lord also says,
"Leave them and stay away!
Don't touch anything
    that is not clean.
Then I will welcome you
    and be your Father.
18You will be my sons
    and my daughters,
as surely as I am God,
    the all-powerful."

Good and evil don't mix
(14) Believers are still in the world, and there is evil all around. Many of the unsaved people we know and live with daily care little for God. Many of them may be living very sinful lives. God doesn't expect us to avoid such people entirely, but someone else's sinful lifestyle can have a bad effect on a believer. When we have a choice, we should seek the company of other believers and help build each other up in faith.

*e*Satan: The Greek text has "Beliar," which is another form of the Hebrew word "Belial," meaning "wicked" or "useless." The Jewish people sometimes used this as a name for Satan.

7 My friends, God has made us these promises. So we should stay away from everything that keeps our bodies and spirits from being clean. We should honor God and try to be completely like him.

The Church Makes Paul Happy

2Make a place for us in your hearts! We haven't mistreated anyone or hurt anyone. We haven't cheated anyone. 3I am not saying this to be hard on you. But, as I have said before, you will always be in our thoughts, whether we live or die. 4I trust you completely.ƒ I am always proud of you, and I am greatly encouraged. In all my trouble I am still very happy.

5After we came to Macedonia, we didn't have any chance to rest. We were faced with all kinds of problems. We were troubled by enemies and troubled by fears. 6But God cheers up people in need, and that is what he did when he sent Titus to us. 7Of course, we were glad to see Titus, but what really made us glad is the way you cheered him up. He told how sorry you were and how concerned you were about me. And this made me even happier.

8I don't feel bad anymore, even though my letterᵍ hurt your feelings. I did feel bad at first, but I don't now. I know that the letter hurt you for a while. 9Now I am happy, but not because I hurt your feelings. It is because God used your hurt feelings to make you turn back to him, and none of you were harmed by us. 10When God makes you feel sorry enough to turn to him and be saved, you don't have anything to feel bad about. But when this world makes you feel sorry, it can cause your death.

11Just look what God has done by making you feel sorry! You sincerely want to prove that you are innocent. You are angry. You are shocked. You are eager to see that jus-

---

Christians flock with Christians
(1) People who are alike attract one another. Christians will want to enjoy the friendship of other Christians. We should, of course, be kind and helpful to non-Christians, but often we will find that their lifestyles are sinful and destructive. It's easy to be influenced badly by them. We should choose our friends carefully because in time we become like them.

Churches sometimes have problems
(8) We see Paul's deep concern for the church at Corinth. He had written an earlier letter to them that hurt their feelings. It could be a lost letter, but some wonder if it may have been 1 Corinthians. That letter had blamed them for tolerating serious sin in the church (1 Corinthians 5.1–5). Let us be thankful for faithful leaders who will kindly but firmly correct us when we fall into sin.

ƒI trust you completely: Or "I have always spoken the truth to you" or "I can speak freely to you." ᵍmy letter: There is no copy of this letter that Paul wrote to the church at Corinth.

tice is done. You have proved that you were completely right in this matter. [12]When I wrote you, it wasn't to accuse the one who was wrong or to take up for the one who was hurt. I wrote, so that God would show you how much you do care for us. [13]And we were greatly encouraged.

Although we were encouraged, we felt even better when we saw how happy Titus was, because you had shown that he had nothing to worry about. [14]We had told him how much we thought of you, and you did not disappoint us. Just as we have always told you the truth, so everything we told him about you has also proved to be true. [15]Titus loves all of you very much, especially when he remembers how you obeyed him and how you trembled with fear when you welcomed him. [16]It makes me really glad to know that I can depend on you.

Generous Giving

8 My friends, we want you to know that the churches in Macedonia[h] have shown others how kind God is. [2]Although they were going through hard times and were very poor, they were glad to give generously. [3]They gave as much as they could afford and even more, simply because they wanted to. [4]They even asked and begged us to let them have the joy of giving their money for God's people. [5]And they did more than we had hoped. They gave themselves first to the Lord and then to us, just as God wanted them to do.

[6]Titus was the one who got you started doing this good thing, so we begged him to have you finish what you had begun. [7]You do everything better than anyone else. You have stronger faith. You speak better and know more. You are eager to give, and you love us better.[i] Now you must give more generously than anyone else.

We should give to God's work

(2) The Macedonians gave gladly to the apostles to support them in their ministry. Our love for God is shown by how much we give of ourselves and our goods to his work. Giving for the spread of the Christian faith is a necessary and joyful habit. We can't take our money to heaven, but we can send it ahead to God by giving to his work now.

[h]*churches in Macedonia*: The churches that Paul had started in Philippi and Thessalonica. The church in Berea is probably also meant. [i]*you love us better*: Some manuscripts have "we love you better."

8I am not ordering you to do this. I am simply testing how real your love is by comparing it with the concern that others have shown. 9You know that our Lord Jesus Christ was kind enough to give up all his riches and become poor, so that you could become rich.

10A year ago you were the first ones to give, and you gave because you wanted to. So listen to my advice. 11I think you should finish what you started. If you give according to what you have, you will prove that you are as eager to give as you were to think about giving. 12It doesn't matter how much you have. What matters is how much you are willing to give from what you have.

13I am not trying to make life easier for others by making life harder for you. But it is only fair 14for you to share with them when you have so much, and they have so little. Later, when they have more than enough, and you are in need, they can share with you. Then everyone will have a fair share, 15just as the Scriptures say,

"Those who gathered
too much
had nothing left.
Those who gathered
only a little
had all they needed."

Titus and His Friends

16I am grateful that God made Titus care as much about you as we do. 17When we begged Titus to visit you, he said he would. He wanted to because he cared so much for you. 18With Titus we are also sending one of the Lord's followers who is well known in every church for spreading the good news. 19The churches chose this follower to travel with us while we carry this gift that will bring praise to the Lord and show how much we hope to help. 20We don't want anyone to find fault with the way we handle your generous gift. 21But we want to do what pleases the Lord and what people think is right.

22We are also sending someone else with

Finish what you started
(11) It's good to give, but it's important to *keep* giving. Sometimes Christians will get generous and give a one-time gift to a ministry. But how would you like to live on a series of uncertain, one-time gifts? God is steady in his giving to us, so we too should be steady in our giving to his work.

Help from Titus
(16) Titus was a young Greek disciple of Paul, the son of Gentile parents. When Titus was converted, Paul took him to Jerusalem where some Jews demanded that Titus must be circumcised according to their Law. But Paul refused (Galatians 2.1–5). As we read here, Titus helped Paul with the problems of the church at Corinth in southern Greece. The last we hear about Titus is during his faithful ministry on the island of Crete, where Paul sent him a letter (see Paul's Letter to Titus).

Titus and the other follower. We approve of this man. In fact, he has already shown us many times that he wants to help. And now he wants to help even more than ever, because he trusts you so much. 23Titus is my partner, who works with me to serve you. The other two followers are sent by the churches, and they bring honor to Christ. 24Treat them in such a way that the churches will see your love and will know why we bragged about you.

The Money for God's People

9 I don't need to write you about the money you plan to give for God's people. 2I know how eager you are to give. And I have proudly told the Lord's followers in Macedonia that you people in Achaia have been ready for a whole year. Now your desire to give has made them want to give. 3That's why I am sending Titus and the two others to you. I want you to be ready, just as I promised. This will prove that we were not wrong to brag about you.

4Some followers from Macedonia may come with me, and I want them to find that you have the money ready. If you don't, I would be embarrassed for trusting you to do this. But you would be embarrassed even more. 5So I have decided to ask Titus and the others to spend some time with you before I arrive. This way they can arrange to collect the money you have promised. Then you will have the chance to give because you want to, and not because you feel forced to.

6Remember this saying,
"A few seeds make
a small harvest,
but a lot of seeds make
a big harvest."

7Each of you must make up your own mind about how much to give. But don't feel sorry that you must give and don't feel that you are forced to give. God loves people who love to give. 8God can bless you with everything you need, and you will always have more than enough to do all kinds of

Be an eager giver
(2) The Corinthians were eager to give, and Paul even boasted about their giving. Maybe he was also trying to tease them a little by comparing them to the church at Macedonia in northern Greece. In Paul's time Christians were very eager to have a part in spreading the good news about Jesus, who had brought them so much happiness. They were strongly aware of how they had been saved from death.

good things for others. 9The Scriptures say,
"God freely gives his gifts
to the poor,
and always does right."
10God gives seed to farmers and provides
everyone with food. He will increase what
you have, so that you can give even more
to those in need. 11You will be blessed in
every way, and you will be able to keep
on being generous. Then many people will
thank God when we deliver your gift.

12What you are doing is much more than
a service that supplies God's people with
what they need. It is something that will
make many others thank God. 13The way
in which you have proved yourselves by
this service will bring honor and praise to
God. You believed the message about
Christ, and you obeyed it by sharing generously with God's people and with everyone
else. 14Now they are praying for you and
want to see you, because God used you to
bless them so very much. 15Thank God for
his gift that is too wonderful for words!

Paul Defends His Work for Christ

10 Do you think I am a coward when I
am with you and brave when I am
far away? Well, I ask you to listen, because
Christ himself was humble and gentle.
2Some people have said that we act like
the people of this world. So when I arrive,
I expect I will have to be firm and forceful
in what I say to them. Please don't make
me treat you that way. 3We live in this world,
but we don't act like its people 4or fight
our battles with the weapons of this world.
Instead, we use God's power that can destroy fortresses. We destroy arguments
5and every bit of pride that keeps anyone
from knowing God. We capture people's
thoughts and make them obey Christ.
6And when you completely obey him, we
will punish anyone who refuses to obey.

7You judge by appearances.j If any of

---

j*You judge by appearances*: Or "Take a close look at
yourselves."

God gives so we can
(10) Paul writes that God
gives to us so we can give
to others. This does not
mean that giving a little will
get us a lot from God, making us rich. It means that
God gives an extra blessing
so we can "pass it on."

Face your opponents
(4) Enemies test the Christian's strength, because a
Christian may not use harsh
language or force to con-
vince people. But, like Paul,
we have to be able to present our case for Christ in a
clear, convincing, and
brave way. Why should
Christians be cowards?
We're children of the mighty
God. So let's arm ourselves
with the knowledge we need
to fight all ignorance.

you think you are the only ones who belong to Christ, then think again. We belong to Christ as much as you do. 8Maybe I brag a little too much about the authority that the Lord gave me to help you and not to hurt you. Yet I am not embarrassed to brag. 9And I am not trying to scare you with my letters. 10Some of you are saying, "Paul's letters are harsh and powerful. But in person, he is a weakling and has nothing worth saying." 11Those people had better understand that when I am with you, I will do exactly what I say in my letters.

12We won't dare compare ourselves with those who think so much of themselves. But they are foolish to compare themselves with themselves. 13We won't brag about something we don't have a right to brag about. We will only brag about the work that God has sent us to do, and you are part of that work. 14We are not bragging more than we should. After all, we did bring the message about Christ to you.

15We don't brag about what others have done, as if we had done those things ourselves. But I hope that as you become stronger in your faith, we will be able to reach many more of the people around you.k That has always been our goal. 16Then we will be able to preach the good news in other lands where we cannot take credit for work someone else has already done. 17The Scriptures say, "If you want to brag, then brag about the Lord." 18You may brag about yourself, but the only approval that counts is the Lord's approval.

Paul and the False Apostles

11 Please put up with a little of my foolishness. 2I am as concerned about you as God is. You were like a virgin bride I had chosen only for Christ. 3But now I fear that you will be tricked, just as Eve was

---

k*we will be able to reach many more of the people around you:* Or "you will praise us even more because of our work among you."

The problem at Corinth
(10) The Greeks, including those at Corinth, were used to hearing powerful speakers who often had a commanding appearance. Paul was not a good speaker, and he seems to have been thin and short. He may also have been badly scarred by beatings and stonings he had received. Many of the people at Corinth looked down on Paul and were embarrassed to have him speak at their church. But Paul soon straightened them out.

Some comedy helps our witness
(1) We don't have to be angry or "dead serious" with those who speak against us. Paul was able to joke about people's low opinion of him. It's as if he were saying, "Go ahead, call me a fool, but listen now to my foolishness." That must have made them blush with shame. Paul's critics in Corinth didn't really hate him—they just didn't know what to make of this little man who didn't look like much.

tricked by that lying snake. I am afraid that you might stop thinking about Christ in an honest and sincere way. 4We told you about Jesus, and you received the Holy Spirit and accepted our message. But you let some people tell you about another Jesus. Now you are ready to receive another spirit and accept a different message. 5I think I am as good as any of those super apostles. 6I may not speak as well as they do, but I know as much. And this has already been made perfectly clear to you.

7Was it wrong for me to lower myself and honor you by preaching God's message free of charge? 8I robbed other churches by taking money from them to serve you. 9Even when I was in need, I still didn't bother you. In fact, some of the Lord's followers from Macedonia brought me what I needed. I have not been a burden to you in the past, and I will never be a burden. 10As surely as I speak the truth about Christ, no one in Achaia can stop me from bragging about this. 11And it isn't because I don't love you. God himself knows how much I do love you.

12I plan to go on doing just what I have always done. Then those people won't be able to brag about doing the same things we are doing. 13Anyway, they are no more than false apostles and dishonest workers. They only pretend to be apostles of Christ. 14And it is no wonder. Even Satan tries to make himself look like an angel of light. 15So why does it seem strange for Satan's servants to pretend to do what is right? Someday they will get exactly what they deserve.

Paul's Sufferings for Christ

16I don't want any of you to think that I am a fool. But if you do, then let me be a fool and brag a little. 17When I do all this bragging, I do it as a fool and not for the Lord. 18Yet if others want to brag about what they have done, so will I. 19And since you are so smart, you will gladly put up with a fool. 20In fact, you let people make

Stick with the pure good news
(14) The Corinthians had been listening to false teachers who made the good news complicated. The teachers had said that Gentiles had to obey Jewish religious customs. Being saved by faith in God's mercy through the sacrifice of Jesus is a simple idea, which people often like to make harder than it has to be.

slaves of you and cheat you and steal from you. Why, you even let them strut around and slap you in the face. [21]I am ashamed to say that we are too weak to behave in such a way.

If they can brag, so can I, but it is a foolish thing to do. [22]Are they Hebrews? So am I. Are they Jews? So am I. Are they from the family of Abraham? Well, so am I. [23]Are they servants of Christ? I am a fool to talk this way, but I serve him better than they do. I have worked harder and have been put in jail more times. I have been beaten with whips more and have been in danger of death more often.

[24]Five times the Jews gave me thirty-nine lashes with a whip. [25]Three times the Romans beat me with a big stick, and once my enemies stoned me. I have been shipwrecked three times, and I even had to spend a night and a day in the sea. [26]During my many travels, I have been in danger from rivers, robbers, Jews, and foreigners. My life has been in danger in cities, in deserts, at sea, and with people who only pretended to be the Lord's followers.

[27]I have worked and struggled and spent many sleepless nights. I have gone hungry and thirsty and often had nothing to eat. I have been cold from not having enough clothes to keep me warm. [28]Besides everything else, each day I am burdened down, worrying about all the churches. [29]When others are weak, I am weak too. When others are tricked into sin, I get angry.[l]

[30]If I have to brag, I will brag about how weak I am. [31]God, the Father of our Lord Jesus, knows I am not lying. And God is to be praised forever! [32]The governor of Damascus at the time of King Aretas had the city gates guarded, so that he could capture me. [33]But I escaped by being let down in a basket through a window in the city wall.

Get to know Paul
(22) Here was a humble-looking man that Christ had called to preach to the Gentiles. He had been cruelly beaten, stoned, left for dead, and even shipwrecked. He had marks in his body that probably embarrassed the Corinthians. They called him a fool. So Paul just uses their own language. Paul is "the fool" who preached the good news about Jesus to them for nothing. That must have made them ashamed.

---

[l]*When others are tricked into sin, I get angry*: Or "When others stumble into sin, I hurt for them."

Visions from the Lord

12 I have to brag. There is nothing to be gained by it, but I must brag about the visions and other things that the Lord has shown me. [2] I know about one of Christ's followers who was taken up into the third heaven fourteen years ago. I don't know if the man was still in his body when it happened, but God surely knows.

[3] As I said, only God really knows if this man was in his body at the time. [4] But he was taken up into paradise,[m] where he heard things that are too wonderful to tell. [5] I will brag about that man, but not about myself, except to say how weak I am.

[6] Yet even if I did brag, I would not be foolish. I would simply be speaking the truth. But I will try not to say too much. That way, none of you will think more highly of me than you should because of what you have seen me do and say. [7] Of course, I am now referring to the wonderful things I saw. One of Satan's angels was sent to make me suffer terribly, so that I would not feel too proud.[n]

[8] Three times I begged the Lord to make this suffering go away. [9] But he replied, "My kindness is all you need. My power is strongest when you are weak." So if Christ keeps giving me his power, I will gladly brag about how weak I am. [10] Yes, I am glad to be weak or insulted or mistreated or to have troubles and sufferings, if it is for Christ. Because when I am weak, I am strong.

Paul's Concern for the Lord's Followers at Corinth

[11] I have been making a fool of myself. But you forced me to do it, when you should

God's kindness is enough for us
(1) Paul had seen many wonderful things, but the best of all was that God's kindness was Paul's continual support. We aren't great or strong because of what we have seen or what we know. Our greatness and strength come directly from God himself. He keeps us going when we fail and even when our friends fail. Jesus said, "I will never leave you."

---

[m]*paradise*: In the Greek translation of the Old Testament, this word is used for the Garden of Eden. In New Testament times it was sometimes used for the place where God's people are happy and at rest, as they wait for the final judgment. [n]*Of course . . . too proud*: Or "Because of the wonderful things that I saw, one of Satan's angels was sent to make me suffer terribly, so that I would not feel too proud."

have been speaking up for me. I may be nothing at all, but I am as good as those super apostles. 12When I was with you, I was patient and worked all the powerful miracles and signs and wonders of a true apostle. 13You missed out on only one blessing that the other churches received. That is, you didn't have to support me. Forgive me for doing you wrong.

14I am planning to visit you for the third time. But I still won't make a burden of myself. What I really want is you, and not what you have. Children are not supposed to save up for their parents, but parents are supposed to take care of their children. 15So I will gladly give all that I have and all that I am. Will you love me less for loving you too much? 16You agree that I was not a burden to you. Maybe that's because I was trying to catch you off guard and trick you. 17Were you cheated by any of those I sent to you? 18I urged Titus to visit you, and I sent another follower with him. But Titus didn't cheat you, and we felt and behaved the same way he did.

19Have you been thinking all along that we have been defending ourselves to you? Actually, we have been speaking to God as followers of Christ. But, my friends, we did it all for your good.

20I am afraid that when I come, we won't be pleased with each other. I fear that some of you may be arguing or jealous or angry or selfish or gossiping or insulting each other. I even fear that you may be proud and acting like a mob. 21I am afraid God will make me ashamed when I visit you again. I will feel like crying because many of you have never given up your old sins. You are still doing things that are immoral, indecent, and shameful.

Final Warnings and Greetings

13 I am on my way to visit you for the third time. And as the Scriptures say, "Any charges must be proved true by at least two or three witnesses." 2During my second visit I warned you that I would pun-

What about the church at Corinth?

(20) The church had grown. But Corinth was one of the most wicked cities in the world of that time. The people who came into the church had a lot of sins to leave behind, but some people seem to have brought their sins with them. That's why Paul had to speak to them so sharply. They needed to wake up and live like Christians.

ish you and anyone else who doesn't stop sinning. I am far away from you now, but I give you the same warning. 3This should prove to you that I am speaking for Christ. When he corrects you, he won't be weak. He will be powerful! 4Although he was weak when he was nailed to the cross, he now lives by the power of God. We are weak, just as Christ was. But you will see that we will live by the power of God, just as Christ does.

5Test yourselves and find out if you really are true to your faith. If you pass the test, you will discover that Christ is living in you. But if Christ isn't living in you, you have failed. 6I hope you will discover that we have not failed. 7We pray that you will stop doing evil things. We don't pray like this to make ourselves look good, but to get you to do right, even if we are failures.

8All we can do is to follow the truth and not fight against it. 9Even though we are weak, we are glad that you are strong, and we pray that you will do even better. 10I am writing these things to you before I arrive. This way I won't have to be hard on you when I use the authority that the Lord has given me. I was given this authority, so that I could help you and not destroy you.

11Good-by, my friends. Do better and pay attention to what I have said. Try to get along and live peacefully with each other.

Now I pray that God, who gives love and peace, will be with you. 12Give each other a warm greeting. All of God's people send their greetings.

13I pray that the Lord Jesus Christ will bless you and be kind to you! May God bless you with his love, and may the Holy Spirit join all your hearts together.

Let's know ourselves

(5) Many of the Corinthians were proud. They thought their love of human wisdom was enough for them. Who needed a Paul to tell them what to believe? We, like they, need to know if Christ can really live in us with an attitude like that. Surely he can't. Saying we're Christians doesn't make it true; living like Christians proves we are.

God doesn't ignore sin

(10) Paul wanted the Corinthians to realize that God does not ignore sin. Paul was God's appointed agent. He warned them that he was not really weak or foolish. He would come personally, in the power of Christ. Then the church would have to get back in line with God's will.

PAUL'S LETTER TO THE CHURCHES IN GALATIA

ABOUT THIS LETTER

From the very beginning of this letter to the churches in the region of Galatia (in central Asia Minor), Paul makes two things clear to his readers: he is a true apostle, and his message is the only true message (1.1–10). These statements were very important, because some people claimed that Paul was a false apostle with a false message.

Paul was indeed a true apostle, and his mission to the Gentiles was given to him by the Lord and approved by the apostles in Jerusalem (1.18—2.10). Paul had even corrected the apostle Peter, when he had stopped eating with Gentile followers who were not obeying the Law of Moses (2.1–18).

Faith is the only way to be saved. Paul insists that this was true already for Abraham, who had received God's promise by faith. And Paul leaves no doubt about what his own faith means to him:

I have been nailed to the cross with Christ. I have died, but Christ lives in me. And I now live by faith in the Son of God, who loved me and gave his life for me. (2.19,20)

A QUICK LOOK AT THIS LETTER

1. A True Apostle and the True Message (1.1–10)
2. God Chose Paul To Be an Apostle (1.11–24)
3. Paul Defends His Message (2.1–21)
4. Faith Is the Only Way To Be Saved (3.1–4.31)
5. Guided by the Spirit and Love (5.1–6.10)
6. Final Warnings (6.11–18)

1 ¹⁻²From the apostle Paul and from all the Lord's followers with me.

I was chosen to be an apostle by Jesus Christ and by God the Father, who raised him from death. No mere human chose or appointed me to this work.

To the churches in Galatia.

³I pray that God the Father and our Lord Jesus Christ will be kind to you and will bless you with peace! ⁴Christ obeyed God our Father and gave himself as a sacrifice for our sins to rescue us from this evil world. ⁵God will be given glory forever and ever. Amen.

The Only True Message

⁶I am shocked that you have so quickly turned from God, who chose you because

What makes a Christian leader?

(2) Does education fit us for Christian service? Not necessarily. Many people have taken training courses but have failed as Christian leaders. Does having the desire to serve as a leader prove that someone has been called to do so? We surely need to desire to work for the Lord. But desire alone doesn't make us able. God proves who his servants are by the way he uses them in his work. Paul was such a God-chosen servant.

of his kindness.a You have believed another message, 7when there is really only one true message. But some people are causing you trouble and want to make you turn away from the good news about Christ. 8I pray that God will punish anyone who preaches anything different from our message to you! It doesn't matter if that person is one of us or an angel from heaven. 9I have said it before, and I will say it again. I hope God will punish anyone who preaches anything different from what you have already believed.

10I am not trying to please people. I want to please God. Do you think I am trying to please people? If I were doing that, I would not be a servant of Christ.

How Paul Became an Apostle

11My friends, I want you to know that no one made up the message I preach. 12It was not given or taught to me by some mere human. My message came directly from Jesus Christ when he appeared to me.

13You know how I used to live as a Jew. I was cruel to God's church and even tried to destroy it. 14I was a much better Jew than anyone else my own age, and I obeyed every law that our ancestors had given us. 15But even before I was born, God had chosen me. He was kind and had decided 16to show me his Son, so that I would announce his message to the Gentiles. I didn't talk this over with anyone. 17I didn't say a word, not even to the men in Jerusalem who were apostles before I was. Instead, I went at once to Arabia, and afterwards I returned to Damascus.

18Three years later I went to visit Peterb in Jerusalem and stayed with him for fifteen days. 19The only other apostle I saw was James, the Lord's brother. 20And in the presence of God I swear I am telling the truth.

Turning aside
(6) Paul had to keep an eye on the churches he helped to start. He would move on only to discover later that the believers he left behind were listening to false teachers. The new believers had to be shown again and again that sinners are saved by God's mercy, not by good works.

God prepares his servants
(17) Sometimes God takes many years to get his servants ready to work for him. Such was the case with Moses in the Old Testament. God also took his time preparing Paul. Be sure that, if God is going to use you in a special way, it will take more than overnight. Some lessons can be learned only by living with God day by day through all of the "ins and outs" of life.

ahis kindness: Some manuscripts have "the kindness of Christ." bPeter: The Greek text has "Cephas," which is an Aramaic name meaning "rock." Peter is the Greek name with the same meaning.

²¹Later, I went to the regions of Syria and Cilicia. ²²But no one who belonged to Christ's churches in Judea had ever seen me in person. ²³They had only heard that the one who had been cruel to them was now preaching the message that he had once tried to destroy. ²⁴And because of me, they praised God.

2 Fourteen years later I went to Jerusalem with Barnabas. I also took along Titus. ²But I went there because God had told me to go, and I explained the good news that I had been preaching to the Gentiles. Then I met privately with the ones who seemed to be the most important leaders. I wanted to make sure that all my work in the past and my future work would not be for nothing.

³Titus went to Jerusalem with me. He was a Greek, but still he was not forced to be circumcised. ⁴We went there because of those who pretended to be followers and had sneaked in among us as spies. They had come to take away the freedom that Christ Jesus had given us, and they were trying to make us their slaves. ⁵But we wanted you to have the true message. That's why we didn't give in to them, not even for a second.

⁶Some of them were supposed to be important leaders, but I didn't care who they were. God doesn't have any favorites! None of these so-called special leaders added anything to my message. ⁷They realized that God had sent me with the good news for Gentiles, and that he had sent Peter with the same message for Jews. ⁸God, who had sent Peter on a mission to the Jews, was now using me to preach to the Gentiles.

⁹James, Peter,ᵇ and John realized that God had given me the message about his kindness. And these men are supposed to be the pillars of the church. They even gave

Sneaking in like spies
(4) Paul did not flatter the false teachers. They were sneaking in like spies, he said, trying to get people who had been saved by faith to put themselves back under the Law. Paul's hard words show how serious the charge was: lives were at stake. The false teachers were getting people to depend on good deeds, which could never save them.

ᵇ*Peter*: The Greek text has "Cephas," which is an Aramaic name meaning "rock." Peter is the Greek name with the same meaning.

Barnabas and me a friendly handshake. This was to show that we would work with Gentiles and that they would work with Jews. 10They only asked us to remember the poor, and that was something I had always been eager to do.

Paul Corrects Peter at Antioch

11When Peter came to Antioch, I told him face-to-face that he was wrong. 12He used to eat with Gentile followers of the Lord, until James sent some Jewish followers. Peter was afraid of the Jews and soon stopped eating with Gentiles. 13He and the other Jews hid their true feelings so well that even Barnabas was fooled. 14But when I saw that they were not really obeying the truth that is in the good news, I corrected Peter and said:

Peter, you are a Jew, but you live like a Gentile. So how can you force Gentiles to live like Jews?

15We are Jews by birth and are not sinners like Gentiles. 16But we know that God accepts only those who have faith in Jesus Christ. No one can please God by simply obeying the Law. So we put our faith in Christ Jesus, and God accepted us because of our faith.

17When we Jews started looking for a way to please God, we discovered that we are sinners too. Does this mean that Christ is the one who makes us sinners? No, it doesn't! 18But if I tear down something and then build it again, I prove that I was wrong at first. 19It was the Law itself that killed me and freed me from its power, so that I could live for God.

I have been nailed to the cross with Christ. 20I have died, but Christ lives in me. And I now live by faith in the Son of God, who loved me and gave his life for me. 21I don't turn my back on God's kindness. If we can be acceptable to God by obeying the Law, it was useless for Christ to die.

Peter was wishy-washy (11) A wishy-washy Christian isn't very convincing. Peter had tried before to be on two sides at the same time, when he said he didn't know Jesus (Matthew 26.69–75). It may be a good thing sometimes just to be quiet and say nothing. But it is never a good thing to live a double life—acting like a Christian sometimes, but pretending not to be one when it suits those around us.

Faith Is the Only Way

3 You stupid Galatians! I told you exactly how Christ was nailed to a cross. Has someone now put an evil spell on you? [2]I want to know only one thing. How were you given God's Spirit? Was it by obeying the Law of Moses or by hearing about Christ and having faith in him? [3]How can you be so stupid? Do you think that by yourself you can complete what God's Spirit started in you? [4]Have you gone through all of this for nothing? Is it all really for nothing? [5]God gives you his Spirit and works miracles in you. But does he do this because you obey the Law of Moses or because you have heard about Christ and have faith in him?

[6]The Scriptures say that God accepted Abraham because Abraham had faith. [7]And so, you should understand that everyone who has faith is a child of Abraham.[c] [8]Long ago the Scriptures said that God would accept the Gentiles because of their faith. That's why God told Abraham the good news that all nations would be blessed because of him. [9]This means that everyone who has faith will share in the blessings that were given to Abraham because of his faith.

[10]Anyone who tries to please God by obeying the Law is under a curse. The Scriptures say, "Everyone who doesn't obey everything in the Law is under a curse." [11]No one can please God by obeying the Law. The Scriptures also say, "The people God accepts because of their faith will live."[d]

[12]The Law is not based on faith. It promises life only to people who obey its commands. [13]But Christ rescued us from the Law's curse, when he became a curse in our place. This is because the Scriptures

Add nothing to the message

(3) Being saved is God's gift that we receive by faith. Jesus alone earned that gift for us by being nailed to the cross. It's good to learn Bible history, and it is also necessary to honor God in our daily lives. But nothing we do or learn will add anything to what Jesus alone could do—and did do—to save sinners.

[c]*a child of Abraham*: God chose Abraham, and so it was believed that anyone who was a child of Abraham was also a child of God. See the note at 3.29.   [d]*The people God accepts because of their faith will live*: Or "The people God accepts will live because of their faith."

say that anyone who is nailed to a tree is under a curse. 14And because of what Jesus Christ has done, the blessing that was promised to Abraham was taken to the Gentiles. This happened so that by faith we would be given the promised Holy Spirit.

The Law and the Promise

15My friends, I will use an everyday example to explain what I mean. Once someone agrees to something, no one else can change or cancel the agreement.e 16That is how it is with the promises that God made to Abraham and his descendant.f The promises were not made to many descendants, but only to one, and that one is Christ. 17What I am saying is that the Law cannot change or cancel God's promise that was made 430 years before the Law was given. 18If we have to obey the Law in order to receive God's blessings, those blessings don't really come to us because of God's promise. But God was kind to Abraham and made him a promise.

19What is the use of the Law? It was given later to show that we sin. But it was only supposed to last until the coming of that descendantg who was given the promise. In fact, angels gave the Law to Moses, and he gave it to the people. 20There is only one God, and the Law did not come directly from him.

Slaves and Children

21Does the Law disagree with God's promises? No, it doesn't! If any law could give life to us, we could become acceptable to God by obeying that law. 22But the Scriptures say that sin controls everyone, so that God's promises will be for anyone who has faith in Jesus Christ.

What good is the Law?
(19) The Law of God, described in the Old Testament, shows people everywhere how much we all need God to save us, because no one can keep the Law and never break it. No one can honestly look at the Law and say, "I deserve eternal life." The Law's purpose is to bring people to faith. It is a "teacher," showing us how holy God is and how much we need his Son Jesus to save us.

eOnce someone . . . cancel the agreement: Or "Once a person makes out a will, no one can change or cancel it." fdescendant: The Greek text has "seed," which may mean one or many descendants. In this verse Paul says it means Christ. gthat descendant: Jesus.

23The Law controlled us and kept us under its power until the time came when we would have faith. 24In fact, the Law was our teacher. It was supposed to teach us until we had faith and were acceptable to God. 25But once a person has learned to have faith, there is no more need to have the Law as a teacher.

26All of you are God's children because of your faith in Christ Jesus. 27And when you were baptized, it was as though you had put on Christ in the same way you put on new clothes. 28Faith in Christ Jesus is what makes each of you equal with each other, whether you are a Jew or a Greek, a slave or a free person, a man or a woman. 29So if you belong to Christ, you are now part of Abraham's family,h and you will be given what God has promised. 1Children who are under age are no better off than slaves, even though everything their parents own will someday be theirs. 2This is because children are placed in the care of guardians and teachers until the time their parents have set. 3That is how it was with us. We were like children ruled by the powers of this world.

4But when the time was right, God sent his Son, and a woman gave birth to him. His Son obeyed the Law, 5so he could set us free from the Law, and we could become God's children. 6Now that we are his children, God has sent the Spirit of his Son into our hearts. And his Spirit tells us that God is our Father. 7You are no longer slaves. You are God's children, and you will be given what he has promised.

Paul's Concern for the Galatians

8Before you knew God, you were slaves of gods that are not real. 9But now you know God, or better still, God knows you. How can you turn back and become the slaves

Christians are free from the curse of the Law
(26) The curse of the Law is that it rightly condemned us for our sins. But now the Judge himself has paid the debt of obedience we owed him. So we are no longer under that curse. As true children of God, not slaves, we love to do the things that please our heavenly Father because we are born again and have a new nature.

How we know we are God's children
(6) Saying we are God's children doesn't make it true. But we now act like God's children. Without the fear we used to have, we now love to obey the commandments of God. Even more than that, we know we are God's children because the Holy Spirit—God himself—now lives within us. The Holy Spirit makes us know we belong to God.

hyou are now part of Abraham's family: Paul tells the Galatians that faith in Jesus Christ is what makes someone a true child of Abraham and of God. See the note at 3.7.

of those weak and pitiful powers?[i] [10]You even celebrate certain days, months, seasons, and years. [11]I am afraid I have wasted my time working with you.

[12]My friends, I beg you to be like me, just as I once tried to be like you. You didn't mistreat me [13]when I first preached to you. No you didn't, even though you knew I had come there because I was sick. [14]My illness must have caused you some trouble, but you didn't hate me or turn me away because of it. You welcomed me as though I were one of God's angels or even Christ Jesus himself. [15]Where is that good feeling now? I am sure that if it had been possible, you would have taken out your own eyes and given them to me. [16]Am I now your enemy, just because I told you the truth?

[17]Those people may be paying you a lot of attention, but it isn't for your good. They only want to keep you away from me, so you will pay them a lot of attention. [18]It is always good to give your attention to something worthwhile, even when I am not with you. [19]My children, I am in terrible pain until Christ may be seen living in you. [20]I wish I were with you now. Then I would not have to talk this way. You really have me puzzled.

Hagar and Sarah

[21]Some of you would like to be under the rule of the Law of Moses. But do you know what the Law says? [22]In the Scriptures we learn that Abraham had two sons. The mother of one of them was a slave, while the mother of the other one had always been free. [23]The son of the slave woman was born in the usual way. But the son of the free woman was born because of God's promise.

[24]All of this has another meaning as well. Each of the two women stands for one of the agreements God made with his people.

Be born of the right "mother"

(22) The truth is, we can't do anything at all to make ourselves Christians. We must be born all over again—this time by the Holy Spirit. Then we will have a whole new outlook on what pleases God. By faith we are born of the "free mother" (the heavenly Jerusalem), not of the "slave mother" (the Law).

[i]powers: Spirits were thought to control human lives and were believed to be connected with the movements of the stars.

Hagar, the slave woman, stands for the agreement that was made at Mount Sinai. Everyone born into her family is a slave. 25Hagar also stands for Mount Sinai in Arabia*j* and for the present city of Jerusalem. She*k* and her children are slaves.

26But our mother is the city of Jerusalem in heaven above, and she isn't a slave. 27The Scriptures say about her,

> "You have never had children,
>> but now you can be glad.
> You have never given birth,
>> but now you can shout.
> Once you had no children,
>> but now you will have
> more children than a woman
> who has been married
>> for a long time."

28My friends, you were born because of this promise, just as Isaac was. 29But the child who was born in the natural way made trouble for the child who was born because of the Spirit. The same thing is happening today. 30The Scriptures say, "Get rid of the slave woman and her son! He won't be given anything. The son of the free woman will receive everything." 31My friends, we are children of the free woman and not of the slave.

Christ Gives Freedom

5 Christ has set us free! This means we are really free. Now hold on to your freedom and don't ever become slaves of the Law again.

2I, Paul, promise you that Christ won't do you any good if you get circumcised. 3If you do, you must obey the whole Law. 4And if you try to please God by obeying the Law, you have cut yourself off from Christ and his kindness. 5But the Spirit makes us sure that God will accept us be-

Rules cannot free us
(1) Paul was talking about the rituals the Jews were required to do daily and at other times, such as circumcising boys soon after birth. The Jewish religion had gotten tangled up in a set of rules. The Jews could never keep them all, and rules could never save them from their sins anyway. Only God could save them. But they let their religious rituals take the place of God. That was wrong.

jHagar also stands for Mount Sinai in Arabia: Some manuscripts have "Sinai is a mountain in Arabia." This sentence would then be translated: "Sinai is a mountain in Arabia, and Hagar stands for the present city of Jerusalem."   *kShe*: "Hagar" or "Jerusalem."

cause of our faith in Christ. [6]If you are a follower of Christ Jesus, it makes no difference whether you are circumcised or not. All that matters is your faith that makes you love others.

[7]You were doing so well until someone made you turn from the truth. [8]And that person was certainly not sent by the one who chose you. [9]A little yeast can change a whole batch of dough, [10]but you belong to the Lord. That makes me certain that you will do what I say, instead of what someone else tells you to do. Whoever is causing trouble for you will be punished.

[11]My friends, if I still preach that people need to be circumcised, why am I in so much trouble? The message about the cross would no longer be a problem, if I told people to be circumcised. [12]I wish that everyone who is upsetting you would not only get circumcised, but would cut off much more!

[13]My friends, you were chosen to be free. So don't use your freedom as an excuse to do anything you want. Use it as an opportunity to serve each other with love. [14]All that the Law says can be summed up in the command to love others as much as you love yourself. [15]But if you keep attacking each other like wild animals, you had better watch out or you will destroy yourselves.

God's Spirit and Our Own Desires

[16]If you are guided by the Spirit, you won't obey your selfish desires. [17]The Spirit and your desires are enemies of each other. They are always fighting each other and keeping you from doing what you feel you should. [18]But if you obey the Spirit, the Law of Moses has no control over you.

[19]People's desires make them give in to immoral ways, filthy thoughts, and shameful deeds. [20]They worship idols, practice witchcraft, hate others, and are hard to get along with. People become jealous, angry, and selfish. They not only argue and cause trouble, but they are [21]envious. They get drunk, carry on at wild parties, and do other evil things as well. I told you before, and I

God's Spirit brings life
(16) The life we were living before the Holy Spirit came to live in us was a sad and dying kind of life. Now that he lives in us, our desires are changed. We no longer wish to do the things that were killing us and dragging us down to hell. This is the kind of life that everybody needs. Then there would be no more hatred, jealousy, or other kinds of sin in the world.

am telling you again: No one who does these things will share in the blessings of God's kingdom. 22God's Spirit makes us loving, happy, peaceful, patient, kind, good, faithful, 23gentle, and self-controlled. There is no law against behaving in any of these ways. 24And because we belong to Christ, we have killed our selfish feelings and desires. 25God's Spirit has given us life, and so we should follow the Spirit. 26But don't be conceited or make others jealous by claiming to be better than they are.

Help Each Other

6 My friends, you are spiritual. So if someone is trapped in sin, you should gently lead that person back to the right path. But watch out, and don't be tempted yourself. 2You obey the law of Christ when you offer each other a helping hand.

3If you think you are better than others, when you really aren't, you are wrong. 4Do your own work well, and then you will have something to be proud of. But don't compare yourself with others. 5We each must carry our own load.

6Share every good thing you have with anyone who teaches you what God has said.

7You cannot fool God, so don't make a fool of yourself! You will harvest what you plant. 8If you follow your selfish desires, you will harvest destruction, but if you follow the Spirit, you will harvest eternal life. 9Don't get tired of helping others. You will be rewarded when the time is right, if you don't give up. 10We should help people whenever we can, especially if they are followers of the Lord.

Final Warnings

11You can see what big letters I make when I write with my own hand.

12Those people who are telling you to get circumcised are only trying to show how important they are. And they don't want to get into trouble for preaching about the

Help others return to Christ

(1) Sometimes Christians forget to keep their promise to Jesus. At those times their Christian friends should help them come back to where they "got off the road." The Galatians had been in danger of getting loaded down with unnecessary laws. Now Paul shows them that they should be helping others get rid of their load of sin. This is the kind of load-bearing that keeps Christ's law of love.

We know this is a letter from Paul

(11) Paul proved this letter was from him by pointing out the "big letters" which he used to write his words. Many people believe Paul had eyesight problems, so he had to write in large handwriting. Eyeglasses had not yet been invented in Paul's time.

cross of Christ. 13They are circumcised, but they don't obey the Law of Moses. All they want is to brag about having you circumcised. 14But I will never brag about anything except the cross of our Lord Jesus Christ. Because of his cross, the world is dead as far as I am concerned, and I am dead as far as the world is concerned.

15It doesn't matter if you are circumcised or not. All that matters is that you are a new person.

16If you follow this rule, you will belong to God's true people. God will treat you with kindness and will bless you with peace.

17On my own body are scars that prove I belong to Christ Jesus. So I don't want anyone to bother me anymore.

18My friends, I pray that the Lord Jesus Christ will be kind to you! Amen.

Be a new creation of God
(15) Being created over again by God is what Paul means by becoming a "new person." That is the main point of his letter. Not marks made on our bodies like circumcision, but a completely new person is God's great answer to our needs. Jesus' answer to Nicodemus is still true: "You must be born from above" (John 3.7).

PAUL'S LETTER TO THE CHURCH IN EPHESUS

ABOUT THIS LETTER

"Praise the God and Father of our Lord Jesus Christ for the spiritual blessings that Christ has brought us from heaven!" (1.3). Paul begins his letter to the Christians in Ephesus with a powerful reminder of the main theme of his message. Christ died on the cross to set us free (1.7,8). But God raised Christ from death, and he now sits at God's right side in heaven, where he rules over this world. And he will rule over the future world as well (1.20,21).

Christ brought Jews and Gentiles together by "breaking down the wall of hatred" that separated them (2.14) and he united them all as part of that holy temple where God's Spirit lives (2.22). This was according to God's eternal plan (3.11).

There is only one Lord, one Spirit of God, and one God, who is the Father of all people (4.4,5). This means that Christians must let the Spirit keep their hearts united, so they can live at peace with each other (4.3). The idea of all Christians being one with Christ is so central to this letter that it occurs twenty times. There is one faith and one baptism by which believers become one body.

Ephesus was a port city on the western shore of Asia Minor (modern-day Turkey). In Paul's time this was the fourth largest city in the Roman empire. It was also an ancient center of nature religion where the goddess Artemis was widely worshiped (Acts 19).

Paul lets the Ephesians know that much is expected of people who are called to a new life (4.17—5.20). Followers of the Lord are God's dear children, and they must do as God does (5.1). They used to live in the dark, but they must now live in the light and make their light shine (5.8,9).

Paul then teaches husbands and wives, children and parents, and slaves and masters how to live as Christians (5.21—6.9).

Paul never forgets how kind God is:

God was merciful! We were dead because of our sins, but God loved us so much that he made us alive with Christ, and God's kindness is what saves you. (2.4,5)

You were saved by faith in God's kindness. This is God's gift to you, and not anything you have done on your own. (2.8)

A QUICK LOOK AT THIS LETTER

1 From Paul, chosen by God to be an apostle of Christ Jesus.

To God's people who live in Ephesus and*a* are faithful followers of Christ Jesus.

alive in Ephesus and: Some manuscripts do not have these words.

2I pray that God our Father and our Lord Jesus Christ will be kind to you and will bless you with peace!

Christ Brings Spiritual Blessings

3Praise the God and Father of our Lord Jesus Christ for the spiritual blessings that Christ has brought us from heaven! 4Before the world was created, God had Christ choose us to live with him and to be his holy and innocent and loving people. 5God was kindb and decided that Christ would choose us to be God's own adopted children. 6God was very kind to us because of the Son he dearly loves, and so we should praise God.

7-8Christ sacrificed his life's blood to set us free, which means that our sins are now forgiven. Christ did this because God was so kind to us. God has great wisdom and understanding, 9and by what Christ has done, God has shown us his own mysterious ways. 10Then when the time is right, God will do all that he has planned, and Christ will bring together everything in heaven and on earth.

11God always does what he plans, and that's why he had Christ choose us. 12He did this so that we Jews would bring honor to him and be the first ones to have hope because of him. 13Christ also brought you the truth, which is the good news about how you can be saved. You put your faith in Christ and were given the promised Holy Spirit to show that you belong to God. 14The Spirit also makes us sure that we will be given what God has stored up for his people. Then we will be set free, and God will be honored and praised.

Paul's Prayer

15I have heard about your faith in the Lord Jesus and your love for all of God's

Jesus stands for us in heaven
(3) Jesus not only brought us blessings from heaven. He is now standing for us in heaven. We enjoy spiritual blessings now because Jesus is in heaven before us. He has given us the Holy Spirit so that we can have some of heaven on earth right now. That's how we know that there is even more and better to come when we join Jesus in the place he has prepared for us.

God chose us
(11) Jesus once reminded his disciples that they had not chosen him, but he chose them (John 15.16). So also he chose each of us who believe, long ago before he created the world. God chose us to believe *and* to be holy and innocent and loving. In that way we would show others in the world how good God is in all his ways. So Christians have a great privilege and a great duty to be like Jesus in the world.

---

bholy and innocent and loving people. 5God was kind: Or "holy and innocent people. God was loving 5and kind."

people. 16So I never stop being grateful for you, as I mention you in my prayers. 17I ask the glorious Father and God of our Lord Jesus Christ to give you his Spirit. The Spirit will make you wise and let you understand what it means to know God. 18My prayer is that light will flood your hearts and that you will understand the hope that was given to you when God chose you. Then you will discover the glorious blessings that will be yours together with all of God's people.

19I want you to know about the great and mighty power that God has for us followers. It is the same wonderful power he used 20when he raised Christ from death and let him sit at his right side*c* in heaven. 21There Christ rules over all forces, authorities, powers, and rulers. He rules over all beings in this world and will rule in the future world as well. 22God has put all things under the power of Christ, and for the good of the church he has made him the head of everything. 23The church is Christ's body and is filled with Christ who completely fills everything.*d*

From Death to Life

2 In the past you were dead because you sinned and fought against God. 2You followed the ways of this world and obeyed the devil. He rules the world, and his spirit has power over everyone who does not obey God. 3Once we were also ruled by the selfish desires of our bodies and minds. We had made God angry, and we were going to be punished.

4-5But God was merciful! We were dead because of our sins, but God loved us so much that he made us alive with Christ, and God's kindness is what saves you. 6God raised us from death to life with Christ Jesus, and he has given us a place beside

cright side: The place of power and honor. *dand is filled with Christ who completely fills everything*: Or "which completely fills Christ and fully completes his work."

What makes us followers of Jesus?
(19) We follow the Lord not simply by our own decision, but by the power of God himself. Paul says that is the same power that raised Jesus from death. We were dead as far as knowing God was concerned. But God "raised us up" to the new life of knowing him, and he used the same power that he used to raise Christ from death.

Don't be a walking dead person
(4) When we don't know God, that's a way of being "dead," even though we're still walking around. But when Christ rose from death, he made it possible for us to live in the same way that he lives—by enjoying the very life of God. By faith we realize that we were dead before Christ came to live in us, but now we're really alive.

Christ in heaven above. 7God did this so that in the future world he could show how truly good and kind he is to us because of what Christ Jesus has done. 8You were saved by faith in God's kindness.e This is God's gift to you, and not anything you have done on your own. 9It isn't something you have earned, so there is nothing you can brag about. 10God planned for us to do good things and to live as he has always wanted us to live. That's why he sent Christ to make us what we are.

United by Christ

11Don't forget that you are Gentiles. In fact, you used to be called "uncircumcised" by Jews, who take pride in being circumcised. 12At that time you did not know about Christ. You were foreigners to the people of Israel, and you had no part in the promises that God had made to them. You were living in this world without hope and without God, 13and you were far from God. But Christ offered his life's blood as a sacrifice and brought you near to God.

14Christ has made peace between Jews and Gentiles, and he has united us by breaking down the wall of hatred that separated us. Christ gave his own body 15to destroy the Law of Moses with all its rules and commands. He even brought Jews and Gentiles together as though we were only one person, when he united us in peace. 16On the cross Christ did away with our hatred for each other. He also made peacef between us and God by uniting Jews and Gentiles in one body. 17Christ came and preached peace to you Gentiles, who were far from God, and peace to us Jews, who were near to God. 18And because of Christ, all of us

Gentiles have been brought into God's family (14) For centuries the Jews enjoyed the friendship of God. They believed him and were his true followers except when they disobeyed, which was often. But now God has also brought Gentiles into that family. Gentiles and Jews now share by faith in the results of the saving work of Jesus Christ. This is what God promised Abraham, the great father of the Jews, two thousand years before Christ was born, saying, "Through you all the families of the earth will be blessed."

eGod's kindness: The Greek word usually rendered "grace" (from gratia of the Latin Vulgate) is often translated in the CEV as "God's kindness" or "God's great kindness" or "God is kind" in order to express in a more contemporary way the overwhelming kindness of God, who treats us far better than we deserve. fHe also made peace: Or "The cross also made peace."

can come to the Father by the same Spirit.

19You Gentiles are no longer strangers and foreigners. You are citizens with everyone else who belongs to the family of God. 20You are like a building with the apostles and prophets as the foundation and with Christ as the most important stone. 21Christ is the one who holds the building together and makes it grow into a holy temple for the Lord. 22And you are part of that building Christ has built as a place for God's own Spirit to live.

Paul's Mission to the Gentiles

3 Christ Jesus made me his prisoner, so that I could help you Gentiles. 2You have surely heard about God's kindness in choosing me to help you. 3In fact, this letter tells you a little about how God has shown me his mysterious ways. 4As you read the letter, you will also find out how well I really do understand the mystery about Christ. 5No one knew about this mystery until God's Spirit told it to his holy apostles and prophets. 6And the mystery is this: Because of Christ Jesus, the good news has given the Gentiles a share in the promises that God gave to the Jews. God has also let the Gentiles be part of the same body.

7God treated me with kindness. His power worked in me, and it became my job to spread the good news. 8I am the least important of all God's people. But God was kind and chose me to tell the Gentiles that because of Christ there are blessings that cannot be measured. 9God, who created everything, wanted me to help everyone understand the mysterious plan that had always been hidden in his mind. 10Then God would use the church to show the powers and authorities above that he has many different kinds of wisdom.

11God did this according to his eternal plan. And he was able to do what he had planned because of all that Christ Jesus our Lord had done. 12Christ now gives us courage and confidence, so that we can come to God by faith. 13That's why you should

God chose Paul to bring the good news
(2) Paul had been an enemy of Christ and his followers. But then one day Jesus appeared to Paul (see Acts 9) when he was still called Saul. Then God gave to Paul a new understanding about why Jesus came. After that time when he met Jesus, Paul became a great missionary to the Gentile world.

not be discouraged when I suffer for you. After all, it will bring honor to you.

Christ's Love for Us

14I kneel in prayer to the Father. 15All beings in heaven and on earth receive their life from him.g 16God is wonderful and glorious. I pray that his Spirit will make you become strong followers 17and that Christ will live in your hearts because of your faith. Stand firm and be deeply rooted in his love. 18I pray that you and all of God's people will understand what is called wide or long or high or deep.h 19I want you to know all about Christ's love, although it is too wonderful to be measured. Then your lives will be filled with all that God is.

20-21I pray that Christ Jesus and the church will forever bring praise to God. His power at work in us can do far more than we dare ask or imagine. Amen.

Unity with Christ

4 As a prisoner of the Lord, I beg you to live in a way that is worthy of the people God has chosen to be his own. 2Always be humble and gentle. Patiently put up with each other and love each other. 3Try your best to let God's Spirit keep your hearts united. Do this by living at peace. 4All of you are part of the same body. There is only one Spirit of God, just as you were given one hope when you were chosen to be God's people. 5We have only one Lord, one faith, and one baptism. 6There is one God who is the Father of all people. Not only is God above all others, but he works by using all of us, and he lives in all of us.

7Christ has generously divided out his gifts to us. 8As the Scriptures say,

"When he went up
　　to the highest place,

Christ's love is great
(19) Paul says you can't measure the love Jesus has for us. We know when ordinary people love us, and we're comforted by that. But when we know Christ's love, we never have to feel unloved again. His love goes on and on, and we're never alone. People cheat themselves of the greatest of all gifts when they fail to accept the love of Jesus.

Paul wrote with a method
(1) If you look carefully you'll see that Paul teaches in Ephesians 1 through 3 mainly about what we should believe, and in chapters 4 through 6 about how we should live. This will help you as you study this great little book. Right Christian believing leads to right Christian living.

---

greceive their life from him: Or "know who they really are because of him." hwhat is called wide or long or high or deep: This may refer to the heavenly Jerusalem or to God's love or wisdom or to the meaning of the cross.

he led away many prisoners
and gave gifts
to people."

9When it says, "he went up," it means
that Christ had been deep in the earth.
10This also means that the one who went
deep into the earth is the same one who
went into the highest heaven, so that he
would fill the whole universe.

11Christ chose some of us to be apostles,
prophets, missionaries, pastors, and teachers, 12so that his people would learn to serve
and his body would grow strong. 13This will
continue until we are united by our faith
and by our understanding of the Son of God.
Then we will be mature, just as Christ is,
and we will be completely like him.*

14We must stop acting like children. We
must not let deceitful people trick us by their
false teachings, which are like winds that
toss us around from place to place. 15Love
should always make us tell the truth. Then
we will grow in every way and be more
like Christ, the head 16of the body. Christ
holds it together and makes all of its parts
work perfectly, as it grows and becomes
strong because of love.

The Old Life and the New Life

17As a follower of the Lord, I order you
to stop living like stupid, godless people.
18Their minds are in the dark, and they are
stubborn and ignorant and have missed out
on the life that comes from God. They no
longer have any feelings about what is right,
19and they are so greedy that they do all
kinds of indecent things.

20-21But that isn't what you were taught
about Jesus Christ. He is the truth, and you
heard about him and learned about him.
22You were told that your foolish desires
will destroy you and that you must give up
your old way of life with all its bad habits.
23Let the Spirit change your way of thinking
24and make you into a new person. You

We are growing up in Christ
(15) Jesus is our head, our leader, and he has given us different gifts and abilities to serve him. The reason for these differences is so that we may help one another grow spiritually and become mature, until we are truly like Christ.

Let the Spirit change your mind
(23) Because we are born into this sinful world, our thinking about God and our lives is twisted by sin. But Christ gives us a new mind, a new understanding, when we are born anew by the Holy Spirit (John 3.3). We must allow the Holy Spirit to keep on changing our minds as long as we live. As our minds change, so do our lives.

---

*and we will be completely like him: Or "and he is com-
pletely perfect."

were created to be like God, and so you must please him and be truly holy.

Rules for the New Life

25We are part of the same body. Stop lying and start telling each other the truth. 26Don't get so angry that you sin. Don't go to bed angry 27and don't give the devil a chance.

28If you are a thief, quit stealing. Be honest and work hard, so you will have something to give to needy people.

29Stop all your dirty talk. Say the right thing at the right time and help others by what you say.

30Don't make God's Spirit sad. The Spirit makes you sure that someday you will be free from your sins.

31Stop being bitter and angry and mad at others. Don't yell at one another or curse each other or ever be rude. 32Instead, be kind and merciful, and forgive others, just as God forgave you because of Christ.

5 Do as God does. After all, you are his dear children. 2Let love be your guide. Christ loved us*j* and offered his life for us as a sacrifice that pleases God.

3You are God's people, so don't let it be said that any of you are immoral or indecent or greedy. 4Don't use dirty or foolish or filthy words. Instead, say how thankful you are. 5Being greedy, indecent, or immoral is just another way of worshiping idols. You can be sure that people who behave in this way will never be part of the kingdom that belongs to Christ and to God.

Living as People of Light

6Don't let anyone trick you with foolish talk. God punishes everyone who disobeys him and says*k* foolish things. 7So don't have anything to do with anyone like that.

8You used to be like people living in the dark, but now you are people of the light

How you talk is important
(6) By "foolish talk" Paul means talk that is not decent. If we are Christians, we have the light of Christ living and shining in us. This should keep us from speaking in a way that brings disgrace on Christ. Filthy talk reveals a filthy mind. This can't be the mind of Christ who lives in the Christian.

j us: Some manuscripts have "you."   *k says*: Or "does."

because you belong to the Lord. So act like people of the light [9]and make your light shine. Be good and honest and truthful, [10]as you try to please the Lord. [11]Don't take part in doing those worthless things that are done in the dark. Instead, show how wrong they are. [12]It is disgusting even to talk about what is done in the dark. [13]But the light will show what these things are really like. [14]Light shows up everything,[l] just as the Scriptures say,

> "Wake up from your sleep
> and rise from death.
> Then Christ will shine
> on you."

[15]Act like people with good sense and not like fools. [16]These are evil times, so make every minute count. [17]Don't be stupid. Instead, find out what the Lord wants you to do. [18]Don't destroy yourself by getting drunk, but let the Spirit fill your life. [19]When you meet together, sing psalms, hymns, and spiritual songs, as you praise the Lord with all your heart. [20]Always use the name of the Lord Jesus Christ to thank God the Father for everything.

Wives and Husbands

[21]Honor the Lord and put others first. [22]A wife should put her husband first, as she does the Lord. [23]A husband is the head of his wife, as Christ is the head and the Savior of the church, which is his own body. [24]Wives should always put their husbands first, as the church puts Christ first.

[25]A husband should love his wife as much as Christ loved the church and gave his life for it. [26]He made the church holy by the power of his word, and he made it pure by washing it with water. [27]Christ did this, so that he would have a glorious and holy church, without faults or spots or wrinkles or any other flaws.

[28]In the same way, a husband should love his wife as much as he loves himself. A hus-

Who will be first?

(22) In our times there is a lot of unhappiness between husbands and wives because either one or both don't follow God's plan for the home. The desire to be "one up" on someone else doesn't come from what God's word tells us. What Paul says about the home is clear. But let us be sure that our love, our desire to serve each other, is sincere. One party should not be doing all the loving and serving. "Love your neighbor" surely must also mean to love the person closest to you.

---

[l]*Light shows up everything*: Or "Everything that is seen in the light becomes light itself."

band who loves his wife shows that he loves himself. 29None of us hate our own bodies. We provide for them and take good care of them, just as Christ does for the church, 30because we are each part of his body. 31As the Scriptures say, "A man leaves his father and mother to get married, and he becomes like one person with his wife." 32This is a great mystery, but I understand it to mean Christ and his church. 33So each husband should love his wife as much as he loves himself, and each wife should respect her husband.

Children and Parents

6 Children, you belong to the Lord, and you do the right thing when you obey your parents. The first commandment with a promise says, 2"Obey your father and your mother, 3and you will have a long and happy life."

4Parents, don't be hard on your children. Raise them properly. Teach them and instruct them about the Lord.

The family teaches life
(1) Children are wise to obey their parents. Later in life they will realize how important this was for them. Living in harmony with others begins by living in harmony with our families.

Slaves and Masters

5Slaves, you must obey your earthly masters. Show them great respect and be as loyal to them as you are to Christ. 6Try to please them at all times, and not just when you think they are watching. You are slaves of Christ, so with your whole heart you must do what God wants you to do. 7Gladly serve your masters, as though they were the Lord himself, and not simply people. 8You know that you will be rewarded for any good things you do, whether you are slaves or free.

9Slave owners, you must treat your slaves with this same respect. Don't threaten them. They have the same Master in heaven that you do, and he doesn't have any favorites.

Be a good Christian worker
(5) We don't have slaves today. But Paul's advice still holds, because just about everybody has to work for somebody else. Christian employees should see the wisdom in Paul's directions about serving. This is Christian love at work in the real world.

The Fight against Evil

10Finally, let the mighty strength of the Lord make you strong. 11Put on all the armor that God gives, so you can defend yourself against the devil's tricks. 12We are not fighting against humans. We are fighting against forces and authorities and against rulers of darkness and spiritual powers in the heavens above. 13So put on all the armor that God gives. Then when that evil day*m* comes, you will be able to defend yourself. And when the battle is over, you will still be standing firm.

14Be ready! Let the truth be like a belt around your waist, and let God's justice protect you like armor. 15Your desire to tell the good news about peace should be like shoes on your feet. 16Let your faith be like a shield, and you will be able to stop all the flaming arrows of the evil one. 17Let God's saving power be like a helmet, and for a sword use God's message that comes from the Spirit.

18Never stop praying, especially for others. Always pray by the power of the Spirit. Stay alert and keep praying for God's people. 19Pray that I will be given the message to speak and that I may fearlessly explain the mystery about the good news. 20I was sent to do this work, and that's the reason I am in jail. So pray that I will be brave and will speak as I should.

Final Greetings

21-22I want you to know how I am getting along and what I am doing. That's why I am sending Tychicus to you. He is a dear friend, as well as a faithful servant of the Lord. He will tell you how I am doing, and he will cheer you up.

23I pray that God the Father and the Lord Jesus Christ will give peace, love, and faith to every follower! 24May God be kind to everyone who keeps on loving our Lord Jesus Christ.

God supplies our weapons
(11) The Christian life is like a war. Our enemy Satan wants to attack us, both from outside and from inside ourselves. Let's think about every weapon and piece of armor that Paul writes about. Then let's pray that we will learn to use each piece well, for the glory of God, as we come up against our daily trials.

Paul the mighty prisoner
(20) Even though Paul had been put in jail for his beliefs, he had strength and wisdom from God, and stayed cheerful and positive about what he was going through. He did some of his greatest writing in chains. Let's remember Paul as our example when we suffer in this life.

m that evil day: Either the present (see 5.16) or "the day of death" or "the day of judgment."

PAUL'S LETTER TO THE CHURCH IN PHILIPPI

ABOUT THIS LETTER

Paul wrote this letter from jail (1.7) to thank the Lord's followers at Philippi for helping him with their gifts and prayers (1.5; 4.10–19). He hopes to be set free, so that he can continue preaching the good news (3.17–19). But he knows that he might be put to death (1.21; 2.17; 3.10).

The city of Philippi is in the part of northern Greece known as Macedonia. It was at Philippi that Paul had entered Europe for the first time, and there he preached the good news and began a church (Acts 16). He now warns the Christians at Philippi that they may have to suffer, just as Christ suffered and Paul is now suffering. If this happens, the Philippians should count it a blessing that comes from having faith in Christ (1.28–30).

There were problems in the church at Philippi, because some of the members claimed that people must obey the law of Moses, or they could not be saved. But Paul has no patience with such members and warns the church, "Watch out for those people who behave like dogs!" (3.2–11). This letter is also filled with joy. Even in jail, Paul is happy because he has discovered how to make the best of a bad situation and because he remembers all the kindness shown to him by the people in the church at Philippi.

Paul reminds them that God's people are to live in harmony (2.2; 4.2,3) and to think the same way that Christ Jesus did:

> *Christ was truly God.*
> *But he did not try to remain*
> *equal with God.*
> *He gave up everything*
> *and became a slave,*
> *when he became*
> *like one of us. (2.6,7)*

A QUICK LOOK AT THIS LETTER

1 From Paul and Timothy, servants of Christ Jesus.

To all of God's people who belong to Christ Jesus at Philippi and to all of your church officials and officers.[a]

²I pray that God our Father and the Lord

---

[a]*church officials and officers*: Or "bishops and deacons."

Jesus Christ will be kind to you and will bless you with peace!

Paul's Prayer for the Church in Philippi

3Every time I think of you, I thank my God. 4And whenever I mention you in my prayers, it makes me happy. 5This is because you have taken part with me in spreading the good news from the first day you heard about it. 6God is the one who began this good work in you, and I am certain that he won't stop before it is complete on the day that Christ Jesus returns.

7You have a special place in my heart. So it is only natural for me to feel the way I do. All of you have helped in the work that God has given me, as I defend the good news and tell about it here in jail. 8God himself knows how much I want to see you. He knows that I care for you in the same way that Christ Jesus does.

9I pray that your love will keep on growing and that you will fully know and understand 10how to make the right choices. Then you will still be pure and innocent when Christ returns. And until that day, 11Jesus Christ will keep you busy doing good deeds that bring glory and praise to God.

What Life Means to Paul

12My dear friends, I want you to know that what has happened to me has helped to spread the good news. 13The Roman guards and all the others know that I am here in jail because I serve Christ. 14Now most of the Lord's followers have become brave and are fearlessly telling the message.*b*

15Some are preaching about Christ because they are jealous and envious of us. Others are preaching because they want to help. 16They love Christ and know that I am here to defend the good news about him. 17But the ones who are jealous of us are

A beautiful way to think
(3) Paul thanked God every time he remembered one of Christ's people. Giving thanks for one another is a good way never to think thoughts of envy or resentment about our Christian brothers and sisters. We have many good memories of the love and kindness of such friends. God is pleased when we give thanks for each one that is so well remembered.

God will finish his work in us
(10) God didn't plan to save us and draw us into his friendship just so he could turn around and throw us away. No—he will complete his good work in us when Jesus comes back to earth. In the meantime, God is doing that work daily—molding and shaping us to be like his Son.

b the message: Some manuscripts have "the Lord's message," and others have "God's message."

not sincere. They just want to cause trouble for me while I am in jail. [18]But that doesn't matter. All that matters is that people are telling about Christ, whether they are sincere or not. That is what makes me glad.

I will keep on being glad, [19]because I know that your prayers and the help that comes from the Spirit of Christ Jesus will keep me safe. [20]I honestly expect and hope that I will never do anything to be ashamed of. Whether I live or die, I always want to be as brave as I am now and bring honor to Christ.

[21]If I live, it will be for Christ, and if I die, I will gain even more. [22]I don't know what to choose. I could keep on living and doing something useful. [23]It is a hard choice to make. I want to die and be with Christ, because that would be much better. [24-25]But I know that all of you still need me. That's why I am sure I will stay on to help you grow and be happy in your faith. [26]Then, when I visit you again, you will have good reason to take great pride in Christ Jesus because of me.c

[27]Above all else, you must live in a way that brings honor to the good news about Christ. Then, whether I visit you or not, I will hear that all of you think alike. I will know that you are working together and that you are struggling side by side to get others to believe the good news.

[28]Be brave when you face your enemies. Your courage will show them that they are going to be destroyed, and it will show you that you will be saved. God will make all of this happen, [29]and he has blessed you. Not only do you have faith in Christ, but you suffer for him. [30]You saw me suffer, and you still hear about my troubles. Now you must suffer in the same way.

True Humility

2 Christ encourages you, and his love comforts you. God's Spirit unites you,

What is your goal in life?
(21) Paul said he lived his life for Christ, and we can easily believe it. The letters to the Ephesians, the Philippians, the Colossians, and Philemon were probably written when Paul was a prisoner in Rome (see Acts 28). But notice Paul's Christlike and generous spirit. When we're set free from selfishness, it's not hard to be cheerful.

Courage says a lot
(28) The believer's courage does two things. First, it shows enemies that they are defeated, even though they might seem to be winning. And it shows the believer that God is in control, and that he saves the soul. No one can truly hurt the believer who has such courage from God.

ctake great pride in Christ Jesus because of me: Or "take great pride in me because of Christ Jesus."

and you are concerned for others. ²Now make me completely happy! Live in harmony by showing love for each other. Be united in what you think, as if you were only one person. ³Don't be jealous or proud, but be humble and consider others more important than yourselves. ⁴Care about them as much as you care about yourselves ⁵and think the same way that Christ Jesus did:ᵈ

⁶Christ was truly God.
But he did not try to remainᵉ
    equal with God.
⁷He gave up everythingᶠ
    and became a slave,
when he became
    like one of us.

⁸Christ was humble.
He obeyed God and even died
    on a cross.
⁹Then God gave Christ
    the highest place
and honored his name
    above all others.

¹⁰So at the name of Jesus
    everyone will bow down,
those in heaven, on earth,
    and under the earth.
¹¹And to the glory
    of God the Father
everyone will openly agree,
    "Jesus Christ is Lord!"

Lights in the World

¹²My dear friends, you always obeyed when I was with you. Now that I am away, you should obey even more. So work with fear and trembling to discover what it really means to be saved. ¹³God is working in you to make you willing to obey him.
¹⁴Do everything without grumbling or ar-

Jesus is our example

(6) Jesus didn't insist on being treated as God—even though he had a right to. He left his royal glory behind to become a servant to people on earth. So what is our "claim to fame"? When we understand what Jesus did to save us from our sins, how can we feel important? The King of glory himself became a man to seek lost people. That ought to make us humble.

We aren't alone

(13) We aren't in a do-it-yourself improvement program. "God is working in you," says Paul. This makes us happy as we realize that we are, after all, God's own workmanship. It is God who is shaping and molding us into the kind of people he wants us to be. Sunshine and rain, good times and hard times, are God's ways of completing his great plan for us.

ᵈ*think the same way that Christ Jesus did*: Or "think the way you should because you belong to Christ Jesus." ᵉ*remain*: Or "become." ᶠ*He gave up everything*: Greek, "He emptied himself."

guing. 15Then you will be the pure and innocent children of God. You live among people
who are crooked and evil, but you must not
do anything that they can say is wrong. Try
to shine as lights among the people of this
world, 16as you hold firmly to g the message
that gives life. Then on the day when Christ
returns, I can take pride in you. I can also
know that my work and efforts were not
useless.

17Your faith in the Lord and your service
are like a sacrifice offered to him. And my
own blood may have to be poured out with
the sacrifice.h If this happens, I will be glad
and rejoice with you. 18In the same way,
you should be glad and rejoice with me.

Timothy and Epaphroditus

19I want to be encouraged by news about
you. So I hope the Lord Jesus will soon let
me send Timothy to you. 20I don't have anyone else who cares about you as much as
he does. 21The others think only about what
interests them and not about what concerns
Christ Jesus. 22But you know what kind of
person Timothy is. He has worked with me
like a son in spreading the good news.
23I hope to send him to you, as soon as I
find out what is going to happen to me.
24I feel sure that the Lord will also let me
come soon.

25I think I ought to send my dear friend
Epaphroditus back to you. He is a follower
and a worker and a soldier of the Lord, just
as I am. You sent him to look after me,
26but now he is eager to see you. He is worried, because you heard he was sick. 27In
fact, he was very sick and almost died. But
God was kind to him, and also to me, and
he kept me from being burdened down with
sorrow.

28Now I am more eager than ever to send
Epaphroditus back again. You will be glad

Be Jesus-minded

(21) Paul praises Timothy
for thinking first about what
concerns Jesus. Life is a lot
simpler and happier for
people who are "Jesus-
minded," who aren't struggling for the sake of their
own interests, but who are
looking out for his.

---

ghold firmly to: Or "offer them."   hmy own blood may
have to be poured out with the sacrifice: Offerings of
water or wine were sometimes poured out when animals were sacrificed on the altar.

to see him, and I won't have to worry any longer. ²⁹Be sure to give him a cheerful welcome, just as people who serve the Lord deserve. ³⁰He almost died working for Christ, and he risked his own life to do for me what you could not.

Being Acceptable to God

3 Finally, my dear friends, be glad that you belong to the Lord. It doesn't bother me to write the same things to you that I have written before. In fact, it is for your own good.

²Watch out for those people who behave like dogs! They are evil and want to do more than just circumcise you. ³But we are the ones who are truly circumcised, because we worship by the power of God's Spiritⁱ and take pride in Christ Jesus. We don't brag about what we have done, ⁴although I could. Others may brag about themselves, but I have more reason to brag than anyone else. ⁵I was circumcised when I was eight days old,^j and I am from the nation of Israel and the tribe of Benjamin. I am a true Hebrew. As a Pharisee, I strictly obeyed the Law of Moses. ⁶And I was so eager that I even made trouble for the church. I did everything the Law demands in order to please God.

⁷But Christ has shown me that what I once thought was valuable is worthless. ⁸Nothing is as wonderful as knowing Christ Jesus my Lord. I have given up everything else and count it all as garbage. All I want is Christ ⁹and to know that I belong to him. I could not make myself acceptable to God by obeying the Law of Moses. God accepted me simply because of my faith in Christ. ¹⁰All I want is to know Christ and the power that raised him to life. I want to suffer and die as he did, ¹¹so that somehow I also may be raised to life.

What really counts

(**7**) Paul had once been the "golden boy" of the Pharisees. He was smart, had lots of energy, and did all of the things that a good Pharisee ought to do. But that was all garbage to Paul once he learned the really important thing—knowing Jesus. How about you? Is there garbage in your life that needs to be taken away?

ⁱ*by the power of God's Spirit*: Or "sincerely." ^j*when I was eight days old*: Jewish boys are circumcised eight days after birth.

Running toward the Goal

12I have not yet reached my goal, and I am not perfect. But Christ has taken hold of me. So I keep on running and struggling to take hold of the prize. 13My friends, I don't feel that I have already arrived. But I forget what is behind, and I struggle for what is ahead. 14I run toward the goal, so that I can win the prize of being called to heaven. This is the prize that God offers because of what Christ Jesus has done. 15All of us who are mature should think in this same way. And if any of you think differently, God will make it clear to you. 16But we must keep going in the direction that we are now headed.

17My friends, I want you to follow my example and learn from others who closely follow the example we set for you. 18I often warned you that many people are living as enemies of the cross of Christ. And now with tears in my eyes, I warn you again 19that they are headed for hell! They worship their stomachs and brag about the disgusting things they do. All they can think about are the things of this world.

20But we are citizens of heaven and are eagerly waiting for our Savior to come from there. Our Lord Jesus Christ 21has power over everything, and he will make these poor bodies of ours like his own glorious body.

4 Dear friends, I love you and long to see you. Please keep on being faithful to the Lord. You are my pride and joy.

Paul Encourages the Lord's Followers

2Euodia and Syntyche, you belong to the Lord, so I beg you to stop arguing with each other. 3And, my true partner,k I ask you to help them. These women have worked together with me and with Clement and with the others in spreading the good news. Their names are now written in the book of life.l

Paul the runner
(12) Paul knew he didn't have to earn forgiveness. But to know Christ better was his goal in life, so he compared himself to a runner. Jesus is worth running for, stretching every nerve and every muscle to "take hold of" the One who is more desirable than all earthly prizes.

What is your real treasure?
(19) Paul was depressed because some who had claimed to be followers of Jesus turned out to be traitors later on. We all see this amazing thing from time to time—people who seemed to have it all, but threw Christ away for a few earthly pleasures that would soon pass away.

---

kpartner: Or "Syzygus," a person's name. lthe book of life: A book in which the names of God's people are written.

4Always be glad because of the Lord! I will say it again: Be glad. 5Always be gentle with others. The Lord will soon be here. 6Don't worry about anything, but pray about everything. With thankful hearts offer up your prayers and requests to God. 7Then, because you belong to Christ Jesus, God will bless you with peace that no one can completely understand. And this peace will control the way you think and feel.

8Finally, my friends, keep your minds on whatever is true, pure, right, holy, friendly, and proper. Don't ever stop thinking about what is truly worthwhile and worthy of praise. 9You know the teachings I gave you, and you know what you heard me say and saw me do. So follow my example. And God, who gives peace, will be with you.

Jesus will return soon
(5) Paul was expecting Jesus to return in his own time, and so should we. It is right to expect Jesus at any time. The years seem long to us, but with God a thousand years are like a moment. That is why Jesus commands us to "watch" (Matthew 24.42). His return is just as likely today as it will be any other day.

Paul Gives Thanks for the Gifts He Was Given

10The Lord has made me very grateful that at last you have thought about me once again. Actually, you were thinking about me all along, but you didn't have any chance to show it. 11I am not complaining about having too little. I have learned to be satisfied with[m] whatever I have. 12I know what it is to be poor or to have plenty, and I have lived under all kinds of conditions. I know what it means to be full or to be hungry, to have too much or too little. 13Christ gives me the strength to face anything.

14It was good of you to help me when I was having such a hard time. 15My friends at Philippi, you remember what it was like when I started preaching the good news in Macedonia.[n] After I left there, you were the only church that became my partner by giving blessings and by receiving them in return. 16Even when I was in Thessalonica, you helped me more than once. 17I am not trying to get something from you, but I want you to receive the blessings that come from giving.

Are you satisfied?
(11) Can Christians usually be satisfied? Yes, they can. We don't expect to be satisfied with what this world has to offer. If our needs are met, we consider ourselves well off. Some people without Christ may have more than they can ever use, but they're never satisfied because they still dream of finding what they want in this world. They never seem to find it. They just keep working and seeking more and more, but happiness is always just out of reach.

[m]be satisfied with: Or "get by on." [n]when I started preaching the good news in Macedonia: Paul is talking about his first visit to Philippi. See Acts 16.12-40.

18I have been paid back everything, and with interest. I am completely satisfied with the gifts that you had Epaphroditus bring me. They are like a sweet-smelling offering or like the right kind of sacrifice that pleases God. 19I pray that God will take care of all your needs with the wonderful blessings that come from Christ Jesus! 20May God our Father be praised forever and ever. Amen.

Final Greetings

21Give my greetings to all who are God's people because of Christ Jesus.

The Lord's followers here with me send you their greetings.

22All of God's people send their greetings, especially those in the service of the Emperor.

23I pray that our Lord Jesus Christ will be kind to you and will bless your life!

Giving to others is giving to God

(18) When we give things to others, we are giving an offering to God. Paul says we are blessed by God for being generous, but our main reason should always be our love toward God, and our desire to serve him by giving to those who are in need.

PAUL'S LETTER TO THE CHURCH IN COLOSSAE

ABOUT THIS LETTER

Colossae was an important city in western Asia Minor, about 100 miles east of the port city of Ephesus. Paul had never been to Colossae, but he was pleased to learn that the Christians there were strong in their faith (1.3–7; 2.6,7). They had heard the good news from a man named Epaphras who had lived there (1.7; 4.12,13), but was in jail with Paul (Philemon 23) at the time that Paul wrote this letter (1.14; 4.3,10,18).

Many of the church members in Colossae were Gentiles (1.27), and some of them were influenced by strange religious ideas and practices (2.16–23). They thought that to obey God fully they must give up certain physical desires and worship angels and other spiritual powers. But Paul wanted them to know that Christ was with God in heaven, ruling over all powers in the universe (3.1). And so, their worship should be directed to Christ.

Paul quotes a beautiful hymn that explains who Christ is:

> Christ is exactly like God,
>> who cannot be seen.
> He is the first-born Son,
>> superior to all creation.
> God himself was pleased
>> to live fully in his Son.
> And God was pleased
>> for him to make peace
> by sacrificing his blood
>> on the cross. (1.15,19,20)

A QUICK LOOK AT THIS LETTER

1. Greetings (1.1,2)
2. A Prayer of Thanks (1.3–8)
3. The Person and Work of Christ (1.9—2.19)
4. New Life with Christ (2.20—4.6)
5. Final Greetings (4.7–18)

1 From Paul, chosen by God to be an apostle of Christ Jesus, and from Timothy, who is also a follower
²To God's people who live in Colossae and are faithful followers of Christ.

I pray that God our Father will be kind to you and will bless you with peace!

A Prayer of Thanks

³Each time we pray for you, we thank God, the Father of our Lord Jesus Christ. ⁴We have heard of your faith in Christ and of your love for all of God's people, ⁵because

what you hope for is kept safe for you in heaven. You first heard about this hope when you believed the true message, which is the good news.

⁶The good news is spreading all over the world with great success. It has spread in that same way among you, ever since the first day you learned the truth about God's kindness ⁷from our good friend Epaphras. He works together with us for Christ and is a faithful worker for you.ᵃ ⁸He is also the one who told us about the love that God's Spirit has given you.

The Person and Work of Christ

⁹We have not stopped praying for you since the first day we heard about you. In fact, we always pray that God will show you everything he wants you to do and that you may have all the wisdom and understanding that his Spirit gives. ¹⁰Then you will live a life that honors the Lord, and you will always please him by doing good deeds. You will come to know God even better. ¹¹His glorious power will make you patient and strong enough to endure anything, and you will be truly happy.

¹²I pray that you will be grateful to God for letting youᵃ have part in what he has promised his people in the kingdom of light. ¹³God rescued us from the dark power of Satan and brought us into the kingdom of his dear Son, ¹⁴who forgives our sins and sets us free.

¹⁵Christ is exactly like God,
  who cannot be seen.
He is the first-born Son,
  superior to all creation.
¹⁶Everything was created by him,
  everything in heaven
    and on earth,
  everything seen and unseen,
  including all forces
    and powers,

Paul loved his people
(9) This is one of the letters Paul wrote when he was a prisoner in Rome. Even as a prisoner Paul's main thoughts were about the people he had won to Christ. Paul was an apostle, but he was also the model pastor. He was careful to teach young Christians the truth, and he also cared for their spiritual well-being.

ᵃyou: Some manuscripts have "us."

and all rulers
and authorities.
All things were created
by God's Son,
and everything was made
for him.

17God's Son was before all else,
and by him everything
is held together.
18He is the head of his body,
which is the church.
He is the very beginning,
the first to be raised
from death,
so that he would be
above all others.

19God himself was pleased
to live fully in his Son.
20And God was pleased
for him to make peace
by sacrificing his blood
on the cross,
so that all beings in heaven
and on earth
would be brought back
to God.

21You used to be far from God. Your thoughts made you his enemies, and you did evil things. 22But his Son became a human and died. So God made peace with you, and now he lets you stand in his presence as people who are holy and faultless and innocent. 23But you must stay deeply rooted and firm in your faith. You must not give up the hope you received when you heard the good news. It was preached to everyone on earth, and I myself have become a servant of this message.

Paul's Service to the Church

24I am glad that I can suffer for you. I am pleased also that in my own body I can continue[b] the suffering of Christ for his body, the church. 25God's plan was to make

All things belong to Christ
(16) Jesus is no longer merely the humble servant he was when he was on earth. Even before he was born in Bethlehem, Jesus was always the everlasting Son of God who created everything. So we all belong to Christ by the fact that we are his creations. All things that we enjoy in the world are provided by him. He holds everything together. So it makes sense to surrender our lives to Jesus.

---

b continue: Or "complete."

me a servant of his church and to send me to preach his complete message to you. 26For ages and ages this message was kept secret from everyone, but now it has been explained to God's people. 27God did this because he wanted you Gentiles to understand his wonderful and glorious mystery. And the mystery is that Christ lives in you, and he is your hope of sharing in God's glory.

28We announce the message about Christ, and we use all our wisdom to warn and teach everyone, so that all of Christ's followers will grow and become mature. 29That's why I work so hard and use all the mighty power he gives me.

2 I want you to know what a struggle I am going through for you, for God's people at Laodicea, and for all of those followers who have never met me. 2I do it to encourage them. Then as their hearts are joined together in love, they will be wonderfully blessed with complete understanding. And they will truly know Christ. Not only is he the key to God's mystery, 3but all wisdom and knowledge are hidden away in him. 4I tell you these things to keep you from being fooled by fancy talk. 5Even though I am not with you, I keep thinking about you. I am glad to know that you are living as you should and that your faith in Christ is strong.

Christ Brings Real Life

6You have accepted Christ Jesus as your Lord. Now keep on following him. 7Plant your roots in Christ and let him be the foundation for your life. Be strong in your faith, just as you were taught. And be grateful.

8Don't let anyone fool you by using senseless arguments. These arguments may sound wise, but they are only human teachings. They come from the powers of this worldᶜ and not from Christ.

ᶜ*powers of this world:* Spirits and unseen forces were thought to control human lives and were believed to be connected with the movements of the stars.

Jesus will live in you

(27) Paul calls this a "mystery." It's something that is revealed to us, that we never could have figured out on our own. The whole purpose of becoming a Christian is so that the Son of God himself may dwell in us forever. This is what really makes us sons and daughters of God.

Don't be fooled

(4) Paul warns us about false teaching. In his day false teachers were claiming to have special knowledge about spiritual things. There are still such false teachers around today, as a look through many bookstores will quickly show. We are not saved by superior knowledge, but by Christ himself who gives us eternal life.

[9]God lives fully in Christ. [10]And you are fully grown because you belong to Christ, who is over every power and authority. [11]Christ has also taken away your selfish desires, just as circumcision removes flesh from the body. [12]And when you were baptized, it was the same as being buried with Christ. Then you were raised to life because you had faith in the power of God, who raised Christ from death. [13]You were dead, because you were sinful and were not God's people. But God let Christ make you[d] alive, when he forgave all our sins.

[14]God wiped out all the charges that were against us for disobeying the Law of Moses. He took them away and nailed them to the cross. [15]There Christ defeated all powers and forces. He let the whole world see them being led away as prisoners when he celebrated his victory.

[16]Don't let anyone tell you what you must eat or drink. Don't let them say that you must celebrate the New Moon festival, the Sabbath, or any other festival. [17]These things are only a shadow of what was to come. But Christ is real!

[18]Don't be cheated by people who make a show of acting humble and who worship angels.[e] They brag about seeing visions. But it is all nonsense, because their minds are filled with selfish desires. [19]They are no longer part of Christ, who is the head of the whole body. Christ gives the body its strength, and he uses its joints and muscles to hold it together, as it grows by the power of God.

Christ Brings New Life

[20]You died with Christ. Now the forces of the universe[f] don't have any power over you. Why do you live as if you had to obey such rules as, [21]"Don't handle this. Don't

Dying with Christ
(12) Different churches have different ways of baptizing. Whatever the method, Paul shows here that being under water in baptism is a picture of being dead and buried with Christ. Then, just as Christ rose again, we are with him in new life as we live for God by the power he gives us.

Christ is our life
(20) Christians are people who have died—in the sense that our disobedient nature was nailed to the cross with Christ. Our true life now comes from Christ who lives in us. We can't make ourselves holy merely by obeying rules. Only Jesus living in us makes it possible for us to live as God's people.

[d]*you*: Some manuscripts have "us."   [e]*worship angels*: Or "worship with angels (in visions of heaven)."   [f]*forces of the universe*: See the note at 2.8.

taste that. Don't touch this."? [22]After these things are used, they are no longer good for anything. So why be bothered with all the rules that humans have made up? [23]Obeying these rules may seem to be the smart thing to do. They appear to make you love God more and to be very humble and to have control over your body. But they don't really have any power over our desires.

3 You have been raised to life with Christ. Now set your heart on what is in heaven, where Christ rules at God's right side.[g] [2]Think about what is up there, not about what is here on earth. [3]You died, which means that your life is hidden with Christ, who sits beside God. [4]Christ gives meaning to your[h] life, and when he appears, you will also appear with him in glory.

[5]Don't be controlled by your body. Kill every desire for the wrong kind of sex. Don't be immoral or indecent or have evil thoughts. Don't be greedy, which is the same as worshiping idols. [6]God is angry with people who disobey him by doing these things.[i] [7]And that is exactly what you did, when you lived among people who behaved in this way. [8]But now you must stop doing such things. You must quit being angry, hateful, and evil. You must no longer say insulting or cruel things about others. [9]And stop lying to each other. You have given up your old way of life with all its habits.

[10]Each of you is now a new person. You are becoming more and more like your Creator, and you will understand him better. [11]It doesn't matter if you are a Greek or a Jew, or if you are circumcised or not. You may even be a barbarian or a Scythian,[j]

Where are your thoughts?
(2) The best way to get rid of evil thoughts is to replace them with good thoughts. We do this by concentrating on the things of heaven where Christ is. When we do that, there is no room left for evil desires that eat away at our happiness.

Christians are new people
(10) We know that Christ has made us new by the things we now love. We used to love things that hurt us and other people. We lived in jealousy and hatred. Now our hearts are being filled with love for others. We are becoming more like God every day in our attitudes and lifestyles.

[g]*right side*: The place of power and honor. [h]*your*: Some manuscripts have "our." [i]*with people who disobey him by doing these things*: Some manuscripts do not have these words. [j]*a barbarian or a Scythian*: Barbarians were people who could not speak Greek and would be in the lower class of society. Scythians were people who were known for their cruelty.

and you may be a slave or a free person. Yet Christ is all that matters, and he lives in all of us.

12God loves you and has chosen you as his own special people. So be gentle, kind, humble, meek, and patient. 13Put up with each other, and forgive anyone who does you wrong, just as Christ has forgiven you. 14Love is more important than anything else. It is what ties everything completely together.

15Each one of you is part of the body of Christ, and you were chosen to live together in peace. So let the peace that comes from Christ control your thoughts. And be grateful. 16Let the message about Christ completely fill your lives, while you use all your wisdom to teach and instruct each other. With thankful hearts, sing psalms, hymns, and spiritual songs to God. 17Whatever you say or do should be done in the name of the Lord Jesus, as you give thanks to God the Father because of him.

Some Rules for Christian Living

18A wife must put her husband first. This is her duty as a follower of the Lord.

19A husband must love his wife and not abuse her.

20Children must always obey their parents. This pleases the Lord.

21Parents, don't be hard on your children. If you are, they might give up.

22Slaves, you must always obey your earthly masters. Try to please them at all times, and not just when you think they are watching. Honor the Lord and serve your masters with your whole heart. 23Do your work willingly, as though you were serving the Lord himself, and not just your earthly master. 24In fact, the Lord Christ is the one you are really serving, and you know that he will reward you. 25But Christ has no favorites! He will punish evil people, just as they deserve.

4 Slave owners, be fair and honest with your slaves. Don't forget that you have a Master in heaven.

Peace is in control
(15) Christians can live together in peace. If Jesus has won the battle against sin, and we are with him in his death and new life, we can stop struggling through life. We can have the peace that God gives and be thankful for what he has done.

Be honest workers
(22) We don't have slaves nowadays. But we do make agreements to serve someone for so much time every day and for so much money. Christian workers should be known for being cheerful and useful, not dishonest. Likewise, Christian employers also honor Christ by treating their employees well and not taking advantage of them.

2Never give up praying. And when you pray, keep alert and be thankful. 3Be sure to pray that God will make a way for us to spread his message and explain the mystery about Christ, even though I am in jail for doing this. 4Please pray that I will make the message as clear as possible.

5When you are with unbelievers, always make good use of the time. 6Be pleasant and hold their interest when you speak the message. Choose your words carefully and be ready to give answers to anyone who asks questions.

Final Greetings

7Tychicus is the dear friend, who faithfully works and serves the Lord with us, and he will give you the news about me. 8I am sending him to cheer you up by telling you how we are getting along. 9Onesimus, that dear and faithful follower from your own group, is coming with him. The two of them will tell you everything that has happened here.

10Aristarchus is in jail with me. He sends greetings to you, and so does Mark, the cousin of Barnabas. You have already been told to welcome Mark, if he visits you. 11Jesus, who is known as Justus, sends his greetings. These three men are the only Jewish followers who have worked with me for the kingdom of God. They have given me much comfort.

12Your own Epaphras, who serves Christ Jesus, sends his greetings. He always prays hard that you may fully know what the Lord wants you to do and that you may do it completely. 13I have seen how much trouble he has gone through for you and for the followers in Laodicea and Hierapolis.

14Our dear doctor Luke sends you his greetings, and so does Demas.

15Give my greetings to the followers at Laodicea, especially to Nympha and the church that meets in her home.

16After this letter has been read to your people, be sure to have it read in the church

Be an effective witness
(4) An effective witness of Jesus Christ is friendly to those around him or her. Also, it's important that our hearers understand what we say. If we are confused in our own thoughts, we will confuse others and our message will not be clear. We need to think carefully about how we can best share Christ with others.

Remember Demas
(14) In his final greetings Paul mentions several of his old friends, some of whom should be familiar to you by now, such as Mark and Luke. But he also sends good wishes from Demas. Later, Paul has to say that Demas deserted him (2 Timothy 4.10). Decide right now never to be a Demas.

at Laodicea. And you should read the letter
that I have sent to them.*k*

17Remind Archippus to do the work that
the Lord has given him to do.

18I am signing this letter myself: PAUL.
Don't forget that I am in jail.
I pray that God will be kind to you.

kthe letter that I have sent to them: This is the only
mention of the letter to the church at Laodicea.

PAUL'S FIRST LETTER TO THE CHURCH IN THESSALONICA

ABOUT THIS LETTER

Paul started the church in Thessalonica (2.13,14), while working hard to support himself (2.9). In this important city of northern Greece, many of the followers had worshiped idols before becoming Christians (1.9). But they were faithful to the Lord, and because of them the Lord's message had spread everywhere in that region (1.8). This letter may have been the first one that Paul wrote, and maybe even the first of all the New Testament writings.

Some people in Thessalonica began to oppose Paul, and he had to escape to Athens. But he sent his young friend Timothy to find out how the Christians were doing (3.1–5). When Timothy returned, he gave Paul good reports of their faith and love (3.6–10).

The church itself had problems. Some of its members had quit working, since they thought that the Lord would soon return (4.11,12). Others were worried because relatives and friends had already died before Christ's return. So Paul tried to explain to them more clearly what would happen when the Lord returns (4.13–15), and then told them how they should live in the meanwhile (5.1–11).

Paul's final instructions are well worth remembering:
Always be joyful and never stop praying. Whatever happens, keep thanking God because of Jesus Christ. This is what God wants you to do. (5.16–18)

A QUICK LOOK AT THIS LETTER

1. Greetings (1.1–3)
2. The Thessalonians' Faith and Example (1.4—3.13)
3. A Life That Pleases God (4.1–12)
4. What to Expect When the Lord Returns (4.13—5.11)
5. Final Instructions and Greetings (5.12–28)

1 From Paul, Silas,*a* and Timothy.
To the church in Thessalonica, the people of God the Father and of the Lord Jesus Christ.

I pray that God will be kind to you and will bless you with peace!

²We thank God for you and always mention you in our prayers. Each time we pray, ³we tell God our Father about your faith and loving work and about your firm hope in our Lord Jesus Christ.

The Thessalonians' Faith and Example

⁴My dear friends, God loves you, and we know he has chosen you to be his people.

aSilas: The Greek text has "Silvanus," which is another form of the name Silas.

The Christian's first work
(2) Paul didn't rush out to preach the good news, but he first reminds us that he prayed for his people and his hearers. That's a good example. We can't do anything for God unless God himself works with us and in the hearts of our hearers. So the first thing to do is to lift up to God the whole matter of our work and the people we are trying to reach.

5When we told you the good news, it was with the power and assurance that come from the Holy Spirit, and not simply with words. You knew what kind of people we were and how we helped you. 6So, when you accepted the message, you followed our example and the example of the Lord. You suffered, but the Holy Spirit made you glad.

7You became an example for all the Lord's followers in Macedonia and Achaia. 8And because of you, the Lord's message has spread everywhere in those regions. Now the news of your faith in God is known all over the world, and we don't have to say a thing about it. 9Everyone is talking about how you welcomed us and how you turned away from idols to serve the true and living God. 10They also tell how you are waiting for his Son Jesus to come from heaven. God raised him from death, and on the day of judgment Jesus will save us from God's anger.

Paul's Work in Thessalonica

2 My friends, you know that our time with you was not wasted. 2As you remember, we had been mistreated and insulted at Philippi. But God gave us the courage to tell you the good news about him, even though many people caused us trouble. 3We didn't have any hidden motives when we won you over, and we didn't try to fool or trick anyone. 4God was pleased to trust us with his message. We didn't speak to please people, but to please God who knows our motives.

5You also know that we didn't try to flatter anyone. God himself knows that what we did was not a cover-up for greed. 6We were not trying to get you or anyone else to praise us. 7But as apostles, we could have demanded help from you. After all, Christ is the one who sent us. We chose to be like children or like a mother[b] nursing her baby. 8We cared so much for you, and you became so dear to us, that we were willing to give

---

[b]*like children or like a mother*: Some manuscripts have "as gentle as a mother."

Example is the best teacher

(7) The Thessalonian people showed by their life-styles that they loved Jesus Christ. Even a quiet Christian reminds people of Jesus. What we are should shout so loudly that people should hardly need to hear what we say. People may not know Jesus themselves, but if they see him in your life they will want to know him.

What is true love?

(8) Is love a warm feeling for others? It may well be so, but love is much more than a feeling. Notice how Paul and his friends gave themselves for the good of others. "We were willing to give our lives for you," he said. And Paul finally did give his life at Rome. Christians are those who have made up their minds that their lives belong to God— to be kept or lost for *him.*

our lives for you when we gave you God's message.

⁹My dear friends, you surely haven't forgotten our hard work and hardships. You remember how night and day we struggled to make a living, so that we could tell you God's message without being a burden to anyone. ¹⁰Both you and God are witnesses that we were pure and honest and innocent in our dealings with you followers of the Lord. ¹¹You also know we did everything for you that parents would do for their own children. ¹²We begged, encouraged, and urged each of you to live in a way that would honor God. He is the one who chose you to share in his own kingdom and glory.

¹³We always thank God that you believed the message we preached. It came from him, and it is not something made up by humans. You accepted it as God's message, and now he is working in you. ¹⁴My friends, you did just like God's churches in Judea and like the other followers of Christ Jesus there. And so, you were mistreated by your own people, in the same way they were mistreated by the Jewish people.

¹⁵Those Jews killed the Lord Jesus and the prophets, and they even chased us away. God doesn't like what they do and neither does anyone else. ¹⁶They keep us from speaking his message to the Gentiles and from leading them to be saved. The Jews have always gone too far with their sins. Now God has finally become angry and will punish them.

Paul Wants to Visit the Church Again

¹⁷My friends, we were kept from coming to you for a while, but we never stopped thinking about you. We were eager to see you and tried our best to visit you in person. ¹⁸We really wanted to come. I myself tried several times, but Satan always stopped us. ¹⁹After all, when the Lord Jesus appears, who else but you will give us hope and joy and be like a glorious crown for us? ²⁰You alone are our glory and joy!

It's hard to have enemies (14) Paul's enemies were people of his own national and religious background—the Jews. Think of how hard this must have been for someone who loved his country as Paul did. Sometimes you may have to suffer mistreatment by those you love the most. That is hard to bear. But remember, that was the path Jesus followed also, and he will help you to follow him with peace in your heart.

3 Finally, we couldn't stand it any longer. We decided to stay in Athens by ourselves 2and send our friend Timothy to you. He works with us as God's servant and preaches the good news about Christ. We wanted him to make you strong in your faith and to encourage you. 3We didn't want any of you to be discouraged by all these troubles. You knew we would have to suffer, 4because when we were with you, we told you this would happen. And we did suffer, as you well know. 5At last, when I could not wait any longer, I sent Timothy to find out about your faith. I hoped that Satan had not tempted you and made all our work useless.

6Timothy has come back from his visit with you and has told us about your faith and love. He also said that you always have happy memories of us and that you want to see us as much as we want to see you.

7My friends, even though we have a lot of trouble and suffering, your faith makes us feel better about you. 8Your strong faith in the Lord is like a breath of new life. 9How can we possibly thank God enough for all the happiness you have brought us? 10Day and night we sincerely pray that we will see you again and help you to have an even stronger faith.

11We pray that God the Father and our Lord Jesus Christ will let us visit you. 12May the Lord make your love for each other and for everyone else grow by leaps and bounds. That's how our love for you has grown. 13And when our Lord comes with all of his people, I pray that he will make your hearts pure and innocent in the sight of God the Father.

A Life That Pleases God

4 Finally, my dear friends, since you belong to the Lord Jesus, we beg and urge you to live as we taught you. Then you will please God. You are already living that way, but try even harder. 2Remember the instructions we gave you as followers of the Lord Jesus. 3God wants you to be holy, so don't

Don't let trouble discourage you
(3) Trouble didn't discourage Paul. It was just what he expected. Everybody who lives in the world has trouble sooner or later. If we have listened to God's word, we know trouble is coming. But we're not discouraged, because we know God is in charge of our lives at all times.

Encourage your leaders
(9) If you belong to a local church (as Christians should), you have a pastor. Perhaps you have elders and deacons too. Do you know that sometimes leaders get lonely? But your faithfulness in your Christian life and duty will encourage them. Leaders are human. They need love and support, perhaps even more than others. Don't be shy about saying a kind word or doing a kind deed for your God-given church leaders. Their work can be a heavy burden, and it's good to let them know they're appreciated.

Dare to be different
(1) A world where all was the same color or all was flat wouldn't be very exciting. Christians should be exciting people because they're different in good

be immoral in matters of sex. 4Respect and honor your wife.c 5Don't be a slave of your desires or live like people who don't know God. 6You must not cheat any of the Lord's followers in matters of sex.d Remember, we warned you that God punishes everyone who does such things. 7God didn't choose you to be filthy, but to be pure. 8So if you don't obey these rules, you are not really disobeying us. You are disobeying God, who gives you his Holy Spirit.

9We don't have to write you about the need to love each other. God has taught you to do this, 10and you already have shown your love for all of his people in Macedonia. But, my dear friends, we ask you to do even more. 11Try your best to live quietly, to mind your own business, and to work hard, just as we taught you to do. 12Then you will be respected by people who are not followers of the Lord, and you won't have to depend on anyone.

ways. They're free from habits that make them get sick and die early. They enjoy living because they know Christ, the author of life. They're true friends of God and of those in need of his love.

The Lord's Coming

13My friends, we want you to understand how it will be for those followers who have already died. Then you won't grieve over them and be like people who don't have any hope. 14We believe that Jesus died and was raised to life. We also believe that when God brings Jesus back again, he will bring with him all who had faith in Jesus before they died. 15Our Lord Jesus told us that when he comes, we won't go up to meet him ahead of his followers who have already died.

16With a loud command and with the shout of the chief angel and a blast of God's trumpet, the Lord will return from heaven. Then those who had faith in Christ before they died will be raised to life. 17Next, all of us who are still alive will be taken up into the clouds together with them to meet the Lord in the sky. From that time on we

Christ's return for his church
(14) Jesus could come back at any time. It's the moment we eagerly look forward to. When Jesus returns he will give glorious new bodies to all of those who have believed in him and have died. The believers who are still alive will join them, also in new bodies, and there will be a great heavenly reunion for God's church. Then we will be with him forever. You'll be there, won't you?

cyour wife: Or "your body."   din matters of sex: Or "in business."

will all be with the Lord forever. [18]Encourage each other with these words.

5 I don't need to write you about the time or date when all this will happen. [2]You surely know that the Lord's return[e] will be as a thief coming at night. [3]People will think they are safe and secure. But destruction will suddenly strike them like the pains of a woman about to give birth. And they won't escape.

[4]My dear friends, you don't live in darkness, and so that day won't surprise you like a thief. [5]All of you belong to the light and live in the day. We don't live in the night or belong to the dark. [6]Others may sleep, but we should stay awake and be alert. [7]People sleep during the night, and some even get drunk. [8]But we belong to the day. So we must stay sober and let our faith and love be like a suit of armor. Our firm hope that we will be saved is our helmet.

[9]God does not intend to punish us, but to have our Lord Jesus Christ save us. [10]Christ died for us, so that we could live with him, whether we are alive or dead when he comes. [11]That's why you must encourage and help each other, just as you are already doing.

Final Instructions and Greetings

[12]My friends, we ask you to be thoughtful of your leaders who work hard and tell you how to live for the Lord. [13]Show them great respect and love because of their work. Try to get along with each other. [14]My friends, we beg you to warn anyone who is not living right. Encourage anyone who feels left out, help all who are weak, and be patient with everyone. [15]Don't be hateful to people, just because they are hateful to you. Rather, be good to each other and to everyone else.

[16]Always be joyful [17]and never stop praying. [18]Whatever happens, keep thanking

When will Christ come?
(1) Paul tells us that Christ's coming will be very sudden and so take many by surprise—like a thief who breaks down the door. But Paul also says that Christians should be so alert that Christ's coming does not surprise them. They will be waiting with great expectation. Let's be filled with joy as we look forward to that great event.

Try to get along
(13) Getting along isn't always easy. Sometimes even believers "rub each other the wrong way." That's when our Christian character must show. If we have been loved by Christ himself, we can afford to accept insults and love people just the same. What do we have to lose but our tempers?

[e]*the Lord's return*: The Greek text has "the day of the Lord."

God because of Jesus Christ. This is what God wants you to do.

19Don't turn away God's Spirit **20**or ignore prophecies. **21**Put everything to the test. Accept what is good **22**and don't have anything to do with evil.

23I pray that God, who gives peace, will make you completely holy. And may your spirit, soul, and body be kept healthy and faultless until our Lord Jesus Christ returns. **24**The one who chose you can be trusted, and he will do this.

25Friends, please pray for us.

26Give all the Lord's followers a warm greeting.

27In the name of the Lord I beg you to read this letter to all his followers.

28I pray that our Lord Jesus Christ will be kind to you!

PAUL'S SECOND LETTER TO THE CHURCH IN THESSALONICA

ABOUT THIS LETTER

In this letter to the believers in Thessalonica, Paul begins by thanking God that their faith and love keep growing all the time (1.3). They were going through a lot of troubles, but Paul insists that this is God's way of testing their faith, not a way of punishing them (1.4,5).

Someone in Thessalonica claimed to have a letter from Paul, saying that the Lord had already returned (2.2). But Paul warns the church not to be fooled! The Lord will not return until after the "wicked one" has appeared (2.3).

Paul also warns against laziness (3.6–10), and he tells the church to guard against any followers who refuse to obey what he has written in this letter.

The letter closes with a prayer:

I pray that the Lord, who gives peace, will keep blessing you with peace no matter where you are. May the Lord be with all of you. (3.16)

A QUICK LOOK AT THIS LETTER

1. Greetings (1.1,2)
2. The Lord's Return Will Bring Justice (1.3–12)
3. The Lord Has Not Returned Yet (2.1–12)
4. Be Faithful (2.13–17)
5. Pray and Work (3.1–15)
6. A Final Prayer (3.16–18)

1 From Paul, Silas,[a] and Timothy.
To the church in Thessalonica, the people of God our Father and of the Lord Jesus Christ.

2I pray that God our Father and the Lord Jesus Christ will be kind to you and will bless you with peace!

When Christ Returns

3My dear friends, we always have good reason to thank God for you, because your faith in God and your love for each other keep growing all the time. **4**That's why we brag about you to all of God's churches. We tell them how patient you are and how you keep on having faith, even though you are going through a lot of trouble and suffering.

Faith and love grow
(3) Anything that lives grows. We're dying if we're not growing. That's true about faith and love, too. Our muscles are strengthened by exercise. So our faith grows by testing, and our love grows by practice.

[a]*Silas*: The Greek text has "Silvanus," which is another form of the name Silas.

5All of this shows that God judges fairly and that he is making you fit to share in his kingdom for which you are suffering. 6It is only right for God to punish everyone who is causing you trouble, 7but he will give you relief from your troubles. He will do the same for us, when the Lord Jesus comes from heaven with his powerful angels 8and with a flaming fire.

Our Lord Jesus will punish anyone who doesn't know God and won't obey his message. 9Their punishment will be eternal destruction, and they will be kept far from the presence of our Lord and his glorious strength. 10This will happen on that day when the Lord returns to be praised and honored by all who have faith in him and belong to him. This includes you, because you believed what we said.

11God chose you, and we keep praying that God will make you worthy of being his people. We pray for God's power to help you do all the good things that you hope to do and that your faith makes you want to do. 12Then, because God and our Lord Jesus Christ are so kind, you will bring honor to the name of our Lord Jesus, and he will bring honor to you.

The Lord's Return

2 When our Lord Jesus returns, we will be gathered up to meet him. So I ask you, my friends, 2not to be easily upset or disturbed by people who claim that the Lordᵇ has already come. They may say that they heard this directly from the Holy Spirit, or from someone else, or even that they read it in one of our letters. 3But don't be fooled! People will rebel against God. Then before the Lord returns, the wickedᶜ one who is doomed to be destroyed will appear. 4He will brag and oppose everything that is holy or sacred. He will even sit in God's temple and claim to be God. 5Don't you remember

*God makes us
what he wants*
(11) God chose us, and so we have a great desire to become like Jesus. By God's power we will reach this goal. From God come both the desire and the ability to be what God plans for us. So we can be comforted as we know we will not fail to be worthy of being called Christians. But this is only because of God's power at work in us.

*There will be an
"Antichrist"*
(3) John later writes about Antichrist in his letters. Paul calls him "the wicked one." So the world is warned and can expect that a wicked leader will arise to lead all the forces of evil on the earth. Then many will be fooled by the false miracles of Satan. It will be a terrible time in history, but God will take his church out of harm's way.

ᵇLord: The Greek text has "day of the Lord."   ᶜwicked: Some manuscripts have "sinful."

that I told you this while I was still with you?

6You already know what is holding this wicked one back until it is time for him to come. 7His mysterious power is already at work, but someone is holding him back. And the wicked one won't appear until that someone is out of the way. 8Then he will appear, but the Lord Jesus will kill him simply by breathing on him. He will be completely destroyed by the Lord's glorious return.

9When the wicked one appears, Satan will pretend to work all kinds of miracles, wonders, and signs. 10Lost people will be fooled by his evil deeds. They could be saved, but they will refuse to love the truth and accept it. 11So God will make sure that they are fooled into believing a lie. 12All of them will be punished, because they would rather do evil than believe the truth.

Be Faithful

13My friends, the Lord loves you, and it is only natural for us to thank God for you. God chose you to be the first ones to be saved.d His Spirit made you holy, and you put your faith in the truth. 14God used our preaching as his way of inviting you to share in the glory of our Lord Jesus Christ. 15My friends, that's why you must remain faithful and follow closely what we taught you in person and by our letters.

16God our Father loves us. He is kind and has given us eternal comfort and a wonderful hope. We pray that our Lord Jesus Christ and God our Father 17will encourage you and help you always to do and say the right thing.

Pray for Us

3 Finally, our friends, please pray for us. This will help the message about the

dGod chose you to be the first ones to be saved: Some manuscripts have "From the beginning God chose you to be saved."

The early Christians are our models

(13) Paul writes that God chose the Thessalonians first. They and many other early believers were the "pioneers" to show the way Christians should think and live. They remained faithful and became our examples. They are gone now, of course, and we don't know any of them personally. But we're thankful to them for showing us the way Christians should walk with God.

Prayer makes a difference

(1) God spreads the good news because we pray. If we don't pray, the good news will still go forward, but probably not where we are. God wants followers who care enough about his work to be continually speaking to him about it. He is pleased by prayer for his honor and glory.

Lord to spread quickly, and others will respect it, just as you do. ²Pray that we may be kept safe from worthless and evil people. After all, not everyone has faith. ³But the Lord can be trusted to make you strong and protect you from harm. ⁴He has made us sure that you are obeying what we taught you and that you will keep on obeying. ⁵I pray that the Lord will guide you to be as loving as God and patient as Christ.

Warnings against Laziness

⁶My dear friends, in the name of*e* the Lord Jesus, I beg you not to have anything to do with any of your people who loaf around and refuse to obey the instructions we gave you. ⁷You surely know that you should follow our example. We didn't waste our time loafing, ⁸and we didn't accept food from anyone without paying for it. We didn't want to be a burden to any of you, so night and day we worked as hard as we could.

⁹We had the right not to work, but we wanted to set an example for you. ¹⁰We also gave you the rule that if you don't work, you don't eat. ¹¹Now we learn that some of you just loaf around and won't do any work, except the work of a busybody. ¹²So, for the sake of our Lord Jesus, we ask and beg these people to settle down and start working for a living. ¹³Dear friends, you must never become tired of doing right.

¹⁴Be on your guard against any followers who refuse to obey what we have written in this letter. Put them to shame by not having anything to do with them. ¹⁵Don't consider them your enemies, but speak kindly to them as you would to any other follower.

Final Prayer

¹⁶I pray that the Lord, who gives peace, will keep blessing you with peace no matter

Christians are not loafers (6) It looks like some of the Thessalonians spent so much time looking for Christ's coming that they had even quit work. But they had the wrong idea. Christians must keep on with whatever God gives them to do until Christ comes. We don't know the day and the hour of Jesus' return, and we must set a good example by not being a burden to others. In fact, if we don't work, other Christians should avoid us. Jesus said, "My father works until now, and I work." So must you and I.

ein the name of: Or "as a follower of."

where you are. May the Lord be with all of you.

17I always sign my letters as I am now doing: PAUL.

18I pray that our Lord Jesus Christ will be kind to all of you.

PAUL'S FIRST LETTER TO TIMOTHY

ABOUT THIS LETTER

Timothy traveled and worked with Paul (Romans 16.21; 1 Corinthians 16.10; Philippians 2.19), and because of their shared faith, Timothy was like a son to Paul (1.2). Timothy became one of Paul's most faithful co-workers, and Paul mentions Timothy in five of his letters.

Although this letter is addressed to Timothy personally, it actually addresses many of the concerns Paul had with the life of the entire church. Guidelines are given for choosing church officials (3.1–7), officers (3.8–13), and leaders (5.17–20).

Christians are to pray for everyone and to remember:

There is only one God,
and Christ Jesus
*   is the only one*
who can bring us
*   to God. (2.5)*

A QUICK LOOK AT THIS LETTER

1. Greetings (1.1,2)
2. Instructions for Church Life (1.3—3.13)
3. The Mystery of Our Religion (3.14—4.5)
4. Paul's Advice to Timothy (4.6—6.21)

1 From Paul.
    God our Savior and Christ Jesus commanded me to be an apostle of Christ Jesus, who gives us hope.

²Timothy, because of our faith, you are like a son to me. I pray that God our Father and our Lord Jesus Christ will be kind and merciful to you. May they bless you with peace!

Warning against False Teaching

³When I was leaving for Macedonia, I asked you to stay on in Ephesus and warn certain people there to stop spreading their false teachings. ⁴You needed to warn them to stop wasting their time on senseless stories and endless lists of ancestors. Such things only cause arguments. They don't help anyone to do God's work that can only be done by faith.

⁵You must teach people to have genuine love, as well as a good conscience and true faith. ⁶There are some who have given up

Timothy became a pastor
(3) Pastoring was the job Paul gave to Timothy at Ephesus. Before, Timothy had traveled with Paul as a missionary. In this letter Paul tells Timothy how to carry on his work of teaching as the pastor at Ephesus. His job was to warn and guide people into the truth.

these for nothing but empty talk. 7They want to be teachers of the Law of Moses. But they don't know what they are talking about, even though they think they do.

8We know that the Law is good, if it is used in the right way. 9We also understand that it was not given to control people who please God, but to control lawbreakers, criminals, godless people, and sinners. It is for wicked and evil people, and for murderers, who would even kill their own parents. 10The Law was written for people who are sexual perverts or who live as homosexuals or are kidnappers or liars or won't tell the truth in court. It is for anything else that opposes the correct teaching 11of the good news that the glorious and wonderful God has given me.

Being Thankful for God's Kindness

12I thank Christ Jesus our Lord. He gives me the strength for my work because he knew that he could trust me. 13I used to say terrible and insulting things about him, and I was cruel. But he had mercy on me because I didn't know what I was doing, and I had not yet put my faith in him. 14Christ Jesus our Lord was very kind to me. He has greatly blessed my life with faith and love just like his own.

15"Christ Jesus came into the world to save sinners." This saying is true, and it can be trusted. I was the worst sinner of all! 16But since I was worse than anyone else, God had mercy on me and let me be an example of the endless patience of Christ Jesus. He did this so that others would put their faith in Christ and have eternal life. 17I pray that honor and glory will always be given to the only God, who lives forever and is the invisible and eternal King! Amen.

18Timothy, my son, the instructions I am giving you are based on what some prophets[a] once said about you. If you follow these instructions, you will fight like a good soldier. 19You will be faithful and have a clear

Paul was the worst of sinners
(15) There were probably lots of people who sinned more kinds of sin than Paul. But Paul called himself the worst of sinners to show what kind of sin God hates the most. Paul had been a self-righteous, stubborn, proud Pharisee. Such people are hard to convince of their sins. A brokenhearted mess of a sinner is usually easier to reach with the good news than a "respectable," unsaved churchgoer.

[a]*prophets*: Probably the Christian prophets referred to in 4.14.

conscience. Some people have made a mess of their faith because they didn't listen to their consciences. 20Two of them are Hymenaeus and Alexander. I have given these men over to the power of Satan, so they will learn not to oppose God.

How to Pray

2 First of all, I ask you to pray for everyone. Ask God to help and bless them all, and tell God how thankful you are for each of them. 2Pray for kings and others in power, so that we may live quiet and peaceful lives as we worship and honor God. 3This kind of prayer is good, and it pleases God our Savior. 4God wants everyone to be saved and to know the whole truth, which is,

5There is only one God,
    and Christ Jesus
        is the only one
    who can bring us
        to God.
Jesus was truly human,
    and he gave himself
        to rescue all of us.
6God showed us this
    at the right time.

7This is why God chose me to be a preacher and an apostle of the good news. I am telling the truth. I am not lying. God sent me to teach the Gentiles about faith and truth.

8I want everyone everywhere to lift innocent hands toward heaven and pray, without being angry or arguing with each other.

9I would like for women to wear modest and sensible clothes. They should not have fancy hairdos, or wear expensive clothes, or put on jewelry made of gold or pearls. 10Women who claim to love God should do helpful things for others, 11and they should learn by being quiet and paying attention. 12They should be silent and not be allowed to teach or to tell men what to do. 13After all, Adam was created before Eve, 14and the man Adam was not the one who was fooled. It was the woman Eve who was com-

Pray for your government
(2) Paul mentions kings "and others in power." The government's decisions often affect the church of God and the peace of society in general. So we should pray, as Paul suggests, that officials will not do anything that will make our lives and our work harder. The government of this world will pass away, but God's kingdom is forever.

Christians believe what God says
(5) There is plenty of teaching all through the Bible, but Paul tells us what we must mainly believe: There is one God, and he sent Jesus his Son to become a man so he could save us from our sins. This is the basic Christian faith. We will be saved if we truly believe in what Jesus did for us.

Service is the main thing
(10) Some women put a lot of effort into making sure they are the center of attention. Paul writes that the main goal of a woman should be to help others humbly, not to be admired for physical beauty. There's truth in this for men, too.

pletely fooled and sinned. [15]But women will be saved by having children,[b] if they stay faithful, loving, holy, and modest.

Church Officials

3 It is true that[c] anyone who desires to be a church official[d] wants to be something worthwhile. [2]That's why officials must have a good reputation and be married only once.[e] They must be self-controlled, sensible, well-behaved, friendly to strangers, and able to teach. [3]They must not be heavy drinkers or troublemakers. Instead, they must be kind and gentle and not love money.

[4]Church officials must be in control of their own families, and they must see that their children are obedient and always respectful. [5]If they don't know how to control their own families, how can they look after God's people?

[6]They must not be new followers of the Lord. If they are, they might become proud and be doomed along with the devil. [7]Finally, they must be well-respected by people who are not followers. Then they won't be trapped and disgraced by the devil.

Church Officers

[8]Church officers[f] should be serious. They must not be liars, heavy drinkers, or greedy for money. [9]And they must have a clear conscience and hold firmly to what God has shown us about our faith. [10]They must first prove themselves. Then if no one has anything against them, they can serve as officers.

[11]Women[g] must also be serious. They

Leaders must be examples
(1) People can't see God, but they can see their pastors and other church leaders. These officers of the church must live in a way that helps people understand what God himself is like. If leaders aren't examples of how a Christian lives, who is? Pastors, teachers, and other leaders must practice what they preach.

[b]*saved by having children*: Or "brought safely through childbirth" or "saved by the birth of a child" (that is, by the birth of Jesus) or "saved by being good mothers."
[c]*It is true that*: These words may be taken with 2.15. If so, that verse would be translated: "It is true that women will be saved . . . holy, and modest." And 3.1 would be translated, "Anyone who desires . . . something worthwhile." [d]*church official*: Or "bishop."
[e]*married only once*: Or "the husbands of only one wife" or "faithful in marriage." [f]*church officers*: Or "deacons." [g]*Women*: Either church officers or the wives of church officers.

must not gossip or be heavy drinkers, and they must be faithful in everything they do.

12Church officers must be married only once.h They must be in full control of their children and everyone else in their home. 13Those who serve well as officers will earn a good reputation and will be highly respected for their faith in Christ Jesus.

The Mystery of Our Religion

14I hope to visit you soon. But I am writing these instructions, 15so that if I am delayed, you will know how everyone who belongs to God's family ought to behave. After all, the church of the living God is the strong foundation of truth.

16Here is the great mystery of our religion:

> Christi came as a human.
> The Spirit proved
>   that he pleased God,
> and he was seen by angels.
>
> Christ was preached
>   to the nations.
> People in this world
>   put their faith in him,
> and he was taken up to glory.

People Will Turn from Their Faith

4 God's Spirit clearly says that in the last days many people will turn from their faith. They will be fooled by evil spirits and by teachings that come from demons. 2They will also be fooled by the false claims of liars whose consciences have lost all feeling. These liars will forbid people 3to marry or to eat certain foods. But God created these foods to be eaten with thankful hearts by his followers who know the truth. 4Everything God created is good. And if you give thanks, you may eat anything. 5What

hmarried only once: See the note at 3.2. iChrist: The Greek text has "he," probably meaning "Christ." Some manuscripts have "God."

How should we behave?
(15) Christianity isn't just what we believe, it is also a special way of living. We aren't expected to figure out this way of living by ourselves. But God has given us his word to show us how to act at all times. We don't have to guess. We should study the Scriptures so we won't fall into lifestyles that hurt us and hurt God's plans for us.

Be faithful
(1) Paul warns Timothy of coming times when "many people will turn from their faith." Why? Because they're fooled into thinking that what they can have from the world is better than what they can have from God. Let's keep our eyes on things that matter. This world will pass away, but our souls will live forever. Our decision now will determine how we will spend eternity. Only God can satisfy our deepest longings.

God has said and your prayer will make it fit to eat.

Paul's Advice to Timothy

6If you teach these things to other followers, you will be a good servant of Christ Jesus. You will show that you have grown up on the teachings about our faith and on the good instructions you have obeyed. 7Don't have anything to do with worthless, senseless stories. Work hard to be truly religious. 8-9As the saying goes,

> "Exercise is good
>   for your body,
> but religion helps you
>   in every way.
> It promises life
>   now and forever."

These words are worthwhile and should not be forgotten. 10We have put our hope in the living God, who is the Savior of everyone, but especially of those who have faith. That's why we work and struggle so hard.*j*

11Teach these things and tell everyone to do what you say. 12Don't let anyone make fun of you, just because you are young. Set an example for other followers by what you say and do, as well as by your love, faith, and purity.

13Until I arrive, be sure to keep on reading the Scriptures in worship, and don't stop preaching and teaching. 14Use the gift you were given when the prophets spoke and the group of church leaders*k* blessed you by placing their hands on you. 15Remember these things and think about them, so everyone can see how well you are doing. 16Be careful about the way you live and about what you teach. Keep on doing this, and you will save not only yourself, but the people who hear you.

Put first things first

(8) It makes sense to keep your body fit. Then you will feel more like living and doing things for the Lord. But it is even more important to exercise your *spiritual* life—that's the part of you that lives forever. Bible reading, prayer, and friendship with other Christians will promote the health of your soul.

---

j struggle so hard: Some manuscripts have "are treated so badly." *k group of church leaders*: Or "group of elders" or "group of presbyters" or "group of priests." This translates one Greek word, and it is related to the one used in 5.17,19.

How to Act toward Others

5 Don't correct an older man. Encourage him, as you would your own father. Treat younger men as you would your own brother, 2and treat older women as you would your own mother. Show the same respect to younger women that you would to your sister.

3Take care of any widow who is really in need. 4But if a widow has children or grandchildren, they should learn to serve God by taking care of her, as she once took care of them. This is what God wants them to do. 5A widow who is really in need is one who does not have any relatives. She has faith in God, and she keeps praying to him night and day, asking for his help.

6A widow who thinks only about having a good time is already dead, even though she is still alive.

7Tell all of this to everyone, so they will do the right thing. 8People who don't take care of their relatives, and especially their own families, have given up their faith. They are worse than someone who doesn't have faith in the Lord.

9For a widow to be put on the list of widows, she must be at least sixty years old, and she must have been married only once.*l* 10She must also be well-known for doing all sorts of good things, such as raising children, giving food to strangers, welcoming God's people into her home,*m* helping people in need, and always making herself useful.

11Don't put young widows on the list. They may later have a strong desire to get married. Then they will turn away from Christ 12and become guilty of breaking their promise to him. 13Besides, they will become lazy and get into the habit of going from house to house. Next, they will start gossip-

Love means respect
(6) Love isn't just a feeling. Love is respect that expresses itself by treating others the way we like to be treated. But people who have no self-respect, like the widows Paul wrote about, need to be corrected. Their lifestyle leads only to ruin.

---

lmarried only once: Or "the wife of only one husband" or "faithful in marriage." *mwelcoming God's people into her home*: The Greek text has "washing the feet of God's people." In New Testament times most people either went barefoot or wore sandals, and a host would often wash the feet of special guests.

ing and become busybodies, talking about things that are none of their business.

¹⁴I would prefer that young widows get married, have children, and look after their families. Then the enemy won't have any reason to say insulting things about us. ¹⁵Look what's already happened to some of the young widows! They have turned away to follow Satan.

¹⁶If a woman who is a follower has any widows in her family, sheⁿ should help them. This will keep the church from having that burden, and then the church can help widows who are really in need.

Church Leaders

¹⁷Church leaders^o who do their job well deserve to be paid^p twice as much, especially if they work hard at preaching and teaching. ¹⁸It is just as the Scriptures say, "Don't muzzle an ox when you are using it to grind grain." You also know the saying, "Workers are worth their pay."

¹⁹Don't listen to any charge against a church leader, unless at least two or three people bring the same charges. ²⁰But if any of the leaders should keep on sinning, they must be corrected in front of the whole group, as a warning to everyone else.

²¹In the presence of God and Christ Jesus and their chosen angels, I order you to follow my instructions! Be fair with everyone, and don't have any favorites.

²²Don't be too quick to accept people into the service of the Lord^q by placing your hands on them.

Don't sin because others do, but stay close to God.

²³Stop drinking only water. Take a little wine to help your stomach trouble and the other illnesses you always have.

²⁴Some people get caught in their sins

Love begins at home
(16) It's a cheap kind of love that pretends to care about a lost world but won't look after one's own family. When Jesus taught us to love our "neighbors" he had in mind those we live closest to. They should benefit most from our caring, and then they too will be able to love others. Love comes from being loved. We love because God first loved us.

Leaders deserve fairness
(19) Here is advice that "cuts both ways." A good leader deserves generous pay. But a leader who sins is to be tried fairly, and then corrected publicly if guilty of repeated sin. Leaders get much honor or much dishonor, depending on their behavior.

ⁿ*woman . . . she*: Some manuscripts have "man . . . he," and others have "man or woman . . . that person." ^o*leaders*: Or "elders" or "presbyters" or "priests." ^p*paid*: Or "honored" or "respected." ^q*to accept people into the service of the Lord*: Or "to forgive people."

right away, even before the time of judgment. But other people's sins don't show up until later. 25It is the same with good deeds. Some are easily seen, but none of them can be hidden.

6 If you are a slave, you should respect and honor your owner. This will keep people from saying bad things about God and about our teaching. 2If any of you slaves have owners who are followers, you should show them respect. After all, they are also followers of Christ, and he loves them. So you should serve and help them the best you can.

False Teaching and True Wealth

These are the things you must teach and tell the people to do. 3Anyone who teaches something different disagrees with the correct and godly teaching of our Lord Jesus Christ. 4Those people who disagree are proud of themselves, but they don't really know a thing. Their minds are sick, and they like to argue over words. They cause jealousy, disagreements, unkind words, evil suspicions, 5and nasty quarrels. They have wicked minds and have missed out on the truth.

These people think religion is supposed to make you rich. 6And religion does make your life rich, by making you content with what you have. 7We didn't bring anything into this world, and we won't*r* take anything with us when we leave. 8So we should be satisfied just to have food and clothes. 9People who want to be rich fall into all sorts of temptations and traps. They are caught by foolish and harmful desires that drag them down and destroy them. 10The love of money causes all kinds of trouble. Some people want money so much that they have given up their faith and caused themselves a lot of pain.

Be content with what you have
(6) People who are discontented have missed the most important kind of wealth: God himself. No matter what our circumstances, we never have a right to complain. God will provide enough for our needs if we will only trust him. But complaining leads to bitterness, and bitterness makes us unable to enjoy any good that comes to us.

r we won't: Some manuscripts have "we surely won't."

Fighting a Good Fight for the Faith

11Timothy, you belong to God, so keep away from all these evil things. Try your best to please God and to be like him. Be faithful, loving, dependable, and gentle. 12Fight a good fight for the faith and claim eternal life. God offered it to you when you clearly told about your faith, while so many people listened. 13Now I ask you to make a promise. Make it in the presence of God, who gives life to all, and in the presence of Jesus Christ, who openly told Pontius Pilate about his faith. 14Promise to obey completely and fully all that you have been told until our Lord Jesus Christ returns.

15The glorious God
  is the only Ruler,
  the King of kings
  and Lord of lords.
At the time that God
  has already decided,
he will send Jesus Christ
  back again.

16Only God lives forever!
And he lives in light
  that no one can come near.
No human has ever seen God
  or ever can see him.
God will be honored,
and his power
  will last forever. Amen.

17Warn the rich people of this world not to be proud or to trust in wealth that is easily lost. Tell them to have faith in God, who is rich and blesses us with everything we need to enjoy life. 18Instruct them to do as many good deeds as they can and to help everyone. Remind the rich to be generous and share what they have. 19This will lay a solid foundation for the future, so that they will know what true life is like.

20Timothy, guard what God has placed in your care! Don't pay any attention to that godless and stupid talk that sounds smart but really isn't. 21Some people have even lost their faith by believing this talk.

I pray that the Lord will be kind to all of you!

Make your promise to God

(13) We shouldn't make promises we can't keep. But it makes good sense to promise God that we'll be faithful to him always. Let that promise to God be the greatest event of your life. Let it be the time at which you can look back and say "That's when I told God I would spend my whole life for him." Otherwise you may just drift along and not live for God at all.

Share the wealth

(17) Some people are gifted by God with the ability to become wealthy. When God does this, he means that such people should use their plenty for him. Any earthly project costs money. That includes the Christian project of spreading the good news. That is the great opportunity for wealthy people to do their part for Christ.

PAUL'S SECOND LETTER TO TIMOTHY

ABOUT THIS LETTER

In his second letter to Timothy Paul is more personal than in his first one. Timothy is like a "dear child" to Paul, and Paul always mentions him in his prayers (1.2,3) because he wants Timothy to be a "good soldier" of Christ Jesus and to learn to endure suffering (2.1,3). Paul mentions Timothy's mother and grandmother by name in this letter and reminds Timothy how he had placed his hands on him as a special sign that the Spirit was guiding his work.

Some who claimed to be followers of the Lord had already been trapped by the devil, and Paul warns Timothy to run from those temptations that often catch young people (2.20–26; 3.1–9). He tells Timothy to keep preaching God's message, even if it is not the popular thing to do (4.2). He should also beware of false teachers.

Paul knows that he will soon die for his faith, but he will be rewarded for his faithfulness (4.6–8), and he reminds Timothy of the true message:

> If we died with Christ,
>> we will live with him.
> If we don't give up,
>> we will rule with him. (2.11,12)

1 From Paul, an apostle of Christ Jesus. God himself chose me to be an apostle, and he gave me the promised life that Jesus Christ makes possible.

2Timothy, you are like a dear child to me. I pray that God our Father and our Lord Christ Jesus will be kind and merciful to you and will bless you with peace!

Do Not Be Ashamed of the Lord

3Night and day I mention you in my prayers. I am always grateful for you, as I pray to the God my ancestors and I have served with a clear conscience. 4I remember how you cried, and I want to see you, because that will make me truly happy. 5I also remember the genuine faith of your mother

Good parents are a great treasure

(5) Timothy's mother and grandmother had been great women of faith. They had taught Timothy the Scriptures, and when he got older their example and teaching paid off in Timothy's life. Parents make the biggest difference in the way their children turn out. They can influence where their children spend eternity. Godly mothers and fathers are the best teachers about Jesus.

Eunice. Your grandmother Lois had the same sort of faith, and I am sure that you have it as well. [6]So I ask you to make full use of the gift that God gave you when I placed my hands on you.[a] Use it well. [7]God's Spirit[b] does not make cowards out of us. The Spirit gives us power, love, and self-control.

[8]Don't be ashamed to speak for our Lord. And don't be ashamed of me, just because I am in jail for serving him. Use the power that comes from God and join with me in suffering for telling the good news.

[9]God saved us and chose us
    to be his holy people.
We did nothing
    to deserve this,
but God planned it
    because he is so kind.
Even before time began
God planned for Christ Jesus
    to show kindness to us.

[10]Now Christ Jesus has come
to show us the kindness
    of God.
Christ our Savior defeated death
and brought us
    the good news.
It shines like a light
and offers life
    that never ends.

[11]My work is to be a preacher, an apostle, and a teacher.[c] [12]That's why I suffer. But I am not ashamed! I know the one I have faith in, and I am sure that he can guard until the last day what he has trusted me with.[d] [13]Now follow the example of the correct teaching I gave you, and let the faith and love of Christ Jesus be your model. [14]You have been trusted with a wonderful treasure. Guard it with the help of the Holy Spirit, who lives within you.

Teach yourself to sing to God

(9) This is one of the little poems or songs that were probably sung by Christians in the days of Paul and Timothy. Their songs didn't have rhyme and rhythm like modern songs. But they expressed great and beautiful thoughts about God. Such songs meant a lot for the faith of the people then. God wants us to sing to him now, too.

---

[a]*when I placed my hands on you*: Church leaders placed their hands on people who were being appointed to preach or teach. See 1 Timothy 4.14. [b]*God's Spirit*: Or "God." [c]*teacher*: Some manuscripts add "of the Gentiles." [d]*what he has trusted me with*: Or "what I have trusted him with."

15You know that everyone in Asia has turned against me, especially Phygelus and Hermogenes.

16I pray that the Lord will be kind to the family of Onesiphorus. He often cheered me up and was not ashamed of me when I was put in jail. 17Then after he arrived in Rome, he searched everywhere until he found me. 18I pray that the Lord Jesus will ask God to show mercy to Onesiphorus on the day of judgment. You know how much he helped me in Ephesus.

A Good Soldier of Christ Jesus

2 Timothy, my child, Christ Jesus is kind, and you must let him make you strong. 2You have often heard me teach. Now I want you to tell these same things to followers who can be trusted to tell others.

3As a good soldier of Christ Jesus you must endure your share of suffering. 4Soldiers on duty don't work at outside jobs. They try only to please their commanding officer. 5No one wins an athletic contest without obeying the rules. 6And farmers who work hard are the first to eat what grows in their field. 7If you keep in mind what I have told you, the Lord will help you understand completely.

8Keep your mind on Jesus Christ! He was from the family of David and was raised from death, just as my good news says. 9And because of this message, I am locked up in jail and treated like a criminal. But God's good news isn't locked in jail, 10and so I am willing to put up with anything. Then God's special people will be saved. They will be given eternal glory because they belong to Christ Jesus. 11Here is a true message:

> "If we died with Christ,
>   we will live with him.
> 12If we don't give up,
>   we will rule with him.
> If we deny
>   that we know him,
> he will deny
>   that he knows us.

Be a good soldier of Christ (3) Being a Christian is no easy life. We have to live in a world that is no friend to Christ. This calls for careful living. A well-known Christian of the 1700's named John Wesley was called a "Methodist" because he and his friends set up a careful method for living a godly life. We, too, can be good soldiers for Christ by making sure we're "in shape" with a life of prayer, study, and useful Christian service.

¹³If we are not faithful,
  he will still be faithful.
Christ cannot deny
  who he is."

An Approved Worker

¹⁴Don't let anyone forget these things.
And with God^e as your witness, you must
warn them not to argue about words. These
arguments don't help anyone. In fact, they
ruin everyone who listens to them. ¹⁵Do
your best to win God's approval as a worker
who does not need to be ashamed and who
teaches only the true message.

¹⁶Keep away from worthless and useless
talk. It only leads people farther away from
God. ¹⁷That sort of talk is like a sore that
won't heal. And Hymenaeus and Philetus
have been talking this way ¹⁸by teaching
that the dead have already been raised to
life. This is far from the truth, and it is destroying the faith of some people.

¹⁹But the foundation that God has laid
is solid. On it is written, "The Lord knows
who his people are. So everyone who worships the Lord must turn away from evil."

²⁰In a large house some dishes are made
of gold or silver, while others are made of
wood or clay. Some of these are special,
and others are not. ²¹That's also how it is
with people. The ones who stop doing evil
and make themselves pure will become special. Their lives will be holy and pleasing
to their Master, and they will be able to
do all kinds of good deeds.

²²Run from temptations that capture
young people. Always do the right thing.
Be faithful, loving, and easy to get along
with. Worship with people whose hearts are
pure. ²³Stay away from stupid and senseless
arguments. These only lead to trouble,
²⁴and God's servants must not be trouble-
makers. They must be kind to everyone,
and they must be good teachers and very
patient.

^eGod: Some manuscripts have "the Lord," and others
have "Christ."

Let's avoid silly arguments
(16) Some people talk as if
their faith depended on winning arguments about things
that don't really matter.
There are things worth
speaking up for, and even
dying for, but a lot of de-
bates about religion are
useless. They often get people more mixed up than they
were before they started
arguing.

Run from temptations
(22) Some Christians think
they can "play with fire" and
not get burned. Paul writes
that we should run when we
see temptation. We
shouldn't assume that we
are so strong that we can't
be drawn away from godly
living. Believers should
strengthen and encourage
each other to live for Jesus.

25Be humble when you correct people who oppose you. Maybe God will lead them to turn to him and learn the truth. 26They have been trapped by the devil, and he makes them obey him, but God may help them escape.

What People Will Be Like in the Last Days

3 You can be certain that in the last days there will be some very hard times. 2People will love only themselves and money. They will be proud, stuck-up, rude, and disobedient to their parents. They will also be ungrateful, godless, 3heartless, and hateful. Their words will be cruel, and they will have no self-control or pity. These people will hate everything that is good. 4They will be sneaky, reckless, and puffed up with pride. Instead of loving God, they will love pleasure. 5Even though they will make a show of being religious, their religion won't be real. Don't have anything to do with such people.

6Some men fool whole families, just to get power over those women, who are slaves of sin and are controlled by all sorts of desires. 7These women always want to learn something new, but they never can discover the truth. 8Just as Jannes and Jambres*f* opposed Moses, these people are enemies of the truth. Their minds are sick, and their faith isn't real. 9But they won't get very far with their foolishness. Soon everyone will know the truth about them, just as Jannes and Jambres were found out.

Paul's Last Instructions to Timothy

10Timothy, you know what I teach and how I live. You know what I want to do and what I believe. You have seen how patient and loving I am, and how in the past I put up with 11trouble and suffering in the

Be aware of evil people
(1) In these days we see a lot of what Paul writes about here concerning the "last days." It would be nice if the world were a sweet place, but it isn't. Paul reminds us that there are a lot of mean and deceitful people in the world. We must be careful to keep our own hearts pure and keep a sharp eye out for the kinds of people Paul describes in this passage. We can get hurt spiritually if we're not careful.

fJannes and Jambres: These names are not found in the Old Testament. But many believe these were the names of the two Egyptian magicians who opposed Moses when he wanted to lead the people of Israel out of Egypt. See Exodus 7.11,22.

cities of Antioch, Iconium, and Lystra. Yet the Lord rescued me from all those terrible troubles. 12Anyone who belongs to Christ Jesus and wants to live right will have trouble from others. 13But evil people who pretend to be what they are not will become worse than ever, as they fool others and are fooled themselves.

14Keep on being faithful to what you were taught and to what you believed. After all, you know who taught you these things. 15Since childhood, you have known the Holy Scriptures that are able to make you wise enough to have faith in Christ Jesus and be saved. 16Everything in the Scriptures is God's Word. All of it is useful for teaching and helping people and for correcting them and showing them how to live. 17The Scriptures train God's servants to do all kinds of good deeds.

4 When Christ Jesus comes as king, he will be the judge of everyone, whether they are living or dead. So with God and Christ as witnesses, I command you 2to preach God's message. Do it willingly, even if it is not the popular thing to do. You must correct people and point out their sins. But also cheer them up, and when you instruct them, always be patient. 3The time is coming when people won't listen to good teaching. Instead, they will look for teachers who will please them by telling them only what they are itching to hear. 4They will turn from the truth and eagerly listen to senseless stories. 5But you must stay calm and be willing to suffer. You must work hard to tell the good news and to do your job well.

6Now the time has come for me to die. My life is like a drink offeringg being poured out on the altar. 7I have fought well. I have finished the race, and I have been faithful. 8So a crown will be given to me for pleasing the Lord. He judges fairly, and on the day of judgment he will give a crown to me and

Teach the children
(14) Here Paul writes that Timothy has known the Scriptures since childhood. Christians who have grown up on God's word often have more wisdom to draw from than those who have not. The greatest good we can do for our young people is to teach them God's word, then show by our lives that we love that word.

Let's be firm but cheerful
(2) This was Paul's last known letter before his execution in Rome. Because of the evils he describes in chapter 3, it's important for all of us to see the needs around us. Sometimes our brothers and sisters in Christ need to be warned. At the same time, let's be cheerful and trust God for a good outcome.

Are you ready to die?
(7) Paul was ready to give up his life here on earth. Let's make up our minds to live every day so that we can say with Paul, "I have fought well." God will help us to get past the things in our lives that hold us back from serving him. Fear is one thing that keeps us back: fear of death, embarrassment, hunger, and other trials. Let's remember Paul the prisoner at such times.

---

gdrink offering: Water or wine was sometimes poured out as an offering when an animal sacrifice was made.

to everyone else who wants him to appear with power.

Personal Instructions

9Come to see me as soon as you can. 10Demas loves the things of this world so much that he left me and went to Thessalonica. Crescens has gone to Galatia, and Titus has gone to Dalmatia. 11Only Luke has stayed with me.

Mark can be very helpful to me, so please find him and bring him with you. 12I sent Tychicus to Ephesus.

13When you come, bring the coat I left at Troas with Carpus. Don't forget to bring the scrolls, especially the ones made of leather.h

14Alexander, the metalworker, has hurt me in many ways. But the Lord will pay him back for what he has done. 15Alexander opposes what we preach. You had better watch out for him.

16When I was first put on trial, no one helped me. In fact, everyone deserted me. I hope it won't be held against them. 17But the Lord stood beside me. He gave me the strength to tell his full message, so that all Gentiles would hear it. And I was kept safe from hungry lions. 18The Lord will always keep me from being harmed by evil, and he will bring me safely into his heavenly kingdom. Praise him forever and ever! Amen.

Final Greetings

19Give my greetings to Priscilla and Aquila and to the family of Onesiphorus. 20Erastus stayed at Corinth.

Trophimus was sick, when I left him at Miletus. 21Do your best to come before winter.

Be ready to stand alone (11) Maybe you've heard that "one with God is a majority." That's a true statement. Paul was finally deserted by his friends. But when he was left alone— that's when he knew best what a friend God is. There is a proverb by Solomon in the Old Testament: "There is a friend who sticks closer than a brother." That friend is Jesus, the Son of God who became a man. With him we are never really alone.

hthe ones made of leather: A scroll was a kind of rolled up book, and it could be made out of paper (called "papyrus") or leather (that is, animal skin) or even copper.

Eubulus, Pudens, Linus, and Claudia send you their greetings, and so do the rest of the Lord's followers.

²²I pray that the Lord will bless your life and will be kind to you.

PAUL'S LETTER TO TITUS

ABOUT THIS LETTER

Paul mentions Titus several times in his letters as someone who worked with him in Asia Minor and Greece (2 Corinthians 2.13; 7.6,13; 8.6,16,23; 12.18; Galatians 2.3). He is told by Paul to appoint church leaders and officials in Crete.

Paul instructs Titus to make sure that church leaders and officials have good reputations (1.5–9) and that all of the Lord's followers keep themselves pure and avoid arguments (1.10—2.9).

Paul includes special instructions for the different groups within the church in Crete. He reminds Titus that a new way of life is possible because of what God has done by sending Jesus Christ: God has saved them, washed them by the power of the Holy Spirit, and given them a fresh start and the hope of eternal life.

Paul also tells how we are saved:

> God our Savior showed us
>   how good and kind he is.
> He saved us because
>   of his mercy,
> and not because
> of any good things
>   that we have done. (3.4,5)

A QUICK LOOK AT THIS LETTER

1. Greetings and a Prayer for Titus (1.1–4)
2. Instructions for Church Officials (1.5–16)
3. Instructions for Church People (2.1—3.11)
4. Personal Advice and Final Greetings (3.12–15)

1 From Paul, a servant of God and an apostle of Jesus Christ.

I encourage God's own people to have more faith and to understand the truth about religion. ²Then they will have the hope of eternal life that God promised long ago. And God never tells a lie! ³So, at the proper time, God our Savior gave this message and told me to announce what he had said.

⁴Titus, because of our faith, you are like a son to me. I pray that God our Father and Christ Jesus our Savior will be kind to you and will bless you with peace!

What Titus Was to Do in Crete

⁵I left you in Crete to do what had been left undone and to appoint leaders*ᵃ* for the

Learn the truth

(1) Jesus said, "The truth will make you free" (John 8.32). That's what Paul is writing here. Our minds have to be changed so that we can appreciate what God wants to teach us. Then we will be made free from everything that keeps us from enjoying all the good things that the Lord wants us to have. Those good things are summed up in the words "eternal life."

ᵃleaders: Or "elders" or "presbyters" or "priests."

churches in each town. As I told you, [6]they must have a good reputation and be married only once.[b] Their children must be followers of the Lord and not have a reputation for being wild and disobedient.

[7]Church officials[c] are in charge of God's work, and so they must also have a good reputation. They must not be bossy, quick-tempered, heavy drinkers, bullies, or dishonest in business. [8]Instead, they must be friendly to strangers and enjoy doing good things. They must also be sensible, fair, pure, and self-controlled. [9]They must stick to the true message they were taught, so that their good teaching can help others and correct everyone who opposes it.

[10]There are many who don't respect authority, and they fool others by talking nonsense. This is especially true of some Jewish followers. [11]But you must make them be quiet. They are after money, and they upset whole families by teaching what they should not. [12]It is like one of their own prophets once said,

"The people of Crete
    always tell lies.
They are greedy and lazy
    like wild animals."

[13]That surely is a true saying. And you should be hard on such people, so you can help them grow stronger in their faith. [14]Don't pay any attention to any of those senseless Jewish stories and human commands. These are made up by people who won't obey the truth.

[15]Everything is pure for someone whose heart is pure. But nothing is pure for an unbeliever with a dirty mind. That person's mind and conscience are destroyed. [16]Such people claim to know God, but their actions prove that they really don't. They are disgusting. They won't obey God, and they are too worthless to do anything good.

---

[b]*married only once*: Or "the husband of only one wife" or "faithful in marriage." [c]*Church officials*: Or "Bishops."

Good leaders

(7) Here is more of the same advice Paul gave to Timothy, about what a good church official is. This was very important information, which Paul didn't mind writing again to Titus. The success or failure of a church often depends on who is leading it. Pastors and other leaders need our prayers.

Keep your heart pure

(15) Everything looks dirty when we look through a dirty window. A heart that is not pure sees evil in things that are not evil. Some people in Paul's day, and in later times, believed that evil comes from having anything to do with the material world. But it isn't the material world that is evil. Sinful people make the world evil by the bad ways they use the good things God made.

Instructions for Different Groups of People

2 Titus, you must teach only what is correct. [2]Tell the older men to have self-control and to be serious and sensible. Their faith, love, and patience must never fail.

[3]Tell the older women to behave as those who love the Lord should. They must not gossip about others or be slaves of wine. They must teach what is proper, [4]so the younger women will be loving wives and mothers. [5]Each of the younger women must be sensible and kind, as well as a good homemaker, who puts her own husband first. Then no one can say insulting things about God's message.

[6]Tell the young men to have self-control in everything.

[7]Always set a good example for others. Be sincere and serious when you teach. [8]Use clean language that no one can criticize. Do this, and your enemies will be too ashamed to say anything against you.

[9]Tell slaves always to please their owners by obeying them in everything. Slaves must not talk back to their owners [10]or steal from them. They must be completely honest and trustworthy. Then everyone will show great respect for what is taught about God our Savior.

God's Kindness and the New Life

[11]God has shown us how kind he is by coming to save all people. [12]He taught us to give up our wicked ways and our worldly desires and to live decent and honest lives in this world. [13]We are filled with hope, as we wait for the glorious return of our great God and Savior Jesus Christ.[d] [14]He gave himself to rescue us from everything that is evil and to make our hearts pure. He wanted us to be his own people and to be eager to do right.

[d]the glorious return of our great God and Savior Jesus Christ: Or "the glorious return of our great God and our Savior Jesus Christ" or "the return of Jesus Christ, who is the glory of our great God and Savior."

Be an example
(7) The best arguments for Christianity are not found in textbooks. The most convincing argument is the life of a Christian. If we talk well but live badly, we only disgrace the name of Jesus. But if we show our love for him by a life of constant goodwill, kindness, and joy, no one can argue with that.

Are you waiting for Jesus?
(13) Political leaders sometimes speak of bringing about a "new world order." Everyone would like to see peace among the nations. But Christians know this great new order will come fully only when Jesus returns to earth to establish his kingdom. In all of our activity for God, let the coming of Jesus be our great desire and inspiration.

¹⁵Teach these things, as you use your full authority to encourage and correct people. Make sure you earn everyone's respect.

Doing Helpful Things

3 Remind your people to obey the rulers and authorities and not to be rebellious. They must always be ready to do something helpful ²and not say cruel things or argue. They should be gentle and kind to everyone. ³We used to be stupid, disobedient, and foolish, as well as slaves of all sorts of desires and pleasures. We were evil and jealous. Everyone hated us, and we hated everyone.

⁴God our Savior showed us
　　how good and kind he is.
⁵He saved us because
　　of his mercy,
and not because
of any good things
　　that we have done.

God washed us by the power
　　of the Holy Spirit.
He gave us new birth
　　and a fresh beginning.
⁶God sent Jesus Christ
our Savior
　　to give us his Spirit.

⁷He did this so that
　　the kindness of Jesus
would make us acceptable
　　to God
and give us the hope
　　of eternal life.
⁸This message is certainly true.

These teachings are useful and helpful for everyone. I want you to insist that the people follow them, so that all who have faith in God will be sure to do good deeds. ⁹But don't have anything to do with stupid arguments about ancestors. And stay away from disagreements and quarrels about the Jewish Law. Such arguments are useless and senseless.

¹⁰Warn troublemakers once or twice. Then don't have anything else to do with

Christians are gentle
(2) Before we were saved we may have been bad-tempered, stubborn, and hostile toward authority. This was because we thought we could save ourselves and our possessions by demanding our personal rights. But this world is dying, and we have no possessions that are really worth fighting about. Christians can afford to be gentle because their treasure is in heaven.

God is our example
(6) God is love, and he proves it by what he does. He saved us from our sins and their result, death, by sending his dear Son to die in our place. If God could do this for us, then we have no excuse for not being like him. Our lives ought to copy his love.

them. 11You know that their minds are twisted, and their own sins show how guilty they are.

Personal Instructions and Greetings

12I plan to send Artemas or Tychicus to you. After they arrive, please try your best to meet me at Nicopolis. I have decided to spend the winter there.

13When Zenas the lawyer and Apollos get ready to leave, help them as much as you can, so they won't have need of anything.

14Our people should learn to spend their time doing something useful and worthwhile.

15Greetings to you from everyone here. Greet all of our friends who share in our faith.

I pray that the Lord will be kind to all of you!

Christians are practical
(14) Being a Christian doesn't mean having our heads in the clouds. We have two countries—earth and heaven. But we prove we are solid citizens of both countries by the way we do the job that is ours to do right now. God has left us here for a reason: to bless those around us and to share the news about his Son.

PAUL'S LETTER TO PHILEMON

ABOUT THIS LETTER

Philemon was a wealthy man who owned slaves and who used his large house for church meetings (2). He probably lived in Colossae, since Paul's letter to the Colossians mentions Onesimus, a slave of Philemon, and Archippus (Colossians 4.9,17).

Paul is writing from jail on behalf of Onesimus, a run-away slave owned by Philemon. Onesimus had become a follower of the Lord and a valuable friend to Paul, and Paul is writing to encourage Philemon to accept Onesimus also as a friend and follower of the Lord.

This letter is an excellent example of the art of letter-writing in the Roman world, and it is the most personal of all Paul's letters. The way the letter is written suggests that Paul and Philemon were close friends.

A QUICK LOOK AT THIS LETTER

1. Greetings to Philemon (1–3)
2. Paul Speaks to Philemon about Onesimus (4–22)
3. Final Greetings and a Prayer (23–25)

1From Paul, who is in jail for serving Christ Jesus, and from Timothy, who is like a brother because of our faith.

Philemon, you have worked with us and are very dear to us. This letter is to you 2and to the church that meets in your home. It is also to our dear friend Apphia and to Archippus, who serves the Lord as we do.

3I pray that God our Father and our Lord Jesus Christ will be kind to you and will bless you with peace!

Philemon's Love and Faith

4Philemon, each time I mention you in my prayers, I thank God. 5I hear about your faith in our Lord Jesus and about your love for all of God's people. 6As you share your faith with others, I pray that they may come to know all the blessings Christ has given us. 7My friend, your love has made me happy and has greatly encouraged me. It has also cheered the hearts of God's people.

Paul Speaks to Philemon about Onesimus

8Christ gives me the courage to tell you what to do. 9But I would rather ask you to

Let's care about individuals
(7) It's easy to say, "I love everybody." But we prove our love by the way we treat individual people. Paul had a large ministry. But, even in prison, he wrote this whole letter about one poor slave. It's a beautiful personal letter from Paul to his friend, Philemon. This letter brings us close to Paul the man, where we can see what he was really like.

do it because of love, since I am a messenger[a] in jail for Christ. [10]So I beg you to help Onesimus,[b] who has been like a son to me here in jail. [11]Before this, he was useless to you, but now he is useful to you and me.

[12]Sending Onesimus to you has made me very sad. [13]I would like to keep him here with me, where he could take your place in helping me spread the good news while I am a prisoner. [14]But I won't do anything unless you agree to it first. I want your act of kindness to come from your heart, and not be something you feel forced to do.

[15]Perhaps Onesimus was taken from you for a little while so that you could have him back for good, [16]but not as a slave. Onesimus is much more than a slave. To me he is a dear friend, but to you he is even more, both as a person and as a follower of the Lord.

[17]If you consider me a friend because of Christ, then welcome Onesimus as you would welcome me. [18]If he has cheated you or owes you anything, charge it to my account. [19]With my own hand I write: I, PAUL, WILL PAY YOU BACK. But don't forget that you owe me your life. [20]My dear friend, I pray that the Lord will make you useful to me and that, as a follower of Christ, you will cheer me up.

[21]I am sure you will do all I have asked, and even more. [22]Please get a room ready for me. I hope your prayers will be answered, and I can visit you.

[23]Epaphras is also here in jail for being a follower of Christ Jesus. He sends his greetings, [24]and so do Mark, Aristarchus, Demas, and Luke, who work together with me.

[25]I pray that the Lord Jesus Christ will be with you!

Carry the burdens of others

(18) Paul didn't just write a kind letter about Onesimus. He was even willing to pay that young slave's debts. It didn't seem to bother Paul at all that he was in prison where he had very little, and he might never see Philemon again. Still he was willing to make this promise. More than most people, Paul was free from selfishness. It seems that his kindness was boundless.

---

[a]*a messenger*: Or "an old man." [b]*Onesimus*: In Greek this name means "useful."

THE LETTER TO THE HEBREWS

ABOUT THIS LETTER

Many religious people in the first century after Jesus' birth, both Jews and Gentiles, had questions about the religion of the early Christians. They were looking for evidence that this new faith was genuine. Jews had the miracle of crossing the Red Sea and the agreement made with God at Mount Sinai to support their faith. But what miracles did Christians have? Jews had beautiful worship ceremonies and a high priest who offered sacrifices in the temple so that the people would be forgiven. But what did Christians have? How could this new Christian faith, centered in Jesus, offer forgiveness of sins and friendship with God?

The letter to the Hebrews was written to answer exactly these kinds of questions. In it the author tells the readers how important Jesus really is. He is greater than any of God's angels (1.5–14), greater than any prophet, and greater even than Moses and Joshua (2.1—4.14). Jesus is the perfect high priest because he never sinned, and by offering his own life he has made the perfect sacrifice for sin once for all time (9.23–10.18). By his death and return from death he has opened the way for all people to come to God (4.14—5.10; 7.1—8.13).

This letter has much to say about the importance of faith. The writer points out that what Jesus offers comes only by faith. And this faith makes his followers sure of what they hope for and gives them proof of things that cannot be seen. The writer praises God's faithful people of the past (11.1–40) and encourages those who follow Jesus now to keep their eyes on him as they run the race (12.1–3).

What does it mean to have a high priest like Jesus?

Jesus understands every weakness of ours, because he was tempted in every way that we are. But he did not sin! So whenever we are in need, we should come bravely before the throne of our merciful God. There we will be treated with kindness, and we will find help. (4.15,16)

1 Long ago in many ways and at many times God's prophets spoke his message to our ancestors. 2But now at last God sent his Son to bring his message to us. God created the universe by his Son, and everything will someday belong to the Son. 3God's Son has all the brightness of God's own glory and is like him in every way.

By his own mighty word he holds the universe together.

After the Son had washed away our sins, he sat down at the right side*a* of the glorious God in heaven. 4He had become much greater than the angels, and the name he was given is far greater than any of theirs.

God's Son Is Greater than Angels

5God has never said
　to any of the angels,
"You are my Son, because today
　I have become your Father!"
Neither has God said
　to any of them,
"I will be his Father,
　and he will be my Son!"

6When God brings his first-born Son*b* into the world, he commands all of his angels to worship him.

7And when God speaks about the angels, he says,

"I change my angels into wind
and my servants
　into flaming fire."

8But God says about his Son,
"You are God,
and you will rule
　as King forever!
Your*c* royal power
　brings about justice.
9You loved justice
　and hated evil,
and so I, your God,
　have chosen you.
I appointed you
and made you happier
　than any of your friends."

10The Scriptures also say,
"Lord, in the beginning
　you were the one

Jesus earned his glory

(3) We know that Jesus came from heaven where he shared equally the glory of his Father. And yet we can say that Jesus earned his glory. Jesus put himself in the position of a servant who had to do a certain work in order to return to heaven. That work was his earthly obedience, his suffering, and his death for our sins. Jesus was again raised to glory after he finished his work.

aright side: The place of honor and power.　*bfirst-born Son*: The first son born into a family had certain privileges that the other children did not have. In 12.23 "first-born" refers to God's special people.　*cYour*: Some manuscripts have "His."

who laid the foundation
of the earth
and created the heavens.
11They will all disappear
and wear out like clothes,
but you will last forever.
12You will roll them up
like a robe
and change them
like a garment.
But you are always the same,
and you will live forever."
13God never said to any
of the angels,
"Sit at my right side
until I make your enemies
into a footstool for you!"
14Angels are merely spirits sent to serve
people who are going to be saved.

This Great Way of Being Saved

2 We must give our full attention to what
we were told, so that we won't drift
away. 2The message spoken by angels
proved to be true, and all who disobeyed
or rejected it were punished as they deserved. 3So if we refuse this great way of
being saved, how can we hope to escape?
The Lord himself was the first to tell about
it, and people who heard the message
proved to us that it was true. 4God himself
showed that his message was true by working all kinds of powerful miracles and wonders. He also gave his Holy Spirit to anyone
he chose to.

The One Who Leads Us to Be Saved

5We know that God did not put the future
world under the power of angels. 6Some-
where in the Scriptures someone says to
God,

"What makes you care
about us humans?
Why are you concerned
for weaklings such as we?
7You made us lower

Christ created all things
(10) Let's not forget that the man Jesus, whom we met in Matthew, Mark, Luke, and John, was hiding his real nature within a body of flesh. But all that time he was still the Son of God, the very One who brought the universe into being. We should adore Jesus even more when we realize how much he humbled himself to become a man with flesh and blood like ours.

than the angels
for a while.
Yet you have crowned us
with glory and honor.d
8And you have put everything
under our power!"

God has put everything under our power
and has not left anything out of our power.
But we still don't see it all under our power.
9What we do see is Jesus, who for a little
while was made lower than the angels. Because of God's kindness, Jesus died for
everyone. And now that Jesus has suffered
and died, he is crowned with glory and
honor!

10Everything belongs to God, and all
things were created by his power. So God
did the right thing when he made Jesus perfect by suffering, as Jesus led many of God's
children to be saved and to share in his
glory. 11Jesus and the people he makes holy
all belong to the same family. That is why
he is not ashamed to call them his brothers
and sisters. 12He even said to God,

"I will tell them your name
and sing your praises
when they come together
to worship."

13He also said,
"I will trust God."
Then he said,
"Here I am with the children
God has given me."

14We are people of flesh and blood. That
is why Jesus became one of us. He died to
destroy the devil, who had power over
death. 15But he also died to rescue all of
us who live each day in fear of dying.
16Jesus clearly did not come to help angels,
but he did come to help Abraham's descendants. 17He had to be one of us, so that he
could serve God as our merciful and faithful
high priest and forgive our sins. 18And now
that Jesus has suffered and was tempted,
he can help anyone else who is tempted.

The power God gives us
(8) Has God really given us
his mighty power? Yes, he
has, through Jesus our great
representative. Through Jesus we have power over sin
and creation. We have not
yet fully realized or understood this power. But one
day believers actually shall
reign as kings on the earth
(see Revelation 1.6). So now
we see what great honors
Christ our King has bought
for us at the price of his own
life.

**Jesus destroyed Satan's
power**
(14) The devil, Satan, had
power over death, and
therefore death was our
great enemy. But Jesus
broke Satan's power by carrying the weight of our sins
on the cross, and then rising
up from death. Now he has
given us as a gift the life he
was raised with. Satan can't
frighten us with death anymore. Jesus said, "I have the
keys to death."

dand honor: Some manuscripts add "and you have
placed us in charge of all you created."

Jesus Is Greater than Moses

3 My friends, God has chosen you to be his holy people. So think about Jesus, the one we call our apostle and high priest! ²Jesus was faithful to God, who appointed him, just as Moses was faithful in serving all of ͤ God's people. ³But Jesus deserves more honor than Moses, just as the builder of a house deserves more honor than the house. ⁴Of course, every house is built by someone, and God is really the one who built everything.

⁵Moses was a faithful servant and told all of God's people what would be said in the future. ⁶But Christ is the Son in charge of God's people. And we are those people, if we keep on being brave and don't lose hope.

A Rest for God's People

⁷It is just as the Holy Spirit says,
"If you hear God's voice today,
8   don't be stubborn!
Don't rebel like those people
who were tested
in the desert.
⁹⁻¹⁰For forty years your ancestors
tested God and saw
the things he did.

"Then God got tired of them
and said,
'You people never
show good sense,
and you don't understand
what I want you to do.'
¹¹God became angry
and told the people,
'You will never enter
my place of rest!'"
¹²My friends, watch out! Don't let evil thoughts or doubts make any of you turn from the living God. ¹³You must encourage

Why Jesus is greater than Moses
(5) Moses was God's ancient lawgiver who told his people of God's commandments. But Moses couldn't give anyone power over the sinfulness that breaks the commandments. Christ, the Lord who gave Moses the Law, is also the One who came and obeyed that Law for us. Then he died to pay for our sins against his Law. So Jesus did what Moses never could have done.

ͤ*all of*: Some manuscripts do not have these words.

one another each day. And you must keep on while there is still a time that can be called "today." If you don't, then sin may fool some of you and make you stubborn. 14We were sure about Christ when we first became his people. So let's hold tightly to our faith until the end. 15The Scriptures say,

> "If you hear his voice today,
> don't be stubborn
> like those who rebelled."

16Who were those people that heard God's voice and rebelled? Weren't they the same ones that came out of Egypt with Moses? 17Who were the people that made God angry for forty years? Weren't they the ones that sinned and died in the desert? 18And who did God say would never enter his place of rest? Weren't they the ones that disobeyed him? 19We see that those people did not enter the place of rest because they did not have faith.

4 The promise to enter the place of rest is still good, and we must take care that none of you miss out. 2We have heard the message, just as they did. But they failed to believe what they heard, and the message did not do them any good. 3Only people who have faith will enter the place of rest. It is just as the Scriptures say,

> "God became angry
> and told the people,
> 'You will never enter
> my place of rest!' "

God said this, even though everything has been ready from the time of creation. 4In fact, somewhere the Scriptures say that God rested on the Sabbath. 5We also read that he later said, "You people will never enter my place of rest!" 6This means that the promise to enter is still good, because those who first heard about it disobeyed and did not enter. 7Much later God told David to make the promise again, just as I have already said,

> "If you hear his voice today,
> don't be stubborn!"

8If Joshua had really given the people rest, there would not be any need for God

Obedience to God

(15) In Old Testament times God tested his people's obedience with many rules. They resisted God by not following him. But even following rules doesn't change hearts. Real obedience is accepting God's plan to save us by what Jesus did for us. It's obedience when we honestly give ourselves to him. Then our hearts are made new, and pleasing God becomes a joy.

What is the rest that God gives?

(3) When we're always working by our own strength to please God, obeying then disobeying, there is no rest for us. But when we have given ourselves to God, then we have rest in him. Rest is knowing we're safely in his everlasting care. Then one day we will enter into his presence, and all of our weariness will pass away. Then we will rest, even though we will still be busy serving God.

to talk about another day of rest. 9But God has promised us a Sabbath when we will rest, even though it has not yet come. 10On that day God's people will rest from their work, just as God rested from his work.

11We should do our best to enter that place of rest, so that none of us will disobey and miss going there, as they did. 12What God has said is not only alive and active! It is sharper than any double-edged sword. His word can cut through our spirits and souls and through our joints and marrow, until it discovers the desires and thoughts of our hearts. 13Nothing is hidden from God! He sees through everything, and we will have to tell him the truth.

Jesus Is the Great High Priest

14We have a great high priest, who has gone into heaven, and he is Jesus the Son of God. That is why we must hold on to what we have said about him. 15Jesus understands every weakness of ours, because he was tempted in every way that we are. But he did not sin! 16So whenever we are in need, we should come bravely before the throne of our merciful God. There we will be treated with kindness, and we will find help.

5 Every high priest is appointed to help others by offering gifts and sacrifices to God because of their sins. 2A high priest has weaknesses of his own, and he feels sorry for foolish and sinful people. 3That is why he must offer sacrifices for his own sins and for the sins of others. 4But no one can have the honor of being a high priest simply by wanting to be one. Only God can choose a priest, and God is the one who chose Aaron.

5That is how it was with Christ. He became a high priest, but not just because he wanted the honor of being one. It was God who told him,

"You are my Son, because today
I have become your Father!"
6In another place, God says,

Christ our great high priest
(14) In Old Testament times the high priest was the spiritual leader of the people. He was the only one who could appear before God once a year to make an offering for the people's sins. The high priest was a picture of the great high priest of the New Testament, Jesus Christ. Instead of the animals that priests sacrificed in the Old Testament, Jesus gave a perfect sacrifice for sins: himself.

Who was Melchizedek?
(6) The Old Testament tells about a meeting of Abraham (the great ancestor of the Hebrew people) with a mysterious high priest called Melchizedek. We're told that Abraham offered a tenth of what he had to God in an act of worship before this strange person,

"You are a priest forever
just like Melchizedek."*f*

7God had the power to save Jesus from
death. And while Jesus was on earth, he
begged God with loud crying and tears to
save him. He truly worshiped God, and God
listened to his prayers. 8Jesus is God's own
Son, but still he had to suffer before he could
learn what it really means to obey God.
9Suffering made Jesus perfect, and now he
can save forever all who obey him. 10This
is because God chose him to be a high priest
like Melchizedek.

Warning against Turning Away

11Much more could be said about this
subject. But it is hard to explain, and all
of you are slow to understand. 12By now
you should have been teachers, but once
again you need to be taught the simplest
things about what God has said. You need
milk instead of solid food. 13People who live
on milk are like babies who don't really
know what is right. 14Solid food is for mature people who have been trained to know
right from wrong.

6 We must try to become mature and start
thinking about more than just the basic
things we were taught about Christ. We
shouldn't need to keep talking about why
we ought to turn from deeds that bring death
and why we ought to have faith in God.
2And we shouldn't need to keep teaching
about baptisms*g* or about the laying on of
hands*h* or about people being raised from
death and the future judgment. 3Let's grow
up, if God is willing.

4-6But what about people who turn away
after they have already seen the light and
have received the gift from heaven and have

whom we never see or hear
from again. This high priest
pointed ahead to the com-
ing of Christ. Melchizedek
means the "king who brings
justice" (see chapter 7).

Jesus was made complete
by suffering

(9) Think of that: even the
Son of God himself had
something he had to do to
be all that God meant him
to be. When we read that
"suffering made Jesus perfect," of course it doesn't
mean that Jesus was ever
sinful. "Perfect" here means
"complete." Jesus could not
complete his work that
saves us without perfectly
obeying his heavenly Father
and suffering for our sins.
In this way Jesus became
complete or perfect as our
Savior.

Christians continue to the
end

(4) Real Christians never
give up. If they do give up
and go back to their old
ways, then they prove that
they don't love Christ at all.
Their hearts are harder than
ever before, and they almost
never come back to Christ.
So let's not have ideas that
we can take Jesus or leave
him depending on what suits
us. If we take Jesus, it must
be for real and it must be
forever.

f Melchizedek: When Melchizedek is mentioned in the
Old Testament, he is described as a priest who lived
before Aaron. Nothing is said about his ancestors or
his death (see 7.3 and Genesis 14.17-20). *g baptisms*:
Or "ceremonies of washing." *h laying on of hands*: This
was a ceremony in which church leaders and others
put their hands on people to show that those people
were chosen to do some special kind of work.

shared in the Holy Spirit? What about those who turn away after they have received the good message of God and the powers of the future world? There is no way to bring them back. What they are doing is the same as nailing the Son of God to a cross and insulting him in public!

7A field is useful to farmers, if there is enough rain to make good crops grow. In fact, God will bless that field. 8But land that produces only thorn bushes is worthless. It is likely to fall under God's curse, and in the end it will be set on fire.

9My friends, we are talking this way. But we are sure that you are doing those really good things that people do when they are being saved. 10God is always fair. He will remember how you helped his people in the past and how you are still helping them. You belong to God, and he won't forget the love you have shown his people. 11We wish that each of you would always be eager to show how strong and lasting your hope really is. 12Then you would never be lazy. You would be following the example of those who had faith and were patient until God kept his promise to them.

God's Promise Is Sure

13No one is greater than God. So he made a promise in his own name when he said to Abraham, 14"I, the Lord, will bless you with many descendants!" 15Then after Abraham had been very patient, he was given what God had promised. 16When anyone wants to settle an argument, they make a vow by using the name of someone or something greater than themselves. 17So when God wanted to prove for certain that his promise to his people could not be broken, he made a vow. 18God cannot tell lies! And so his promises and vows are two things that can never be changed.

We have run to God for safety. Now his promises should greatly encourage us to take hold of the hope that is right in front of us. 19This hope is like a firm and steady anchor for our souls. In fact, hope reaches

God gave Abraham a great family
(14) The "many descendants" God promised Abraham in the Old Testament includes all those who put their faith in Jesus now. This was a very solemn promise that God made to Abraham. We can see this promise of God as an anchor that rests on our Savior's love and can never be moved.

behind the curtain[i] and into the most holy place. [20]Jesus has gone there ahead of us, and he is our high priest forever, just like Melchizedek.[j]

The Priestly Family of Melchizedek

7 Melchizedek was both king of Salem and priest of God Most High. He was the one who went out and gave Abraham his blessing, when Abraham returned from killing the kings. [2]Then Abraham gave him a tenth of everything he had.

The meaning of the name Melchizedek is "King Who Brings Justice." But since Salem means "peace," he is also "King Who Brings Peace." [3]We are not told that he had a father or mother or ancestors or beginning or end. He is like the Son of God and will be a priest forever.[k]

[4]Notice how great Melchizedek is! Our famous ancestor Abraham gave him a tenth of what he had taken from his enemies. [5]The Law teaches that even Abraham's descendants must give a tenth of what they possess. And they are to give this to their own relatives, who are the descendants of Levi and are priests. [6]Although Melchizedek was not a descendant of Levi, Abraham gave him a tenth of what he had. Then Melchizedek blessed Abraham, who had been given God's promise. [7]Everyone agrees that a person who gives a blessing is greater than the one who receives the blessing.

[8]Priests are given a tenth of what people earn. But all priests die, except Melchizedek, and the Scriptures teach that he is alive. [9]Levi's descendants are now the ones who receive a tenth from people. We could even say that when Abraham gave Melchizedek a tenth, Levi also gave him a tenth. [10]This is because Levi was born later into the fam-

Just who was this king?
(1) We have seen in chapter 5 that the name of Melchizedek means the "the king who brings justice." Now we see that he was also the king of Salem. Salem was an ancient name for Jerusalem. Jerusalem means "city of peace," while Salem means simply "peace." So Melchizedek was both the king of justice and peace, as well as being that mysterious priest who visited Abraham, the great ancestor of the Jews. Melchizedek points toward Jesus, our true and everlasting King of justice and peace.

[i]*behind the curtain*: In the tent that was used for worship, a curtain separated the "holy place" from the "most holy place," which only the high priest could enter. [j]*Melchizedek*: See the note at 5.6. [k]*will be a priest forever*: See the note at 5.6.

ily of Abraham, who gave a tenth to Melchizedek.

¹¹Even though the Law of Moses says that the priests must be descendants of Levi, those priests cannot make anyone perfect. So there needs to be a priest like Melchizedek, rather than one from the priestly family of Aaron.ˡ ¹²And when the rules for selecting a priest are changed, the Law must also be changed.

¹³The person we are talking about is our Lord, who came from a tribe that had never had anyone to serve as a priest at the altar. ¹⁴Everyone knows he came from the tribe of Judah, and Moses never said that priests would come from that tribe.

¹⁵All of this becomes clearer, when someone who is like Melchizedek is appointed to be a priest. ¹⁶That person was not appointed because of his ancestors, but because his life can never end. ¹⁷The Scriptures say about him,

> "You are a priest forever,
>   just like Melchizedek."

¹⁸In this way a weak and useless command was put aside, ¹⁹because the Law cannot make anything perfect. At the same time, we are given a much better hope, and it can bring us close to God.

²⁰⁻²¹God himself made a promise when this priest was appointed. But he did not make a promise like this when the other priests were appointed. The promise he made is,

> "I, the Lord, promise that you
>   will be a priest forever!
> And I will never
>   change my mind!"

²²This means that Jesus guarantees us a better agreement with God. ²³There have been a lot of other priests, and all of them have died. ²⁴But Jesus will never die, and so he will be a priest forever! ²⁵He is forever

Jesus is a priest forever
(17) Whoever Melchizedek was, he was indeed like Jesus who would come two thousand years later. So God calls his Son "a priest forever, just like Melchizedek." As our priest, Jesus stands for us in heaven. There he presents his own body as our true and only sacrifice for sins.

ˡ*descendants of Levi . . . from the priestly family of Aaron:* Levi was the ancestor of the tribe from which priests and their helpers (called "Levites") were chosen. Aaron was the first high priest.

able to save[m] the people he leads to God, because he always lives to speak to God for them.

26Jesus is the high priest we need. He is holy and innocent and faultless, and not at all like us sinners. Jesus is honored above all beings in heaven, 27and he is better than any other high priest. Jesus does not need to offer sacrifices each day for his own sins and then for the sins of the people. He offered a sacrifice once for all, when he gave himself. 28The Law appoints priests who have weaknesses. But God's promise, which came later than the Law, appoints his Son. And he is the perfect high priest forever.

A Better Promise

8 What I mean is that we have a high priest who sits at the right side[n] of God's great throne in heaven. 2He also serves as the priest in the most holy place[o] inside the real tent there in heaven. This tent of worship was set up by the Lord, not by humans.

3Since all priests must offer gifts and sacrifices, Christ also needed to have something to offer. 4If he were here on earth, he would not be a priest at all, because here the Law appoints other priests to offer sacrifices. 5But the tent where they serve is just a copy and a shadow of the real one in heaven. Before Moses made the tent, he was told, "Be sure to make it exactly like the pattern you were shown on the mountain!" 6Now Christ has been appointed to serve as a priest in a much better way, and he has given us much assurance of a better agreement.

7If the first agreement with God had been all right, there would not have been any need for another one. 8But the Lord found fault with it and said,

"I tell you the time will come,
     when I will make
         a new agreement

One true sacrifice
(27) Because Jesus is the Son of God, his own death on the cross was all the sacrifice any believer would ever need. Killing animals on an altar was just a sign to point to Jesus. We don't have to do that now.

The tent in heaven
(2) In Old Testament times, before a stone temple was built, God commanded Moses to raise a tent where the sacrifices for sin were made. A tent was used because, at that time, the people were wandering in the desert. In that tent there was a special section called the most holy place. The high priest went there once a year to make a special offering for the people's sins. But now Christ himself is our high priest forever in heaven, and his own crucified but living body is the real payment for our sins.

God makes a new agreement
(8) The Old Testament prophet Jeremiah described this new agreement that would cancel the old agreement. Now the Law of God would be in our minds and hearts, not on stone or any other material. Only Jesus himself, the Son of God, was

[m]*forever able to save*: Or "able to save forever." [n]*right side*: See the note at 1.3. [o]*most holy place*: See the note at 6.19.

with the people of Israel
and the people of Judah.
9It won't be like the agreement
that I made
with their ancestors,
when I took them by the hand
and led them out of Egypt.
They broke their agreement
with me,
and I stopped caring
about them!

10"But now I tell the people
of Israel
this is my new agreement:
'The time will come
when I, the Lord,
will write my laws
on their minds and hearts.
I will be their God,
and they will be
my people.
11Not one of them
will have to teach another
to know me, their Lord.'

"All of them will know me,
no matter who they are.
12I will treat them
with kindness,
even though they
are wicked.
I will surely forget
their sins."
13When the Lord talks about a new agreement, he means that the first one is out of date. And anything that is old and useless will soon disappear.

able to be the sacrifice to pay for our sins. This was something neither we nor anyone else could do. Because of Jesus, we can have friendship with God.

The Tent in Heaven

9 The first promise that was made included rules for worship and a tent for worship here on earth. 2The first part of the tent was called the holy place, and a lampstand, a table, and the sacred loaves of bread were kept there.

3Behind the curtain was the most holy place. 4The gold altar that was used for

The things in the tent
(2) In the part of the tent called "the holy place" there were three main things: the lampstand, which stands for the light-giving presence of God's Spirit; the gold altar of incense, which was a symbol of the prayers of the people rising up to heaven; and the table of

burning incense was in this holy place. The gold-covered sacred chest was also there, and inside it were three things. First, there was a gold jar filled with manna.p Then there was Aaron's walking stick that sprouted.q Finally, there were the flat stones with the Ten Commandments written on them. 5On top of the chest were the glorious creatures with wingsr opened out above the place of mercy.s

Now is not the time to go into detail about these things. 6But this is how everything was when the priests went each day into the first part of the tent to do their duties. 7However, only the high priest could go into the second part of the tent, and he went in only once a year. Each time he carried blood to offer for his sins and for any sins that the people had committed without meaning to.

8All of this is the Holy Spirit's way of saying that no one could enter the most holy place while the tent was still the place of worship. 9This also has a meaning for today. It shows that we cannot make our consciences clear by offering gifts and sacrifices. 10These rules are merely about such things as eating and drinking and ceremonies for washing ourselves. And rules about physical things will last only until the time comes to change them for something better.

11Christ came as the high priest of the good things that are now here.t He also went into a much better tent that was not made by humans and that does not belong to this world. 12Then Christ went once for all into

bread, which meant God was the life of his people. Then "the most holy place," behind a heavy curtain, contained a gold-covered chest that contained God's Law. Now, all of these things have been replaced by Jesus Christ himself.

---

pmanna: When the people of Israel were wandering through the desert, the Lord provided them with food that could be made into thin wafers. This food was called manna, which in Hebrew means "What is it?" qAaron's walking stick that sprouted: According to Numbers 17.1-11, Aaron's walking stick sprouted and produced almonds to show that the Lord was pleased with him and Moses. rglorious creatures with wings: Two of these creatures (called "cherubim" in Hebrew and Greek) with outspread wings were on top of the sacred chest and were symbols of God's throne. splace of mercy: The lid of the sacred chest, which was thought to be God's throne on earth. tthat are now here: Some manuscripts have "that were coming."

the most holy place and freed us from sin forever. He did this by offering his own blood instead of the blood of goats and bulls.

13According to the Jewish religion, those people who become unclean are not fit to worship God. Yet they will be considered clean, if they are sprinkled with the blood of goats and bulls and with the ashes of a sacrificed calf. 14But Christ was sinless, and he offered himself as an eternal and spiritual sacrifice to God. That's why his blood is much more powerful and makes our[u] consciences clear. Now we can serve the living God and no longer do things that lead to death.

15Christ died to rescue those who had sinned and broken the old agreement. Now he brings his chosen ones a new agreement with its guarantee of God's eternal blessings! 16In fact, making an agreement of this kind is like writing a will. This is because the one who makes the will must die before it is of any use. 17In other words, a will does not go into effect as long as the one who made it is still alive.

18Blood was also used[v] to put the first agreement into effect. 19Moses told the people all that the Law said they must do. Then he used red wool and a hyssop plant to sprinkle the people and the book of the Law with the blood of bulls and goats[w] and with water. 20He told the people, "With this blood God makes his agreement with you." 21Moses also sprinkled blood on the tent and on everything else that was used in worship. 22The Law says that almost everything must be sprinkled with blood, and no sins can be forgiven unless blood is offered.

Christ's Great Sacrifice

23These things are only copies of what is in heaven, and so they had to be made holy by these ceremonies. But the real

Why did someone need to die?

(15) It's helpful to look at it this way: We are made immune to certain diseases by serums made from the dead remains of those diseases. Like a disease, sin causes the death of sinners. So you might say someone had to die in a way that would "kill the disease of sin" and make us immune to it. The death of animals couldn't do this. It took the death of the sinless Son of God to destroy sin and to overcome death.

Blood is needed

(22) Blood stands for life. Our natural bodies couldn't live without blood in our veins. When Jesus' blood was shed on the cross, it stood for the new life we could have by believing in him and his perfect sacrifice for us.

---

[u]*our*: Some manuscripts have "your," and others have "their." [v]*Blood was also used*: Or "There also had to be a death." [w]*blood of bulls and goats*: Some manuscripts do not have "and goats."

things in heaven must be made holy by something better. ²⁴This is why Christ did not go into a tent that had been made by humans and was only a copy of the real one. Instead, he went into heaven and is now there with God to help us.

²⁵Christ did not have to offer himself many times. He was not like a high priest who goes into the most holy place each year to offer the blood of an animal. ²⁶If he had offered himself every year, he would have suffered many times since the creation of the world. But instead, near the end of time he offered himself once and for all, so that he could be a sacrifice that does away with sin.

²⁷We die only once, and then we are judged. ²⁸So Christ died only once to take away the sins of many people. But when he comes again, it will not be to take away sin. He will come to save everyone who is waiting for him.

10 The Law of Moses is like a shadow of the good things to come. This shadow is not the good things themselves, because it cannot free people from sin by the sacrifices that are offered year after year. ²If there were worshipers who already have their sins washed away and their consciences made clear, there would not be any need to go on offering sacrifices. ³⁻⁴But the blood of bulls and goats cannot take away sins. It only reminds people of their sins from one year to the next.

⁵When Christ came into the world, he said to God,

> "Sacrifices and offerings
>   are not what you want,
> but you have given me
>   my body.
> ⁶No, you are not pleased
>   with animal sacrifices
>   and offerings for sin."

⁷Then Christ said,
> "And so, my God,
>   I have come to do
> what you want,
>   as the Scriptures say."

We needed one sacrifice for sin

(5) In Old Testament times, sacrifices were made every day. There were also special times of sacrifice, festivals held once a year. By making sacrifices the people were able to see the horrible cost of sin. But the sacrifices were also signs that pointed ahead to Jesus Christ. His one death paid the whole price of sin for believers forever. His death made the Old Testament sacrifices unnecessary.

8The Law teaches that offerings and sacrifices must be made because of sin. But why did Christ mention these things and say that God did not want them? 9Well, it was to do away with offerings and sacrifices and to replace them. That is what he meant by saying to God, "I have come to do what you want." 10So we are made holy because Christ obeyed God and offered himself once for all.

11The priests do their work each day, and they keep on offering sacrifices that can never take away sins. 12But Christ offered himself as a sacrifice that is good forever. Now he is sitting at God's right side,x 13and he will stay there until his enemies are put under his power. 14By his one sacrifice he has forever set free from sin the people he brings to God.

15The Holy Spirit also speaks of this by telling us that the Lord said,

16"When the time comes,
I will make an agreement
with them.
I will write my laws
on their minds and hearts.
17Then I will forget
about their sins
and no longer remember
their evil deeds."

18When sins are forgiven, there is no more need to offer sacrifices.

Encouragement and Warning

19My friends, the blood of Jesus gives us courage to enter the most holy place 20by a new way that leads to life! And this way takes us through the curtain that is Christ himself.

21We have a great high priest who is in charge of God's house. 22So let's come near to God with pure hearts and a confidence that comes from having faith. Let's keep our hearts pure, our consciences free from evil, and our bodies washed with clean wa-

We can enter the most holy place
(19) In Old Testament times the people could not come directly before God. The high priest alone could do this only once a year. But now, Jesus himself is our high priest. When Jesus died, the curtain that hid the most holy place was opened (see Matthew 27.51). Now we can all come into God's presence.

xright side: See the note at 1.3.

ter. 23We must hold tightly to the hope that we say is ours. After all, we can trust the one who made the agreement with us. 24We should keep on encouraging each other to be thoughtful and to do helpful things. 25Some people have gotten out of the habit of meeting for worship, but we must not do that. We should keep on encouraging each other, especially since you know that the day of the Lord's coming is getting closer.

26No sacrifices can be made for people who decide to sin after they find out about the truth. 27They are God's enemies, and all they can look forward to is a terrible judgment and a furious fire. 28If two or more witnesses accused someone of breaking the Law of Moses, that person could be put to death. 29But it is much worse to dishonor God's Son and to disgrace the blood of the promise that made us holy. And it is just as bad to insult the Holy Spirit, who shows us mercy. 30We know that God has said he will punish and take revenge. We also know that the Scriptures say the Lord will judge his people. 31It is a terrible thing to fall into the hands of the living God!

32Don't forget all the hard times you went through when you first received the light. 33Sometimes you were abused and mistreated in public, and at other times you shared in the sufferings of others. 34You were kind to people in jail. And you gladly let your possessions be taken away, because you knew you had something better, something that would last forever.

35Keep on being brave! It will bring you great rewards. 36Learn to be patient, so that you will please God and be given what he has promised. 37As the Scriptures say,

"God is coming soon!
It won't be very long.
38The people God accepts
will live because
of their faith.y

Be brave

(35) Let's not turn back, but be brave. There is only one sacrifice for sin. That is the sacrifice made by Jesus. If we turn back from him, we have no hope. God loves his Son, so we must understand how serious it is to reject Jesus after we have promised to follow him.

yThe people God accepts will live because of their faith: Or "The people God accepts because of their faith will live."

> But he is not pleased
> with anyone
> who turns back."

39We are not like those people who turn back and get destroyed. We will keep on having faith until we are saved.

The Great Faith of God's People

11 Faith makes us sure of what we hope for and gives us proof of what we cannot see. 2It was their faith that made our ancestors pleasing to God.

3Because of our faith, we know that the world was made at God's command. We also know that what can be seen was made out of what cannot be seen.

4Because Abel had faith, he offered God a better sacrifice than Cain did. God was pleased with him and his gift, and even though Abel is now dead, his faith still speaks for him.

5Enoch had faith and did not die. He pleased God, and God took him up to heaven. That's why his body was never found. 6But without faith no one can please God. We must believe that God is real and that he rewards everyone who searches for him.

7Because Noah had faith, he was warned about something that had not yet happened. He obeyed and built a boat that saved him and his family. In this way the people of the world were judged, and Noah was given the blessings that come to everyone who pleases God.

8Abraham had faith and obeyed God. He was told to go to the land that God had said would be his, and he left for a country he had never seen. 9Because Abraham had faith, he lived as a stranger in the promised land. He lived there in a tent, and so did Isaac and Jacob, who were later given the same promise. 10Abraham did this, because he was waiting for the eternal city that God had planned and built.

11Even when Sarah was too old to have children, she had faith that God would do what he had promised, and she had a son.

Faith is proof

(1) Seeing is believing, but only if we dare to believe what we see. We believe in God because the Holy Spirit makes us able to know him. That is the way faith works, by trusting what God has promised.

Where did our world come from?

(3) Some people like to think that the world just happened without any cause. It takes a lot of nerve to believe that. We know that there is a cause for everything that happens around us. Why should the world be any different? It makes sense to believe that the world was brought into being by a very powerful God.

12Her husband Abraham was almost dead, but he became the ancestor of many people. In fact, there are as many of them as there are stars in the sky or grains of sand along the beach.

13Every one of those people died. But they still had faith, even though they had not received what they had been promised. They were glad just to see these things from far away, and they agreed that they were only strangers and foreigners on this earth. 14When people talk this way, it is clear that they are looking for a place to call their own. 15If they had been talking about the land where they had once lived, they could have gone back at any time. 16But they were looking forward to a better home in heaven. That's why God was not ashamed for them to call him their God. He even built a city for them.

17-18Abraham had been promised that Isaac, his only son,z would continue his family. But when Abraham was tested, he had faith and was willing to sacrifice Isaac, 19because he was sure that God could raise people to life. This was just like getting Isaac back from death.

20Isaac had faith, and he promised blessings to Jacob and Esau. 21Later, when Jacob was about to die, he leaned on his walking stick and worshiped. Then because of his faith he blessed each of Joseph's sons. 22And right before Joseph died, he had faith that God would lead the people of Israel out of Egypt. So he told them to take his bones with them.

23Because Moses' parents had faith, they kept him hidden until he was three months old. They saw that he was a beautiful child, and they were not afraid to disobey the king's orders.a 24Then after Moses grew up, his faith made him refuse to be called Pha-

"They still had faith"
(13) This chapter includes a great "hall of fame" of faithful men and women who lived during Old Testament times. It's a very exciting story. You should read about these lives in a translation of the Old Testament. See how these believing people overcame very difficult challenges just by continuing to trust God. Sometimes they died without ever seeing all of what they had been promised, but their faith stood firm.

---

zhis only son: Although Abraham had a son by a slave woman, his son Isaac was considered his only son, because he was born as a result of God's promise to Abraham. athe king's orders: The king of Egypt ordered all Israelite baby boys to be left outside of their homes, so they would die or be killed.

raoh's grandson. 25He chose to be mistreated with God's people instead of having the good time that sin could bring for a little while. 26Moses knew that the treasures of Egypt were not as wonderful as what he would receive from suffering for the Messiah,b and he looked forward to his reward.

27Because of his faith, Moses left Egypt. Moses had seen the invisible God and was not afraid of the king's anger. 28His faith also made him celebrate Passover. He sprinkled the blood of animals on the first-born sons of the people of Israel, so that they would not be killed by the destroying angel.

29Because of their faith, the people walked through the Red Sea on dry land. But when the Egyptians tried to do it, they were drowned.

30God's people had faith, and when they had walked around the city of Jericho for seven days, its walls fell down.

31Rahab had been an immoral woman, but she had faith and welcomed the spies. So she was not killed with the people who disobeyed.

32What else can I say? There is not enough time to tell about Gideon, Barak, Samson, Jephthah, David, Samuel, and the prophets. 33Their faith helped them conquer kingdoms, and because they did right, God made promises to them. They closed the jaws of lions 34and put out raging fires and escaped from the swords of their enemies. Although they were weak, they were given the strength and power to chase foreign armies away.

35Some women received their loved ones back from death. Many of these people were tortured, but they refused to be released. They were sure that they would get a better reward when the dead are raised to life. 36Others were made fun of and beaten with whips, and some were chained in jail. 37Still others were stoned to death or sawed in twoc or killed with swords. Some had

God's reward for his people was sure

(26) God promised the people of the Old Testament that a Savior would come and die for their sins. But they never lived to see it. Abraham, Isaac, and Jacob were to be the ancestors of the Messiah. Moses would point to him. But it would take years and years to happen—with many troubles and heartaches along the way. But in Jesus we have seen the fulfillment of God's great promise. So we have no excuse for not trusting him.

Suffering may come

(35) Many who have loved God over the years have been treated very badly, even tortured. We are no better than they. We also might be called upon to suffer for Jesus. But God has never forgotten his brave believers, and he will remember us too.

---

bthe Messiah: Or "Christ." csawed in two: Some manuscripts have "tested" or "tempted."

nothing but sheep skins or goat skins to wear. They were poor, mistreated, and tortured. 38The world did not deserve these good people, who had to wander in deserts and on mountains and had to live in caves and holes in the ground.

39All of them pleased God because of their faith! But still they died without being given what had been promised. 40This was because God had something better in store for us. And he did not want them to reach the goal of their faith without us.

A Large Crowd of Witnesses

12 Such a large crowd of witnesses is all around us! So we must get rid of everything that slows us down, especially the sin that just won't let go. And we must be determined to run the race that is ahead of us. 2We must keep our eyes on Jesus, who leads us and makes our faith complete. He endured the shame of being nailed to a cross, because he knew that later on he would be glad he did. Now he is seated at the right side*d* of God's throne! 3So keep your mind on Jesus, who put up with many insults from sinners. Then you won't get discouraged and give up.

4None of you have yet been hurt*e* in your battle against sin. 5But you have forgotten that the Scriptures say to God's children,
"When the Lord punishes you,
  don't make light of it,
and when he corrects you,
  don't be discouraged.
6The Lord corrects the people
  he loves
and disciplines those
  he calls his own."

7Be patient when you are being corrected! This is how the Lord treats his children. Don't all parents correct their children? 8God corrects all of his children, and if he doesn't correct you, then you don't really belong to him. 9Our earthly fathers

Run your race for Christ
(1) A Christian is like a runner. Athletes can't follow a lifestyle of sin. Their strength would give out, their muscles would get soft, and their health would fail. Runners can't carry any extra weight in a race, because it would slow them down. Christians, too, must live so that they aren't weakened or slowed down by sin.

---

dright side: See the note at 1.3.   *ehurt*: Or "killed."

correct us, and we still respect them. Isn't it even better to be given true life by letting our spiritual Father correct us?

10Our human fathers correct us for a short time, and they do it as they think best. But God corrects us for our own good, because he wants us to be holy, as he is. 11It is never fun to be corrected. In fact, at the time it is always painful. But if we learn to obey by being corrected, we will do right and live at peace.

12Now stand up straight! Stop your knees from shaking 13and walk a straight path. Then lame people will be healed, instead of getting worse.

Warning against Turning from God

14Try to live at peace with everyone! Live a clean life. If you don't, you will never see the Lord. 15Make sure that no one misses out on God's kindness. Don't let anyone become bitter and cause trouble for the rest of you. 16Watch out for immoral and ungodly people like Esau, who sold his future blessingᶠ for only one meal. 17You know how he later wanted it back. But there was nothing he could do to change things, even though he begged his father and cried.

18You have not come to a place like Mount Sinaiᵍ that can be seen and touched. There is no flaming fire or dark cloud or storm 19or trumpet sound. The people of Israel heard a voice speak. But they begged it to stop, 20because they could not obey its commands. They were even told to kill any animal that touched the mountain. 21The sight was so frightening that Moses said he shook with fear.

22You have now come to Mount Zion and to the heavenly Jerusalem. This is the city of the living God, where thousands and

We need to be corrected
(10) Only the foolish say they never make mistakes and never need to be corrected. As parents correct children when they are wrong, God corrects us, too, as a loving father. We should be glad he does. If he didn't, we would hurt ourselves badly.

The heavenly city lasts forever
(22) All around us we see proof daily that everything in this world passes away. It must pass away if God's plan is to be carried out. It's important for this present world to disappear at last so that the everlasting world of God can take its place.

ᶠsold his future blessing: As the firstborn son, Esau had certain privileges that were known as a "birthright." ᵍa place like Mount Sinai: The Greek text has "a place," but the writer is referring to the time that the Lord spoke to the people of Israel from Mount Sinai (Exodus 19.16-25).

thousands of angels have come to celebrate. 23Here you will find all of God's dearest children,^h whose names are written in heaven. And you will find God himself, who judges everyone. Here also are the spirits of those good people who have been made perfect. 24And Jesus is here! He is the one who makes God's new agreement with us, and his sprinkled blood says much better things than the blood of Abel.ⁱ

25Make sure that you obey the one who speaks to you. The people of Israel did not escape, when they refused to obey the one who spoke to them at Mount Sinai. Do you think you can possibly escape, if you refuse to obey the one who speaks to you from heaven? 26When God spoke the first time, his voice shook only the earth. This time he has promised to shake the earth once again, and heaven too.

27The words "once again" mean that these created things will someday be shaken and removed. Then what cannot be shaken will last. 28We should be grateful that we were given a kingdom that cannot be shaken. And in this kingdom we please God by worshiping him and by showing him great honor and respect. 29Our God is like a destructive fire!

Service That Pleases God

13 Keep being concerned about each other as the Lord's followers should.

2Be sure to welcome strangers into your home. By doing this, some people have welcomed angels as guests, without even knowing it.

3Remember the Lord's people who are in jail and be concerned for them. Don't forget those who are suffering, but imagine that you are there with them.

4Have respect for marriage. Always be

Christians care about everyone

(2) Whether they are friends or strangers, all people are God's creations for whom Christ died. We owe all people our love and care even if we don't know them.

---

^h*all of God's dearest children*: The Greek text has "the gathering of the first-born children." See the note at 1.6. ⁱ*blood of Abel*: Cain and Abel were the two sons of Adam and Eve. Cain murdered Abel (Genesis 4.1-16).

faithful to your partner, because God will punish anyone who is immoral or unfaithful in marriage.

⁵Don't fall in love with money. Be satisfied with what you have. The Lord has promised that he will not leave us or desert us. ⁶That should make you feel like saying,

"The Lord helps me!
Why should I be afraid
of what people can do
to me?"

⁷Don't forget about your leaders who taught you God's message. Remember what kind of lives they lived and try to have faith like theirs.

⁸Jesus Christ never changes! He is the same yesterday, today, and forever. ⁹Don't be fooled by any kind of strange teachings. It is better to receive strength from God's kindness than to depend on certain foods. After all, these foods don't really help the people who eat them. ¹⁰But we have an altar where even the priests who serve in the place of worship have no right to eat.

¹¹After the high priest offers the blood of animals as a sin offering, the bodies of those animals are burned outside the camp. ¹²Jesus himself suffered outside the city gate, so that his blood would make people holy. ¹³That's why we should go outside the camp to Jesus and share in his disgrace. ¹⁴On this earth we don't have a city that lasts forever, but we are waiting for such a city.

¹⁵Our sacrifice is to keep offering praise to God in the name of Jesus. ¹⁶But don't forget to help others and to share your possessions with them. This too is like offering a sacrifice that pleases God.

¹⁷Obey your leaders and do what they say. They are watching over you, and they must answer to God. So don't make them sad as they do their work. Make them happy. Otherwise, they won't be able to help you at all.

¹⁸Pray for us. Our consciences are clear, and we always try to live right. ¹⁹I especially want you to pray that I can visit you again soon.

Christians are satisfied people

(5) Believers aren't looking for more than they need, and they know God will supply what they must have. So they don't worry about money. Some of us need to pray for God to help us with our complaining attitude.

Jesus is always the same

(8) As we read about his life in Matthew, Mark, Luke, and John, we should know that Jesus is still with us today. He said, "I will never leave you." As we pray, let us ask the Holy Spirit to help us realize that Jesus is always at our side. He grieves when we sin, and he wants to help us in all our troubles.

We need earthly leaders

(17) We wouldn't get far without leadership. That's why God gives us pastors, teachers, and others to guide and advise us about our Christian life. If we don't listen to the earthly leaders God gives us, then we probably won't obey God either. Just like earthly families, we need the spiritual family and the leaders of the church.

Final Prayers and Greetings

20God gives peace, and he raised our Lord Jesus Christ from death. Now Jesus is like a Great Shepherd whose blood was used to make God's eternal agreement with his flock.*j* **21**I pray that God will make you ready to obey him and that you will always be eager to do right. May Jesus help you do what pleases God. To Jesus Christ be glory forever and ever! Amen.

22My friends, I have written only a short letter to encourage you, and I beg you to pay close attention to what I have said.

23By now you surely must know that our friend Timothy is out of jail. If he gets here in time, I will bring him with me when I come to visit you.

24Please give my greetings to your leaders and to the rest of the Lord's people.

His followers from Italy send you their greetings.

25I pray that God will be kind to all of you!*k*

Faith is eager to do right
(21) To please God, we are eager to do right. We do right not so we can earn our way into heaven, but because we love God. We know Jesus has saved us, and we are grateful, so we want God to be happy. Saving faith is what makes believers so eager to please.

---

*j*whose blood was used to make God's eternal agreement with his flock: See 9.18-22.   *k*to all of you!: Some manuscripts add "Amen."

A LETTER FROM JAMES

ABOUT THIS LETTER

This is a good example of a general letter, because it is addressed to Christians scattered throughout the Roman empire. Though written as a letter, it is more like a short book of instructions for daily living.

For James faith means action! In fact, the entire book is a series of examples that show faith in action in wise and practical ways.

His advice was clear and to the point: If you are poor, don't despair! Don't give up when your faith is being tested. Don't get angry quickly. Don't favor the rich over the poor. Do good things for others. Control your tongue and desires. Surrender to God and rely on his wisdom. Resist the devil. Don't brag about what you are going to do. If you are rich, use your money to help the poor. Be patient and kind, and pray for those who need God's help.

1 From James, a servant of God and of our Lord Jesus Christ. Greetings to the twelve tribes scattered all over the world.[a]

Faith and Wisdom

²My friends, be glad, even if you have a lot of trouble. ³You know that you learn to endure by having your faith tested. ⁴But you must learn to endure everything, so that you will be completely mature and not lacking in anything.

⁵If any of you need wisdom, you should ask God, and it will be given to you. God is generous and won't correct you for asking. ⁶But when you ask for something, you must have faith and not doubt. Anyone who doubts is like an ocean wave tossed around in a storm. ⁷⁻⁸If you are that kind of person,

Who was James?

(1) This is the James we met personally in Acts 15. Matthew mentions him in his Gospel, chapter 13, verse 35. So the author of this letter is probably the half-brother of Jesus. James was the son of Joseph and Mary; but Jesus is the Son of God, born of Mary. Notice how James calls himself "a servant of God, and our Lord Jesus Christ." He humbly refuses to claim his family tie to Jesus.

---

[a]*twelve tribes scattered all over the world*: James is saying that the Lord's followers are like the tribes of Israel that were scattered everywhere by their enemies.

you can't make up your mind, and you surely can't be trusted. So don't expect the Lord to give you anything at all.

Poor People and Rich People

⁹Any of God's people who are poor should be glad that he thinks so highly of them. ¹⁰But any who are rich should be glad when God makes them humble. Rich people will disappear like wild flowers ¹¹scorched by the burning heat of the sun. The flowers lose their blossoms, and their beauty is destroyed. That is how the rich will disappear, as they go about their business.

Trials and Temptations

¹²God will bless you, if you don't give up when your faith is being tested. He will reward you with a glorious life,ᵇ just as he rewards everyone who loves him.

¹³Don't blame God when you are tempted! God cannot be tempted by evil, and he doesn't use evil to tempt others. ¹⁴We are tempted by our own desires that drag us off and trap us. ¹⁵Our desires make us sin, and when sin is finished with us, it leaves us dead.

¹⁶Don't be fooled, my dear friends. ¹⁷Every good and perfect gift comes down from the Father who created all the lights in the heavens. He is always the same and never makes dark shadows by changing. ¹⁸He wanted us to be his own special people,ᶜ and so he sent the true message to give us new birth.

Hearing and Obeying

¹⁹My dear friends, you should be quick to listen and slow to speak or to get angry.

ᵇ*a glorious life*: The Greek text has "the crown of life." In ancient times an athlete who had won a contest was rewarded with a crown of flowers as a sign of victory. ᶜ*his own special people*: The Greek text has "the first of his creatures." The Law of Moses taught that the firstborn of all animals and the first part of the harvest were special and belonged to the Lord.

It's okay to be poor
(9) Being poor isn't punishment. Jesus was a poor young man who grew up working with his hands. Not having a lot of riches helps us to keep our eyes on the things of God. The fewer possessions Christians have, the more they depend on the Lord. The rich are tempted to trust their wealth and the power it gives them over others. But "you can't take it with you."

Are you listening?
(19) Solomon wrote in one of his wise sayings that even fools are considered wise if they don't talk much. Or, as you may have heard, "Better to be quiet and be thought a fool, than to open your mouth and remove all doubt." These are strong words but good advice.

20If you are angry, you cannot do any of the good things that God wants done. 21You must stop doing anything immoral or evil. Instead be humble and accept the message that is planted in you to save you.

22Obey God's message! Don't fool yourselves by just listening to it. 23If you hear the message and don't obey it, you are like people who stare at themselves in a mirror 24and forget what they look like as soon as they leave. 25But you must never stop looking at the perfect law that sets you free. God will bless you in everything you do, if you listen and obey, and don't just hear and forget.

26If you think you are being religious, but can't control your tongue, you are fooling yourself, and everything you do is useless. 27Religion that pleases God the Father must be pure and spotless. You must help needy orphans and widows and not let this world make you evil.

Warning against Having Favorites

2 My friends, if you have faith in our glorious Lord Jesus Christ, you won't treat some people better than others. 2Suppose a rich person wearing fancy clothes and a gold ring comes to one of your meetings. And suppose a poor person dressed in worn-out clothes also comes. 3You must not give the best seat to the one in fancy clothes and tell the one who is poor to stand at the side or sit on the floor. 4That is the same as saying that some people are better than others, and you would be acting like a crooked judge.

5My dear friends, pay attention. God has given a lot of faith to the poor people in this world. He has also promised them a share in his kingdom that he will give to everyone who loves him. 6You mistreat the poor. But isn't it the rich who boss you around and drag you off to court? 7Aren't they the ones who make fun of your Lord?

8You will do all right, if you obey the

Show and tell
(25) Although much talking about religion may deceive others and ourselves, only *doing* impresses God. In his book *The Pilgrim's Progress,* John Bunyan describes a man he calls Talkative. The man bored his listeners with great talk, then came to a bad end because talking was all he could do. We ought to be able to *show* the truth as well as we tell it.

What does God expect?
(8) God doesn't expect the impossible, but love does a lot. We show true love when we are kind to people who may not be able to pay us back. Our love is really working when we care about those closest to us, such as family members. But if we say we're Christians and don't even care about our wives and husbands, then we aren't telling the truth about ourselves.

most important law^d in the Scriptures. It is the law that commands us to love others as much as we love ourselves. 9But if you treat some people better than others, you have done wrong, and the Scriptures teach that you have sinned.

10If you obey every law except one, you are still guilty of breaking them all. 11The same God who told us to be faithful in marriage also told us not to murder. So even if you are faithful in marriage, but murder someone, you still have broken God's Law.

12Speak and act like people who will be judged by the law that sets us free. 13Do this, because on the day of judgment there will be no pity for those who have not had pity on others. But even in judgment, God is merciful!^e

Faith and Works

14My friends, what good is it to say you have faith, when you don't do anything to show that you really do have faith? Can that kind of faith save you? 15If you know someone who doesn't have any clothes or food, 16you shouldn't just say, "I hope all goes well for you. I hope you will be warm and have plenty to eat." What good is it to say this, unless you do something to help? 17Faith that doesn't lead us to do good deeds is all alone and dead!

18Suppose someone disagrees and says, "It is possible to have faith without doing kind deeds."

I would answer, "Prove that you have faith without doing kind deeds, and I will prove that I have faith by doing them." 19You surely believe there is only one God. That's fine. Even demons believe this, and it makes them shake with fear.

20Does some stupid person want proof that faith without deeds is useless? 21Well,

Good deeds are important
(15) Christian faith is not just an "other-worldly" thing. Believers cannot just close their eyes to the needs and suffering of others. Our love toward God must also be love toward others, which shows itself in real acts of kindness.

^dmost important law: The Greek text has "royal law," meaning the one given by the king (that is, God).
^eBut even in judgment, God is merciful!: Or "So be merciful, and you will be shown mercy on the day of judgment."

our ancestor Abraham pleased God by putting his son Isaac on the altar to sacrifice him. 22Now you see how Abraham's faith and deeds worked together. He proved that his faith was real by what he did. 23This is what the Scriptures mean by saying, "Abraham had faith in God, and God was pleased with him." That's how Abraham became God's friend.

24You can now see that we please God by what we do and not only by what we believe. 25For example, Rahab had been an immoral woman. But she pleased God when she welcomed the spies and sent them home by another way.

26Anyone who doesn't breathe is dead, and faith that doesn't do anything is just as dead!

The Tongue

3 My friends, we should not all try to become teachers. In fact, teachers will be judged more strictly than others. 2All of us do many wrong things. But if you can control your tongue, you are mature and able to control your whole body.

3By putting a bit into the mouth of a horse, we can turn the horse in different directions. 4It takes strong winds to move a large sailing ship, but the captain uses only a small rudder to make it go in any direction. 5Our tongues are small too, and yet they brag about big things.

It takes only a spark to start a forest fire! 6The tongue is like a spark. It is an evil power that dirties the rest of the body and sets a person's entire life on fire with flames that come from hell itself. 7All kinds of animals, birds, reptiles, and sea creatures can be tamed and have been tamed. 8But our tongues get out of control. They are restless and evil, and always spreading deadly poison.

9-10My dear friends, with our tongues we speak both praises and curses. We praise our Lord and Father, and we curse people who were created to be like God, and this is not right. 11Can clean water and dirty

Real faith works

(22) Paul told us in his letter to the Romans that God accepted Abraham because he had faith. That's true. But a living faith doesn't exist all by itself, just as an acorn doesn't exist forever by itself. The acorn either becomes an oak tree, or else it dies. Abraham had faith in God and he acted on that faith. You can see people's faith by the things they do. Like the acorn, faith dies if it doesn't work. But real faith always works.

Where do we go wrong?

(6) The tongue causes a lot of mischief for such a small muscle. The tongue's bad words begin with bad thoughts. But if we check those thoughts before they become words, then the wrong words don't come out. Notice that bad words are often the beginning of bad actions. Before we speak let's ask, "Does this remark honor God, and will it really help those who hear me?"

water both flow from the same spring?
12Can a fig tree produce olives or a grapevine produce figs? Does fresh water come
from a well full of salt water?

Wisdom from Above

13Are any of you wise or sensible? Then
show it by living right and by being humble
and wise in everything you do. 14But if your
heart is full of bitter jealousy and selfishness, don't brag or lie to cover up the truth.
15That kind of wisdom doesn't come from
above. It is earthly and selfish and comes
from the devil himself. 16Whenever people
are jealous or selfish, they cause trouble
and do all sorts of cruel things. 17But the
wisdom that comes from above leads us to
be pure, friendly, gentle, sensible, kind,
helpful, genuine, and sincere. 18When
peacemakers plant seeds of peace, they will
harvest justice.

Friendship with the World

4 Why do you fight and argue with each
other? Isn't it because you are full of
selfish desires that fight to control your
body? 2You want something you don't have,
and you will do anything to get it. You will
even kill! But you still cannot get what you
want, and you won't get it by fighting and
arguing. You should pray for it. 3Yet even
when you do pray, your prayers are not
answered, because you pray just for selfish
reasons.

4You people aren't faithful to God! Don't
you know that if you love the world, you
are God's enemies? And if you decide to
be a friend of the world, you make yourself
an enemy of God. 5Do you doubt the Scriptures that say, "God truly cares about the
Spirit he has put in us"?ƒ 6In fact, God treats

What is wisdom?

(13) Wisdom isn't just the
ability to amaze people with
our clever talk. Wisdom re-
flects God's own life at work
in us. This wisdom results in
actions that bring peace and
happiness to those around
us. That which gives glory
to God and love to others
is truly wise.

*Are you "a friend of the
world"?*

(4) James surely doesn't
want us to think we shouldn't
be friendly. If a Christian is
anything, he is certainly a
friend. But James is speaking about being friendly to
the ways of the evil world
system which people have
made. Christians should
want to avoid and discourage everything that is evil
in the world.

ƒ*God truly cares about the Spirit he has put in us*: The
meaning of the Greek text is unclear, and other translations are possible, such as, "The Spirit that God put
in us truly cares."

us with even greater kindness, just as the Scriptures say,

"God opposes everyone
    who is proud,
but he is kind to everyone
    who is humble."

7Surrender to God! Resist the devil, and he will run from you. 8Come near to God, and he will come near to you. Clean up your lives, you sinners. Purify your hearts, you people who can't make up your mind. 9Be sad and sorry and weep. Stop laughing and start crying. Be gloomy instead of glad. 10Be humble in the Lord's presence, and he will honor you.

Saying Cruel Things about Others

11My friends, don't say cruel things about others! If you do, or if you condemn others, you are condemning God's Law. And if you condemn the Law, you put yourself above the Law and refuse to obey either it 12or God who gave it. God is our judge, and he can save or destroy us. What right do you have to condemn anyone?

Warning against Bragging

13You should know better than to say, "Today or tomorrow we'll go to the city. We'll do business there for a year and make a lot of money!" 14What do you know about tomorrow? How can you be so sure about your life? It is nothing more than mist that appears for only a little while before it disappears. 15You should say, "If the Lord lets us live, we will do these things." 16Yet you are stupid enough to brag, and it is wrong to be so proud. 17If you don't do what you know is right, you have sinned.

Warning to the Rich

5 You rich people should cry and weep! Terrible things are going to happen to you. 2Your treasures have already rotted, and moths have eaten your clothes. 3Your money has rusted, and the rust will be evi-

Put your life in God's hands
(13) We're asking for disappointment and misery when we imagine we can control our futures. Only God is in charge of what is to be. We do well to make wise plans, but let's give those plans to God and let him decide what is best. We may plan our way, but God actually directs our steps.

We must account for our wealth
(1) God has entrusted some of us with more money than others. That means he expects us to use our wealth for his glory and the good of others. If we hoard our money, and even cheat people out of what we owe them, that is a very bad sign about our relationship with God. He sees our greed, and religion can't cover it up.

dence against you, as it burns your body
like fire. Yet you keep on storing up wealth
in these last days. 4You refused to pay the
people who worked in your fields, and now
their unpaid wages are shouting out against
you. The Lord All-Powerful has surely
heard the cries of the workers who harvested your crops.

5While here on earth, you have thought
only of filling your own stomachs and having a good time. But now you are like fat
cattle on their way to be butchered. 6You
have condemned and murdered innocent
people, who couldn't even fight back.

Be Patient and Kind

7My friends, be patient until the Lord returns. Think of farmers who wait patiently
for the spring and summer rains to make
their valuable crops grow. 8Be patient like
those farmers and don't give up. The Lord
will soon be here! 9Don't grumble about
each other or you will be judged, and the
judge is right outside the door.

10My friends, follow the example of the
prophets who spoke for the Lord. They were
patient, even when they had to suffer.
11In fact, we praise the ones who endured
the most. You remember how patient Job
was and how the Lord finally helped him.
The Lord did this because he is so merciful
and kind.

12My friends, above all else, don't take
an oath. You must not swear by heaven or
by earth or by anything else. "Yes" or "No"
is all you need to say. If you say anything
more, you will be condemned.

13If you are having trouble, you should
pray. And if you are feeling good, you
should sing praises. 14If you are sick, ask
the church leadersg to come and pray for
you. Ask them to put olive oilh on you in
the name of the Lord. 15If you have faith
when you pray for sick people, they will

Patiently wait for Jesus
(7) The Lord will return,
maybe in our own lifetimes,
and we should wait patiently
for him. But that waiting
shouldn't be a *do-nothing*
kind of waiting, but a *do-
something* kind. The farmer
who waits for the rain to
make things grow is not just
sitting around. There is a lot
of work to be done daily.
Let's get busy. Jesus has left
us much with which to oc-
cupy ourselves until he
comes.

gchurch leaders: Or "elders" or "presbyters" or
"priests." holive oil: The Jewish people used olive oil
for healing.

get well. The Lord will heal them, and if they have sinned, he will forgive them.

16If you have sinned, you should tell each other what you have done. Then you can pray for one another and be healed. The prayer of an innocent person is powerful, and it can help a lot. 17Elijah was just as human as we are, and for three and a half years his prayers kept the rain from falling. 18But when he did pray for rain, it fell from the skies and made the crops grow.

19My friends, if any followers have wandered away from the truth, you should try to lead them back. 20If you turn sinners from the wrong way, you will save them from death, and many of their sins will be forgiven.

Prayer works

(16) We should pray for the needs of our brothers and sisters in Christ. If anyone is sick or has a problem with sin, they should share their need for healing. Then Christians can join together in prayer. God has promised to hear our prayers and honor them according to his love and wisdom.

PETER'S FIRST LETTER

ABOUT THIS LETTER

In this letter Peter has much to say about suffering. He shows how it can be a way of serving the Lord, of sharing the faith, and of being tested. The letter was written to Christians scattered all over the northern part of Asia Minor. In this part of the Roman empire many Christians had already suffered unfair treatment from people who did not believe in Jesus. And they could expect to suffer even more.

Peter was quick to offer encouragement. His letter reminds the readers that some of the Lord's followers may have to go through times of hard testing. But this should make them glad, Peter declares, because it will strengthen their faith and bring them honor on the day when Jesus Christ returns (1.6,7).

Peter reminds them that Christ suffered here on earth, and when his followers suffer for doing right they are sharing his sufferings (2.18–25; 4.12–17). In fact, Christians should expect to suffer for their faith (3.8—4.19).

But because of who God is and because of what God has done by raising Jesus Christ from death, Christians can have hope in the future. Just as Christ suffered before he received honor from God, so will Christians be tested by suffering before they receive honor when the Lord returns. Peter uses poetic language to remind his readers of what Christ has done:

Christ died once for our sins.
An innocent person died
for those who are guilty.
Christ did this
to bring you to God,
when his body
was put to death
and his spirit
was made alive. (3.18)

1 From Peter, an apostle of Jesus Christ. To God's people who are scattered like foreigners in Pontus, Galatia, Cappadocia, Asia, and Bithynia.

²God the Father decided to choose you as his people, and his Spirit has made you

Christians are chosen
(2) It's good to know that God has chosen every person who has faith in him. We did not force ourselves on God, but he selected each believer personally. Surely God will never forget any of us. We are his by his own will.

holy. You have obeyed Jesus Christ and are sprinkled with his blood.[a]

I pray that God will be kind to you and will keep on giving you peace!

A Real Reason for Hope

3Praise God, the Father of our Lord Jesus Christ. God is so good, and by raising Jesus from death, he has given us new life and a hope that lives on. 4God has something stored up for you in heaven, where it will never decay or be ruined or disappear.

5You have faith in God, whose power will protect you until the last day.[b] Then he will save you, just as he has always planned to do. 6On that day you will be glad, even if you have to go through many hard trials for a while. 7You will be like gold that has been tested in a fire. And these trials will prove that your faith is worth much more than gold that can be destroyed. They will show that you will be given praise and honor and glory when Jesus Christ returns.

8You have never seen Jesus, and you don't see him now. But still you love him and have faith in him, and no words can tell how glad and happy 9you are to be saved. That's why you have faith.

10Some prophets told how kind God would be to you, and they searched hard to find out more about the way you would be saved. 11The Spirit of Christ was in them and was telling them how Christ would suffer and would then be given great honor. So they searched to find out exactly who Christ would be and when this would happen. 12But they were told that they were serving you and not themselves. They preached to you by the power of the Holy Spirit, who was sent from heaven. And their

We love a Savior we have never seen
(8) We have never looked on the face of Jesus. In fact the Bible says very little about what he looked like on earth. Yet we can know Jesus even better than we know anyone else. Jesus is alive, and he is as close to us as it is possible to be.

[a]*sprinkled with his blood*: According to Exodus 24.3-8 the people of Israel were sprinkled with the blood of cows to show they would keep their agreement with God. Peter says that it is the blood of Jesus that seals the agreement between God and his people. See Hebrews 9.18-21. [b]*the last day*: When God will judge all people.

message was only for you, even though angels would like to know more about it.

Chosen to Live a Holy Life

13Be alert and think straight. Put all your
hope in how kind God will be to you when
Jesus Christ appears. 14Behave like obedient children. Don't let your lives be controlled by your desires, as they used to be.
15Always live as God's holy people should,
because God is the one who chose you, and
he is holy. 16That's why the Scriptures say,
"I am the holy God, and you must be holy
too."

17You say that God is your Father, but
God does not have favorites! He judges all
people by what they do. So you must honor
God while you live as strangers here on
earth. 18You were rescued from the useless
way of life that you learned from your ancestors. But you know that you were not
rescued by such things as silver or gold that
don't last forever. 19You were rescued^c by
the precious blood of Christ, that spotless
and innocent lamb. 20Christ was chosen
even before the world was created, but because of you, he did not come until these
last days. 21And when he did come, it was
to lead you to have faith in God, who raised
him from death and honored him in a glorious way. That's why you have put your faith
and hope in God.

22You obeyed the truth,^d and your souls
were made pure. Now you sincerely love
each other. But you must keep on loving
with all your heart. 23Do this because God
has given you new birth by his message
that lives on forever. 24The Scriptures say,
> "Humans wither like grass,
>   and their glory fades
>   like wild flowers.
> Grass dries up,

---

^crescued: The Greek word often, though not always,
means payment of a price to free a slave or prisoner.
^dYou obeyed the truth: Some manuscripts add "by the
power of the Spirit."

Thinking straight
(13) Before we were saved
our thoughts were crooked.
For one thing, we were always "cutting corners" to
get away from God and to
avoid confessing our sins.
We tried to cover up by satisfying ourselves with a
lifestyle that would only lead
to ruin. But we started to
think straight when we began seeing ourselves from
God's point of view. W
started thinking G
thoughts, acco   g to his
way of looking at things.

God's word never fails
(24) Today's hot news is tomorrow's waste paper, but
the word of God is just as
fresh today as the day it was
written down. The Bible
stands forever, inspired by
God himself, telling us the
truth about the past, the
present, and the future.

and flowers fall
    to the ground.
25But what the Lord has said
    will stand forever."
Our good news to you is what the Lord
has said.

A Living Stone and a Holy Nation

2 Stop being hateful! Quit trying to fool
people, and start being sincere. Don't
be jealous or say cruel things about others.
2Be like newborn babies who are thirsty
for the pure spiritual milk that will help you
grow and be saved. 3You have already
found out how good the Lord really is.

4Come to Jesus Christ. He is the living
stone that people have rejected, but which
God has chosen and highly honored. 5And
now you are living stones that are being
used to build a spiritual house. You are also
a group of holy priests, and with the help
of Jesus Christ you will offer sacrifices that
please God. 6It is just as God says in the
Scriptures,

"Look! I am placing in Zion
a choice and precious
    cornerstone.
No one who has faith
in that one
    will be disappointed."

7You are followers of the Lord, and that
stone is precious to you. But it isn't precious
to those who refuse to follow him. They are
the builders who tossed aside the stone that
turned out to be the most important one
of all. 8They disobeyed the message and
stumbled and fell over that stone, because
they were doomed.

9But you are God's chosen and special
people. You are a group of royal priests and
a holy nation. God has brought you out of
darkness into his marvelous light. Now you
must tell all the wonderful things that he
has done. The Scriptures say,

10"Once you were nobody.
    Now you are God's people.
At one time no one
    had pity on you.

Be a living stone
(4) God doesn't live in
buildings of brick and stone.
But God is building a great
living house to dwell in. That
house is made up of people
who love Christ and have
built their lives on him. Christ
is the living foundation of
that great house of God. He
wants to live in us forever.

Now God has treated you
with kindness.

Live as God's Servants Should

11Dear friends, you are foreigners and
strangers on this earth. So I beg you not
to surrender to those desires that fight
against you. 12Always let others see you behaving properly, even though they may still
accuse you of doing wrong. Then on the
day of judgment they will honor God by
telling the good things they saw you do.

13The Lord wants you to obey all human
authorities, especially the Emperor, who
rules over everyone. 14You must also obey
governors, because they are sent by the Emperor to punish criminals and to praise good
citizens. 15God wants you to silence stupid
and ignorant people by doing right. 16You
are free, but still you are God's servants,
and you must not use your freedom as an
excuse for doing wrong. 17Respect everyone
and show special love for God's people.
Honor God and respect the Emperor.

*Let's be law-abiding
citizens*
(13) Christians have less at
stake in this world than others. Our main citizenship is
in the kingdom of God. Yet
Christians should be known
as people who obey the
laws of the land they live in.
Many people who don't
know Jesus are always in
trouble with the law. But we
will give ourselves and
Christ a good name by our
law-abiding lifestyle.

The Example of Christ's Suffering

18Servants, you must obey your masters
and always show respect to them. Do this,
not only to those who are kind and thoughtful, but also to those who are cruel. 19God
will bless you, even if others treat you un-
fairly for being loyal to him. 20You don't
gain anything by being punished for some
wrong you have done. But God will bless
you, if you have to suffer for doing something good. 21After all, God chose you to
suffer as you follow in the footsteps of
Christ, who set an example by suffering for
you.

22Christ did not sin
or ever tell a lie.
23Although he was abused,
he never tried to get even.
And when he suffered,
he made no threats.
Instead, he had faith in God,
who judges fairly.

Life isn't always fair
(19) If we're not careful, we
may resent being treated
badly in the world. That very
resentment can hurt our
souls. The world isn't always
fair, but it wasn't fair to Jesus when it nailed him to a
cross. The world is just "doing its thing" when it is being
unfair to Christians. The
world is not neutral—peo-
ple either love Christ or they
hate him. That means they
must either love or hate
Christ's people too.

²⁴Christ carried the burden
of our sins.
He was nailed to the cross,
so that we would stop sinning
and start living right.
By his cuts and bruises
you are healed.
²⁵You had wandered away
like sheep.
Now you have returned
to the one
who is your shepherd
and protector.

Wives and Husbands

3 If you are a wife, you must put your husband first. Even if he opposes our message, you will win him over by what you do. No one else will have to say anything to him, ²because he will see how you honor God and live a pure life. ³Don't depend on things like fancy hairdos or gold jewelry or expensive clothes to make you look beautiful. ⁴Be beautiful in your heart by being gentle and quiet. This kind of beauty will last, and God considers it very special.

⁵Long ago those women who worshiped God and put their hope in him made themselves beautiful by putting their husbands first. ⁶For example, Sarah obeyed Abraham and called him her master. You are her true children, if you do right and don't let anything frighten you.

⁷If you are a husband, you should be thoughtful of your wife. Treat her with honor, because she is not as strong as you are, and she shares with you in the gift of life. Then nothing will stand in the way of your prayers.

Suffering for Doing Right

⁸Finally, all of you should agree and have concern and love for each other. You should also be kind and humble. ⁹Don't be hateful and insult people just because they are hateful and insult you. Instead, treat everyone

Who will be first?
(1) In these days there is a lot of quiet quarreling, and some not so quiet, about who will be given first place in society and in the home. That conflict is one way in which Satan can destroy our happiness. It's good that as Christians we don't have to worry about being first and "getting ours" in this world.

Christians can be polite
(9) Sometimes people who believe in Christ are a little rude the way they witness for him. As the saying goes, "you catch more flies with honey than with vinegar." It's nice to be important, but it's more important to be nice. Courtesy costs nothing, and it goes a long way toward gaining attention for the good news about Jesus.

with kindness. You are God's chosen ones,
and he will bless you. The Scriptures say,

10"Do you really love life?
   Do you want to be happy?
   Then stop saying cruel things
   and quit telling lies.
11Give up your evil ways
   and do right,
   as you find and follow
   the road that leads
   to peace.
12The Lord watches over
   everyone who obeys him,
   and he listens
   to their prayers.
   But he opposes everyone
   who does evil."

13Can anyone really harm you for being
eager to do good deeds? 14Even if you have
to suffer for doing good things, God will
bless you. So stop being afraid and don't
worry about what people might do. 15Honor
Christ and let him be the Lord of your life.

Always be ready to give an answer when
someone asks you about your hope. 16Give
a kind and respectful answer and keep your
conscience clear. This way you will make
people ashamed for saying bad things about
your good conduct as a follower of Christ.
17You are better off to obey God and suffer
for doing right than to suffer for doing
wrong.

18Christ died once for our sins.
   An innocent person died
   for those who are guilty.
   Christ did this
   to bring you to God,
   when his body
   was put to death
   and his spirit
   was made alive.
19Christ then preached to the spirits that
were being kept in prison. 20They had disobeyed God while Noah was building the
boat, but God had been patient with them.
Eight people went into that boat and were
brought safely through the flood.

21Those flood waters were like baptism
that now saves you. But baptism is more

Be ready to answer
(15) We shouldn't be trying to start a debate wherever we go—but we ought to be ready to answer questions. It's sad when Christians can't explain what Jesus has done for us. We need to be able to tell the good news about Jesus to another person any time we're called on to do so.

than just washing your body. It means turning to God with a clear conscience, because Jesus Christ was raised from death. 22Christ is now in heaven, where he sits at the right side*e* of God. All angels, authorities, and powers are under his control.

Being Faithful to God

4 Christ suffered here on earth. Now you must be ready to suffer as he did, because suffering shows that you have stopped sinning. 2It means you have turned from your own desires and want to obey God for the rest of your life. 3You have already lived long enough like people who don't know God. You were immoral and followed your evil desires. You went around drinking and partying and carrying on. In fact, you even worshiped disgusting idols. 4Now your former friends wonder why you have stopped running around with them, and they curse you for it. 5But they will have to answer to God, who judges the living and the dead. 6The good news has even been preached to the dead,*f* so that after they have been judged for what they have done in this life, their spirits will live with God.

7Everything will soon come to an end. So be serious and be sensible enough to pray.

8Most important of all, you must sincerely love each other, because love wipes away many sins.

9Welcome people into your home and don't grumble about it.

10Each of you has been blessed with one of God's many wonderful gifts to be used in the service of others. So use your gift well. 11If you have the gift of speaking, preach God's message. If you have the gift of helping others, do it with the strength that God supplies. Everything should be done in a way that will bring honor to God

Former friends
(1) Christians need to be ready to suffer for the sake of Jesus. Here's a warning: our enemies might be people we once counted as friends. Sometimes unsaved people are bitter when a friend turns to Jesus. They might not feel comfortable around the saved person. They might not be happy to know they are sinners who need Jesus too. But keep praying—many of them get saved later.

What is your gift?
(10) Peter repeats what Paul also says about Christian gifts. Note that Peter says these gifts are for serving others. When you use your gift from God, then people are blessed and God is honored in the world. How do you serve others with your gifts?

e right side: The place of honor and power. *f the dead*: Either people who died after becoming followers of Christ or the people of Noah's day (3.19).

because of Jesus Christ, who is glorious and powerful forever. Amen.

Suffering for Being a Christian

12Dear friends, don't be surprised or shocked that you are going through testing that is like walking through fire. 13Be glad for the chance to suffer as Christ suffered. It will prepare you for even greater happiness when he makes his glorious return.

14Count it a blessing when you suffer for being a Christian. This shows that God's glorious Spirit is with you. 15But you deserve to suffer if you are a murderer, a thief, a crook, or a busybody. 16Don't be ashamed to suffer for being a Christian. Praise God that you belong to him. 17God has already begun judging his own people. And if his judgment begins with us, imagine how terrible it will be for those who refuse to obey his message. The Scriptures say,

18"If good people barely escape,
　　what will happen to sinners
　and to others
　　who don't respect God?"

19If you suffer for obeying God, you must have complete faith in your faithful Creator and keep on doing right.

Suffer for a good reason
(14) Again we see that life isn't always fair. Christians often suffer for their goodness. The godless world is jealous of our happiness in Christ. But be sure you're not suffering because of faults in your behavior. A pure Christian life of love and kindness produces a clear conscience that can help us bear much trouble.

Helping Christian Leaders

5 Church leaders,g I am writing to encourage you. I too am a leader, as well as a witness to Christ's suffering, and I will share in his glory when it is shown to us.

2Just as shepherds watch over their sheep, you must watch over everyone God has placed in your care. Do it willingly in order to please God, and not simply because you think you must. Let it be something you want to do, instead of something you do merely to make money. 3Don't be bossy to those people who are in your care, but set an example for them. 4Then when Christ

Where has God placed you?
(1) Are you a mechanic, a student, or perhaps a teacher? Let those around you know it is your greatest pleasure to be doing what God has assigned to you. Are you a young person? Use this time of your life to learn from others who have gone before you. God looks for people who are serious and sincere workers for him.

gChurch leaders: Or "Elders" or "Presbyters" or "Priests."

the Chief Shepherd returns, you will be given a crown that will never lose its glory.

5All of you young people should obey your elders. In fact, everyone should be humble toward everyone else. The Scriptures say,

> "God opposes proud people,
> but he helps everyone
> who is humble."

6Be humble in the presence of God's mighty power, and he will honor you when the time comes. 7God cares for you, so turn all your worries over to him.

8Be on your guard and stay awake. Your enemy, the devil, is like a roaring lion, sneaking around to find someone to attack. 9But you must resist the devil and stay strong in your faith. You know that all over the world the Lord's followers are suffering just as you are. 10But God shows kindness to everyone. That's why he had Christ Jesus choose you to share in his eternal glory. You will suffer for a while, but God will make you complete, steady, strong, and firm. 11God will be in control forever! Amen.

Final Greetings

12Silvanus helped me write this short letter, and I consider him a faithful follower of the Lord. I wanted to encourage you and tell you how kind God really is, so that you will keep on having faith in him.

13Greetings from the Lord's followers in Babylon.*h* They are God's chosen ones.

Mark, who is like a son to me, sends his greetings too.

14Give each other a warm greeting. I pray that God will give peace to everyone who belongs to Christ.*i*

hBabylon: This may be a secret name for the city of Rome.   *iChrist*: Some manuscripts add "Amen."

God cares for you

(10) If you can remember at all times that *God cares*, life will not discourage you. The Lord is in charge of your life, and he knows about everything that comes your way. The key to happiness in this world is *trust*. You'll see that God always makes a way through every problem, even if the way is sometimes hard to see or a long time in coming.

PETER'S SECOND LETTER

ABOUT THIS LETTER

The writer of this letter wants the readers to know that Christians must live in a way that pleases God (1.3) and hold firmly to the truth they were given (1.12).

He warns them that false prophets and teachers had entered the Christian community and were trying to lead the Lord's followers away from the truth. But they will be punished for their evil deeds (2.1–22). When false teachers are at work, Christians must stick to their faith and be examples for others of right living. They must have understanding, self-control and patience, and they should show love for God and all people.

The readers must never forget that the Lord's return is certain, no matter what others may say (3.1–18):

Don't forget that for the Lord one day is the same as a thousand years, and a thousand years is the same as one day. The Lord isn't slow about keeping his promises, as some people think he is. In fact, God is patient, because he wants everyone to turn from sin and no one to be lost. (3.8,9)

1 From Simon Peter, a servant and an apostle of Jesus Christ. To everyone who shares with us in the privilege of believing that our God and Savior Jesus Christ will do what is just and fair.[a]

2I pray that God will be kind to you and will let you live in perfect peace! May you keep learning more and more about God and our Lord Jesus.

Living as the Lord's Followers Should

3We have everything we need to live a life that pleases God. It was all given to us by God's own power, when we learned that he had invited us to share in his wonderful goodness. 4God made great and marvelous promises, so that his nature would become

---

[a]*To everyone who . . . just and fair*: Or "To everyone whose faith in the justice and fairness of our God and Savior Jesus Christ is as precious as our own faith."

God himself lives in us
(4) Some religions are just a set of ideas. But Christians aren't merely religious people who hold certain opinions about God that they can't be sure about. God himself comes to live in us. We know him by personal experience. Because God reveals himself to us by the Holy Spirit in us, we are changed more and more to be like him.

part of us. Then we could escape our evil desires and the corrupt influences of this world.

5Do your best to improve your faith. You can do this by adding goodness, understanding, 6self-control, patience, devotion to God, 7concern for others, and love. 8If you keep growing in this way, it will show that what you know about our Lord Jesus Christ has made your lives useful and meaningful. 9But if you don't grow, you are like someone who is nearsighted or blind, and you have forgotten that your past sins are forgiven.

10My friends, you must do all you can to show that God has really chosen and selected you. If you keep on doing this, you won't stumble and fall. 11Then our Lord and Savior Jesus Christ will give you a glorious welcome into his kingdom that will last forever.

12You are holding firmly to the truth that you were given. But I am still going to remind you of these things. 13In fact, I think I should keep on reminding you until I leave this body. 14And our Lord Jesus Christ has already told me that I will soon leave it behind. 15That is why I am doing my best to make sure that each of you remembers all of this after I am gone.

The Message about the Glory of Christ

16When we told you about the power and the return of our Lord Jesus Christ, we were not telling clever stories that someone had made up. But with our own eyes we saw his true greatness. 17God, our great and wonderful Father, truly honored him by saying, "This is my own dear Son, and I am pleased with him." 18We were there with Jesus on the holy mountain and heard this voice speak from heaven.

19All of this makes us even more certain that what the prophets said is true. So you should pay close attention to their message, as you would to a lamp shining in some dark place. You must keep on paying attention until daylight comes and the morning

Follow the light
(19) Peter tells us the word of God is like a lamp in a dark place. The dark place is the world we now live in. We need that light because of the confusing messages we hear in the darkened world. God's word is the true message and the true light that leads us to the dawn of God's coming day. Then the darkness will pass away, and God's light of truth will remain.

star rises in your hearts. [20]But you need to realize that no one alone can understand any of the prophecies in the Scriptures. [21]The prophets did not think these things up on their own, but they were guided by the Spirit of God.

False Prophets and Teachers

2 Sometimes false prophets spoke to the people of Israel. False teachers will also sneak in and speak harmful lies to you. But these teachers don't really belong to the Master who paid a great price for them, and they will quickly destroy themselves. [2]Many people will follow their evil ways and cause others to tell lies about the true way. [3]They will be greedy and cheat you with smooth talk. But long ago God decided to punish them, and God does not sleep.

[4]God did not have pity on the angels that sinned. He had them tied up and thrown into the dark pits of hell until the time of judgment. [5]And during Noah's time God did not have pity on the ungodly people of the world. He destroyed them with a flood, though he did save eight people, including Noah, who preached the truth.

[6]God punished the cities of Sodom and Gomorrah[b] by burning them to ashes, and this is a warning to anyone else who wants to sin.

[7-8]Lot lived right and was greatly troubled by the terrible way those wicked people were living. He was a good man, and day after day he suffered because of the evil things he saw and heard. So the Lord rescued him. [9]This shows that the Lord knows how to rescue godly people from their sufferings and to punish evil people while they wait for the day of judgment.

[10]The Lord is especially hard on people who disobey him and don't think of anything except their own filthy desires. They are reckless and proud and are not afraid

God doesn't tolerate evil
(6) Some misguided people would like us to think their evil lifestyles are merely "different" and not evil at all. But even common sense shows that their so-called different lifestyles, including sexual immorality, cause great unhappiness and ruin people's lives. God destroyed the two cities of Sodom and Gomorrah (told of in the Old Testament book of Genesis) to show how much he hates sin.

[b]*Sodom and Gomorrah*: During the time of Abraham the Lord destroyed these cities because the people there were so evil. See Genesis 19.24.

of cursing the glorious beings in heaven.
[11]Although angels are more powerful than
these evil beings,[c] even the angels don't
dare to accuse them to the Lord.

[12]These people are no better than senseless animals that live by their feelings and
are born to be caught and killed. They speak
evil of things they don't know anything
about. But their own corrupt deeds will destroy them. [13]They have done evil, and they
will be rewarded with evil.

They think it is fun to have wild parties
during the day. They are immoral, and the
meals they eat with you are spoiled by the
shameful and selfish way they carry on.[d]
[14]All they think about is having sex with
someone else's husband or wife. There is
no end to their wicked deeds. They trick
people who are easily fooled, and their
minds are filled with greedy thoughts. But
they are headed for trouble!

[15]They have left the true road and have
gone down the wrong path by following the
example of the prophet Balaam. He was the
son of Beor and loved what he got from
being a crook. [16]But a donkey corrected him
for this evil deed. It spoke to him with a
human voice and made him stop his
foolishness.

[17]These people are like dried up water
holes and clouds blown by a windstorm.
The darkest part of hell is waiting for them.
[18]They brag out loud about their stupid nonsense. And by being vulgar and crude, they
trap people who have barely escaped from
living the wrong kind of life. [19]They promise
freedom to everyone. But they are merely
slaves of filthy living, because people are
slaves of whatever controls them.

[20]When they learned about our Lord and
Savior Jesus Christ, they escaped from the
filthy things of this world. But they are again

A speaking donkey

(15) Balaam was a strange
prophet (see the book of
Numbers in the Old Testa-
ment). The enemies of Israel
offered him money to
preach against the people
of God. When Balaam
seemed to go along with the
plan, his own donkey told
him off. It was funny but sad
that the Lord had to use a
dumb animal to speak
God's word to a foolish
prophet. Balaam is a warning to us that giving in to
evil will hurt us in the end.

---

[c]*evil beings:* Or "evil teachers."   [d]*and the meals they
eat with you are spoiled by the shameful and selfish
way they carry on:* Some manuscripts have "and the
meals they eat with you are spoiled by the shameful
way they carry on during your feasts of Christian love."

caught up and controlled by these filthy things, and now they are in worse shape than they were at first. 21They would have been better off if they had never known about the right way. Even after they knew what was right, they turned their backs on the holy commandments that they were given. 22What happened to them is just like the true saying,

"A dog will come back
    to lick up its own vomit.
A pig that has been washed
    will roll in the mud."

The Lord Will Return

3 My dear friends, this is the second letter I have written to encourage you to do some honest thinking. I don't want you to forget 2what God's prophets said would happen. You must never forget what the holy prophets taught in the past. And you must remember what the apostles told you our Lord and Savior has commanded us to do.

3But first you must realize that in the last days some people won't think about anything except their own selfish desires. They will make fun of you 4and say, "Didn't your Lord promise to come back? Yet the first leaders have already died, and the world hasn't changed a bit."

5They will say this because they want to forget that long ago the heavens and the earth were made by God's command. The earth came out of water and was made from water. 6Later it was destroyed by the waters of a mighty flood. 7But God has commanded the present heavens and earth to remain until the day of judgment. Then they will be set on fire, and ungodly people will be destroyed.

8Dear friends, don't forget that for the Lord one day is the same as a thousand years, and a thousand years is the same as one day. 9The Lord isn't slow about keeping his promises, as some people think he is. In fact, God is patient, because he wants

God has warned the world
(5) Imagine Noah building his ship as he looked for the great flood that God had promised. Think of how Noah's neighbors would have laughed at him: "When is it going to rain, Noah?" But Noah just went on building. We know that God is going to judge the world. The tragedy is that many don't take God seriously.

God has lots of time
(8) A thousand or even a million years are no time at all to God. In God's eternity time doesn't matter. He has forever to do what he plans. Therefore, we do well not to be anxious about God's timetable. But we ought to live each day as if it were our last. When all is said and done, we will be with God, and he will deal with what people have done or not done in this present age.

everyone to turn from sin and no one to be lost.

¹⁰The day of the Lord's return will surprise us like a thief. The heavens will disappear with a loud noise, and the heat will melt the whole universe.^e Then the earth and everything on it will be seen for what they are.^f

¹¹Everything will be destroyed. So you should serve and honor God by the way you live. ¹²You should look forward to the day when God judges everyone, and you should try to make it come soon.^g On that day the heavens will be destroyed by fire, and everything else will melt in the heat. ¹³But God has promised us a new heaven and a new earth, where justice will rule. We are really looking forward to that!

¹⁴My friends, while you are waiting, you should make certain that the Lord finds you pure, spotless, and living at peace. ¹⁵Don't forget that the Lord is patient because he wants people to be saved. This is also what our dear friend Paul said when he wrote you with the wisdom that God had given him. ¹⁶Paul talks about these same things in all his letters, but part of what he says is hard to understand. Some ignorant and unsteady people even destroy themselves by twisting what he said. They do the same thing with other Scriptures too.

¹⁷My dear friends, you have been warned ahead of time! So don't let the errors of evil people lead you down the wrong path and make you lose your balance. ¹⁸Let the kindness and the understanding that come from our Lord and Savior Jesus Christ help you to keep on growing. Praise Jesus now and forever! Amen.^h

---

^e*the whole universe*: Probably the sun, moon, and stars, or the elements that everything in the universe is made of. ^f*will be seen for what they are*: Some manuscripts have "will go up in flames." ^g*and you should try to make it come soon*: Or "and you should eagerly desire for that day to come." ^h*Amen*: Some manuscripts do not have "Amen."

What will God's world be like?
(13) The Lord has promised a new heaven and a new earth after the present world has passed away. Peter writes that justice will rule there. Also there will be no more sorrow, or pain, or sickness, or death. But we will live with God himself, and we will be his people. The question is, are you God's person right now?

Don't twist the Scriptures
(16) Some things in God's word are not as easy to understand as others. The important thing is to believe and obey what we do understand. As time goes by, the rest will become clear. Let the Holy Spirit reveal the truth to you as you compare one passage with another. But beware of "reading into" the Bible your own opinions.

JOHN'S FIRST LETTER

ABOUT THIS LETTER

John wants Christian believers to know that when we tell God about our sins, God will forgive us and take them away (1.9).

The true test of faith is love for each other (3.11–24). Because God is love, his people must be like him (4.1–21). For a complete victory over sin, we must not only love others, but we must believe that Jesus, the Son of God, is truly Christ, and that his death for us was real (5.1–12).

Remember:

> The Word that gives life
> was from the beginning,
> and this is the one
> our message is about. (1.1)

1 The Word that gives life
   was from the beginning,
and this is the one
   our message is about.

Our ears have heard,
   our own eyes have seen,
and our hands touched
   this Word.

²The one who gives life appeared! We saw it happen, and we are witnesses to what we have seen. Now we are telling you about this eternal life that was with the Father and appeared to us. ³We are telling you what we have seen and heard, so that you may share in this life with us. And we share in it with the Father and with his Son Jesus Christ. ⁴We are writing to tell you these things, because this makes us[a] truly happy.

John saw and touched Jesus

(1) Jesus' disciples saw and touched him when he came back from death, as the four Gospels tell us. John was not writing here about something he had only heard about. He had seen and touched Jesus, whom John calls "the Word" (see also John 1.1). We ourselves have not yet been able to see and touch the risen Lord Jesus, but we have the statements of honest witnesses who have.

Jesus shares eternal life with us

(3) John describes the risen Jesus as the one who has eternal life. Jesus had overcome death and was alive forever with a glory that must have been wonderful

[a]*us*: Some manuscripts have "you."

God Is Light

5Jesus told us that God is light and doesn't have any darkness in him. Now we are telling you.

6If we say that we share in life with God and keep on living in the dark, we are lying and are not living by the truth. 7But if we live in the light, as God does, we share in life with each other. And the blood of his Son Jesus washes all our sins away. 8If we say that we have not sinned, we are fooling ourselves, and the truth is not in our hearts. 9But if we tell God about our sins, he can always be trusted to forgive us and take our sins away.

10If we say that we have not sinned, we make God a liar, and his message is not in our hearts.b

Christ Helps Us

2 My children, I am writing this so that you will not sin. But if you do sin, Jesus Christ always does the right thing, and he will speak to the Father for us. 2Christ is the sacrifice that takes away our sins and the sins of all the world's people.

3When we obey God, we are sure that we know him. 4But if we claim to know him and don't obey him, we are lying and the truth is not in our hearts. 5We truly love God only when we obey him as we should, and then we know that we belong to him. 6If we say we are his, we must follow the example of Christ.

The New Commandment

7My dear friends, I am not writing to give you a new commandment. It is the same one you were first given, and it is the message you heard. 8But it really is a new commandment, and you know its true meaning, just as Christ does. You can see the darkness fading away and the true light already shining.

band his message is not in our hearts: Or "because we have not accepted his message."

to see. But remember, Jesus is now able to give us eternal life too. We believe in him and are saved, and the Holy Spirit dwells in us. Believers have eternal life straight from God himself.

Let's live in God's light
(7) Living in constant darkness would be a gloomy existence. In fact, we would die very soon, because we need light to live. John tells us to live in God's own light. To live in God's light is to have life that lasts forever and can't fade away. God's light is the truth that sets us free from our sins.

Jesus prays for us
(1) If we truly love the Lord Jesus, we also hate our sins. But we still sin at times. When that happens, it's important not to try to hide or forget our sins. We should bring them to Jesus, and he will ask his Father to forgive us. The best thing is to love Jesus so much, and to be so filled with the Holy Spirit, that sin will not control our thoughts and actions.

The true light is shining
(8) It was a dark time before Jesus came. People had very little hope for the future. But now that Jesus has come, we can have great hope and joy. Jesus has

⁹If we claim to be in the light and hate someone, we are still in the dark. ¹⁰But if we love others, we are in the light, and we don't cause problems for them.c ¹¹If we hate others, we are living and walking in the dark. We don't know where we are going, because we can't see in the dark.

¹²Children, I am writing you,
because your sins
have been forgiven
in the name of Christ.
¹³Parents, I am writing you,
because you have known
the one who was there
from the beginning.
Young people, I am writing you,
because you have defeated
the evil one.
¹⁴Children, I am writing you,
because you have known
the Father.
Parents, I am writing you,
because you have known
the one who was there
from the beginning.
Young people, I am writing you,
because you are strong.
God's message is firm
in your hearts,
and you have defeated
the evil one.

¹⁵Don't love the world or anything that belongs to the world. If you love the world, you cannot love the Father. ¹⁶Our foolish pride comes from this world, and so do our selfish desires and our desire to have everything we see. None of this comes from the Father. ¹⁷The world and the desires it causes are disappearing. But if we obey God, we will live forever.

The Enemy of Christ

¹⁸Children, this is the last hour. You heard that the enemy of Christ would ap-

opened heaven's doors. Now eternal life and light come streaming toward us, and the darkness is past.

Christ's enemy is coming
(18) Sometimes this person is called "the man of sin" or "the Antichrist." John also calls him "the beast" in Revelation 17.11. He will some day arise in the world to defy God's authority, and he will torment God's people. But in the end he will be destroyed (Revelation 20.10).

---

cand we don't cause problems for them: Or "and we can see anything that might make us fall."

pear at this time, and many of Christ's enemies have already appeared. So we know
that the last hour is here. [19]These people
came from our own group, yet they were
not part of us. If they had been part of us,
they would have stayed with us. But they
left, which proves that they did not belong
to our group.

[20]Christ, the Holy One,[d] has blessed[e] you,
and now all of you understand.[f] [21]I did not
need to write you about the truth, since you
already know it. You also know that liars
do not belong to the truth. [22]And a liar is
anyone who says that Jesus isn't truly
Christ. Anyone who says this is an enemy
of Christ and rejects both the Father and
the Son. [23]If we reject the Son, we reject
the Father. But if we say that we accept
the Son, we have the Father. [24]Keep thinking about the message you first heard, and
you will always be one in your heart with
the Son and with the Father. [25]The Son[g]
has promised us[h] eternal life.

[26]I am writing to warn you about those
people who are misleading you. [27]But Christ
has blessed you with the Holy Spirit.[i] Now
the Spirit stays in you, and you don't need
any teachers. The Spirit is truthful and
teaches you everything. So stay one in your
heart with Christ, just as the Spirit has
taught you to do.

The Holy Spirit teaches us
(27) We are never alone.
The Holy Spirit is the real
presence of God who
dwells in us when we have
put our trust in Jesus. That
same Spirit continually comforts us, reminding us that
we will belong to Christ forever. The Holy Spirit also
speaks God's truth to us as
we read the Scriptures.

[d]Christ, the Holy One: The Greek text has "the Holy
One" which may refer either to Christ or to God the
Father. [e]blessed: This translates a word which means
"to pour olive oil on (someone's head)." In Old Testament times it was the custom to pour olive oil on a
person's head when that person was chosen to be a
priest or a king. Here the meaning is not clear. It may
refer to the ceremony of pouring olive oil on the followers of the Lord right before they were baptized or it
may refer to the gift of the Holy Spirit which they were
given at baptism (see verse 27). [f]now all of you understand: Some manuscripts have "you understand all
things." [g]The Son: The Greek text has "he" and may
refer to God the Father. [h]us: Some manuscripts have
"you." [i]Christ has blessed you with the Holy Spirit:
The Greek text has "You received a pouring on of olive
oil from him" (see verse 20). The "pouring on of olive
oil" is here taken to refer to the gift of the Holy Spirit,
and "he" may refer either to Christ or to the Father.

Children of God

28Children, stay one in your hearts with Christ. Then when he returns, we will have confidence and won't have to hide in shame. 29You know that Christ always does right and that everyone who does right is a child of God.

3 Think how much the Father loves us. He loves us so much that he lets us be called his children, as we truly are. But since the people of this world did not know who Christ[j] is, they don't know who we are. 2My dear friends, we are already God's children, though what we will be has not yet been seen. But we do know that when Christ returns, we will be like him, because we will see him as he truly is. 3This hope makes us keep ourselves holy, just as Christ[k] is holy.

4Everyone who sins breaks God's law, because sin is the same as breaking God's law. 5You know that Christ came to take away sins. He isn't sinful, 6and people who stay one in their hearts with him won't keep on sinning. If they do keep on sinning, they don't know Christ, and they have never seen him.

7Children, don't be fooled. Anyone who does right is good, just like Christ himself. 8Anyone who keeps on sinning belongs to the devil. He has sinned from the beginning, but the Son of God came to destroy all that he has done. 9God's children cannot keep on being sinful. His life-giving power[l] lives in them and makes them his children, so that they cannot keep on sinning. 10You can tell God's children from the devil's children, because those who belong to the devil refuse to do right or to love each other.

Love Each Other

11From the beginning you were told that we must love each other. 12Don't be like

We will be like Jesus

(2) Have you watched a leafless tree in the springtime? It looks dry and dead. Then the branches begin to send out buds, and we begin to hope that the tree will live again. One morning we get up, and there the tree is covered with beautiful leaves. It's all new. One day we, too, will wake up in God's morning, and we will bloom with new life from above.

When believers sin

(9) Believers do not keep living in sin. Does this mean that we are not saved any more if we sin? No, we are still saved, and God will forgive us when we ask him. But for those who have faith, sin is no longer a way of life. When we sin, we feel bad, and we can't wait to get things right with God again. That includes asking forgiveness from someone we might have hurt.

[j]Christ: The Greek text has "he" and may refer to God.
[k]Christ: The Greek text has "that one" and may refer to God.   [l]His life-giving power: The Greek text has "his seed."

Cain, who belonged to the devil and murdered his own brother. Why did he murder him? He did it because his brother was good, and he was evil. 13My friends, don't be surprised if the people of this world hate you. 14Our love for each other proves that we have gone from death to life. But if you don't love each other, you are still under the power of death.

15If you hate each other, you are murderers, and we know that murderers do not have eternal life. 16We know what love is because Jesus gave his life for us. That is why we must give our lives for each other. 17If we have all we need and see one of our own people in need, we must have pity on that person, or else we cannot say we love God. 18Children, you show love for others by truly helping them, and not merely by talking about it.

19When we love others, we know that we belong to the truth, and we feel at ease in the presence of God. 20But even if we don't feel at ease, God is greater than our feelings, and he knows everything. 21Dear friends, if we feel at ease in the presence of God, we will have the courage to come near to him. 22He will give us whatever we ask, because we obey him and do what pleases him. 23God wants us to have faith in his Son Jesus Christ and to love each other. This is also what Jesus taught us to do. 24If we obey God's commandments, we will stay one in our hearts with him, and he will stay one with us. The Spirit that he has given us is proof that we are one with him.

God Is Love

4 Dear friends, don't believe everyone who claims to have the Spirit of God. Test them all to find out if they really do come from God. Many false prophets have already gone out into the world, 2and you can know which ones come from God. His Spirit says that Jesus Christ had a truly human body. 3But when someone does not say this about Jesus, you know that person has

The importance of love
(19) Joy, peace, and patience are kinds of goodness too. But love is the kind of goodness that gives life. Hatred brings about death. Love is shown by the way we care. Even plants and animals live well when we care for them. But most of all, people need love, or their lives aren't worth living. God's love brings life, and believers share God's love with others.

Remember who Jesus is
(3) After Jesus went back to heaven, some people in New Testament times were saying that Jesus was really like a ghost that had no body. They said this because they wrongly believed that any physical body always has to be evil. Their opinion seemed very religious to them, but Jesus could not have died for our sins unless he had a body that could die.

a spirit that does not come from God and is the enemy of Christ. You knew that this enemy was coming into the world and now is already here.

4Children, you belong to God, and you have defeated these enemies. God's Spirit*m* is in you and is more powerful than the one that is in the world. 5These enemies belong to this world, and the world listens to them, because they speak its language. 6We belong to God, and everyone who knows God will listen to us. But the people who don't know God won't listen to us. That's how we can tell the Spirit that speaks the truth from the one that tells lies.

7My dear friends, we must love each other. Love comes from God, and when we love each other, it shows that we have been given new life. We are now God's children, and we know him. 8God is love, and anyone who doesn't love others has never known him. 9God showed his love for us when he sent his only Son into the world to give us life. 10Real love is not our love for God, but his love for us. God sent his Son to be the sacrifice by which our sins are forgiven. 11Dear friends, since God loved us this much, we must love each other.

12No one has ever seen God. But if we love each other, God lives in us, and his love is truly in our hearts.

13God has given us his Spirit. That is how we know that we are one with him, just as he is one with us. 14God sent his Son to be the Savior of the world. We saw his Son and are now telling others about him. 15God stays one with everyone who openly says that Jesus is the Son of God. That's how we stay one with God 16and are sure that God loves us.

God is love. If we keep on loving others, we will stay one in our hearts with God, and he will stay one with us. 17If we truly love others and live as Christ did in this world, we won't be worried about the day of judgment. 18A real love for others will

How does true love happen?
(11) One of the greatest things about God is love, and all love flows from him. When you meet people who are full of hate, it is because they have never known or accepted love for themselves. When God's love is poured into us, then our response is to love him and to love others.

---

*m*God's Spirit: The Greek text has "he" and may refer to the Spirit or to God or to Jesus.

chase those worries away. The thought of being punished is what makes us afraid. It shows that we have not really learned to love.

19We love because God loved us first. 20But if we say we love God and don't love each other, we are liars. We cannot see God. So how can we love God, if we don't love the people we can see? 21The two commandments that God has given us are: "Love God and love each other!"

Victory over the World

5 If we believe that Jesus is truly Christ, we are God's children. Everyone who loves the Father will also love his children. 2If we love and obey God, we know that we will love his children. 3We show our love for God by obeying his commandments, and they are not hard to follow.

4Every child of God can defeat the world, and our faith is what gives us this victory. 5No one can defeat the world without having faith in Jesus as the Son of God.

Who Jesus Is

6Water and blood came out from the side of Jesus Christ. It was not just water, but water and blood.n The Spirit tells about this, because the Spirit is truthful. 7In fact, there are three who tell about it. 8They are the Spirit, the water, and the blood, and they all agree.

9We believe what people tell us. But we can trust what God says even more, and God is the one who has spoken about his Son. 10If we have faith in God's Son, we have believed what God has said. But if we

Why we love God

(1) We are not naturally loving people—we are born sinners. But God loves us first, and then we are able to love him. God loved us by creating us. Then God gave his Son to die for us and save us from our sinful selves. His love gives us eternal life, which sin cannot destroy. It's sad that there are still so many people who fear God and wish he didn't exist. God loves the world and wants everyone to come back to him.

nWater and blood came out from the side of Jesus Christ. It was not just water, but water and blood: See John 19.34. It is also possible to translate, "Jesus Christ came by the water of baptism and by the blood of his death! He was not only baptized, but he bled and died." The purpose of the verse is to tell that Jesus was truly human and that he really died.

don't believe what God has said about his Son, it is the same as calling God a liar. 11God has also said that he gave us eternal life and that this life comes to us from his Son. 12And so, if we have God's Son, we have this life. But if we don't have the Son, we don't have this life.

Knowing about Eternal Life

13All of you have faith in the Son of God, and I have written to let you know that you have eternal life. 14We are certain that God will hear our prayers when we ask for what pleases him. 15And if we know that God listens when we pray, we are sure that our prayers have already been answered.

16Suppose you see one of our people commit a sin that is not a deadly sin. You can pray, and that person will be given eternal life. But the sin must not be one that is deadly. 17Everything that is wrong is sin, but not all sins are deadly.

18We are sure that God's children do not keep on sinning. God's own Son protects them, and the devil cannot harm them.

19We are certain that we come from God and that the rest of the world is under the power of the devil.

20We know that Jesus Christ the Son of God has come and has shown us the true God. And because of Jesus, we now belong to the true God who gives eternal life.

21Children, you must stay away from idols.

The Son is the difference
(12) Having eternal life or not having it depends on what we believe about Jesus. Some people say they believe in God, but they try to make Jesus into a "great teacher" instead of God's Son. It doesn't work that way. We are saved by believing that Jesus is the Son of God who died and rose again, who alone has the authority to forgive sins. Rejecting him is not only foolish, it's deadly.

Under the devil's power
(19) In this age, we live in a world over which the devil has power. It won't always be that way. Jesus will return and claim the earth for himself. But for now, the devil has power, and we can see the results all around us.

JOHN'S SECOND LETTER

ABOUT THIS LETTER

John writes again about the importance of love in a Christian's life. He points out that truth and love must go together. We must also believe that Christ was truly human, and we must love each other.

¹From the church leader.ᵃ

To a very special woman and her children.ᵇ I truly love all of you, and so does everyone else who knows the truth. ²We love you because the truth is now in our hearts, and it will be there forever.

³I pray that God the Father and Jesus Christ his Son will be kind and merciful to us! May they give us peace and truth and love.

Truth and Love

⁴I was very glad to learn that some of your children are obeying the truth, as the Father told us to do. ⁵Dear friend, I am not writing to tell you and your children to do something you have not done before. I am writing to tell you to love each other, which is the first thing you were told to do. ⁶Love means that we do what God tells us. And from the beginning, he told you to love him.

⁷Many liars have gone out into the world. These deceitful liars are saying that Jesus Christ did not have a truly human body. But they are liars and the enemies of Christ. ⁸So be sure not to lose what weᶜ have

Who was this "special woman"?

(1) It could be that the "woman" was really a congregation of God's people in a certain area. So it would be John's loving way of speaking to the church. Notice that he says, "Some of your children are obeying the truth." All in that church might not have been living faithfully. They might not have been doing as God commanded.

The big lie

(7) As in his first letter, John writes against the false teaching that said that although Jesus came, he didn't have a real body. That was the devil's clever way of attacking the good news that Jesus died for our sins. A spirit without a body wouldn't be able to die.

ᵃchurch leader: Or "elder" or "presbyter" or "priest."
ᵇvery special woman and her children: A group of the Lord's followers who met together for worship. "The children of your . . . sister" (verse 13) is another group of followers. "Very special" (here and verse 13) probably means "chosen (by the Lord)." ᶜwe: Some manuscripts have "you."

worked for. If you do, you won't be given your full reward. 9Don't keep changing what you were taught about Christ, or else God will no longer be with you. But if you hold firmly to what you were taught, both the Father and the Son will be with you. 10If people won't agree to this teaching, don't welcome them into your home or even greet them. 11Greeting them is the same as taking part in their evil deeds.

Final Greetings

12I have much more to tell you, but I don't want to write it with pen and ink. I want to come and talk to you in person, because that will make us*d* really happy.

13Greetings from the children of your very special sister.*e*

---

*d*us: Some manuscripts have "you." *e*sister: See the note at verse 1.

JOHN'S THIRD LETTER

ABOUT THIS LETTER

In this letter the writer reminds Christian readers that they should help support those who go to other parts of the world to tell others about the Lord. The letter is written to an important church member named Gaius, who had been very helpful to Christians who traveled around and preached the good news.

A QUICK LOOK AT THIS LETTER

1. Greetings to Gaius (1–4)
2. The Importance of Working Together (5–12)
3. Final Greetings   (13–15)

1From the church leader.*a*
To my dear friend Gaius.

I love you because we follow the truth, 2dear friend, and I pray that all goes well for you. I hope that you are as strong in body, as I know you are in spirit. 3It makes me very happy when the Lord's followers come by and speak openly of how you obey the truth. 4Nothing brings me greater happiness than to hear that my children*b* are obeying the truth.

Working Together

5Dear friend, you have always been faithful in helping other followers of the Lord, even the ones you didn't know before. 6They have told the church about your love. They say you were good enough to welcome them and to send them on their mission in a way that God's servants deserve. 7When they left to tell others about the Lord, they decided not to accept help from anyone who was not a follower. 8We must support people like them, so that we can take part in what they are doing to spread the truth.

9I wrote to the church. But Diotrephes likes to be the number-one leader, and he won't pay any attention to us. 10So if I come,

One well spoken of
(3) Gaius had a valuable treasure called a good reputation. People told of his obedience to God's truth. It's good to be known for loving God and doing his will. It's not that we want glory for ourselves, but for the Lord Jesus and what he has done.

There is only one "number one"
(9) God is number one. Poor Diotrephes (pronounced dye-AH-tra-fees) thought his purpose in life was to get ahead of everyone else. You meet a lot of people like this. Often they just get discouraged and quit. The main thing is to remember who God is, and that we are his servants. God doesn't need more bosses, he needs more workers.

---

*a*church leader: Or "elder" or "presbyter" or "priest."
*b*children: Probably persons that the leader had led to be followers of the Lord.

I will remind him of how he has been attacking us with gossip. Not only has he been doing this, but he refuses to welcome any of the Lord's followers who come by. And when other church members want to welcome them, he puts them out of the church.

11Dear friend, don't copy the evil deeds of others! Follow the example of people who do kind deeds. They are God's children, but those who are always doing evil have never seen God.

12Everyone speaks well of Demetrius, and so does the true message that he teaches. I also speak well of him, and you know what I say is true.

Final Greetings

13I have much more to say to you, but I don't want to write it with pen and ink. 14I hope to see you soon, and then we can talk in person.

15I pray that God will bless you with peace!

Your friends send their greetings. Please give a personal greeting to each of our friends.

Be a Demetrius
(12) Pronounce his name de-MEE-tree-us. You can just imagine how different he was from Diotrephes. Demetrius loved the truth, and he was everybody's friend. People knew they could trust him to show them the path of life and help solve their problems. He was a good and faithful teacher.

A LETTER FROM JUDE

ABOUT THIS LETTER

Jude has much to say about false teachers. They are evil! God will punish them, and Christians should not follow their teaching or imitate the way they live.

Jude ends with a beautiful prayer-like blessing:

Offer praise to God our Savior because of our Lord Jesus Christ! Only God can keep you from falling and make you pure and joyful in his glorious presence. Before time began and now and forevermore, God is worthy of glory, honor, power, and authority. Amen. (24,25)

1From Jude, a servant of Jesus Christ and the brother of James.

To all who are chosen and loved by God the Father and are kept safe by Jesus Christ.

2I pray that God will greatly bless you with kindness, peace, and love!

False Teachers

3My dear friends, I really wanted to write you about God's saving power at work in our lives. But instead, I must write and ask you to defend the faith that God has once for all given to his people. 4Some godless people have sneaked in among us and are saying, "God is kind, and so it is all right to be immoral." They even deny that we must obey Jesus Christ as our only Master and Lord. But long ago the Scriptures warned that these godless people were doomed.

5Don't forget what happened to those people the Lord rescued from Egypt. Some of them did not have faith, and he destroyed them. 6You also know about the angels[a] who didn't do their work and left their proper places. God chained them with ever-

Know God's enemies

(4) Jude describes in great detail the enemies of the truth. They live loose lives and they disobey Christ. They laugh at authority. They let their desires run their lives. You can see how believers must be different from the crowd. Our lives should reflect the beauty of Jesus, so others in this sinful world might also be saved.

[a]*angels*: This may refer to the angels who liked the women on earth so much that they came down and married them (Genesis 6.2).

lasting chains and is now keeping them in dark pits until the great day of judgment. 7We should also be warned by what happened to the cities of Sodom and Gomorrah[b] and the nearby towns. Their people became immoral and did all sorts of sexual sins. Then God made an example of them and punished them with eternal fire.

8The people I am talking about are behaving just like those dreamers who destroyed their own bodies. They reject all authority and insult angels. 9Even Michael, the chief angel, didn't dare to insult the devil, when the two of them were arguing about the body of Moses.[c] All Michael said was, "The Lord will punish you!"

10But these people insult powers they don't know anything about. They are like senseless animals that end up getting destroyed, because they live only by their feelings. 11Now they are in for real trouble. They have followed Cain's example[d] and have made the same mistake that Balaam[e] did by caring only for money. They have also rebelled against God, just as Korah did.[f] Because of all this, they will be destroyed.

12These people are filthy minded, and because of their shameful and selfish actions they spoil the meals you eat together. They are like clouds blown along by the wind, but never bringing any rain. They are like leafless trees, uprooted and dead, and unable to produce fruit. 13Their shameful deeds show up like foam on wild ocean waves. They are like wandering stars forever doomed to the darkest pits of hell.

---

[b]*Sodom and Gomorrah*: During the time of Abraham the Lord destroyed these cities because the people there were so evil. [c]*Michael . . . the body of Moses*: This refers to what was said in an ancient Jewish book about Moses. [d]*Cain's example*: Cain murdered his brother Abel. [e]*Balaam*: According to the biblical account, Balaam refused to curse the people of Israel for profit (Numbers 22.18; 24.13), though he led them to be unfaithful to the Lord (Numbers 25.1-3; 31.16). But by New Testament times, some Jewish teachers taught that Balaam was greedy and did accept money to curse them. [f]*just as Korah did*: Together with Dathan and Abiram, Korah led a rebellion against Moses and Aaron (Numbers 16.1-35; 26.9, 10).

14Enoch was the seventh person after Adam, and he was talking about these people when he said:

Look! The Lord is coming with thousands and thousands of holy angels 15to judge everyone. He will punish all those ungodly people for all the evil things they have done. The Lord will surely punish those ungodly sinners for every evil thing they have ever said about him.

16These people grumble and complain and live by their own selfish desires. They brag about themselves and flatter others to get what they want.

More Warnings

17My dear friends, remember the warning you were given by the apostles of our Lord Jesus. 18They told you that near the end of time, selfish and godless people would start making fun of God. 19And now these people are already making you turn against each other. They think only about this life, and they don't have God's Spirit.

20Dear friends, keep building on the foundation of your most holy faith, as the Holy Spirit helps you to pray. 21And keep in step with God's love, as you wait for our Lord Jesus Christ to show how kind he is by giving you eternal life. 22Be helpful to*g* all who may have doubts. 23Rescue any who need to be saved, as you would rescue someone from a fire. Then with fear in your own hearts, have mercy on everyone who needs it. But hate even the clothes of those who have been made dirty by their filthy deeds.

Final Prayer

24-25Offer praise to God our Savior because of our Lord Jesus Christ! Only God can keep you from falling and make you pure and joyful in his glorious presence. Before time began and now and forevermore, God is worthy of glory, honor, power, and authority. Amen.

gBe helpful to: Some manuscripts have "Correct."

Stuck in this world
(16) Jude writes that while God's enemies care little for God, they care a great deal about this world and its things. Their whole life seems devoted to pleasure. They flatter and "wheel and deal" to get what they want, and they are miserable when they don't get it. Of course, they are never satisfied. How sad. If these people had Jesus they would have everything that is really valuable.

A good prayer to learn
(24) Jude's prayer contains the great truths of our faith. God is our Savior by his Son, our Lord Jesus Christ. He keeps us from falling back into our sinful ways and brings us at last to himself. This is the eternal God, and he deserves all glory, honor, power, and authority. He should be the very center of our lives.

REVELATION

ABOUT THIS BOOK

This book tells what John had seen in a vision about God's message and about what Jesus Christ had said and done (1.2). The message has three main parts: (1) There are evil forces at work in the world, and Christians may have to suffer and die; (2) Jesus is Lord, and he will conquer all people and powers who oppose God; and (3) God has wonderful rewards in store for his faithful people, who remain faithful to him, especially for those who lose their lives in his service.

This was a powerful message of hope for those early Christians who had to suffer or die for their faith. In this book they learned that, in spite of the cruel power of the Roman empire, the Lamb of God would win the final victory. And this gave them the courage to be faithful.

Because this book is so full of visions that use ideas and word pictures from the Old Testament, it was like a book with secret messages for the early Christians. The book could be passed around and be understood by Christians, but an official of the Roman empire would not be able to understand it. For example, when the fall of Babylon is described (chapter 18), the early Christians knew that this pointed to the fall of the Roman empire. This knowledge gave them hope.

At the beginning of this book there are seven letters to seven churches. These letters show what different groups of the Lord's followers will do in times of persecution (2.1—3.22).

The author uses many powerful images to describe God's power and judgment. The vision of God's throne (4.1–11) and of the scroll and the Lamb (5.1–14) show that God and Christ are in control of all human and supernatural events. Opening seven seals (6.1—8.5), blowing the seven trumpets (8.6—11.19), and emptying the seven bowls (16.1–21) are among the visions that show God's fierce judgment on the world.

After the suffering has ended, God's faithful people will receive the greatest blessing of all:

God's home is now with his people. He will live with them, and they will be his own. Yes, God will make his home among his people. He will wipe all tears from their eyes, and there will be no more death, suffering, crying, or pain. These things of the past are gone forever. (21.3,4)

A QUICK LOOK AT THIS BOOK

1 This is what God showed to Jesus Christ, so that he could tell his servants what must happen soon. Christ then sent his angel with the message to his servant John. 2And John told everything that he had seen about God's message and about what Jesus Christ had said and done.

3God will bless everyone who reads this prophecy to others,*a* and he will bless everyone who hears and obeys it. The time is almost here.

4From John to the seven churches in Asia.*b*

I pray that you
　　will be blessed
with kindness and peace
from God, who is and was
　　and is coming.
May you receive
　　kindness and peace
from the seven spirits
　　before the throne of God.
5May kindness and peace
　　be yours
from Jesus Christ,
　　the faithful witness.

Jesus was the first
　　to conquer death,
and he is the ruler
　　of all earthly kings.
Christ loves us,
　　and by his blood
he set us free
　　from our sins.
6He lets us rule as kings
and serve God his Father
　　as priests.
To him be glory and power
　　forever and ever! Amen.
7Look! He is coming
　　with the clouds.
Everyone will see him,

You really ought to read this book

(3) You won't understand all of this amazing book, but you will get a look behind the scenes at God's great plans for the future. This reading will be a happy experience if you are trusting in Jesus and watching for his return. John writes, "The time is almost here." The time until Jesus comes could be very short. We ought to pay attention to what God has to say about the last days of the society we live in.

awho reads this prophecy to others: A public reading, in a worship service.　*bAsia*: The section 1.4—3.22 is in the form of a letter. Asia was in the eastern part of the Roman empire and is present day Turkey.

even the ones who stuck
    a sword through him.
All people on earth
    will weep because of him.
        Yes, it will happen! Amen.

⁸The Lord God says, "I am Alpha and Omega,ᶜ the one who is and was and is coming. I am God All-Powerful!"

A Vision of the Risen Lord

⁹I am John, a follower together with all of you. We all suffer because Jesus is our king, but he gives us the strength to endure. I was sent to Patmos Island,ᵈ because I had preached God's message and had told about Jesus. ¹⁰On the Lord's dayᵉ the Spirit took control of me, and behind me I heard a loud voice that sounded like a trumpet. ¹¹The voice said, "Write in a book what you see. Then send it to the seven churches in Ephesus, Smyrna, Pergamum, Thyatira, Sardis, Philadelphia, and Laodicea."ᶠ

¹²When I turned to see who was speaking to me, I saw seven gold lampstands. ¹³There with the lampstands was someone who seemed to be the Son of Man.ᵍ He was wearing a robe that reached down to his feet, and a gold cloth was wrapped around his chest. ¹⁴His head and his hair were white as wool or snow, and his eyes looked like flames of fire. ¹⁵His feet were glowing like bronze being heated in a furnace, and his voice sounded like the roar of a waterfall. ¹⁶He held seven stars in his right hand, and a sharp double-edged sword was coming from his mouth. His face was shining as bright as the sun at noon.

¹⁷When I saw him, I fell at his feet like a dead person. But he put his right hand on me and said:

God is eternal
(8) These words, a way of saying "the beginning and the end" in Greek, tell us that the Lord Jesus Christ was the One who brought in the beginning of time and will bring about the end of time. In fact Christ himself is God the Creator of time (see Colossians 1.16). Humans should remember that all of history is in God's hands. He started it and he will end it when he is ready.

Jesus showed his real glory
(14) In this book we see Jesus Christ as he really is. During his short time on earth the Son of God humbled himself as a servant and went about doing good. Then he died like a criminal on a cross. But he rose from death and is now back where he came from, in heaven. John got to see the Lord Jesus in his real glory.

ᶜ*Alpha and Omega*: The first and last letters of the Greek alphabet, which sometimes mean "first" and "last." ᵈ*Patmos Island*: A small island where prisoners were sometimes kept by the Romans. ᵉ*Lord's day*: Sunday, the day when Jesus was raised from death, and when Christians worship. ᶠ*Ephesus . . . Laodicea*: Ephesus was in the center with the six other cities forming a half-circle around it. ᵍ*Son of Man*: That is, Jesus.

Don't be afraid! I am the first, the last, [18]and the living one. I died, but now I am alive forevermore, and I have the keys to death and the world of the dead.[h] [19]Write what you have seen and what is and what will happen after these things. [20]I will explain the mystery of the seven stars that you saw at my right side and the seven gold lampstands. The seven stars are the angels [i] of the seven churches, and the lampstands are the seven churches.

The Letter to Ephesus

2 This is what you must write to the angel of the church in Ephesus:

I am the one who holds the seven stars in my right hand, and I walk among the seven gold lampstands. Listen to what I say.

[2]I know everything you have done, including your hard work and how you have endured. I know you won't put up with anyone who is evil. When some people pretended to be apostles, you tested them and found out that they were liars. [3]You have endured and gone through hard times because of me, and you have not given up.

[4]But I do have something against you! And it is this: You don't have as much love as you used to. [5]Think about where you have fallen from, and then turn back and do as you did at first. If you don't turn back, I will come and take away your lampstand. [6]But there is one thing you are doing right. You hate what the Nicolaitans[j] are doing, and so do I.

[7]If you have ears, listen to what the

"Don't be afraid"
(17) These are the comforting words that the risen Savior spoke to John. It's no wonder John was afraid. He had to struggle to describe what he saw and heard. This surely was a different view of Jesus than John ever had before. Now we, too, can be unafraid as we realize that all nature and our own lives are in the hands of a great Savior.

Let's keep our love warm
(1) The Christians at Ephesus had let their love grow cold. Ephesus had been John's home church, and it is interesting that the first of seven letters is sent there. They had kept their faith, but they had not continued to be excited about Jesus. Loving Christ is not just having correct ideas about him. Our service for him proves our faith is sincere.

Be a Christian all through
(6) As suggested in the footnote, it is believed there was a group at Ephesus who followed a certain Nicolaus. Some think he may have been a false teacher who led people to believe they could lead an immoral life and still be true Christians. It is a mistake to imagine we can say we are Christians and live like the worst members of our society.

[h]*keys to death and the world of the dead*: That is, power over death and the world of the dead.   [i]*angels*: Perhaps guardian angels that represent the churches, or they may be church leaders or messengers sent to the churches.   [j]*Nicolaitans*: Nothing else is known about these people, though it is possible that they claimed to be followers of Nicolaus from Antioch (Acts 6.5).

Spirit says to the churches. I will let everyone who wins the victory eat from the life-giving tree in God's wonderful garden.

The Letter to Smyrna

[8]This is what you must write to the angel of the church in Smyrna:

I am the first and the last. I died, but now I am alive! Listen to what I say.

[9]I know how much you suffer and how poor you are, but you are rich. I also know the cruel things being said about you by people who claim to be Jews. But they are not really Jews. They are a group that belongs to Satan.

[10]Don't worry about what you will suffer. The devil will throw some of you into jail, and you will be tested and made

Run for the prize
(8) This is what Jesus told the Christians at Smyrna. They had suffered much. But their Lord promised them a life after death that would be glorious if they would just be faithful to him. The second death he refers to is to be thrown into the lake of fire (see chapter 20, verse 15).

The Seven Churches of Revelation

to suffer for ten days. But if you are faithful until you die, I will reward you with a glorious life.[k]

11If you have ears, listen to what the Spirit says to the churches. Whoever wins the victory will not be hurt by the second death.[l]

The Letter to Pergamum

12This is what you must write to the angel of the church in Pergamum:

I am the one who has the sharp double-edged sword! Listen to what I say.

13I know that you live where Satan has his throne.[m] But you have kept true to my name. Right there where Satan lives, my faithful witness Antipas[n] was taken from you and put to death. Even then you did not give up your faith in me.

14I do have a few things against you. Some of you are following the teaching of Balaam.[o] Long ago he told Balak to teach the people of Israel to eat food that had been offered to idols and to be immoral. 15Now some of you are following the teaching of the Nicolaitans.[p] 16Turn back! If you don't, I will come quickly and fight against these people. And my words will cut like a sword.

17If you have ears, listen to what the Spirit says to the churches. To everyone who wins the victory, I will give some of the hidden food.[q] I will also give each

Eat the hidden food

(17) The footnote tells you where this idea comes from. Also, Jesus called himself the "bread that gives life" (see John 6.35). He is the one whose life we need to feed on every day. He is the true bread who came down from heaven and gave his life to us. When we feed on Christ through his word and the Holy Spirit, we have real nourishment.

[k]*a glorious life*: The Greek text has "a crown of life." In ancient times an athlete who had won a contest was rewarded with a crown of flowers as a sign of victory. [l]*second death*: The first death is physical death, and the "second death" is eternal death. [m]*where Satan has his throne*: The meaning is uncertain, but it may refer to the city as a center of pagan worship or of Emperor worship. [n]*Antipas*: Nothing else is known about this man, who is mentioned only here in the New Testament. [o]*Balaam*: According to Numbers 22—24, Balaam refused to disobey the Lord. But in other books of the Old Testament, he is spoken of as evil (Deuteronomy 23.4,5; Joshua 13.22; 24.9,10; Nehemiah 13.2). [p]*Nicolaitans*: See the note at verse 6. [q]*hidden food*: When the people of Israel were going through the desert, the Lord provided a special food for them. Some

one a white stone[r] with a new name[s] written on it. No one will know that name except the one who is given the stone.

The Letter to Thyatira

[18]This is what you must write to the angel of the church in Thyatira:

I am the Son of God! My eyes are like flames of fire, and my feet are like bronze. Listen to what I say.

[19]I know everything about you, including your love, your faith, your service, and how you have endured. I know that you are doing more now than you have ever done before. [20]But I still have something against you because of that woman Jezebel.[t] She calls herself a prophet, and you let her teach and mislead my servants to do immoral things and to eat food offered to idols. [21]I gave her a chance to turn from her sins, but she did not want to stop doing these immoral things.

[22]I am going to strike down Jezebel. Everyone who does these immoral things with her will also be punished, if they don't stop. [23]I will even kill her followers.[u] Then all the churches will see that I know everyone's thoughts and feelings. I will treat each of you as you deserve.

[24]Some of you in Thyatira don't follow Jezebel's teaching. You don't know

Watch out for Jezebels
(20) The people at Thyatira were listening to a woman called Jezebel who was leading them into immoral living. Today, there are a lot of "Jezebels" in and out of the church. We are easily misled by tempting voices on television, in movies, and in other places. We hear the message that sin is fun, that it's not so bad. That's a lie. Don't let Jezebels lead you away from the Lord Jesus.

of this was placed in a jar and stored in the sacred chest (Exodus 16). According to later Jewish teaching, the prophet Jeremiah rescued the sacred chest when the temple was destroyed by the Babylonians. He hid the chest in a cave, where it would stay until God came to save his people. [r]*white stone*: The meaning of this is uncertain, though it may be the same as a ticket that lets a person into God's banquet where the "hidden food" is eaten. Or it may be a symbol of victory. [s]*a new name*: Either the name of Christ or God or the name of the follower who is given the stone. [t]*Jezebel*: Nothing else is known about her. This may have been her real name or a name that was given to her because she was like Queen Jezebel, who opposed the Lord (1 Kings 19.1,2; 21.1-26). [u]*her followers*: Or "her children."

anything about what her followers call the "deep secrets of Satan." So I won't burden you down with any other commands. 25But until I come, you must hold firmly to the teaching you have.

26I will give power over the nations to everyone who wins the victory and keeps on obeying me until the end. 27-28I will give each of them the same power that my Father has given me. They will rule the nations with an iron rod and smash those nations to pieces like clay pots. I will also give them the morning star.v

29If you have ears, listen to what the Spirit says to the churches.

The Letter to Sardis

3 This is what you must write to the angel of the church in Sardis:

I have the seven spirits of God and the seven stars. Listen to what I say.

I know what you are doing. Everyone may think you are alive, but you are dead. 2Wake up! You have only a little strength left, and it is almost gone. So try to become stronger. I have found that you are not completely obeying God. 3Remember the teaching that you were given and that you heard. Hold firmly to it and turn from your sins. If you don't wake up, I will come when you least expect it, just as a thief does.

4A few of you in Sardis have not dirtied your clothes with sin. You will walk with me in white clothes, because you are worthy. 5Everyone who wins the victory will wear white clothes. Their names will not be erased from the book of life,w and I will tell my Father and his angels that they are my followers.

6If you have ears, listen to what the Spirit says to the churches.

Listen to the Spirit
(29) All seven of Jesus' letters to the churches contain the command to "listen to the Spirit." There are so many voices in the world that it is easy to tune out the Holy Spirit. That is why you should read the word of God every day to hear what the Spirit is saying.

Let's be living Christians
(2) That's what Jesus said to the people at Sardis. We can go around talking a good religion, but Christ may not be living in us. Words don't make us Christians. We may fool a lot of people, but God sees what we are inside. If Christ truly lives in us, we are truly clean.

vthe morning star: Probably thought of as the star that signals the end of night and the beginning of day. In 22.16 Christ is called the "morning star." wbook of life: The book in which the names of God's people are written.

The Letter to Philadelphia

7This is what you must write to the angel of the church in Philadelphia:

I am the one who is holy and true, and I have the keys that belonged to David.*x* When I open a door, no one can close it. And when I close a door, no one can open it. Listen to what I say.

8I know everything you have done. And I have placed before you an open door that no one can close. You were not very strong, but you obeyed my message and did not deny that you are my followers.*y* 9Now you will see what I will do with those people who belong to Satan's group. They claim to be Jews, but they are liars. I will make them come and kneel down at your feet. Then they will know that I love you.

10You obeyed my message and endured. So I will protect you from the time of testing that everyone in all the world must go through. 11I am coming soon. So hold firmly to what you have, and no one will take away the crown that you will be given as your reward.

12Everyone who wins the victory will be made into a pillar in the temple of my God, and they will stay there forever. I will write on each of them the name of my God and the name of his city. It is the new Jerusalem that my God will send down from heaven. I will also write on them my own new name.

13If you have ears, listen to what the Spirit says to the churches.

The Letter to Laodicea

14This is what you must write to the angel of the church in Laodicea:

I am the one called Amen!*z* I am the faithful and true witness and the

We have an open door
(8) The open door is Jesus (John 10.7). He has eternal life. No one can close the door that he has opened, and all we have to do is walk through that door. This means that we accept Jesus as the only Savior, who opens the way to a satisfying life, and then finally the way to heaven with him.

---

x the keys that belonged to David: The keys stand for authority over David's kingdom. *y did not deny that you are my followers*: Or "did not say evil things about me." *z Amen*: Meaning "Trustworthy."

source*a* of God's creation. Listen to what I say.

15I know everything you have done, and you are not cold or hot. I wish you were either one or the other. 16But since you are lukewarm and neither cold nor hot, I will spit you out of my mouth. 17You claim to be rich and successful and to have everything you need. But you don't know how bad off you are. You are pitiful, poor, blind, and naked.

18Buy your gold from me. It has been refined in a fire, and it will make you rich. Buy white clothes from me. Wear them and you can cover up your shameful nakedness. Buy medicine for your eyes, so that you will be able to see.

19I correct and punish everyone I love. So make up your minds to turn away from your sins. 20Listen! I am standing and knocking at your door. If you hear my voice and open the door, I will come in and we will eat together. 21Everyone who wins the victory will sit with me on my throne, just as I won the victory and sat with my Father on his throne.

22If you have ears, listen to what the Spirit says to the churches.

Worship in Heaven

4 After this, I looked and saw a door that opened into heaven. Then the voice that had spoken to me at first and that sounded like a trumpet said, "Come up here! I will show you what must happen next." 2Right then the Spirit took control of me, and there in heaven I saw a throne and someone sitting on it. 3The one who was sitting there sparkled like precious stones of jasper*b* and carnelian.*c* A rainbow that looked like an emerald*d* surrounded the throne.

4Twenty-four other thrones were in a circle around that throne. And on each of these

A lukewarm drink is unpleasant

(16) It's better not to be baked at all than to be half-baked. A lukewarm or half-hearted Christian may be fooled into thinking everything is okay. But Jesus doesn't want halfway followers. What joy can there be in a half faith that wants to be half saved and half lost? That's a two-faced, dishonest way to live.

Jesus is knocking at your door

(20) God's Son wants to come in and be your friend forever. Eating a meal together is a beautiful picture of friendship. But you must open the door of your life, and say, "Come in, Jesus. Be my honored guest and the Lord of my life."

John went up to heaven

(1) Up to here, John had been writing about things seen and heard on earth. Here we see him taken up to heaven itself, where he saw a great throne. Because of the rainbow, like a veil surrounding the throne, John couldn't see clearly the One sitting there. But we know that this is a vision of God. As we read John's words we share in the beauty of what he saw.

---

*a*source: Or "beginning."   *b*jasper: Usually green or clear.   *c*carnelian: Usually deep-red or reddish-white. *d*emerald: A precious stone, usually green.

thrones there was an elder dressed in white clothes and wearing a gold crown. ⁵Flashes of lightning and roars of thunder came out from the throne in the center of the circle. Seven torches, which are the seven spirits of God, were burning in front of the throne. ⁶Also in front of the throne was something that looked like a glass sea, clear as crystal.

Around the throne in the center were four living creatures covered front and back with eyes. ⁷The first creature was like a lion, the second one was like a bull, the third one had the face of a human, and the fourth was like a flying eagle. ⁸Each of the four living creatures had six wings, and their bodies were covered with eyes. Day and night they never stopped singing,

"Holy, holy, holy is the Lord,
    the all-powerful God,
who was and is
    and is coming!"

⁹The living creatures kept praising, honoring, and thanking the one who sits on the throne and who lives forever and ever. ¹⁰At the same time the twenty-four elders kneeled down before the one sitting on the throne. And as they worshiped the one who lives forever, they placed their crowns in front of the throne and said,

¹¹"Our Lord and God,
    you are worthy
to receive glory,
    honor, and power.
You created all things,
and by your decision they are
    and were created."

The Scroll and the Lamb

5 In the right hand of the one sitting on the throne I saw a scroll^e that had writing on the inside and on the outside. And it was sealed in seven places. ²I saw a mighty angel ask with a loud voice, "Who is worthy to open the scroll and break its seals?"

---

^e scroll: A roll of paper or special leather used for writing on. Sometimes a scroll would be sealed on the outside with one or more pieces of wax.

We can come only so near
(6) John was separated from the throne by a sea. We are separated from God by his majesty. We can't grasp all that is God because we are creations of the infinite Creator. But we see his glory in Christ who is God the Son. It is more than enough for us that we have the friendship of Jesus.

Heavenly beings worship God
(9) We have never seen these beings that John describes in God's throne room. They seem superior to God's other creations. Yet they never cease to worship God. Do you think our worship on earth should in many ways be like their worship? If we know God as he really is, how can we not worship him continually?

The scroll of future history
(1) We shall see that the scroll unfolds the events that are to come. It is God's history book written beforehand. We get comfort from knowing that the story of mankind is not just "a happening." God himself is the grand director of the drama of the ages. All things are under the control of God, who created time itself. Good must win over evil.

3No one in heaven or on earth or under the earth was able to open the scroll or see inside it.

4I cried hard because no one was found worthy to open the book or see inside it. 5Then one of the elders said to me, "Stop crying and look! The one who is called both the 'Lion from the Tribe of Judah'ᶠ and 'King David's Great Descendant'ᵍ has won the victory. He will open the book and its seven seals."

6Then I looked and saw a Lamb standing in the center of the throne that was surrounded by the four living creatures and the elders. The Lamb looked as if it had once been killed. It had seven horns and seven eyes, which are the seven spiritsʰ of God, sent out to all the earth.

7The Lamb went over and took the scroll from the right hand of the one who sat on the throne. 8After he had taken it, the four living creatures and the twenty-four elders kneeled down before him. Each of them had a harp and a gold bowl full of incense,ᶦ which are the prayers of God's people. 9Then they sang a new song,

> "You are worthy
>   to receive the scroll
> and open its seals,
>   because you were killed.
> And with your own blood
>   you bought for God
> people from every tribe,
>   language, nation, and race.
> 10You let them become kings
>   and serve God as priests,
> and they will rule on earth."

11As I looked, I heard the voices of a lot of angels around the throne and the voices of the living creatures and of the elders.

The Lion of Judah

(5) A picture of the lion, which stood for the ancient tribe of Judah in Israel, was on King David's banner. The lion spoken of here is David's very great Grandson, the Lord Jesus Christ himself. But he is also called "the Lamb." This is the word that John the Baptist used for Jesus (John 1.29). It tells us a lot about Jesus that he is called both Lion and Lamb. He is both strong and gentle.

The Lamb can open the scroll

(9) Of course—Jesus, the Lamb of God, is able to open the scroll and unlock the meaning of time and history. He died to free the world from sin's slavery, and he is able to unfold before our eyes that work of setting free. Jesus has the key that unlocks all secrets. Time has meaning only as it points to God's eternal plan for the ages.

ᶠ'*Lion from the Tribe of Judah*': In Genesis 49.9 the tribe of Judah is called a young lion, and King David was from Judah.   ᵍ'*King David's Great Descendant*': The Greek text has "the root of David" which is a title for the Messiah based on Isaiah 11.1,10.   ʰ*the seven spirits*: Some manuscripts have "the spirits."   ᶦ*incense*: A material that produces a sweet smell when burned. Sometimes it is a symbol for the prayers of God's people.

There were millions and millions of them,
12and they were saying in a loud voice,

> "The Lamb who was killed
> is worthy to receive power,
> riches, wisdom, strength,
> honor, glory, and praise."

13Then I heard all beings in heaven and
on the earth and under the earth and in
the sea offer praise. Together, all of them
were saying,

> "Praise, honor, glory,
> and strength
> forever and ever
> to the one who sits
> on the throne
> and to the Lamb!"

14The four living creatures said "Amen,"
while the elders kneeled down and worshiped.

Opening the Seven Seals

6 At the same time that I saw the Lamb
open the first of the seven seals, I heard
one of the four living creatures shout with
a voice like thunder. It said, "Come out!"
2Then I saw a white horse. Its rider carried
a bow and was given a crown. He had already won some victories, and he went out
to win more.

3When the Lamb opened the second seal,
I heard the second living creature say,
"Come out!" 4Then another horse came out.
It was fiery red. And its rider was given
the power to take away all peace from the
earth, so that people would slaughter one
another. He was also given a big sword.

5When the Lamb opened the third seal,
I heard the third living creature say, "Come
out!" Then I saw a black horse, and its rider
had a balance scale in one hand. 6I heard
what sounded like a voice from somewhere
among the four living creatures. It said, "A
quart of wheat will cost you a whole day's
wages! Three quarts of barley will cost you
a day's wages too. But don't ruin the olive
oil or the wine."

7When the Lamb opened the fourth seal,
I heard the voice of the fourth living creature

Death is the story of life
(1) The first four seals
opened by Christ reveal a
time of death, warfare, and
destruction. As the years go
by, wars are only more
mammoth and deadly, as
millions of people can be
destroyed in a few moments.
The Prince of Peace alone
can bring an end to war. Until then, death of all kinds
is continually present to remind the world that sin still
carries a high price (Ro-
mans 6.23).

say, "Come out!" [8]Then I saw a pale green horse. Its rider was named Death, and Death's Kingdom followed behind. They were given power over one fourth of the earth, and they could kill its people with swords, famines, diseases, and wild animals.

[9]When the Lamb opened the fifth seal, I saw under the altar the souls of everyone who had been killed for speaking God's message and telling about their faith. [10]They shouted, "Master, you are holy and faithful! How long will it be before you judge and punish the people of this earth who killed us?"

[11]Then each of those who had been killed was given a white robe and told to rest for a little while. They had to wait until the complete number of the Lord's other servants and followers would be killed.

[12]When I saw the Lamb open the sixth seal, I looked and saw a great earthquake. The sun turned as dark as sackcloth,[j] and the moon became as red as blood. [13]The stars in the sky fell to earth, just like figs shaken loose by a windstorm. [14]Then the sky was rolled up like a scroll,[k] and all mountains and islands were moved from their places.

[15]The kings of the earth, its famous people, and its military leaders hid in caves or behind rocks on the mountains. They hid there together with the rich and the powerful and with all the slaves and free people. [16]Then they shouted to the mountains and the rocks, "Fall on us! Hide us from the one who sits on the throne and from the anger of the Lamb. [17]That terrible day has come! God and the Lamb will show their anger, and who can face it?"

The 144,000 Are Marked for God

7 [1-2]After this I saw four angels. Each one was standing on one of the earth's four

The world kills God's messengers
(9) God's people are not silent. They are his witnesses. But when we witness for God, the world is often hostile to that witness. The witnesses are often put to death, especially in parts of the world where the good news about Jesus is very unwelcome. But the Lord knows when you suffer for him, and his judgment is coming to a world that rejects him and his messengers.

God will judge the world
(16) Expect tremendous things to happen as God gets ready to judge the world. The order of nature will be disturbed. As unsaved people, great and small, begin to realize what is happening to them, they will cry out in horror in the presence of God's justice. Those who have not known God as Savior will know him as their Judge.

[j]*sackcloth*: A rough, dark-colored cloth made from goat or camel hair and used to make grain sacks. It was worn in times of trouble or sorrow. [k]*scroll*: See the note at 5.1.

corners. The angels held back the four winds, so that no wind would blow on the earth or on the sea or on any tree. These angels had also been given the power to harm the earth and the sea. Then I saw another angel come up from where the sun rises in the east, and he was ready to put the mark of the living God on people. He shouted to the four angels, 3"Don't harm the earth or the sea or any tree! Wait until I have marked the foreheads of the servants of our God."

4Then I heard how many people had been marked on the forehead. There were one hundred forty-four thousand, and they came from every tribe of Israel:

5 12,000 from the tribe
of Judah,
12,000 from the tribe
of Reuben,
12,000 from the tribe
of Gad,
6 12,000 from the tribe
of Asher,
12,000 from the tribe
of Naphtali,
12,000 from the tribe
of Manasseh,
7 12,000 from the tribe
of Simeon,
12,000 from the tribe
of Levi,
12,000 from the tribe
of Issachar,
8 12,000 from the tribe
of Zebulun,
12,000 from the tribe
of Joseph, and
12,000 from the tribe
of Benjamin.

People from Every Nation

9After this, I saw a large crowd with more people than could be counted. They were from every race, tribe, nation, and language, and they stood before the throne and before the Lamb. They wore white robes and held

Israel has not been forgotten
(4) When you are reading the Old Testament you will see, over and over, that God made some very special promises to ancient Israel. Many faithful Israelites will be saved from the time of trouble to come. In God's new order, the believing nation of Israel will receive her promised blessings. At that time, Israel will no longer be the victim of wars and the hatred of the nations that surround her.

Countless saved people
(9) John saw a crowd in heaven so large that no one could count them, from every nation on earth. Such a thing could happen because of men and women who carried the good news about Jesus to every place in the world. Blessed are those who have gone to faraway places to share the news about Jesus with every tribe and race.

palm branches in their hands, ¹⁰as they shouted,

> "Our God, who sits
> upon the throne,
> has the power
> to save his people,
> and so does the Lamb."

¹¹The angels who stood around the throne kneeled in front of it with their faces to the ground. The elders and the four living creatures kneeled there with them. Then they all worshiped God ¹²and said,

> "Amen! Praise, glory, wisdom,
> thanks, honor, power,
> and strength belong to our God
> forever and ever! Amen!"

¹³One of the elders asked me, "Do you know who these people are that are dressed in white robes? Do you know where they come from?"

¹⁴"Sir," I answered, "you must know." Then he told me:

> "These are the ones
> who have gone through
> the great suffering.
> They have washed their robes
> in the blood of the Lamb
> and have made them white.
> ¹⁵And so they stand
> before the throne of God
> and worship him in his temple
> day and night.
> The one who sits on the throne
> will spread his tent
> over them.
> ¹⁶They will never hunger
> or thirst again,
> and they won't be troubled
> by the sun
> or any scorching heat.

> ¹⁷The Lamb in the center
> of the throne
> will be their shepherd.
> He will lead them to streams
> of life-giving water,
> and God will wipe all tears
> from their eyes."

God's people suffer

(13) The crowd John saw in heaven was made up of those who suffered on earth because they loved Christ more than the wickedness of the world. Even today we see that sin divides people, so that those who don't love Christ usually resent people who do. God is healing the world through the suffering of his Son—and his people are sometimes called on to share in that suffering.

The Lamb who is also a Shepherd

(17) Jesus is "the Lamb" we have seen before in this book, and now the elder says that the Lamb is also a "Shepherd." David the King called the Lord his Shepherd a thousand years before John wrote this book (see Psalm 23). We are the "sheep" that Jesus tends and cares for now and forever, in fields where flowers never fade.

The Seventh Seal Is Opened

8 When the Lamb opened the seventh seal, there was silence in heaven for about half an hour. 2I noticed that the seven angels who stood before God were each given a trumpet.

3Another angel, who had a gold container for incense,[l] came and stood at the altar. This one was given a lot of incense to offer with the prayers of God's people on the gold altar in front of the throne. 4Then the smoke of the incense, together with the prayers of God's people, went up to God from the hand of the angel.

5After this, the angel filled the incense container with fire from the altar and threw it on the earth. Thunder roared, lightning flashed, and the earth shook.

The Trumpets

6The seven angels now got ready to blow their trumpets.

7When the first angel blew his trumpet, hail and fire mixed with blood were thrown down on the earth. A third of the earth, a third of the trees, and a third of all green plants were burned.

8When the second angel blew his trumpet, something like a great fiery mountain was thrown into the sea. A third of the sea turned to blood, 9a third of the living creatures in the sea died, and a third of the ships was destroyed.

10When the third angel blew his trumpet, a great star fell from heaven. It was burning like a torch, and it fell on a third of the rivers and on a third of the springs of water. 11The name of the star was Bitter, and a third of the water turned bitter. Many people died because the water was so bitter.

12When the fourth angel blew his trumpet, a third of the sun, a third of the moon, and a third of the stars were struck. They each lost a third of their light. So during a

Prayer is a sweet aroma
(3) Sometimes prayer seems hard for us, but the sincere prayers of his people please God very much. The fact that we personally take time to spend with God shows that we genuinely love him. Just as a father enjoys quiet talks with his children, so much more God loves the time we spend speaking with him about our joys, concerns, and troubles.

Hard times are coming
(7) World history is a story of small amounts of peace followed by great trouble. It is dangerous to think that such trouble just "happens." By allowing trouble, God warns the world that it loves the wrong things. This passage shows that the last round of trouble will the worst ever by far. Yet people still turn their backs on God.

[l]incense: See the note at 5.8.

third of the day there was no light, and a third of the night was also without light.

13Then I looked and saw a lone eagle flying across the sky. It was shouting, "Trouble, trouble, trouble to everyone who lives on earth! The other three angels are now going to blow their trumpets."

9 When the fifth angel blew his trumpet, I saw a star[m] fall from the sky to earth. It was given the key to the tunnel that leads down to the deep pit. 2As it opened the tunnel, smoke poured out like the smoke of a great furnace. The sun and the air turned dark because of the smoke. 3Locusts came out of the smoke and covered the earth. They were given the same power that scorpions have.

4The locusts were told not to harm the grass on the earth or any plant or any tree. They were to punish only those people who did not have God's mark on their foreheads. 5The locusts were allowed to make them suffer for five months, but not to kill them. The suffering they caused was like the sting of a scorpion. 6In those days people will want to die, but they will not be able to. They will hope for death, but it will escape from them.

7These locusts looked like horses ready for battle. On their heads they wore something like gold crowns, and they had human faces. 8Their hair was like a woman's long hair, and their teeth were like those of a lion. 9On their chests they wore armor made of iron. Their wings roared like an army of horse-drawn chariots rushing into battle. 10Their tails were like a scorpion's tail with a stinger that had the power to hurt someone for five months. 11Their king was the angel in charge of the deep pit. In Hebrew his name was Abaddon, and in Greek it was Apollyon.[n]

12The first horrible thing has now happened! But wait. Two more horrible things will happen soon.

The deep pit will send forth evil

(1) This passage, with its references to the deep pit, locusts, and the angel of destruction, reminds us that Satan and his demons are quite real and able to do much harm. Even though Jesus has won the victory over sin and death, we still ought to take the devil very seriously.

---

*m*star: In the ancient world, stars were often thought of as living beings, such as angels. *n*Abaddon . . . Apollyon: The Hebrew word "Abaddon" and the Greek word "Apollyon" each mean "destruction."

13Then the sixth angel blew his trumpet. I heard a voice speak from the four corners of the gold altar that stands in the presence of God. 14The voice spoke to this angel and said, "Release the four angels who are tied up beside the great Euphrates River." 15The four angels had been prepared for this very hour and day and month and year. Now they were set free to kill a third of all people.

16By listening, I could tell there were more than two hundred million of these war horses. 17In my vision their riders wore fiery-red, dark-blue, and yellow armor on their chests. The heads of the horses looked like lions, with fire and smoke and sulphur coming out of their mouths. 18One third of all people were killed by the three terrible troubles caused by the fire, the smoke, and the sulphur. 19The horses had powerful mouths, and their tails were like poisonous snakes that bite and hurt.

20The people who lived through these terrible troubles did not turn away from the idols they had made, and they did not stop worshiping demons. They kept on worshiping idols that were made of gold, silver, bronze, stone, and wood. Not one of these idols could see, hear, or walk. 21No one stopped murdering or practicing witchcraft or being immoral or stealing.

The Angel and the Little Scroll

10 I saw another powerful angel come down from heaven. This one was covered with a cloud, and a rainbow was over his head. His face was like the sun, his legs were like columns of fire, 2and with his hand he held a little scrollo that had been unrolled. He stood there with his right foot on the sea and his left foot on the land. 3Then he shouted with a voice that sounded like a growling lion. Thunder roared seven times.

4After the thunder stopped, I was about to write what it had said. But a voice from

oscroll: See the note at 5.1.

Suffering comes up from hell

(16) We have read and heard about the horrible suffering in wars that have taken place in our own lifetime. We are reminded that there seems to be no limit to the ugly ways ungodly people can torment their neighbors. Right up until the time of the Lord's return to judge the world, mankind will suffer from terrible wars. Force cannot change human nature, but people can be changed if only they will turn to Jesus.

Angels are God's agents

(1) We meet these personalities all through the Bible. The word "angel" comes from a Greek word meaning "messenger." So an angel is a messenger of God. Angels are God's spiritual agents who announce his plans and serve him as he wishes. The angel in John's vision announces that all the plans God told the ancient prophets would soon be carried out. Count on it: every promise God has made will come true.

heaven shouted, "Keep it secret! Don't write these things."

5The angel I had seen standing on the sea and the land then held his right hand up toward heaven. 6He made a promise in the name of God who lives forever and who created heaven, earth, the sea, and every living creature. The angel said, "You won't have to wait any longer. 7God told his secret plans to his servants the prophets, and it will all happen by the time the seventh angel sounds his trumpet."

8Once again the voice from heaven spoke to me. It said, "Go and take the open scroll from the hand of the angel standing on the sea and the land."

9When I went over to ask the angel for the little scroll, the angel said, "Take the scroll and eat it! Your stomach will turn sour, but the taste in your mouth will be as sweet as honey." 10I took the little scroll from the hand of the angel and ate it. The taste was as sweet as honey, but my stomach turned sour.

11Then some voices said, "Keep on telling what will happen to the people of many nations, races, and languages, and also to kings."

The Two Witnesses

11 An angel gave me a measuring stick and said:

Measure around God's temple. Be sure to include the altar and everyone worshiping there. 2But don't measure the courtyard outside the temple building. Leave it out. It has been given to those people who don't know God, and they will trample all over the holy city for forty-two months. 3My two witnesses will wear sackcloth,p while I let them preach for one thousand two hundred sixty days.

4These two witnesses are the two olive trees and the two lampstands that stand in the presence of the Lord who rules the earth.

psackcloth: See the note at 6.12.

God's plan is judgment
(9) That's why the scroll John ate was bitter after it entered his stomach. God's word may be pleasant to read at first, and it has sweet comfort for those who are saved by faith. Yet the carrying out of that word will be very unpleasant for those who don't love the true God but love their own sinful ways instead.

"Keep on telling"
(11) Our job is to be faithful in telling people about God's plans for the future. Then some of them will believe us and be saved from the great judgment to come. Some will not want to hear us, but we must warn them.

5Any enemy who tries to harm them will be destroyed by the fire that comes out of their mouths. 6They have the power to lock up the sky and to keep rain from falling while they are prophesying. And whenever they want to, they can turn water to blood and cause all kinds of terrible troubles on earth.

7After the two witnesses have finished preaching God's message, the beast that lives in the deep pit will come up and fight against them. It will win the battle and kill them. 8Their bodies will be left lying in the streets of the same great city where their Lord was nailed to a cross. And that city is spiritually like the city of Sodom or the country of Egypt.

9For three and a half days the people of every nation, tribe, language, and race will stare at the bodies of these two witnesses and refuse to let them be buried. 10Everyone on earth will celebrate and be happy. They will give gifts to each other, because of what happened to the two prophets who caused them so much trouble. 11But three and a half days later, God will breathe life into their bodies. They will stand up, and everyone who sees them will be terrified.

12The witnesses then heard a loud voice from heaven, saying, "Come up here." And while their enemies are watching, they were taken up to heaven in a cloud. 13At that same moment there was a terrible earthquake that destroyed a tenth of the city. Seven thousand people were killed, and the rest were frightened and praised the God who rules in heaven.

14The second horrible thing has now happened! But the third one will be here soon.

The Seventh Trumpet

15At the sound of the seventh trumpet, loud voices were heard in heaven. They said,

> "Now the kingdoms
>   of this world
> belong to our Lord
>   and to his Chosen One!

Can people be so blind?
(7) Here John tells beforehand how God's two witnesses will be treated. Yet it seems that nobody will care that the witnesses are murdered. The people of the world are strangely careless about the terrible things they have done. But as godless ways increase, so does ignorance of God's warnings. We see such ignorance every day, even though more people than ever can read and hear the word of God.

God's kingdom is near
(15) The seventh trumpet announces the coming of Christ to rule the world. We need this comfort as we read about God's frightening judgments. As one of the Psalms says, "weeping may last for a night, but joy comes in the morning." At the end of the dark night of sin and its trouble comes the dawn of the Son of God's wonderful reign.

And he will rule
    forever and ever!"

16Then the twenty-four elders, who were seated on thrones in God's presence, kneeled down and worshiped him. 17They said,

"Lord God All-Powerful,
you are and you were,
    and we thank you.
You used your great power
    and started ruling.
18When the nations got angry,
    you became angry too!
Now the time has come
for the dead
    to be judged.
It is time for you to reward
    your servants the prophets
and all of your people
who honor your name,
    no matter who they are.
It is time to destroy everyone
who has destroyed
    the earth."

19The door to God's temple in heaven was then opened, and the sacred chest*q* could be seen inside the temple. I saw lightning and heard roars of thunder. The earth trembled and huge hailstones fell to the ground.

The Woman and the Dragon

12 Something important appeared in the sky. It was a woman whose clothes were the sun. The moon was under her feet, and a crown made of twelve stars was on her head. 2She was about to give birth, and she was crying because of the great pain.

3Something else appeared in the sky. It was a huge red dragon with seven heads and ten horns, and a crown on each of its seven heads. 4With its tail, it dragged a third of the stars from the sky and threw them down to the earth. Then the dragon turned

The sacred chest in heaven
(19) The footnote tells what this chest was. Now we see that God has never forgotten his ancient agreement. The happiness promised in the agreement God made with his people was based on the keeping of the God-given Law, the Ten Commandments, a copy of which was put in the sacred chest. Christ himself kept that Law by living a sinless life and dying for us on the cross.

qsacred chest: In Old Testament times the sacred chest was kept in the tent used for worship. It was the symbol of God's presence with his people and also of his agreement with them.

toward the woman, because it wanted to eat her child as soon as it was born.

5The woman gave birth to a son, who would rule all nations with an iron rod. The boy was snatched away. He was taken to God and placed on his throne. 6The woman ran into the desert to a place that God had prepared for her. There she would be taken care of for one thousand two hundred sixty days.

Michael Fights the Dragon

7A war broke out in heaven. Michael and his angels were fighting against the dragon and its angels. 8But the dragon lost the battle. It and its angels were forced out of their places in heaven 9and were thrown down to the earth. Yes, that old snake and his angels were thrown out of heaven! That snake, who fools everyone on earth, is known as the devil and Satan. 10Then I heard a voice from heaven shout,

"Our God has shown
his saving power,
    and his kingdom has come!
God's own Chosen One
    has shown his authority.
Satan accused our people
in the presence of God
    day and night.
Now he has been thrown out!

11Our people defeated Satan
    because of the bloodr
of the Lamb
    and the message of God.
They were willing
    to give up their lives.

12The heavens should rejoice,
together with everyone
    who lives there.
But pity the earth
    and the sea,
because the devil

God saves his Son

(5) In John's vision of the dragon we see the birth of Jesus all over again (see Matthew 1 and 2 with Luke 1 and 2). Satan, who is called "the dragon," began trying to destroy the Christ child as soon as he was born. But we know the rest. Jesus was killed and buried but rose again, and then he returned to heaven. So Satan could not destroy God's plan to save us. The woman is more than just the mother of Jesus. She stands for God's people Israel, whom he protects until Satan is finally defeated forever.

---

rblood: Or "death."

was thrown down
  to the earth.
He knows his time is short,
  and he is very angry."

13When the dragon realized that it had been thrown down to the earth, it tried to make trouble for the woman who had given birth to a son. 14But the woman was given two wings like those of a huge eagle, so that she could fly into the desert. There she would escape from the snake and be taken care of for a time, two times, and half a time.

15The snake then spit out water like a river to sweep the woman away. 16But the earth helped her and swallowed the water that had come from the dragon's mouth. 17This made the dragon terribly angry with the woman. So it started a war against the rest of her children. They are the people who obey God and are faithful to what Jesus did and taught. 18The dragons stood on the beach beside the sea.

The Two Beasts

13 I looked and saw a beast coming up from the sea. This one had ten horns and seven heads, and a crown was on each of its ten horns. On each of its heads were names that were an insult to God. 2The beast that I saw had the body of a leopard, the feet of a bear, and the mouth of a lion. The dragon handed over its own power and throne and great authority to this beast. 3One of its heads seemed to have been fatally wounded. but now it was well. Everyone on earth marveled at this beast, 4and they worshiped the dragon who had given its authority to the beast. They also worshiped the beast and said, "No one is like this beast! No one can fight against it."

5The beast was allowed to brag and claim to be God, and for forty-two months it was allowed to rule. 6The beast cursed God, and it cursed the name of God. It even cursed

Satan is on earth
(13) Satan doesn't live in hell, as some wrongly think. He is a spiritual being who was thrown out of heaven and lives in this world. Although he knows he can't win his war against the Lord, his insane desire is to destroy the Lord's people. If we are careful to listen to God's word, we know that Satan's cause is hopeless.

Antichrist
(1) The beast is "Antichrist," which means what the word says, a spirit opposed to Christ, or here, a particular person who opposes Christ in the last years before his return. Antichrist will even pretend to be a savior for the world. He will be very attractive, and many will follow his leadership. John writes about this person in his first letter (1 John 2.3). Paul also writes about him in 2 Thessalonians 2.

---

sThe dragon: The text has "he," and some manuscripts have "I."

the place where God lives, as well as everyone who lives in heaven with God. 7It was allowed to fight against God's people and defeat them. It was also given authority over the people of every tribe, nation, language, and race. 8The beast was worshiped by everyone whose name was not written before the time of creation in the book of the Lamb who was killed.*t*

9If you have ears,
   then listen!
10If you are doomed
   to be captured,
      you will be captured.
If you are doomed
   to be killed by a sword,
   you will be killed
      by a sword.

This means that God's people must learn to endure and be faithful!

11I now saw another beast. This one came out of the ground. It had two horns like a lamb, but spoke like a dragon. 12It worked for the beast whose fatal wound had been healed. And it used all its authority to force the earth and all its people to worship that beast. 13It worked miracles, and while people watched, it even made fire come down from the sky.

14This second beast fooled people on earth by working miracles for the first one. Then it talked them into making an idol in the form of the beast that did not die after being wounded by a sword. 15It was allowed to put breath into the idol, so that it could speak. Everyone who refused to worship the idol of the beast was put to death. 16All people were forced to put a mark on their right hand or forehead. Whether they were powerful or weak, rich or poor, free people or slaves, 17they all had to have this mark, or else they could not buy or sell anything. This mark stood for the name of the beast and for the number of its name.

18You need wisdom to understand the number of the beast! But if you are smart

The second beast
(11) John writes of another beast who appears and works for the first one. He does miracles and gets people to worship the first beast as if he were God. False religion will be this second beast's specialty. Many people will actually adore Antichrist as if he were God.

---

tnot written . . . was killed: Or "not written in the book of the Lamb who was killed before the time of creation."

enough, you can figure this out. Its number is six hundred sixty-six, and it stands for a person.

The Lamb and His 144,000 Followers

14 I looked and saw the Lamb standing on Mount Zion!u With him were a hundred forty-four thousand, who had his name and his Father's name written on their foreheads. 2Then I heard a sound from heaven that was like a roaring flood or loud thunder or even like the music of harps. 3And a new song was being sung in front of God's throne and in front of the four living creatures and the elders. No one could learn that song, except the one hundred forty-four thousand who had been rescued from the earth. 4All of these are pure virgins, and they follow the Lamb wherever he leads. They have been rescued to be presented to God and the Lamb as the most precious peoplev on earth. 5They never tell lies, and they are innocent.

The Messages of the Three Angels

6I saw another angel. This one was flying across the sky and had the eternal good news to announce to the people of every race, tribe, language, and nation on earth. 7The angel shouted, "Worship and honor God! The time has come for him to judge everyone. Kneel down before the one who created heaven and earth, the oceans, and every stream."

8A second angel followed and said, "The great city of Babylon has fallen! This is the city that made all nations drunk and immoral. Now God is angry, and Babylon has fallen."

9Finally, a third angel came and shouted:
Here is what will happen if you worship the beast and the idol and have

Praise for the promise-keeping God
(1) We met this crowd of 144,000 before, in chapter 7. There we were told they represent the saved from the nation of Israel at this time. Once again we are reminded of the wonderful goodness of God who always keeps his promises. Israel was his first love, and he promised their ancestors, such as Abraham, that he would be their protector forever. The 144,000 will sing a new song to their Savior. Even now, we too should have a song of love to Christ in our hearts.

What do you live for?
(9) What you worship is what you live for. If you live for the satisfaction of your body and all that this world has to offer, that is what you worship—and the result will be very ugly indeed. It is part of what the angel calls worshiping "the beast and the idol." If you serve the devil you get back all that the devil gives—hatred, heartache, and sorrow. False worship pays bitter wages.

uMount Zion: Another name for Jerusalem. vthe most precious people: The Greek text has "the first people." The Law of Moses taught that the firstborn of all animals and the first part of the harvest were special and belonged to the Lord.

the mark of the beast on your hand or forehead. 10You will have to drink the wine that God gives to everyone who makes him angry. You will feel his mighty anger, and you will be tortured with fire and burning sulphur, while the holy angels and the Lamb look on.

11If you worship the beast and the idol and accept the mark of its name, you will be tortured day and night. The smoke from your torture will go up forever and ever, and you will never be able to rest.

12God's people must learn to endure. They must also obey his commands and have faith in Jesus.

13Then I heard a voice from heaven say, "Put this in writing. From now on, the Lord will bless everyone who has faith in him when they die."

The Spirit answered, "Yes, they will rest from their hard work, and they will be rewarded for what they have done."

The Earth Is Harvested

14I looked and saw a bright cloud, and someone who seemed to be the Son of Manw was sitting on the cloud. He wore a gold crown on his head and held a sharp sicklex in his hand. 15An angel came out of the temple and shouted, "Start cutting with your sickle! Harvest season is here, and all crops on earth are ripe." 16The one on the cloud swung his sickle and harvested the crops.

17Another angel with a sharp sickle then came out of the temple. 18After this, an angel with power over fire came from the altar and shouted to the angel who had the sickle. He said, "All grapes on earth are ripe! Harvest them with your sharp sickle." 19The angel swung his sickle on earth and cut off its grapes. He threw them into a pity where

The Lord will be your Shepherd
(13) Have you ever watched the restful scene of a flock of sheep in a pasture? This is, in a way, a picture of the peace that waits for God's people beyond death. Those who die with faith in the Lord have the comfort of knowing that he will take them into his eternal fields where there will be no more dying, or sorrow, or pain. We will be with our great Shepherd forever.

This harvest will be awful
(18) When the grapes are ripe, the owner of the vineyard harvests them. Likewise, the world will come to a time when it is "ripe and ready for harvesting." But this will not be a joyful harvest—it will be a sad one with much suffering. God will finally deal with the evil world that has refused to accept his Son.

---

wSon of Man: See the note at 1.13. xsickle: A knife with a long curved blade, used to cut grain and other crops. ypit: It was the custom to put grapes in a pit (called a wine press) and stomp on them to make juice that would later turn to wine.

they were stomped on as a sign of God's anger. [20]The pit was outside the city, and when the grapes were mashed, blood flowed out. The blood turned into a river that was about two hundred miles long and almost deep enough to cover a horse.

The Last of the Terrible Troubles

15 After this, I looked at the sky and saw something else that was strange and important. Seven angels were bringing the last seven terrible troubles. When these are ended, God will no longer be angry.

[2]Then I saw something that looked like a glass sea mixed with fire, and people were standing on it. They were the ones who had defeated the beast and the idol and the number that tells the name of the beast. God had given them harps, [3]and they were singing the song that his servant Moses and the Lamb had sung. They were singing,

"Lord God All-Powerful,
you have done great
and marvelous things.
You are the ruler
of all nations,
and you do what is
right and fair.
[4]Lord, who does not honor
and praise your name?
You alone are holy,
and all nations will come
and worship you,
because you have shown
that you judge
with fairness."

[5]After this, I noticed something else in heaven. The sacred tent used for a temple was open. [6]And the seven angels who were bringing the terrible troubles were coming out of it. They were dressed in robes of pure white linen and wore belts made of pure gold. [7]One of the living creatures gave each of the seven angels a bowl made of gold. These bowls were filled with the anger of God who lives forever and ever. [8]The temple quickly filled with smoke from the glory and power of God. No one could enter it

There will be singing in heaven
(3) Before the bowls of God's anger are poured out, there will be worship in heaven. Listen to the beautiful words of the song. Consider all of the glorious things the choir will sing about God. He is "All-Powerful," the "ruler of all nations," and he does "what is right and fair." Don't listen to people who belittle the Lord. Because he is God, he always does what is right.

until the seven angels had finished pouring out the seven last troubles.

The Bowls of God's Anger

16 From the temple I heard a voice shout to the seven angels, "Go and empty the seven bowls of God's anger on the earth."

2The first angel emptied his bowl on the earth. At once ugly and painful sores broke out on everyone who had the mark of the beast and worshiped the idol.

3The second angel emptied his bowl on the sea. Right away the sea turned into blood like that of a dead person, and every living thing in the sea died.

4The third angel emptied his bowl into the rivers and streams. At once they turned to blood. 5Then I heard the angel, who has power over water, say,

"You have always been,
and you always will be
the holy God.
You had the right
to judge in this way.
6They poured out the bloodz
of your people
and your prophets.
So you gave them blood
to drink, as they deserve!"
7After this, I heard
the altar shout,
"Yes, Lord God All-Powerful,
your judgments are honest
and fair."

8The fourth angel emptied his bowl on the sun, and it began to scorch people like fire. 9Everyone was scorched by its great heat, and all of them cursed the name of God who had power over these terrible troubles. But no one turned to God and praised him.

10The fifth angel emptied his bowl on the throne of the beast. At once darkness covered its kingdom, and its people began bit-

What are these seven bowls?
(1) Beginning in chapter 5 we saw Christ the Lamb begin to open the seven seals of the future. This scene ends with the sounding of the seven trumpets in chapters 8 through 11. (The seven trumpets are included in the seventh seal.) Now we read the conclusion of this review of future history. In this chapter the seven bowls picture the judgments of God at the end of this age. The number "seven" throughout Scripture often suggests completeness. The age of sin and sorrow will be completed, and then Jesus will return to rule.

---

zThey poured out the blood: A way of saying, "They murdered."

ing their tongues in pain. ¹¹And because of their painful sores, they cursed the God who rules in heaven. But still they did not stop doing evil things.

¹²The sixth angel emptied his bowl on the great Euphrates River, and it completely dried up to make a road for the kings from the east. ¹³An evil spirit that looked like a frog came out of the mouth of the dragon. One also came out of the mouth of the beast, and another out of the mouth of the false prophet. ¹⁴These evil spirits had the power to work miracles. They went to every king on earth, to bring them together for a war against God All-Powerful. But that will be the day of God's great victory.

¹⁵Remember that Christ says, "When I come, it will surprise you like a thief! But God will bless you, if you are awake and ready. Then you won't have to walk around naked and be ashamed."

¹⁶Those armies came together in a place that in Hebrew is called Armagedon.ᵃ

¹⁷As soon as the seventh angel emptied his bowl in the air, a loud voice from the throne in the temple shouted, "It's done!" ¹⁸There were flashes of lightning, roars of thunder, and the worst earthquake in all history. ¹⁹The great city of Babylon split into three parts, and the cities of other nations fell. So God made Babylon drink from the wine cup that was filled with his anger. ²⁰Every island ran away, and the mountains disappeared. ²¹Hailstones, weighing about a hundred pounds each, fell from the sky on people. Finally, the people cursed God, because the hail was so terrible.

The Immoral Woman and the Beast

17 One of the seven angels who had emptied the bowls came over and said to me, "Come on! I will show you how God will punish that shameless and immoral woman who sits on many oceans.

ᵃ*Armagedon:* The Hebrew form of the name would be "Har Megeddo," meaning "Hill of Megeddo," where many battles were fought in ancient times (see Judges 5.19; 2 Kings 23.29,30).

Armagedon

(16) At the end of this great time of trouble, the armies of the world will gather one last time to try to defeat the Lord. They will come together to fight at a place called Armagedon. But they will not be able to overcome the All-Powerful God. It looks foolish that they could try such a thing. But there are people now who fight God every day.

Some people never change

(21) John Milton's great poem, *Paradise Lost,* quotes Satan as saying, "Better to reign in hell than serve in heaven." In spite of the judgments that will happen before Christ comes again, people will curse God. All that God can do will make no difference to them. God even sent his Son into the world to die for sinners. Then he waited many centuries for people to believe in him. But right up to the end, there will be people who would rather die than turn from their sins.

Evil likes to look good

(1) The immoral woman in John's vision doesn't want to look ugly. Even prostitutes like to "look nice." That's their trap. The immoral woman here is trapping a lot of people too. While trying to look like the beautiful "bride of Christ" in chapter 21, she is really a deceiver and "drunk on the blood of God's people." But in the end the very world powers that she serves will destroy her.

²Every king on earth has slept with her, and her shameless ways are like wine that has made everyone on earth drunk."

³With the help of the Spirit, the angel took me into the desert, where I saw a woman sitting on a red beast. The beast was covered with names that were an insult to God, and it had seven heads and ten horns. ⁴The woman was dressed in purple and scarlet robes, and she wore jewelry made of gold, precious stones, and pearls. In her hand she held a gold cup filled with the filthy and nasty things she had done. ⁵On her forehead a mysterious name was written:

I AM THE GREAT CITY OF BABYLON,
THE MOTHER OF EVERY IMMORAL
AND FILTHY THING ON EARTH.

⁶I could tell that the woman was drunk on the blood of God's people who had given their lives for Jesus. This surprising sight amazed me, ⁷and the angel said:

Why are you so amazed? I will explain the mystery about this woman and about the beast she is sitting on, with its seven heads and ten horns. ⁸The beast you saw is one that used to be and no longer is. It will come back from the deep pit, but only to be destroyed. Everyone on earth whose names were not written in the book of lifeᵇ before the time of creation will be amazed. They will see this beast that used to be and no longer is, but will be once more.

⁹Anyone with wisdom can figure this out. The seven heads that the woman is sitting on stand for seven hills. These heads are also seven kings. ¹⁰Five of the kings are dead. One is ruling now, and the other one has not yet come. But when he does, he will rule for only a little while.

¹¹You also saw a beast that used to be and no longer is. That beast is one of the seven kings who will return as

Filthy, rotten Babylon
(5) Babylon was an ancient city that contained all forms of evil. It was destroyed years ago, never to be built again. The name is a way of speaking of the world's immorality. A system of evil exists around the world, which God will finally destroy.

ᵇ*book of life:* The book in which the names of God's people are written.

the eighth king, but only to be destroyed.

12The ten horns that you saw are ten more kings, who have not yet come into power, and they will rule with the beast for only a short time. 13They all think alike and will give their power and authority to the beast. 14These kings will go to war against the Lamb. But he will defeat them, because he is Lord over all lords and King over all kings. His followers are chosen and special and faithful.

15The oceans that you saw the immoral woman sitting on are crowds of people from all races and languages. 16The ten horns and the beast will start hating the shameless woman. They will strip off her clothes and leave her naked. Then they will eat her flesh and throw the rest of her body into a fire. 17God is the one who made these kings all think alike and decide to give their power to the beast. And they will do this until what God has said comes true.

18The woman you saw is the great city that rules over all kings on earth.

The Fall of Babylon

18 I saw another angel come from heaven. This one had great power, and the earth was bright because of his glory. 2The angel shouted,

"Fallen! Powerful Babylon
        has fallen
and is now the home
        of demons.
It is the den
        of every filthy spirit
and of all unclean birds,
and every dirty
        and hated animal.
3Babylon's evil and immoral wine
        has made all nations drunk.
Every king on earth
        has slept with her,
and every merchant on earth

Evil allies

(12) The ten horns stand for ten nations that will follow the beast. Notice how they will turn on the immoral woman. There's a saying that "there is no honor among thieves." Those who band together to do evil cannot even trust each other.

is rich because of
her evil desires."

4Then I heard another voice
from heaven shout,
"My people, you must escape
from Babylon.
Don't take part in her sins
and share her punishment.
5Her sins are piled
as high as heaven.
God has remembered the evil
she has done.
6Treat her as she
has treated others.
Make her pay double
for what she has done.
Make her drink twice as much
of what she mixed
for others.
7That woman honored herself
with a life of luxury.
Reward her now
with suffering and pain.

"Deep in her heart
Babylon said,
'I am the queen!
Never will I be a widow
or know what it means
to be sad.'
8And so, in a single day
she will suffer the pain
of sorrow, hunger, and death.
Fire will destroy
her dead body,
because her judge
is the powerful Lord God."
9Every king on earth who slept with her
and shared in her luxury will mourn. They
will weep, when they see the smoke from
that fire. 10Her sufferings will frighten them,
and they will stand at a distance and say,
"Pity that great
and powerful city!
Pity Babylon!
In a single hour
her judgment has come."
11Every merchant on earth will mourn,

Get out of Babylon
(4) Living in the world has always been hard for those who love Christ, because the world's ways are not God's ways. For now there is no escape from living in the world, except death. Until the Lord comes back to change everything, he warns those who love him to avoid bad lifestyles and evil cooperation with the sinful world.

The world loves Babylon
(10) "Pity that great and powerful city." The center of the world's wickedness in John's time was the city of Rome. Now the evils are more modern, and are spread all over the so-called "civilized world." Those evils have also gotten into the very church of God. Many people accept religion if it will just agree to bless their evil doings.

because there is no one to buy their goods.
¹²There won't be anyone to buy their gold,
silver, jewels, pearls, fine linen, purple
cloth, silk, scarlet cloth, sweet-smelling
wood, fancy carvings of ivory and wood,
as well as things made of bronze, iron, or
marble. ¹³No one will buy their cinnamon,
spices, incense, myrrh, frankincense,ᶜ wine,
olive oil, fine flour, wheat, cattle, sheep,
horses, chariots, slaves, and other humans.

> ¹⁴Babylon, the things
>   your heart desired
> have all escaped
>   from you.
> Every luxury
> and all your glory
>   will be lost forever.
> You will never
>   get them back.

¹⁵The merchants had become rich because of her. But when they saw her sufferings, they were terrified. They stood at a
distance, crying and mourning. ¹⁶Then they
shouted,

> "Pity the great city
>   of Babylon!
> She dressed in fine linen
> and wore purple
>   and scarlet cloth.
> She had jewelry
>   made of gold
> and precious stones
>   and pearls.
> ¹⁷Yet in a single hour
>   her riches disappeared."

Every ship captain and passenger and
sailor stood at a distance, together with
everyone who does business by traveling
on the sea. ¹⁸When they saw the smoke from
her fire, they shouted, "This was the greatest city ever!"

¹⁹They cried loudly, and in their sorrow
they threw dust on their heads, as they said,

ᶜ*myrrh, frankincense*: Myrrh was a valuable sweet-
smelling powder often used in perfume. Frankincense
was a valuable powder that was burned to make a sweet
smell.

What do you value in life?
(19) Notice that people will
mourn when the world sys-
tem called "Babylon" falls.
It's easy to imagine that material goods are what life is
really all about. The mistake
here is our failure to realize
that the world's little joys
pass away at last. If we set
our hearts on them, we end
up losers when they're gone.
Those "things" are just an
empty, false god.

"Pity the great city
of Babylon!
Everyone who sailed the seas
became rich
from her treasures.
But in a single hour
the city was destroyed.
20 The heavens should be happy
with God's people
and apostles and prophets.
God has punished her
for them."

21 A powerful angel then picked up a huge stone and threw it into the sea. The angel said,

"This is how the great city
of Babylon
will be thrown down,
never to rise again.
22 The music of harps and singers
and of flutes and trumpets
will no longer be heard.
No workers will ever
set up shop in that city,
and the sound
of grinding grain
will be silenced forever.
23 Lamps will no longer shine
anywhere in Babylon,
and couples will never again
say wedding vows there.
Her merchants ruled
the earth,
and by her witchcraft
she fooled all nations.
24 On the streets of Babylon
is found the blood
of God's people
and of his prophets,
and everyone else."

19 After this, I heard what sounded like a lot of voices in heaven, and they were shouting,

"Praise the Lord!
To our God belongs
the glorious power to save,
2 because his judgments
are honest and fair.
That filthy, immoral woman

Christians pay a price
(24) Of course, if you don't crave the joys of this world, the world will be glad to see that you don't get them. They say "the race is to the swift." You may have to make a clever deal now and then if you're going to get a big share of the world's goods. But is it worth it?

There will be joy in heaven
(1) All who love God will be glad to see the vicious system described above destroyed. Right now, dishonesty and immorality seem to be the rule. The world is mean to you if you don't join the crowd and become part of the system. But this system will pass away, and then we will be glad when we see our Lord win his victory.

ruined the earth
  with shameful deeds.
But God has judged her
  and made her pay
the price for murdering
  his servants.''

³Then the crowd shouted,
  ''Praise the Lord!
Smoke will never stop rising
  from her burning body.''
⁴After this, the twenty-four elders and
the four living creatures all kneeled before
the throne of God and worshiped him. They
said, ''Amen! Praise the Lord!

The Marriage Supper of the Lamb

⁵From the throne a voice said,
  ''If you worship
    and fear our God,
  give praise to him,
    no matter who you are.''
⁶Then I heard what seemed to be a large
crowd that sounded like a roaring flood and
loud thunder all mixed together. They were
saying,

    ''Praise the Lord!
    Our Lord God All-Powerful
      now rules as king.
  ⁷So we will be glad and happy
    and give him praise.
  The wedding day of the Lamb
  is here,
    and his bride is ready.
  ⁸She will be given
    a wedding dress
  made of pure
    and shining linen.
  This linen stands
  for the good things
    God's people have done.''
⁹Then the angel told me, ''Put this in writ-
ing. God will bless everyone who is invited
to the wedding feast of the Lamb.'' The angel also said, ''These things that God has
said are true.''

¹⁰I kneeled at the feet of the angel and
began to worship him. But the angel said,

A royal wedding

(7) The world has seen some royal weddings, but none to match this. The King Jesus, the Lamb of God, will be the royal bridegroom, and those who have been saved will be the bride, clothed in a gown that stands for the goodness that comes from him.

"Don't do that! I am a servant, just like you and everyone else who tells about Jesus. Don't worship anyone but God. Everyone who tells about Jesus does it by the power of the Spirit."

The Rider on the White Horse

11I looked and saw that heaven was open, and a white horse was there. Its rider was called Faithful and True, and he is always fair when he judges or goes to war. 12He had eyes like flames of fire, and he was wearing a lot of crowns. His name was written on him, but he was the only one who knew what the name meant.

13The rider wore a robe that was covered withd blood, and he was known as "The Word of God." 14He was followed by armies from heaven, which rode on horses and were dressed in pure white linen. 15From his mouth a sharp sword went out to attack the nations. He will rule them with an iron rod and will show the fierce anger of God All-Powerful by stomping the grapes in the pit where wine is made. 16On the part of the robe that covered his thigh was written, "KING OF KINGS AND LORD OF LORDS."

17I then saw an angel standing on the sun, and he shouted to all the birds flying in the sky, "Come and join in God's great feast! 18You can eat the flesh of kings, rulers, leaders, horses, riders, free people, slaves, important people, and everyone else."

19I also saw the beast and all kings of the earth come together. They fought against the rider on the white horse and against his army. 20But the beast was captured and so was the false prophet. This is the same prophet who had worked miracles for the beast, so that he could fool everyone who had the mark of the beast and worshiped the idol. The beast and the false prophet were thrown alive into a lake of

Christ the King will make war
(13) Jesus Christ will ride against the beast and his armies in a tremendous battle. There can be only one certain outcome of this great war of the ages. Christ is the King of kings. His enemies will realize that they never really had a chance against his authority.

dcovered with: Some manuscripts have "sprinkled with."

burning sulphur. 21But the rest of their army was killed by the sword that came from the mouth of the rider on the horse. Then birds stuffed themselves on the dead bodies.

The Thousand Years

20 I saw an angel come down from heaven, carrying the key to the deep pit and a big chain. 2He chained the dragon for a thousand years. It is that old snake, who is also known as the devil and Satan. 3Then the angel threw the dragon into the pit. He locked and sealed it, so that a thousand years would go by before the dragon could fool the nations again. But after that, it would have to be set free for a little while.

4I saw thrones, and sitting on those thrones were the ones who had been given the right to judge. I also saw the souls of the people who had their heads cut off because they had told about Jesus and preached God's message. They were the same ones who had not worshiped the beast or the idol, and they had refused to let its mark be put on their hands or foreheads. They will come to life and rule with Christ for a thousand years.

5-6These people are the first to be raised to life, and they are especially blessed and holy. The second death*e* has no power over them. They will be priests for God and Christ and will rule with them for a thousand years.

No other dead people were raised to life until a thousand years later.

Satan Is Defeated

7At the end of the thousand years, Satan will be set free. 8He will fool the countries of Gog and Magog, which are at the far ends of the earth, and their people will follow him into battle. They will have as many followers as there are grains of sand along the beach, 9and they will march all the way

Christ will reign on earth (4) The ones who loved Jesus and suffered for him will be raised up from death by his power, and will reign with him when he wins his victory. That was always the right outcome of the conflict between God and Satan, between good and evil. It was never possible that the hopeless dreams of the devil and his followers could come true. While evil seems to run the world we are sometimes discouraged, but in God's time we will see Jesus reign in mighty power.

esecond death: The first death is physical death, and the "second death" is eternal death.

across the earth. They will surround the camp of God's people and the city that his people love. But fire will come down from heaven and destroy the whole army. [10]Then the devil who fooled them will be thrown into the lake of fire and burning sulphur. He will be there with the beast and the false prophet, and they will be in pain day and night forever and ever.

The Judgment at the Great White Throne

[11]I saw a great white throne with someone sitting on it. Earth and heaven tried to run away, but there was no place for them to go. [12]I also saw all the dead people standing in front of that throne. Every one of them was there, no matter who they had once been. Several books were opened, and then the book of life[f] was opened. The dead were judged by what those books said they had done.

[13]The sea gave up the dead people who were in it, and death and its kingdom also gave up their dead. Then everyone was judged by what they had done. [14]Afterwards, death and its kingdom were thrown into the lake of fire. This is the second death.[g] [15]Anyone whose name was not written in the book of life was thrown into the lake of fire.

The New Heaven and the New Earth

21 I saw a new heaven and a new earth. The first heaven and the first earth had disappeared, and so had the sea. [2]Then I saw New Jerusalem, that holy city, coming down from God in heaven. It was like a bride dressed in her wedding gown and ready to meet her husband.

[3]I heard a loud voice shout from the throne:

God's home is now with his people.
He will live with them, and they will
be his own. Yes, God will make his home

God will punish evil
(10) It is an unpleasant subject. Nevertheless, the warnings are clear that everlasting punishment in hell, the "lake of fire," awaits Satan, his antichrist, and their willing followers. Evil is not something people follow blindly, and they have been warned that evil cannot exist along with God's eternal goodness. So they will have the evil they chose, along with evil's natural and tragic results.

God's everlasting order will arrive
(1) Time itself will pass away, and eternity will begin. The old order will fall away like a worn-out suit of clothes. The tree that was bare and dry will burst forth with healthy leaves and fruit. The kingdom of God will come. Good people have long dreamed and spoken of a "new order," but God always had this in mind. God himself will live with his people.

among his people. 4He will wipe all tears from their eyes, and there will be no more death, suffering, crying, or pain. These things of the past are gone forever.

5Then the one sitting on the throne said:

I am making everything new. Write down what I have said. My words are true and can be trusted. 6Everything is finished! I am Alpha and Omega,h the beginning and the end. I will freely give water from the life-giving fountain to everyone who is thirsty. 7All who win the victory will be given these blessings. I will be their God, and they will be my people.

8But I will tell you what will happen to cowards and to everyone who is unfaithful or dirty-minded or who murders or is sexually immoral or uses witchcraft or worships idols or tells lies. They will be thrown into that lake of fire and burning sulphur. This is the second death.i

The New Jerusalem

9I saw one of the seven angels who had the bowls filled with the seven last terrible troubles. The angel came to me and said, "Come on! I will show you the one who will be the bride and wife of the Lamb." 10Then with the help of the Spirit, he took me to the top of a very high mountain. There he showed me the holy city of Jerusalem coming down from God in heaven.

11The glory of God made the city bright. It was dazzling and crystal clear like a precious jasperj stone. 12The city had a high

There will be a new city of God

(10) A great Christian named Augustine long ago wrote a book called *The City of God.* Believers have always tried to picture what God's new Jerusalem will be like. Old Jerusalem was a poor shadow of the city God plans for the future. Look at the size of it (verse 16). An Old Testament prophet tells us that the name of the city will be "The Lord Is There." God himself will be the beauty and glory of his eternal city.

---

hAlpha and Omega: See the note at 1.8.   isecond death: See the note at 20.6.   jjasper: The precious and semiprecious stones mentioned in verses 19,20 are of different colors. Jasper is usually green or clear; sapphire is blue; agate has circles of brown and white; emerald is green; onyx has different bands of color; carnelian is deep-red or reddish-white; chrysolite is olive-green; beryl is green or bluish-green; topaz is yellow; chrysoprase is apple-green; jacinth is reddish-orange; and amethyst is deep purple.

and thick wall with twelve gates, and each one of them was guarded by an angel. On each of the gates was written the name of one of the twelve tribes of Israel. [13]Three of these gates were on the east, three were on the north, three more were on the south, and the other three were on the west. [14]The city was built on twelve foundation stones. On each of the stones was written the name of one of the Lamb's twelve apostles.

[15]The angel who spoke to me had a gold measuring stick to measure the city and its gates and its walls. [16]The city was shaped like a cube, because it was just as high as it was wide. When the angel measured the city, it was about fifteen hundred miles high and fifteen hundred miles wide. [17]Then the angel measured the wall, and by our measurements it was about two hundred sixteen feet high.

[18]The wall was built of jasper,[j] and the city was made of pure gold, clear as crystal. [19]Each of the twelve foundations was a precious stone. The first was jasper, the second was sapphire, the third was agate, the fourth was emerald, [20]the fifth was onyx, the sixth was carnelian, the seventh was chrysolite, the eighth was beryl, the ninth was topaz, the tenth was chrysoprase, the eleventh was jacinth, and the twelfth was amethyst. [21]Each of the twelve gates was a solid pearl. The streets of the city were made of pure gold, clear as crystal.

[22]I did not see a temple there. The Lord God All-Powerful and the Lamb were its temple. [23]And the city did not need the sun or the moon. The glory of God was shining on it, and the Lamb was its light.

---

[j]*jasper*: The precious and semiprecious stones mentioned in verses 19,20 are of different colors. *Jasper* is usually green or clear; *sapphire* is blue; *agate* has circles of brown and white; *emerald* is green; *onyx* has different bands of color; *carnelian* is deep-red or reddish-white; *chrysolite* is olive-green; *beryl* is green or bluish-green; *topaz* is yellow; *chrysoprase* is apple-green; *jacinth* is reddish-orange; and *amethyst* is deep purple.

²⁴Nations will walk by the light of that city, and kings will bring their riches there. ²⁵Its gates are always open during the day, and night never comes. ²⁶The glorious treasures of nations will be brought into the city. ²⁷But nothing unworthy will be allowed to enter. No one who is dirty-minded or who tells lies will be there. Only those whose names are written in the Lamb's book of life*ᵏ* will be in the city.

22 The angel showed me a river that was crystal clear, and its waters gave life. The river came from the throne where God and the Lamb were seated. ²Then it flowed down the middle of the city's main street. On each side of the river are trees*ˡ* that grow a different kind of fruit each month of the year. The fruit gives life, and the leaves are used as medicine to heal the nations.

³God's curse will no longer be on the people of that city. He and the Lamb will be seated there on their thrones, and its people will worship God ⁴and will see him face to face. God's name will be written on the foreheads of the people. ⁵Never again will night appear, and no one who lives there will ever need a lamp or the sun. The Lord God will be their light, and they will rule forever.

The Coming of Christ

⁶Then I was told:

These words are true and can be trusted. The Lord God controls the spirits of his prophets, and he is the one who sent his angel to show his servants what must happen right away. ⁷Remember, I am coming soon! God will bless everyone who pays attention to what this book tells about the future.

⁸My name is John, and I am the one who heard and saw these things. Then after I had heard and seen all this, I kneeled down and began to worship at the feet of the angel who had shown it to me.

ᵏbook of life: A book in which the names of God's people are written. *ˡtrees:* The Greek has "tree," which is used in a collective sense of trees on both sides of the heavenly river.

Who will live in the city?
(27) "The bride," the ones who love Jesus and are saved by him, whose names are in the book of life, will live in God's city. But even now, if you love Jesus, he will come to live in you. Have you given your life to Jesus? It's the only reasonable thing to do with your life. God made you for himself. So you can be happy only when you have given your life to him.

When will Jesus come?
(7) The child asks, "When will Daddy come home?" The answer is usually, "Soon." So the child waits, at times a little impatiently. But when the father returns the child forgets all about the waiting. The return of Jesus for his church is like that. He is coming "soon," but that includes some waiting—how long, we cannot say. The main thing is to watch and live in a way that will make us glad to see Jesus when he appears.

9But the angel said,

Don't do that! I am a servant, just like you. I am the same as a follower or a prophet or anyone else who obeys what is written in this book. God is the one you should worship.

10Don't keep the prophecies in this book a secret. These things will happen soon.

11Evil people will keep on being evil, and everyone who is dirty-minded will still be dirty-minded. But good people will keep on doing right, and God's people will always be holy.

12Then I was told:

I am coming soon! And when I come, I will reward everyone for what they have done. 13I am Alpha and Omega,m the first and the last, the beginning and the end.

14God will bless all who have washed their robes. They will each have the right to eat fruit from the tree that gives life, and they can enter the gates of the city. 15But outside the city will be dogs, witches, immoral people, murderers, idol worshipers, and everyone who loves to tell lies and do wrong.

16I am Jesus! And I am the one who sent my angel to tell all of you these things for the churches. I am David's Great Descendant,n and I am also the bright morning star.o

17The Spirit and the bride say, "Come!" Everyone who hears thisp should say, "Come!"

If you are thirsty, come! If you want life-giving water, come and take it. It's free!

18Here is my warning for everyone who hears the prophecies in this book:

If you add anything to them, God will make you suffer all the terrible troubles written in this book. 19If you take any-

---

mAlpha and Omega: See the note at 1.8. nDavid's Great Descendant: See the note at 5.5. othe bright morning star: Probably thought of as the brightest star. See 2.27,28. pwho hears this: The reading of the book of Revelation in a service of worship.

Be honest with God's word

(18) Some people might like to cut out or add to some of the things John wrote down in Revelation. Yes, there are some very shocking words in this book. But a Christian believes that God himself gave John these visions, just as surely as God gave us the rest of the Bible. By what God has spoken, we can know what he promises and what he expects. So let's pay serious attention to all that God says in his word, the Bible.

thing away from these prophecies, God will not let you have part in the life-giving tree and in the holy city described in this book.

20The one who has spoken these things says, "I am coming soon!"

So, Lord Jesus, please come soon!

21I pray that the Lord Jesus will be kind to all of you.

Word List

Aaron The brother of Moses. Only he and his descendants were to serve as priests and offer sacrifices for the people of Israel.

Abel The second son of Adam and Eve and the younger brother of Cain, who killed him, after God accepted Abel's offering and refused Cain's.

Abijah A descendant of Aaron. King David divided the priests into twenty-four groups, and Abijah was head of the eighth group.

Abraham The husband of Sarah and the father of Isaac. God promised Abraham that he would be a blessing to everyone on earth, because Abraham had faith in him.

Adam The first man and the husband of Eve.

Agrippa (1) Herod Agrippa was king of Judea A.D. 41–44 and mistreated Christians (Acts 12.1–5). (2) Agrippa II was the son of Herod Agrippa and ruled Judea A.D. 44–53. He and his sister Bernice listened to Paul defend himself (Acts 25.13–26,32).

aloes A sweet-smelling spice that was mixed with myrrh and used as a perfume.

amen A Hebrew word used after a prayer or a blessing and meaning, "Let it be that way."

ancestor Someone born one or more generations earlier in a family line, such as a grandparent or great-grandparent.

angel A supernatural being who tells God's messages or protects God's people.

Antipas The father of Herod the Great and ruler of Judea 55–43 B.C. He was also known as Antipater.

apostle A person chosen by Christ to take his message to others.

Aramaic A language closely related to Hebrew. It was spoken by many Jews including Jesus during New Testament times.

Augustus This is the title meaning "honored" that the Romans gave to Octavian when he began ruling the Roman world in 27 B.C. He was Emperor when Jesus was born (Luke 2.1).

barley A grain something like wheat and used to make bread.

Cain The first son of Adam and Eve and the brother of Abel.

Christ A Greek word meaning "the Chosen One" and used to translate the Hebrew word "Messiah." It is used in the New Testament both as a title and a name for Jesus.

circumcise To cut off the foreskin from the male organ. This is done for Jewish boys as part of a religious ceremony eight days after they are born to show that they belong to God's people. God's command to Abraham

(Genesis 17.9–14) was to circumcise all males on the eighth day. Jesus' circumcision on the eighth day is reported in Luke 2.21.

citizen   A person who is given special rights and privileges by a nation or state. In return, a citizen was expected to be loyal to that nation or state.

commandments   God's rules for his people to live by.

council   A leading group of Jewish men who were allowed by the Roman government to meet and make certain decisions for their people.

cumin   A plant with small seeds used for seasoning food.

David   The most famous ancestor of the Jewish people and the most powerful king Israel ever had. They hoped that one of his descendants would always be their king.

Day of Atonement   The one day each year (the tenth day after the Jewish new year's day in the fall) when the high priest went into the most holy part of the temple and sprinkled some of the blood of a sacrificed bull on the sacred chest. This was done so that the people's sins would be forgiven. This holy day is called Yom Kippur in Hebrew.

demons and **evil spirits**   Supernatural beings that do harmful things to people and sometimes cause them to do bad things. In the New Testament they are sometimes called "unclean spirits," because people under their power were thought to be unclean and unfit to worship God.

descendant   Someone born one or more generations later in a family line, such as a grandchild or great-grandchild.

devil   The chief of the demons and evil spirits, also known as "Satan."

disciple   Someone who was a follower of Jesus and learned from him.

elders   Men whose age and wisdom made them respected leaders.

Elijah   A prophet who spoke for God in the ninth century B.C. Many Jews in later centuries thought Elijah would return to get things ready for the coming of the Lord.

Emperor   The ruler who lived in the city of Rome and governed all the land around the Mediterranean Sea.

Epicureans   People who followed the teachings of a man named Epicurus, who taught that happiness should be a person's main goal in life.

eternal life   Life that is the gift of God and never ends.

evil spirits   See "demons."

exile   The time in Jewish history (597–539 B.C.) when the Babylonians took away most of the people of Jerusalem and Judah as prisoners of war and made them live in Babylonia.

Feast of Thin Bread   The days after Passover when Jews eat a kind of thin, flat bread made without yeast to remember how God freed the people of Israel from slavery in Egypt and gave them a fresh start.

Felix   The Roman governor of Judea A.D. 52–60, who listened to Paul speak and kept him in jail.

Festival of Shelters   This festival celebrates the period of forty years when the people of Israel walked through the desert and lived in small shelters. This happy celebration takes place each year in connection with the fall harvest season. Its name in Hebrew is Sukkoth.

Festus   The Roman governor after Felix, who sent Paul to stand trial in Rome.

Gentile   Someone who is not a Jew.

God's kingdom   God's rule over people, both in this life and in the next.

God's Law   God's rules for his people to live by. They are found in the Old Testament, especially in the first five books.

God's tent   The tent where the people of Israel worshiped God before the temple was built.

Greek   The language in which the New Testament was written.

Hagar   A personal servant of Sarah, the wife of Abraham. When Sarah could not have any children, she followed the ancient custom of letting her husband have a child by Hagar, her servant woman. The boy's name was Ishmael.

Hebrew   The language used by the people of Israel and for the writing of most of the Old Testament.

Hermes   The Greek god of skillful speaking and the messenger of the other Greek gods.

Herod   (1) Herod the Great was the king of all Palestine 37–4 B.C. He ruled Judea at the time Jesus was born. (2) Herod Antipas was the son of Herod the Great and the ruler of Galilee 4 B.C.–A.D. 39, during the time of John the Baptist and Jesus. (3) Herod Agrippa I, the grandson of Herod the Great, ruled Palestine A.D. 41–44.

high priest   See "priest."

Holy One   A name for the Savior that God had promised to send. See "Savior."

incense   A material that makes a sweet smell when burned and is used in the worship of God.

Isaac   The son of Abraham and Sarah and the father of Esau and Jacob. Abraham, Isaac, and Jacob are three of the most famous ancestors of the Jewish people.

Isaiah   A prophet from Jerusalem, who lived during the eighth century B.C. He served as a prophet during the rule of four different kings of Judah, between the years 740–700 B.C.

Jacob   The son of Isaac and Rebecca. He is better known by the name Israel, which God gave to him. See "Isaac."

judges   Leaders chosen by the Lord for the people of Israel after the time of Joshua and before the time of the kings.

Law and the Prophets   The sacred writings of the Jews in Jesus' day (the first two of the three sections of the Old Testament).

Law of Moses and **Law of the Lord**   Usually refers to the first five books of the Old Testament, but sometimes to the entire Old Testament.

Levite   A member of the tribe of Levi, from which priests were chosen. Men from this tribe who were not priests helped with the work in the temple.

Messiah   A Hebrew word meaning "the Chosen One." See "Christ."

mint   A garden plant used for seasoning and medicine.

Moses   The leader of the people of Israel when God rescued them from Egypt.

myrrh   A valuable sweet-smelling powder used in perfume.

Nazarenes   A name that was sometimes used for the followers of Jesus, who came from the small town of Nazareth.

Noah   When God destroyed the world by a flood, Noah and his family were kept safe in a big boat that God had told him to build.

paradise   The place where God's people go when they die, often understood as another name for heaven.

Passover   A day each year in the spring when Jews celebrate the time God rescued them from slavery in Egypt.

Pentecost   A Jewish festival fifty days after Passover to celebrate the wheat harvest.

Pharisees   A large group of Jews who thought they could best serve God by strictly obeying the laws of the Old Testament as well as their own teachings.

pit or **deep pit**   The place of punishment for demons and evil spirits.

priest   A man who led the worship in the temple and offered sacrifices. Some of the more important priests were called "chief priests," and the most important priest was called the "high priest."

Promised One   A title for the Savior that God promised to send. See "Savior."

prophesy   See "prophet."

prophet   Someone who speaks God's message and tells what will happen in the future. To speak as a prophet is thus to "prophesy."

rue   A garden plant used for seasoning and medicine.

Sabbath   The seventh day of the week when Jews worship and do not work, in obedience to the third commandment.

Sadducees   A small and powerful group of Jews who were closely connected with the high priests and who accepted only the first five books of the Old Testament as their Bible. They also did not believe in life after death.

Samaria A district between Judea and Galilee. The people of Samaria, called Samaritans, worshiped God differently from the Jews and did not get along with them.

Sarah The wife of Abraham and the mother of Isaac. When she was very old, God promised her that she would have a son.

Satan See "devil."

save To rescue people from the power of evil, to give them new life, and to place them under God's care. See "Savior."

Savior The one who rescues people from the power of evil, gives them new life, and places them under God's care. See "save."

Scriptures The sacred writings known as the Old Testament. These were first written in Hebrew and Aramaic, then translated into Greek about two centuries before the birth of Jesus. This Greek translation, known as the Septuagint, was used both by Jews and Christians in the first century.

Son of Man A name often used by Jesus to refer to himself. It is also found in the book of Daniel and refers to the one to whom God has given the power to rule.

Stoics Followers of a man named Zeno, who believed that nature was controlled by the gods and who taught that people should learn self-control.

taxes and **tax collectors** Special fees collected by rulers, usually part of the value of a citizen's crops, property, or income. There were also market taxes to be paid, and customs taxes were collected at ports and border crossings. The wealthy Zacchaeus (Luke 19.1–10) was a tax collector who collected taxes at a border crossing near Jericho. Jews hired by the Roman government to collect taxes from other Jews were hated by their own people.

temple A building used as a place of worship. The Jewish temple was in Jerusalem.

Temple Festival In 165 B.C. the Jewish people recaptured the Jerusalem temple from their enemies and made it fit for worship again. They celebrate this event in December of each year by a festival which they call "dedication" (Hanukkah). In the New Testament it is mentioned only in John 10.22.

Theophilus The name means "someone God loves" and is found only in Luke 1.3 and Acts 1.1. Nothing else is known about him.

Way In the book of Acts the Christian religion is sometimes called "the Way" or "the Way of the Lord" or "God's Way."

Zeus The chief god of the Greeks.

HOW TO READ THROUGH YOUR NEW TESTAMENT IN A YEAR

Date	Chapter	Reading
		MATTHEW TELLS THE GOOD NEWS
Jan. 1	1	The Ancestors of Jesus; The Birth of Jesus
Jan. 2	2	The Wise Men; The Escape to Egypt; The Killing of the Children; The Return from Egypt
Jan. 3	3	The Preaching of John the Baptist; The Baptism of Jesus
Jan. 4	4	Jesus and the Devil; Jesus Begins His Work; Jesus Chooses Four Fishermen; Jesus Preaches, Teaches, and Heals
Jan. 5	5	The Sermon on the Mount; Blessings; Salt and Light; The Law of Moses; Anger
Jan. 6	5	Marriage; Divorce; Promises; Revenge; Love
Jan. 7	6	Giving; Prayer; Worshiping God by Going without Eating
Jan. 8	6	Treasures in Heaven; Light; Money; Worry
Jan. 9	7	Judging Others; Ask, Search, Knock; The Narrow Gate; A Tree and Its Fruit; A Warning; Two Builders
Jan. 10	8	Jesus Heals a Man; Jesus Heals an Army Officer's Servant; Jesus Heals Many People
Jan. 11	8	Some Who Wanted to Go with Jesus; A Storm; Two Men with Demons in Them
Jan. 12	9	Jesus Heals a Crippled Man; Jesus Chooses Matthew; People Ask about Going without Eating
Jan. 13	9	A Dead Girl and a Sick Woman; Jesus Heals Two Blind Men; Jesus Heals a Man Who Could Not Talk; Jesus Has Pity on People
Jan. 14	10	Jesus Chooses His Twelve Apostles; Instructions for the Twelve Apostles; Warning about Trouble
Jan. 15	10	The One to Fear; Telling Others about Christ; Not Peace, but Trouble; Rewards
Jan. 16	11	John the Baptist; The Unbelieving Towns; Come to Me and Rest
Jan. 17	12	A Question about the Sabbath; A Man with a Crippled Hand; God's Chosen Servant
Jan. 18	12	Jesus and the Ruler of the Demons; A Tree and Its Fruit; A Sign from Heaven; Return of an Evil Spirit; Jesus' Mother and Brothers

Date	Chapter	Reading
Feb. 10	25	The Final Judgment
Feb. 11	26	The Plot to Kill Jesus; At Bethany; Judas and the Chief Priests; Jesus Eats the Passover Meal with His Disciples
Feb. 12	26	The Lord's Supper; Peter's Promise; Jesus Prays
Feb. 13	26	Jesus Is Arrested; Jesus Is Questioned by the Jewish Council; Peter Says He Does Not Know Jesus
Feb. 14	27	Jesus Is Taken to Pilate; The Death of Judas; Pilate Questions Jesus; The Death Sentence
Feb. 15	27	Soldiers Make Fun of Jesus; Jesus Is Nailed to a Cross
Feb. 16	27	The Death of Jesus; Jesus Is Buried
Feb. 17	28	Jesus Is Alive; Report of the Guard; What Jesus' Followers Must Do

MARK TELLS THE GOOD NEWS

Date	Chapter	Reading
Feb. 18	1	The Preaching of John the Baptist; The Baptism of Jesus; Jesus and Satan; Jesus Begins His Work; Jesus Chooses Four Fishermen
Feb. 19	1	A Man with an Evil Spirit; Jesus Heals Many People; Jesus Heals a Man
Feb. 20	2	Jesus Heals a Crippled Man; Jesus Chooses Levi; People Ask about Going without Eating; A Question about the Sabbath
Feb. 21	3	A Man with a Crippled Hand; Large Crowds Come to Jesus; Jesus Chooses His Twelve Apostles
Feb. 22	3	Jesus and the Ruler of Demons; Jesus' Mother and Brothers
Feb. 23	4	A Story about a Farmer; Why Jesus Used Stories; Jesus Explains the Story about the Farmer
Feb. 24	4	Light; Another Story about Seeds; A Mustard Seed; The Reason for Teaching with Stories; A Storm
Feb. 25	5	A Man with Evil Spirits
Feb. 26	5	A Dying Girl and a Sick Woman
Feb. 27	6	The People of Nazareth Turn against Jesus; Instructions for the Twelve Apostles; The Death of John the Baptist
Feb. 28	6	Jesus Feeds Five Thousand; Jesus Walks on the Water; Jesus Heals Sick People in Gennesaret
Feb. 29	7	The Teaching of the Ancestors
Mar. 1	7	What Really Makes People Unclean; A Woman's Faith; Jesus Heals a Man Who Was Deaf and Could Hardly Talk
Mar. 2	8	Jesus Feeds Four Thousand; A Sign from Heaven; The Yeast of the Pharisees and of Herod
Mar. 3	8–9	Jesus Heals a Blind Man at Bethsaida; Who Is Jesus?; Jesus Speaks about His Suffering and Death
Mar. 4	9	The True Glory of Jesus; Jesus Heals a Boy

JOHN TELLS THE GOOD NEWS

Date	Chapter	Reading

THE ACTS OF THE APOSTLES

Date	Chapter	Reading
July 12	17	Paul in Athens
July 13	18	Paul in Corinth; Paul Returns to Antioch in Syria; Apollos in Ephesus
July 14	19	Paul in Ephesus; The Sons of Sceva
July 15	19	The Riot in Ephesus
July 16	20	Paul Goes Through Macedonia and Greece; Paul's Last Visit to Troas; The Voyage from Troas to Miletus
July 17	20	Paul Says Good-by to the Church Leaders of Ephesus
July 18	21	Paul Goes to Jerusalem
July 19	21	Paul Visits James; Paul Is Arrested
July 20	21–22	Paul Speaks to the Crowd; Paul and the Roman Army Commander
July 21	22–23	Paul Is Tried by the Council
July 22	23	A Plot to Kill Paul; Paul Is Sent to Felix the Governor
July 23	24	Paul Is Accused in the Court of Felix; Paul Defends Himself; Paul Is Kept Under Guard
July 24	25	Paul Asks to Be Tried by the Roman Emperor; Paul Speaks to Agrippa and Bernice
July 25	26	Paul's Defense before Agrippa
July 26	27	Paul Is Taken to Rome; The Storm at Sea (to verse 26)
July 27	27	The Storm at Sea (from verse 27); The Shipwreck
July 28	28	On the Island of Malta; From Malta to Rome; Paul in Rome

PAUL'S LETTER TO THE CHURCH IN ROME

Date	Chapter	Reading
July 29	1	Greeting; A Prayer of Thanks; The Power of the Good News; Everyone Is Guilty
July 30	2–3	God's Judgment Is Fair; The Jews and the Law
July 31	3	No One Is Good; God's Way of Accepting People
Aug. 1	4	The Example of Abraham; The Promise Is for All Who Have Faith
Aug. 2	5	What It Means to Be Acceptable to God; Adam and Christ
Aug. 3	6	Dead to Sin but Alive because of Christ; Slaves Who Do What Pleases God
Aug. 4	7	An Example from Marriage; The Battle with Sin
Aug. 5	8	Living by the Power of God's Spirit
Aug. 6	8	A Wonderful Future for God's People; God's Love
Aug. 7	9	God's Choice of Israel
Aug. 8	9–10	God's Anger and Mercy; Israel and the Good News
Aug. 9	10	Anyone Can Be Saved
Aug. 10	11	God Has Not Rejected His People; Gentiles Will Be Saved (to verse 16)
Aug. 11	11	Gentiles Will Be Saved (from verse 17); The People of Israel Will Be Brought Back
Aug. 12	12	Christ Brings New Life; Rules for Christian Living
Aug. 13	13	Obey Rulers; Love; The Day When Christ Returns

Date	Chapter	Reading
Sep. 18	11	Paul and the False Apostles
Sep. 19	11	Paul's Sufferings for Christ
Sep. 20	12	Visions from the Lord; Paul's Concern for the Lord's Followers at Corinth
Sep. 21	13	Final Warnings and Greetings

PAUL'S LETTER TO THE CHURCHES IN GALATIA

Date	Chapter	Reading
Sep. 22	1	Greeting; The Only True Message; How Paul Became an Apostle (to verse 24)
Sep. 23	2	How Paul Became an Apostle (from verse 1); Paul Corrects Peter at Antioch
Sep. 24	3–4	Faith Is the Only Way; The Law and the Promise; Slaves and Children
Sep. 25	4	Paul's Concern for the Galatians; Hagar and Sarah
Sep. 26	5	Christ Gives Freedom; God's Spirit and Our Own Desires
Sep. 27	6	Help Each Other; Final Warnings

PAUL'S LETTER TO THE CHURCH IN EPHESUS

Date	Chapter	Reading
Sep. 28	1	Greeting; Christ Brings Spiritual Blessings; Paul's Prayer
Sep. 29	2	From Death to Life; United by Christ
Sep. 30	3	Paul's Mission to the Gentiles; Christ's Love for Us
Oct. 1	4	Unity with Christ; The Old Life and the New Life
Oct. 2	4–5	Rules for the New Life; Living as People of Light
Oct. 3	5–6	Wives and Husbands; Children and Parents; Slaves and Masters
Oct. 4	6	The Fight against Evil; Final Greetings

PAUL'S LETTER TO THE CHURCH IN PHILIPPI

Date	Chapter	Reading
Oct. 5	1	Greeting; Paul's Prayer for the Church in Philippi; What Life Means to Paul
Oct. 6	2	True Humility; Lights in the World; Timothy and Epaphroditus
Oct. 7	3–4	Being Acceptable to God; Running toward the Goal
Oct. 8	4	Paul Encourages the Lord's Followers; Paul Gives Thanks for the Gifts He Was Given; Final Greetings

PAUL'S LETTER TO THE CHURCH IN COLOSSAE

Date	Chapter	Reading
Oct. 9	1	Greeting; A Prayer of Thanks; The Person and Work of Christ
Oct. 10	1–2	Paul's Service to the Church; Christ Brings Real Life
Oct. 11	2–3	Christ Brings New Life
Oct. 12	3–4	Some Rules for Christian Living; Final Greetings

PAUL'S FIRST LETTER TO THE CHURCH IN THESSALONICA

Date	Chapter	Reading
Oct. 13	1	Greeting; The Thessalonians' Faith and Example
Oct. 14	2	Paul's Work in Thessalonica

Date	Chapter	Reading
Nov. 6	3	Jesus Is Greater than Moses; A Rest for God's People (to verse 19)
Nov. 7	4	A Rest for God's People (from verse 1)
Nov. 8	4–5	Jesus Is the Great High Priest
Nov. 9	5–6	Warning against Turning Away; God's Promise Is Sure
Nov. 10	7	The Priestly Family of Melchizedek
Nov. 11	8	A Better Promise
Nov. 12	9	The Tent in Heaven; Christ's Great Sacrifice (to verse 28)
Nov. 13	10	Christ's Great Sacrifice (from verse 1)
Nov. 14	10	Encouragement and Warning
Nov. 15	11	The Great Faith of God's People (to verse 19)
Nov. 16	11	The Great Faith of God's People (from verse 20)
Nov. 17	12	A Large Crowd of Witnesses; Warning against Turning from God
Nov. 18	13	Service That Pleases God; Final Prayers and Greetings

A LETTER FROM JAMES

Date	Chapter	Reading
Nov. 19	1	Greeting; Faith and Wisdom; Poor People and Rich People; Trials and Temptations; Hearing and Obeying
Nov. 20	2	Warning against Having Favorites; Faith and Works
Nov. 21	3	The Tongue; Wisdom from Above
Nov. 22	4	Friendship with the World; Saying Cruel Things about Others; Warning against Bragging
Nov. 23	5	Warning to the Rich; Be Patient and Kind

PETER'S FIRST LETTER

Date	Chapter	Reading
Nov. 24	1	Greeting; A Real Reason for Hope; Chosen to Live a Holy Life
Nov. 25	2	A Living Stone and a Holy Nation; Live as God's Servants Should; The Example of Christ's Suffering
Nov. 26	3	Wives and Husbands; Suffering for Doing Right
Nov. 27	4	Being Faithful to God; Suffering for Being a Christian
Nov. 28	5	Helping Christian Leaders; Final Greetings

PETER'S SECOND LETTER

Date	Chapter	Reading
Nov. 29	1	Greeting; Living as the Lord's Followers Should; The Message about the Glory of Christ
Nov. 30	2	False Prophets and Teachers
Dec. 1	3	The Lord Will Return

JOHN'S FIRST LETTER

Date	Chapter	Reading
Dec. 2	1	Greeting; God Is Light
Dec. 3	2	Christ Helps Us; The New Commandment; The Enemy of Christ
Dec. 4	2–3	Children of God; Love Each Other
Dec. 5	4	God Is Love